BARGAINING WITH INCOMPLETE INFORMATION

This is a volume in
ECONOMIC THEORY, ECONOMETRICS,
AND MATHEMATICAL ECONOMICS

A Series of Monographs and Textbooks

Consulting Editor: Karl Shell, *Cornell University*

A list of recent titles in this series appears at the end of this volume.

BARGAINING WITH INCOMPLETE INFORMATION

Edited by

PETER B. LINHART

AT&T Bell Laboratories
Murray Hill, New Jersey

ROY RADNER

AT&T Bell Laboratories
Murray Hill, New Jersey

MARK A. SATTERTHWAITE

Kellogg Graduate School of Management
Northwestern University
Evanston, Illinois

ACADEMIC PRESS, INC.

Harcourt Brace Jovanovich, Publishers

San Diego   New York   Boston   London   Sydney   Tokyo   Toronto

Academic Press Rapid Manuscript Reproduction

This book is printed on acid-free paper. ∞

Academic Press, Inc.
1250 Sixth Avenue, San Diego, California 92101-4311

United Kingdom Edition published by
Academic Press Limited
24–28 Oval Road, London NW1 7DX

Library of Congress Cataloging-in-Publication Data

Bargaining with incomplete information / edited by Peter B. Linhart,
   Roy Radner, Mark A. Satterthwaite.
      p.   cm. – (Economic theory, econometrics, and mathematical
   economics)
   Includes index.
   ISBN 0-12-451050-7
   1. Negotiation–Mathematical models.   2. Uncertainty–Mathematical
models.   I. Linhart, Peter B.   II. Radner, Roy, date
III. Satterthwaite, Mark A.   IV. Series.
HD58.6.B37   1992
302.3–dc20   92-11473
                                                            CIP

PRINTED IN THE UNITED STATES OF AMERICA
92 93 94 95 96 97   QW   9 8 7 6 5 4 3 2 1

Contents

Preface

Most of the papers in this volume were published in the June 1989 issue of *Journal of Economic Theory* as a symposium on noncooperative bargaining. Ten papers that were not in that issue have been added and are reprinted here: Admati and Perry on strategic delay; Ausubel and Deneckere on reputational equilibria; Chatterjee and Samuelson on an equilibrium with linear strategies in the sealed-bid double auction; two papers by Gresik on *ex post* individual rationality's relationship to interim individual rationality; Gul, Sonnenschein, and Wilson on the difficulties a monopoly seller has in committing to a monopoly price; Myerson and Satterthwaite on the necessity of inefficiency in situations with incomplete information; Rob on pollution claims settlements under private information; Rubinstein on a bargaining situation in which incomplete information exists with respect to the buyer's rate of time preference; and Satterthwaite and Williams on the rate at which strategic misrepresentation vanishes within the sealed-bid double auction as the number of traders grows large. These papers have been added to make the resulting collection more complete and more self-contained than the journal issue, which was constrained by the requirement that papers in it not be previously published.

C 78
D8 3

βκ Title:

Introduction

PETER LINHART AND ROY RADNER*

AT&T Bell Laboratories
Murray Hill, New Jersey 07974

AND

MARK A. SATTERTHWAITE[†]

Kellogg Graduate School of Management
Northwestern University
Evanston, Illinois 60208

According to a dictionary [2], to bargain is "to negotiate the terms of a sale, exchange, or other agreement." Understanding of bargaining is fundamental to economics. Without bargaining, transactions cannot occur, and without transactions, economics is limited to the study of Robinson Crusoe economies. Any complete theory of the functioning and efficiency of markets must have at its base a theory of how bargaining determines who trades what at what prices.

Adequate theories of bargaining exist only for the degenerate, polar cases of perfect competition and monopoly, in which respectively no agent has any bargaining power and all bargaining power is concentrated with a single agent. If each agent has significant bargaining power in the sense that his rejection of a proposed agreement substantially reduces the other agents' utilities, then the available theories, with a few notable exceptions, are generally not fully satisfactory. Bilateral bargaining is the classic example of this: each agent has bargaining power, and adequate theories have not been developed, except for Rubinstein's analysis [10] of the special case of alternating-offer sequential bargaining with complete information and discounting of gains.

The pioneer of modern bargaining theory in economics was Nash [8, 9]. According to him [8], "A two-person bargaining situation involves two individuals

*The views expressed here are those of the authors and not necessarily those of AT&T Bell Laboratories.

[†]This material is based upon work supported by the National Science Foundation under Grants SES-8520247, SES-8721283, and SES-9009546.

1

who have the opportunity to collaborate for mutual benefit in more than one way."
More explicitly, in Nash's definition bargaining has two characteristics:

1. There is a status quo or "threat point" (cf. Nash [9]).

2. In addition to the status quo, there are alternative agreements or outcomes, all Pareto-superior to the status quo.

This definition seems to include all voluntary agreements and is broader than the dictionary definition.

Of course "bargaining" in the present book means something a good deal narrower than what is defined by characteristics 1 and 2 above. In almost all the chapters:

3. Outcomes are reallocations of goods and money.

4. Some or all of the traders have incomplete information about each other's values and costs (i.e., about each other's preferences or the nature of what is being traded).

5. There is transferable utility.

6. Behavior is noncooperative within a given set of rules governing the process of negotiation.

Characteristic 6 implies that all chapters within this book fall within what has become known as the "Nash program" (after Nash's paper [9]). This program suggests that the proper way to understand bargaining outcomes is to model various rules for bargaining as noncooperative games and solve for the corresponding equilibria. Several groups of questions then arise:

1. Does an equilibrium exist? Is it unique, or are there at least only finitely many? Do the equilibria change continuously with the parameters of the model, at least for most values?

2. Can these equilibria be interpreted, at least in some approximate or qualitative sense, as describing observed bargaining behavior, either in laboratory experiments or in the field?

3. What are the welfare (efficiency) properties of these equilibrium outcomes, and how do these welfare properties depend on the rules under which the bargaining is carried out and on the distribution of information?

The chapters included here cannot claim, individually and collectively, to solve all the theoretical problems that bargaining (even in the narrow sense) poses, but they do illuminate aspects of the problem that heretofore have been poorly understood and that further theoretical progress will have to acknowledge and deal with. In this Introduction we seek to give a short description of each chapter's main contribution. In addition to this, we attempt informally to cross-reference the chapters with respect to (i) the underlying model used, (ii) the specific questions asked, and (iii) the strength of the results obtained. Our hope is that this will help the reader to integrate the individual chapters into his or her theoretical understanding of bargaining in simple economic situations.

A BASIC MODEL, INDIVIDUAL RATIONALITY, INCENTIVE CONSTRAINTS, AND THREE MECHANISMS

The model that underlies the majority of the chapters is of a particular bilateral bargaining situation. The seller has a single object that he may sell to the buyer if an acceptable price, p, is agreed upon. The seller's reservation value for the object is C and the buyer's reservation value is V. If trade occurs without delay, then the gains from trade are $p - C$ and $V - p$ for the seller and buyer, respectively. If negotiations fail, then neither party incurs any cost and the gain for each is zero. More generally, if the traders incur a delay of t units of time before agreeing to trade, then their gains from trade are respectively $e^{-\delta t}(p - C)$ and $e^{-\delta t}(V - p)$, where δ is the traders' discount rate, the same for both.

Incomplete information may exist in this situation. It is modeled as follows. Each trader's reservation value is a random variable whose value is in some interval, e.g., $[0, 1]$. C and V are independently drawn from the distributions F and G, respectively.[1] The distributions F and G are common knowledge to the traders. If the incompleteness of information is two-sided, then the realization of C is private to the seller and the realization of V is private to the buyer. For one-sided incomplete information, the value C or V (but not both) is common knowledge to both seller and buyer. For the certainty case, both C and V are common knowledge. The majority of the book's chapters concern two-sided uncertainty.

A trading mechanism is a set of rules that governs the process of trade. Several mechanisms are considered in the chapters. The sealed-bid double auction is the simplest of these mechanisms. Its rules are that simultaneously the seller submits an offer c and the buyer submits a bid v. Trade occurs with no delay at price $(c + v)/2$ if $v \geq c$; if $v < c$, then negotiations are broken off.[2] Given this mechanism, a pure strategy for the seller is a function $S(\cdot)$ that specifies an offer $c = S(C)$ for each of his possible reservation values. Likewise $B(\cdot)$ is a strategy for the buyer. A pair of strategies (S, B) is an equilibrium if B is a best response to S and S is a best response to B. S is a best response to B if, conditional on the seller's knowledge of the distribution of G, the strategy B, and the realization of C, $S(C)$ maximizes his expected gain from trade for each value of C.

The best known example of an equilibrium for the double auction with two-sided incomplete information is the linear equilibrium that Chatterjee and Samu-

---

[1] More generally, C and V could be statistically dependent.

[2] More generally, in the sealed-bid double auction the price is set at $kc + (1 - k)v$, where k, a number between zero and one, is a parameter of the mechanism.

elson (Chapter 2) constructed. Their paper was the first exploration of the nature of equilibria in the double auction and established properties that all equilibria must satisfy. In the example they constructed, F and G are each the uniform distribution on [0, 1] and, on the region where trade takes place, $S(C) = \frac{2}{3}C + \frac{1}{4}$ and $B(V) = \frac{2}{3}V + \frac{1}{12}$. Direct calculation shows that each trader's *ex ante* expected gain from trade in this equilibrium (the C-S equilibrium henceforth) is 0.0703, i.e., before his reservation value is drawn from [0, 1], 0.0703 is his expected gain, given that both he and his bargaining partner play the linear C-S strategies. It is easy to verify that trade occurs ($c \leq v$) if and only if $C + \frac{1}{4} \leq V$.

Ex post efficiency requires that the bargaining process result in trade if and only if $V \geq C$, i.e., it requires that bargaining exhaust all available gains from trade.[3] Clearly the C-S equilibrium is not *ex post* efficient because some available gains from trade will be lost whenever $C \leq V < C + \frac{1}{4}$, an event with probability $\frac{7}{32}$. Myerson and Satterthwaite (Chapter 3) showed that this type of inefficiency is necessary. Specifically, for two-sided incomplete information, they proved that if a particular equilibrium of a given mechanism satisfies interim individual rationality (interim IR hereafter), then its equilibrium allocations cannot always be *ex post* efficient.[4] An equilibrium of a mechanism is interim IR for a trader if, after he learns the realization of his reservation value and before he begins bargaining, his expected gain from trade is nonnegative for each of his possible reservation values. This expected gain, conditional on his reservation value, is called his interim expected utility.

Interim IR captures the idea that bargaining is a voluntary activity; if it holds, then each trader wants to participate no matter what the realization of his reservation value. Note that in the double auction each trader can guarantee interim IR for himself by choosing his strategy such that $v \leq V$ if he is a buyer and $c \geq C$ if he is a seller. In fact, this guarantees a strong form of IR, *ex post* IR, because such a strategy ensures that his realized gain from trade is either zero or positive.[5] Interim IR only guarantees nonnegative gains in expectation. Of the two conditions, *ex post* IR is the more desirable for a mechanism to satisfy because it, unlike interim IR, never gives a trader an incentive to renege on carrying out a trade or payment that the mechanism prescribes.

---

[3] Our nomenclature for different forms of efficiency does not quite match that of Holmstrom and Myerson [6]. Our *ex post* efficiency is their *ex post* classical efficiency, our *ex ante* efficiency (see below) is their *ex ante* incentive efficiency, and our interim efficiency (again see below) is their interim incentive efficiency.

[4] This result depends critically on the nature of the underlying uncertainty. The hypothesis Myerson and Satterthwaite employ is that F has a positive probability density over the interval $[a_1, b_1]$, G has a positive probability density over $[a_2, b_2]$, and the interiors of the two intervals have a nonempty intersection.

[5] *Ex ante* IR can also be defined. It requires that each trader's expected utility, before his reservation value is revealed to him, be nonnegative. D'Aspremont and Gerard-Varet [4] showed that if a mechanism is required only to satisfy *ex ante* IR instead of interim IR, then achievement of *ex post* efficiency can be guaranteed.

Gresik (Chapters 4 and 5) explored the extent that *ex post* IR is more restrictive than interim IR in bargaining situations. Define a trader's type to be his reservation value. Given a mechanism m and pair of equilibrium strategies e for m, let $u_S(m, e|C)$ be the interim expected utility of a type C seller, $u_B(m, e|V)$ be the interim expected utility of a type V buyer, $u_S(m, e|C, V)$ be the realized utility (i.e., *ex post* utility) of a type C seller who is matched with a type V buyer, etc. Gresik proved and illustrated that, for commonly considered pairs of prior distributions (F, G), if the pair (m, e) is interim IR, then a mechanism m' and equilibrium e' for m' exist such that (i) the pair (m', e') is *ex post* IR and (ii) the interim expected utilities (m, e) yields are identical to the interim expected utilities (m', e') yields. More precisely, if (m, e) is interim IR, then a (m', e') exists such that, for all pairs (C, V), (i) both $u_S(m', e'|C, V) \geq 0$ and $u_B(m', e'|C, V) \geq 0$ and (ii) $u_S(m, e|C) = u_S(m', e'|C)$ and $u_B(m, e|V) = u_B(m', e'|V)$.

Myerson and Satterthwaite's result that *ex post* efficiency cannot be guaranteed by any interim IR mechanism in situations of two-sided uncertainty follows from the fact that each trader's reservation value is private. Conditional on his private reservation value and the other trader's strategy, a trader can (and presumably will) select whatever action maximizes his expected utility. This selected action may not be the action that satisfies some notion of efficiency. Generally, a central planner or other authority is powerless to compel the trader to select the efficient choice. The reason is that the efficient choice of actions generally depends on all the traders' reservation values. These values are private and inaccessible to the planner, making it impossible for him — no matter what his powers for coercion — to guarantee an efficient outcome. This inability to force traders to behave in any other way than a maximizing way is called the incentive constraint (IC). By definition, all equilibrium outcomes necessarily satisfy it.

IC's bite can be seen in the double auction. *Ex post* efficiency would be achieved if traders would truthfully announce their reservation values. In equilibrium, of course, a trader does shade his offer/bid upward if he is a seller (downward if a buyer) because the favorable effect on the price more than offsets the unfavorable effect on the probability that a profitable trade will be foregone. This shading of offers/bids so that $C < c$ and $V > v$ is what produces *ex post* inefficient outcomes.

Since IC and interim (or, equivalently, *ex post*) IR together may make *ex post* efficiency unachievable, two alternative standards considered in some of the chapters are *ex ante* efficiency and interim efficiency. If m is a mechanism and e is a pair of equilibrium strategies for m, then the pair (m, e) is *ex ante* efficient if no other pair (m', e') gives both traders at least as great *ex ante* gains from trade and one trader a greater *ex ante* expected gain. For example, Myerson and Satterthwaite showed that if F and G are each the uniform distribution on $[0, 1]$, then the C-S equilibrium for the double auction is *ex ante* efficient. Specifically, no mechanism and equilibrium exist that give one trader an *ex ante* expected gain greater than 0.0703 while giving the other an *ex ante* expected gain of at least 0.0703. If *ex post* efficiency were achievable, then each trader's *ex ante* expected gains would be

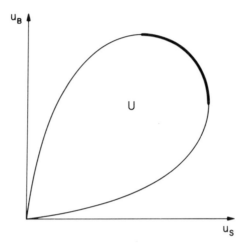

FIG. 1. U is the set of allocations of *ex ante* utility that are attainable in equilibrium. The upper right frontier (drawn as a heavy line) is the set of *ex ante* efficient allocations.

0.0833; the difference of 0.0130 represents the cost that IC and interim IR impose on the traders.

Figure 1 illustrates the concept of *ex ante* efficiency. Let $u_S(m, e)$ and $u_B(m, e)$ represent the *ex ante* expected gains from trade (utilities) that equilibrium e of mechanism m produces for the seller and buyer respectively. For a given preference and information structure, the set U in the figure is the set of utility pairs that satisfy both interim IR and IC. In other words, as IC requires, for each point (u_S, u_B) in U a mechanism m and an equilibrium e exist such that $(u_S(m, e), u_B(m, e)) = (u_S, u_B)$ and, as interim IR requires, $u_S \geq 0$ and $u_B \geq 0$. The upper right frontier of U is the set of *ex ante* efficient allocations. The C-S equilibrium generates a point on that frontier.

Interim efficiency is a somewhat weaker form of efficiency.[6] The mechanism–equilibrium pair (m, e) is interim efficient if no other pair (m', e') exists such that,

1. for all C, $u_S(m', e'|C) \geq u_S(m, e|C)$,

2. for all V, $u_B(m', e'|V) \geq u_B(m, e|V)$; and

3. for some C or V, either $u_S(m', e'|C) > u_S(m, e|C)$ or $u_B(m', e'|V) > u_B(m, e|V)$.

In essence, interim efficiency applies the Pareto criterion to each type of buyer and seller, while *ex ante* efficiency applies it averaged across all types of buyers and all types of sellers. This distinction will arise again below.

_____

[6]Holmstrom and Myerson [6] observe that *ex ante* efficiency implies interim efficiency, but not the reverse. Neither *ex ante* efficiency nor interim efficiency imply *ex post* efficiency.

Two mechanisms besides the double auction receive substantial attention in this book. The first is sequential bargaining, as studied by Rubinstein [10] for the full information case. In sequential bargaining traders follow a predetermined order in making offers back and forth until one or the other accepts an offer and bargaining terminates. To be more specific, suppose uncertainty is two-sided. In seller's-offer sequential bargaining, the seller makes an offer that the buyer can accept or reject. If the buyer accepts, trade occurs. If the buyer rejects, the seller makes another offer after a given delay. This process continues until either the traders reach agreement or they become convinced that no gains from trade exist and negotiations cease. (In the abstract model it is also possible for bargaining to continue without end.) If trade occurs after a delay of t units of time, then each trader's gain is discounted by $e^{-\delta t}$.

Strategies for this game are quite complicated. The buyer's strategy is an infinite sequence of functions $(B_1(h_1, V), B_2(h_2, V), B_3(h_3, V), \ldots)$ whose ranges are the set (accept, reject, break off) and whose arguments are h_j, the history of the seller's first j offers, and V, his reservation value. The seller's strategy is also an infinite sequence of functions $(S_1(C), S_2(C, h_1), S_3(C, h_2), \ldots)$ that specifies the series of price offers he will make to the buyer as a function of his reservation value and his previous offers. The equilibrium concept for sequential bargaining is a modification of Kreps and Wilson's sequential equilibrium [5] that accommodates the infinite nature of sequential bargaining games. It requires traders to exhibit sequential rationality in their choices of strategies and to update their beliefs concerning their trading partner's reservation value using Bayes's rule whenever possible.

Sequential bargaining is attractive to study for two reasons. First, casual observation suggests that it resembles methods commonly used in practice. Second, sequential bargaining exhibits sequential rationality in a way that a one-shot mechanism such as the double auction does not. In particular, consider again the linear C-S equilibrium. If $C = \frac{3}{8}$ and $V = \frac{1}{2}$ (trade should occur), then $c = \frac{1}{2}$ and $v = \frac{5}{12}$ (trade does not occur). Because the C-S strategies are invertible, it is common knowledge between the buyer and seller after they fail to trade that some unrealized gains from trade exist (provided each learns the other's bid). They therefore have an incentive, contrary to the rules of the double auction, to engage in another round of bargaining. Consequently, if bargaining is regarded as a voluntary activity, the double auction rule that bargaining is restricted to a single offer/bid pair lacks credibility.

If additional rounds of bargaining were permitted in the double auction, making it into another variety of sequential bargaining, then *ex post* efficiency would not be achieved in the second round. The reason is that the traders would anticipate that additional rounds are available and would no longer play the C-S linear strategies in the first round. In fact, generally they would play strategies in the first round that are not fully invertible. If they did play invertible strategies, then their reservation values would be revealed and an equilibrium in round two would exist that realizes all available gains from trade. If the time period between rounds were sufficiently short, then the delay would be trivial and this outcome would be essentially *ex post* efficient. In particular, each trader's *ex ante* expected gain from trade would be almost 0.0833. This, however, is impossible because such a result would violate Myerson and Satterthwaite's result that the C-S equilibrium, which gives each trader an *ex ante* expected gain of 0.0703, is *ex ante* efficient. (Their result applies to sequential bargaining as well as to the double auction.) In sequential bargaining the cost associated with interim IR and IC shows up as delay in trading, not as failure to trade.

The third type of mechanism that appears in several of the chapters is the optimal revelation mechanism, as introduced into bargaining theory by Myerson and Satterthwaite. Given distributions F and G, an optimal mechanism is one that satisfies IC and interim IR and is designed to be *ex ante* efficient. In a revelation mechanism each trader submits his cost C or value V as his offer/bid. Since traders' costs/values are private, every trader has the choice of making either a truthful or misrepresented report. As a function of the costs and values that the traders report, the mechanism specifies whether trade occurs and what payment the buyer should make to the seller. If it specifies no trade, negotiations are terminated.

Let r denote a revelation mechanism and t denote the pair of strategies in which the players' bids/offers are equal to their reservation values, i.e., the strategy pair t specifies that each trader truthfully reveal his reservation value. Suppose that, given the distributions F and G, t is an equilibrium for r. Then r is an optimal revelation mechanism if the pair (r, t) satisfies both *ex ante* efficiency and interim IR. It follows from the Revelation Principle that, if any pair (m, e) exists that is *ex ante* efficient, then an optimal revelation mechanism exists that gives each trader the same interim expected utility as does (m, e).[7] Optimal revelation mechanisms are analytically useful because they delineate the limits of achievable performance within a particular setting. As a set of rules for conducting actual bargaining they are not useful because an optimal mechanism's rules change as the underlying distributions F and G vary. The rules that are actually used in a realistic bargaining situation generally do not vary with the priors of the participants.

This discussion should make Table 1 understandable. It outlines the most salient aspects of the models used in the chapters contained in this volume. Inspection of the table shows that they can be classified without too much arbitrariness into four main groups. The first set of chapters investigates the nature of equilibria for the bilateral sealed-bid double auction. Issues of existence, multiplicity, and efficiency of equilibria are considered. Chapters by Broman; Chatterjee and Samuelson; Gresik; Leininger, Linhart, and Radner; Linhart and Radner; Myerson and Sat-

---

[7]The Revelation Principle states that for every mechanism–equilibrium pair (m, e) there exists a mechanism r for which the strategy t of truth telling is an equilibrium, and for which the pair (r, t) results in payoffs to each trader identical to those resulting from (m, e). See Myerson [7] for a complete statement and discussion.

terthwaite; Radner and Schotter; and Satterthwaite and Williams constitute this group. The second set of chapters focuses on equilibrium within bilateral sequential bargaining situations. This set includes chapters by Admati and Perry; Ausubel and Deneckere; Gul, Sonnenschein, and Wilson; Rubinstein; and Vincent.

The third set of chapters explores the effects of preplay communication. Preplay communication is nonbinding conversation between the traders that occurs before any of them takes any payoff-relevant action. It is inconsequential in the real sense that it has no direct costs or benefits to the traders. Yet, as the chapters show, it can increase the set of equilibria that exists for a particular bargaining situation and, paradoxically, it can play a role in selecting among a multiplicity of possible equilibria. The chapters by Farrell and Gibbons, Matthews and Postlewaite, and Myerson are in this group. The fourth set consists of chapters by Gresik and Satterthwaite; Rob; and Satterthwaite and Williams. These three chapters investigate the effect that increasing the number of agents from two to many has on the efficiency of equilibria.

BILATERAL SEALED-BID DOUBLE AUCTION

Chatterjee and Samuelson (Chapter 2) and Myerson and Satterthwaite (Chapter 3) are discussed above. This section discusses the five remaining chapters whose focus is primarily the bilateral sealed-bid double auction. The first three of them are negative in their implications: an extraordinary number of equilibria exists, almost none of which can be guaranteed to have attractive efficiency properties. The final two are more positive and indicate that the multiplicity problem may not in fact be as severe as Bayesian theory implies.

Leininger, Linhart, and Radner (Chapter 6) explore the variety of equilibria that can occur in the double auction with two-sided incomplete information. They first consider equilibria in which the strategies $S(\cdot)$ and $B(\cdot)$ are differentiable and symmetric and show that a one-parameter continuum of such equilibria exists whenever the (F, G) pair belongs to a parametric class of distributions that includes the uniform. For the case of uniform F and G, these equilibria range in performance from the *ex ante* efficiency of the C-S linear equilibria to the complete inefficiency of no trade. They also show that if $S(\cdot)$ and $B(\cdot)$ are permitted to be step functions, then a similarly large family of step-function equilibria exists. In fact, each equilibrium that has differentiable strategies can be approximated arbitrarily closely by step-function equilibria.

Satterthwaite and Williams (Chapter 7) also investigate the multiplicity of differentiable equilibria for the bilateral double auction, though without any assumption of symmetry. They show that, for any (F, G) pair from a broad class of distributions, a two-parameter continuum of differentiable equilibria exists. Their geometric representation of this two-parameter family illustrates the broad range

TABLE 1. Structure of the Models

Chapter	Mechanism	Preferences	Information
2. Chatterjee & Samuelson	Double auction	Reservation values drawn independently from F and G on [0, 1]. Special attention given to uniform case.	Buyer's and seller's values are private. F and G are common knowledge.
3. Myerson & Satterthwaite	Optimal revelation mechanism	Reservation values drawn independently from F and G on [0, 1].	Buyer's and seller's values are private. F and G are common knowledge.
4. Gresik	Optimal revelation mechanism	Reservation values drawn independently from F and G on [0, 1].	Buyer's and seller's values are private. F and G are common knowledge.
5. Gresik	Optimal revelation mechanism	Reservation values drawn independently from F and G on [0, 1].	Buyer's and seller's values are private. F and G are common knowledge.
6. Leininger, Linhart, & Radner	Double auction	Reservation values drawn independently from F and G on [0, 1]. Special attention given to uniform case.	Buyer's and seller's values are private. F and G are common knowledge.
7. Satterthwaite & Williams	Double auction	Reservation values drawn independently from F and G on [0, 1].	Buyer's and seller's values are private. F and G are common knowledge.
8. Broman	Double auction	Reservation values drawn independently from F and G on [0, 1]. Both F and G are permitted to be degenerate, with all their mass at 0 and 1 respectively.	Buyer's and seller's values are private. F and G are common knowledge.
9. Radner & Schotter	Double auction; experimental study	Reservation values drawn independently from F and G on [0, 1].	Buyer's and seller's values are private. F and G are common knowledge.

10. Linhart & Radner	Double auction with multiple units and dimensions	Reservation values drawn independently from F and G on $[0, 1]$. Each trader minimizes his maximal regret where regret is the difference between his gains from trade actually realized and the gains that he could have realized with perfect foresight.	Buyer's and seller's values are private. F and G are common knowledge. Both F and G are permitted to be degenerate with all their mass at 0 and 1 respectively.
11. Rubinstein	Alternating offer sequential bargaining	Two players split a pie of size one. Player 1 has fixed discount factor. Player 2 has either high or low discount factor.	Player 1's discount value and probabilities of player 2's discount factor being high or low are common knowledge. Player 2's discount value is private.
12. Gul, Sonnenschein, & Wilson	Seller-offer sequential bargaining. Buyer's acceptance strategy depends only on his reservation value and the current offer. Time interval between offers approaches zero.	Seller has reservation value 0. Buyer has positive reservation value drawn from distribution G. Delay reduces gains from trade exponentially.	Seller's value, G, and discount rate are common knowledge. Buyer's value is private.
13. Ausubel & Deneckere	Seller-offer sequential bargaining. Time interval between offers approaches zero.	Seller has reservation value 0. Buyer has nonnegative reservation value drawn from distribution G. Delay reduces gains from trade exponentially.	Seller's value, G, and discount rate are common knowledge. Buyer's value is private.
14. Admati & Perry	Alternating offer sequential bargaining with a minimum time between bids/offers. A trader can delay in making a bid/offer beyond the minimum time if he desires.	Seller has reservation value 0. Buyer has positive reservation value that is either high or low. Delay reduces gains from trade exponentially.	Seller's value, probabilities of buyer's value being high or low, and discount rate are common knowledge. Buyer's value is private.

(continues)

11

TABLE 1 (*Continued*)

Chapter	Mechanism	Preferences	Information
15. Ausubel & Deneckere	Seller-offer, alternating offer, and buyer-offer sequential bargaining. Time interval between bids/offers approaches zero.	Seller has reservation value 0. Buyer value drawn from distribution G on $[0, 1]$. Delay reduces gains from trade exponentially.	Seller's value, G, and discount rate are common knowledge. Buyer's value is private.
16. Vincent	Buyer offer sequential bargaining	Buyer's value is $v(q)$ and seller's value is $f(q)$, where q is a uniform random variable and f and v are functions such that $v(q) - f(q) > 0$. Delay reduces gains from trade exponentially.	Seller's value is private. Functions v and f, uniformity of q, and discount rates are common knowledge. Buyer may be ignorant of his value.
17. Farrell & Gibbons	Double auction with restricted pre-play communication	Reservation values drawn independently from F and G on $[0, 1]$.	Buyer's and seller's values are private. F and G are common knowledge.
18. Matthews & Postlewaite	Double auction with unrestricted preplay communication	Reservation values drawn independently from F and G on $[0, 1]$.	Buyer's and seller's reservation values are private. F and G are common knowledge.

19. Myerson	General normal form incomplete information game in which one player is permitted preplay communication	General utility function whose arguments are the agent's type and the vector of actions taken.	Agents' types are private. Distribution of types and utility functions are common knowledge.
20. Gresik & Satterthwaite	Optimal mechanism with n sellers and n buyers	Reservation values drawn independently from F and G on $[0, 1]$.	Buyers' and sellers' reservation values are private. F and G are common knowledge.
21. Satterthwaite & Williams	Buyer's bid double auction with n sellers and n buyers	Reservation values drawn independently from F and G on $[0, 1]$.	Buyers' and sellers' reservation values are private. F and G are common knowledge.
22. Rob	Optimal mechanism for a single firm planning to build a polluting plant and its n neighbors	Firm's profits from building and operating the plant are R. The cost imposed on each neighbor is drawn independently from distribution F on $[0, 1]$.	The firm's profits and the distribution F are common knowledge. Each neighbor's pollution costs are private.

of performance that is possible with smooth equilibria. They then investigate the efficiency of these equilibria and show that, for a generic (F, G) pair, no equilibrium exists that is *ex ante* efficient. In other words, if for some (F, G) pair an *ex ante* efficient equilibrium of the double auction happens to exist, then for almost any distribution pair $(F_\varepsilon, G_\varepsilon)$ no *ex ante* efficient equilibrium exists, where $(F_\varepsilon, G_\varepsilon)$ is an arbitrary perturbation of (F, G). This directly implies that for uniform (F, G) the *ex ante* efficiency of the linear C-S equilibrium is a special, knife-edge case. On a more positive note, they also show that the interim efficiency of the C-S equilibrium when (F, G) are uniform is not a knife-edge case, thus establishing that the double auction is not generically interim inefficient.

Broman (Chapter 8) is concerned with the behavior of the equilibrium set of the two-sided incomplete information double auction as the pair (F, G) of distributions approach certainty. Specifically, suppose a sequence of distribution pairs (F_k, G_k) converge to $(\bar{F}, \bar{G})$, the certainty case, in which $\bar{F}$'s mass is concentrated on 0 and $\bar{G}$'s mass is concentrated on 1. She first shows that, for $(\bar{F}, \bar{G})$ and any finite set $\{a_1, \ldots, a_n\}$ such that $0 < a_1 < \ldots < a_n < 1$, a mixed strategy equilibrium exists whose support is $\{a_1, \ldots, a_n\}$. She then shows that a sequence of equilibria corresponding to the sequence (F_k, G_k) exists that converges to the certainty equilibrium with support $\{a_1, \ldots, a_n\}$.

Radner and Schotter (Chapter 9) report on an experimental study that used students to explore the empirical properties of the double auction with two-sided incomplete information. The (F, G) pair for each experiment was picked so that a linear equilibrium with good efficiency properties can be found among the continuum of equilibria that exist. The results they obtained stand in contrast to the theoretical results reported just above. Rather than observing a great variety of different equilibria with widely varying efficiency properties, the experimental results show a strong tendency for the students to play linear strategies that attain reasonably efficient performance. The strategies sellers tended to use were close to the linear equilibrium strategies. The buyers, however, tended not to shave their bids under their reservation values as much as the linear equilibrium predicts they should.

Linhart and Radner's chapter (Chapter 10) on minimax regret and the double auction can be seen as seeking a way out of the difficulty posed by the multiplicity of equilibria in the double auction with incomplete information. Regret is defined to be the difference between (i) the gain from trade that a trader would have realized if he had known before the fact what the other trader was going to bid, and (ii) the gain he actually realized. Linhart and Radner show that if a trader minimizes his maximum regret, conditional on his reservation value, then the resulting strategy is linear in his reservation value. Thus if both traders adopt the minimax regret criterion, then the multiplicity of "solutions" in the Bayesian–Nash equilibrium approach to analyzing double auctions is eliminated. Moreover, within a particular parametric class of distributions (F, G), the minimax strategies show reasonably good performance in terms of the *ex ante* expected gains from trade they realize.

SEQUENTIAL BARGAINING

Sequential bargaining, we argued above, is intuitively more attractive in bilateral situations than is the sealed-bid double auction because sequential bargaining does not require the buyer and seller to break off negotiations after they have revealed that gains from trade in fact exist. Sequential bargaining, however, is more difficult to analyze than the double auction because its strategies are much more complex and depend critically on the assumptions that are made about how each trader's beliefs about the other trader's preferences evolve as a function of the game's history. An indication of this difficulty is that all six chapters in this section concern one-sided uncertainty. Unlike the double auction chapters in the previous section that have incomplete information on both sides of the market, typically in these chapters the seller's reservation value C is common knowledge and only the buyer's value B is private. This simpler information structure means that Myerson and Satterthwaite's result concerning the necessity of *ex post* inefficiency does not hold; full *ex post* efficiency can be obtained by adopting the convention that price is always fixed equal to the seller's cost, which is common knowledge.

Rubinstein (Chapter 11) considers alternating-offer bargaining within a somewhat different model than those used in the other chapters within the book. The two players are bargaining over the division of a pie, i.e., they must agree on an $s \in$ [0, 1] that represents the proportion of the pie that player 1 receives. Player 2 receives $1 - s$ of the pie. Player 1 begins the bargaining by proposing an s. If player 2 rejects this offer, then he makes a counteroffer. This process continues until agreement is reached. Player i's preferences are represented by $u(x_i)(\delta_i)^t$, where u is a concave utility function, x_i is the player's share of the pie, $\delta_i \in (0, 1)$ is his discount factor, and t is the number of periods it takes to reach agreement. Incomplete information in this model exists only with respect to player 2's discount factor: he is either strong ($\delta_2 = \delta_s$) or weak ($\delta_2 = \delta_w$) where $\delta_s > \delta_w$. Note that if player 2 is strong (denoted by 2_s), then he is more patient (in the sense that delay is less costly) than if he were weak (2_w). Player 1's prior belief is that player two is 2_w with probability ω_0.

Rubinstein's main result is that if a plausible restriction is made on how player 1 updates his beliefs about player 2's type, then a unique sequential equilibrium exists to this game. When ω_0 is greater than some cutoff value ω^*, then the equilibrium involves player 1 offering $s = P_1$, player 2 accepting P_1 if he is 2_w, player 2 counteroffering $s = P_2 < P_1$ if he is 2_s, and player 1 accepting the counteroffer P_2. P_1 and P_2 are the equilibrium shares because they are the only two divisions of the pie such that:

(i) Player 1 is indifferent between "P_2 today" and the lottery of "P_1 tomorrow" with probability ω_0 and "P_2 after tomorrow" with probability $1 - \omega_0$;
(ii) Player 2_w is indifferent between "P_1 today" and "P_2 tomorrow." (Rubinstein, Chapter 11)

Note that player 2_s prefers "P_2 tomorrow" to "P_1 today." The uniqueness of this equilibrium depends critically on the following assumption on how player 1 revises his beliefs about player 2's type: if player 2 rejects some offer P_1 and counteroffers with P_2 where the offers are such that player 2_w prefers "P_1 today" to "P_2 tomorrow" and player 2_s prefers "P_2 tomorrow" to "P_1 today," then player 1 infers that player 2 is strong for certain.

Gul, Sonnenschein, and Wilson's chapter (Chapter 12) is ostensibly about dynamic monopoly, but as they point out (and is well known) the dynamic monopoly problem is formally equivalent to the standard seller-offer sequential bilateral bargaining problem with one-sided incomplete information. Thus the seller's reservation value C is commonly known to be zero, the buyer's private reservation value V is drawn from the distribution G, and the seller makes offers to the buyer until agreement is reached. They show that if (i) the exogenously given time between the seller's offers is short and (ii) the buyer's acceptance strategy is stationary in the sense that it is conditional only on his value V and the price that the seller is currently offering, then in all sequential equilibria to the game the seller's offers are always close to zero.

The seller would like to exploit his monopoly power as the price-setter by making the optimal take-it-or-leave-it offer P_M. Given such a strategy, the best response for a buyer with value V is to accept immediately if $V > P_M$ and to break-off negotiations if $V \leq P_M$. The seller, however, can not commit to a take-it-or-leave-it strategy. To see why this is so, suppose (contrary to the result) a sequential equilibrium did exist in which the seller maintained price at P_M. In the first period the seller offers the monopoly price P_M. If his offer is rejected, then that signals to him that $V \leq P_M$. Sequential rationality then implies that in period 2 the seller should deviate from the equilibrium by reducing his offer for the purpose of making the sale and securing some gains from trade. But this gives the buyer for whom $V > P_M$ an incentive to deviate from his equilibrium strategy of accepting P_M immediately: by rejecting P_M he causes the seller to reduce his price at the cost of a short delay. Unless the offer is already close to zero it always pays for the buyer to delay and force another reduction. Consequently the seller is better off to offer a low price starting right from period 1, i.e., the seller is unable to exert his potential monopoly power.

Gul, Sonnenschein, and Wilson's result, as the next two chapters show, is sensitive both to their requirement that strategies be stationary and to the details of the rules they specify for governing the bargaining. Ausubel and Deneckere (Chapter 13), who follow the former approach, adopt Gul, Sonnenschein, and Wilson's model unmodified with the exception of the requirement that strategies be stationary. Abandoning stationarity permits them to construct a reputational equilibrium in which the seller fully exercises his potential monopoly power. Specifically, the seller's equilibrium strategy is initially to make an offer at or near the monopoly price and then slowly to reduce this offer in subsequent periods if necessary. If the seller sticks to this equilibrium sequence of offers, then the buyer sets a cutoff value that is a function of his reservation value and accepts the first offer that is less than this cutoff value.

If, however, the seller deviates from his equilibrium sequence of slowly declining price offers, then he loses his reputation for being a tough bargainer, and the buyer revises his cutoff downward and only accepts offers that are near the seller's cost C. The seller, with his reputation lost, has little choice but to make an offer close enough to C that the buyer accepts it. This outcome punishes the seller for deviating: instead of receiving almost the monopoly price, the seller receives little more than C. Consequently the seller does not deviate. Note that the buyer's strategy here is nonstationary because his cutoff value is conditional on the seller's obedience to his own equilibrium strategy.

Admati and Perry (Chapter 14) make a plausible change in Gul, Sonnenschein, and Wilson's rules of bargaining and show a second way in which the seller can exert monopoly power. They consider the alternating-offer sequential bargaining problem in which the seller's reservation value is known and the buyer either has a high reservation value (V_h) or a low reservation value (V_l). The novel feature of the game is that a trader who has received an offer cannot counteroffer more quickly than one unit of time but can delay indefinitely before counteroffering. The possibility of delay means that if a buyer rejects the seller's initial offer P_M, then the buyer can use delay beyond the required one unit of time to show that his value is in fact $V_l < P_M$.

Admati and Perry show an equilibrium with just this behavior. The seller makes an original offer P_1. If the buyer's value is V_h he accepts immediately. Otherwise he delays for an additional time interval before making a counteroffer P_2, which the seller immediately accepts. The equilibrium works because delay is less costly for a buyer with value V_l than for a buyer with value V_h; i.e., a buyer with V_h prefers "P_1 now" to "P_2 with delay" while the buyer with V_l prefers "P_2 with delay" to "P_1 now."

Ausubel and Deneckere (Chapter 15) consider the standard bilateral sequential bargaining problem with one-sided uncertainty in which the seller's reservation value is commonly known to be zero and the buyer's value has distribution G on [0, 1]. For this problem they characterize the full set of equilibrium outcomes by using optimal-revelation-mechanism theory to define the feasible set of outcomes with which the outcomes of sequential bargaining can be compared. All sequential bargaining equilibria must satisfy *ex post* IR and IC. Specifically, let the interim expected utility of the seller be $u_S(m, e|C)$, which is identical to $u_S(m, e)$ because $C = 0$ with certainty, and let the interim expected utility of the buyer be $u_B(m, e|V)$. Let $W = \{(u_S(m, e), u_B(m, e)|\cdot): m$ and e satisfy IC and *ex post* IR$\}$. Clearly W contains all outcomes that sequential bargaining can generate.

Given this setup, Ausubel and Deneckere prove the following. If the sequential bargaining is structured as seller-offer sequential bargaining in which only the seller is permitted to make offers and if the time interval between offers is shrunk to zero, then W_{SO} is identical to W where $W_{SO} = \{(u_S(m, e), u_B(m, e|\cdot): m = $ seller-offer sequential bargaining and e is a sequential equilibrium}.[8] Thus any outcome that can be achieved by an *ex post* IR equilibrium of some arbitrary mechanism can also be achieved by seller-offer sequential bargaining. If the bargaining is structured as alternating offers, then W_{AO} is strictly contained in W where W_{AO}, analogous to W_{SO}, is the set of outcomes alternating-offer sequential bargaining generates. Finally, for buyer-offer sequential bargaining, W_{BO} is the set in W that awards all expected gains from trade to the buyer and no gains to the seller. These results demonstrate two things. First, the rules of bargaining shape the outcome of a negotiation and, more specifically, a trader's power to make offers is important in obtaining a favorable split of the gains from trade. Second, as with the sealed-bid double auction, a great multiplicity of equilibria exists in sequential bargaining.

Vincent (Chapter 16) studies the sequential bargaining mechanism within a different structure of preferences and information. The value the seller places on the object is a random variable and privately known to him. The buyer does not know his own reservation value; he only knows that the object is more valuable to him than to the seller (gains from trade are certain) and how his value is correlated with the seller's value. This, for instance, is the preference structure that a buyer of a used car may face, i.e., Vincent's setup includes Akerlof's famous "lemons" problem [1] as a particular case. If trade is to take place, as it should, the seller must convince the buyer how valuable the object is; otherwise the buyer may be unwilling to pay the seller's reservation value. Delay is the means available to the buyer to test what value the seller actually places on the object. Vincent shows that if the mechanism is buyer-offer sequential bargaining and the buyer is at least as patient as the seller, then a unique equilibrium exists and leads to trade occurring in finite time. For many correlated preference structures the equilibrium involves some, but not infinite, delay.

PREPLAY COMMUNICATION

Farrell and Gibbons (Chapter 17) develop an example of a sealed-bid double auction with two-sided uncertainty in which the rules are modified to allow each trader simultaneously to send a preliminary message of "keen" or "not keen" to the other before submitting his bid/offer. Both traders' reservation values are independently drawn from the uniform distribution on [0, 1]. Trade is then governed by the bilateral sealed-bid double auction. In the equilibrium Farrell and Gibbons construct, a buyer is keen if and only if his value V is greater than 0.795

---

[8]It should be emphasized that Ausubel and Deneckere look at the full set of sequential equilibria. They do not refine the set by putting conditions beyond Bayes's rule on how the seller makes inferences concerning the buyer's value and they do not restrict traders' acceptance/rejection strategies to be a function only of the current offer/bid price.

and a seller is keen if his cost C is less than 0.205. Conditional on which of the four possible pairs of messages is realized, each trader selects a strategy for making his bid/offer as a function of his reservation value.

Each strategy has the property (as it must since it is an equilibrium) that it is a best response to the strategy selected by the other. Thus, if both the buyer and seller say they are keen, then the seller's offer is conditional both on the buyer's value being distributed uniformly on [0.795, 1] and on the buyer using his "keen–keen" strategy. Farrell and Gibbons show that the resulting equilibrium is distinct from any equilibrium for the double auction without preplay communication. Thus preplay communication of a plausible sort expands the equilibrium set.

Matthews and Postlewaite (Chapter 18) demonstrate the degree to which preplay communication expands the equilibrium set within the double auction. Specifically, consider a game in which the buyer and seller, first, simultaneously exchange messages chosen from a sufficiently rich space and, second, play the sealed-bid double auction. They show that any allocation that satisfies two properties, *ex post* IR and IC*, is an equilibrium outcome of the game. IC* is a strengthening of IC; it together with the *ex post* IR condition can be thought of as giving each trader at the conclusion of the double auction the ability to enact the no-trade option rather than the trade prescribed by the auction's outcome. Matthews and Postlewaite show that this set of allocations satisfying *ex post* IR and IC* is very large in the sense that it does not exclude any allocations that are equilibrium outcomes of those specific trading mechanisms that have been studied in the literature. In fact, Gresik's result (Chapter 4) that *ex post* IR is no more restrictive than interim IR is applicable. Therefore, allowing preplay communication appears to expand the double auction's equilibrium set to include every equilibrium allocation of every individually rational mechanism.

Myerson (Chapter 19) seeks to turn the effect of preplay communication around by investigating how it can promote cooperation among rational traders. The idea is this: Suppose one trader, called the negotiator, is exogenously given the right to communicate with the other trader(s) through a mediator. The negotiator makes a statement that consists of three parts: an allegation that describes his private information (e.g., his reservation value), a promise that says how he intends to act, and a request that states how he wishes the other trader to act. Myerson analyzes conditions under which the negotiator's statement is credible. Clearly a necessary condition for credibility is that obeying the negotiator's request be in the other trader's best interests, if the negotiator in fact carries out his promise.

But, in addition, the negotiator's allegations about his own private information should be consistent with his promises and requests: given that his allegations are truthful, another set of promises and requests should not exist that would make him better off. Thus for the negotiator's statement to be credible it must be maximal in an appropriate sense. While Myerson does not prove that this analysis leads to a unique prescription for the statement the negotiator should make, he does sketch an argument that generically only finitely many statements are fully credible.

MULTIPLE TRADERS

Gresik and Satterthwaite (Chapter 20) examine the bargaining problem for a market composed of n buyers and n sellers. Each seller has an object that he is willing to sell if he receives a payment greater than his reservation value, and each buyer wishes to purchase an object if he makes a payment less than his reservation value. Each trader's reservation value is private; each seller's value is drawn from F, each buyer's value is drawn from G, and all draws are independent. *Ex post* efficiency could be achieved if reservation values were common knowledge by setting a market clearing price. Since this cannot be done, the bids and offers of the traders, who act strategically, must be used to set payments and decide who trades.

Gresik and Satterthwaite investigate the speed with which an optimal mechanism approaches *ex post* efficiency as n, the number of traders on each side of the market, increases. Recall that in the bilateral double auction case with uniform (F, G), the C-S equilibrium is optimal inasmuch as it is *ex ante* efficient. It is not *ex post* efficient, however, because under it a necessary condition for trade to occur is that $V - C > \frac{1}{4}$. The quantity $\frac{1}{4}$ is the "wedge" between the buyer and seller reservation values that causes the inefficiency. Gresik and Satterthwaite show that this wedge shrinks rapidly as n increases; its magnitude is at most $O((\ln n)^{1/2}/n)$. In other words as n becomes large, interim IR and IC, which are the source of the wedge, become less and less binding.

Satterthwaite and Williams (Chapter 21) further study the question of the rate of convergence to *ex post* efficiency as the number of traders on each side of the market increases. Rather than using optimal mechanism theory, they examine the convergence of a particular sealed-bid double auction, the buyer's bid double auction (BBDA). In their model, reservation values are generated as in Gresik and Satterthwaite (Chapter 20). The BBDA's rules are that all n buyers and n sellers simultaneously submit offers and bids. These offers/bids determine a closed interval in which a market clearing price can be selected; the BBDA selects the highest price in this interval. Trade then occurs between those buyers whose bids are at least as great as the price and those sellers whose offers are strictly less than the price. These rules imply that each seller has a dominant strategy of submitting an offer c equal to his reservation value C and each buyer has an incentive to submit a bid v that is strictly less than his value V. Satterthwaite and Williams show that for this game all equilibrium strategies $B(\cdot)$ have the property that $V - B(V)$ is $O(1/n)$. The difference $V - B(V)$ is the amount by which buyers misrepresent their values when they bid; when strictly positive it is the wedge that causes *ex post* inefficiency. The rate $O(1/n)$ is quite fast (it improves on the lower bound that Gresik and Satterthwaite identified for an optimal mechanism's rate), which means that the BBDA converges rapidly to full efficiency as n grows.

Rob (Chapter 22) addresses much the same question, but does it in the context of public rather than private goods. He considers a model in which a manufacturing plant, if it is allowed to operate, will earn profits R. It will, however, damage each of its n neighbors through pollution. The damage to neighbor i is C_i, where each

C_i is independently drawn from a distribution F. Knowledge of the cost C_i is private to neighbor i. *Ex post* efficiency requires that the plant be allowed to operate if and only if $\Sigma_i C_i < R$. This, however, is not directly observable and the decision must be made on the basis of the neighbors' self-reports of their individual costs.

Rob constructs an optimal revelation mechanism for eliciting this information. It maximizes the firm's *ex ante* expected profit subject to the interim IR and IC constraints. He shows that as the number of neighbors increases the performance of this mechanism worsens, i.e., it deviates increasingly from realizing *ex post* efficiency. This result indicates that Coase's famous argument [3] that bargaining can resolve problems of externalities is dependent both on the structure of available information and on the number of agents involved. When compared with Gresik and Satterthwaite's result, it confirms the old intuition that increasing the number of agents improves performance when private goods are involved and worsens performance when public goods are involved.

An interesting sidelight is that a modified form of Rob's public goods problem is exactly the same mathematically as the bilateral sealed-bid double auction. A bridge, of unit cost, is to be built if and only if two parties are willing to finance it. Party i ($i = 1, 2$) submits a sealed offer to pay amount a_i toward the construction. The bridge will be built if and only if $\Sigma_i a_i \geq 1$. If it is built, the excess, $\Sigma_i a_i - 1$, is split in two and returned to the contributors.

It is easy to see that this scheme is mathematically equivalent to the double auction; a mapping between them is:

$$v \sim a_1,$$
$$c \sim 1 - a_2.$$

This formal identity between the private goods problem and the public goods problem breaks down if the number of parties is increased beyond two. The reason is that in the public goods case nonexcludability implies that unanimity among the parties remains necessary. In the private goods case all traders need not agree on all trades; unanimity is necessary only in the case of a single buyer and a single seller. With two buyers and two sellers unanimity is not necessary; one of the buyers and one of the sellers can trade and exclude the other two parties.

CONCLUSION

Substantial progress has been made technically in analyzing bargaining situations within the Bayesian–Nash equilibrium framework. This work, however, has created somewhat of an impasse: the theory permits an extremely wide range of behavior,[9] while the scanty empirical evidence suggests that regularities do exist.

---

[9]The generalization that the theory permits a wide range of behavior breaks down in some situations when one party (e.g., the seller) has a passive role that only involves accepting or rejecting the other party's proposals. See, for example, Satterthwaite and Williams' analysis (Chapter 5) of sealed-bid double auctions in which only the buyer has any influence on price.

The chapters in this book suggest three directions that may be productive avenues for breaking the impasse. First, Linhart and Radner (Chapter 10) demonstrate that approaches other than Bayesian–Nash equilibrium may be more fruitful in generating theory that rules out enough possible behavior so as to be testable (i.e., refutable). Second, Myerson (Chapter 19) suggests that a full understanding of preplay communication may allow successful selection among the plethora of equilibria that exist in bargaining problems. Third, Gresik and Satterthwaite (Chapter 20) and Williams and Satterthwaite (Chapter 21) suggest that embedding individual bargaining situations within a larger market context may greatly restrict equilibrium behavior in all types of bargaining by effectively making the market large.

REFERENCES

1. G. AKERLOF, The market for lemons: Qualitative uncertainty and the market mechanism. *Quart. J. Econ.* **84** (1970), 488–500.

2. *American Heritage Dictionary of the English Language*, Houghton Mifflin, New York, 1973.

3. R. COASE, The problem of social cost, *J. Law Econ.* **3** (1960), 1–44.

4. C. D'ASPREMONT AND L. GERARD-VARET, Incentives and incomplete information, *J. Public Econ.* **11** (1979), 25–45.

5. D. KREPS AND R. WILSON, Sequential equilibria, *Econometrica* **50** (1982), 863–894.

6. B. HOLMSTROM AND R. MYERSON, Efficient and durable decision rules with incomplete information, *J. Econ. Theory* **58** (1983), 1799–1820.

7. R. MYERSON, Incentive compatibility and the bargaining problem, *Econometrica* **47** (1979), 61–73.

8. J. NASH, The bargaining problem, *Econometrica* **18** (1950), 155–162.

9. J. NASH, Two-person cooperative games, *Econometrica* **21** (1953), 128–140.

10. A. RUBINSTEIN, Perfect equilibrium in a bargaining model, *Econometrica* **50** (1982), 411–426.

CP , D42
D83,
D82   23 - 39

[1983]

Bargaining under Incomplete Information

KALYAN CHATTERJEE

Pennsylvania State University, University Park, Pennsylvania

WILLIAM SAMUELSON

Boston University, Boston, Massachusetts

(Received July 1981; revised April 1982; accepted April 1983)

This paper presents and analyzes a bargaining model of bilateral monopoly under uncertainty. Under the bargaining rule proposed, the buyer and the seller each submit sealed offers that determine whether the good in question is sold and the transfer price. The Nash equilibrium solution of this bargaining game implies an offer strategy of each party that is monotonic in its own reservation price and depends on its assessment of the opponent's reservation price. Issues of relative bargaining advantage and efficiency are examined for a number of special cases. Finally, we discuss the appropriateness of the Nash solution concept.

THIS PAPER presents a simple model of two-person bargaining under incomplete information. Applications of the model range from the settlement of a claim out of court, to union-management negotiations, to the purchase and sale of a used automobile. The common feature shared by these examples is that each bargainer, while certain of the potential value it places on the transaction, has only probabilistic information concerning the potential value of the other. For instance, in haggling over the price of a used car, neither buyer nor seller knows the other's walk-away price.

Our principal aim is to investigate equilibrium bargaining behavior under uncertainty and to study how the parties fare, individually and collectively, under a simple class of bargaining procedures. A main result is that, given incomplete information, not all mutually beneficial agreements can be attained via bargaining. Even when the buyer values the good more highly than the seller, a successful sale may be impossible. Additionally, we present a number of results characterizing the players' optimal bargaining strategies and give explicit solutions for a number of examples. These examples provide useful comparative statics results—indicating the effect on bargaining behavior of changes in the negotiation

Subject classification: 231 bargaining, 232 bargaining.

23

ground rules, the information available to the players, and the degree of the players' risk aversion.

Complete vs. Incomplete Information. Most game-theoretic literature on bargaining has assumed that the participants possess complete information about the negotiation situation. Important contributions are provided by Nash [1950], Harsanyi [1956], Schelling [1960], Cross [1969], and Roth [1979]. Young [1975] provides an excellent summary and critique of the most important literature on the bargaining problem. In two-person bargains (to which our discussion will be limited), it is customary to stipulate that the set of possible actions of the parties and the player payoffs from any combination of actions are common knowledge. In the model of bilateral monopoly considered here, with the presumption of complete information, each bargainer, seller and buyer, knows the other's walk-away price. Then the bargainers negotiate a final price in the known range of mutually acceptable prices (i.e. between the seller's minimum and the buyer's maximum acceptable prices). Since any price in this range can be supported as an equilibrium outcome, bargaining solutions are usually determined either by specifying a concession mechanism leading to a distinct outcome, or a set of axioms that a "reasonable" outcome should satisfy.

Despite its many insights, the complete information approach fails to mirror key features of actual negotiations: 1) the fact that each bargainer is uncertain about its adversary's payoff, and 2) the occurrence of "unreasonable" bargaining outcomes—breakdowns in negotiations, strikes, and work stoppages—when mutually beneficial agreements are possible. A bargaining model that embraces these features carries a number of noteworthy implications. First, each party's bargaining strategy will depend directly on the information it possesses about his adversary's possible payoffs. For instance, as shown in later examples, the more optimistic a player's assessment of his opponent's stake in the negotiation, the more aggressive it can afford to be when bargaining. Second, as has been recently noted by Samuelson [1980] and Crawford [1982], the employment of optimal bargaining strategies may result in the breakdown of negotiations altogether—this despite the fact that a mutually beneficial agreement may exist ex post. Bargaining under uncertainty will, in general, fail to be Pareto efficient.

The present paper examines these issues by modeling bargaining as a game of incomplete information following the pioneering approach of Harsanyi [1967–1968]. The application of these ideas to the bargaining problem is found in Harsanyi and Selten [1972]. Like Harsanyi and Selten, we frame the bargaining situation as a noncooperative game and focus on the resulting set of equilibrium outcomes. In other respects, however, our methods differ. First, we substitute a single stage bargaining procedure for the multistage representation of Harsanyi and Selten. Acting independently and without prior communication, the bargainers submit price offers. If these offers are compatible (in a sense to be defined later), a transaction is concluded at a price that depends on the offers; if they are not, then no transaction takes place. Though abstracting from the dynamics of the negotiation process, the single stage bargaining procedure emphasizes the basic strategy trade-off faced by each player. By making a more aggressive price offer, a player earns a greater profit in the event of an agreement but, at the same time, increases the risk of a disagreement (i.e. that his offer is unacceptable to the other).

Second, our approach employs continuous distributions to summarize the probability beliefs of the bargainers whereas Hansanyi and Selten focus on discrete distributions. Our aim is to investigate player bargaining strategies—that is, the mapping between the continuum of possible values that a player might hold and its price offers. The use of continuous distributions allows us to characterize a class of equilibria in which these bargaining strategies are well-behaved (i.e. differentiable). Additionally, the assumption facilitates the presentation of comparative statics results for specific examples.

Recently, a number of authors (Rosenthal [1978], Myerson [1979], and Myerson and Satterthwaite [1981] have examined the performance of arbitration procedures in the bargaining context. While our model offers predictions about the frequency of negotiation breakdown, bargaining efficiency, and relative bargaining advantage, our emphasis is on individual bargaining strategy and not on arbitration performance.

1. THE BASIC MODEL

Our analysis investigates bargaining behavior in the well-known case of bilateral monopoly. Suppose that a single seller of an indivisible good faces a single potential buyer. A successful bargain is concluded if and only if the good is transferred at a mutually acceptable price. Let v_s denote the seller's reservation price—the smallest monetary sum he will accept in exchange for the good (independent of his level of income). Similarly, let v_b denote the buyer's reservation price (the greatest sum he is willing to pay for the good). Since a bargain is struck only when it is agreeable to both parties, the sale price P must satisfy $v_s \leq P \leq v_b$ if such an interval exists.

Incomplete information of the bargainers is modeled by the following assumption: Each party knows his own reservation price, but is uncertain about his adversary's, assessing a subjective probability distribution over the range of possible values that his opponent might hold. Specifically, the buyer regards v_s as a random variable possessing a cumulative distribution function $F_b(v_s)$ satisfying $F_b(\underline{v}_s) = 0$ and $F_b(\bar{v}_s) = 1$, and which is strictly increasing and differentiable on $[\underline{v}_s, \bar{v}_s]$. The seller's knowledge of v_b is summarized by $F_s(v_b)$ which satisfies $F_s(\underline{v}_b) = 0$ and $F_s(\bar{v}_b) = 1$, and which is strictly increasing and differentiable on $[\underline{v}_b, \bar{v}_b]$. These distribution functions are common knowledge in the sense of Aumann [1976]—that is, each side knows these distributions, knows that they are known by the other side, knows that the latter knowledge is known, and so forth.

In this framework, bargaining behavior depends on a player's reservation price v_i, his assessment of the opponent's reservation price, $F_i(v_j)$, and the knowledge of the opponent's assessment, $F_j(v_i)$, for $i = s, b$.

We will consider the following simple bargaining procedure:

Bargaining Rule. Seller and buyer submit sealed offers, s and b respectively. If $b \geq s$, a bargain is enacted and the good is sold at price, $P = kb + (1 - k)s$, where $0 \leq k \leq 1$. If $b < s$, there is no sale and no money trades hands.

Special cases of this rule are of some interest. When k equals 1, the rule is equivalent to granting the buyer the right to make a first and final offer that the seller can accept or reject. In this instance, the sale price is determined solely by the buyer's offer, while the seller's offer serves only to determine whether there is an agreement or not. The seller's optimal strategy is to submit offers $s = v_s$ for all v_s (i.e. his reservation price), and an agreement is reached if and only if $b \geq s$. Similarly, setting $k = 0$ effectively grants the seller the first-offer right. Finally, when $k = \frac{1}{2}$, the rule determines a final sale price by splitting the difference between the player offers. Both offers carry equal weight in determining the sale price.

Framing the single stage bargain as a noncooperative game, we will characterize the resulting Nash or Bayesian equilibrium solutions. In the event of an agreement, each player earns a profit measured by the difference between the agreed price and his reservation price ($P - v_s$ for the seller and $v_b - P$ for the buyer); in the event of no agreement, each earns a zero profit. Additionally, we assume that each bargainer makes offers to maximize his expected profit. The notation $b = B(v_b)$ and $s = S(v_s)$ indicates that the players' price offers depend on their respective reservation prices. The functions $B(\ )$ and $S(\ )$ will be referred to as the player offer strategies. Then, the expected profit of the buyer is given by

$$\pi_b(b, v_b) = \int_s^b (v_b - P)g_b(s)ds \quad \text{if} \quad b \geq s$$

$$= 0 \quad \text{if} \quad b < s,$$

(1)

where $g_b(s)$ is the density function of seller offers induced by the offer strategy $S(\ )$ and the underlying distribution of values $F_b(v_s)$. The upper and lower supports of the offer distribution are $\bar{s}$ and $\underline{s}$, respectively. Similarly, the expected profit of a seller with value v_s who makes offer s and faces a potential buyer using offer strategy $B(\ )$ is

$$\pi_s(s, v_s) = \int_s^{\bar{b}} (P - v_s)g_s(b)db \quad \text{if} \quad s \leq \bar{b},$$

$$= 0 \quad \text{if} \quad s > \bar{b}.$$

Conditional on v_s, the seller's offer s^* is a best response against $B(\ )$ if $\pi_s(s^*, v_s) \geq \pi_s(s, v_s)$, for all s. Similarly, a buyer holding v_b makes offer b^* that is a best response against $S(\ )$ if $\pi_b(b^*, v_b) \geq \pi_b(b, v_b)$, for all b. Then player i employs a best response strategy if for each v_i his offer is a best response against his opponent's strategy. A pair of best response offer strategies constitute a Nash (or Bayesian) equilibrium. By definition, neither player can increase his expected profit by unilaterally altering his chosen strategy.

2. PROPERTIES OF EQUILIBRIUM STRATEGIES

This section presents a number of results characterizing the equilibrium offer strategies of the bargaining game. Offer strategies satisfying $S(v_s) > \bar{v}_b$ and $B(v_b) < \underline{v}_s$ for all v_s and v_b constitute a no trade equilibrium. Obviously, these offer strategies are not very interesting. The results in this section describe equilibria in which an agreement occurs with a positive probability.

A fundamental property of equilibrium offer strategies for which trades occur is that they are increasing in the individual reservation prices. The higher the value placed on the good by the seller (buyer), the higher the price he demands (offers). The proof of this result requires no special assumptions about the offer strategies (e.g. continuity or differentiability).

THEOREM 1. *Under the sealed offer bargaining rule, the equilibrium bargaining strategies of the buyer and seller are increasing in the respective reservation prices.*

Proof. We present the proof for only the buyer offer function $B(\ )$; the seller proof is analogous. Consider v_b and v_b' such that $v_b \neq v_b'$ and let b and b' be the buyer's optimal offers for these respective values. Then by assumption, $\pi_b(b, v_b) \geq \pi_b(b', v_b)$, and $\pi_b(b', v_b') \geq \pi_b(b, v_b')$. Combining these inequalities, we find

$$\pi_b(b, v_b) - \pi_b(b', v_b) + \pi_b(b', v_b') - \pi_b(b, v_b') \geq 0. \tag{2}$$

The expression for the buyer's expected profit in (1) implies that $\pi_b(b, v_b') - \pi_b(b, v_b) = G_b(b)(v_b' - v_b)$ where $G_b(b)$ is the cumulative distribution function of s. In turn, it follows that $\pi_b(b', v_b') - \pi_b(b', v_b) = G_b(b')(v_b' - v_b)$. Substituting these expressions into (2) yields $[G_b(b') - G_b(b)][v_b' - v_b] \geq 0$. For $v_b' > v_b$, then $G_b(b') \geq G_b(b)$. Since $G_b(\ )$ is a distribution function, $b' \geq b$ when the strict inequality holds. If $G_b(b') = G_b(b)$, the buyer's profit maximization behavior ensures that $b' \geq b$. If b' were smaller than b, a buyer holding v_b could lower his offer to b' and increase his profit in the event of a bargain without affecting the probability of a bargain. This would imply that b' and not b was optimal for v_b—a contradiction. This illustrates the basic principle that a player should never place an offer in an interval where the other player makes no offer.

Our principal objective is to characterize the class of equilibria for which player offer strategies are well-behaved. We shall consider the family $\underline{A}$ of equilibria for which the following assumption is met: Each offer strategy is bounded above and below and is strictly increasing and differentiable except possibly at these offer bounds. Theorems 2 and 3 that follow characterize class $\underline{A}$ equilibria.

THEOREM 2. *In a class $\underline{A}$ equilibrium, over intervals of reservation prices for which the offer strategies are strictly increasing, $S(\ )$ and $B(\ )$ must satisfy the linked differential equations*

$$kF_b(y)S'(y) + f_b(y)S(y) = B^{-1}(S(y))f_b(y) \qquad (3a)$$

$$(1 - k)(1 - F_s(x))B'(x) - f_s(x)B(x) = -S^{-1}(B(x))f_s(x). \qquad (3b)$$

Proof. Start with the buyer's equilibrium strategy. His expected profit is

$$\pi_b(b, v_b) = \int_s^b [v_b - kb - (1 - k)s] \, g_b(s)ds.$$

The first order condition for a maximum is

$$\partial \pi_b/\partial b = (v_b - b)g_b(b) - kG_b(b) = 0.$$

Note that $G_b(b) = F_b(S^{-1}(b))$, where S^{-1} is the inverse offer function, i.e. $v_s = S^{-1}(b)$. Equivalently, $G_b(b) = F_b(y)$, where y is a dummy variable defined so that $b = S(y)$. After noting that $g_b(b) = f_b(y)/S'(y)$ and $v_b = B^{-1}(Sy))$, we can rewrite the first order condition as

$$[B^{-1}(S(y)) - S(y)]f_b(b) - kS'(y)F_b(y) = 0,$$

which, after some rearrangement, is identical to (3a).

Similarly, the seller's first order condition is

$$\partial \pi_s/\partial s = (v_s - s)g_s(s) + (1 - k)(1 - G_s(s)) = 0.$$

Then by employing the dummy variable $x = B^{-1}(s)$ and making the appropriate substitutions, we arrive at (3b).

Equations 3a and 3b are "linked" differential equations indicating that the player strategies are interdependent. The equations are a precise expression of the fact that a player's optimal price offer depends not only on v_i and $F_i(v_j)$, but also indirectly on $F_j(v_i)$ since the latter influences the opponent's strategy.

We can now characterize the equilibrium strategies at the offer bounds. For reference purposes, we denote the solutions to (3a) and (3b) over an unrestricted range of reservation prices by $\hat{S}(\ )$ and $\hat{B}(\ )$ respectively. We denote the corresponding inverse functions similarly. Since these functions are strictly increasing, the maximum and minimum price offers are $\hat{S}(\bar{v}_s)$ and $\hat{S}(\underline{v}_s)$ for the seller and $\hat{B}(\bar{v}_b)$ and $\hat{B}(\underline{v}_b)$ for the buyer.

To illustrate the nature of the boundary solutions consider the case when $\hat{B}(\bar{v}_b) > \hat{S}(\bar{v}_s)$ and $\hat{B}(\underline{v}_b) < \hat{S}(\underline{v}_s)$. In this case, $\hat{B}(\ )$ describes the buyer's optimal strategy only for the interval of reservation prices where the probability of a successful bargain is positive but smaller than unity. When the buyer employs $\hat{B}(\ )$, a bargain first becomes a certainty when $\hat{B}(v_b) = \hat{S}(\bar{v}_s)$—when the buyer's offer just matches the greatest possible seller offer. Equivalently, this occurs at value $v_b = \hat{B}^{-1}(\hat{S}(\bar{v}_s))$. Clearly, the buyer improves upon $\hat{B}(\ )$ by employing the constant offer strategy $B(v_b) = \hat{S}(\bar{v}_s)$, for $v_b > \hat{B}^{-1}(\hat{S}(\bar{v}_s))$, since he increases his profit in instances when he knows a successful bargain is certain. In this case, $\hat{S}(\bar{v}_s)$ establishes the upper bound for both the buyer and seller offers.

It is straightforward to check that the seller's best response strategy is unchanged with this modification in the buyer's optimal strategy. Against the buyer's modified strategy, the seller's expected profit is

$$\pi_s(s, v_s) = k \int_s^{\bar{i}} b g_s(b)\,db + k \int_{\bar{i}}^{\bar{b}} \hat{S}(\bar{v}_s) g_s(b)\,db$$

$$+ \int_s^{\bar{b}} [(1 - k)s - v_s]\,g_s(b)\,db.$$

Differentiating this expression with respect to s yields precisely the first order condition of Theorem 2.

Similarly, in the case that $\hat{B}(\underline{v}_b) < \hat{S}(\underline{v}_s)$, a bargain is impossible for sufficiently low buyer reservation prices. For lower and lower buyer values, the probability of a bargain first goes to zero at $v_b = \hat{S}(\underline{v}_s)$. (At a reservation price greater than this, it is suboptimal for the buyer to match the lowest seller offer since by bidding instead in the interval $(\hat{S}(\underline{v}_s), v_b)$, he can earn a positive profit. Thus, the buyer makes the truthful offer $B(v_b) = v_b$ only at $v_b = \hat{S}(\underline{v}_s)$.) For $v_b < \hat{S}(\underline{v}_s)$, the buyer's precise offer strategy is largely irrelevant since in equilibrium no bargain will ever be concluded. A buyer with v_b in this range faces only one restriction—that his offer be smaller than $\hat{B}(v_b)$ in order to preserve the zero profit equilibrium. If this restriction failed to hold, the buyer would earn negative expected profits against the seller's best response.

In sum, the pair $\hat{S}(\ )$ and $\tilde{B}(\ )$ of Theorem 2 describe class A equilibria except at boundary conditions that occur as follows:

THEOREM 3. *In a class A equilibrium, boundary conditions are*:
   1) *If $\tilde{B}(\bar{v}_b) > \hat{S}(\bar{v}_s)$, then $B(v_b) = \hat{S}(\bar{v}_s)$ for $v_b > \tilde{B}^{-1}(\hat{S}(\bar{v}_s))$.*
   2) *If $\tilde{B}(\bar{v}_b) < \hat{S}(\bar{v}_s)$, then $S(v_s) \geq \hat{S}(\bar{v}_s)$ for $v_s > \tilde{B}(\bar{v}_b)$.*
   3) *If $\tilde{B}(\underline{v}_b) > \hat{S}(\underline{v}_s)$, then $S(v_s) = \tilde{B}(\underline{v}_b)$ for $v_s < \hat{S}^{-1}(\tilde{B}(\underline{v}_b))$.*
   4) *If $\tilde{B}(\underline{v}_b) < \hat{S}(\underline{v}_s)$, then $B(v_b) \leq \tilde{B}(\underline{v}_b)$ for $v_b < \hat{S}(\underline{v}_s)$.*

Thus, the range of "serious" offers is bounded from below by $\max[\hat{S}(\underline{v}_s), \tilde{B}(\underline{v}_b)]$ and from above by $\min[\hat{S}(\bar{v}_s), \tilde{B}(\bar{v}_b)]$.

3. ANALYSIS OF SPECIAL CASES

While Theorems 2 and 3 characterize equilibrium strategies that are well-behaved, this by no means exhausts the set of all equilibrium solutions. For instance, it is possible to construct other equilibria involving discontinuous offer strategies that place probability masses on specific offer values. Furthermore, even the linked differential equations of Theorem 2 resist analytic solutions for all but the most elementary distribution functions. The examples that follow are limited to distributions belonging to the uniform family. We begin with an examination of "identical" bargains—cases in which $F_s(\ ) = F_b(\ )$.

Example 1. Suppose the parties bargain under the sealed offer rule with $F_s(v) = F_b(v) = v/\bar{v}$. We have the following results:
   a) The equilibrium offer strategies, $S(\ )$ and $B(\ )$, are given by:

$$S(v_s) = v_s/(2 - k) + ((1 - k)/2)\bar{v} \quad \text{for} \quad 0 \leq v_s \leq ((2 - k)/2)\bar{v}$$

$$S(v_s) \geq v_s/(2 - k) + ((1 - k)/2)\bar{v} \quad \text{for} \quad ((2 - k)/2)\,\bar{v} < v_s \leq \bar{v}$$

$$B(v_b) \leq v_b/(1 + k) + (k(1 - k)/2(1 + k))\bar{v} \quad \text{for} \quad 0 \leq v_b < ((1 - k)/2)\bar{v}$$

$$B(v_b) = v_b/(1 + k) + (k(1 - k)/2(1 + k))\bar{v} \quad \text{for} \quad ((1 - k)/2)\,\bar{v} \leq v_b \leq \bar{v}.$$

   b) The probability that a bargain is reached equals $(-k^2 + k + 2)/8$ and achieves it maximum value, 9/32, at $k = \frac{1}{2}$.
   c) i) The seller's expected profit is $\pi_s(k) = (\bar{v}/48)(2 - k)^2(1 + k)$ which is strictly decreasing in k.
      ii) The buyer's expected profit is $\pi_b(k) = (\bar{v}/48)(1 + k)^2(2 - k)$ which is strictly increasing in k.
      iii) The sum of the parties' profits is $\pi_s + \pi_b = (\bar{v}/16)(1 + k)(2 - k)$, which has a maximum of $(9/64)\bar{v}$, at $k = \frac{1}{2}$.

By simple inspection one can check that linear offer strategies above constitute solutions of Equations 3a and 3b when both distribution functions are linear. Once the equilibrium strategies have been established, the results in parts b and c follow from straightforward computations. Note that part c describes each player's ex ante profit prior to the "draw" of either reservation price.

For easy reference, Figure 1 plots the equilibrium strategies for the

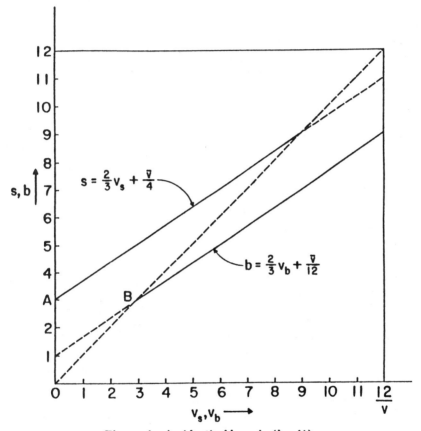

Figure 1. An identical bargain ($k = \frac{1}{2}$).

split-the-difference rule, $k = \frac{1}{2}$. Regardless of the specific rule, however, the equilibria of Example 1 satisfy a number of general properties. The buyer "shades" his offer below his true reservation price except when the probability of a bargain just becomes zero. (In Figure 1, the buyer strategy intersects the 45° line precisely at the seller's lowest offer; point B is level with point A.) Similarly, the optimal seller strategy calls for a "mark up." The combination of linear distributions, offer strategies, and bargaining rule imply that the buyer's (seller's) conditional expected profit increases (decreases) as the square of his reservation price.

The employment of shading and mark up strategies in equilibrium precludes sales in many circumstances when mutually beneficial bargains exist. A bargain is possible provided $v_s \leq v_b$ but will only be concluded when $s \leq b$, or when $v_s \leq ((2 - k)/(1 + k))v_b - ((1 - k)(2 - k)/2(1 + k))\bar{v}$, using the results in part a. To put this another way, the probability of a successful bargain would be ½ if both parties made truthful offers (since $F_s = F_b$). The maximum attainable probability when optimal offer strategies are used is 9/32. Similarly, expected group profit under truthful offers is 1/6; under the equilibrium strategies it is at most 9/64.

One conclusion of Example 1 is that one's intuitive notion of who gains from different kinds of compromises can be mistaken. Suppose that the bargaining rule is $k = \frac{1}{2}$. A suggestion is made to change the rule to $k = \frac{3}{4}$, so that the sale price is determined according to $P = (\frac{3}{4})b + (\frac{1}{4})s$. In whose interest, buyer or seller, is such a change? It would appear at first blush that this change benefits the seller and harms the buyer. Since a sale is made only when there is some "bargaining space" between the two offers (i.e., when $b - s \geq 0$), the move would seem to signify a surrender of this space by the buyer. Should not the switch signify an increase in profit for the seller and a reduction for the buyer?

The answer is no. The fallacy of this line of reasoning is that it implicitly assumes that the bargaining strategies are unaffected by the rule change. It is true that the seller would gain and the buyer would lose if the strategies employed for $k = \frac{1}{2}$ were continued to be used for $k = \frac{3}{4}$. This is not the case, however, as the formulas of Example 1 demonstrate. When k increases, both the buyer and the seller shade their offers, the seller moving closer to his reservation price, the buyer toward a greater understatement. The net result is to confer an advantage on the buyer.

In Example 1, the bargain is identical ($F_s = F_b$) and, furthermore, the probability distribution is symmetric. In this instance, the bargaining rule that calls for splitting the difference ($k = \frac{1}{2}$) has a natural appeal. It is efficient (i.e., it maximizes expected group profit), and it treats the parties symmetrically. In fact, Myerson and Satterthwaite show that the split-the-difference bargaining rule is an *optimal* mechanism—that is, it attains the greatest group expected profit of all possible bargaining procedures. For these reasons splitting the difference between offers is attractive for bargains that are identical and symmetric.

The next example characterizes the equilibrium strategies for nonidentical bargains when the buyer and seller distributions are uniform.

Example 2. Suppose that v_s is uniformly distributed on the interval [0,

$\bar{v}_s$] and that v_b is uniformly distributed on $[\underline{v}_b, \bar{v}_b]$, where $0 \le \underline{v}_b \le \bar{v}_s \le \bar{v}_b$. Then we have the following results:

a) The equilibrium offer strategy of the seller is specified by:

$$S(v_s) = \underline{v}_b/(1 + k) + (k(1 - k)/2(1 + k))\bar{v}_b$$

$$\text{for} \quad 0 \le v_s < ((2 - k)/(1 + k))\bar{v}_b$$

$$- ((1 - k)(2 - k)/2(1 + k))\bar{v}_b$$

$$S(v_s) = v_s/(2 - k) + ((1 - k)/2)\bar{v}_b$$

$$\text{for} \quad ((2 - k)/(1 + k))\bar{v}_b$$

$$- ((1 - k)(2 - k)/2(1 + k))\bar{v}_b \le v_s \le ((2 - k)/2)\bar{v}_b$$

$$S(v_s) \ge v_s/(2 - k) + ((1 - k)/2)\bar{v}_b \quad \text{for} \quad ((2 - k)/2)\, \bar{v}_b < v_s \le \bar{v}_s.$$

b) The equilibrium offer strategy of the buyer is specified by:

$$B(v_b) \le v_b/(1 + k) + (k(1 - k)/2(1 + k))\bar{v}_b$$

$$\text{for} \quad 0 \le v_b < ((1 - k)/2)\bar{v}_b$$

$$B(v_b) = v_b/(1 + k) + (k(1 - k)/2(1 + k))\bar{v}_b$$

$$\text{for} \quad ((1 - k)/2)\bar{v}_b \le v_b \le ((1 + k)/(2 - k))\bar{v}_s + ((1 - k)/2)\bar{v}_b$$

$$B(v_b) = \bar{v}_s/(1 - k) + ((1 - k)/2)\bar{v}_b$$

$$\text{for} \quad ((1 + k)/(2 - k))\bar{v}_s + ((1 - k)/2)\bar{v}_b < v_b \le \bar{v}_b.$$

The offer strategies are sensitive to changes in the underlying distributions in the natural way. Other things equal, increases in $\underline{v}_b$, $\bar{v}_s$, and $\bar{v}_b$ imply larger (or no smaller) buyer and seller offers—that is, a shift to uniformly higher possible buyer or seller reservation prices (in the sense of stochastic dominance) results in higher offers. As a second example consider a player's offer response to a mean preserving spread in the distribution of his opponent's reservation price. For instance, if the seller becomes more uncertain about the buyer's value (such that $\Delta \bar{v}_b = -\Delta \underline{v}_b > 0$), the range of his offers increases in equilibrium (i.e. he makes higher (lower) offers than before when he holds sufficiently large (small) reservation prices). Furthermore, a simple calculation shows that, with the increase in uncertainty, the seller on average is worse off than before. An analogous result holds for an uncertain buyer. Figures 2 and 3 illustrate a pair of typical equilibria.

A number of points concerning the efficiency of the sealed offer bargaining rule can be summarized. First, in the nonidentical setting the rule of thumb of splitting the difference between offers will no longer maximize expected group profit (except coincidentally). When the distributions $F_s(\ )$ and $F_b(\ )$ differ, the seller and buyer obviously play asymmetric roles. Clearly then, the expected group profit as a function of the bargaining rule k will vary with $\underline{v}_s$, $\bar{v}_s$, $\underline{v}_b$, and $\bar{v}_b$. To take an extreme case, suppose there is no uncertainty surrounding the buyer's reservation price. The bargaining rule that calls for the seller to make the first and final offer ($k = 0$) extracts 100% of the potential group

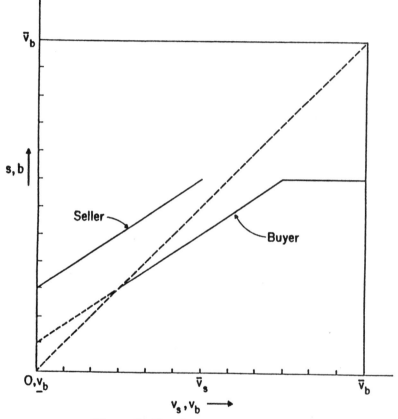

Figure 2. Nonidentical bargain, $k = \frac{1}{2}$.

profit (since the seller offers $s = v_b$ when $v_s \leq v_b$). But a buyer who makes a first and final offer ($k = 1$) will shade his offer below his true value; consequently, a number of mutually beneficial bargains will be missed. Here, a seller's first offer is superior to any other bargaining rule. In short, the bargaining rule that maximizes group profit must be determined on a case-by-case basis.

Second, a tedious but straightforward calculation can confirm that the expected profit of the seller (buyer) is decreasing (increasing) in k. This result, which held in the identical bargain example, continues to hold for nonidentical uniformly distributed bargains.

Player Risk Aversion. Additional insight into the nature of the bargaining equilibrium can be gained by relaxing the assumption that the bargainers are risk neutral. Suppose that the seller and the buyer,

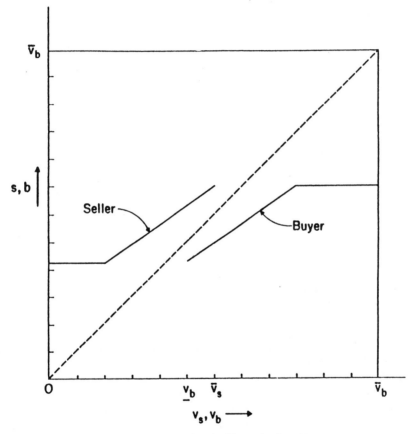

Figure 3. Nonidentical bargain, $k = \frac{1}{2}$.

respectively, earn von Neumann-Morgenstern utilities $u_s(P - v_s)$ and $u_b(v_b - P)$ in the event of an agreement and zero utilities otherwise. Then it is easy to check that the new first order conditions are

$$u_b(v_b - b) - k \int_s^b u_b(v_b - kb - (1 - k)s)g_b(s)ds = 0,$$

and

$$u_s(s - v_s) - (1 - k) \int_s^{\bar{b}} u_s(kb + (1 - k)s - v_s)g_s(b)db = 0.$$

With these expressions, we can present equilibria in the case that: 1) the players' utility functions display constant relative risk aversion, $u(y) = y^\alpha$, where $0 < \alpha < 1$, and 2) the underlying distributions are uniform. As a simple illustration, suppose the players have the same degree of risk aversion, the underlying distributions are both uniform on $[0, 1]$, and the bargaining rule is $k = \frac{1}{2}$. Then the equilibrium strategies are linear:

$$s = (\beta - \frac{1}{2})/(2\beta^2 - \frac{1}{2}) + [1 - (1/2\beta)]v_s$$

$$b = (1 - \frac{1}{2}\beta)/(4\beta^2 - 1) + [1 - (1/2\beta)]v_b$$

where $\beta = 2^{1/\alpha} - \frac{1}{2}$. In this symmetric example, the offer strategies have the same slope, and the buyer's intercept is smaller than the seller's. Consider the effect on the bargaining strategies as the players become increasingly risk averse: As α decreases, β increases causing the slope of each offer strategy to increase (and the intercept to fall). The result is generally lower seller offers and higher buyer offers. The intuition underlying this result is that, with risk aversion, the marginal increment in profit associated with a slighty more agressive offer (a higher seller offer or a lower buyer offer) is weighted less heavily than the possible loss, if as a result of the change, an agreement is precluded ($b < s$). This fact leads risk-averse bargainers to make offers closer to their true values than their risk-neutral counterparts. In the limit as α approaches 0 (i.e. the players become infinitely risk averse), the equilibrium strategies approach the strategies $s = v_s$ and $b = v_b$ for all v_s and v_b. Consequently, $b \geq s$ if and only if $v_b \geq v_s$, and so all mutually beneficial agreements are attained. Short of this extreme case, however, potentially beneficial bargains will be lost.

In the case of differing degrees of risk aversion, one can show that, other things equal, an increase in the risk aversion of the seller (buyer) implies uniformly lower (higher) offers by *both* parties in equilibrium. Not surprisingly, the opponent's best response to more truthful bids by the player who has become more risk averse is to make more aggressive offers himself.

4. CONCLUDING REMARKS

In what respects do the equilibria described in Theorems 2 and 3 provide an accurate representation of bargaining under uncertainty? Since the conclusions of any model depend on its premises, it is well to examine the extent to which the model's assumptions capture or approximate the actual bargaining conditions. First, uncertainty concerning the opponent's walk away price is frequently encountered in bargaining situations. It is the task of each bargainer to assess the likely reservation price of his opponent. Indeed, the better the bargainer's information about his opponent, the better he can expect to fare in the negotiations. For instance, the man on the street is better equipped to bargain with a car dealer if he possesses the "book" that lists the prices the dealer himself has paid for various models and if he has assessed the current state of demand for automobiles.

Probability assessment becomes more complicated in an environment with stochastic dependence between the player values. For instance, suppose that each bargainer's value for the good depends on future (unknown) market conditions as well as on his personal characteristics. Additionally, suppose that each bargainer possesses differential information bearing on the good's potential value. Then, based on this information, each player must estimate his opponent's value *and* his own value in the event there is an agreement or not. In particular, the fact that the players would conclude an agreement (or not) is informative of the good's ultimate value.

While the single-stage bargaining rule fails to capture the pattern of reciprocal concessions observed in everyday practice, it is a useful idealization and a starting point for other investigations. A more general model would allow the bargainers multiple rounds in which to exchange offers (potentially incurrng "transaction" costs in the process). To the extent that the exchange of offers conveys information about the reservation prices, one would expect agreements to become more frequent. For example, when a bargain is unsuccessful at the initial stage, each party could revise his probability assessment of the other's reservation price and could make a concession in his next offer. These kinds of multistage bargains can be properly analyzed within our framework and deserve further attention. (For an example, see Sobel and Takahashi [1980].)

In our view, there are strong arguments for the monotonic equilibria of Theorems 2 and 3 even when other equilibria may exist. An individual is likely to accept the following proposition as reasonable: "The higher the seller's value the more he demands for the good; the higher the buyer's value the more he is willing to offer." Accepting this principle and believing firmly that any bargaining opponent will accept it as well, the individual then seeks a best monotonic offer strategy.

Monotonic offer strategies may also provide a focal point for the bargaining process. As a simple example, suppose the buyer's reservation price is uniformly distributed on the interval [0.5, 1] and the seller's price is similarly distributed on the interval [0, 0.5]. In this case, the constant offers $S(v_s) = B(v_b) = 0.5$ constitute an equilibrium and guar antee that the players always concluded a bargain. Each party chooses not to push further its demand, nor to retreat, expecting his opponent to feel the same way. One must not overlook, however, the existence of a second equilibrium in monotonic strategies. In this case, both parties make offers that are smaller than 0.5 for sufficiently low reservation prices and offers greater than 0.5 for high prices. Thus, it is prudent for a buyer who values the good highly to make a generous offer, thereby increasing the likelihood of an agreement when facing a seller who may not cooperate with an offer of $S(v_s) = 0.5$.

Equilibrium theory can furnish no definitive conclusion indicating which outcome represents the "more logical" bargaining focal point. Observe, however, that the monotonic equilibrium is responsive to changes in the underlying distributions F_s and F_b, while the constant strategy equilibrium is not. If, for instance, the buyer's value is drawn uniformly from the interval [0.5, 5] instead of [0.5, 1], the constant strategy equilibrium $S(v_s) = B(v_b) = 0.5$ becomes much less compelling. Is this a logical resting point—a position from which neither player expects the other to retreat? It would seem that the buyer could be expected to concede (settling for a smaller but still substantial profit) if the seller insisted. The monotonic equilibrium is free from these criticisms since it depends explicitly on the underlying distributions. With the shift in possible buyer values, the offers of the buyer become more generous and those of the seller more demanding. This response is consistent with the expectation that such a shift should benefit both parties (not just the buyer).

Finally, when $\bar{v}_s > \underline{v}_b$, there is no guarantee that a mutually beneficial agreement is always available. In this case of a "close" bargain, there is no constant strategy equilibrium. Indeed, the case of an identical bargain $F_s = F_b$ points out the main difficulty with a constant offer strategy. The employment of an aggressive offer will likely preclude an agreement, while an offer making too great a concession will be unprofitable. In short, players will adopt monotonic strategies because they are more efficient.

We would argue that close bargains occur most frequently in actual practice. In most bargaining situations, the opportunity for the seller or the buyer to cease negotiations and to consider a third-party transaction is available, at least implicitly. It is unusual for the buyer to be the only potential customer for the good or for the seller to have a monopoly position. In this instance, each party's reservation price will reflect, at least partially, the price (net of search transaction costs) that he could expect to obtain elsewhere. To the extent to which beliefs about the prices available from third parties transactions differ, or access to these parties differs, the reservation prices of the buyer and seller will diverge. Nevertheless, one would expect such an opportunity to minimize the gap between the possible reservation prices of the parties. This suggests that close bargains may be of the greatest practical importance.

ACKNOWLEDGMENT

We would like to thank Jerry Green, Takao Kobayashi, and John Pratt for helpful comments and especially Howard Raiffa for suggesting the problem.

REFERENCES

AUMANN, R. J. 1976. Agreeing to Disagree. *Ann. Statist.* **4**, 1236–1239.

CRAWFORD, V. P. 1982. A Theory of Disagreement in Bargaining. *Econometrica* **50**, 602–637.

CROSS, J. G. 1969. *The Economics of Bargaining.* Basic Books, New York.

HARSANYI, J. C. 1956. Approaches to the Bargaining Problem Before and After the Theory of Games. *Econometrica* **24**, 144–157.

HARSANYI, J. C. 1967–1968. Games with Incomplete Information Played by Bayesian Players. *Mgmt. Sci.* **14**, 159–182, 321–334, 486–502.

HARSANYI, J. C., AND R. SELTEN. 1972. A Generalized Nash Solution for Two-Person Bargaining Games with Incomplete Information. *Mgmt. Sci.* **18**, P80–P106.

MYERSON, R. B. 1979. Incentive Compatibility and the Bargaining Problem. *Econometrica* **47**, 61–73.

MYERSON, R. B., AND M. SATTERTHWAITE. 1981. Efficient Mechanisms for Bilateral Trading," Discussion Paper 469S, Northwestern Universtiy.

NASH, J. C. 1950. The Bargaining Problem. *Econometrica* **18**, 151–162.

ROSENTHAL, R. W. 1978. Arbitration of Two-Party Disputes under Uncertainty. *Rev. Econ. Studies* **45**, 595–604.

ROTH, A. E. 1979. *Axiomatic Models of Bargaining.* Springer-Verlag.

SAMUELSON, W. 1980. First-Offer Bargains. *Mgmt. Sci.* **26**, 155–164.

SCHELLING, T. 1960. *The Strategy of Conflict.* Harvard University Press, Cambridge, Mass.

SOBEL, J., AND I. TAKAHASHI. 1980. A Multi-Stage Model of Bargaining, Discussion Paper 80-25, University of California, San Diego.

YOUNG, O. R. (ED.) 1975. *Bargaining: Formal Theories of Negotiations.* University of Illinois Press, Champaign-Urbana, Ill.

JOURNAL OF ECONOMIC THEORY 29, 265–281 (1983)

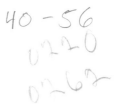

Efficient Mechanisms for Bilateral Trading*

ROGER B. MYERSON AND MARK A. SATTERTHWAITE

*J. L. Kellogg Graduate School of Management, Northwestern University,
Evanston, Illinois 60201*

Received June 8, 1981; revised December 7, 1981

We consider bargaining problems between one buyer and one seller for a single object. The seller's valuation and the buyer's valuation for the object are assumed to be independent random variables, and each individual's valuation is unknown to the other. We characterize the set of allocation mechanisms that are Bayesian incentive compatible and individually rational, and show the general impossibility of ex post efficient mechanisms without outside subsidies. For a wide class of problems we show how to compute mechanisms that maximize expected total gains from trade, and mechanisms that can maximize a broker's expected profit. *Journal of Economic Literature* Classification Number: 026.

1. INTRODUCTION

Vickrey [7] showed the fundamental impossibility of designing a mechanism for negotiating the terms of trade in such a way that (i) honest revelation of supply and demand curves is a dominant strategy for all individuals, (ii) no outside subsidy is needed, and (iii) the final allocation of goods is always Pareto-efficient ex post. D'Aspremont and Gerard-Varet [3] weakened the incentive criterion from dominant-strategy to Bayesian Nash equilibrium, and showed that Bayesian incentive-compatible mechanisms could achieve efficient allocations without outside subsidies. However, the mechanisms of D'Aspremont and Gerard-Varet may give negative expected gains from trade to some individuals. That is, an individual who already knows his true preferences (but still does not know the preferences of the other individuals) may expect to do worse in the D'Aspremont-Gerard-Varet mechanism than if no trade took place. In this paper we prove some results relating to the efficiency properties of Bayesian incentive-compatible mechanisms that are individually rational, in the sense that each individual expects nonnegative gains from trade in any state of his preferences. We restrict our attention here to the simplest trading problems, where two

---

* Research for this paper was supported by the Kellogg Center for Advanced Study in Managerial Economics and by the National Science Foundation.

individuals, one of whom has a single indivisible object to sell to the other, attempt to agree on an exchange of the object for money.

Chatterjee and Samuelson [2] have studied this two-person trading problem. For some specific bargaining games, they characterized the Bayesian equilibria. Chatterjee [1] has also studied the impossibility of simple mechanisms satisfying efficiency and individual rationality. In this paper we analyze a more general class of mechanisms, using some techniques similar to those developed in Myerson [6] to analyze optimal auction design. We show, as an application of our results, that if the traders' priors about each other's reservation prices are symmetric and uniform, then one of the games studied by Chatterjee and Samuelson [2] has equilibria that result in maximal expected gains from trade.

In the context of public goods economies, Laffont and Maskin [4] have also studied Bayesian incentive-compatible mechanisms that achieve ex post efficiency. Using a differentiability assumption (that the efficient level of the public goods depends differentiably on the consumers' types), they have shown for a very general class of problems that ex post efficiency and individual rationality may be incompatible. Although their differentiability assumption cannot be used in the trading problems which we study here, we derive an impossibility result (Corollary 1) that is closely related to this result.

The plan of this paper is as follows. In Section 2, we first define the formal structure of the bilateral trading problem. We then present a general characterization of all rules for transferring the object (as a function of the traders' valuations) that can be implemented by incentive-compatible individually-rational mechanisms. In Section 3, we show it is generally impossible to have a mechanism that is incentive-compatible, individually-rational, and ex post efficient, in the sense that it transfers the object to the buyer if and only if his valuation for the object is higher. In proving this result, we also show how to compute the smallest lump-sum subsidy that would be required from an outside party to make such an ex post efficient mechanism possible. In Section 4, we show how to construct mechanisms which maximize the expected total gains from trade, subject to the constraints of individual rationality and incentive compatibility. In Section 5, we consider the case where the traders are intermediated by a broker, who may either subsidize or exploit their desire to trade. We characterize the incentive-compatible individually rational trading mechanisms feasible with a broker, and we show how to construct mechanisms that maximize the broker's expected profit.

2. Incentive Compatibility and Individual Rationality

Let us consider a trading problem where individual #1 owns an object that individual #2 wants to buy. We let $\tilde{V}_1$ and $\tilde{V}_2$ denote the values of the object to the seller (#1) and the buyer (#2), respectively, and assume that these two valuations are independent random variables, with each $\tilde{V}_i$ distributed over a given interval from a_i to b_i. Let $f_1(\cdot)$ and $f_2(\cdot)$ be the probability density functions for $\tilde{V}_1$ and $\tilde{V}_2$, respectively. We assume that each $f_i(\cdot)$ is continuous and positive on its domain $[a_i, b_i]$. We let $F_1(\cdot)$ and $F_2(\cdot)$ be the cumulative distribution functions corresponding to f_1 and f_2 (so $f_i = F_i'$).

We assume that each individual knows his own valuation at the time of bargaining, but he considers the other's valuation as a random variable, distributed as above. Thus, to guarantee that each individual is willing to participate in a bargaining mechanism, the appropriate individual rationality constraint is that the mechanism gives each individual i nonnegative expected gains from trade in the mechanism, regardless of his given valuation $\tilde{V}_i$. Finally, we assume that the individuals are risk neutral and have additively separable utility for money and the object.

These two individuals are going to participate in some bargaining game or mechanism to determine, first, whether the object should be transferred from the seller to the buyer and, second, how much the buyer should pay to the seller. Our general question is: what kinds of bargaining mechanisms can be designed that have good economic efficiency properties?

A *direct bargaining mechanism* is one in which each individual simultaneously reports his valuation to a coordinater or broker who then determines whether the object is transferred, and how much the buyer must pay. A direct mechanism is thus characterized by two *outcome functions*, denoted by $p(\cdot, \cdot)$ and $x(\cdot, \cdot)$, where $p(v_1, v_2)$ is the probability that the object is transferred to the buyer and $x(v_1, v_2)$ is the expected payment from buyer to seller if v_1 and v_2 are the reported valuations of the seller and buyer. A direct mechanism is (*Bayesian*) *incentive-compatible* if honest reporting forms a Bayesian Nash equilibrium. That is, in an incentive-compatible mechanism, each individual can maximize his expected utility by reporting his true valuation, given that the other is expected to report honestly.

We can, without any loss of generality, restrict our attention to incentive-compatible direct mechanisms. This is because, for any Bayesian equilibrium of any bargaining game, there is an equivalent incentive-compatible direct mechanism that always yields the same outcomes (when the individuals play the honest equilibrium). This result, which is well known and very general, is called the *revelation principle*. The essential idea is that, given any equilibrium of any bargaining game, we can construct an equivalent incentive-compatible direct mechanism by first asking the buyer and seller each to confidentially report his valuation, then computing what each would have done in the given equilibrium strategies with these valuations, and then implementing the outcome (transfer of money and object) as in the given game for this computed behavior. If either individual had any incentive to lie to us in this direct mechanism, then he would have had an incentive to lie to himself in the original game, which is a contradiction of the premise that he was in equilibrium in the original game. (For more on this revelation principle, see Myerson [5] and [6].)

Given a direct mechanism with outcome functions (p, x), we define that following quantities:

$$\bar{x}_1(v_1) = \int_{a_2}^{b_2} x(v_1, t_2) f_2(t_2)\, dt_2, \qquad \bar{x}_2(v_2) = \int_{a_1}^{b_1} x(t_1, v_2) f_1(t_1)\, dt_1,$$

$$\bar{p}_1(v_1) = \int_{a_2}^{b_2} p(v_1, t_2) f_2(t_2)\, dt_2, \qquad \bar{p}_2(v_2) = \int_{a_1}^{b_1} p(t_1, v_2) f_1(t_1)\, dt_1,$$

$$U_1(v_1) = \bar{x}_1(v_1) - v_1 \bar{p}_1(v_1), \qquad U_2(v_2) = v_2 \bar{p}_2(v_2) - \bar{x}_2(v_2).$$

Thus $U_1(v_1)$ is the expected gains from trade for the seller if his valuation is v_1, since $\bar{x}_1(v_1)$ is his expected revenue and $\bar{p}_1(v_1)$ is his probability of losing the object given $\tilde{V}_1 = v_1$. Similarly, $U_2(v_2)$ is the expected gains from trade for the buyer, $\bar{x}_2(v_2)$ is the buyer's expected payment, and $\bar{p}_2(v_2)$ is the buyer's probability of getting the object, if his valuation is v_2.

In our formal notation, we say that (p, x) is *incentive-compatible* (in the Bayesian sense) iff for every v_1 and $\hat{v}_1$ in $[a_1, b_1]$,

$$U_1(v_1) \geqslant \bar{x}_1(\hat{v}_1) - v_1 \bar{p}_1(\hat{v}_1),$$

and for every v_2 and $\hat{v}_2$ in $[a_2, b_2]$,

$$U_2(v_2) \geqslant v_2 \bar{p}_2(\hat{v}_2) - \bar{x}_2(\hat{v}_2).$$

These two inequalities assert that neither individual should expect to gain by reporting valuation $\hat{v}_i$ when v_i is true. The mechanism (p, x) is *individually rational* iff

$$U_1(v_1) \geqslant 0 \quad \text{and} \quad U_2(v_2) \geqslant 0$$

for every v_1 in $[a_1, b_1]$ and for every v_2 in $[a_2, b_2]$. That is, individual rationality requires that each individual have nonnegative expected gains from trade after he knows his own valuation, but before he learns the other's valuation. (We do not require

$$x(v_1, v_2) - v_2 p(v_1, v_2) \geqslant 0 \quad \text{or} \quad v_2 p(v_1, v_2) - x(v_1, v_2) \geqslant 0 \quad \text{ex post.})$$

We can now state and prove our main result.

THEOREM 1.   *For any incentive-compatible mechanism,*

$$U_1(b_1) + U_2(a_2) = \underset{v_1 \epsilon [a_1, b_1]}{\text{minimum}} (U_1(v_1)) + \underset{v_2 \epsilon [a_2, b_2]}{\text{minimum}} (U_2(v_2))$$

$$= \int_{a_2}^{b_2} \int_{a_1}^{b_1} \left(\left[v_2 - \frac{1 - F_2(v_2)}{f_2(v_2)} \right] - \left[v_1 + \frac{F_1(v_1)}{f_1(v_1)} \right] \right)$$

$$\times p(v_1, v_2) f_1(v_1) f_2(v_2) \, dv_1 \, dv_2. \tag{1}$$

Furthermore, if $p(\cdot, \cdot)$ is any function mapping $[a_1, b_1] \times [a_2, b_2]$ into $[0, 1]$, then there .exists a function $x(\cdot, \cdot)$ such that (p, x) is incentive-compatible and individually-rational if and only if $\bar{p}_1(\cdot)$ is weakly decreasing, $\bar{p}_2(\cdot)$ is weakly increasing, and

$$0 \leqslant \int_{a_2}^{b_2} \int_{a_1}^{b_1} \left(\left[v_2 - \frac{1 - F_2(v_2)}{f_2(v_2)} \right] - \left[v_1 + \frac{F_1(v_1)}{f_1(v_1)} \right] \right)$$

$$\times p(v_1, v_2) f_1(v_1) f_2(v_2) \, dv_1 \, dv_2. \tag{2}$$

Proof of Theorem 1.   Suppose first that we are given an incentive-compatible mechanism (p, x). By incentive compatibility, we know that, for any two possible valuations v_1 and $\hat{v}_1$ for the seller,

$$U_1(v_1) = \bar{x}_1(v_1) - v_1 \, \bar{p}_1(v_1) \geqslant \bar{x}_1(\hat{v}_1) - v_1 \, \bar{p}_1(\hat{v}_1),$$

and

$$U_1(\hat{v}_1) = \bar{x}_1(\hat{v}_1) - \hat{v}_1 \, \bar{p}_1(\hat{v}_1) \geqslant \bar{x}_1(v_1) - \hat{v}_1 \, \bar{p}_1(v_1).$$

These two inequalities imply that

$$(\hat{v}_1 - v_1) \, \bar{p}_1(v_1) \geqslant U_1(v_1) - U_1(\hat{v}_1) \geqslant (\hat{v}_1 - v_1) \, \bar{p}_1(\hat{v}_1). \tag{3}$$

Thus, if $\hat{v}_1 > v_1$, we must have $\bar{p}_1(\hat{v}_1) \leqslant \bar{p}_1(v_1)$, so $\bar{p}_1(\cdot)$ is decreasing. Furthermore, since $\bar{p}_1(\cdot)$ is decreasing, it is Riemann integrable, and so (3) implies that $U_1'(v_1) = -\bar{p}_1(v_1)$ at almost every v_1 and

$$U_1(v_1) = U_1(b_1) + \int_{v_1}^{b_1} \bar{p}_1(t_1) \, dt_1. \tag{4}$$

A similar argument for the buyer shows that

$$(\hat{v}_2 - v_2) \, \bar{p}_2(\hat{v}_2) \geqslant U_2(\hat{v}_2) - U_2(v_2) \geqslant (\hat{v}_2 - v_2) \, \bar{p}_2(v_2).$$

Thus, $\bar{p}_2(\cdot)$ is increasing, $U_2'(v_2) = \bar{p}_2(v_2)$ almost everywhere, and

$$U_2(v_2) = U_2(a_2) + \int_{a_2}^{v_2} \bar{p}_2(t_2) \, dt_2. \tag{5}$$

Equations (4) and (5) imply that $U_1(\cdot)$ is decreasing and $U_2(\cdot)$ is increasing. Furthermore, we get:

$$\int_{a_2}^{b_2} \int_{a_1}^{b_1} (v_2 - v_1) \, p(v_1, v_2) f_1(v_1) f_2(v_2) \, dv_1 \, dv_2$$

$$= \int_{a_1}^{b_1} U_1(v_1) f_1(v_1) \, dv_1 + \int_{a_2}^{b_2} U_2(v_2) f_2(v_2) \, dv_2$$

$$= U_1(b_1) + \int_{a_1}^{b_1} \int_{v_1}^{b_1} \bar{p}_1(t_1) \, dt_1 f_1(v_1) \, dv_1$$

$$+ U_2(a_2) + \int_{a_2}^{b_2} \int_{a_2}^{v_2} \bar{p}_2(t_2) \, dt_2 \, f_2(v_2) \, dv_2$$

$$= U_1(b_1) + U_2(a_2) + \int_{a_1}^{b_1} F_1(t_1) \bar{p}_1(t_1) \, dt_1$$

$$+ \int_{a_2}^{b_2} (1 - F_2(t_2)) \, \bar{p}_2(t_2) \, dt_2$$

$$= U_1(b_1) + U_2(a_2)$$

$$+ \int_{a_2}^{b_2} \int_{a_1}^{b_1} (F_1(t_1) f_2(t_2)$$

$$+ (1 - F_2(t_2)) f_1(t_1)) p(t_1, t_2) \, dt_1 \, dt_2.$$

Equating the first and last of these expressions gives us Eq. (1) of Theorem 1, which in turn implies inequality (2) when the mechanism is individually-rational. Thus, we have proven the first sentence and the "only if" part of the second sentence in Theorem 1.

To complete the proof of Theorem 1, suppose now that $p(\cdot, \cdot)$ satisfies (2), $\bar{p}_1(\cdot)$ is decreasing, and $\bar{p}_2(\cdot)$ is increasing. We must construct the payment function $x(\cdot, \cdot)$ so that (p, x) is an individually rational, incentive-compatible mechanism. There are many such functions which could be used; we shall consider a function defined as follows:

$$x(v_1, v_2) = \int_{t_2=a_2}^{v_2} t_2 \, d[\bar{p}_2(t_2)] - \int_{t_1=a_1}^{v_1} t_1 \, d[-\bar{p}_1(t_1)]$$

$$+ a_2 \bar{p}_2(a_2) + \int_{t_1=a_1}^{b_1} t_1(1 - F_1(t_1)) \, d[-\bar{p}_1(t_1)]. \tag{6}$$

Notice that, since $\bar{p}_2(\cdot)$ and $-\bar{p}_1(\cdot)$ are monotone increasing, each integral in (6) is a nonnegative quantity (assuming $a_1 \geq 0$ and $a_2 \geq 0$). The first term in (6) depends only on v_2, the second term depends only on v_1, and the last two terms represent a constant chosen to give

$$U_2(a_2) = a_2 \bar{p}_2(a_2) - \int_{a_1}^{b_1} x(v_1, a_2) f_1(v_1)\, dv_1 = 0.$$

(Notice that $x(v_1, v_2)$ is paid by the buyer even if he does not get the object.) To check incentive-compatibility of (6), observe that

$$(v_2 \bar{p}_2(v_2) - v_2 \bar{p}_2(\hat{v}_2)) - (\bar{x}_2(v_2) - \bar{x}_2(\hat{v}_2))$$

$$= v_2 \int_{t_2=\hat{v}_2}^{v_2} d[\bar{p}_2(t_2)] - \int_{t_2=\hat{v}_2}^{v_2} t_2\, d[\bar{p}_2(t_2)]$$

$$= \int_{t_2=\hat{v}_2}^{v_2} (v_2 - t_2)\, d[\bar{p}_2(t_2)] \geq 0.$$

So the buyer would do better reporting v_2 rather than $\hat{v}_2$ if his true valuation is v_2. (This argument holds even if $\hat{v}_2 > v_2$, in which case the integrand is negative, but the direction of integration is backwards, giving a nonnegative integral overall.) The proof of incentive-compatibility for the seller is analogous.

Thus, since (p, x) is incentive-compatible, (1) applies. Because $U_2(a_2) = 0$, and because we have assumed (2), we must have $U_1(b_1) \geq 0$. By the monotonicity properties of $U_1(\cdot)$ and $U_2(\cdot)$, it suffices to check individual-rationality for the buyer's lowest valuation and the seller's highest valuation. Thus, our proof of Theorem 1 is complete. ∎

3. Ex Post Efficiency

A mechanism (p, x) is *ex post efficient* iff

$$p(v_1, v_2) = 1 \qquad \text{if} \quad v_1 < v_2,$$

$$= 0 \qquad \text{if} \quad v_1 > v_2.$$

That is, in an ex post efficient mechanism, the buyer gets the object whenever his valuation is higher, and the seller keeps the object whenever his valuation is higher. For such a mechanism, $\bar{p}_1(v_1) = 1 - F_2(v_1)$, which is decreasing, and $\bar{p}_2(v_2) = F_1(v_2)$, which is increasing. Thus, to check whether ex post efficient mechanisms are feasible, it only remains to check whether inequality

(2) in Theorem 1 holds for this $p(\cdot, \cdot)$. In fact, for an ex post efficient mechanism, we get:

$$\int_{a_2}^{b_2} \int_{a_1}^{b_1} \left(\left[v_2 - \frac{1 - F_2(v_2)}{f_2(v_2)} \right] - \left[v_1 + \frac{F_1(v_1)}{f_1(v_1)} \right] \right) p(v_1, v_2) f_1(v_1) f_2(v_2) \, dv_1 \, dv_2$$

$$= \int_{a_2}^{b_2} \int_{a_1}^{\min\{v_2, b_1\}} [v_2 f_2(v_2) + F(v_2) - 1] f_1(v_1) \, dv_1 \, dv_2$$

$$- \int_{a_2}^{b_2} \int_{a_1}^{\min\{v_2, b_1\}} [v_1 f_1(v_1) + F_1(v_1)] \, dv_1 f_2(v_2) \, dv_2$$

$$= \int_{a_2}^{b_2} [v_2 f_2(v_2) + F_2(v_2) - 1] F_1(v_2) \, dv_2$$

$$- \int_{a_2}^{b_2} \min\{v_2 F_1(v_2), b_1\} f_2(v_2) \, dv_2$$

$$= -\int_{a_2}^{b_2} (1 - F_2(v_2)) F_1(v_2) \, dv_2 + \int_{b_1}^{b_2} (v_2 - b_1) f_2(v_2) \, dv_2$$

$$= -\int_{a_2}^{b_2} (1 - F_2(v_2)) F_1(v_2) \, dv_2 - \int_{b_1}^{b_2} (F_2(v_2) - 1) \, dv_2$$

$$= -\int_{a_2}^{b_1} (1 - F_2(t)) F_1(t) \, dt.$$

Thus, if $a_2 < b_1$ and $a_1 < b_2$, so that the two valuation-intervals properly intersect, then any Bayesian incentive-compatible mechanism which is ex post efficient must give

$$U_1(b_1) + U_2(a_2) = -\int_{a_2}^{b_1} (1 - F_2(t)) F_1(t) \, dt < 0, \tag{7}$$

and so it cannot be individually rational. Thus, this quantity

$$\int_{a_2}^{b_1} (1 - F_2(t)) F_1(t) \, dt$$

is the smallest lump-sum subsidy required from an outside party to create a Bayesian incentive-compatible mechanism which is both ex post efficient and individually rational. (Thus far in this paper we have been assuming that no such subsidy is actually available. We will consider the case of trading with a broker more generally in Section 5.)

To summarize, we have shown the following result.

COROLLARY 1. *If the seller's valuation is distributed with positive probability density over the interval* $[a_1, b_1]$, *and the buyer's valuation is distributed with positive probability density over the interval* $[a_2, b_2]$, *and if the interiors of these intervals have a nonempty intersection, then no incentive-compatible individually rational trading mechanism can be ex post efficient.*

It should be noted that our proofs have used the assumption that the valuations have positive density over their respective intervals. Without this assumption the corollary is untrue. For example, suppose that $[a_1, b_1] = [1, 4]$ and $[a_2, b_2] = [0, 3]$, but all the probability mass is concentrated at the endpoints, with

$$\Pr(\tilde{V}_1 = 1) = \Pr(\tilde{V}_1 = 4) = \tfrac{1}{2} = \Pr(\tilde{V}_2 = 0) = \Pr(\tilde{V}_2 = 3).$$

Then the mechanism "sell at price 2 if both are willing (otherwise no trade)" is incentive-compatible, individually-rational, and ex post efficient. But if we admit any small positive probability density over the whole of these intersecting intervals, then neither this mechanism nor any other feasible mechanism can satisfy ex post efficiency.

To apply this theory, consider the case where $\tilde{V}_1$ and $\tilde{V}_2$ are both uniformly distributed on $[0, 1]$. Then, each $F_i(v_i) = v_i$ and $f_i(v_i) = 1$ on this interval, and the constraint (2) becomes

$$0 \leqslant \int_0^1 \int_0^1 ([2v_2 - 1] - [2v_1]) \, p(v_1, v_2) \, dv_1 \, dv_2$$

$$= 2 \int_0^1 \int_0^1 (v_2 - v_1 - \tfrac{1}{2}) \, p(v_1, v_2) \, dv_1 \, dv_2.$$

Thus, conditional on the individuals reaching an agreement to trade, the expected difference in their valuations must be at least 1/2. This conclusion holds when these traders use rational equilibrium strategies, no matter what the rules of their bargaining game might be (provided only that either trader could refuse to participate if his expected gains from trade were negative, so that individual rationality is guaranteed). Conditional on the buyer's valuation being higher than the seller's, the expected difference $\tilde{V}_2 - \tilde{V}_1$ would be only

$$\int_0^1 \int_0^{v_2} 2(v_2 - v_1) \, dv_1 \, dv_2 = \frac{1}{3}$$

in this problem. Thus, ex post efficiency cannot be achieved by any individually-rational mechanism, unless some outsider is willing to provide a subsidy of at least

$$\int_0^1 (1-t)t \, dt = \frac{1}{6}$$

to the traders for participating in the bargaining game.

4. Maximizing Expected Total Gains from Trade

The expected total gains from trade in a mechanism is just

$$\int_{a_1}^{b_1} U_1(v_1) f_1(v_1) \, dv_1 + \int_{a_2}^{b_2} U_2(v_2) f_2(v_2) \, dv_2$$

$$= \int_{a_2}^{b_2} \int_{a_1}^{b_1} (v_2 - v_1) p(v_1, v_2) f_1(v_1) f_2(v_2) \, dv_1 \, dv_2.$$

Since ex post efficiency is unattainable, it is natural to seek a mechanism that maximizes expected total gains from trade, subject to the incentive-compatibility and individual-rationality constraints. (Of course, other collective objective functions could also be considered, but here we shall just consider the problem of maximizing expected gains from trade.) With a bit of machinery, we can show how to solve this problem for a wide class of examples.

First, we define some new functions. For any number $\alpha \geqslant 0$, let

$$c_1(v_1, \alpha) = v_1 + \alpha \frac{F_1(v_1)}{f_1(v_1)}, \qquad c_2(v_2, \alpha) = v_2 - \alpha \frac{1 - F_2(v_2)}{f_2(v_2)}.$$

Let $p^\alpha(\cdot, \cdot)$ be defined by

$$p^\alpha(v_1, v_2) = 1 \quad \text{if } c_1(v_1, \alpha) \leqslant c_2(v_2, \alpha),$$
$$= 0 \quad \text{if } c_1(v_1, \alpha) > c_2(v_2, \alpha).$$

Notice that p^0 is the ex post efficient outcome function (transferring the object iff $v_1 \leqslant v_2$), whereas p^1 maximizes the integral in inequality (2).

Theorem 2. *If there exists an incentive-compatible mechanism (p, x) such that $U_1(b_1) = U_2(a_2) = 0$ and $p = p^\alpha$ for some α in $[0, 1]$, then this mechanism maximizes the expected total gains from trade among all incentive-compatible individually-rational mechanisms. Furthermore, if $c_1(\cdot, 1)$ and $c_2(\cdot, 1)$ are increasing functions on $[a_1, b_1]$ and $[a_2, b_2]$, respec-*

tively, and if the interiors of these two intervals have a nonempty intersection, then such a mechanism must exist.

Proof of Theorem 2. Consider the problem to choose $p: [a_1, b_1] \times [a_2, b_2] \to [0, 1]$ to maximize

$$\int_{a_2}^{b_2} \int_{a_1}^{b_1} (v_2 - v_1) p(v_1, v_2) f_1(v_1) f_2(v_2) \, dv_1 \, dv_2$$

subject to constraint (2), that is,

$$\int_{a_2}^{b_2} \int_{a_1}^{b_1} (c_2(v_2, 1) - c_1(v_1, 1)) p(v_1, v_2) f_1(v_1) f_2(v_2) \, dv_1 \, dv_2 \geqslant 0$$

If the solution to this problem happens to give us $\bar{p}_1(\cdot)$ and $\bar{p}_2(\cdot)$, which are monotone decreasing and increasing, respectively, then by Theorem 1, this $p(\cdot, \cdot)$ function will be associated with a mechanism which maximizes the expected gains from trade among all incentive-compatible individually rational mechanisms. If we multiply the integral in the constraint by $\lambda \geqslant 0$ and add it to the objective function, then we get the Lagrangian for this problem; this Lagrangian equals

$$\iint (v_2 + \lambda c_2(v_2, 1) - v_1 - \lambda c_1(v_1, 1)) p(v_1, v_2) f_1(v_1) f_2(v_2) \, dv_1 \, dv_2$$

$$= (1 + \lambda) \iint \left(c_2 \left(v_2, \frac{\lambda}{1 + \lambda} \right) - c_1 \left(v_1, \frac{\lambda}{1 + \lambda} \right) \right)$$
$$\times p(v_1, v_2) f_1(v_1) f_2(v_2) \, dv_1 \, dv_2.$$

Any $p(\cdot, \cdot)$ function that satisfies the constraint with equality and maximizes the Lagrangian for some $\lambda \geqslant 0$ must be a solution for our problem. But the Lagrangian is maximized by p^α, when $\alpha = \lambda/(1 + \lambda)$; and the constraint (2) will be satisfied with equality if $U_1(b_1) = U_2(a_2) = 0$. This proves the first sentence in Theorem 2.

Now, suppose that $c_1(\cdot, 1)$ and $c_2(\cdot, 1)$ are both increasing. Then for every α between 0 and 1, $c_1(\cdot, \alpha)$ and $c_2(\cdot, \alpha)$ are increasing functions, which, in turn, implies that $p^\alpha(v_1, v_2)$ is increasing in v_2 and decreasing in v_1. So all $\bar{p}_1^\alpha$ and $\bar{p}_2^\alpha$ have the necessary monotonicity properties.

Let

$$G(\alpha) = \int_{a_2}^{b_2} \int_{a_1}^{b_1} (c_2(v_2, 1) - c_1(v_1, 1)) p^\alpha(v_1, v_2) f_1(v_1) f_2(v_2) \, dv_1 \, dv_2.$$

Clearly, $G(1) \geqslant 0$, since p^1 is positive only when $c_2(v_2, 1) \geqslant c_1(v_1, 1)$. Furthermore, $G(\alpha)$ is increasing in α. To prove this, observe that

$$c_2(v_2, \alpha) - c_1(v_1, \alpha) = (v_2 - v_1) - \alpha \left(\frac{1 - F_2(v_2)}{f_2(v_2)} + \frac{F_1(v_1)}{f_1(v_1)} \right),$$

which is decreasing in α, so $p^\alpha(v_1, v_2)$ is decreasing in α. Thus, for $\alpha < \beta$, $G(\beta)$ differs from $G(\alpha)$ only because $0 = p^\beta(v_1, v_2) < p^\alpha(v_1, v_2) = 1$ for some (v_1, v_2) where $c_2(v_2, \beta) < c_1(v_1, \beta)$ and so $c_2(v_2, 1) < c_1(v_1, 1)$. Thus, $G(\cdot)$ is increasing.

To prove that $G(\cdot)$ is continuous, observe that, if each $c_i(v_i, 1)$ is increasing in v_i, then each $c_i(v_i, \alpha)$ is strictly increasing in v_i, for any $\alpha < 1$. So given v_2 and α, the equation $c_1(v_1, \alpha) = c_2(v_2, \alpha)$ has at most one solution in v_1, and this solution varies continuously in v_2 and α. Thus, we may write

$$G(\alpha) = \int_{a_2}^{b_2} \int_{a_1}^{g(v_2, \alpha)} (c_2(v_2, 1) - c_1(v_1, 1)) f_1(v_1) f_2(v_2) \, dv_1 \, dv_2,$$

where $g(v_2, \alpha)$ is continuous in v_2 and α. So $G(\cdot)$ is continuous, increasing, and $G(1) \geqslant 0$. But $G(0) < 0$, because otherwise p^0 would be an ex post efficient individually-rational mechanism, which is impossible by Corollary 1. Thus there must be some α in $(0, 1]$ such that $G(\alpha) = 0$ and p^α can satisfy the conditions in Theorem 2. This completes the proof of Theorem 2. ∎

For an example, consider again the case where $\tilde{V}_1$ and $\tilde{V}_2$ are both uniform random variables on $[0, 1]$. Then,

$$c_1(v_1, \alpha) = v_1 + \alpha v_1 = (1 + \alpha) v_1$$

and

$$c_2(v_2, \alpha) = v_2 - \alpha(1 - v_2) = (1 + \alpha) v_2 - \alpha.$$

Both of these functions are monotone increasing when $\alpha = 1$, so we know that the expected gains from trade are maximized by $p = p^\alpha$ for some α between 0 and 1. To get $U_1(b_1) = U_2(a_2) = 0$ for $p = p^\alpha$, we must have (by Eq. (1))

$$0 = \int_0^1 \int_0^1 ([2v_2 - 1] - [2v_2]) p^\alpha(v_1, v_2) \, dv_1 \, dv_2.$$

But in this case

$$p^\alpha(v_1, v_2) = 1 \quad \text{if} \quad (1 + \alpha) v_1 \leqslant (1 + \alpha) v_2 - \alpha,$$
$$= 0 \quad \text{if} \quad (1 + \alpha) v_1 > (1 + \alpha) v_2 - \alpha.$$

So the above equation becomes

$$0 = \int_{a/(1+a)}^{1} \int_{0}^{v_2 - a/(1+a)} [2v_2 - 1 - 2v_1] \, dv_1 \, dv_2 = \frac{3a - 1}{6(1 + a)^3}.$$

So we must have $a = 1/3$, and then $p = p^a$ implies

$$p(v_1, v_2) = 1 \text{ if } v_1 \leqslant v_2 - \tfrac{1}{4},$$
$$= 0 \text{ if } v_1 > v_2 - \tfrac{1}{4}.$$

So the expected gains from trade are maximized by a mechanism which transfers the object iff the buyer's valuation exceeds the seller's by at least 1/4.

Such a mechanism has indeed been found for this example. Chatterjee and Samuelson [2] have studied a bargaining game with the following rules. The buyer and seller each simultaneously propose a price. If the buyer's price is higher than the seller's, then the object is sold at the average of the two; otherwise the seller keeps the object. This mechanism is *not* incentive-compatible. In fact, Chatterjee and Samuelson have shown that in the equilibrium strategies for this example, the seller proposes price $2/3 v_1 + 1/4$ and the buyer proposes price $2/3 v_2 + 1/12$. Thus, the object is sold iff

$$\frac{2}{3} v_1 + \frac{1}{4} \leqslant \frac{2}{3} v_2 + \frac{1}{12} \quad \text{or} \quad v_1 \leqslant v_2 - \frac{1}{4},$$

and the sale price is

$$\frac{1}{2} \left(\frac{2}{3} v_1 + \frac{1}{4} \right) + \frac{1}{2} \left(\frac{2}{3} v_2 + \frac{1}{12} \right) = \frac{1}{3} \left(v_1 + v_2 + \frac{1}{2} \right).$$

In this equilibrium, there is no possibility of trade if $\tilde{V}_1 = 1$ or $\tilde{V}_2 = 0$, so $U_1(1) = U_2(0) = 0$. Thus, this equilibrium of this split-the-difference game gives the highest expected total gains from trade among all equilibria of all bargaining games satisfying individual-rationality for this symmetric-uniform trading problem.

To illustrate the revelation principle, we may point out that the incentive-compatible direct mechanism equivalent to the Chatterjee-Samuelson equilibrium for this example is to have

$$p(v_1, v_2) = 1 \quad \text{if} \quad v_1 \leqslant v_2 - \tfrac{1}{4},$$
$$= 0 \quad \text{otherwise},$$

$$x(v_1, v_2) = (v_1 + v_2 + .5)/3 \quad \text{if} \quad v_1 \leqslant v_2 - \tfrac{1}{4},$$
$$0 \quad \text{otherwise}.$$

That is, the direct mechanism simply implements what the original game would have done after the players used their equilibrium strategies.

5. Trading with a Broker

Thus far, we have assumed that the payments from the buyer must equal the payments to the seller, because there is no outside source (or sink) of funds. Let us now drop this assumption, and allow a third party to either subsidize or exploit the buyer and seller. We shall refer to this third party as the *broker*.

Let us assume that the broker can be a net source or sink of money, but he cannot himself own the object. Thus, a trading mechanism with a broker is characterized by three outcome functions (p, x_1, x_2), where $p(v_1, v_2)$ is the probability that the object is transferred from the seller to the buyer, $x_1(v_1, v_2)$ is the expected payment from broker to seller, and $x_2(v_1, v_2)$ is the expected payment from buyer to broker, if v_1 and v_2 are the reported valuations of seller and buyer. Given such a mechanism, we define $\bar{x}_1(v_1)$, $\bar{x}_2(v_2)$, $\bar{p}_1(v_1)$, $\bar{p}_2(v_2)$, $U_1(v_1)$ and $U_2(v_2)$ exactly as in Section 2, except that we must modify the definitions of $\bar{x}_1(v_1)$ and $\bar{x}_2(v_2)$ to:

$$\bar{x}_1(v_1) = \int_{a_2}^{b_2} x_1(v_1, t_2) f_2(t_2) \, dt_2,$$

$$\bar{x}_2(v_2) = \int_{a_1}^{b_1} x_2(t_1, v_2) f_1(t_1) \, dt_1.$$

In addition, we let U_0 denote the expected net profit for the broker, so that

$$U_0 = \int_{a_2}^{b_2} \int_{a_1}^{b_1} (x_2(t_1, t_2) - x_1(t_1, t_2)) f_1(t_1) f_2(t_2) \, dt_1 \, dt_2.$$

The definitions of incentive-compatibility and individual-rationality for a trading mechanism with broker are the same as in Section 2: neither buyer nor seller should ever expect to gain by lying about his valuation, and both traders should get nonnegative expected gains from trade in the mechanism. As before, there is no loss of generality in restricting our attention to incentive-compatible mechanisms, because any Bayesian equilibrium of any trading game with broker can be simulated by an equivalent incentive-compatible direct mechanism.

For any v_1 and v_2, let

$$C_1(v_1) = c_1(v_1, 1) = v_1 + \frac{F_1(v_1)}{f_1(v_1)},$$

$$C_2(v_2) = c_2(v_2, 1) = v_2 - \frac{1 - F_1(v_1)}{f_2(v_2)}.$$

With this formulation we can extend Theorem 1, as follows.

THEOREM 3. *For any incentive-compatible mechanism with a broker,* $\bar{p}_1(\cdot)$ *is weakly decreasing,* $\bar{p}_2(\cdot)$ *is weakly increasing, and*

$$U_0 + U_1(b_1) + U_2(a_2) = U_0 + \underset{v_1\epsilon[a_1,b_1]}{\text{minimum}}\ (U_1(v_1)) + \underset{v_2\epsilon[a_2,b_2]}{\text{minimum}}\ (U_2(v_2))$$

$$= \int_{a_2}^{b_2} \int_{a_1}^{b_1} (C_2(v_2) - C_1(v_1))\, p(v_1, v_2)\, f_1(v_1)\, f_2(v_2)\, dv_1\, dv_2. \tag{8}$$

Proof of Theorem 3.   The proof is exactly the same as the proof of Theorem 1 except that the string of equalities after Eq. (5) must begin with

$$\int_{a_2}^{b_2} \int_{a_1}^{b_1} (v_1 - v_2)\, p(v_1, v_2)\, f_1(v_1)\, f_2(v_2)\, dv_1\, dv_2 - U_0$$

$$= \int_{a_1}^{b_1} U_1(v_1)\, f_1(v_1)\, dv_1 + \int_{a_2}^{b_2} U_2(v_2)\, f_2(v_2)\, dv_2.$$

(That is, the expected gains from trade minus the expected net profit to the broker must equal the expected gains to buyer and seller.) With this one change, the proof goes through exactly as before. ∎

Extending the results in Section 3, Theorem 3 implies that, for any ex post efficient mechanism with broker,

$$U_0 + U_1(b_1) + U_2(a_2) = -\int_{a_2}^{b_1} (1 - F_2(t))\, F_1(t)\, dt.$$

Thus, the minimum expected subsidy required from the broker, to achieve ex post efficiency with individual-rationality, is

$$\int_{a_2}^{b_1} (1 - F_2(t))\, F_1(t)\, dt,$$

even if the subsidy is not lump-sum.

Another interesting question is to ask for the mechanism which maximizes the expected profit to the broker, subject to incentive compatibility and individual rationality for the two traders. That is, if the buyer and seller can only trade through the broker, then what is the optimal mechanism for the broker?

THEOREM 4.   *Suppose $C_1(\cdot)$ and $C_2(\cdot)$ are monotone increasing functions on $[a_1, b_1]$ and $[a_2, b_2]$, respectively. Then among all incentive-compatible, individually-rational mechanisms, the broker's expected profit is maximized by a mechanism in which the object is transferred to the buyer if and only if $C_2(\tilde{V}_2) \geqslant C_1(\tilde{V}_1)$.*

Proof of Theorem 4.   From Theorem 3 we get

$$U_0 = \iint (C_2(v_2) - C_1(v_1))\, p(v_1, v_2) f_1(v_1) f_2(v_2)\, dv_1\, dv_2 - U_1(b_1) - U_2(a_2),$$

for any incentive-compatible mechanism. To maximize this expression subject to individual rationality, we want

$$p(v_1, v_2) = 1 \qquad \text{if} \quad C_2(v_2) \geqslant C_1(v_1)$$
$$= 0 \qquad \text{if} \quad C_2(v_2) < C_1(v_1),$$

and $U_1(b_1) = U_2(a_2) = 0$. It only remains to construct x_1 and x_2 such that (p, x_1, x_2) satisfies these conditions and incentive compatibility. There are many ways to do this; one is to let

$$x_2(v_1, v_2) = p(v_1, v_2) \cdot \min\{t_2 | t_2 \geqslant a_2 \text{ and } C_2(t_2) \geqslant C_1(v_1)\},$$
$$x_1(v_1, v_2) = p(v_1, v_2) \cdot \max\{t_1 | t_1 \leqslant b_1 \text{ and } C_1(t_1) \leqslant C_2(v_2)\}.$$

That is, if there is a trade, then the broker charges the buyer the lowest valuation he could have quoted and still gotten the object (given the seller's valuation), and the broker pays to the seller the highest valuation which he could have quoted and still sold the object (given the buyer's valuation). If there is no trade, then there are no payments.

It is straightforward to show that this mechanism is incentive-compatible if the $C_1(\cdot)$ and $C_2(\cdot)$ functions are monotone, following the argument used by Vickrey [7] to show the incentive-compatibility of the second price auction. For example, if the seller reported a valuation higher than the truth, he would not affect the price he gets when he sells, but he would lose some opportunities to sell when he could have done so profitably in the mechanism. Similarly, if the seller reported a valuation lower than the truth, then he would only add possibilities of selling below his valuation. It is also straightforward to check that $U_1(b_1) = 0$ and $U_2(a_2) = 0$ in this mechanism, since it gives

$$x_1(b_1, v_2) = p(b_1, v_2)\, b_1, \qquad x_2(v_1, a_2) = p(v_1, a_2)\, a_2. \quad \blacksquare$$

For the case where $\tilde{V}_1$ and $\tilde{V}_2$ are both uniform on $[0, 1]$, the broker's optimal mechanism transfers the object if and only if

$$C_2(\tilde{V}_2) = 2\tilde{V}_2 - 1 \geqslant 2\tilde{V}_1 = C_1(\tilde{V}_1), \qquad \text{or} \quad \tilde{V}_2 - \tilde{V}_1 \geqslant \tfrac{1}{2}.$$

So the broker should offer to buy from the seller for $\tilde{V}_2 - 1/2$, and should offer to sell to the buyer for $\tilde{V}_1 + 1/2$, and trade occurs if and only if the traders are both willing to trade at these prices.

Comparing Theorems 2 and 4, we see that the broker's optimal trading mechanism has strictly less trading than the mechanism which maximizes the expected total gains from trade. In this symmetric-uniform example, the maximum expected total gains from trade is achieved by a mechanism in which the object is transferred whenever the buyer's valuation exceeds the seller's by at least $1/4$, but the broker's optimal mechanism does not transfer the object unless the buyer's valuations exceeds the seller's by at least $1/2$. That is, if a broker is to profitably exploit his control over the trading channel, he must actually restrict trade to some extent.

In both Theorems 2 and 4, monotonicity of the $C_i(\cdot)$ functions is required. This assumption is satisfied for a very wide class of distributions, but it is a restriction. The general case can be analyzed using the methods developed in Myerson [6] to construct optimal auctions in the general (nonmonotone) case.

REFERENCES

1. K. CHATTERJEE, Incentive compatibility in bargaining under uncertainty, mimeograph, Pennsylvania State University, 1980. To appear in *Quarterly Journal of Economics.*
2. K. CHATTERJEE AND W. SAMUELSON, "The Simple Economics of Bargaining," mimeographed, Pennsylvania State University and Boston University, 1979. To appear in *Operations Research.*
3. C. D'ASPREMONT AND L. GERARD-VARET, Incentives and incomplete information. *J. Pub. Econom.* **11** (1979), 25–45.
4. J.-J. LAFFONT AND E. MASKIN, A differential approach to expected utility maximizing mechanisms, *in* "Aggregation and Revelation of Preferences," (J.-J. Laffont, Ed.), pp. 289–308, North-Holland, Amsterdam, 1979.
5. R. B. MYERSON, Incentive compatibility and the bargaining problem, *Econometrica* **47** (1979), 61–73.
6. R. B. MYERSON, Optimal auction design, *Math. Oper. Res.* **6** (1981), 58–73.
7. W. VICKREY, Counterspeculation, auctions, and competitive sealed tenders. *J. Finance* **16** (1961), 8–37.

JOURNAL OF ECONOMIC THEORY **53**, 131–145 (1991)

Ex Ante Efficient, Ex Post Individually Rational Trade

THOMAS A. GRESIK*

*John M. Olin School of Business, Washington University,
St. Louis, Missouri 63130*

Received July 21, 1989

Consider a bilateral-trade model with two-sided incomplete information. For a general set of independent beliefs, an *ex post* individually rational mechanism generating the same level of *ex ante* expected gains from trade as an *ex ante* efficient, interim individually rational mechanism is constructed. Thus, imposing the stronger notion of *ex post* individual rationality on this mechanism design problem generates no loss of efficiency. *Journal of Economic Literature* Classification Numbers: 026, 024. © 1991 Academic Press, Inc.

1. INTRODUCTION

One of the major research programs of the last 10 years involves understanding why a significant proportion of commercial trade is transacted through a seemingly small number of trading institutions. For instance, Wilson [15, p. 36] reports that a few simple rules such as auctions, double auctions, bid–ask markets, and specialist trading account for most institutional exchange. The mechanism design approach, with its formal foundations in Myerson [11], has had only limited success in advancing this line of study, in part because the theoretically optimal mechanisms differ from the above institutions in important ways.

One particular discrepancy between the derived rules of trade and the observed rules involves their individual rationality properties. The standard in mechanism design is interim individual rationality. It ensures that each trader's expected utility conditional on his private information is non-negative. On the other hand, in most markets each trader has the ability to refuse to trade when the "best" negotiated terms give him negative

* I have benefitted greatly from discussions with Bob Wilson and participants at Northwestern's Theory Seminar, especially Mark Satterthwaite and Steve Williams. I also thank Larry Samuelson and Don Coursey for their comments. I am solely responsible for all errors.

FIG. 1. A trading process defined *ex ante* and the points in the process beyond which *ex ante*, interim, and *ex post* individual rationality prohibit reneging, respectively.

utility.[1] That is, the rules of trade used by many institutions, including those Wilson mentions, are *ex post* individually rational. This is a much stronger rationality property than interim individual rationality.

The basic difference between the standard notions of individual rationality (*ex ante*, interim, and *ex post*) involves the point in the trading process beyond which no trader can drop out. Figure 1 illustrates the sequence of events that make up a trading process in which traders use the same rule repeatedly. *Ex ante* individual rationality requires that all traders commit to the trading process after learning the rules of trade but before receiving any private information. Interim individual rationality allows a trader to drop out after learning his type but before submitting a bid or an offer. *Ex post* individual rationality, on the other hand, allows a trader to first learn the terms of trade before deciding whether or not to consummate the deal.

D'Aspremont and Gerard-Varet [2] prove the existence of (Bayesian–Nash) incentive compatible, *ex ante* individually rational, *ex post* efficient mechanisms. Myerson and Satterthwaite [12] in turn show that in independent, private value markets with a continuum of trader types there exists no incentive compatible, interim individually rational, *ex post* efficient mechanism. Thus, requiring a mechanism to be interim individually rational generates efficiency losses. In this paper, I investigate the potential efficiency losses associated with *ex post* individually rational mechanisms in the Myerson and Satterthwaite model.

The first part of the paper, Section 2, reviews the characterization of bilateral-trade mechanisms that are incentive compatible, interim

---

[1] Actually, *ex post* individual rationality requires each trader's expected utility from participating, conditional on all traders' types, to be non-negative. If the commodity being traded is itself a random variable, e.g. a futures contract, then even trades executed via an *ex post* individually rational mechanism can give a trader negative utility. However, *ex post* individually rational mechanisms do guarantee that any realized trading loss will only be due to some unresolved uncertainty at the time of trade. Such uncertainty is not explicitly modelled in this paper.

individually rational, and *ex ante* efficient.[2] Particular emphasis is given to the restrictions placed upon a mechanism's payment rule. Sections 3 and 4 then construct a trading mechanism that not only satisfies these three desiderata but, for a large class of environments, is also *ex post* individually rational. This class includes most of the environments considered in the mechanism design literature. Consequently, in those environments, imposing this stronger rationality condition generates no welfare losses. As a result, employing *ex post* individually rational mechanisms dominates the alternative of using contracts to bind traders to the outcomes proposed by any interim individually rational mechanism. Since writing and enforcing such contracts is costly, their use renders the associated trading mechanism *ex ante* inefficient.

2. CHARACTERIZING *EX ANTE* INCENTIVE EFFICIENT MECHANISMS

Consider the problem of a risk-neutral buyer and seller negotiating the trade of a single, indivisible good when each trader's valuation is private information. Regard the buyer's valuation, v_b, and the seller's valuation, v_s, as being drawn independently from the distributions $F_b(\cdot)$ and $F_s(\cdot)$, respectively. The corresponding densities, $f_b(\cdot)$ and $f_s(\cdot)$, are continuous with non-zero support on $[0, 1]$. Let F_b (F_s) represent the seller's (buyer's) beliefs about the other's valuation. These beliefs are common knowledge.

Direct mechanisms, which require the traders to simultaneously report their valuations, provide a way for setting the terms of trade. However, the private nature of each trader's valuation means there is no way to verify the veracity of any report. Denote the buyer's report by b and the seller's report by s. A direct mechanism, then, consists of a trading rule $p(b, s)$: $[0, 1]^2 \rightarrow [0, 1]$ that determines the probability that trade occurs and a payment rule $x(b, s)$: $[0, 1]^2 \rightarrow R$ that assesses any money transfers from the buyer to the seller. Denote a direct mechanism by (p, x).

Given reports (b, s) and valuations (v_b, v_s), the buyer's utility from participating in this process is $v_b\, p(b, s) - x(b, s)$ and the seller's is $x(b, s) - v_s\, p(b, s)$. Each trader selects a report that maximizes his interim expected utility. Without loss of generality, the Revelation Principle allows us to restrict the set of feasible mechanisms to those that are (interim) incentive compatible. A mechanism is incentive compatible if it supports a Bayesian–Nash equilibrium in which every trader honestly reports his valuation.

To define the traders' interim expected utilities, first let

---

[2] See Myerson and Satterthwaite [12] or Gresik and Satterthwaite [5] for a detailed discussion.

$$p_b(b) = \int_{v_s=0}^{1} p(b, v_s) f_s(v_s) \, dv_s,$$

$$p_s(s) = \int_{v_b=0}^{1} p(v_b, s) f_b(v_b) \, dv_b,$$

$$x_b(b) = \int_{v_s=0}^{1} x(b, v_s) f_s(v_s) \, dv_s,$$

and

$$x_s(s) = \int_{v_b=0}^{1} x(v_b, s) f_b(v_b) \, dv_b.$$

Then, given that the other trader reports honestly, the buyer's interim expected utility from reporting b and the seller's from reporting s are

$$U(b, v_b) = v_b \, p_b(b) - x_b(b) \qquad \text{and} \qquad V(s, v_s) = x_s(s) - v_s \, p_s(s),$$

respectively. Therefore, a mechanism is incentive compatible if for all v_b and b, $U(v_b) \equiv U(v_b, v_b) \geq U(b, v_b)$ and for all v_s and s, $V(v_s) \equiv V(v_s, v_s) \geq V(s, v_s)$.

In addition, we restrict consideration to interim individually rational mechanisms. An incentive compatible mechanism is interim individually rational if for all v_b, $U(v_b) \geq 0$ and for all v_s, $V(v_s) \geq 0$. These constraints ensure that participation is always optimal. A mechanism that is both incentive compatible and interim individually rational is said to be incentive feasible.

Finally, consider the set of direct mechanisms that are incentive feasible and that maximize *ex ante* expected gains from trade. This objective is consistent with the notion of designing rules of trade which the buyer and the seller expect to use repeatedly. The *ex ante* expected gains from trade generated by an incentive feasible mechanism equal

$$\int_{v_b=0}^{1} U(v_b) f_b(v_b) \, dv_b + \int_{v_s=0}^{1} V(v_s) f_s(v_s) \, dv_s.^3 \qquad (2.01)$$

Any incentive feasible trading mechanism that maximizes (2.01) is called *ex ante* incentive efficient.[4]

---

[3] Williams [14] solves a more general design problem by maximizing an arbitrarily weighted sum of the traders' *ex ante* expected payoffs. Allowing the welfare weights to be unequal does not affect this paper's qualitative results.

[4] See Holmström and Myerson [7] for a complete discussion of the various notions of incentive efficiency.

For a certain nice class of beliefs, *ex ante* incentive efficient mechanisms have a simple characterization. To define this class, let

$$c_b(v_b, \alpha) = v_b + \alpha(F_b(v_b) - 1)/f_b(v_b) \tag{2.02}$$

and

$$c_s(v_s, \alpha) = v_s + \alpha F_s(v_s)/f_s(v_s), \tag{2.03}$$

where $0 \leqslant \alpha \leqslant 1$. Adopting Myerson's [10] terminology, $c_b(\cdot, \alpha)$ and $c_s(\cdot, \alpha)$ are the buyer's and the seller's virtual reservation valuations, respectively. Also define

$$p^\alpha(v_b, v_s) = \begin{cases} 1 & \text{if} \quad c_b(v_b, \alpha) \geqslant c_s(v_s, \alpha) \\ 0 & \text{if} \quad c_b(v_b, \alpha) < c_s(v_s, \alpha), \end{cases} \tag{2.04}$$

$$W(p) = \int_{v_b = 0}^{1} \int_{v_s = 0}^{1} [c_b(v_b, 1) - c_s(v_s, 1)]$$
$$\times p(v_b, v_s) f_b(v_b) f_s(v_s) \, dv_s \, dv_b, \tag{2.05}$$

and let $\alpha^* = \min\{\alpha \mid W(p^\alpha) \geqslant 0\}$.[5] Finally, call (F_b, F_s) regular if $c_b(\cdot, \alpha^*)$ and $c_s(\cdot, \alpha^*)$ are increasing.[6] Theorem 1 characterizes the set of *ex ante* incentive efficient mechanisms for regular beliefs.

THEOREM 1 (Myerson and Satterthwaite [12], Gresik and Satterthwaite [5]). *Let (F_b, F_s) be regular. Then (p^{α^*}, x) is* ex ante *incentive efficient if, and only if,*

$$x_b(v_b) = \int_{t = 0}^{v_b} t \, dp_b(t) \tag{2.06}$$

and

$$x_s(v_s) = -\int_{t = v_s}^{1} t \, dp_s(t).^7 \tag{2.07}$$

Gresik and Satterthwaite [5] offer one solution to (2.06) and (2.07). It is

---

[5] Gresik and Satterthwaite [5] show that this minimum is well-defined.

[6] Myerson [11] and Satterthwaite and Williams [13] call a trading problem regular if $c_b(\cdot, 1)$ and $c_s(\cdot, 1)$ are non-decreasing. Because α^* is always strictly less than one, their notion of regularity is more restrictive than the definition used in this paper.

[7] Myerson and Satterthwaite [12] prove the sufficiency of (2.06) and (2.07). Gresik and Satterthwaite [5] prove necessity.

$$x(v_b, v_s) = \int_{t=0}^{v_b} t \, dp_b(t) - \int_{t=v_s}^1 t \, dp_s(t) - \int_{t=0}^1 tF_s(t) \, dp_s(t).^8 \qquad (2.08)$$

Equation (2.08) is typical of the solutions to (2.06) and (2.07) found in other papers in that it mandates payments in the absence of trade and with positive probability, it gives some types of sellers negative utility when trade occurs. Traders facing such outcomes have an incentive to reject the proposed trade. The ability to reject a proposed trade, however, affects a mechanism's incentive properties in a way that Theorem 1 does not reflect. Consider then the problem of designing an *ex ante* incentive efficient mechanism for which

    (a)   money transfers equal zero in the absence of trade; and

    (b)   each trader's utility is non-negative when trade occurs.

Such a mechanism is *ex post* individually rational because it guarantees that each trader's utility is always non-negative.

The approach employed here involves finding a solution to (2.06) and (2.07) that satisfies properties (a) and (b). To begin, rewrite Eqs. (2.06) and (2.07) as Riemann–Stieltjes integrals. Namely,

$$x_b(v_b) = \int_{v_s=0}^1 \int_{t=0}^{v_b} t \, dp(t, v_s) f_s(v_s) \, dv_s \qquad (2.09)$$

and

$$x_s(v_s) = -\int_{v_b=0}^1 \int_{t=v_s}^1 t \, dp(v_b, t) f_b(v_b) \, dv_b. \qquad (2.10)$$

Recall that Eq. (2.04) specifies the functional form of an optimal trading rule. Because of the monotonicity properties regularity requires, the trading rule from an incentive efficient mechanism is a step function with a single step. Thus, the only non-zero contribution to the right-hand side of Eq. (2.09) occurs when $v_s \leqslant c_s^{-1}(1, \alpha^*)$ and $t = b(v_s, \alpha^*) \equiv c_b^{-1}(c_s(v_s, \alpha^*), \alpha^*)$. Similarly, for Eq. (2.10) the only non-zero contribution occurs when $v_b \geqslant c_b^{-1}(0, \alpha^*)$ and $t = s(v_b, \alpha^*) \equiv c_s^{-1}(c_b(v_b, \alpha^*), \alpha^*).^9$

Both $b(v_s)$ and $s(v_b)$ have straightforward economic interpretations. When the seller reports v_s, $b(v_s)$ represents the smallest trade-generating report the buyer could have submitted. Likewise, when the buyer reports v_b, $s(v_b)$ represents the largest trade-generating report the seller could have made.

---

[8] Myerson and Satterthwaite [12] use a payment rule that differs from (2.08) only in its constant term.

[9] Except in those instances where ambiguities may arise, the reference to α^* as the second argument of $b(v_s, \cdot)$ and $s(v_b, \cdot)$ will be omitted.

3. Zero Money Transfers in the Absence of Trade

Incorporating property (a) into Eqs. (2.09) and (2.10) yields three conditions on the payment rule. They are

$$x(v_b, v_s) = 0 \text{ if } c_b(v_b, \alpha^*) < c_s(v_s, \alpha^*), \tag{3.01}$$

$$\int_{v_s = 0}^{s(v_b)} x(v_b, v_s) f_s(v_s) \, dv_s = \int_{v_s = 0}^{s(v_b)} b(v_s) f_s(v_s) \, dv_s, \tag{3.02}$$

and

$$\int_{v_b = b(v_s)}^{1} x(v_b, v_s) f_b(v_b) \, dv_b = \int_{v_b = b(v_s)}^{1} s(v_b) f_b(v_b) \, dv_b \tag{3.03}$$

if $c_b(v_b, \alpha^*) \geqslant c_s(v_s, \alpha^*)$. Theorem 2 proves that a solution to (3.01)–(3.03) exists for all regular beliefs.

THEOREM 2. *Let* (F_b, F_s) *be regular. There exists an incentive efficient trading mechanism that prescribes zero money transfers in the absence of trade.*

A lemma is needed to prove Theorem 2. To state this lemma, define

$$\theta_1(v_s) = F_s(v_s) \frac{db(v_s)}{dv_s} \{ [v_s - b(v_s)] f_b[b(v_s)] + 1 - F_b[b(v_s)] \} \tag{3.04}$$

and

$$g(v_s) = - \int_{t = v_s}^{s(1)} \theta_1(t) \, dt. \tag{3.05}$$

LEMMA 1. $g(0) = g[s(1)] = 0.$

The proof of Lemma 1 is in the appendix.

Proof of Theorem 2. Define

$$\theta_2(v_s) = \frac{g(v_s) f_s(v_s)}{(1 - F_b[b(v_s)]) F_s(v_s)^2 \, db(v_s)/dv_s}. \tag{3.06}$$

and

$$x^*(v_b, v_s) = \begin{cases} b(v_s) - \dfrac{g(v_s)}{(1 - F_b[b(v_s)]) F_s(v_s)} + \displaystyle\int_{t = b(v_s)}^{v_b} \theta_2[s(t)] \, dt \\ \quad \text{if } c_b(v_b, \alpha^*) \geqslant c_s(v_s, \alpha^*) \\ 0 \quad \text{otherwise.} \end{cases} \tag{3.07}$$

This proof will show that (3.07) satisfies (3.02) and (3.03). To begin, consider solutions of the form $x(v_b, v_s) = \phi(v_b) + \gamma(v_s)$. For such solutions (3.02) and (3.03) become

$$\phi(v_b) F_s[s(v_b)] + \int_{v_s=0}^{s(v_b)} \gamma(v_s) f_s(v_s) \, dv_s = \int_{v_s=0}^{s(v_b)} b(v_s) f_s(v_s) \, dv_s \quad (3.08)$$

and

$$\gamma(v_s)(1 - F_b[b(v_s)]) + \int_{v_b=b(v_s)}^{1} \phi(v_b) f_b(v_b) \, dv_b$$

$$= \int_{v_b=b(v_s)}^{1} s(v_b) f_b(v_b) \, dv_b. \quad (3.09)$$

Payment rule (3.07) is generated by the following steps:

(i)   differentiate (3.08) with respect to v_b,

(ii)   differentiate (3.09) with respect to v_s,

(iii)   substitute $v_b = b(v_s)$ into the equation from step (i) and solve for $\gamma(v_s)$,

(iv)   differentiate $\gamma(v_s)$ from step (iii) with respect to v_s, and

(v)   substitute the equations from steps (iii) and (iv) into the equation from step (ii).

Step (iii) yields

$$\gamma(v_s) = b(v_s) - \phi[b(v_s)] - \phi'[b(v_s)] \frac{F_s(v_s)}{f_s(v_s)} \frac{db(v_s)}{dv_s} \quad (3.10)$$

while step (v) produces the differential equation

$$\phi''[b(v_s)](1 - F_b[b(v_s)]) \frac{F_s(v_s)}{f_s(v_s)} \left(\frac{db(v_s)}{dv_s} \right)^2$$

$$+ \phi'[b(v_s)] \left\{ (1 - F_b[b(v_s)]) \right.$$

$$\times \left[\frac{F_s(v_s)}{f_s(v_s)} \frac{d^2 b(v_s)}{dv_s^2} + \frac{db(v_s)}{dv_s} \left[2 - \frac{F_s(v_s) f_s'(v_s)}{f_s(v_s)^2} \right] \right]$$

$$\left. - \frac{F_s(v_s)}{f_s(v_s)} f_b[b(v_s)] \left(\frac{db(v_s)}{dv_s} \right)^2 \right\}$$

$$= \left\{ [v_s - b(v_s)] f_b[b(v_s)] + (1 - F_b[b(v_s)]) \right\} \frac{db(v_s)}{dv_s}. \quad (3.11)$$

The non-homogeneous solution to Eq. (3.11) is

$$\phi(v_b) = \int_{t=0}^{v_b} \theta_2 [s(t)] \, dt. \tag{3.12}$$

Given (3.12), (3.10) admits a solution for γ which together with (3.12) yields x^*.

Finally, l'Hôpital's Rule and Lemma 1 imply that x^* is well-defined at $v_s = 0$ and at $v_s = s(1)$. Q.E.D.

EXAMPLE 1. Uniform beliefs—$F_b(t) = F_s(t) = t$. Eq. (3.07) becomes

$$x^*(v_b, v_s) = \begin{cases} (v_b + v_s + \frac{1}{3})/2 & \text{if } v_b \geqslant v_s + \frac{1}{4} \\ 0 & \text{if } v_b < v_s + \frac{1}{4}. \end{cases}$$

Thus, the above technique produces the mechanism which Myerson and Satterthwaite show not only maximizes *ex ante* expected gains from trade in the uniform case but is also equivalent to the linear equilibrium of Chatterjee and Samuelson's split-the-difference game [1].

EXAMPLE 2. More generally, consider the class of beliefs where, for $\beta, \rho > 0$, $F_b(t) = 1 - (1 - t)^\rho$ and $F_s(t) = t^\beta$. This class of beliefs generates linear virtual valuations (Eqs. (2.02) and (2.03)). Leininger, Linhart, and Radner [8] also show that this is the class for which the split-the-difference game admits linear equilibria. Finally, Gresik [3] shows that for each member of this class, there exists a $k \in (0, 1)$ such that the linear equilibrium of the k-double auction achieves *ex ante* incentive efficient performance.

For this example, (3.07) reduces to a payment rule of the form

$$x^*(v_b, v_s) = \begin{cases} a_1 v_b + a_2 v_s + a_3 & \text{if } c_b(v_b, \alpha^*) \geqslant c_s(v_s, \alpha^*) \\ 0 & \text{otherwise,} \end{cases}$$

where a_1, a_2, and a_3 are functions of β and ρ. Their explicit values are derived in Gresik [3, Theorem 1].

4. NON-NEGATIVE PAYOFFS FROM TRADE

A payment rule having been constructed that requires zero money transfers when no trade occurs, the next step is to check whether such a rule also guarantees non-negative utility to each trader when trade does occur. If it does,. then the resultant trading mechanism is *ex post* individually rational.

Lemma 2 shows that the payment rule $x = x^*$ defines non-negative payoffs if it is non-decreasing in both arguments. First, let $x_1(v_b, v_s)$ and $x_2(v_b, v_s)$ denote the partial derivatives of $x(\cdot, \cdot)$. Then given Eq. (3.07), $x_1(v_b, v_s) = \theta_2[s(v_b)]$ and

$$x_2(v_b, v_s) = \frac{-f_b[b(v_s)]\{g(v_s) + [v_s - b(v_s)]\, F_s(v_s)(1 - F_b[b(v_s)])\}}{(1 - F_b[b(v_s)])^2\, F_s(v_s)} \frac{db(v_s)}{dv_s}.$$

$$(4.01)$$

LEMMA 2. *Let* $x = x^*$. *If for all* v_b *and* v_s, $x_1(v_b, v_s) \geqslant 0$ *and* $x_2(v_b, v_s) \geqslant 0$, *then* $v_s \leqslant x(v_b, v_s) \leqslant v_b$.

Proof of Lemma 2. Observe that $x_1(v_b, v_s) \geqslant 0$ if, and only if,

$$g[s(v_b)] \geqslant 0; \tag{4.02}$$

and $x_2(v_b, v_s) \geqslant 0$ if, and only if,

$$g(v_s) + [v_s - b(v_s)]\, F_s(v_s)(1 - F_b[b(v_s)]) \leqslant 0. \tag{4.03}$$

Next fix v_b. Since $x_2(v_b, v_s) \geqslant 0$, $x(v_b, v_s)$ is maximized by maximizing v_s. The largest value of v_s for which trade will occur is $s(v_b)$. Then

$$x(v_b, s(v_b)) = v_b - \frac{g[s(v_b)]}{(1 - F_b(v_b))\, F_s[s(v_b)]} \leqslant v_b$$

since $x_1(v_b, v_s) \geqslant 0$ implies that $g[s(v_b)] \geqslant 0$.

Finally, fix v_s. Since $x_1(v_b, v_s) \geqslant 0$, $x(v_b, v_s)$ is minized by minimizing v_b. Given v_s, the smallest value of v_b for which trade will occur is $b(v_s)$ and

$$x(b(v_s), v_s) = b(v_s) - \frac{g(v_s)}{(1 - F_b[b(v_s)])\, F_s(v_s)} \geqslant v_s$$

since $x_2(v_b, v_s) \geqslant 0$ implies (4.03). Q.E.D.

The conditions under which (4.02) and (4.03) hold are related to the number of zeros of

$$c_b(v_b, 1) - s(v_b, \alpha^*) \tag{4.04}$$

and of

$$c_s(v_s, 1) - b(v_s, \alpha^*). \tag{4.05}$$

Since (4.04) is strictly positive at $v_b = 1$ and strictly negative at $v_b = b(0, \alpha^*)$, it must have at least one zero. Similarly, (4.05) is strictly positive at $v_s = s(1, \alpha^*)$ and it is strictly negative at $v_s = 0$. Thus, it too must have at least one zero. Call a regular set of beliefs (F_b, F_s) *unimodular* if (4.04) and (4.05) each have exactly one zero.

Theorem 3 states that unimodularity is a sufficient condition for payment rule (3.07) to generate non-negative payoffs when trade occurs.

THEOREM 3. *Let the* (F_b, F_s) *be unimodular. Then, the incentive efficient trading mechanism* $(p^{\alpha*}, x^*)$ *is* ex post *individually rational.*

Proof of Theorem 3. It is possible to relate conditions (4.02) and (4.03) to the condition $W(p^{\alpha}) \geqslant 0$, which is the primary incentive constraint from Section 2. Starting with (4.02), recall that Eq. (3.05) defines $g(\cdot)$. Change the variable of integration so that $w = b(t)$. Then

$$g[s(v_b)] = \int_{w = v_b}^{1} F_s[s(w)] f_b(w)\{c_b(w, 1) - s(w)\} \, dw. \qquad (4.06)$$

When $v_b = b(0)$, (4.06) equals $W(p^{\alpha})$.

In a similar fashion, (4.03) can be rewritten as

$$\int_{w = v_s}^{s(1)} f_s(w)(1 - F_b[b(w)])\{c_s(w, 1) - b(w)\} \, dx \geqslant 0 \qquad (4.07)$$

When $v_s = 0$, the left-hand side of (4.07) equals $W(p^{\alpha})$.

By unimodularity, (4.04) and (4.05) each have only one zero. Thus, (4.06) and (4.07) are positive except at their endpoints where they equal zero. So by Lemma 2, x^* generates non-negative utility when trade occurs.

Q.E.D.

Theorem 3 is a strong result because unimodularity is a weak restriction. As Proposition 1 proves, unimodularity includes beliefs for which the inverse hazard rates $(F_b - 1)/f_b$ and F_s/f_s are increasing. Since increasing inverse hazard rates is a commonly imposed condition, Theorem 3 has wide applicability.

PROPOSITION 1. *Let* (F_b, F_s) *be regular. If* $(F_b - 1)/f_b$ *and* F_s/f_s *are increasing, then* (F_b, F_s) *is unimodular.*

Proof of Proposition 1. By definition,

$$b(v_s, \alpha^*) + \alpha^* \left(\frac{F_b[b(v_s, \alpha^*)] - 1}{f_b[b(v_s, \alpha^*)]} \right) = c_s(v_s, \alpha^*).$$

Thus, (4.05) equals

$$(1 - \alpha^*) \frac{F_s(v_s)}{f_s(v_s)} + \alpha^* \left(\frac{F_b[b(v_s, \alpha^*)] - 1}{f_b[b(v_s, \alpha^*)]} \right)$$

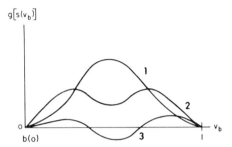

FIG. 2.   The function $g[s(v_b)]$ given beliefs that are (1) unimodular, (2) non-unimodular but support *ex post* individually rational trade, and (3) non-unimodular and preclude *ex post* individually rational trade.

and

$$\frac{d}{dv_s}[c_s(v_s, 1) - b(v_s, \alpha^*)]$$

$$= (1 - \alpha^*)\left(\frac{F_s(v_s)}{f_s(v_s)}\right)' + \alpha^*\left(\frac{F_b - 1}{f_b}\right)' (b(v_s, \alpha^*))\frac{db(v_s, \alpha^*)}{dv_s}$$

which is non-negative by assumption. Thus, (4.05) has exactly one zero. A similar argument shows that the same is true for (4.04).   Q.E.D.

To help explain the role unimodularity plays in this section, Fig. 2 illustrates three possible graphs of $g(s[\cdot])$. Unimodular beliefs generate graphs similar to curve 1. Curves 2 and 3 are two possible representations arising from non-unimodular beliefs when (4.04) has three zeros. However, only the beliefs associated with curve 3 lead to a violation of *ex post* individual rationality. Thus, unimodularity is not a necessary condition as small perturbations of the set of unimodular beliefs also clearly support *ex post* individual rationality.

At the same time, unimodularity is a strictly stronger condition than regularity. Regularity only requires that $c_b(\cdot, \alpha^*)$ and $c_s(\cdot, \alpha^*)$ be increasing. This condition in turn implies that $s(\cdot, \alpha^*)$ and $b(\cdot, \alpha^*)$ are increasing. Strengthening the definition of regularity so that $c_b(\cdot, 1)$ and $c_s(\cdot, 1)$ are increasing is also not sufficient to ensure that (4.04) and (4.05) each have only one zero. Even so, I conjecture that regularity is sufficient to support *ex post* individually rational trade.[10]

Theorem 3 also resolves an open question put forth by Matthews and Postlewaite [9]. They show that the range of equilibrium outcomes arising

[10] Gresik [4] provides a counter-example to this conjecture when the traders' beliefs are statistically dependent. To my knowledge no counter-example exists for the independent-belief case with continuous support.

from the use of a sealed-bid double auction preceded by a period of simultaneous communication between the buyer and the seller includes those that can be generated by all monotonic, deterministic, *ex post* individually rational, and incentive feasible trading rules. They ask whether this set also contains all the equilibrium outcomes obtained from the set of *ex ante* incentive efficient trading rules.

Their deterministic condition requires that the trading rule assume only the values 0 or 1. The monotonicity condition requires that the trading rule be non-decreasing in the buyer's valuation and non-increasing in the seller's valuation. Moreover, monotonicity requires that the payment rule be non-decreasing in both traders' valuations. According to Theorem 3, (p^{α^*}, x^*) clearly satisfies these conditions for all unimodular beliefs. Thus, we have the following corollary to Theorem 3.

COROLLARY 1. *For all unimodular beliefs, Matthews and Postlewaite's sealed-bid double auction with unmediated communication weakly implements* (p^{α^*}, x^*).

5. CONCLUSION

For a fairly general set of bilateral trading problems, I have shown how to weakly implement an *ex ante* efficient, interim individually rational allocation with an *ex post* individually rational mechanism. This means that the *ex ante* incentive efficiency frontier defined by Williams [14] is the appropriate benchmark to use when studying trading rules that are inherently *ex post* individually rational such as the k-double auctions Satterthwaite and Williams [13] and Leininger, Linhart, and Radner [8] consider. To apply this result to larger markets, an understanding of how the number of traders affects the performance of a market's incentive constraints is needed. Gresik and Satterthwaite [6] show that these constraints weaken as the number of traders grows. Thus, it should be most difficult to construct an *ex ante* incentive efficient, *ex post* individually rational trading mechanism precisely in the case I considered: bilateral trade. As a result, this paper's results should apply to larger markets as well.

APPENDIX

Proof of Lemma 1. $g[s(1)] = 0$ follows directly from Eq. (3.05). Showing that $g(0) = 0$ requires some extra work. Begin by changing the variable of integration so that $v_b = b(t)$, which also implies $s(v_b) = t$.

Equation (3.05) becomes

$$\int_{v_s = 0}^{s(1)} \theta_1(v_s)\, dv_s = \int_{v_b = b(0)}^{1} F_s[s(v_b)]\{1 - F_b(v_b)$$
$$- v_b f_b(v_b) + s(v_b) f_b(v_b)\}\, dv_b. \tag{A.01}$$

Recall that both $b(\cdot)$ and $s(\cdot)$ are implicitly evaluated at $\alpha = \alpha^*$, where α^* is the solution to $W(p^\alpha) = 0$. Substituting (2.04) into (2.05) with $\alpha = \alpha^*$ and integrating over v_s yields

$$\int_{v_b = b(0)}^{1} \{[v_b f_b(v_b) + F_b(v_b) - 1]\, F_s[s(v_b)]$$
$$- s(v_b)\, F_s[s(v_b)]\, f_b(v_b)\}\, dv_b = 0. \tag{A.02}$$

Simple inspection shows that (A.01) is just the negative of the left-hand side of (A.02). Thus, $g(0) = 0$.   Q.E.D.

REFERENCES

1. K. CHATTERJEE AND W. SAMUELSON, Bargaining under incomplete information, *Oper. Res.* **31** (1983), 835–851.
2. C. D'ASPREMONT AND L. GERARD-VARET, Incentives and incomplete information, *J. Public. Econ.* **11** (1979), 25–45.
3. T. GRESIK, The efficiency of linear equilibria of sealed-bid double auctions, *J. Econ. Theory* **53** (1991), 173–184.
4. T. GRESIK, Efficient bilateral trade with statistically dependent beliefs, *J. Econ. Theory* **53** (1991), 199–205.
5. T. GRESIK AND M. SATTERTHWAITE, "The Number of Traders Required to Make a Market Competitive: The Beginnings of a Theory," CMSEMS D. P. No. 551, Northwestern University, 1983.
6. T. GRESIK AND M. SATTERTHWAITE, The rate at which a simple market converges to efficiency as the number of traders increases: An asymptotic result for optimal trading mechanisms, *J. Econ. Theory* **48** (1989), 304–332.
7. B. HOLMSTRÖM AND R. MYERSON, Efficient and durable decision rules with incomplete information, *Econometrica* **51** (1983), 1799–1820.
8. W. LEININGER, P. LINHART, AND R. RADNER, The sealed-bid mechanism for bargaining with incomplete information, *J. Econ. Theory* **48** (1989), 63–106.
9. S. MATTHEWS AND A. POSTLEWAITE, Pre-play communication in two-person sealed-bid double auctions, *J. Econ. Theory* **48** (1989), 238–263.
10. R. MYERSON, Incentive compatibility and the bargaining problem, *Econometrica* **47** (1979), 61–73.
11. R. MYERSON, Optimal auction design, *Math. Oper. Res.* **6** (1981), 58–73.
12. R. MYERSON AND M. SATTERTHWAITE, Efficient mechanisms for bilateral trading, *J. Econ. Theory* **29** (1983), 265–281.

13. M. SATTERTHWAITE AND S. WILLIAMS, Bilateral trade with the sealed-bid double auction: Existence and efficiency, *J. Econ. Theory* **48** (1989), 107–133.
14. S. WILLIAMS, Efficient performance in two agent bargaining, *J. Econ. Theory* **41** (1987), 154–172.
15. R. WILSON, Game-theoretic analyses of trading processes, *in* "Advances in Economic Theory, Fifth World Congress" (T. Bewley, Ed.), pp. 33–70, Cambridge Univ. Press, Cambridge, MA, 1987.

JOURNAL OF ECONOMIC THEORY **53**, 173–184 (1991)

The Efficiency of Linear Equilibria of Sealed-Bid Double Auctions

THOMAS A. GRESIK*

John M. Olin School of Business, Washington University,
St. Louis, Missouri 63130

Received January 21, 1988; revised March 6, 1990

This paper modifies Myerson and Satterthwaite's (*J. Econ. Theory* **29** (1983), 265–281) analysis of direct bilateral-trade mechanisms with two-sided incomplete information by developing a new technique for analyzing their payment rule restrictions. For each member of a narrow class of beliefs, this new technique defines a mechanism that is both *ex ante* efficient and *ex post* individually rational. Moreover, the resulting allocation is shown to be equivalent to that generated by the linear equilibrium of a *k*-double auction. *Journal of Economic Literature* Classification Number(s): 026, 024. © 1991 Academic Press, Inc.

1. INTRODUCTION

Myerson and Satterthwaite (MS) [10] show that when trader beliefs are uniform, the linear equilibrium of Chatterjee and Samuelson's (CS) [1] split-the-difference bargaining game achieves *ex ante* incentive efficient performance.[1] Unfortunately, the indirect approach they employ in drawing this association provides no general technique for understanding the relationship between efficient direct mechanisms and commonly studied static bargaining rules when trader beliefs are non-uniform. The basic problem involves finding economically plausible solutions to the incentive compatibility restrictions on a mechanism's payment rules. Although these restrictions have multiple solutions, the solutions identified in the literature (e.g., [4, 10]) all share certain undesirable characteristics such as payments that leave one trader or the other worse off from trading.

* I thank Don Coursey, Jim Little, Steve Matthews, Mark Satterthwaite, and Steve Williams for their comments and Elisabeth Case for her editorial assistance. In addition, this journal's referees provided comments that greatly improved this paper. All errors are my responsibility.

[1] MS did not recognize the existence of multiple equilibria. I have restated their result to reflect this problem.

72

This paper modifies the analysis in [10] and, for an interesting family of beliefs, identifies payment rules that, unlike earlier rules, prohibit money transfers in the absence of trade and set a price between the buyer's and the seller's valuations when trade does occur. Mechanisms that employ payment rules with such features are *ex post* individually rational. Moreover, it turns out that when used to construct an *ex ante* incentive-efficient direct mechanism, this approach defines an allocation equivalent to the one generated via the linear equilibrium of a k-double auction.[2] This family of beliefs is the same family which Leininger, Linhart, and Radner (LLR) [6] show supports linear equilibria in CS's game and it is the family that yields linear virtual valuations.

Related studies include Hagerty and Rogerson [5] and Williams [12]. Hagerty and Rogerson show that posted-price mechanisms are the only ones that satisfy dominant-strategy incentive compatibility and *ex post* individual rationality. Williams shows that the seller's-offer (buyer's-bid) double auction maximizes *ex ante* expected gains to the seller (buyer). Our analysis is very much in the spirit of William's work except that we weight expected gains to the buyer and to the seller equally.

2. THE MODEL

We use an independent, private-value, bilateral-trade model. The seller owns one unit of an indivisible good. The buyer has an inelastic demand for one unit at any price at or below his reservation valuation.

The buyer's valuation, v_B, and the seller's, v_S, are drawn independently[3] from the distributions $F_B(\cdot)$ and $F_S(\cdot)$ with continuous densities, $f_B(\cdot)$ and $f_S(\cdot)$, and non-zero support on $[0, 1]$.[4] Each trader's valuation is private information and F_B (F_S) represents the seller's (buyer's) beliefs about the other's valuation. Thus, we refer to (F_B, F_S) as the trading problem. It is common knowledge.

Trade is determined by a mechanism that solicits a bid, b, from the

---

[2] A k-double auction is a generalized split-the-difference mechanism with k ranging from 0 to 1. k equal to $\frac{1}{2}$ yields the split-the-difference mechanism. A formal definition is provided in Section 4.

[3] Statistically independent trader valuations is a strong condition. McAfee and Reny [7] have recently extended the work of Milgrom and Weber [8] and Crémer and McLean [2] on "single-sided" auctions with dependent beliefs to the case of double auctions but they require a weak budget-balancing condition. Gresik [3] provides some results about the behavior of optimal double auction mechanisms when trader valuations are affiliated and strict budget-balancing is required. These results, however, rely on discrete valuation distributions.

[4] The results that follow are valid for any compact interval support.

buyer and an offer, s, from the seller. The mechanism consists of an trading rule $p(b, s)$ and a payment rule $x(b, s)$. The trading rule represents the probability that the buyer will receive the object. Hence, $0 \leqslant p(b, s) \leqslant 1$ for all (b, s). The payment rule represents the amount of money that the buyer will pay the seller. Define the buyer's utility from trade to be $v_B p(b, s) - x(b, s)$ and the seller's to be $x(b, s) - v_S p(b, s)$.

Each trader selects a bid (offer) so as to maximize his or her interim expected utility. Some additional notation will simplify their definitions. Let

$$p_B(b) = \int_{v_S=0}^{1} p(b, v_S) f_S(v_S) \, dv_S,$$

$$p_S(s) = \int_{v_B=0}^{1} p(v_B, s) f_B(v_B) \, dv_B,$$

$$x_B(b) = \int_{v_S=0}^{1} x(b, v_S) f_S(v_S) \, dv_S,$$

and

$$x_S(s) = \int_{v_B=0}^{1} x(v_B, s) f_B(v_B) \, dv_B.$$

Therefore, when the buyer bids b with valuation v_B and the seller honestly offers v_S, the buyer's interim expected utility is

$$U(b, v_B) = v_B p_B(b) - x_B(b).$$

Similarly, when the buyer honestly bids v_B and the seller offers s with valuation v_S, the seller's interim expected utility is

$$V(s, v_S) = x_S(s) - v_S p_S(s).$$

We will restrict attention to incentive compatible mechanisms which, given the Revelation Principle, incurs no loss of generality. A mechanism is incentive compatible if there exists a Bayesian–Nash equilibrium in which every trader honestly reports his or her private information. Formally, incentive compatibility requires that for all v_B and b, $U(v_B) \equiv U(v_B, v_B) \geqslant U(b, v_B)$, and for all v_S and s, $V(v_S) \equiv V(v_S, v_S) \geqslant V(s, v_S)$.

We also require trading mechanisms to be interim individually rational so that participation is optimal. An incentive compatible mechanism is interim individually rational if for all v_B, $U(v_B) \geqslant 0$; and if for all v_S, $V(v_S) \geqslant 0$. A stronger property, *ex post* individual rationality, obtains (i) when payments occur only in conjunction with a trade, and (ii) when if trade occurs, the buyer never pays more than his reservation value and the seller never receives less than hers. Initially, however, we will restrict our discussion to interim individually rational mechanisms.

Our objective is to select a trading mechanism that maximizes *ex ante* expected gains from trade. This measure is consistent with the notion that the traders except to use a given trading rule repeatedly.[5] The *ex ante* expected gains from trade that a mechanism achieves are defined by

$$\int_{v_B=0}^1 U(v_B) f_B(v_B)\, dv_B + \int_{v_S=0}^1 V(v_S) f_S(v_S)\, dv_S. \qquad (2.01)$$

An incentive compatible, interim individually rational mechanism that maximizes (2.01) is said to be *ex ante* incentive efficient.[6]

To help characterize the set of incentive efficient mechanisms, for $\alpha \in [0, 1]$ define

$$c_B(v_B, \alpha) = v_B + \alpha(F_B(v_B) - 1)/f_B(v_B)$$

and

$$c_S(v_S, \alpha) = v_S + \alpha F_S(v_S)/f_S(v_S).$$

Following Myerson [9], call $c_B(\cdot, \alpha)$ and $c_S(\cdot, \alpha)$ α-virtual reservation valuations. Also define

$$p^\alpha(v_B, v_S) = \begin{cases} 1 & \text{if} \quad c_B(v_B, \alpha) \geqslant c_S(v_S, \alpha) \\ 0 & \text{if} \quad c_B(v_B, \alpha) < c_S(v_S, \alpha), \end{cases} \qquad (2.02)$$

and

$$W(p) = \int_{v_B=0}^1 \int_{v_S=0}^1 [c_B(v_B, 1) - c_S(v_S, 1)]$$
$$\times p(v_B, v_S) f_B(v_B) f_S(v_S)\, dv_S\, dv_B.$$

Let $\alpha^* = \min\{\alpha \geqslant 0 \mid W(p^\alpha) \geqslant 0\}$.[7] Finally, we will need the two constraints

$$x_B(v_B) = \int_{t=0}^{v_B} t\, dp_B(t) + x_B(0), \qquad (2.03)$$

---

[5] Adopting it assumes that recontracting in any one trading period be either cost prohibitive or otherwise impractical.

[6] Since this paper will not consider the concepts of interim or *ex post* incentive efficiency, the modifier "*ex ante*" will be dropped.

[7] Under very general conditions, this minimum exists.

and

$$x_S(v_S) = -\int_{t=v_S}^{1} t \, dp_S(t) + x_S(1).^{8} \qquad (2.04)$$

Theorem 0 characterizes the set of incentive efficient trading mechanisms by summarizing results from MS and Gresik and Satterthwaite [4].

THEOREM 0. *Let* (F_B, F_S) *be the trading problem. If* $c_B(\cdot, \alpha^*)$ *and* $c_S(\cdot, \alpha^*)$ *are non-decreasing, then* (p^{α^*}, x) *is incentive efficient if, and only if,* $x(\cdot, \cdot)$ *satisfies* (2.03) *and* (2.04) *with* $x_B(0) = x_S(1) = 0.^9$

3. THE PAYMENT RULE RESTRICTIONS

For a trading problem with non-decreasing α-virtual valuations (with $\alpha = \alpha^*$), Williams [12] shows that all incentive efficient mechanisms share the same trading rule. Equations (2.03) and (2.04), however, have multiple solutions. The solutions vary by the extent to which they employ entry fees and subsidies and according to the money transfers set when trade does occur. In some cases, these variations can affect a mechanism's individual rationality properties.

For instance, consider the example from MS. With uniform beliefs, the trading rule that achieves incentive efficient performance is

$$p^{(\alpha^* = 1/3)} = \begin{cases} 1 & \text{if } v_B - v_S \geq \frac{1}{4} \\ 0 & \text{if } v_B - v_S < \frac{1}{4}. \end{cases}$$

Of the two payment rules MS use, the first is their Eq. (6). The payment rule it describes is:

$$x(v_B, v_S) = \begin{cases} (v_B^2 - v_S^2)/2 + 7/64 & \text{if } v_B \geq \frac{1}{4} \text{ and } v_S \leq \frac{3}{4} \\ 9/64 - v_S^2/2 & \text{if } v_B < \frac{1}{4} \text{ and } v_S \leq \frac{3}{4} \\ v_B^2/2 - 11/64 & \text{if } v_B \geq \frac{1}{4} \text{ and } v_S > \frac{3}{4} \\ -9/64 & \text{if } v_B < \frac{1}{4} \text{ and } v_S > \frac{3}{4}. \end{cases} \qquad (3.01)$$

(3.01) employs both entry fees and participation subsidies. Also in the event of a trade, the buyer always pays less than v_B; with positive probability, the seller receives less than v_S.

---

[8] Solving $\partial U(b, v_B)/\partial b = 0$ with $b = v_B$ yields $v_B p_1'(v_B) = x_1'(v_B)$. Integrating this expression gives us (2.03). Equation (2.04) is obtained in a similar fashion.

[9] Interim individual rationality requires that $x_B(0)$, $x_S(1) \geq 0$. Efficiency requires that $x_B(0) = x_S(1) = 0$.

The second payment rule they use is

$$x(v_B, v_S) = \begin{cases} (v_B + v_S + \frac{1}{2})/3 & \text{if} \quad v_B - v_S \geq \frac{1}{4} \\ 0 & \text{if} \quad v_B - v_S < \frac{1}{4}. \end{cases} \tag{3.02}$$

It supports *ex post* individually rational trade. MS construct this rule by appealing to CS's calculations for the split-the-difference mechanism. Unfortunately, the manner in which this rule was constructed cannot be generalized to the case of non-uniform beliefs.

A more general approach can be developed and it begins by rewriting equations (2.03) and (2.04) as

$$x_B(v_B) = \int_{v_S=0}^{1} \int_{t=0}^{v_B} t \, dp(t, v_S) \, f_S(v_S) \, dv_S \tag{3.03}$$

and

$$x_S(v_S) = -\int_{v_B=0}^{1} \int_{t=v_S}^{1} t \, dp(v_B, t) \, f_B(v_B) \, dv_B. \tag{3.04}$$

Both equations, then, consist of Riemann–Stieltjes integrals where $dp(t, \cdot)$ represents the differential change in $p(t, \cdot)$ with respect to changes in t. To simplify the analysis, we now restrict attention even further to those trading problems for which the α-virtual valuations with $\alpha = \alpha^*$ are strictly increasing.

Given the definition of an optimal trading rule in (2.02), $dp(\cdot, \cdot)$ is zero almost everywhere. As long as $p(\cdot, \cdot)$ is monotonic in both arguments, for the buyer $dp(t, \cdot) = 1$ at at most one point, and for the seller $dp(\cdot, t) = -1$ at at most one point.[10] Now consider Eq. (3.03). Fix a value of $v_S \in [0, 1]$. The only non-zero contribution to the integral occurs when $c_B(t, \alpha^*) = c_S(v_S, \alpha^*)$. So define $\bar{v}_B(v_S, \alpha^*) = c_B^{-1}(c_S(v_S, \alpha^*), \alpha^*)$ and $\bar{v}_S(v_B, \alpha^*) = c_S^{-1}(c_B(v_B, \alpha^*), \alpha^*)$. Given a seller with valuation v_S, $\bar{v}_B(v_S, \cdot)$ is the lowest profitable winning bid the buyer could have submitted. For a fixed buyer valuation v_B, the highest profitable trade-generating offer the seller could have made is $\bar{v}_S(v_B, \cdot)$. These observations and definitions allow us to rewrite (3.03) as

$$x_B(v_B) = \int_{v_S=0}^{\max[0, \bar{v}_S(v_B, \alpha^*)]} \bar{v}_B(v_S, \alpha^*) \, f_S(v_S) \, dv_S. \tag{3.05}$$

For the seller, we can rewrite (3.04) as

$$x_S(v_S) = \int_{v_B=\min[\bar{v}_B(v_S, \alpha^*), 1]}^{1} \bar{v}_S(v_B, \alpha^*) \, f_B(v_B) \, dv_B. \tag{3.06}$$

[10] The antecedents of Theorem 0 guarantee that these monotonicity properties exist.

Written in this manner, it becomes clear that (3.05) and (3.06) (and hence (2.03)–(2.04)) require that, given no trade, the buyer's interim expected payment and the seller's interim expected receipt are zero, and that conditional on trade occuring, i.e., $p(v_B, v_S) = 1$, the buyer's interim expected payment (seller's interim expected receipt) equals the lowest bid (highest offer) with which trade would have still taken place.

Returning to our example, we can now generate payment rule (3.02) directly by imposing an additional restriction on the set of feasible payment rules: $\chi(v_B, v_S) = 0$ if $p(v_B, v_S) = 0$. This constraint insures that no payments are made in the absence of trade and thereby captures the idea that if the buyer and the seller cannot agree to a trade, they simply walk away.

Equations (3.05) and (3.06) now become

$$\int_{v_S = 0}^{v_B - 1/4} x(v_B, v_S)\, dv_S = v_B^2/2 - 1/32 \tag{3.07}$$

for $v_B \geq \frac{1}{4}$ and

$$\int_{v_B = v_S + 1/4}^{1} x(v_B, v_S)\, dv_B = 9/32 - v_S^2/2 \tag{3.08}$$

for $v_S \leq \frac{3}{4}$. For $v_B < \frac{1}{4}$ or $v_S > \frac{3}{4}$, our new restriction requires that $\chi(v_B, v_S) = 0$. Thus, we need only concern ourselves with solutions to (3.07) and (3.08) when $p(\cdot, \cdot) > 0$.

A cursory inspection of (3.07) and (3.08) reveals that $x(v_B, v_S)$ must have a linear term both in v_B and in v_S. Payment rule (3.02) is the linear solution to this system. However, this rule is neither the unique solution nor the unique *ex post* individually rational solution. For example, consider

$$x(v_B, v_S) = (v_B + v_S + 0.5)/3$$
$$- (2/3)(v_B^2 + v_S^2 - 8v_B v_S/3 - v_B + 5v_S/3 + 3/16)$$

when $v_B - v_S \geq \frac{1}{4}$; otherwise, $x(v_B, v_S) = 0$. This payment rule also supports *ex post* individually rational trade.

4. LINEAR VIRTUAL VALUATIONS AND k-DOUBLE AUCTIONS

This section illustrates the way in which this new formulation can be applied to questions about k-double auctions. A k-double auction dictates trade if, and only if, the bid exceeds or equals the offer; and in the event of a trade, requires the buyer to pay the seller k times the bid plus $(1 - k)$

times the offer. When a trading problem induces linear α-virtual valuations, finding a "no-trade, no-pay" solution to (3.05) and (3.06) is straightforward and these solutions always support *ex post* individually rational trade. Moreover, for each such trading problem, there exists a linear equilibrium of a k-double auction that achieves incentive efficiency.

LLR characterize the family of trading problems that have linear equilibrium strategies for the split-the-difference game. That family is identical to the one that generates linear virtual valuations.[11]

LEMMA 1. *The trading problem (F_B, F_S) yields linear virtual valuations if, and only if, for $\beta, \rho > 0$, $F_B(v_B) = 1 - (1 - v_B)^\rho$ and $F_S(v_S) = v_S^\beta$.*

Lemma 1 defines a subset of the beta family. F_B and F_S are uniform distributions when $\beta = \rho = 1$. For trading problems in this family,

$$\bar{v}_B(v_S, \alpha) = [\rho(\beta + \alpha) v_S + \alpha\beta] / [(\alpha + \rho)\beta]$$

and

$$\bar{v}_S(v_B, \alpha) = \beta[(\rho + \alpha) v_B - \alpha] / [\rho(\beta + \alpha)].$$

If we define

$$C_1(v_B) = \{(\rho + \alpha)v_B - \alpha\}^\beta \, \beta^\beta / [(\alpha + \rho) \rho^\beta (\beta + \alpha)^\beta (\beta + 1)]$$

and

$$C_2(v_S) = \rho^\rho [\beta - (\beta + \alpha) v_S]^\rho / [(\alpha + \rho)^\rho \beta^\rho (\beta + \alpha)(\rho + 1)],$$

then under the "no-trade, no-pay" restriction, Eqs. (3.05) and (3.06) become

$$\int_{v_S = 0}^{\bar{v}_S(v_B, \alpha)} x(v_B, v_S) f_S(v_S) \, dv_S = C_1(v_B)[\beta(\rho + \alpha) v_B + \alpha] \qquad (4.01)$$

and

$$\int_{v_B = \bar{v}_B(v_S, \alpha)}^{1} x(v_B, v_S) f_B(v_B) \, dv_B = C_2(v_S)[\beta + \rho(\beta + \alpha) v_S]. \qquad (4.02)$$

Finally, Theorem 0 requires that we calculate α^*.

---

[11] One advantage of our characterization is its focus on the functional form of the traders' virtual valuations rather than that of the traders' strategies. A trader's virtual valuation is unique while k-double auctions have multiple equilibria.

Straightforward calculations yield:

$$\alpha^* = [(\beta\rho(\beta + 1)(\rho + 1))^{1/2} - \beta\rho]/(\beta + \rho + 1). \qquad (4.03)$$

We can now state and prove this section's two main results.

THEOREM 1.   *Let* (F_B, F_S) *induce linear virtual valuations. There exists an incentive efficient trading mechanism* (p, x) *such that* $p(\cdot,\cdot) = 0$ *(no trade) implies that* $x(\cdot,\cdot) = 0$ *(no money transfer).*

Proof of Theorem 1.   By Lemma 1, select β and ρ. Then define α^* using (4.03). The linearity of the virtual valuations insures that $p = p^{\alpha^*}$ satisfies conditions (a) and (b) of Theorem 0. Let

$$x(v_B, v_S) = \begin{cases} \omega_1 v_B + \omega_2 v_S + \omega_3 & \text{if } c_B(v_B, \alpha^*) \geqslant c_S(v_S, \alpha^*) \\ 0 & \text{otherwise.} \end{cases} \qquad (4.04)$$

Substitute (4.04) into (4.01) and (4.02). After some simplification the left-hand side of (4.01) is proportional to $C_1(v_B)$ and the left-hand side of (4.02) is proportional to $C_2(v_S)$. Cancellation transforms (4.01) and (4.02) into equations that are linear in v_B and v_S, respectively. Matching coefficients yields four equations in $(\omega_1, \omega_2, \omega_3)$. These equations are consistent if, and only if, $\alpha = \alpha^*$. When $\alpha = \alpha^*$,

$$\omega_1 = \beta[\alpha^*(\rho + 1) + \beta(1 - \alpha^*)]/[(\beta + \alpha^*)(\rho + \beta + 1)],$$

$$\omega_2 = (\beta + \alpha^*)\rho[\beta - (\beta + 1)\omega_1]/[\beta^2(\alpha^* + \rho)], \quad \text{and} \qquad (4.05)$$

$$\omega_3 = \alpha^*[1 - \omega_1]/(\alpha^* + \rho)$$

is the unique solution to the coefficient equations. Thus, the payment rule defined by (4.04) and (4.05) solves (4.01) and (4.02). As a result, (p, χ) is incentive efficient and $p(\cdot,\cdot) = 0$ implies $\chi(\cdot,\cdot) = 0$.   Q.E.D.

Like most direct-revelation trading mechanisms, the one defined by Eqs. (2.02) and (4.03)–(4.05) bears little resemblance to real-world market rules. Theorem 2 shows that, in fact, this mechanism can be implemented with a trading mechanism of the form

$$p(b, s) = \begin{cases} 1 & \text{if } b \geqslant s \\ 0 & \text{if } b < s \end{cases} \qquad (4.06)$$

and

$$x(b, s) = \begin{cases} kb + (1 - k)s & \text{if } b \geqslant s \\ 0 & \text{if } b < s \end{cases} \qquad (4.07)$$

for some $k \in [0, 1]$. The trading mechanism defined by equations (4.06) and (4.07) is a k-double auction.

THEOREM 2.   *Let (F_B, F_S) induce linear virtual valuations. There exist a unique $k \in (0, 1)$ and a unique linear equilibrium of the corresponding k-double auction that achieves incentive efficient performance.*

Proof of Theorem 2.   By Lemma 1, select β and ρ. Call the mechanism defined by Eqs. (2.02) and (4.03)–(4.05), (p^*, x^*).

From LLR we know that there exist equilibrium bid and offer strategies for the k-double auction of the form

$$b^0(v_B) = a_0 + a_1 v_B \qquad \text{and} \qquad s^0(v_S) = a_2 + a_3 v_S.$$

Substituting these strategies into Eq. (4.07) yields

$$x^0(v_B, v_S) = \begin{cases} ka_0 + ka_1 v_B + (1-k) a_2 + (1-k) a_3 v_S & \text{if } b^0(v_B) \geqslant s^0(v_S) \\ 0 & \text{if } b^0(v_B) < s^0(v_S). \end{cases}$$

Equating $x^0(v_B, v_S)$ with $x^*(v_B, v_S)$ generates three equations with five unknowns (a_0, a_1, a_2, a_3, and k). Two more equations arise from noting that $b^0(v_B) \geqslant s^0(v_S)$ must define the same region as $c_B(v_B, \alpha^*) \geqslant c_S(v_S, \alpha^*)$. Solving this system uniquely results in

$$a_0 = \alpha^*[\alpha^*(\rho - \beta + 1) + \beta]/[(\beta + \alpha^*)(\rho + \alpha^*)(\rho + \beta + 1)], \quad (4.08)$$

$$a_1 = \beta(\rho + \beta + 2\alpha^*)/[(\beta + \alpha^*)(\rho + \beta + 1)], \tag{4.09}$$

$$a_2 = \alpha^*/(\alpha^* + \rho), \tag{4.10}$$

$$a_3 = \rho(\rho + \beta + 2\alpha^*)/[(\rho + \alpha^*)(\rho + \beta + 1)], \tag{4.11}$$

and

$$k = [\alpha^*(\rho - \beta + 1) + \beta]/(\rho + \beta + 2\alpha^*). \tag{4.12}$$

Note that $k = (\alpha^*\rho + (1 - \alpha^*)\beta + \alpha^*)/(\rho + \beta + 2\alpha^*)$. Thus, ρ and β positive and $0 < \alpha^* < 1$ imply that $0 < k < 1$.

Finally, we need to check that (b^0, s^0) is in fact a Bayesian–Nash equilibrium. (b^0, s^0), as defined by Eqs. (4.08)–(4.11), is an equilibrium strategy for the k-double auction with k defined by equation (4.12) if, and only if, it satisfies

$$b^{-1}(s(v_S)) = s(v_S) + ks'(v_S) F_S(v_S)/f_S(v_S) \tag{4.13}$$

and

$$s^{-1}(b(v_B)) = b(v_B) + (1 - k) \, b'(v_B)(F_B(v_B) - 1)/f_B(v_B).^{12} \qquad (4.14)$$

Setting $b = b^0$ and $s = s^0$ solves Eqs. (4.13) and (4.14) given (4.03) and (4.12). Thus, (4.08)–(4.11) define a Bayesian–Nash equilibrium of a k-double auction.   Q.E.D.

In their study of the efficiency of the *linear* equilibria of the ($\frac{1}{2}$)-double auction LLR conjecture that, for each pair of priors defined by Lemma 1, the *linear* equilibrium they consider is the most efficient. However, by Theorem 2, (4.08)–(4.12) uniquely define the linear equilibrium of the k-double auction that achieves efficient performance and $k = \frac{1}{2}$ if, and only if, $\beta = \rho$. So when $\beta = \rho$, their conjecture is correct. However, when $\beta \neq \rho$ there exists a $k \neq \frac{1}{2}$ such that an equilibrium of that k-double auction outperforms the linear equilibrium of the ($\frac{1}{2}$)-double auction. Moreover, by the Revelation Principle no other equilibrium of any other mechanism can outperform the linear equilibrium of the appropriate k-double auction. Still Theorem 2 does not completely invalidate their conjecture as it remains unclear whether LLR employ the most efficient equilibrium for the double auction with $k = \frac{1}{2}$. However, if we are willing to allow k to vary with changes in (F_B, F_S), then the range of efficient performance across trading problems defined by Lemma 1 is narrower than that observed by LLR.

5. CONCLUSION

This paper presents a technique for imposing restrictions stronger than interim individual rationality upon the choice of an optimal payment schedule. Such restrictions compel the solutions arising from our model to more closely parallel the observed structure of real-world trading rules.

Given Satterthwaite and Williams's (SW) [11] result on the generic inefficiency of k-double auctions, it is important that our results on k-double auctions be viewed primarily as illustrations of the general methodology developed in Section 3. At the same time, the results do point to the generic non-linearity of the traders' virtual valuations as a possible explanation for the generic inefficiency of k-double auctions with their linear sharing rules.

An additional caveat in interpreting the results on k-double auctions concerns the problem of multiple equilibria as shown by SW and LLR. Direct-revelation mechanisms also have multiple equilibria. We have analyzed the properties of the most efficient of all these equilibria. That is, no non-sincere equilibrium of (p^{α^*}, x) can outperform its sincere equi-

---

[12] CS prove necessity; SW prove sufficiency.

librium. These multiple-equilibria problems notwithstanding, this paper's characterization of incentive efficient, k-double auctions provides us with a better understanding of the nature of the pathologies SW identify in the k-double auction model.

REFERENCES

1. K. CHATTERJEE AND W. SAMUELSON, Bargaining under incomplete information, *Oper. Res.* **31** (1983), 835–851.
2. J. CRÉMER AND R. MCLEAN, Optimal selling strategies under uncertainty for a discriminating monopolist when demands are interdependent, *Econometrica* **53** (1985), 345–362.
3. T. GRESIK, Efficient bilateral trade with statistically dependent beliefs, *J. Econ. Theory* **53** (1991), 199–205.
4. T. GRESIK AND M. SATTERTHWAITE, "The number of traders required to make a market competitive: The beginnings of a theory," CMSEMS D.P. No. 551, Northwestern University, 1983.
5. K. HAGERTY AND W. ROGERSON, Robust trading mechanisms, *J. Econ. Theory* **42** (1987), 94–107.
6. W. LEININGER, P. LINHART, AND R. RADNER, The sealed-bid mechanism for bargaining with incomplete information, *J. Econ. Theory* **48** (1989), 63–106.
7. R. MCAFEE AND P. RENY, "Correlated Information and Mechanism Design," working paper, University of Western Ontario, 1989.
8. P. MILGROM AND R. WEBER, A theory of auctions and competitive bidding, *Econometrica* **50** (1982), 1089–1122.
9. R. MYERSON, Incentive compatibility and the bargaining problem, *Econometrica* **47** (1979), 61–73.
10. R. MYERSON AND M. SATTERTHWAITE, Efficient mechanisms for bilateral trading, *J. Econ. Theory* **29** (1983), 265–281.
11. M. SATTERTHWAITE AND S. WILLIAMS, Bilateral trade with the sealed-bid double auction: Existence and efficiency, *J. Econ. Theory* **48** (1989), 107–133.
12. S. WILLIAMS, Efficient performance in two agent bargaining, *J. Econ. Theory* **41** (1987), 154–172.

JOURNAL OF ECONOMIC THEORY **48**, 63–106 (1989)

Equilibria of the Sealed-Bid Mechanism for Bargaining with Incomplete Information*, †

W. LEININGER

Universität Bonn, D-5300 Bonn, West Germany

P. B. LINHART

AT & T Bell Laboratories, Murray Hill, New Jersey 07974

AND

R. RADNER

*AT & T Bell Laboratories, Murray Hill, New Jersey 07974,
and New York University, New York, New York 10003*

Received January 1, 1987; received July 1, 1988

We study the Nash equilibria of the sealed-bid bargaining mechanism with incomplete information, a nonzero-sum game. For the case of uniform priors, we describe two uncountably numerous families of equilibria: the first has differentiable strategies; in the second the strategies are step-functions. The efficiencies of these equilibria range from "second best" to zero. For independent nonuniform priors, we show that a similar situation obtains. These results seem discouraging with regard to using the sealed-bid mechanism in practice. The mechanism might be salvaged, however, if bargainers turn out to confine themselves to linear-strategy equilibria. *Journal of Economic Literature* Classification Number: 026.   © 1989 Academic Press, Inc.

1. INTRODUCTION AND SUMMARY

The study of structured bargaining procedures arises naturally in the context of the so-called "transfer price problem," i.e., the problem of designing mechanisms for the pricing of goods and services that are transferred from one division of a firm to another. A typical feature of this situation is that the relevant data, e.g., the costs to the supplier division and the

---

*The views expressed in this paper are the authors', not necessarily those of AT & T Bell Laboratories.

† The authors are indebted to Frank Sinden for a number of very helpful discussions of this problem.

84

benefits to the customer division, are not equally well known to the participants. For example, it would be normal for the supplier's costs to be better known to the supplier than to the customer, and for the customer's benefits to be better known to the customer than to the supplier.

A bargaining procedure of particular interest is the *sealed-bid mechanism*. Consider the case in which the potential buyer (customer) and seller are bargaining over the price at which the seller will deliver a single "object" to the buyer. (This "object" might be a batch of integrated circuits with certain specifications, a batch of optical fiber, or a design and prototype for a new component.) The buyer and the seller independently make sealed bids; these bids are opened simultaneously. If the buyer's bid is at least as large as the seller's bid, then the transaction takes place at a price equal to the average of the two bids; otherwise there is no trade.

The sealed-bid mechanism is a special case of the determination of price by equating supply and demand. In the standard case, in which both quantity and price may vary continuously, the supply curve slopes upward and the demand curve slopes downward (see Fig. 1a). The market-clearing

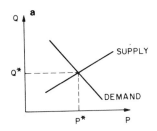

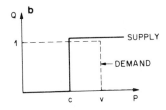

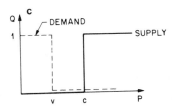

FIG. 1. Bargaining and market equilibrium.

price P^* and quantity Q^* are determined by the intersection of the two curves. In the present case of bargaining over a single object, the quantity can only be 0 or 1. If the supplier's bid is c, then the "supply curve" is a step-function that jumps up from 0 to 1 at the price c. Similarly, if the buyer's bid is v, then the "demand curve" is a step-function that jumps down from 1 to 0 at the price v. If v exceeds c, then the two curves "intersect" over an entire interval (c, v) of prices at which the quantity is 1 (see Fig. 1b). The sealed-bid mechanism picks out the midpoint of this interval as the price at which the transaction takes place. If v is less than c, then the two "curves" intersect over an interval (v, c) of prices at which the quantity is 0 (see Fig. 1c). In this case there is no transaction.

Note that the sealed-bid mechanism is a special case of a *double auction*, in which there is only one bidder on each side. Other bargaining mechanisms are conceivable. For example, the seller could be required to make a single bid, which the buyer must accept or reject. Or, the bargainers could be allowed to bid alternately until one of the bids is accepted by the other party.

The current theoretical approach to the study of bargaining mechanisms in the present context is to model the situation as a noncooperative game with incomplete information. Following Harsanyi [6], the beliefs of the players about each other's benefits and/or costs are modelled as a prior probability distribution. (For a survey of recent work on this topic, see Rubinstein, [10].) One imagines that "Nature" first chooses the benefit and cost according to this distribution, and then reveals the benefit to the buyer and the cost to the seller, but not vice versa. The buyer and seller then simultaneously choose their respective bids. The buyer's strategy is thus a function mapping his observed benefit into his bid v, and the seller's strategy is likewise a function mapping his observed cost into his bid c. A *Nash equilibrium* (or just *equilibrium* for short) is a pair of strategies such that neither player can increase his expected profit by *unilaterally* changing his own strategy.[1]

From the point of view of the firm as a whole, an equilibrium of the sealed-bid game (with incomplete information) is *efficient* if trade occurs whenever the benefit exceeds the cost and does not occur when the cost exceeds the benefit.[2] One can show that, if both of these inequalities have

---

[1] In the context of a game with incomplete information, this is sometimes called a Bayesian-Nash equilibrium.

[2] In this statement, "benefit" and "cost" should be interpreted as "opportunity benefit" and "opportunity cost," respectively. For example, if the supplier division can produce the object at a cost K and can sell it externally for a price F, which is greater than K, then the opportunity cost of transferring it internally is F, not K. A similar consideration applies to the customer division.

positive probability, then no equilibrium of the sealed-bid game is efficient. Indeed, Myerson and Satterthwaite [8] have shown that, under fairly general conditions, there is no bargaining mechanism whose equilibria can be guaranteed to be efficient.

We shall concentrate most of our analysis of the special case in which the benefit and cost are independently and identically distributed, uniformly on the unit interval. For this case, Chatterjee and Samuelson [2] demonstrated the existence of an equilibrium in which each player's bid is a linear function of his observation. (Cox *et al.* [4] had used similar methods to study equilibrium bidding strategies in auctions with heterogeneous bidders.) Furthermore, Myerson and Satterthwaite [8] showed that this equilibrium had the highest expected gains from trade of any equilibrium of any (suitably restricted) bargaining mechanism. In other words, the linear-strategy equilibrium of the sealed-bid mechanism is "second-best" (for the uniform prior distribution).

We shall show (Section 3) that, for the uniform case, the sealed-bid game has a very large set of equilibria. In fact, not only is there a continuum of equilibria, but the set of equilibrium strategy-pairs has infinitely many degrees of freedom. Furthermore, the expected gains from trade for the set of equilibria range from second best to zero!

We have confined our search to pure-strategy equilibria, and we do not know whether we have found them all. One family of equilibria (Section 3.3) has differentiable strategies (including the linear-strategy equilibrium). In the other family we have studied, the strategies are step-functions, and equilibrium strategies can have arbitrarily many jumps (Section 3.4). For example, for any positive integer n, there is an open set of equilibria for which the jumps occur at all multiples of $1/n$. In each family of strategies, the expected gains from trade range between zero and second best.

All of the step-function equilibria are in a certain sense perfect (Section 3.5). Roughly speaking, this means that these equilibria have a certain kind of structural stability with respect to low-probability mistakes in the players' bids. We do not know whether the differentiable equilibria are perfect (beeing handicapped here by the lack of explicit expressions for these equilibria). However, we conjecture that every differentiable equilibrium can be approximated by a sequence of step-function equilibria, and we can demonstrate this for the linear equilibrium.

We also consider the case of general independent distributions of benefits and costs. Three qualitative propositions about equilibria can be demonstrated (Section 4.1; see also Chatterjee and Samuelson); roughly speaking, these propositions apply only to the range of bids for which there is a positive probability that trade will take place. For this range of bids, in equilibrium, (1) a player's strategy is a nondecreasing function of his observation (benefit or cost), (2) the buyer's bid will not exceed his benefit, and the seller's bid will not be less than his cost, and (3) the distributions of the buyer's and seller's bids have the same support.

We do not give as thorough an analysis of the set of equilibria for the case of general independent priors as we do for the uniform case, but we do demonstrate the existence of both differentiable and step-function equilibria (Sections 4.2 and 4.4). One striking result is: for any finite set of points in the unit interval there is a pair of priors and a step-function equilibrium such that the support of the distributions of bids is exactly the given set of points.

Multiplicity of equilibria is, of course, a frequent phenomenon in game theory. For example, if the benefit and cost are both known to *both* players, and the benefit exceeds the cost, then the sealed-bid mechanism has a continuum of equilibria, corresponding to all the possible divisions of the surplus between the two players. Also, multiplicity of equilibria is common in sequential games with incomplete information. What is impressive about the present game is that (although it is not sequential), the set of equilibria is so large that its predictions about equilibrium behavior are extremely weak. Even worse, the *equilibria in the uniform distribution case range from second best to worthless, so that equilibrium theory provides no basis for recommending the sealed-bid mechanism in practice.* In our opinion, this is a strong indictment of the theory of equilibrium with incomplete information as it is currently formulated.

Since the sealed-bid mechanism studied here is a special case of a double auction, our results suggest, but do not prove, a similar multiplicity of equilibria for double auctions with finitely many participants and incomplete information. We have not, however, explored this question.

To conclude this summary on a more positive note, recall that in the case of a uniform distribution of benefits and costs on the unit square, the linear equilibrium is "second best." We study a family of independent priors with linear equilibria (Section 4.3). There is a one-parameter family of priors corresponding to each player. Each family includes the uniform distribution as a special case, and also includes the extreme special cases in which all the probability is concentrated at 0 and 1, respectively. For each pair of such priors, one for each player, there is an equilibrium in linear strategies (among many other equilibria) Let the *efficiency* of an equilibrium be defined as the ratio of the expected gains from trade (in that equilibrium) to the potential maximum expected gains from trade. (The latter would be realized if each player bid his true benefit or cost.) We derive a simple formula for the efficiency of the linear equilibrium for any pair of priors in this family, and show that this efficiency is quite high for all pairs of priors. Thus, for all pairs of priors in which the expectation of the buyer's true value is at least as large as the expectation of the seller's true cost, the efficiency ranges from $27/32 = 0.84375$ in the uniform case (second-best) to 1 in the case in which the benefit is 1 or the cost is zero with certainty. The minimum efficiency over all pairs of priors in this family is $(2/e) = 0.7358$. Experimental studies of one-sided auctions indicate that the players' strategies are usually close to linear (Cox *et al.* [3]). Recent experimental results (Radner and Schotter [9]) for the sealed-bid mechanism also seem to show linear behavior; if this result is robust, it should lend support to the mechanism as a practical procedure, in spite of the multiplicity of equilibria that could theoretically arise.

2. THE SEALED-BID GAME

A potential buyer B and a potential seller S are bargaining over the terms of a possible trade of a single object. If the object is traded, the value of B is V and the cost to S is C. (The seller incurs no cost if there is no trade.) The *sealed-bid mechanism* works as follows: B and S simultaneously choose bids, v and c, respectively. If $v \geqslant c$, then trade takes place, and B pays S the price

$$P = \frac{v + c}{2},$$

i.e., the average of the two bids. If $v < c$, then no trade takes place and B pays S nothing.

Suppose that at the time of bidding, B knows V but not C, and S knows C but not V. This situation is modelled by supposing that V and C are random variables with a joint probability distribuion, called the *prior*, which is known to both parties. Before the bidding takes place, B observes V but not C, and S observes C but not V. B's *strategy* is a function β that determines his bid v for each value of V, and S's *strategy* is a function γ that determines his bid c for each value of C. Thus

$$v = \beta(V),$$
$$c = \gamma(C). \tag{2.1}$$

The buyer's and seller's *profits* are, respectively,

$$\Phi_B = \begin{cases} V - (v + c)/2, & v \geqslant c, \\ 0, & v < c, \end{cases}$$

$$\Phi_S = \begin{cases} (v + c)/2 - C, & v \geqslant c, \\ 0, & v < c. \end{cases} \tag{2.2}$$

Suppose that the parties are risk-neutral, so that, for a given pair of strategies β and γ, the respective *expected utilities* are

$$\pi_B(\beta, \gamma) = E\Phi_B,$$
$$\pi_S(\beta, \gamma) = E\Phi_S,$$

(2.3)

where the expectation is taken with respect to the prior distribution of V and C. Equations (2.1)–(2.3) determine a noncooperative game; as usual, an *equilibrium* of the game is a pair of strategies such that neither player can increase his expected utility (expected profit) by unilaterally changing his strategy.[3]

3. The "Uniform Prior" Case

3.1. *Introduction*

Suppose that, in the sealed-bid game of Section 2, the prior distribution of V and C is uniform on the unit square; in other words, V and C are independent and each is uniformly distributed on the unit interval $[0, 1]$. In this case, for strategies β and γ, the respective expected profits (ex ante) are

$$\pi_B(\beta, \gamma) = \int_0^1 \int_0^1 I(v, c)[V - P(v, c)]\, dV\, dC,$$

(3.1)

$$\pi_S(\beta, \gamma) = \int_0^1 \int_0^1 I(v, c)[P(v, c) - C]\, dV\, dC,$$

where

$$v = \beta(V), \qquad c = \gamma(C),$$

and

$$I(v, c) = \begin{Bmatrix} 1 \\ 0 \end{Bmatrix} \qquad \text{as} \quad v \begin{Bmatrix} \geq \\ < \end{Bmatrix} c,$$

$$P(v, c) = \frac{v + c}{2}.$$

(3.2)

There are infinitely many equilibria of this game, although it is not known to us what the entire set of equilibria is. We shall describe here two

---

[3] See Myerson and Satterthwaite [8]. The linear equilibrium of the sealed-bid game was first identified by Chatterjee and Samuelson [2]. Myerson and Satterthwaite include consideration of mechanisms for which the function $I(v, c)$ is the probability that trade takes place, and hence can take any value in $[0, 1]$.

families of equilibria, one in which the strategies satisfy (over an interval) a certain pair of differential equations, and a second family in which the strategies are step-functions.

In the first family there is a particular equilibrium in which the strategies are linear over an interval; we shall call this the *linear equilibrium*. The linear equilibrium is noteworthy because it has been shown that, in the present uniform prior case, the linear equilibrium achieves the maximum expected gains from trade ($\pi_B + \pi_S$) for any equilibrium of any bargaining mechanism. Roughly speaking, a bargaining mechanism is defined by a pair of functions I and P, as in (3.1), that determine when trade takes place and at what price. Thus the functions I and P in (3.2) define the sealed-bid mechanism.

3.2. Optimal Responses to Distribution of Bids

As a preliminary to calculating various equilibria of the sealed-bid game in the uniform-prior case, we shall present a method of fairly general applicability.

For a given strategy of the seller, let G denote the cumulative distribution function (cdf) of the seller's bids. Given the buyer's true value V and his bid v, his conditional expected profit is

$$\Pi_B = \int_{c=0}^{v} (V - P)\, dG(c). \tag{3.3}$$

At points where the derivatives exist,

$$\frac{\partial \Pi_B}{\partial v} = (V - v)\, G'(v) - \left(\frac{1}{2}\right) G(v), \tag{3.4}$$

$$\frac{\partial^2 \Pi_B}{\partial v^2} = (V - v)\, G''(v) - \left(\frac{3}{2}\right) G'(v). \tag{3.5}$$

Equation (3.4) expresses the fact that slightly increasing the buyer's bid adds to his profit by marginally increasing the set of possible transactions, but subtracts from his profit by decreasing the price on all possible transactions. Setting (3.4) equal to zero at points v where $G'(v) > 0$ gives

$$V = v + \left(\frac{1}{2}\right) \frac{G(v)}{G'(v)}, \tag{3.6}$$

and evaluating (3.5) at (3.6) gives

$$\frac{\partial^2 \Pi_B}{\partial v^2} = \left(\frac{1}{2G'(v)}\right) [G(v)\, G''(v) - 3(G'(v))], \tag{3.7}$$

so that at such points

$$\frac{\partial^2 \Pi_B}{\partial v^2} < 0$$

if and only if

$$3[G'(v)]^2 - G(v)\,G''(v) > 0. \tag{3.8}$$

Hence (3.8) is a sufficient condition that (3.6) characterize a local maximum of Π_B. Note also that (3.8) is a necessary and sufficient condition for the right-hand side of (3.6) to be strictly increasing, so that if (3.8) holds then (3.6) determines the inverse function β^{-1}, where β is the buyer's optimal response to G (i.e., to the seller's strategy), and β is strictly increasing. Finally, (3.6) shows that $\beta(V) < V$ in this case. Note that *individual rationality* requires $\beta(V) \leqslant V$, and also $\gamma(C) \geqslant C$.

Corresponding calculations derive the conditions for the seller's optimal strategy,

$$C = c - \left(\frac{1}{2}\right) \frac{[1 - F(c)]}{F'(c)} \equiv \gamma^{-1}(c), \tag{3.9}$$

$$3[F'(c)]^2 + [1 - F(c)]\,F''(c) > 0, \tag{3.10}$$

which correspond to (3.6) and (3.8), respectively. (Here F denotes the cdf of the buyer's bids.)

3.3. Differentiable Equilibria[4]

Now observe that, since β is strictly monotone and the prior is uniform,

$$F[\beta(x)] = \Pr[\beta(V) \leqslant \beta(x)]$$
$$= \Pr[V \leqslant x]$$
$$= x,$$

so that

$$F = \beta^{-1}. \tag{3.11}$$

Similarly,

$$G = \gamma^{-1}. \tag{3.12}$$

---

[4] Since our research on differentiable equilibria was done, Satterthwaite and Williams [11] have come out with a more thorough investigation of the solutions of the coupled differential equations (3.13), below. Nonetheless, this section is included to emphasize the multiplicity, and the seriousness of the multiplicity, of differentiable equilibria.

If we denote β^{-1} and γ^{-1} by b and g, respectively, then we have from (3.6), (3.9), (3.10), and (3.12),

$$b(v) = v + \left(\frac{1}{2}\right) \frac{g(v)}{g'(v)},$$

$$g(c) = c - \left(\frac{1}{2}\right) \frac{[1 - b(c)]}{b'(c)}. \tag{3.13}$$

We are thus led to look for solutions of (3.13) to determine equilibria of the game with differentiable strategies.

One such solution is

$$V = b(v) = \left(\tfrac{3}{2}\right) v - \tfrac{1}{8},$$

$$C = g(c) = \left(\tfrac{3}{2}\right) c - \tfrac{3}{8}. \tag{3.14}$$

Inverting these linear functions yields

$$v = \left(\tfrac{2}{3}\right) V + \tfrac{1}{12},$$

$$c = \left(\tfrac{2}{3}\right) C + \tfrac{1}{4}. \tag{3.15}$$

This is the "linear equilibrium" referred to in Section 3.1. Note that $v \geqslant c$ (trade takes place) if and only if

$$V \geqslant C + \tfrac{1}{4}. \tag{3.16}$$

By (3.16), one can modify the strategies for $0 \leqslant V < \tfrac{1}{4}$ and $\tfrac{3}{4} < C \leqslant 1$, without changing the outcome of the game, in any way such that

$$v < \tfrac{1}{4} \quad \text{for} \quad V < \tfrac{1}{4},$$

$$c > \tfrac{3}{4} \quad \text{for} \quad C > \tfrac{3}{4}. \tag{3.17}$$

For example, take

$$\beta(V) = \begin{cases} V, & 0 \leqslant V \leqslant \tfrac{1}{4}, \\ \left(\tfrac{2}{3}\right) V + \tfrac{1}{12}, & \tfrac{1}{4} \leqslant V \leqslant 1, \end{cases} \tag{3.18}$$

$$\gamma(C) = \begin{cases} \left(\tfrac{2}{3}\right) C + \tfrac{1}{4}, & 0 \leqslant C \leqslant \tfrac{3}{4} \\ C, & \tfrac{3}{4} \leqslant C \leqslant 1. \end{cases} \tag{3.19}$$

(See Fig. 2.)

The linear functions (3.15) constitute one of a one-parameter family of *symmetric* solutions to the pair of differential equations (3.13). Here the natural symmetry condition is

$$\beta(x) = 1 - \gamma(1 - x), \tag{3.20}$$

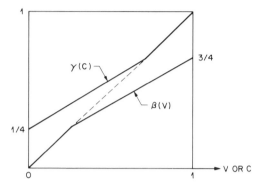

FIG. 2. "Linear equilibrium" strategies.

or equivalently

$$b(x) = 1 - g(1 - x).$$ (3.21)

(That is, the curve γ is obtained from the curve β by rotation through 180°, as in Fig. 2, and similarly for their inverses.) In a symmetric equilibrium, the seller overbids, when his cost is C, by the same amount that the buyer underbids when his value is $V = 1 - C$. [To prove that (3.20) and (3.21) are equivalent, solve (3.20) to get

$$x = b[1 - \gamma(1 - x)].$$

Let

$$y = 1 - \gamma(1 - x);$$

then

$$\gamma(1 - x) = 1 - y,$$
$$1 - x = g(1 - y),$$
$$x = 1 - g(1 - y),$$

and so

$$b(y) = 1 - g(1 - y),$$

which is (3.21).]

With the symmetry condition, (3.13) becomes

$$g'(x) = \left(\frac{1}{2}\right) \frac{g(x)}{1 - x - g(1 - x)}.$$ (3.22)

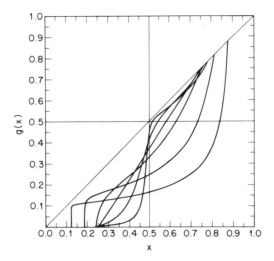

FIG. 3. Symmetric differentiable equilibria with uniform prior (inverse of Seller's strategy).

Note that at any point x, the derivative of g is determined by the value of g at both x and the "symmetric" point $(1 - x)$. In particular,

$$g'(\tfrac{1}{2}) = \left(\frac{1}{2}\right) \frac{g(\tfrac{1}{2})}{\tfrac{1}{2} - g(\tfrac{1}{2})}.$$

Starting from any value of $g(\tfrac{1}{2})$ one can solve (3.22) by working one's way out from $x = \tfrac{1}{2}$ in both directions at once. The linear solution corresponds to taking $g(\tfrac{1}{2}) = \tfrac{3}{8}$. Although closed-form expressions for the other solutions are not known to us, those solutions can be calculated numerically.

Some of these solutions are illustrated in Fig. 3. We may note the following[5]:

  (i) There can be no polynomial solutions of (3.22), other than the linear one, (3.14). This follows easily from the inhomogeneous nature of (3.22).

  (ii) Solutions are defined over a domain symmetrically placed around $x = \tfrac{1}{2}$, say from $x = a$ to $x = 1 - a$; trade cannot take place for $C < a$ nor for $V > 1 - a$. At $x = a$, $g(x) = 0$. At $x = 1 - a$, $g(x)$ hits the diagonal: $g(x) = x$. For the linear solution $a = \tfrac{1}{4}$. (Warning! The symbol a has different meanings in different sections of this paper.)

[5] We thank H. J. Landau and B. F. Logan for Fig. 3 and for points (i) and (ii) noted below.

(iii) The gains from trade are maximized by the linear solution. For any solution, they are given by

$$\text{gains from trade} = a^2(1-a) + \frac{1}{2}\int_a^{1-a} g(\gamma)\,d\gamma. \tag{3.23}$$

This expression is derived in the Appendix.

Further progress in understanding the solutions of the coupled differential equations (3.13) has been reported by Satterthwaite and Williams [11].

3.4. Step-Function Equilibria

In this section we investigate the class of equilibria which uses only a *finite* number of different (potential) bids. These equilibria imply that buyers (sellers) with *different* valuations (costs) may post the *same* bids. They are not only of interest as a subclass of equilibria in the general sealed-bid game outlined in Section 2, but also have particular relevance for real world situations in which bids are required to be in full dollars (hundreds of dollars, etc.).

The simplest case is illustrated by the following strategies:

(i) *One-step equilibria.* Let $a \in (0, 1)$ be arbitrary and define

$$\beta(V) = \begin{cases} 0, & 0 \leqslant V < a, \\ a, & a \leqslant V \leqslant 1, \end{cases}$$

$$\gamma(C) = \begin{cases} a, & 0 \leqslant C \leqslant a, \\ 1, & a < C \leqslant 1. \end{cases} \tag{3.24}$$

(β, γ) form a pair of equilibrium strategies for any a. This may be seen as follows: Clearly, with strategies restricted to 1-step functions the only way to meet the individual-rationality constraint for low-valuation buyers (high-cost sellers) is to have the lower potential bid of the buyer (the higher potential bid of the seller) equal to zero (one). (This already imposes monotonicity on *equilibrium* strategies in this case.) We refer to these as "marginal" bids. If the higher (i.e., nonmarginal) bid of the buyer equals a the seller's optimal response is to set his nonmarginal bid equal to a. Any bid c above a results in no trade taking place (so the seller should only consider such a bid if $C > a$); any bid c below a results in trade with probability $(1-a)$, but this situation is dominated by the bid $c = a$ which also results in trade with probability $(1-a)$ but at a higher price (and thus higher expected profits). Moreover, bidding $c = a$ makes sense as long as $C \leqslant a$. The analogous argument holds for the buyer. Also note that the only equilibrium of this family which is symmetric in the sense of (3.20) is the one with $a = \frac{1}{2}$ (where the possible bids $\{0, \frac{1}{2}, 1\}$ are equidistant).

(ii) *n-step equilibria.* We now allow strategies to be *n*-step functions. Two features of the 1-step case generalize immediately. First, the lowest bid of the buyer (highest bid of the seller) has to be marginal, i.e., zero (one). Secondly, it is never an optimal response to place a nonmarginal bid in a region which lies outside the set of potential bids of the other player (see Lemma 4.2, below). One may add that it is easy to show that equilibrium strategies are monotonically nondecreasing with respect to valuation (buyer) and cost (seller) (see Lemma 4.1). These facts are used in the formulation of the following proposition that *completely* characterizes *n*-step equilibria.

PROPOSITION 3.1. *Let n be any natural number and suppose that the pair of strategies (γ, β) form an equilibrium of the sealed-bid game where*

$$
\gamma(C) = \begin{cases} c_1, & 0 \leqslant C \leqslant x_1, \\ c_2, & x_1 < C \leqslant x_2, \\ \vdots & \\ c_n, & x_{n-1} < C \leqslant x_n, \\ 1, & x_n < C \leqslant 1, \end{cases} \tag{3.25}
$$

with $0 < c_1 < c_2 < \cdots < c_n < 1$ and $0 < x_1 < x_2 < \cdots < x_n < 1$, and

$$
\beta(V) = \begin{cases} 0, & 0 \leqslant V < z_1, \\ v_1, & z_1 \leqslant V < z_2, \\ v_2, & z_2 \leqslant V < z_3, \\ \vdots & \vdots \\ v_n, & z_n \leqslant V \leqslant 1, \end{cases} \tag{3.26}
$$

with $0 < v_1 < v_2 < \cdots < c_n < 1$ and $0 < z_1 < z_2 < \cdots < z_n < 1$. Then the following relations hold:

(i) $c_i = v_i = a_i$ for $i = 1, ..., n,$

(ii) $z_1 = a_1,$

$$
z_i = a_i + \frac{x_{i-1}}{(x_i - x_{i-1})} \frac{(a_i - a_{i-1})}{2} \qquad for \quad i = 2, ..., n, \tag{3.27}
$$

(iii) $x_i = a_i - \frac{(1 - z_{i+1})}{(z_{i+1} - z_i)} \frac{(a_{i+1} - a_i)}{2} \qquad for \quad i = 1, ..., n-1,$

$$
x_n = a_n. \tag{3.28}
$$

Proof. See Appendix.

The interpretation of Proposition 3.1 is as follows: If we—for convenience—define $x_0 = r_0 = 0$ and $z_{n+1} = c_{n+1} = 1$, (3.25) and (3.26) state that buyers with valuation $V \in [z_i, z_{i+1})$ (resp. sellers with cost $C \in (x_{i-1}, x_i])$ bid v_i(resp. c_i). Alternatively, the probability of a bid v_i by the buyer (c_i by the seller) is $(z_{i+1} - z_i)$ (resp. $(x_i - x_{i-1})$). Conclusion (i) then says that in equilibrium the supports of the two bid distributions have to coincide while conclusions, (ii) and (iii) give the precise relationship between the probability weights. Note that with $c_i = r_i = a_i$ (ii) and (iii) imply that $x_i < a_i < z_i$, $i = 2, ..., n-1$, indicating "shading" on both sides of the market. Roughly speaking, the extent of shading employed by a bidder—given the other bidder's strategy—depends on the differences of "adjacent" bids, which determine price changes, and the sizes of the "market segments" of bidders who make the same bid, which determine changes in the probability of trade taking place. For a detailed discussion and derivation of (ii) and (iii) we refer to the Appendix.

Proposition 3.1 reduces the existence issue for n-step equilibria to the solvability of the recursive system (difference equations) (3.27) and (3.28) subject to the constraints

$$0 < a_i < a_{i+1} < 1, \quad 0 < z_i < z_{i+1} < 1, \quad 0 < x_i < x_{i+1} < 1, \quad i = 1, ..., n-1.$$
$$(3.29)$$

It is apparent that for $n \geq 2$ existence of n-step equilibria will crucially depend on the vector of potential bids $a = (a_1, ..., a_n)$. It is not true—as in the case $n = 1$—that for any $a = (a_1, ..., a_n)$ such that $0 < a_1 < \cdots < a_n < 1$ there is an n-step equilibrium.

Consider for example the case $n = 2$: Equilibrium exists (by Proposition 3.1) if the following equations admit a solution:

$$z_2 = a_2 + \frac{x_1}{(a_2 - x_1)} \frac{(a_2 - a_1)}{2}; \qquad x_1 = a_1 - \frac{(1 - z_2)}{(z_2 - a_1)} \frac{(a_2 - a_1)}{2}. \quad (3.30)$$

However, (3.30) does not admit a general solution $(z_2(a_1, a_2), x_1(a_1, a_2))$. Choose a_2 very close to 1, e.g., $\frac{9}{10}$. Then, if z_2 is to lie between a_2 and 1, z_2 is even closer to 1. Thus by the second equation of (3.30) $x_1 \approx a_1$ and the first equation becomes $z_2 \approx a_2 + (a_1/2)$ which is only compatible with $z_2 < 1$ if $a_1 < 2(1 - a_2)$. That is, a_1 has to be very small (close to 0). Thus, for example, there is no solution for $a = (\frac{1}{2}, \frac{9}{10})$. The reason for this is simple. As $a_2 \to 1$ almost all buyers bid a_1 (or 0) and the potential gains of a bid a_2, namely, $(x_2 - x_1)(V - a_2)$, will vanish, since the maximal valuation of a buyer is $1(V \leq 1)$. The cost of a bid of a_2, namely, $x_1((a_2 - a_1)/2)$, does not go to zero if $a_1 > 0$ is kept constant. There are always low-cost sellers $(c < a_1)$ who prefer a bid of a_1 (and trade with probability $> (a_2 - a_1)$) over a bid of a_2 (and trade with probability $<(1-a_2)$). On trades with these types of sellers the buyer incurs a substantial loss if he bids a_2 due to the sharp resulting price increase. Consequently if sellers who bid $c < a_1$ are reasonably probable (a_1 not close to zero), then no buyer would be willing to submit a bid of a_2, because the expected price increase would be too costly.

However, if we require the support of the distribution of potential bids to be *symmetric*, in the sense of (3.20), i.e., $a_1 = 1 - a_2$, it is easily seen that there always exists an equilibrium supporting this distribution. Set $x_1 = 1 - z_2$ and (3.30) reduces to the single equation

$$x_1 = a_1 - \frac{x_1}{(1 - x_1 - a_1)} \frac{(1 - 2a_1)}{2}, \tag{3.31}$$

which has a unique solution for any $a_1 \in (0, \frac{1}{2})$. There also exist numerous *nonsymmetric* equilibria as any slight perturbation of a symmetric support distribution of bids is still compatible with (3.30).

These exercises suggest that the more the distribution of potential bids reflects the dual roles of buyer and seller (given the uniform priors) the more likely it is to be sustainable in an equilibrium of the sealed-bid game. For this reason we now adopt the symmetry condition (3.20) which for n-step functions translates into the requirements

$$a_i = 1 - a_{n-(i-1)}, \qquad i = 1, ..., n, \tag{3.32}$$

and

$$x_i = 1 - z_{n-(i-1)}, \qquad i = 1, ..., n. \tag{3.33}$$

It is interesting to observe that (3.33) is implied by (3.32) if the solution to (3.27) and (3.28) (for a given $a = (a_1, ..., a_n)$ satisfying (3.32)) is unique.

LEMMA 3.2. *Suppose $a = (a_1, ..., a_n)$ satisfies (3.32) and let y^- denote the vector $(y_n, y_{n-1}, ..., y_1)$ when $y = (y_1, ..., y_n)$. Then (x, z) is a solution of (3.27), (3.28) if and only if $(\bar{x}, \bar{z}) = (1 - z^-, 1 - x^-)$ is a solution of (3.27), (3.28). (Here $1 \equiv (1, 1, ..., 1)$.)*

Proof. Elementary.

It is not clear whether a solution to (3.27), (3.28) subject to (3.32) is always unique. However, numerical calculations of equilibria using (3.32) strongly suggest that (3.32) already implies uniqueness (and hence symmetry) of the solution to (3.27), (3.28).

An important consequence of Lemma 3.2 is that any *symmetric* solution to (3.27) (resp. (3.28)) is also a solution to (3.28) (resp. (3.27)). Hence we are led to study (3.27) subject to (3.32) and (3.33).

Solving (3.27) for x_i results in

$$x_i = x_{i-1} + \frac{x_i - 1}{(z_i - a_i)} \frac{(a_i - a_{i-1})}{2}, \qquad i = 2, ..., n,$$

$$z_1 = a_1, \tag{3.34}$$

and the application of (3.32) and (3.33) then yields

$$x_i = x_{i-1} + \frac{x_{i-1}}{(1 - x_{n-(i-1)} - a_i)} - \frac{(a_i - a_{i-1})}{2}, \qquad i = 2, ..., n,$$

$$x_n = 1 - a_1 = a_n \tag{3.35}$$

which we use in the form of

$$x_i = x_{i-1} + \frac{x_{i-1}}{(a_{n-(i-1)} - x_{n-(i-1)})} \frac{(a_i - a_{i-1})}{2}$$

$$= \left(1 + \frac{(a_i - a_{i-1})}{2[a_{n-(i-1)} - x_{n-(i-1)}]} \right) x_{i-1},$$

$$x_n = a_n, \qquad i = 2, ..., n. \tag{3.36}$$

To make further progress we now specify the symmetric distribution of bids as follows: Let $b \in (0, \frac{1}{2})$ and consider the interval $[b, 1-b] \subset [0, 1]$. Define

$$a_i = b + \frac{(i-1)}{n-1}(1 - 2b), \qquad i = 1, ..., n, \tag{3.37}$$

i.e., $a_1 = b$ and $a_n = 1 - b$. Then

$$\frac{1}{2}(a_i - a_{i-1}) = \frac{(1 - 2b)}{2(n-1)} = \text{const.} = B \tag{3.38}$$

and (3.36) becomes the following set of n equations:

$$x_2 = \left(1 + \frac{B}{(a_{n-1} - x_{n-1})} \right) x_1, \tag{3.39, 1}$$

$$x_3 = \left(1 + \frac{B}{(a_{n-2} - x_{n-2})} \right) x_2, \tag{3.39, 2}$$

$$\vdots$$

$$x_i = \left(1 + \frac{B}{(a_{n-(i-1)} - x_{n-(i-1)})} \right) x_{i-1}, \tag{3.39, i-1}$$

$$\vdots$$

$$x_{n-1} = \left(1 + \frac{B}{(a_2 - x_2)}\right) x_{n-2},$$ (3.39, n-2)

$$x_n = \left(1 + \frac{B}{(a_1 - x_1)}\right) x_{n-1},$$ (3.39, n-1)

$$x_n = 1 - b.$$ (3.39, n)

So, if we substitute $x_n = 1 - b$ into (3.39, $n-1$) and *choose* x_1 from $(0, a_1)$ that equation will determine x_{n-1}. Given x_1 and x_{n-1} equation 1 of (3.39) will determine (x_2, x_{n-1}) and x_2 will determine x_{n-2} from (3.39, $n-2$), etc.; eventually the "middle" equation has to be satisfied. Alternatively, one could start in the middle by choosing $x_{n/2}$ or $x_{(n+1)/2}$ (depending on whether n is even or odd) and work "outwards" to determine x_n. The equilibrium condition then is given by Eq. (3.39, n): $x_n = 1 - b$ (and the inequalities $x_i < a_i$, $i = 1, ..., n$). Note that the choice of b in (3.37) determines the "boundary condition" expressed by equation n and the vector $a = (a_1, ..., a_n)$. Our first result is concerned with the case $b = 0$, i.e., (after relabelling) $a_i = i/(n+1)$, $i = 1, ..., n$.

PROPOSITION 3.3.   *Let n be any natural number and set $a = (1/(n+1), ..., n/(n+1))$. Then there exists a solution to (3.39). Moreover, any sequence of n-step equilibria $(\beta_n, \gamma_n)_{n=1}^{\infty}$ converges to the pair of functions $\beta(V) \equiv 0$ and $\gamma(C) \equiv 1$ as $n \to \infty$.*

The proof of Proposition 3.3., which is relegated to the Appendix, shows that the "perverse" convergence behavior to the "trivial" equilibrium in

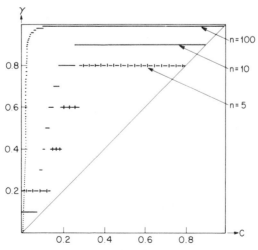

FIG 4. Equilibrium strategies of Seller with symmetric support of distribution of bids over [0, 1] (for $n = 5$, 10, and 100).

which the seller always bids 1 and the buyer always bids 0 with no trade taking place, is *solely* due to the particular choice of the support of the bid distribution, namely, that $b = 0$ was used in (3.37). This case is illustrated in Fig. 4 which shows equilibrium strategies of the seller for various n. However, if we choose $b > 0$ in (3.37) n-step equilibria do not converge to the trivial equilibrium. Moreover, raising b ($= a_1$) and thus lowering the starting value of the recursion, $x_n = 1 - b$, makes it easier to satisfy (3.39).

The next proposition shows that the "linear equilibrium" of Section 3.2 arises as a limit of a sequence of n-step equilibria for $n \to \infty$.

PROPOSITION 3.4.   *There exists a sequence of n-step equilibria* (β_n, γ_n) *such that*

$$(\beta_n, \gamma_n) \to (\tfrac{2}{3}V + \tfrac{1}{12}, \tfrac{2}{3}C + \tfrac{1}{4}) \qquad as \quad n \to \infty.$$

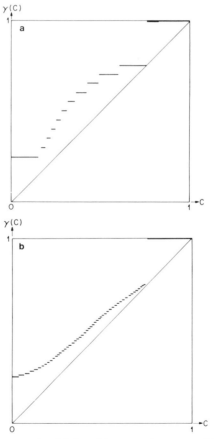

FIG. 5. Equilibrium strategies of Seller with symmetric support of distribution of bids over [1/4, 3/4], (a) for $n = 10$ and (b) for $n = 50$.

Proof. See Appendix.

Figures 5a and 5b illustrate convergence to the linear equilibrium if $b = \frac{1}{4}$ is chosen in (3.37) by graphing the seller's equilibrium strategies for $n = 10$ and $n = 50$, respectively.

Proposition 3.3 and 3.4 in a sense describe the "extremes" of possible convergence behavior of n-step equilibria. As is shown in the Appendix there also exist n-step equilibria for other values of b. Figures 6a and 6b shows equilibrium strategies if $b = 0.15$ for $n = 15$ and $n = 70$. We presume from additional numerical calculations that convergence is now to symmetric differentiable solutions of (3.22) as depicted in Fig. 3 (note that Fig. 3 graphs the *inverse* of the seller's strategy).

The family of n-step equilibria contains elements yielding total gains from trade as close as one wishes to the second-best level produced by the "linear" equilibrium. To see this consider the sequence of n-step equilibria constructed in Proposition 3.4 that converges to this equilibrium. They are determined, for $n = 1, 2,...,$ by (3.25)–(3.28), (3.32), (3.33), and (3.37) with

$$b_n = \frac{1}{4} + \frac{\frac{3}{4}}{2n+1} \quad \text{and} \quad x_i = i \cdot \frac{3}{2} \cdot \frac{1 - 2b_n}{n-1}.$$

Let (β_n, γ_n) denote the buyer's and seller's strategy pair in the equilibrium

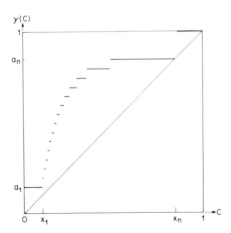

FIG. 6a. Equilibrium strategies of Seller with symmetric support of distribution of bids over [0.15, 0.85] (for $n = 15$). In the limit, the "slope" of γ becomes infinite at x_1. These solutions approximate curves like those in Fig. 3 (which, however, shows the *inverse* of the equilibrium strategy).

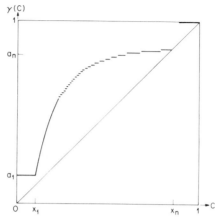

FIG. 6b. Equilibrium strategies of Seller with symmetric support of distribution of bids over [0.15, 0.85] (for $n = 70$).

with n steps. Trade occurs if and only if $\beta_n(V) \geqslant \gamma_n(C)$ which—after some tedious calculations—results in

$$\beta_n(V) \geqslant \gamma_n(C)$$

$$\Leftrightarrow \begin{cases} V - C \geqslant \dfrac{\frac{1}{2}n + \frac{3}{2}i - \frac{1}{2}}{2n+1} - \dfrac{3}{2} \cdot i \, \dfrac{1}{2n+1} + \dfrac{3}{2} \dfrac{1}{2n+1} = \dfrac{1}{4} + \dfrac{\frac{3}{4}}{2n+1} \\[2ex] \text{or} \\[1ex] \{V = 1 - x_{n-(i-1)} \text{ and } C = x_i \text{ for } i \in \{1, ..., n\} \text{ and } V \geqslant C\}. \end{cases}$$

(3.40)

This requires some comment. $\frac{3}{2} \cdot 1/(2n+1)$ is the length of the half-open intervals $(x_j, x_{j+1}]$ and $[1 - x_{n-(j-1)}, 1 - x_{n-j})$ over which the seller's and the buyer's bid is *constant*. To make sure that $\beta_n(V) \geqslant \gamma_n(C)$ one has to add this quantity to the difference "$\beta_n^{-1}(a_i) - \gamma_n^{-1}(a_i)$" unless this difference is exactly taken at x_{j+1}, the *upper* boundary of $(x_j, x_{j+1}]$, and $1 - x_{n(j-1)}$, the *lower* boundary of $[1 - x_{n-(j-1)}, 1 - x_{n-j})$. But this can happen only $(n-1)$ times.

COROLLARY. *For n large enough the equilibria* (β_n, γ_n) *are approximately* *(second-best) optimal.*

We close this section by observing that the arguments given in the proof of Proposition 3.1. imply that the differentiable equilibria of Sections 3.2 and 3.3 arise from *global* (and not just local) maximizers if they are limits of (globally maximizing) n-step equilibria.

3.5. Perfection of n-Step Equilibria

All these n-step equilibria are "perfect," in a certain sense that we shall define below. Selten [12] defined for *finite* games the notion of a perfect (often called "trembling-hand perfect") equilibrium. Such an equilibrium is the limit of some sequence of equilibria in completely mixed strategies, where a completely mixed strategy is one in which every feasible strategy appears with positive probability.

For the infinite game we are discussing, the space of feasible strategies is so large that it is not clear how to define a probability measure on it in a natural way. We therefore prefer to consider complete mixtures not of strategies but of bids. It will be as if the buyer's or seller's bid were transmitted through a noisy channel, so that with small but positive probability the received bid may take any value on [0, 1].

Selten shows (Theorem 7) that for finite games an equilibrium is perfect if and only if it is "substitute perfect." In the present context this would mean that the buyer's (seller's) pure equilibrium strategy is a best response to each of a sequence of seller's (buyer's) bid distributions that have trembled, where the sequence converges (pointwise) to the seller's (buyer's) pure equilibrium strategy. Our perfection property will be similar (but not identical) to this latter notion.

Consider the one-step equilibrium of Eq. (3.24). From (3.11) and (3.12), the corresponding bid distributions are

$$F(c) = \begin{cases} a & \text{if} \quad 0 \leqslant v < a, \\ 1 & \text{if} \quad a \leqslant v \leqslant 1, \end{cases}$$

$$G(c) = \begin{cases} 0 & \text{if} \quad 0 \leqslant c < a, \\ a & \text{if} \quad a \leqslant c < 1, \\ 1 & \text{if} \quad c = 1. \end{cases} \tag{3.43}$$

Let us now perturb these bid distributions as follows:

$$F_\varepsilon(v) = (1 - \varepsilon) F(v) + \varepsilon \bar{F}(v), \tag{3.44}$$

where

$$\bar{F}(v) = \begin{cases} (1 - k) v & \text{if} \quad 0 \leqslant v < 1, \\ 1 & \text{if} \quad v = 1, \end{cases}$$

and $0 < k < 1$. Also,

$$G_\varepsilon(c) = (1 - \varepsilon) G(c) + \varepsilon \bar{G}(c), \tag{3.45}$$

where

$$\bar{G}(c) = k + (1 - k) c, \qquad 0 \leqslant c \leqslant 1.$$

(Note that $\bar{F}(v)$ and $\bar{G}(c)$ are symmetric, in the sense of (3.20).) Equation (3.45) says that the seller whose cost is C succeeds with probability $1 - \varepsilon$

in bidding according to (3.24), but with probability ε trembles; if he trembles, he bids zero with (conditional) probability k, while with (conditional) probability $(1-k)$ his bid is spread uniformly over $(0, 1]$.

We now show that, except for a small neighborhood of $V = a$, $\beta(V)$, given by (3.24), is a best response to $G_\varepsilon(c)$ for any ε sufficiently small, and for appropriately chosen k. Let the buyer's expected profit be Π_B:

$$\Pi_B = (1-\varepsilon)\,\Pi_B^0(v, V, a) + \varepsilon\Pi_B^T(v, V). \tag{3.46}$$

Here Π_B^0 is the expected profit of a buyer with value V and bid v if the seller's bid distribution is G, while Π_B^T (T for tremble) is the expected profit of the same buyer if the seller's bid distribution is $\bar{G}$.

It is easy to calculate Π_B^T:

$$\Pi_B^T(v, V) = k\left(V - \frac{v}{2}\right) + (1-k)\int_{c=0}^{v}\left(V - \frac{v+c}{2}\right)dc$$

$$= k\left(V - \frac{v}{2}\right) + (1-k)\left(Vv - \frac{3}{4}v^2\right). \tag{3.47}$$

We shall require Π_B^T decreasing in v for $V < a$:

$$\frac{\partial \Pi_B^T}{\partial v} = \frac{k}{2} + (1-k)\left(V - \frac{3}{2}v\right) < 0. \tag{3.48}$$

It is necessary and sufficient that (3.48) be satisfied at $V = a, v = 0$; this implies

$$k > \frac{a}{a + \frac{1}{2}}, \tag{3.49}$$

so we now choose k in this range.

As to Π_B^0, we have

$$\Pi_B^0 = \begin{cases} 0, & \text{if } v < a, \\ \left(V - \dfrac{v+a}{2}\right)a, & \text{if } v \geqslant a. \end{cases} \tag{3.50}$$

We can calculate the buyer's best strategy. For $V < a$ we must have $v < a$; hence, from (3.46) and (3.50), the buyer's profit in this case is

$$\Pi_B = \varepsilon\Pi_B^T.$$

Thus, in light of (3.48), his best bid is $v = 0$.

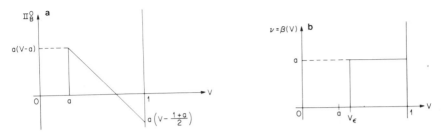

FIG. 7. (a) Buyer's profit as a function of his bid, when seller plays pure one-step strategy. (b) Buyer's best response to an ε-perturbed bid distribution by the seller.

For $V \geqslant a$, Π_B^0 is as shown in Fig. 7a. It is evident that for small ε, and in view of (3.48), the buyer's best bid is either $v = 0$ or $v = a$, whichever leads to the greater profit. For $v = 0$, we have

$$\Pi_B = \varepsilon \Pi_B^T(0, V) = \varepsilon k V. \tag{3.51}$$

For $v = a$,

$$\Pi_B = (1 - \varepsilon) a(V - a) + \varepsilon \left[k \left(V - \frac{a}{2} \right) + (1 - k) \left(Va - \frac{3}{4} a^2 \right) \right]. \tag{3.52}$$

The buyer's profit at $v = 0$ exceeds that at $v = a$ if

$$V > \frac{a + \varepsilon/(1 - \varepsilon)[k/2 + (1 - k) \, 3/4a]}{1 + \varepsilon/[(1 - \varepsilon)(1 - k)]} \equiv V_\varepsilon, \qquad \text{say.} \tag{3.53}$$

Clearly V_ε approaches V as ε approaches zero, and it is easy to show that $V_\varepsilon > a$ if k satisfies (3.49). Hence the buyer's best response is as shown in Fig. 7b.

An exactly symmetric argument applies to the seller's best response to a perturbed distribution of bids by the buyer. Moreover, similar results can be obtained by similar methods for the n-step case (we omit the details). In this way we obtain:

PROPOSITION 3.6. *Every n-step equilibrium $(\beta^0(V), \gamma^0(C))$ is perfect in the following sense*:

For every $\delta > 0$, there is an $\varepsilon_0 > 0$, such that the buyer's best response to an ε-perturbed strategy of the seller (where $\varepsilon < \varepsilon_0$) is $\beta^0(V)$, except on a V-set of measure $< \delta$.

This proposition is important for two reasons: First, it suggests that differentiable equilibria that arise as limits of n-step equilibria, too, share the perfection property (although, in the absence of explicit expressions for the differentiable strategies, we cannot show this). And secondly, it indicates that there is no easy way to discriminate among the multitude of equilibria of this game unearthed in the previous sections.[6]

4. GENERAL INDEPENDENT PRIORS

4.1. *Preliminaries*

It would be interesting to compare the performance of the sealed-bid mechanism with nonuniform priors to that with the uniform prior, where it is known to be the optimal mechanism. In this section we consider priors that are nonuniform but (for tractability) independent:

$$P\{V \leqslant v, C \leqslant c\} \equiv M(v) N(c). \tag{4.1}$$

As in Section 3, the buyer's optimal response strategy is determined by the seller's bid distribution. This distribution is jointly determined by the seller's prior and his strategy, N and γ, respectively, Similarly, the seller's optimal response is to the buyer's bid distribution, which is jointly determined by *his* prior and strategy, M and β. The situation can be represented schematically as in Fig. 8; for an equilibrium, the system of causal arrows and functions in this picture must be related in a consistent way.

As before, the buyer's and seller's bid distributions, F and G, respectively, are defined by

$$F(v) \equiv \text{Prob}\{\beta(V) \leqslant v\},$$

$$G(c) \equiv \text{Prob}\{\gamma(C) \leqslant c\}.$$

As in Section 3.3, given the seller's bid distribution G, and given the buyer's true value V and bid v, the buyer's conditional expected profit is

$$\Pi_B(V, v) = \int_{c=0}^{v} \left(V - \frac{v+c}{2} \right) dG(c).$$

Similarly, the seller's conditional expected profit is

$$\Pi_S(C, c) = \int_{v=c}^{1} \left(\frac{v+c}{2} - C \right) dF(c).$$

---

[6] It is also unlikely that "dominance" relations between equilibria based on extended notions of Pareto efficiency (like Holmström and Myerson's [7] notion of "durability" of decision rules) can be established: e.g., a comparison between the linear equilibrium (Fig. 1) and the 100-step equilibrium of Fig. 4 shows that the types that never take part in trades under the linear equilibrium (i.e., those buyers with $V < 1/4$ and those sellers with $C > 3/4$) have the highest probabilities of attracting trades in the 100-step equilibrium, whereas the types that have the best chances of getting trades in the linear equilibrium have the worst odds of finding a trading partner in the 100-step equilibrium.

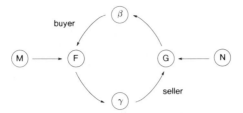

FIG. 8.   Equilibrium with nonuniform priors.

The following lemma *almost* shows that an optimal response of one player to the other player's bid distribution is a monotone nondecreasing strategy.[7]

LEMMA 4.1. (Chatterjee and Samuelson [2]). *Let G be any distribution of the seller's bids, and let v and v' be optimal bids for the buyer corresponding to the true values V and V', respectively; then*

$$V > V' \qquad implies \qquad G(v) \geqslant G(v').$$

A corresponding statement holds for the seller.

Proof.   Since v is optimal for V and v' is optimal for V',

$$\Pi_{\mathrm{B}}(V, v) \geqslant \Pi_{\mathrm{B}}(V, v'),$$

$$\Pi_{\mathrm{B}}(V', v') \geqslant \Pi_{\mathrm{B}}(V', v),$$

and hence

$$\Pi_{\mathrm{B}}(V, v) - \Pi_{\mathrm{B}}(V, v') + \Pi_{\mathrm{B}}(V', v') - \Pi_{\mathrm{B}}(V', v) \geqslant 0.$$

One can easily verify that

$$\Pi_{\mathrm{B}}(V, v) - \Pi_{\mathrm{B}}(V', v) = (V - V') \, G(v),$$

$$\Pi_{\mathrm{B}}(V', v') - \Pi_{\mathrm{B}}(V, v') = (V' - V) \, G(v').$$

Hence

$$(V - V') \, G(v) + (V' - V) \, G(v') \geqslant 0,$$

or

$$(V - V')[G(v) - G(v')] \geqslant 0,$$

from which the conclusion of the lemma immediately follows.

[7] Results similar to Lemmas 4.1 and 4.2 can be found in Chatterjee [1] and Chatterjee and Samuelson [2]; nevertheless, for the reader's convenience, we give brief statements and proofs of these Lemmas here.

Notice that, in the circumstances of Lemma 4.1, if $G(v) > G(v')$ then $v > v'$, since G is a cumulative distribution function. On the other hand, $G(v) = G(v')$ is consistent with $v < v'$. However, this possibility will be ruled out, for optimal responses, by Lemma 4.2.

Recall that the support of a probability measure is the smallest closed set with probability one. For two sets A and B, let $A \backslash B$ denote the set of points that are in A but not in B, and let $A < B$ mean that every element of A is less than every element of B. Finally, let supp(F) and supp(G) denote the supports of the bidding distributions F and G, respectively.

The next lemma states that, except for bids for which no trade is possible, mutually optimal bidding distributions have a common support.

LEMMA 4.2 ("Common support lemma"). *Let* (β, γ) *be an equilibrium, and let* (F, G) *be the corresponding bidding distributions; then*

$$\text{supp}(F) \backslash \text{supp}(G) < \text{supp}(G),$$

$$\text{supp}(G) \backslash \text{supp}(F) > \text{supp}(F).$$

Proof. Consider a buyer's bid v that is not in supp(G). We shall show by contradiction that $G(v) = 0$. Since v is not in supp(G), there is an open interval around v such that, for all v' in the interval, $G(v') = G(v)$. Suppose $G(v) > 0$; then if the buyer lowers his bid from v to some $v' < v$ in the interval, he will not lose any trades and he will increase his profit on each trade. Hence such a bid v cannot be optimal. A corresponding argument proves the second statement in the conclusion of the lemma.

Note that if $v < \text{supp}(G)$ then there will be no trade if the buyer bids v. The linear equilibrium of (3.18) and (3.19) provides an example of a case in which supp(F) and supp(G) are not identical. In that case the intersection of the two supports is the interval $[\frac{1}{4}, \frac{3}{4}]$.

The final lemma in this subsection shows that in equilibrium, except where no trade takes place, the buyer's bid will not exceed his value, and the seller's bid will not be less than his cost.

LEMMA 4.3. *Let* (β, γ) *be an equilibrium; then*

$$G(V) > 0 \quad implies \quad \beta(V) \leqslant V,$$

$$F(C) < 1 \quad implies \quad \gamma(C) \geqslant C.$$

Proof. We prove only the first conclusion. Suppose $G(V) > 0$ and $v > V$; we shall show that it is better for the buyer to bid V than v.

$$\Pi_B(V, V) - \Pi_B(V, v)$$

$$= \int_0^V \left(V - \frac{V+c}{2} \right) dG(c) - \int_0^v \left(V - \frac{v+c}{2} \right) dG(c)$$

$$= \int_0^V \left(\frac{v-V}{2} \right) dG(c) - \int_V^v \left(V - \frac{v+c}{2} \right) dG(c)$$

$$= \left(\frac{v-V}{2} \right) G(V) + \int_V^v \left(\frac{v+c}{2} - V \right) dG(c).$$

It is clear that if $v > V$ and $G(V) > 0$ then the first term is strictly positive and the second term is nonnegative; this completes the proof.

4.2. Differentiable Equilibria

We now discuss differentiable equilibria for general independent priors. Rather than give a complete treatment, we limit ourselves to deriving the differential equations that characterize the equilibrium strategies, and to presenting a family of examples that have linear equilibria.

Analogously to Section 3.3, we have

$$F(\beta(x)) = \Pr\{\beta(V) \leq \beta(x)\}$$
$$= \Pr\{V \leq x\} = M(x),$$

or

$$F(x) = M(\beta^{-1}(x)). \qquad (4.2)$$

Similarly,

$$G(x) = N(\gamma^{-1}(x)). \qquad (4.3)$$

Equations (3.6) and (3.9), which express the way each player's bid distribution is determined by the other's strategy, still hold. From (3.6) and (4.2), we have

$$F(x) = M\left[x + \frac{1}{2} \frac{G(x)}{G'(x)} \right]. \qquad (4.4)$$

From (3.9) and (4.3) we have

$$G(x) = N\left[x - \frac{1}{2} \frac{1 - F(x)}{F'(x)} \right]. \qquad (4.5)$$

Equations (4.4) and (4.5) express the first-order equilibrium conditions without reference to strategies, for the case of independent priors.

If we want to find explicit analytic expressions for equilibrium strategies, the right-hand sides of Eqs. (3.6) and (3.9) must be simple invertible functions. A particularly easy case is that in which

$$\frac{G(v)}{G'(v)}$$

is a linear function of v, and

$$\frac{1 - F(c)}{F'(c)}$$

is a linear function of c. This is achieved if $F(x)$ and $1 - G(x)$ are functions of the form

$$k(x - a)^r, \tag{4.6}$$

where k, a, and γ are positive constants. In the next section, we give examples which exploit this property.

4.3. Examples

To establish the formalism we first amplify somewhat on the case of uniform priors discussed in Section 3. Following that, we shall work the problem for a class of nonuniform priors yielding bid distributions of the type (4.6).

UNIFORM PRIORS.   In this case we had

$$M(x) = N(x) = x, \qquad 0 \leqslant x \leqslant 1, \tag{4.7}$$

as shown in Figs. 9e and 9f.

Equilibrium strategies in this case are given by Eqs. (3.18) and (3.19), and are illustrated in Figs. 9a and 9b. Note that the buyer never overbids, while the seller never underbids:

$$\begin{aligned} \beta(V) &\leqslant V, \\ \gamma(C) &\geqslant C. \end{aligned} \tag{4.8}$$

In light of Lemma 4.2, and because the strategies are linear, the range of trade is as shown in Fig. 9g.

From Figs. 9a and 9b we can, for the case of uniform priors, read off the bid distributions. These are

$$F(x) = \begin{cases} x, & 0 \leqslant x \leqslant \frac{1}{4}, \\ \frac{3}{2}x - \frac{1}{8}, & \frac{1}{4} \leqslant x \leqslant \frac{3}{4}, \\ 1, & \frac{3}{4} \leqslant x \leqslant 1, \end{cases} \tag{4.9}$$

$$G(x) = \begin{cases} 0, & 0 \leqslant x \leqslant \frac{1}{4}, \\ \frac{3}{2}x - \frac{3}{8}, & \frac{1}{4} \leqslant x \leqslant \frac{3}{4}, \\ x, & \frac{3}{4} \leqslant x \leqslant 1. \end{cases} \tag{4.10}$$

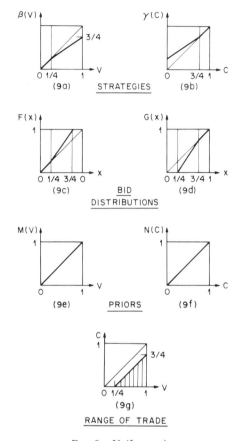

FIG. 9. Uniform priors.

These bid distributions are shown in Figs 9c and 9d. It is easy to verify that these strategies, bid distributions, and priors satisfy Eqs. (3.6), (3.9), (4.4), and (4.5). Note that the symmetry of this example extends to the bid distributions, as well as the strategies.

The total gains from trade for this equilibrium, defined as

$$K(\beta, \gamma) \equiv \pi_B(\beta, \gamma) + \pi_S(\beta, \gamma) = \int_0^1 \int_0^1 I(v, c)(V - C) \, dM(V) \, dN(C), \qquad (4.11)$$

are easily calculated to be $\frac{9}{64}$. This is to be compared to the potential (truth-telling) gains from trade, defined as

$$J \equiv \int_0^1 \int_0^1 I(V, C)(V - C) \, dM(V) \, dN(C) \qquad (4.12)$$

whose value in this case is $\frac{1}{6}$.

In comparing the efficiency of equilibria with differing priors, it is not sufficient to compare gains from trade, $K(\beta, \gamma)$. Some allowance must be made for differences in potential gains from trade, J. We could compare efficiency only of equilibria supported by priors whose potential gains from trade are equal, but this would give only a partial ordering. We adopt the following definition:

$$\text{Efficiency} \equiv \eta \equiv \frac{K(\beta, \gamma)}{J}. \tag{4.13}$$

For the present example,

$$\eta = \frac{27}{32} = 0.84375.$$

NONUNIFORM PRIORS AND A GENERAL EXAMPLE. In searching for equilibria, we can start anywhere in the diagram of Fig. 8. We choose to start with the priors and with the assumption that the strategies are linear, and to infer the bid distributions and the parameters of the linear strategies. (Of course these priors, like the uniform ones, will also have many equilibria in strategies that are not linear.)

In this example we do not confine ourselves to symmetrical cases (in the sense of Eq. (3.20)).

Taking a hint from Eq. (4.6), let us take the buyer's and seller's priors to be, respectively,

$$M(V) = 1 - (1 - V)^{r_1},$$
$$N(C) = C^{r_2}. \tag{4.14}$$

These priors are illustrated, for $r_1 < 1$, $r_2 < 1$, in Figs. 10e and 10f. The expected values of the buyer's value and the seller's cost are given, respectively, by:

$$\bar{V} \equiv \int_0^1 V \, dM(V) = \frac{1}{1 + r_1}$$

and

$$\bar{C} = \int_0^1 C \, dN(C) = \frac{r_2}{1 + r_2}. \tag{4.15}$$

The more natural cases, perhaps, are those in which $\bar{V} \geqslant \bar{C}$, that is,

$$r_1 r_2 \leqslant 1. \tag{4.16}$$

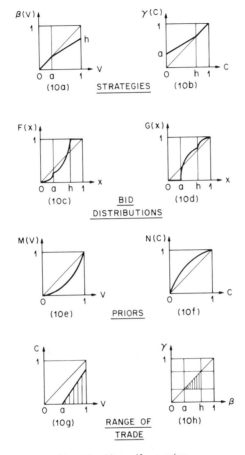

FIG. 10.   Nonuniform priors.

Let us further assume linear strategies with bids confined to the interval $[a, h]$, as in Figs. 10a and 10b; from these diagrams, one reads off the equations

$$\beta(V) = \begin{cases} V, & 0 \leqslant V \leqslant a, \\ a + \dfrac{(h-a)}{1-a}(V-a), & a \leqslant V \leqslant 1. \end{cases}$$

$$\gamma(C) = \begin{cases} a + \dfrac{h-a}{h}C, & 0 \leqslant C \leqslant h, \\ C, & h \leqslant C \leqslant 1, \end{cases}$$

(4.17)

where we have made the same arbitrary choices for the strategies outside the region of trade as in Eqs. (3.18) and (3.19).

Equations (4.2) and (4.3) now determine the bid distributions, which are shown in Figs. 10c and 10d. Their equations are

$$
F(x) = \begin{cases}
1 - (1-x)^{r_1}, & 0 \leqslant x \leqslant a, \\
1 - \left[1 - a - \dfrac{(1-a)(x-a)}{h-a} \right]^{r_1}, & a \leqslant x \leqslant h, \\
1, & h \leqslant x \leqslant 1,
\end{cases}
$$

$$
G(x) = \begin{cases}
0, & 0 \leqslant x \leqslant a, \\
\left[\dfrac{h(x-a)}{h-a} \right]^{r_2}, & a \leqslant x \leqslant h, \\
x^{r_2}, & h \leqslant x \leqslant 1.
\end{cases}
$$
(4.18)

Only the forms of these distributions on the interval $[a, h]$ are pertinent, however.

We next make use of Eqs. (4.4) and (4.5). It is straightforward to show that the priors and bid distributions given by Eqs. (4.14) and (4.18) satisfy (4.4) and (4.5) if, and only if,

$$
a = \frac{r_2}{r_1 + r_2 + 2r_1 r_2},
$$
(4.19)

$$
h = \frac{r_2(1 + 2r_1)}{r_1 + r_2 + 2r_1 r_2},
$$
(4.20)

We now calculate the potential (first-best) and actual (second-best) gains from trade, as defined in Eqs. (4.11) and (4.12). The range of trade is shown in Fig. 10g.

From (4.12), the potential gains from trade are

$$
J = \int_{V=0}^{1} \int_{C=0}^{V} (V - C)\, dM(V)\, dN(C).
$$
(4.21)

Using (4.14), we can find

$$
J = \frac{r_1}{1 + r_2} \int_{V=0}^{1} (1 - V)^{r_1 - 1} V^{r_2 + 1}\, dV.
$$
(4.22)

The integral in Eq. (4.22) has the form of the so-called complete beta-function, and is given by

$$\frac{(r_1 - 1)!(r_2 + 1)!}{(r_1 + r_2 + 1)!}$$

(where of course the factorial is understood, for noninteger r_1, r_2, in the sense $n! = \Gamma(n + 1)$). Thus

$$J = \frac{r_1! r_2!}{(1 + r_1 + r_2)!}. \tag{4.23}$$

A somewhat more elaborate calculation leads to the expression for the actual gains from trade:

$$K = r_1 r_2 h^{r_2}(1 - a)^{r_1} \frac{r_1! r_2!}{(r_1 + r_2)!} \left[-\frac{1 - a}{r_2(1 + r_1 + r_2)} - \frac{h}{r_1(1 + r_1 + r_2)} + \frac{1}{r_1 r_2} \right]. \tag{4.24}$$

Dividing (4.24) by (4.23) we get an expression for the efficiency; using also (4.19) and (4.20), this is

$$\eta = h^{r_2}(1 - a)^{r_1} \frac{r_1 + r_2 + 4 r_1 r_2}{r_1 + r_2 + 2 r_1 r_2} \tag{4.25}$$

J is symmetrical in r_1 and r_2; slightly less obviously, so are K and η.

J, K, and η have been calculated for a wide range of priors, as parameterized by r_1 and r_2; their values are shown in Tables I, II, and III.

TABLE I

Actual Gains from Trade, K

$r_2 \backslash r_1$	0	1/4	1/2	3/4	1	3/2	2	∞
0	1	0.8000	0.6667	0.5714	0.5000	0.4000	0.3333	0
1/4	0.8000	0.5745	0.4546	0.3744	0.3170	0.2404	0.1920	0
1/2	0.6667	0.4546	0.3491	0.2813	0.2313	0.1683	0.1296	0
3/4	0.5714	0.3744	0.2813	0.2192	0.1773	0.1242	0.09252	0
1	0.5000	0.3170	0.2313	0.1773	0.1406	0.09506	0.06032	0
3/2	0.4000	0.2404	0.1683	0.1242	0.09506	0.06032	0.04122	0
2	0.3333	0.1920	0.1296	0.09252	0.06872	0.04122	0.02679	0
∞	0	0	0	0	0	0	0	0

TABLE II

Potential Gains from Trade, J

$r_2 \backslash r_1$	0	1/4	1/2	3/4	1	3/2	2	∞
0	1	0.8000	0.6667	0.5714	0.5000	0.4000	0.3333	0
1/4	0.8000	0.6182	0.4994	0.4165	0.3556	0.2724	0.2188	0
1/2	0.6667	0.4994	0.3927	0.3195	0.2667	0.1963	0.1524	0
3/4	0.5714	0.4165	0.3195	0.2542	0.2078	0.1475	0.1108	0
1	0.5000	0.3556	0.2667	0.2078	0.1667	0.1143	0.08333	0
3/2	0.4000	0.2724	0.1963	0.1475	0.1143	0.07363	0.05079	0
2	0.3330	0.2188	0.1524	0.1108	0.08333	0.05079	0.03333	0
∞	0	0	0	0	0	0	0	0

In preparing these tables, we have made use of the following formula, which can be obtained from (4.25), using (4.19) and (4.20): for $r_2 = \infty$,

$$\eta = \left(\frac{2r_1}{1 + 2r_1} \right)^{r_1} \frac{1 + 4r_1}{1 + 2r_1} \exp \left(\frac{r_1}{1 + 2r_1} \right),$$

and similarly (symmetrically) for $r_1 = \infty$. When both r_1 and $r_2 = \infty$, it can be shown that $\eta = 2/e$, and this is the smallest value that η can assume, for this family of priors (see Appendix).

From the tables, we observe that using linear strategies in the sealed-bid mechanism seems to be quite robust, in the sense that the efficiency, as defined by (4.13), varies very little over a wide range of priors and a correspondingly wide range of potential and actual gains from trade. In fact, for the family of priors considered here, the full range of η is from 1.0 to $2/e$ (i.e., 0.7358), and for the natural situation $\bar{V} \geqslant \bar{C}$ (i.e., according to Eq. (4.16), $r_1 r_2 \leqslant 1$) the range of η is from 1.0 to $\frac{27}{32}$ (i.e., 0.84735). Unfortunately, we do not know how representative the behavior of this class of priors (of monotone density) is, among all possible priors.

TABLE III

Efficiency, η

$r_2 \backslash r_1$	0	1/4	1/2	3/4	1	3/2	2	∞
0	1	1	1	1	1	1	1	1
1/4	1	0.9292	0.9103	0.8990	0.8917	0.8827	0.8775	0.8573
1/2	1	0.9103	0.8889	0.8805	0.8675	0.8572	0.8507	0.8260
3/4	1	0.8990	0.8805	0.8625	0.8532	0.8419	0.8350	0.8080
1	1	0.8917	0.8675	0.8532	0.8437	0.8318	0.8247	0.7961
3/2	1	0.8827	0.8572	0.8419	0.8318	0.8192	0.8116	0.7812
2	1	0.8775	0.8507	0.8350	0.8247	0.8116	0.8038	0.7722
∞	1	0.8573	0.8260	0.8080	0.7961	0.7812	0.7722	0.7358

It must be recalled, however, that although it seems natural to assume that the equilibria we have been discussing are the most efficient ones for their respective priors, and correspond to the linear equilibrium for the uniform prior, this has not been shown.[8]

4.4. *Step-Function Equilibria*

Allowing general independent priors does not change the characterization of n-step equilibria given in Section 3.4 in any essential way. The Support Lemma implies that the supports of the two (nonmarginal) bid distributions have to be the same and it is then straightforward to show that with priors M (buyer) and N (seller) formulas (3.27) and (3.28) take the form

$$z_1 = a_1,$$

$$z_i = a_i + \frac{N(x_{i-1})}{N(x_i) - N(x_{i-1})} \frac{(a_i - a_{i-1})}{2}, \qquad i = 2,..., n,$$

$$x_i = a_i - \frac{1 - M(z_{i+1})}{M(z_{i+1}) - M(z_i)} \frac{(a_{i+1} - a_i)}{2}, \qquad i = 1, ..., n-1,$$

$$x_n = a_n.$$

(4.26)

The existence problem is now, of course, more complex. However, we observe from (4.16) that the one-parameter family of 1-step functions defined by (3.24) represents equilibria of the sealed-bid game with respect to *any* pair of priors (M, N). It is also not difficult to see that for any natural number n and any given support of the distribution of bids, $a = (a_1, ..., a_n)$ such that $0 < a_1 < \cdots < a_n < 1$ there exist priors (M, N) on $[0, 1]$ such that (4.26) is satisfied. One simply has to choose *numbers* n_i, $i = 1, ..., n$, and m_i, $i = 1, ..., n$, such that $0 < n_i < n_{i+1} < 1$, $0 < m_i < m_{i+1} < 1$, that produce z_is and x_i's satisfying (3.33). (One has $2(n-1)$ equations in $4n - 2$ unknowns.) Any pair of vectors $(z, n) = (z_1, ..., z_n; n_1, ..., n_n)$ can then be related to each other via a prior N such that $n_i = N(z_i)$, $i = 1, ..., n$. Since the priors are assumed to be independent one can treat the two systems of equations separately. This shows

PROPOSITION 4.1. *For any natural number n and any* $a = (a_1, ..., a_n)$ *such that* $0 < a_1 < \cdots < a_n < 1$ *there exist priors* (M, N) *on* $[0, 1]$ *such that a is*

---

[8] In fact, since this paper was written, it has been shown (Gresik [5]) that for this class of nonuniform priors the most efficient equilibrium is not in general achieved by the split-the-difference rule, $p = (v + c)/2$. Furthermore, it is known (Satterthwaite and Williams [11]) that the sealed-bid mechanism has second-best (*ex-ante* efficient) equilibria for only a "small" set of priors; however, this does not rule out the possibility that—relative to the second-best—linear equilibria (when they exist) of the sealed-bid mechanism show, for "most" priors, only a small percentage loss in efficiency.

the support of the bid distributions of an n-step equilibrium on the sealed bid game.

This is to say that any discrete support for the distribution of bids of the sealed bid game is *rationalizable* in the sense that it may result from equilibrium play of the game.

Appendix

1. Gains from Trade—Uniform Prior

We now derive Eq. (3.23) for actual gains from trade in a differentiable equilibrium, for the case of a uniform prior. We start by rewriting Eq. (3.1) for this case

$$K(\beta, \gamma) \equiv \pi_B + \pi_S = \iint_{\gamma(C) \leqslant \beta(V)} (V - C) \, dV \, dC. \tag{A1.1}$$

We shall change the variables of integration from (V, C) to (β, γ). The range of integration in $\beta\gamma$-space is the shaded are in Fig. 9h. Thus

$$K(\beta, \gamma) = \left\{ \int_{\beta=a}^{h} \int_{\gamma=a}^{\beta} \text{ or } \int_{\gamma=a}^{h} \int_{\beta=\gamma}^{h} \right\} [b(\beta) - g(\gamma)] \, b'(\beta) \, g'(\gamma) \, d\beta \, d\gamma$$

$$= \int_{\beta=a}^{h} b(\beta) \, b'(\beta) \, d\beta \int_{\gamma=a}^{\beta} g'(\gamma) \, d\gamma - \int_{\gamma=a}^{h} g(\gamma) \, g'(\gamma) \, d\gamma \int_{\beta=\gamma}^{\beta} b'(\beta) \, d\beta$$

$$= \int_{\beta=a}^{h} \{ b(\beta) \, b'(\beta) \, g(\beta) - g(\beta) \, g'(\beta)[1 - b(\beta)] \} \, d\beta. \tag{A1.2}$$

Using Eqs. (3.13), (A1.2) becomes

$$K(\beta, \gamma) = \int_{\beta=a}^{h} \left\{ b(\beta)[\beta b'(\beta) - \frac{1}{2}(1 - b(\beta))] \right.$$

$$\left. - (1 - \beta) \, g(\beta) \, g'(\beta) + \frac{1}{2}[h(\beta)]^2 \right\} d\beta. \tag{A1.3}$$

Now note that

$$\int_a^h \beta b(\beta) \, b'(\beta) \, d\beta = \frac{1}{2} \int_a^h bd[b(\beta)]^2$$

$$= \frac{1}{2} \beta[b(\beta)]^2 \Big|_a^h - \frac{1}{2} \int_a^h [b(\beta)]^2 \, d\beta$$

$$= \frac{1}{2} h - \frac{1}{2} a^3 - \frac{1}{2} \int_a^h [b(\beta)]^2 \, d\beta, \tag{A1.4}$$

where we have recalled that $b(a) = a$, $b(h) = 1$. Similarly

$$\int_a^h (1 - \beta) g(\beta) g'(\beta) \, d\beta = \frac{1}{2} (1 - h) h^2 + \frac{1}{2} \int_a^h [g(\beta)]^2 \, d\beta, \quad (A1.5)$$

using $g(a) = 0$, $g(h) = h$. Substituting (A1.4) and (A1.5) in (A1.3),

$$K(\beta, \gamma) = \frac{1}{2} (h - h^2 + h^3 - a^3) - \frac{1}{2} \int_a^h f(\beta) \, d\beta. \quad (A1.6)$$

In the symmetric case, where $a + h = 1$ and $f(\beta) = 1 - g(1 - \beta)$, (A1.6) reduces to (3.23).

2. Step-Function Equilibria

Proof of Proposition 3.1. Since the set of (potential) nonmarginal bids of the buyer has to be contained in the set of nonmarginal bids of the seller and vice versa if they behave rationally, it follows that these two sets must coincide in equilibrium, that is, $c_i = v_i$ for $i = 1, ..., n$.

Since $a_1 > 0$ a bid $\beta(V) = 0$ is optimal for the buyer if $V < a_1$ and no trade takes place. If $V \geq a_1$ the bid $\beta(V) = 0$ is *not* optimal since there is a positive probability (a_1 is offered by some types of sellers) of trade and positive profits if $\beta(V) = a_1$. The buyer with valuation $V = a_1$ is indifferent between the bids $v = 0$ and $v = a_1$: both result in zero (expected) profits for him. For buyers with valuation $V \in (a_1, a_2)$ the bid $\beta(V) = a_1$ must also be optimal; this proves that $z_1 = a_1$.

In general the "marginal" type of buyer who is indifferent between bids a_i and a_{i+1}, $i = 2, ..., n - 1$, is determined as follows:

For a buyer to be indifferent between bids a_i and a_{i+1} we must have $V > a_{i+1}$. Suppose such a buyer switches from bid $v = a_i$ to bid $v = a_{i+1}$. Then his expected gains and losses are as follows:

exp. gains:
$$(x_{i+1} - x_i) \left(V - \frac{a_{i+1} + a_{i+1}}{2} \right) = (x_{i+1} - x_i)(V - a_{i+1}), \quad (A2.1)$$

exp. losses:
$$\sum_{j=1}^i \left[(x_j - x_{j-1}) \left(V - \frac{a_i + a_j}{2} \right) - (x_j - x_{j-1}) \left(V - \frac{a_{i+1} + a_j}{2} \right) \right]$$

$$= \sum_{j=1}^i (x_j - x_{j-1}) \frac{(a_{i+1} - a_i)}{2}$$

$$= x_i \frac{(a_{i+1} - a_i)}{2} \quad \text{(with } x_0 = 0\text{).} \quad (A2.2)$$

The gains stem from "winning" the new market segment $(x_i, x_{i+1}]$ for potential trade; the losses stem from paying a higher price in all market segments that were already available for potential trade under the bid $c = a_i$, i.e., the segments $[0, x_1]$, $(x_1, x_2]$,..., $(x_{i-1}, x_i]$. Note that these losses only depend on the seller's offer strategy and *not* on the buyer's true valuation V that determines the (expected) gains. This allows us to solve explicitly for the "marginal" buyer's valuation at which the gains just equal the losses:

$$(x_{i+1} - x_i)(V - a_{i+1}) = x_i \frac{(a_{i+1} - a_i)}{2}$$

$$\Rightarrow z_{i+1} = V_{i+1} = \frac{x_i}{(x_{i+1} - x_i)} \frac{(a_{i+1} - a_i)}{2} + a_{i+1}. \quad (A2.3)$$

This is (3.27). A similar calculation yields (3.28) for the seller's optimal response.

The bids a_i, $i = 1, ..., n$, that prevail over the intervals $[z_i, z_{i+1})$ resp. $(x_{i-1}, x_i]$ (with $z_{n+1} = 1$ and $x_0 = 0$), are not just local profit maxima but global ones. This is seen as follows: Let $V(i+1)$ denote a buyer who prefers bid a_{i+1} over bids a_i and a_{i+2} and let $\Pi_{a_j}^{V(i+1)}$ denote the profit of buyer $V(i+1)$ if he bids a_j, $i = 1, ..., n-1$ and $j = 1, ..., i$. Then the following relationship holds: For all $i = 1, ..., n-1$

$$\Pi_{a_j}^{V(i+1)} = \Pi_{a_j}^{V(j)} + x_j(V_{i+1} - V_j), \qquad j = 1, ..., i. \quad (A2.4)$$

Hence

$$\Pi_{a_{i+1}}^{V(i+1)} > \Pi_{a_i}^{V(i+1)} = \Pi_{a_i}^{V(i)} + x_i(V_{i+1} - V_i)$$
$$> \Pi_{a_{i-1}}^{V(i)} + x_i(V_{i+1} - V_i)$$
$$= \Pi_{a_{i-1}}^{V(i-1)} + x_{i-1}(V_i - V_{i-1}) + x_i(V_{i+1} - V_i)$$
$$= \Pi_{a_{i-1}}^{V(i-1)} + x_{i-1}(V_{i+1} - V_{i-1}) + (x_i - x_{i-1})(V_{i+1} - V_i)$$
$$= \Pi_{a_{i-1}}^{V(i+1)} + (x_i - x_{i-1})(V_{i+1} - V_i)$$
$$> \Pi_{a_{i-1}}^{V(i+1)}.$$

Repetition of this argument proves that $\Pi_{a_{i+1}}^{V(i+1)} > \Pi_{a_j}^{V(i+1)}$ for all $j = 1, ..., i$ and all $i = 2, ..., n-1$. This completes the proof of the proposition. ∎

Proof of Proposition 3.3. Let $x_n = n/(n+1)$ in (3.39). We will argue that, for any n, there is a choice of x_1 that generates a sequence of x_{n-i}'s (backwards from x_n) that will eventually contain elements *smaller* than the originally chosen x_1; and there is a choice of x_1 such that the backwardly generated sequence $\{x_{n-i}\}$ will only contain elements *greater* than the chosen x_1. Hence there must exist (by continuity) an x_1 such that x_1 is exactly reproduced by the backwards recursion (which then coincides with the forward recursion). This recursion generates a solution to (3.39).

(i)   Choose $\bar{x}_1 < a_1$ arbitrarily close to $a_1 = 1/(n+1)$. Then x_{n-1} will become arbitrarily small and so will all subsequently generated x_{n-i}'s Clearly, all inequalities $x_i < a_i$ are satisfied.

(ii)   Now choose $\bar{x}_1$ arbitrarily close to zero. Then (from Eq. $(n-1)$ of (3.39))

$$\frac{B}{a_1 - x_1} \approx \frac{1}{2} \quad \text{and so} \quad x_{n-1} \approx \frac{2}{3} x_n = \frac{2}{3} \frac{n}{n+1}.$$

This produces in turn a multiplier

$$\left(1 + \frac{B}{(a_{n-1} - x_{n-1})}\right)$$

in (3.39, 1) that is close to 1 and hence x_2 will be arbitrarily close to zero. As a consequence $x_{n-2} \approx \frac{4}{5} x_{n-1}$ (from (3.39), $n-1$)); etc. An estimate for x_{n-i} is then given by

$$x_{n-i} \approx \left(\prod_{j=1}^{i} \frac{2j}{2j+1}\right) \cdot \frac{n}{n+1}. \tag{A2.5}$$

But

$$\prod_{j=1}^{n-1} \frac{2j}{2j+1} > \frac{1}{n} \quad \text{for all} \quad n \geq 2$$

and thus

$$x_1 = x_{n-(n-1)} \approx \left(\prod_{j=1}^{n-1} \frac{2j}{2j+1}\right) \cdot \frac{n}{n+1} > \frac{1}{n+1} = a_1.$$

Since the first violation of the set of inequalities $x_{n-i} < a_{n-i}$, $i = 1, ..., n-1$, through the x_{n-i}'s generated in this backwards fashion for $\bar{x}_1 \to 0$ will occur for $x_{n-(n-1)} = x_1$, it is also clear that the solution that must exist for an intermediate value of $\bar{x}_1$ satisfies all of these inequalities. Hence it is an equilibrium.

Convergence.   Let $(\gamma_n, \beta_n)_{n=1}^{\infty}$ be a sequence of n-step equilibria. As $x_1 < a_1 = 1/(n+1)$, $n \to \infty$ not only implies that $x_1 \to 0$ but also $(a_1 - x_1) \to 0$ and hence (from (3.39), $(n-1)$ $x_{n-1} \to 0$. But this means that the bid $(n-1)/n$ (that prevails for $C \in (x_{n-1}, x_n]$) is submitted for all $C \in T[\varepsilon_n, (n-1)/n]$. As $n \to \infty$, $[\varepsilon_n, (n-1)/n] \to [0,1]$ and $(n-1)/n \to 1$. ∎

Proof of Proposition 3.4.   We show that for any n there exists a support of the distribution of potential bids satisfying (3.38) such that (3.39) has a solution with $x_{i+1} - x_i = \text{const}$ for $i = 1, ..., n-1$. From (3.39) it follows that for $i = 1, ..., n-1$

$$x_{i+1} - x_i = x_i - x_{i-1} \Leftrightarrow \frac{x_i}{a_{n-i} - x_{n-i}} = \frac{x_{i-1}}{a_{n-(i-1)} - x_{n-(i-1)}} \quad \text{(A2.6)}$$

and hence

$$\frac{x_i}{x_{i-1}} = \frac{a_{n-i} - x_{n-i}}{a_{n-(i-1)} - x_{n-(i-1)}}. \quad \text{(A2.7)}$$

But from (3.39, $i-1$), Eq. $(i-1)$, we also have that

$$\frac{x_i}{x_{i-1}} = 1 + \frac{B}{(a_{n-(i-1)} - x_{n-(i-1)})} = \frac{a_{n-(i-1)} - x_{n-(i-1)} + B}{a_{n-(i-1)} - x_{n-(i-1)}} \quad \text{(A2.8)}$$

(A2.7) and (A2.8) imply

$$a_{n-i} - x_{n-i} = a_{n-(i-1)} - x_{n-(i-1)} + B \quad \text{(A2.9)}$$

or

$$x_{n-(i-1)} - x_{n-i} = a_{n-(i-1)} - a_{n-i} + B = \tfrac{3}{2}(a_{n-(i-1)} - a_{n-i}) \quad \text{(A2.10)}$$

as

$$B = \frac{a_i - a_{i-1}}{2} = \frac{a_{n-(i-1)} - a_{n-i}}{2} = \frac{1 - 2b_n}{2(n-1)}$$

from (3.38). Now choose b_n in such a way that $x_i = i \cdot 3B = i \cdot \tfrac{3}{2} \cdot$ (step-size), $i = 1, ..., n$, is a solution to (3.39).

$$x_n = 1 - b_n \Leftrightarrow n \cdot \frac{3}{2} \cdot \frac{(1 - 2b_n)}{(n-1)} = 1 - b_n$$

i.e.

$$b_n = \frac{\tfrac{1}{2}n + 1}{2n + 1} = \frac{1}{4} + \frac{\tfrac{3}{4}}{2n + 1}. \quad \text{(A2.11)}$$

It is now trivial to check that for

$$a_i = b_n + \frac{(i-1)}{(n-1)}(1 - 2b_n) \quad x_i = i \cdot \frac{3}{2} \frac{(1 - 2b_n)}{(n-1)}, \qquad i = 1, ..., n.$$

is a solution to (3.39) that satisfies all the inequalities required by (3.29). This solution defines, for any n, symmetric strategies γ_n (through (3.25)) and β_n (through (3.33)).

Equation (A2.10) implies that

$$\lim_{n \to \infty} \frac{\gamma_n(x_{i+1}) - \gamma_n(x_i)}{x_{i+1} - x_i} = \lim_{x_{i+1} - x_i} \frac{a_{i+1} - a_i}{x_{i+1} - x_i} = \frac{2}{3} \qquad \text{for all} \quad (x_{i+1}, x_i);$$

and

$$\lim_{n \to \infty} \gamma_n(0) = \lim_{n \to \infty} \gamma_n(x_1) = \lim_{n \to \infty} b_n = \frac{1}{4}$$

(from A2.11). This proves that $\lim_{n \to \infty} \gamma_n(C) = \frac{2}{3}C + \frac{1}{4}$ for al $C \in [0, \frac{3}{4}]$. As we pointed out in Section 3.2 this fully determines the outcome of the game as one can change $\gamma(C)$ for $\frac{3}{4} < C \leqslant 1$ arbitrarily without affecting the play of the game. Applying (3.33) yields

$$\lim_{n \to \infty} \beta_n(V) = \lim_{n \to \infty} (1 - \gamma_n(1 - V)) = \frac{2}{3} V + \frac{1}{12} \qquad \text{for all} \quad v \in \left[\frac{1}{4}, 1\right].$$

This competes the proof. ∎

One can also show that a sequence of n-step equilibria that converges to the linear equilibrium can be generated by keeping $b = \frac{1}{4}$ fixed and increasing n. Convergence then, however, is not "uniform" as with the construction used in the proof of Proposition 3.4. Figures 5a and 5b show equilibria for $n = 10$ and $n = 50$, respectively, in that case.

n-step equilibria with $b \notin \{0, \frac{1}{4}\}$. The argument given in the proof of Proposition 3.3 can in fact be extended to prove existence of n-step equilibria for arbitrarily large n's in a whole neighborhood of $b = \frac{1}{4}$. Choose any $b \in (0, \frac{1}{2})$ and determine the set of potential bids according to (3.37). Then part (i) of the proof of Proposition 3.3 carries over literally. The estimate for x_{n-i} generated by the backwards induction in part (ii) if $\bar{x}_1$ is chosen arbitrarily close to 0 can now be shown to be

$$x_{n-i} \approx \prod_{j=1}^{i} \left[\frac{a_i}{a_i + B}\right] \cdot (1 - b) = \prod_{j=1}^{i} \left[\frac{b + (i-1 \Delta}{b + (i-1)\Delta + \frac{1}{2}\Delta}\right] \cdot (1 - b)$$

$$= \prod_{j=1}^{i} \left[\frac{b + (i-1)\Delta}{b + (i - \frac{1}{2})\Delta}\right] \cdot (1 - b)$$

$$\text{with} \quad \Delta = \frac{1 - 2b}{n - 1} = \text{step-size, and} \quad B = \frac{\Delta}{2}. \tag{A2.12}$$

Hence

$$x_1 = x_{n-(n-1)} \approx \prod_{j=1}^{n-1} \left[\frac{b + (i-1)\Delta}{b + (i - \frac{1}{2})\Delta}\right] > \left[\frac{b}{b + \frac{1}{2}\Delta}\right]^{n-1}$$

$$= \left[\frac{b}{b + (1 - 2b)/2(n - 1)}\right]^{n-1}. \tag{A2.13}$$

As $n \to \infty$,

$$\left[\frac{b}{b + (1 - 2b)/2(n - 1)} \right]^{n-1} \to \exp\left(-\frac{1 - 2b}{2b} \right) > 0,$$

and

$$\exp\left(-\frac{1 - 2b}{2b} \right) \cdot (1 - b) > b = a_1$$

in a neighborhood of $b = \frac{1}{4}$ by continuity, since

$$\exp\left(-\frac{1 - 2 \cdot \frac{1}{4}}{2 \cdot \frac{1}{4}} \right) = e^{-1} > \frac{\frac{1}{4}}{1 - \frac{1}{4}} = \frac{1}{3}.$$

If we now pick a sequence of n-step equilibria $(n = 1, 2, ...)$ for b chosen from this neighborhood, convergence is neither to the linear nor to the trivial equilibrium, but to the nonlinear symmetric solutions of the differential equations as graphed in Fig. 3. Figures 6a and 6b show solutions for $b = 0.15$ that correspond to a continuous curve of the type depicted in Fig. 3.

3. *Nonuniform Priors—Efficiency When* $(r_1, r_2) \to (\infty, \infty)$

When $r_1 = r_2 \equiv r$, then from Eqs. (4.19) and (4.20),

$$a = \frac{1}{2(1 + r)}, \tag{A3.1}$$

$$h = \frac{1 + 2r}{2(1 + r)}, \tag{A3.2}$$

so that $a + h = 1$. Substituting (A3.1) and (A3.2) in (4.25),

$$\eta = 2 \left[\frac{1 + 2r}{2(1 + r)} \right]^{2r+1} \tag{A3.3}$$

$$= 2 \cdot \frac{2(1 + r)}{1 + 2r} \left[1 - \frac{1}{2(1 + r)} \right]^{2(1 + r)} \tag{A3.4}$$

It follows directly from (A3.4) that

$$\lim_{r \to \infty} \eta = 2/e. \tag{A3.5}$$

It is easy to show that η is monotone decreasing in r on $[0, \infty]$: From (A3.3)

$$\frac{d\eta}{dr} = \eta \left\{ \frac{1}{1+r} + 2 \ln \left[\frac{1+2r}{2(1+r)} \right] \right\}. \tag{A3.6}$$

It suffices to show that the coefficient of η in (A3.6) is negative. Using the series

$$\ln(1-x) = -\left(x + \frac{x^2}{2} + \frac{x^3}{3} + \cdots \right),$$

we have

$$\frac{1}{1+r} + 2 \ln \left[\frac{1+2r}{2(1+r)} \right] = \frac{1}{1+r} + 2 \ln \left[1 - \frac{1}{2(1+r)} \right]$$

$$= \frac{1}{1+r} - 2 \left[\frac{1}{2(1+r)} + \frac{1}{2 \cdot 2^2 (1+r)^2} + \frac{1}{3 \cdot 2^3 (1+r)^3} + \cdots \right] < 0,$$

as desired.

REFERENCES

1. K. CHATTERJEE, doctoral thesis, Harvard University, 1979.
2. K. CHATTERJEE AND W. SAMUELSON, Bargaining under incomplete information, *Oper. Res.* **31** (1983), 835–851.
3. J. C. COX, V. L. SMITH, AND J. M. WALKER, Auction market theory of heterogeneous bidders, *Econ. Lett.* **9** (1982), 319–325.
4. J. C. COX, V. L. SMITH, AND J. M. WALKER, "Theory and Individual Behavior of First Price Auctions," unpublished manuscript, University of Arizona, May 1986.
5. T. A. GRESIK, "The Efficiency of Linear Equilibria of Sealed-Bid Double Auctions," Graduate School of Business Administration, Washington University, 1987.
6. J. HARSANYI, Games with incomplete information played by Bayesian players, Parts I, II, and III, *Management Sci.* **14** (1967–68), 159–182, 320–334, 486–502.
7. B. HOLMSTRÖM AND R. B. MYERSON, Efficient and durable decision rules with incomplete information, *Econometrica* **51** (1983), 1799–1819.
8. R. B. MYERSON AND M. A. SATTERTHWAITE, Efficient mechanism for bilateral trading, *J. Econ. Theory* **29** (1983), 265–281.
9. R. RADNER AND A. SCHOTTER, The sealed-bid mechanism: An experimental study, *J. Econ. Theory* **48** (1989), 179–220.
10. A. RUBINSTEIN, A bargaining model with incomplete information, *Econometrica* **53** (1985), 1151–1172.
11. M. A. SATTERTHWAITE AND S. R. WILLIAMS, Bilateral trade with the sealed bid k-double auction, *J. Econ. Theory* **48** (1989), 107–133.
12. R. SELTEN, Re-examination of the perfectness concept for equilibrium points in extensive games, *Int. J. Game Theory* **4** (1975), 25–55.

JOURNAL OF ECONOMIC THEORY **48**, 107–133 (1989)

Bilateral Trade with the Sealed Bid k-Double Auction: Existence and Efficiency*

MARK A. SATTERTHWAITE

*Kellogg Graduate School of Management,
Northwestern University, Evanston, Illinois 60608*

AND

STEVEN R. WILLIAMS

*Department of Economics, Northwestern University,
Evanston, Illinois 60608*

Received March 11, 1987; revised April 7, 1988

For k in the unit interval, the k-double auction determines the terms of trade when a buyer and a seller negotiate transfer of an item. The buyer submits a bid b and the seller submits an offer s. Trade occurs if b exceeds s, at price $kb + (1 - k)s$. We model trade as a Bayesian game in which each trader privately knows his reservation value, but only has beliefs about the other trader's value. Existence of a multiplicity of equilibria is proven for a class of traders' beliefs. For generic beliefs, however, these equilibria are shown to be ex ante inefficient. *Journal of Economic Literature* Classification Numbers: 026, 024. © 1989 Academic Press, Inc.

1. INTRODUCTION

This paper concerns *sealed bid k-double auctions*, a one-parameter family of rules for determining the terms of trade when a single buyer and a single seller voluntarily negotiate the transfer of an indivisible item. The buyer submits a sealed bid b, while the seller submits a sealed offer s. Trade occurs if and only if $b \geqslant s$, and the buyer pays the seller $kb + (1 - k)s$ when trade occurs. The choice of k in $[0, 1]$ determines a particular member of the family that we study. For example, if $k = 0.5$, we refer to the mechanism as the 0.5-double auction. A value of k in $(0, 1)$ means that both the buyer

* We thank Michael Chwe, Tom Gresik, Roger Myerson, and three anonymous reviewers for their help. This material is based upon work supported by the National Science Foundation Nos. SES–8520247 and SES–8705649. We also acknowledge the support of Northwestern University's Research Grants Committee and its Center for Advanced Study in Managerial Economics and Decision Sciences.

128

and the seller influence the price at which trade occurs. If $k = 0$, then the seller sets price unilaterally; we call this the *seller's offer* double auction. At the other extreme, if $k = 1$, then the buyer sets price unilaterally; we call this the *buyer's bid* double auction.

The value a trader places on the item is his *reservation value*. Focus on either trader. We assume that (i) he alone knows his reservation value, (ii) his utility is the sum of his reservation value (if he possesses the item) plus any transfer payment (positive or negative) that is part of the terms of trade, and (iii) his beliefs concerning the other trader's reservation value are described by a prior probability distribution that is independent of his own reservation value. The strategic problem the traders face is modeled as a Bayesian game, as formulated by Harsanyi [5]. Our main goals are to examine the existence and qualitative nature of the traders' differentiable equilibrium strategies, and to investigate the efficiency of these equilibria.

We study bilateral k-double auctions for two main reasons. First, some markets are inherently small. Consider, for example, the problem of determining the terms of trade for the transfer of an item between two divisions of the same firm. One wants to understand how the choice of the rules for bargaining in such situations affects both (i) the proportion of the potential gains from trade actually realized through bargaining, and (ii) the division of the realized gains between the traders. The k-double auctions are extremely simple procedures that can actually be used to determine the terms of trade. They can be analyzed because they are simple, and yet we can gain insight into how the choice of the rules for bargaining affects the outcome because we can analyze an entire family of procedures. While bargaining in small markets typically follows more complicated procedures than k-double auctions, a thorough analysis of such simple procedures is a step toward the development of a deeper theory of small markets.

Second, k-double auctions may be an appropriate foundation for a noncooperative theory of large markets. Wilson [18], for example, proposes this view. Though this paper considers only the one seller, one buyer, one item case, we believe that the results and methods that we develop are applicable to k-double auctions with multiple sellers and buyers. An alternative approach, exemplified by Gale [4], is to model the microstructure of large markets as a sequence of interactions between individual buyers and sellers. These interactions may be modeled as bilateral k-double auctions, provided that the equilibria of these procedures are understood in detail.

Our results fall into three categories: existence, ex ante efficiency, and interim efficiency. In each category the results fall into two groups: results for k-double auctions when $k \in (0, 1)$, and results for the seller's offer/ buyer's bid double auctions. Throughout the paper we assume that the traders' reservation values are independently drawn from distributions that satisfy a well-known monotonicity property. This property has been frequently used in the auction literature to guarantee the existence of differentiable equilibria.

Consider our existence results first. An equilibrium pair of strategies is *regular* if (roughly) each strategy is differentiable and monotone increasing at each reservation value where the conditional expected probability of trade is positive. For all k-double auctions, regular equilibria exist, though their number depends critically on the value of k. For each $k \in (0, 1)$ and each pair of prior distributions of traders' reservation values, Theorem 3.2 characterizes all of the regular equilibria as a two-parameter family. In addition to establishing the existence of this continuum of equilibria, we develop a geometric representation of their qualitative nature. If, on the other hand, $k \in \{0, 1\}$ (the seller's offer or buyer's bid double auction), then the unique dominant strategy of the trader who cannot affect price is to trutfully report his reservation value. The other trader's best response to truthful revelation defines a regular equilibrium.

With the existence of equilibria established, we turn to questions of efficiency. Throughout this paper, the Holmstrom and Myerson [7] taxonomy of efficiency for games with incomplete information is used. Myerson and Satterthwaite [13, Corollary 1] showed that the private information and individual incentives of the two traders implies that neither the k-double auction nor any other trading mechanism can be ex post classical efficient: no rules for bilateral trade permit equilibrium behavior in which trade occurs whenever the buyer's reservation value exceeds the seller's reservation value.[1] Intuitively, ex post classical efficiency is not realized in the k-double auctions because if a trader's bid/offer affects price as well as the likelihood of trade, then he has an incentive to misrepresent his true reservation value. The buyer bids less than his reservation value in order to drive the price down and the seller makes an offer greater than his reservation value in order to force the price up. The unfotunate result of this strategizing is that some trades that should take place do not, for a bid may be less than an offer even though the buyer's reservation value is greater than the seller's reservation value.

Since ex post classical efficiency is impossible, we turn to ex ante efficiency and interim efficiency.[2] These standards take into account the limits on performance that are caused by private information and

---

[1] Myerson and Satterthwaite assume that participation in trade is voluntary, i.e., individually rational. If this assumption is dropped, then ex post efficient mechanisms do exist for bilateral trade. See d'Aspremont and Gerard-Varet [3].

[2] In the precise language of Holmstrom and Myerson [7], we analyze the ex ante incentive efficiency and the interim incentive efficiency of k-double auctions. Interim efficiency in our own paper is the same as "incentive efficiency" in Wilson [18].

individual incentives. Each applies the Pareto standard to the traders' expected gains from trade. Their difference lies in the timing of the welfare analysis: ex ante efficiency evaluates performance according to each trader's expected gain from trade before he learns his reservation value, while interim efficiency is based upon the expected gain to the trader conditioned upon his realized reservation value. Which standard is appropriate depends on the particular problem at hand. Interim efficiency, for example, is appropriate if the traders themselves choose rules for bargaining after each has learned his own reservation value. Ex ante efficiency is appropriate if the traders will trade many times, each time with an independently drawn reservation value. Note that interim efficiency is the weaker standard: an outcome of bargaining is interim efficient if it is ex ante efficient. Finally, for a given k and a given pair of prior distributions, we say that a k-double auction achieves *ex ante efficient performance* if at least one of its equilibria is ex ante efficient. *Interim efficient performance* is defined similarly.

Our main result with respect to ex ante efficiency is Theorem 5.1. It states (subject to some technical restrictions) that if $k \in (0, 1)$, then for a generic pair of prior distributions ex ante efficient performance cannot be achieved with the k-double auction. This result contrasts sharply with an example in Myerson and Satterthwaite [13] that concerns uniformly distributed reservation values. They showed that the linear equilibrium in the 0.5-double auction that Chatterjee and Samuelson [2] identified is ex ante efficient. Our theorem implies that the efficiency of this equilibrium is exceptional and does not generalize to a generic perturbation of the prior distributions away from the uniform.

The generic inefficiency of the k-double auction when $k \in (0, 1)$ is reversed for the seller's offer/buyer's bid auctions where $k \in \{0, 1\}$. Theorem 5.2, which is from Myerson [10] and Williams [17], states that the buyer's bid/seller's offer auction achieves ex ante efficient performance for all pairs of distributions in the specified class. Neither auction, however, has much to offer with respect to equity. The seller's offer auction maximizes the seller's expected gain from trade and places zero welfare weight on the buyer's expected gain from trade. The buyer's bid auction reverses the weights to the buyer's favor.

The final standard of performance we consider is interim efficiency. The seller's offer/buyer's bid auctions are interim efficient because they are ex ante efficient; consequently, our results concern the $k \in (0, 1)$ case where both traders jointly determine the price. Theorem 6.1 is a necessary condition for interim efficiency. Together with the existence result of Theorem 3.2, it implies that for every $k \in (0, 1)$ and every pair of prior distributions there exists an open family of equilibria that are interim inefficient. It shows that any statement about the interim efficiency of a k-double auction must be conditioned upon the choice of the equilibrium.

Furthermore, any theory that asserts that k-double auctions are interim efficient must explain how the traders select the strategies that implement interim efficient performance.

Theorem 6.2 adapts Wilson's [18] sufficient conditions for interim efficiency to our setting. Theorem 6.3 uses these conditions to establish that, for each $k \in (0, 1)$, there exists an open set of pairs of prior distributions over which the k-double auction achieves interim efficient performance. In this limited sense we are able to show that interim efficient performance in a k-double auction is robust over some class of distributions. We have not, however, been able to determine the size of this class.

This paper builds on the insights of other papers. Three of the most important are cited above. Chatterjee and Samuelson [2] first examined Bayesian equilibria within the k-double auction. Myerson and Satterthwaite [13] applied to double auctions with two-sided uncertainty the techniques Myerson [10] developed for analyzing the performance of auctions with one-sided uncertainty. Wilson [18] established that as the number of traders grows large the k-double auction achieves interim efficient performance if well-behaved equilibria exist. In addition, see Wilson [19] for a nice discussion of the equilibria of k-double auctions. Finally, Leininger et al. [9] use different techniques to explore the equilibria in the bilateral k-double auction. Remarkably they show the existence of a large class of equilibria that involve step-function strategies. This contrasts with our paper, which focuses on differentiable equilibrium strategies.

2. Notation and Preliminaries

Basic Structure

The seller is trader one and the buyer is trader two. Trader i's reservation value (or type) $v_i \in [0, 1]$ is drawn from the distribution F_i. Its density f_i is positive over $(0, 1)$. Both traders are risk neutral, expected utility maximizers. Traders' utility functions are normalized so that if no trade takes place their utility is zero. When trade occurs at price p, the seller's utility is $p - v_1$ and the buyer's utility is $v_2 - p$. The rules of the k-double auction, the value of the parameter k, the distributions F_1 and F_2, and the traders' utility functions are common knowledge. Only the reservation values are private.

Restrictions on Distributions

Define

$$R(v_1) = F_1(v_1)/f_1(v_1), \tag{2.01}$$

$$T(v_2) = [F_2(v_2) - 1]/f_2(v_2), \tag{2.02}$$

$$c_1(v_1) = v_1 + R(v_1), \tag{2.03}$$

$$c_2(v_2) = v_2 + T(v_2). \tag{2.04}$$

R and T are inverse hazard rates and, in the terminology of Myerson [11], c_1 and c_2 are virtual reservation values. These functions arise naturally in the first-order conditions for traders' equilibrium strategies and in the characterization of ex ante and interim efficiency.

Throughout this paper, we assume that F_1 and F_2 satisfy

$$R \text{ and } T \text{ are } C^1 \text{ on } [0, 1], \tag{2.05}$$

$$R > 0 \text{ on } (0, 1] \quad \text{and} \quad R(0) = 0, \tag{2.06}$$

$$T < 0 \text{ on } [0, 1) \quad \text{and} \quad T(1) = 0, \tag{2.07}$$

$$c_1 \text{ and } c_2 \text{ are strictly increasing on } [0, 1]. \tag{2.08}$$

A pair (F_1, F_2) is *admissible* if it satisfies (2.05)–(2.08). Since (F_1, F_2) are recoverable from any pair (R, T) that satisfies (2.05)–(2.07), we use (R, T) interchangeably with (F_1, F_2).[3] Note that (2.05)–(2.07) are quite general: over a proper subinterval $[\varepsilon, 1 - \varepsilon]$ of $[0, 1]$, R can be any positive C^1 function, and T can be any negative C^1 function. The monotonicity condition (2.08), while common in the auction design literature, is genuinely restrictive.

Let H^n be the set of admissible (R, T) pairs that are also C^n. We topologize H^n with the induced Whitney C^n topology. Under this topology two functions are close if and only if, at every point in their common domain, both their values are close and their first n derivatives are close. Note that H^1 is the space of all admissible pairs.

Equilibria in k-Double Auctions

A *strategy* for a trader is a real-valued function on $[0, 1]$ that describes his bid/offer as a function of his reservation value. Let S and B denote the seller's and buyer's respective strategies. Given a strategy pair (S, B), we call $\{(v_1, v_2) | S(v_1) = B(v_2)\}$ the *trading boundary*; it divides those pairs (v_1, v_2) for which trade occurs from those for which trade does not occur.

Consider a pair of strategies (S, B). The seller's strategy S is a best response to the buyer's strategy B if, for all $v_1 \in [0, 1]$, the offer $S(v_1)$ maxi-

---

[3] Rewrite the definition of $R(v_1)$ as $f_1(v_1)/F_1(v_1) = 1/R(v_1)$. Consequently, $\int d(\ln F_1(v_1)) = \int 1/R(v_1) \, dv_1 + C$, which, coupled with appropriate boundary conditions, gives F_1. Note that condition (2.05) guarantees that the solution process yields a function while (2.06)–(2.07) ensure that the solution can be interpreted as a distribution.

mizes type v_1 seller's expected utility given that (i) the buyer's strategy is B and (ii) the buyer's reservation value has distribution F_2. The definition of a best response to S is parallel. A strategy pair (S, B) is a *Bayesian–Nash equilibrium* if and only if B is a best response to S and S is a best response to B.

Several properties of an equilibrium (S, B) can be stated immediately. Chatterjee and Samuelson [2, Th. 1] proved that each of these strategies is nondecreasing over the set of those reservation values at which the conditional probability of trade is positive. Similar arguments show that (i) $S(v_1) \geq v_1$ unless the conditional probability of trade at v_1 is zero, and (ii) $B(v_2) \leq v_2$ unless the conditional probability of trade at v_2 is zero. If $v_1 \geq B(1)$, then the conditional probability of trade at v_1 is zero and the value of $S(v_1)$ can be modified arbitrarily within the interval $[B(1), 1]$ without breaking the equilibrium. A similar statement holds for B on the interval $[0, S(0)]$.

We focus on differentiable equilibrium strategies. This focus, together with the above properties of equilibrium strategies, leads us to impose the following restrictions upon the equilibria we consider:

$$S \text{ and } B \text{ are continuous and strictly increasing,} \tag{2.09}$$

$$v_1 \leq S(v_1) \leq 1 \quad \text{for all} \quad v_1 \in [0, 1], \tag{2.10}$$

$$0 \leq B(v_2) \leq v_2 \quad \text{for all} \quad v_2 \in [0, 1], \tag{2.11}$$

$$S(v_1) = v_1 \quad \text{whenever} \quad v_1 \geq B(1), \tag{2.12}$$

$$B(v_2) = v_2 \quad \text{whenever} \quad v_2 \leq S(0), \tag{2.13}$$

$$S \text{ is } C^1 \text{ on } [0, B(1)], \tag{2.14}$$

$$B \text{ is } C^1 \text{ on } [S(0), 1]. \tag{2.15}$$

A strategy pair is *regular* if it satisfies (2.09)–(2.15) and an equilibrium is *regular* if its strategies are regular. Requirements (2.12)–(2.13) pin down each strategy over the interval in which the best response is indeterminate.

Allocation Rules

Evaluating the efficiency of k-double auctions involves comparing their outcomes with all conceivable outcomes of arbitrary bargaining procedures. Formally, an outcome of bargaining is an *allocation rule*. An allocation rule is a pair (p, x) where p (the *trading rule*) is a function from $[0, 1]^2 \rightarrow [0, 1]$ whose value at (v_1, v_2) is the probability that trade occurs at that pair, and x (the *payment rule*) is a real-valued function on $[0, 1]^2$ whose values at (v_1, v_2) is the payment from the buyer to the seller at these values. We impose two condition on the class of allocation rules that we consider—incentive compatibility and individual rationality. Each is discussed in turn.

An allocation rule (p, x) is *incentive compatible* if (p, x) is the outcome of some Bayesian game when a pair of Bayesian–Nash equilibrium strategies are chosen. Note that an equilibrium (S, B) in the k-double auction defines the following incentive compatible allocation rule:

$$p(v_1, v_2) = \begin{cases} 1 & \text{if } B(v_2) \geqslant S(v_1), \\ 0 & \text{otherwise,} \end{cases} \tag{2.16}$$

and

$$x(v_1, v_2) = \begin{cases} kB(v_2) + (1-k) S(v_1) & \text{if } B(v_2) \geqslant S(v_1), \\ 0 & \text{otherwise.} \end{cases} \tag{2.17}$$

For an incentive compatible allocation rule (p, x), the interim expected utility of a seller of type v_1 is

$$U_1(v_1; p, x) = \int_0^1 [x(v_1, v_2) - v_1 \, p(v_1, v_2)] \, dF_2(v_2). \tag{2.18}$$

The ex ante expected utility of a seller is

$$\bar{U}_1(p, x) = \int_0^1 U_1(v_1; p, x) \, dF_1(v_1). \tag{2.19}$$

Finally, the probability that a type v_1 seller will trade is

$$p_1(v_1) = \int_0^1 p(v_1, v_2) \, dF_2(v_2). \tag{2.20}$$

Similar formulas apply to the buyer. Because any equilibrium (S, B) in the k-double auction implements an incentive compatible allocation rule (p, x) as in (2.16)–(2.17), we can without ambiguity write a type v_i trader's interim expected utility under this equilibrium as $U_i(v_i; S, B) = U_i(v_i; p, x)$. $\bar{U}_i(S, B)$ and $p_i(v_i; S, B)$ are defined analogously.

An allocation rule (p, x) is *individually rational* if, for all $i \in \{1, 2\}$ and all $v_i \in [0, 1]$, $U_i(v_i; p, x) \geqslant 0$. The allocation rules defined by k-double auctions are individually rational because in equilibrium each trader's strategy guarantees that he never incurs a loss. Individual rationality is a natural requirement, for the essence of a free market is that trade is voluntary. An allocation rule that is both incentive compatible and individually rational is *incentive feasible*. The allocation rule (p, x) that an equilibrium pair (S, B) defines is thus incentive feasible.

In order to evaluate the outcomes of k-double auctions against all other incentive feasible allocation rules, we need to know which pairs (p, x) are incentive feasible. Define $\Gamma(p)$ as the following function of a trading rule p:

$$\Gamma(p) = \int_0^1 \int_0^1 \{c_2(v_2) - c_1(v_1)\}\, p(v_1, v_2)\, dF_1(v_1)\, dF_2(v_2). \quad (2.21)$$

Using an approach first formulated by Myerson [10], Myerson and Satterthwaite [13, Th. 1] characterized all incentive feasible allocation rules.

THEOREM 2.1.   *Let (R, T) be admissible. If (p, x) is an incentive feasible allocation rule, then*

$$p_1 \text{ is nonincreasing and } p_2 \text{ is nondecreasing on } [0, 1], \quad (2.22)$$

$$\Gamma(p) = U_1(1; p, x) + U_2(0; p, x) \geq 0, \quad (2.23)$$

$$U_1(v_1; p, x) = m + \int_{v_1}^1 p_1(y)\, dy, \quad (2.24)$$

$$U_2(v_2; p, x) = \Gamma(p) - m + \int_0^{v_2} p_2(y)\, dy \quad (2.25)$$

where $m \in [0, \Gamma(p)]$. Conversely, if $p: [0, 1]^2 \to [0, 1]$ is a function satisfying (2.22)–(2.23), then a function $x: [0, 1]^2 \to \Re$ exists such that (p, x) is incentive feasible.

Efficiency criteria.   An incentive feasible allocation rule (p^*, x^*) is ex ante efficient if no incentive feasible allocation rule (p, x) exists such that, for $i \in \{1, 2\}$, $\bar{U}_i(p, x) \geq \bar{U}_i(p^*, x^*)$ and, for some i, $\bar{U}_i(p, x) > \bar{U}(p^*, x^*)$. Ex ante efficiency means that the seller on average cannot be made better off without making the buyer on average worse off, and vice versa. Williams [17, Th. 2] characterized all ex ante efficient incentive feasible allocation rules.

THEOREM 2.2.   *Let (R, T) be admissible. An incentive feasible allocation rule (p, x) is ex ante efficient if and only if (i) $\Gamma(p) = 0$ and (ii) scalars $t, s \in [0, 1]$ exist such that*

$$p(v_1, v_2) = \begin{cases} 1 & \text{if } v_2 + sT(v_2) \geq v_1 + tR(v_1), \\ 0 & \text{otherwise.} \end{cases} \quad (2.26)$$

Thus, ex ante efficiency requires that the trading boundary consists of solutions to the equation $v_2 + sT(v_2) = v_1 + tR(v_1)$ for some choice of $s, t \in [0, 1]$.

An incentive feasible allocation rule (p^*, x^*) is *interim efficient* if no incentive feasible allocation rule (p, x) exists such that, for all $i \in \{1, 2\}$ and all $v_i \in [0, 1]$, $U_i(v_i; p, x) \geq U_i(v_i; p^*, x^*)$ and, for some i and v_i, $U_i(v_i; p, x) > U_i(v_i; p^*, x^*)$. Interim efficiency means that, without leaving the class of incentive feasible allocation rules, a type v_i trader cannot be made better off unless a trader of another type is made worse off. Under interim efficiency each type buyer and each type seller is a distinct person whose interests must be respected.

THEOREM 2.3. *Let (R, T) be admissible. An incentive feasible allocation rule (p, x) is interim efficient if* (i) $\Gamma(p) = 0$ *and* (ii) *functions* $(\tilde{\alpha}_1(v_1), \tilde{\alpha}_2(v_2))$: $[0, 1]^2 \to [0, 1]^2$ *exist such that*

$$(d/dv_1)[F_1(v_1) \tilde{\alpha}_1(v_1)] \geq 0, \tag{2.27}$$

$$(d/dv_2)[(1 - F_2(v_2)) \tilde{\alpha}_2(v_2)] \leq 0, \tag{2.28}$$

$$p(v_1, v_2) = \begin{cases} 1 & \text{if } v_2 + (1 - \tilde{\alpha}_2(v_2)) T(v_2) \geq v_1 + (1 - \tilde{\alpha}_1(v_1)) R(v_1), \\ 0 & \text{otherwise.} \end{cases}$$
$$\tag{2.29}$$

This theorem is a corollary of Lemma 3 in Wilson [18]. See the Appendix for details.

3. EXISTENCE OF EQUILIBRIA

The first step in showing existence of regular equilibria is the development of necesary and sufficient conditions for their existence.

THEOREM 3.1. *Let (R, T) be admissible. If (S, B) form a regular equilibrium in a k-double auction, then they satisfy the following two differential equations whenever $v_2 \geq S(0)$ and $v_1 \leq B(1)$:*

$$B^{-1}[S(v_1)] = S(v_1) + kS'(v_1) R(v_1) \tag{3.01}$$

and

$$S^{-1}[B(v_2)] = B(v_2) + (1 - k) B'(v_2) T(v_2). \tag{3.02}$$

Conversely, if (S, B) is a regular strategy pair such that, for all $v_1 \leq B(1)$ and $v_2 \geq S(0)$, (3.01)–(3.02) are satisfied, then (S, B) is a regular equilibrium.

Chatterjee and Samuelson [2, Th. 2] showed the theorem's necessary part. To our knowledge, the sufficient part is new; its proof is in the Appendix. Given Theorem 3.1, demonstration that regular equilibria exist in a

k-double auction is straightforward if the $k \in (0, 1)$ and the $k \in \{0, 1\}$ cases are considered separately. Theorem 3.2 states the result for $k \in (0, 1)$.

THEOREM 3.2.   *If (R, T) is admissible and $k \in (0, 1)$, then the regular equilibria in the k-double auction form a two-parameter family.*

This theorem's proof is central to understanding the nature of equilibria in k-double auctions; consequently we include it here instead of relegating it to the Appendix.

Let b, the bid/offer of a trader, be regarded as a parameter. Regard each v_i ($i \in \{1, 2\}$) as a function of the parameter b by inverting trader i's strategy; $v_i(b)$ therefore describes the reservation value at which trader i makes the bid/offer b. Let $\dot{v}_i \equiv dv_i/db$. Then $v_1 = S^{-1}(b)$, $v_2 = B^{-1}(b)$, $S'(v_1) = 1/\dot{v}_1$, and $B'(v_2) = 1/\dot{v}_2$. Substitution into (3.01)–(3.02) gives

$$\dot{v}_1 = kR(v_1)/(v_2 - b) \tag{3.03}$$

and

$$\dot{v}_2 = (1 - k) \, T(v_2)/(v_1 - b). \tag{3.04}$$

If (3.03)–(3.04) are supplemented with the tautology

$$\dot{b} = 1, \tag{3.05}$$

then (3.03)–(3.05) define a vector field at each point in the tetrahedron $0 \leqslant v_1 \leqslant b \leqslant v_2 \leqslant 1$ within $\mathfrak{R}^3$ where the axes are labeled v_1, v_2, and b. This tetrahedron is illustrated in Fig. 3.1. Note that $\dot{v}_1$, $\dot{v}_2$, and $\dot{b}$ are strictly positive at each interior point. A standard theorem from the theory of differential equations (e.g., see Arnold [1, Th. 7.1]) asserts that a solution to

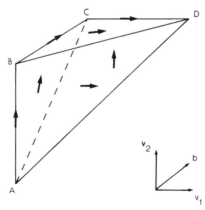

FIG. 3.1.   Tetrahedron $0 \leqslant v_1 \leqslant b \leqslant v_2 \leqslant 1$ that contains solutions. The arrows indicate the limit of the normalized vector field on the tetrahedron's faces and edges.

(3.03)–(3.05) exists through any point in the interior of the tetrahedron. Though some solution curve passes through each point in the interior, the family of all solutions can be indexed with any planar surface that is transverse to this family. This completes the proof.

The second existence theorem considers regular equilibria for the seller's offer auction $(k = 0)$ and buyer's bid auction $(k = 1)$.

THEOREM 3.3. *If (R, T) is admissible and if $k \in \{0, 1\}$, then a regular equilibrium exists. For the seller's offer double auction $(k = 0)$, the truthful strategy $B(v_2) = v_2$ is the unique, dominant strategy for the buyer. The seller's best response S to this strategy is unique, differentiable, and satisfies $c_2[S(v_1)] = v_1$. Similarly, for the buyer's bid double auction $(k = 1)$, the truthful strategy $S(v_1) = v_1$ is the unique dominant strategy for the seller. The buyer's best response B to this strategy is unique, differentiable, and satisfies $c_1[B(v_2)] = v_2$.*

A proof can be found in Williams [17, Th. 5].

4. GEOMETRY OF SOLUTIONS WHEN $k \in (0,1)$

Specific Examples

Equations (3.03)–(3.05) are useful not only in proving existence, but also in numerically calculating equilibria. The computational procedure is as follows. Pick a point (v_1, v_2, b) within the tetrahedron. The vector $(\dot{v}_1, \dot{v}_2, \dot{b})$ points along the solution through this point. Compute, using a small step, a second solution point by moving in the direction of the vector. Repeat this process until the path leaves the tetrahedron. Return to the initial point and repeat the process moving in the opposite direction of the vector field until the path again leaves the tetrahedron. The resulting path approximates a complete solution. We used this procedure to compute the numerical examples that are graphed in this paper.

Figures 4.1 and 4.2 illustrate an equilibrium in the 0.5-double auction. Figure 4.1 shows, within the tetrahedron, the solution that passes through the point $(v_1, v_2, b) = (0.375, 0.625, 0.45)$. Note that the solution enters the tetrahedron at point $E = (0.0, 0.285, 0.285)$ on edge AC and leaves the tetrahedron at point $F = (0.791, 1.0, 0.791)$ on edge BD. In this equilibrium $S(0) = 0.285$ and $B(0.285) = 0.285$. Thus, a type 0 seller distorts his offer upward to 0.285, while a type 0.285 buyer bids his value 0.285. Buyers of types $v_2 \leqslant 0.285$ bid truthfully, but have zero probability of trading because a seller's offer always exceeds 0.285.

Figure 4.2 shows this same solution projected three different ways into the unit square. The seller's strategy $S(v_1) = b$ is obtained by projecting

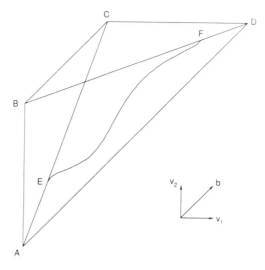

FIG. 4.1.   Solution through $(v_1, v_2, b) = (0.375, 0.625, 0.45)$ shown within tetrahedron. The solution enters the tetrahedron at point E and exits through point F.

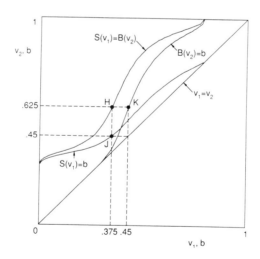

FIG. 4.2.   Solution   through $(v_1, v_2, b) = (0.375, 0.625, 0.45)$.   Point $H = (v_1, v_2) = (0.375, 0.625)$ is   on   the   trading   boundary   where $S(0.375) = B(0.625) = 0.45$.   Point $J = (v_1, S(v_1)) = (0.375, 0.45)$ is on the graph of the seller's strategy. Point $K = (B(v_2), v_2) = (0.45, 0.625)$ is on the graph of the buyer's strategy. The ex ante expected utility is 0.0654 for the seller and 0.0725 for the buyer.

the solution onto the tetrahedron's top face BCD, the buyer's strategy $B(v_2) = b$ is obtained by projecting the solution onto the side face ABC, and the trading boundary $B(v_2) = S(v_1)$ is obtained by projecting the solution onto the plane at the front of the tetrahedron defined by the v_1 and v_2 axes.

Figure 4.3 shows, for $k = 0.5$, the well-known linear Chatterjee–Samuelson [2] solution. It passes through point $(0.375, 0.625, 0.5)$, has equilibrium strategies $S(v_1) = (\frac{2}{3}) v_1 + \frac{1}{4}$ and $B(v_2) = (\frac{2}{3}) v_2 + \frac{1}{12}$, and has a linear trading boundary $v_2 = v_1 + \frac{1}{4}$ (i.e., trade only occurs if the buyer's reservation value is at least $\frac{1}{4}$ greater than the seller's reservation value). Myerson and Satterthwaite [13] showed that the Chatterjee–Samuelson equilibrium is ex ante efficient because it maximizes the total expected gains from trade. Under this equilibrium each trader's ex ante expected utility is 0.0703. These ex ante utilities should be compared with the ex ante utilities generated by the equilibrium shown in Figs. 4.1 and 4.2. That equilibrium gives the seller ex ante utility of 0.0654 and the buyer 0.0725. While this equilibrium is ex ante inefficient, it is ex ante preferred by the buyer. Equilibria of k-double auctions generally cannot be Pareto ordered, and traders may have conflicting preferences over them.

The Chatterjee–Samuelson solution is one example of how each ex ante efficient allocation rule in the uniform distribution case can be implemented through a properly chosen k-double auction. Williams [17, Section 3] showed that the ex ante efficient trading boundaries in the uniform case are given by $v_2 = dv_1 + c$, where $c \in [0, \frac{1}{2}]$ and $d = 2(1 - c)/(2c + 1)$. For a given c, the welfare weights assigned to the seller and buyer are $4c/(2c + 1)$ and

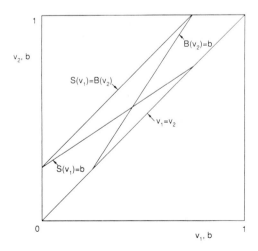

FIG. 4.3. Chatterjee–Samuelson linear solution. It passes through $(v_1, v_2, b) = (0.375, 0.625, 0.50)$. The ex ante expected utility of each trader is 0.0703.

$(1 - 2c)/(1 - c)$, respectively. By solving (3.01)–(3.02) directly, it can be shown that for each choice of c (and therefore of the welfare weights), there is a unique k-double auction ($k = 1 - 2c$) and a regular equilibrium

$$S(v_1) = dv_1/(1 + k) + c \qquad (4.01)$$

and

$$B(v_2) = v_2/(1 + k) + ck/(1 + k) \qquad (4.02)$$

that implements the ex ante efficient allocation rule associated with c. Note that $c = \frac{1}{4}$ gives the Chatterjee–Samuelson equilibrium. This family of ex ante efficient equilibria plays an important role in the proof of Theorem 6.3.

General Features

Examination of the limiting values that (3.03)–(3.05) assign to the vector field $(\dot{v}_1, \dot{v}_2, \dot{b})$ on the faces and edges of the tetrahedron allows us to deduce a number of qualitative features of regular equilibria. On each face and each edge $\dot{v}_1$ and $\dot{v}_2$ equals either zero or infinity. To avoid the problems that values of infinity create, we look at the normalization of the vector field. (Recall that a vector is normalized by reducing its length to unity and leaving its direction unchanged.) Normalization has no effect on solutions to (3.03)–(3.05) because the solution curves are fully determined by the vector field's direction at each point, not by its magnitude. The limits of the normalized field are summarized in Table I, and they are also depicted in Fig. 3.1. Note that the normalized vector field is indeterminate along the edges *AC*, *BD*, and *AD*.

TABLE I

Direction of the Vector Field on the Faces and Edges of the Tetrahedron

	$\dot{v}_1$	$\dot{v}_2$	$\dot{b}$
Face			
ABD	0	1	0
ABC	0	>0	>0
BCD	>0	0	>0
ACD	1	0	0
Edge			
AB	0	1	0
BC	0	0	1
CD	1	0	0
AD		Undefined	
BD		Undefined	
AC		Undefined	

A striking regularity of Table I is that the normalized vector field on each face lies within that face. This means that a solution curve to the field can enter and exit the tetrahedron only along the edges AC and BD; the curves flow up from the edge AC through the tetrahedron and out the edge BD. This illustrates an important property of equilibrium auction strategies: at the seller's smallest offer, $S(0)$ on face ABC, the buyer's strategy converges to truthful revelation. A similar result holds for the seller's strategy.

Not only can solution curves enter only along the edge AC and exit through edge BD, curves can only enter and exit through specific subintervals of those edges. Consider the case of edge BD in detail by examining the behavior of the vector field near a point $\bar{q} = (v_1, v_2, b)$ on BD where $v_1 = b = \bar{v}_1$ and $v_2 = 1$. The limit of the field is not well defined at $\bar{q}$ because $\dot{v}_2(\bar{q})$ is a $0/0$ indeterminate form that can be made to converge to any positive number by properly choosing the direction in which the limit is taken. The limit of the $\dot{v}_1$ term, however, is well defined at $\bar{q}$:

$$\dot{v}_1(\bar{q}) = kR(\bar{v}_1)/(1 - \bar{v}_1). \tag{4.04}$$

If $\dot{v}_1(\bar{q})$ is less than $\dot{b} = 1$, then no solution curve can exit through $\bar{q}$ because (regardless of the value of $\dot{v}_2$) near $\bar{q}$ the vector field points back into the tetrahedron rather than toward the boundary BD. Consequently, a necessary and sufficient condition for solution curves to exit at point $\bar{q}$ on BD is that $\dot{v}_1(\bar{q}) > \dot{b} \equiv 1$. This condition depends solely on the values of k, $\bar{v}_1$, and $R(\bar{v}_1)$, and is independent of T. An analogous condition can be derived for points of entry on edge AC.

If $\dot{v}_1 \geq 1$ so that solution curves can exit from the tetrahedron at $\bar{q}$, then a one-parameter family of curves exits at $\bar{q}$. This is true because $\dot{v}_2(\bar{q})$ is indeterminate and can assume any positive limiting value. It is intuitively suggested by the fact that a two-dimensional family of solutions exists that must enter and exit through edges that are one dimensional.

Because R is differentiable, the condition $\dot{v}_1(\bar{q}) \geq 1$ partitions the edge BD into subintervals where solution curves can and cannot terminate. For instance, in the standard example where F_1 and F_2 are both uniform and $k = 0.5$, solution curves cannot exit at points on BD unless $v_1 \geq \frac{2}{3}$, and solution curves cannot enter at points on AC unless $v_2 \leq \frac{1}{3}$.

Table I indicates that the normalized vector field has the limiting values (i) $(\dot{v}_1, \dot{v}_2, \dot{b}) = (1, 0, 0)$ on face ACD and (ii) $(0, 1, 0)$ on face ABD. These limiting values trace out the following one-parameter family of step-function equilibria:

$$S_\delta(v_1) = \begin{cases} \delta & \text{if } v_1 \leq \delta, \\ 1 & \text{otherwise,} \end{cases} \tag{4.05}$$

and

$$B_\delta(v_2) = \begin{cases} 0 & \text{if} \quad v_2 \leqslant \delta, \\ \delta & \text{otherwise,} \end{cases}$$

where $\delta \in (0, 1)$. The equilibrium a given δ determines corresponds to a solution curve that crosses from the point $(0, \delta, \delta)$ on AC, along the bottom face ACD of the tetrahedron to (δ, δ, δ) on AD, and then up the face ABD to $(\delta, 1, \delta)$ on BD. These are the simplest of the many step-function equilibria Leininger *et al.* [9] found.

5. Ex Ante Efficiency

For generic distributions the only k-double auctions that achieve ex ante efficiency are the seller's offer and the buyer's bid double auctions. When both traders influence price the k-double auction is generically ex ante inefficient.

THEOREM 5.1. *An open, dense subset $X \subset H^6$ exists such that, for $(R, T) \in X$ and $k \in (0, 1)$, the k-double auction is ex ante inefficient.*

Recall that H^n is the admissible pairs (R, T) that have continuous nth-order derivatives. We explain the intuition here; the formal proof is in the Appendix.

Suppose $(R, T) \in H^n$ and (S, B) is a regular equilibrium. As before let $v_1(b) \equiv S^{-1}(b)$ and $v_2(b) \equiv B^{-1}(b)$. The first-order conditions (3.03)–(3.05) can be rewritten as

$$R[v_1(b)] = \dot{v}_1(b)[v_2(b) - b]/k \tag{5.01}$$

and

$$T[v_2(b)] = \dot{v}_2(b)[v_1(b) - b]/(1 - k). \tag{5.02}$$

Note that if the inverse strategies (v_1, v_2) are perturbed slightly (while respecting monotonicity and boundary conditions), then the perturbed strategies are a regular equilibrium for the perturbed pair (R', T') obtained through (5.01)–(5.02).

Suppose a pair of inverse strategies (v_1, v_2) is an ex ante efficient equilibrium for (R, T). Theorem 2.2 states that constants $s, t \in [0, 1]$ exist such that

$$v_2(b) + sT(v_2(b)) = v_1(b) + tR(v_1(b)) \tag{5.03}$$

for all $b \in [S(0), B(1)]$. Use (5.01)–(5.02) to substitute for R and T in (5.03):

$$v_2 + s\dot{v}_2(v_1 - b)/(1 - k) = v_1 + t\dot{v}_1(v_2 - b)/k. \tag{5.04}$$

Equation (5.04) is noteworthy because it is a necessary condition for ex ante efficiency on $v_1(b)$ and $v_2(b)$. It is immediate that a generic perturbation of (v_1, v_2) defines an ex ante inefficient equilibrium for (R', T'), because (5.04) will not be solvable for constants s and t as b varies. This useful observation, however, does not complete our argument because some other element of the two-parameter family of equilibria that exists for (R', T') could be efficient.

We must show for a generic pair (R, T) that none of its equilibria is ex ante efficient. To show this we consider all pairs of functions $v_1(b)$ and $v_2(b)$ that solve (5.04) for some constants s, t, and k. When these solutions are substituted into (5.01)–(5.02), do they generate all admissible pairs (R, T), as they must if every admissible (R, T) has an ex ante efficient equilibrium? No, for the following reason. Equation (5.04) shows that the selection of $v_1(b)$ and the constants s, t, k determine $v_2(b)$ up to a constant of integration K. The four scalars s, t, k, K, and one functional parameter $v_1(b)$ cannot generate the two independent functional parameters R and T. This suggests that the set of (R, T) for which at least one ex ante efficient equilibrium exists is small relative to the entire set of admissible (R, T).

To describe precisely the sense in which this subset is small, we consider the nth-order Taylor polynomials of $v_1(b)$, $v_2(b)$, $R(v_1)$, and $T(v_2)$. Equations (5.01)–(5.02) can be rewritten in terms of the coefficients of these polynomials. We show that, for an open dense subset of the coefficients of the sixth-order Taylor polynomials of R and T, (5.01)–(5.02) are not solvable for appropriate coefficients of the Taylor polynomials of $v_1(b)$ and $v_2(b)$. An ex ante efficient equilibrium therefore does not exist for a generic pair $(R, T) \in H^6$.

To understand this theorem, it is helpful to apply it in the context of the family of ex ante efficient, regular equilibria that (4.01)–(4.02) describe for the uniform case in which $(R, T) \equiv (v_1, 1 - v_2) \in H^6$. Perturb (R, T) slightly to create $(R', T') \in H^6$. Theorem 5.1 states that, for any $k \in (0, 1)$, no ex ante efficient equilibrium exists for the generic perturbed pair (R', T'). This means that the ex ante efficiency of the family of equilibria in (4.01)–(4.02) is a knife-edge phenomenon.

Ex ante efficient performance is achievable when only one trader influences price. The cost of achieving this efficiency is a welfare weight of zero on the trader who cannot influence price.

THEOREM 5.2. *For all admissible (R, T) the regular equilibrium specified* *in Theorem* 3.3 *of the seller's offer auction* ($k = 0$) *is ex ante efficient and maximizes the seller's ex ante expected utility. Similarly, the regular equilibrium of the buyer's bid auction* ($k = 1$) *is ex ante efficient and maximizes the buyer's ex ante expected utility.*

For proofs, see Williams [17, Th. 5] and Myerson [10, cf. pp. 66–68].

6. INTERIM EFFICIENCY

When both traders can affect price, ex ante efficient equilibria generically do not exist. This leads to the following question: Do interim efficient equilibria exist for k-double auctions when $k \in (0, 1)$? We are unable to answer this question definitively, but we do provide some partial answers and insights.

Our first result is a necessary condition for interim efficient performance.

THEOREM 6.1. *Let* (R, T) *be admissible. If* (S, B) *is a regular equilibrium that is interim efficient, then under* (S, B) *trade occurs with probability one in the region* $A(R, T) \equiv \{(v_1, v_2) | c_2(v_2) > c_1(v_1)\}$.

Proofs of this and the remaining theorems are in the Appendix.

To illustrate this theorem, consider the uniform case in which $c_1(v_1) = 2v_1$ and $c_2(v_2) = 2v_2 - 1$. Within the square $0 \leqslant v_1, v_2 \leqslant 1$ the region $A(R, T)$ is the area above and to the left of the line $v_2 - v_1 = 0.5$. If an equilibrium (S, B) generates a trading boundary that enters the region $A(R, T)$, then trade does not occur for some (v_1, v_2) pairs within $A(R, T)$; consequently the equilibrium is interim inefficient.

More generally, because $c_2(1) = 1 > 0 = c_1(0)$ for any admissible pair (R, T), the region $A(R, T)$ always contains a nonempty open set in the upper left corner of the square $0 \leqslant v_1, v_2 \leqslant 1$. This determines a "tube" in the tetrahedron that contains the edge BC ($v_1 = 0$, $v_2 = 1$, and $b \in [0, 1]$). Any solution curve to (3.03)–(3.05) that passes through this tube is an interim inefficient equilibrium. Consequently, for every $k \in (0, 1)$, the k-double auction has an open set of regular equilibria that are interim inefficient. In this sense interim inefficient performance of the k-double auction is robust over the set of admissible pairs, the scalar k, and the choice of the equilibrium strategy pair.

The second result of the section is a sufficient condition for interim efficiency. The theorem assumes that R, T are C^2 in order to ensure that the regular equilibrium strategies are also C^2.

THEOREM 6.2. *Suppose* $(R, T) \in H^2$ *and* (S, B) *is a regular equilibrium for a k-double auction with* $k \in (0, 1)$. *If, for all pairs* $v_1 < B(1)$ *and* $v_2 > S(0)$,

$$1 - kS'(v_1) \in [0, 1], \tag{6.01}$$

$$1 - (1 - k) B'(v_2) \in [0, 1], \tag{6.02}$$

$$d/dv_1 [F_1(v_1)(1 - kS'(v_1))] \geqslant 0, \tag{6.03}$$

$$d/dv_2 [(1 - F_2(v_2))(1 - (1 - k) B'(v_2))] \leqslant 0, \tag{6.04}$$

then the equilibrium pair is interim efficient.

The proof is a direct application of Theorem 2.3.

Theorem 6.2 is used to prove our final result, which establishes the existence of an interim efficient equilibrium for all (R, T) pairs that are close enough to the uniform case. This contrasts with the statement in Theorem 5.1 that generically ex ante efficient performance is unachievable.

THEOREM 6.3.   *For each $k \in (0, 1)$, an open subset $X_k \subset H^1$ exists such that the k-double auction achieves interim efficient performance for every (R, T) in X_k. For each k, X_k contains the pair $(v_1, 1 - v_2) \in H^1$.*

7. Remarks

1.   Myerson [12] considered the situation where (i) the buyer and seller trade only once and (ii) each F_i is the uniform distribution on $[0, 1]$. Each trader knows his reservation value from the outset of the bargaining process, and is concerned with maximizing his interim expected utility. Therefore their ex ante expected utilities are irrelevant. Myerson argued that the Chatterjee–Samuelson linear equilibrium to the 0.5-double auction is both positively and normatively an inappropriate outcome to the bargaining process. As an alternative he suggests the *neutral bargaining solution*—originally defined in Myerson [11]—that gives rise to the trading boundary M shown on Fig. 7.1. This solution concept incorporates what Myerson calls the "arrogance of strength" that naturally arises in situations in which a seller's realized reservation value is high or a buyer's realized reservation value is low.

Superimposed on trading boundary M is trading boundary T, which is generated by the regular equilibrium of the 0.5-double auction that passes through the point $(v_1, v_2, b) = (0.25, 0.75, 0.5)$. Because T approximates the boundary M, this equilibrium gives both traders approximately the same interim expected utilities as Myerson's neutral bargaining solution.

This illustrates a general point: the multiplicity of equilibria in the k-double auction may enable it to implement many different allocation rules approximately. Our work, however, provides no basis for selecting

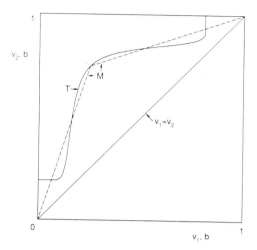

Fig. 7.1. Double auction vs neutral bargaining solution. Curve M is the trading boundary that Myerson's neutral bargaining solution generates. Curve T is the trading boundary of the 0.5-double auction equilibrium that passes through $(v_1, v_2, b) = (0.25, 0.75, 0.50)$.

among the possible equilibria, nor for explaining regularities that are observed in experiments with double auctions.[4]

2.   Wilson [18] showed that the k-double auction achieves interim efficient performance when the number of traders becomes large. His result assumes the existence of a sequence of equilibria indexed by the size of the market such that (i) in each equilibrium the buyers' strategies are identical and the sellers' strategies are identical and (ii) the strategies are differentiable and their derivatives are uniformly bounded in both the traders' reservation values and the total number of traders. Our Theorem 6.2 shows that if equilibrium strategies in the bilateral case obey certain bounds on their derivatives, then the equilibrium is interim efficient. While Wilson's assumptions on strategies are not simply an extension of the bounds given in our Theorem 6.2, our theorem does suggest that his assumptions on the derivatives of the equilibrium strategies play a central role in his proof. Thus an important problem that remains is to prove that sequences of equilibria that satisfy Wilson's hypotheses actually exist.

Appendix

Proof of Theorem 2.3.   The correspondence between our notation and Wilson's notation is as follows. In Wilson's paper v_1 is $v(t)$, v_2 is $u(t)$, $F_1(v_1)$

---

[4] See, e.g., Smith *et al.* [15] and Radner and Schotter [14].

and $F_2(v_2)$ are t, $\tilde{\alpha}_1(v_1)$ is $\tilde{\alpha}_j(t)$, and $\tilde{\alpha}_2(v_2)$ is $\tilde{\alpha}_i(t)$. Wilson's Lemma 3 takes as given both the set of welfare weights α and the conditional welfare weights $\tilde{\alpha}$ that the weights α imply. It then states conditions on the conditional weights that are sufficient to guarantee that the trading rule is interim efficient. Our theorem takes as given a set of conditional welfare weights $\tilde{\alpha}$. It states conditions on these weights that are sufficient to guarantee (i) the existence of imputed, nonnegative welfare weights α and (ii) the interim efficiency of the trading rule.

Three observations establish the theorem. Our condition $\Gamma(p) = 0$ implies Wilson's requirement $V_h(1) = 0$. Inequalities (2.27)–(2.28) guarantee the nonnegativity of the imputed welfare weights α. Equation (2.29) is equivalent to maximization of Wilson's expression (9).

Proof of Theorem 3.1. We begin with Chatterjee and Samuelson's derivation of Eq. (3.01). Suppose (S, B) is a regular equilibrium. Define

$$V_1(b) = \begin{cases} S^{-1}(b) & \text{if } 1 \geqslant b \geqslant S(0), \\ 0 & \text{if } S(0) > b \geqslant 0. \end{cases} \tag{A.01}$$

V_1 is increasing and differentiable for all $b > S(0)$ because of the properties of S. Given a bid b by the buyer, trade occurs only if the seller's reservation value v_1 is less than $V_1(b)$. Consequently, the type v_2 buyer's expected utility as a function of his bid b is

$$U_2(b; v_2, S) = \int_0^{V_1} [v_2 - kb - (1-k) S(v_1)] \, dF_1(v_1)$$

$$= (v_2 - kb) F_1(V_1) - (1-k) \int_0^{V_1} S(v_1) \, dF_1(v_1). \tag{A.02}$$

The buyer selects b to maximize $U_2(b; v_2, S)$. If $v_2 \leqslant S(0)$, then the buyer cannot make an advantageous trade. If $v_2 > S(0)$, then the first-order condition for selecting b is

$$dU_2/db = -kF_1(V_1) + (v_2 - kb) f_1(V_1) \dot{V}_1 - (1-k) S(V_1) f_1(V_1) \dot{V}_1$$

$$= f_1(V_1)[-kR(V_1) + (v_2 - b) \dot{V}_1] = 0 \tag{A.03}$$

where $\dot{V}_1 \equiv dV_1(b)/db = 1/S'[V_1(b)]$. Because $B(v_2)$ is a bid that maximizes a type v_2 buyer's expected utility, (A.03) is satisfied when $v_2 = B^{-1}(b)$. The definition of V_1 implies that $S(V_1) = b$. Substituting into (A.03) gives

$$f_1(V_1)[-kR(V_1) S'(V_1) + B^{-1}(S(V_1)) - S(V_1)]/S'(V_1) = 0. \tag{A.04}$$

Replacing V_1 with v_1, the term in brackets implies Eq. (3.01). Derivation of Eq. (3.02) is analogous.

We now prove that (3.01)–(3.02) are sufficient. Suppose (S, B) is a regular strategy pair that satisfies (3.01)–(3.02) for all $v_1 \leqslant B(1)$ and $v_2 \geqslant S(0)$. Let v_2 be the buyer's reservation value. We show that his optimal bid b is $B(v_2)$. A similar argument shows that S is optimal for the seller.

If $v_2 \leqslant S(0)$, then the buyer cannot make an advantageous trade; $b = B(v_2) = v_2$ achieves zero as his expected utility level. Suppose instead that $v_2 > S(0)$. Up to the second line of (A.03), the derivation of dU_2/db does not change. Factor $\dot{V}_1 = 1/S'(V_1)$ from the expression in brackets to obtain

$$\frac{dU_2}{db} = [-kR(V_1)S'(V_1) + (v_2 - b)]f_1(V_1)\,\dot{V}_1. \tag{A.05}$$

For bids $b \in [S(0), B(1)]$ we can use (3.01) to substitute for $-kR(V_1)S'(V_1)$; simplifying we obtain

$$dU_2/db = [v_2 - B^{-1}(b)]f_1(V_1)\,\dot{V}_1. \tag{A.06}$$

At $b = B(v_2)$ this expression equals zero. As b increases dU_2/db changes from positive to negative because (i) B is increasing, (ii) f_1 is positive on the interval $(0, 1)$, and (iii) $\dot{V}_1$ is positive on $(0, B(1))$. Therefore $b = B(v_2)$ is the optimal bid in $[S(0), B(1)]$.

It remains to be shown that the buyer would not want to choose b within $[B(1), 1]$. We establish this by showing that dU_2/db is nonpositive in $[B(1), 1]$. For bids in this interval $\dot{V}_1 = 1/S'(V_1) = 1$ because the seller's offer equals his reservation value when it exceeds $B(1)$. Substituting this into (A.05) gives

$$dU_2/db = [v_2 - (b + kR(b))]f_1(V_1). \tag{A.07}$$

The term $b + kR(b)$ is increasing because R is admissible. It is therefore sufficient to show that

$$v_2 - [B(1) + kR(B(1))] \tag{A.08}$$

is nonpositive. Any regular solution to the Chatterjee–Samuelson equations has the geometry we described in Section 4. The solution we are considering exits the tetrahedron at the point $v_1 = B(1)$, $v_2 = 1$, $b = B(1)$. At this point $\dot{v}_1 \geqslant 1$. Using (3.03) we obtain

$$1 \leqslant \dot{v}_1 = kR(v_1)/(v_2 - b), \tag{A.09}$$

which implies

$$1 - [B(1) + kR(B(1))] \leqslant 0. \tag{A.10}$$

Expression (A.08) is therefore nonpositive for all $v_2 \leqslant 1$, which completes the proof.

Proof of Theorem 5.1. A q-jet space is a topological space that represents all possible Taylor polynomials of order q for a particular class of functions. Specifically, the q-jet of an admissible R at $v_1 \in [0, 1]$ is the $(q + 2)$-tuple $(v_1, R(v_1), R'(v_1), R''(v_1), ..., R^{(q)}(v_1))$. The q-jet of an admissible pair (R, T) at (v_1, v_2) is the $(2q + 4)$-tuple obtained by concatenating the q-jets of R at v_1 and T at v_2. For $q \leqslant n$, the q-jet space of admissible pairs $(R, T) \in H^n$ is therefore a $(2q + 4)$-dimensional subset of $[0, 1]^2 \times \Re^{2q + 2}$. Let J^q denote this space. Note that J^q is the union of an open subset of $[0, 1]^2 \times \Re^{2q + 2}$, which is determined by the monotonicity condition (2.08), and a boundary set that is determined by (2.06)–(2.07). We also consider the q-jet of an inverse strategy pair $(v_1(b), v_2(b))$: $(b, v_1(b), v_2(b), ..., v_1^{(q)}(b), v_2^{(q)}(b))$. Let I^q denote the space of all such $(2q + 3)$-tuples; it is a subset of $[0, 1]^3 \times \Re^{2q}$. See Hirsch [6, pp. 60–61] for further discussion of jet spaces.

The first goal in the proof is to describe at the n-jet level the set of s, t, k, b, $v_1(b)$, and $v_2(b)$ that satisfy the necessary condition (5.04) for ex ante efficiency. For $1 \leqslant q \leqslant n$, differentiating (5.04) $q - 1$ times permits the derivation of a formula for the qth derivative of $v_2(b)$ in terms of the variables s, t, k, b, the value of $v_2(b)$ and its derivatives of order $q - 1$ and smaller, and the value of $v_1(b)$ and its derivatives of order q and smaller. Sequential substitution for the first derivative of $v_2(b)$, its second derivative, etc., eliminates the derivatives of $v_2(b)$ that are of order less than q from the formula for the qth derivative of $v_2(b)$. The result of this exercise is a system of algebraic equations on $[0, 1]^2 \times (0, 1) \times I^n$ in the variables s, t, k, b, and the n-jet of $(v_1(b), v_2(b))$. The solution set of this system has dimension $6 + n$ (i.e., the three variables s, t, k, the value of b, the value of $v_1(b)$ and its first n derivatives, and the value of $v_2(b)$). Let V^n denote this solution set. A necessary condition for a pair $(v_1(b), v_2(b))$ to achieve ex ante efficient performance is that an s, t, k, and b exist such that they, together with the n-jet of $(v_1(b), v_2(b))$ at b, define an element of V^n.

Each element of V^n determines through (5.01)–(5.02) an element of $\Re^{2n + 2}$, which also contains the $(n - 1)$-jets of all admissible pairs (R, T). Formally, (5.01)–(5.02) can be differentiated repeatedly with respect to b to obtain algebraic formulas for the first $n - 1$ derivatives of $R(v_1)$ with respect to v_1 and of $T(v_2)$ with respect to v_2 as functions of s, t, k, b, the values of $v_1(b)$ and $v_2(b)$, and their derivatives of order less than or equal to n. This defines a mapping τ^n from $[0, 1]^2 \times (0, 1) \times I^n$ into $\Re^{2n + 2}$. Note that $\tau^n(V^n)$ is contained in a union of submanifolds of $\Re^{2n + 2}$, each of which is of dimension no greater than $n + 6$, the dimension of V^n.[5]

---

[5] See Jacobson [8, p. 312, Th. 16] and Whitney [16, Ths. 1 and 2] for details.

The set $\tau''(V^n)$ is significant because if ex ante efficiency is achievable for an admissible (R, T), then the $(n-1)$-jet of (R, T) at some point (v_1, v_2) is an element of $\tau''(V^n)$. We now show that, for $n > 6$ and any (R, T) within some open dense subset of H^{n-1}, no such point exists. Ex ante efficiency is therefore not achievable for a generic (R, T). Formally, the $(n-1)$-jet of any admissible (R, T) defines a compact 2-dimensional submanifold of $\mathfrak{R}^{2n+2}$ as (v_1, v_2) varies. Standard transversality arguments (e.g., see Hirsch [6]) imply that the 2-dimensional manifold determined by any (R, T) pair within some open dense subset of H^{n-1} will not intersect the $(n+6)$-dimensional (or smaller) submanifolds of $\tau''(V^n)$ whenever $2 + (n+6) < 2n + 2$, i.e., whenever $n > 6$. This completes the proof.

Proof of Theorem 6.1. Contrary to the theorem, assume that there exists some subset of $A(R, T)$ of positive measure where trade des not occur under the interim efficient, regular equilibrium (S, B). We show that the allocation rule (p, x) defined by (S, B) is dominated by the allocation rule we construct below.

The pair (S, B) defines the trading boundary $v_2 = B^{-1}S(v_1)$. Define a new trading boundary $\beta: [0, 1] \to [0, 1]$ by the formula $\beta(v_1) = \min(B^{-1}S(v_1), c_2^{-1}c_1(v_1))$. Since $B^{-1}S$ and $c_2^{-1}c_1$ are increasing, β is increasing. Define a trading rule $\phi: [0, 1]^2 \to [0, 1]$ by the formula

$$\phi(v_1, v_2) = \begin{cases} 1 & \text{if } v_2 \geq \beta(v_1), \\ 0 & \text{otherwise.} \end{cases} \tag{A.11}$$

Note that the support of ϕ is the disjoint union of (i) the support of the trading rule p defined by (S, B), (ii) a set of positive measure where $c_2(v_2) > c_1(v_1)$, and (iii) a set where $c_2(v_2) = c_1(v_1)$.

We now verify that ϕ satisfies conditions (2.22) and (2.23) of Theorem 2.1. Because β is nondecreasing, condition (2.22) is satisfied. To show that $\Gamma(\phi)$ is positive, we first note that $\Gamma(p) = 0$; the inequality then follows by considering the integrand in Γ, and the relationship between the supports of ϕ and p. The second part of Theorem 2.1 therefore implies that a payment rule χ exists such that (ϕ, χ) is an incentive feasible allocation rule.

Because (ϕ, χ) is incentive feasible, (2.23)–(2.25) apply and may be used to calculate the interim expected utility $U_i(v_i; \phi, \chi)$ of each trader type. This calculation shows that, for all $v_i \in [0, 1]$ and $i \in \{1, 2\}$, $U_i(v_i; \phi, \chi) \geq U_i(v_i; p, x)$ because the support of ϕ contains the support of p. We must also have strict inequality for some v_i because $\Gamma(\phi) > 0$. Therefore (ϕ, χ) interim dominates (p, x), which means that (S, B) is an interim inefficient equilibrium.

Proof of Theorem 6.2. This theorem is a direct application of Theorem

2.3, which provides sufficient conditions for interim efficiency. Let (p, x) be the allocation rule defined by the regular equilibrium (S, B). The first requirement of Theorem 2.3 is that $\Gamma(p) = 0$. As pointed out in Section 4, this is satisfied because $U_1(1; p, x) = U_2(0; p, x) = 0$ for every regular equilibrium of the k-double auction. Let $\tilde{\alpha}_1(v_1) = 1 - kS'(v_1)$ and $\tilde{\alpha}_2(v_2) \equiv 1 - (1 - k) B'(v_2)$. The hypothesis of the theorem we are proving then guarantees that, as Theorem 2.3 requires, (i) $\tilde{\alpha}_1$ and $\tilde{\alpha}_2$ have ranges within the unit interval and (ii) inequalities (2.27)–(2.28) are satisfied.

All that remains to be shown is that the trading rule p satisfies Eq. (2.29). It is satisfied if at every point (v_1, v_2) on the trading boundary

$$v_1 + [1 - \tilde{\alpha}_1(v_1)] R(v_1) = v_2 + [1 - \tilde{\alpha}_2(v_2)] T(v_2). \qquad \text{(A.12)}$$

This follows from (3.01)–(3.02), which are true for every point on the trading boundary of a regular equilibrium. Specifically, the Chatterjee–Samuelson equations (3.01)–(3.02) may be rewritten as

$$v_2 = S(v_1) + kS'(v_1) R(v_1) \qquad \text{(A.13)}$$

and

$$v_1 = B(v_2) + (1 - k) B'(v_2) T(v_2) \qquad \text{(A.14)}$$

at point (v_1, v_2) on the trading boundary $S(v_1) = B(v_2)$. Equation (A.12) is then obtained by solving (A.13), (A.14) for $S(v_1)$ and $B(v_2)$, respectively, and then equating these expressions.

Proof of Theorem 6.3. Fix k in $(0, 1)$. In Section 4, for the case of uniformly distributed reservation values (where $R(v_1) = v_1$ and $T(v_2) = 1 - v_2$), we demonstrated an equilibrium with linear strategies that is ex ante efficient. Inspection of this equilibrium shows that it satisfies the requirements of Theorem 6.2 with slack. Therefore, if an admissible (R', T') is sufficiently near $(R, T) = (v_1, 1 - v_2)$, an equilibrium exists for (R', T') that also satisfies the requirements of Theorem 6.2.

REFERENCES

1. V. I. ARNOLD, "Ordinary Differential Equations," MIT Press, Cambridge, MA, 1973.
2. K. CHATTERJEE AND W. SAMUELSON, Bargaining under incomplete information, *Oper. Res.* **31** (1983), 835–851.
3. C. D'ASPREMONT AND L. GERARD-VARET, Incentives and incomplete information, *J. Pub. Econ.* **11** (1979), 25–45.
4. D. GALE, Bargaining and competition, Part I: Characterization, *Econometrica* **54** (1986), 785–806.
5. J. HARSANYI, Games with incomplete information played by Bayesian players: Parts I, II, and III, *Management Sci.* **14** (1967–1968), 159–182, 320–334, 486–502.

6. M. W. Hirsch, "Differential Topology," Springer-Verlag, New York, 1976.
7. B. Holmstrom and R. Myerson, Efficient and durable decision rules with incomplete information, *Econometrica* **51** (1983), 1799–1820.
8. N. Jacobson, "Lectures in Abstract Algebra: III. Theory of Fields and Galois Theory," Springer-Verlag, New York, 1964.
9. W. Leininger, P. Linhart, and R. Radner, Equilibria of the sealed-bid mechanism for bargaining with incomplete information, *J. Econ. Theory* **48** (1989), 63–106.
10. R. Myerson, Optimal auction design, *Math. Oper. Res.* **6** (1981), 58–73.
11. R. Myerson, Two-person bargaining problems with incomplete information, *Econometrica* **52** (1984), 461–488.
12. R. Myerson, Analysis of two bargaining problems with incomplete information, *in* "Game-Theoretic Models of Bargaining," (A. Roth, Ed.), Cambridge Univ. Press, Cambridge, 1985.
13. R. Myerson and M. Satterthwaite, Efficient mechanisms for bilateral trading, *J. Econ. Theory* **29** (1983), 265–281.
14. R. Radner and A. Schotter, The sealed bid mechanism: An experimental study, *J. Econ. Theory* **48** (1989), 179–220.
15. V. Smith, A. Williams, K. Bratton, and V. Vannoni, Competitive market institutions: Double auctions vs. sealed bid-offer auctions, *Amer. Econ. Rev.* **72** (1982), 58–77.
16. H. Whitney, Elementary structure of real algebraic varieties, *Ann. of Math.* **66** (1957), 545–555.
17. S. Williams, Efficient performance in two agent bargaining, *J. Econ. Theory* **41** (1987), 154–172.
18. R. Wilson, Incentive efficiency of double auctions, *Econometrica* **53** (1985), 1101–1115.
19. R. Wilson, Efficient trading, *in* "Issues in Contemporary Microeconomics and Welfare" (G. Feiwel, Ed.), Macmillan, New York, 1985.

JOURNAL OF ECONOMIC THEORY **48**, 134–151 (1989)

155 – 72
0262
C 7 8, D42,   0226

The Bilateral Monopoly Model: Approaching Certainty under the Split-the-Difference Mechanism*

ELIZABETH M. BROMAN[†]

Department of Mathematical Sciences, The Johns Hopkins University, Baltimore, Maryland 21218

Received February 12, 1987; revised October 9, 1987

This paper describes a bilateral monopoly model in which two players trading an object submit bids from which a bargaining mechanism determines the transfer price and the probability of trade. The buyer knows only her own benefit from the trade and the probability distribution of the seller's cost. The paper first examines the equilibria of the model under certainty. It is shown that, if restricted to mixed strategies over finite sets, the equilibrium correspondence is lower hemi-continuous at continuity and upper hemi-continuous if restricted to pure strategies and finite prior distributions. *Journal of Economic Literature* Classification Number: 026. © 1989 Academic Press, Inc.

1. INTRODUCTION

In many corporations, one division makes a product that another uses. Often, such a company would like the producing division to sell the product to the consuming one. The firm must determine when this trade should take place and at what price. One way to do this is through a bargaining mechanism: the buyer and seller submit a bid, based on the true benefit or cost, to company headquarters where the mechanism determines the probability of transfer and the transfer price, given the two bids.

This situation is a bilateral monopoly with incomplete information: the buyer knows her benefit but does not know the seller's cost; instead she knows the probability distribution of possible costs. One trade mechanism that is often studied is the "split-the-difference" mechanism [3, 6]. Under this mechanism, trade takes place when the buyer's bid exceeds the seller's, and the price is the average of the two bids. The bilateral monopoly under this mechanism can be interpreted as a noncooperative game.

---

* The author would like to thank Harold Kuhn, Wolfgang Leininger, Peter Linhart, and Roy Radner for their help with this paper.

† This paper was written while the author was a student at Princeton University and a consultant at AT&T Bell Laboratories.

155

This paper will examine what happens to the equilibria of the game as the distribution of benefits and costs approaches certainty: is the correspondence of equilibria continuous at certainty? We find that it is continuous, given certain restrictions on strategies and priors. The question of continuity is important for several reasons. First, it was the certainty case that was originally considered by Nash so that case is interesting in itself. Furthermore, because many equilibria exist in the case of uncertainty [5], we would like to know if this is a result of the uncertainty. Without continuity of the equilibrium correspondence, the multiple equilibria could collapse into a single equilibrium under certainty. However, as we will see, there are multiple equilibria in the certainty case as well, which agrees with the continuity result. In the case of uncertainty, the equilibria range from being second-best to being worthless [5], while under certainty, all equilibria are efficient except one. Thus, although the equilibrium correspondence is continuous at certainty (in certain cases), inefficiency of equilibria is introduced gradually as uncertainty increases.

In Section 2, I formally present the bilateral monopoly model and the split-the-difference mechanism. In Section 3, the equilibria under certainty, both pure and mixed, are explored thoroughly: over any finite set of bids, there is a unique completely mixed equilibrium, there are countable sets which are supports of mixed strategy equilibria (though not all are), and no uncountable set is the support of a mixed strategy equilibrium (except possibly one which has a singular part). Lower hemi-continuity of the equilibrium correspondence is investigated in Section 4: are there, for all sequences of distributions approaching certainty, corresponding sequences of equilibria approaching each equilibrium under certainty? If we are restricted to finite mixed strategies, lower hemi-continuity can be proved. Finally, Section 5 examines the issue of whether or not the equilibrium correspondence is upper hemi-continuous at certainty, using a generalization of Berge's Maximum Theorem. It is proved that the correspondence is upper hemicontinuous when restricted to pure strategies and finite distributions.

2. The Model

There are two players, one who wishes to buy some fixed object from the other. The buyer receives benefit V from buying the item; it costs the seller C to provide it. V and C are each distributed on a compact set Ω, with a σ-algebra of measurable sets. There is a prior σ, a probability measure on $\Omega \times \Omega$, endowed with the product σ-algebra of measurable sets. This prior is known to each player. However, after V and C have been chosen by Nature, V is known only to the buyer and C only to the seller.

The buyer has a set of strategies $\{\beta\}$ which consists of all measurable functions from Ω to Ω: the strategy tells how she will bid given her actual benefit. Similarly, the seller has a set of strategies $\{\gamma\}$. Thus, each player chooses a strategy and then, after learning his true benefit or cost, makes the bid $v = \beta(V)$ or $c = \gamma(C)$.

A trade mechanism ρ consist of two matrices: ϕ_{vc}, the probability that trade takes place, and τ_{vc}, the transfer price at which trade occurs. Constraints on $\rho = (\varphi, \tau)$ are, for a given v and c,

$$0 \leqslant \phi_{vc} \leqslant 1, \tag{2.1}$$

and

$$c \leqslant \tau_{vc} \leqslant v. \tag{2.2}$$

Thus the split-the-difference mechanism consists of

$$\phi_{vc} = \begin{cases} 1 & \text{for} \quad v \geqslant c, \\ 0 & \text{for} \quad v < c, \end{cases} \tag{2.3}$$

$$\tau_{vc} = \begin{cases} (v + c)/2 & \text{for} \quad v \geqslant c, \\ 0 & \text{for} \quad v < c. \end{cases} \tag{2.4}$$

The buyer's expected profit, given σ and ρ, is

$$\pi_B(\beta, \gamma) = \int_{V,C} \phi_{\beta(V),\gamma(C)} (V - \tau_{\beta(V),\gamma(C)}) \, d\sigma, \tag{2.5}$$

while the seller's expected profit is

$$\pi_S(\beta, \gamma) = \int_{V,C} \phi_{\beta(V),\gamma(C)} (\tau_{\beta(V),\gamma(C)} - C) \, d\sigma. \tag{2.6}$$

We assume each player is risk-neutral and, hence, would like to maximize his expected profit for a given mechanism. Thus, a Nash equilibrium for the model will be a pair of strategies (β^*, γ^*), such that, for all β and γ,

$$\pi_B(\beta^*, \gamma^*) \geqslant \pi_B(\beta, \gamma^*), \tag{2.7}$$

and

$$\pi_S(\beta^*, \gamma^*) \geqslant \pi_S(\beta^*, \gamma). \tag{2.8}$$

Because a positive linear transformation of Ω does not change the equilibria of the model, one can let Ω be $[0, 1]$ without loss of generality. We let "certainty" be defined as $V = 1$ and $C = 0$, without loss of generality.

Given a distribution σ, we define $E(\sigma)$ to be the set of all Nash equilibria of the split-the-difference mechanism under σ. E is nonempty-valued because the following pair of strategies is an equilibrium for all σ:

$$\beta(V) = 0 \qquad \text{for all } V,$$

and

$$\gamma(C) = 1 \qquad \text{for all } C.$$

This is called the *trivial* equilibrium because trade does not take place.

There are several characteristics common to all equilibrium strategies under the split-the-difference mechanism, for any distribution. First, an equilibrium strategy for the buyer or seller is nondecreasing in V or C [3]. Second, in order for a strategy to be individually rational (i.e., not weakly dominated), $\beta(V) \leqslant V$ for all V and $\gamma(C) \geqslant C$ for all C—it never pays the buyer to bid more than her value [5]. A third property is that the supports of the buyer's and seller's strategies must be identical, except for the buyer's bids which are below all possible seller's bids and seller's bids above all possible buyer's bids. [5]

3. EQUILIBRIA UNDER CERTAINTY

The prior of certainty will be denoted by $\bar{\sigma}$: the buyer's benefit is always 1 and the seller's cost is always 0. The buyer's strategies are all bids v in $[0, 1]$ and her profit is

$$\phi_{vc}(1 - \tau_{vc}).$$

The seller's strategies are analogous. Here ϕ_{vc} and τ_{vc} are that of the split-the-difference mechanism.

3.1. *Pure Strategy Equilibria*

Under certainty, a pure strategy is any v for the buyer or c for the seller in the interval $[0, 1]$. By the Common Support Lemma, an equilibrium of pure strategies must consist of the buyer and seller both bidding some $x \in [0, 1]$. Gains from trade are $1 - x$ for the buyer and x for the seller. One exception to this is the trivial equilibrium discussed before in which the buyer bids 0 and the seller 1.

3.2. *Mixed Strategy Equilibria over Finite Sets*

To find a completely mixed strategy over a finite set of bids, it is possible to form the corresponding bimatrix game in which pure strategies are the bids in the set and compute its completely mixed equilibrium. In solving for an equilibrium over two bids a_i and a_j with $0 < a_i < a_j < 1$, one finds that the buyer's probabilities for bidding a_i and a_j, respectively, are

$$P_1(a_i, a_j) = \frac{a_j - a_i}{a_j + a_i}, \tag{3.1}$$

and

$$P_2(a_i, a_j) = \frac{2a_j}{a_j + a_i}. \tag{3.2}$$

Similarly, one finds for the seller,

$$Q_1(a_i, a_j) = \frac{2 - 2a_j}{2 - a_j a_i}, \tag{3.3}$$

and

$$Q_2(a_i, a_j) = \frac{a_j - a_i}{2 - a_j - a_i}. \tag{3.4}$$

For a general set of bids we have the following proposition:

PROPOSITION 1. *The buyer's completely mixed strategy over a set* $\{a_1, ..., a_n\}$, *with* $0 < a_1 < \cdots < a_n < 1$, *is*

$p_1 = P_1(a_1, a_2)$,

$p_k = P_1(a_k, a_{k+1}) P_2(a_1, a_2) \cdots P_2(a_{k-1}, a_k)$, *for all k*, $1 < k < n$,

and

$p_n = P_2(a_1, a_2) \cdots P_2(a_{n-1}, a_n). \tag{3.5}$

The seller's completely mixed strategy over the set is

$q_1 = Q_1(a_1, a_2) \cdots Q_1(a_{n-1}, a_n)$,

$q_k = Q_2(a_{k-1}, a_k) Q_1(a_k, a_{k+1}) \cdots Q_1(a_{n-1}, a_n)$, *for all k*, $1 < k < n$,

and

$q_n = Q_2(a_{n-1}, a_n). \tag{3.6}$

The buyer's value, using these mixed strategies, is

$$\frac{2^{n-1}(1 - a_1) \cdots (1 - a_n)}{(2 - a_1 - a_2) \cdots (2 - a_{n-1} - a_n)}. \tag{3.7}$$

Similarly, the seller's value is

$$\frac{2^{n-1}a_1 \cdots a_n}{(a_1 + a_2) \cdots (a_{n-1} + a_n)}. \tag{3.8}$$

Given a set of bids $\{a_1, \ldots, a_n\}$ which contains neither 0 or 1, any pair of equilibrium mixed strategies over a subset of this set gives an equilibrium using bids from the set. Thus, there are $2^n - 1$ Nash equilibria (pure and mixed) whose strategies have support in the set of nonempty subsets of $\{a_1, \ldots, a_n\}$. If 0 or 1 is in the set, $c = 1$ or $v = 0$ will dominate all other strategies for the seller or buyer.

3.3. Mixed Strategy Equilibria over Countable Sets

We are not able to solve explicitly for all mixed strategy equilibria of the split-the-difference mechanism, under certainty, whose strategies have (infinitely) countable supports. However, it is possible to show that certain countable sets are not supports of any mixed equilibrium strategy, and to give an example of an equilibrium defined on a countable set.

The following propositions state that no limit point of a countable set is played in equilibrium, and, if the supremum or infimum of a countable set is a limit point or there is a finite number of points above the greatest limit point or below the least limit point, then there is no completely mixed equilibrium over the set. The proofs are in Appendix B.

PROPOSITION 2. *Given a countable set* $\{a_n\}$ *with a subsequence* $\{a_{n_k}\}$ *converging to* a^* *and an equilibrium mixed strategy pair* (p, q) *each having a given subset of* $\{a_n\}$ *as support. Then,* $p_{a^*} = q_{a^*} = 0$, *unless* $a^* = \sup_n\{a_n\}$, *in which case* q_{a^*} *could be nonzero or,* $a^* = \inf_n\{a_n\}$, *in which case* p_{a^*} *could be nonzero.*

PROPOSITION 3. *Given a countable set* $S = \{a_n\}$. *Let* $\bar{a} = \sup S$ *and* $\underline{a} = \inf S$. *If* $\bar{a}$ *or* $\underline{a}$ *is a limit point of some subsequence of* $\{a_n\}$, *then there is no completely mixed strategy equilibrium over* S.

PROPOSITION 4. *Given a set* S *with the number of points above the highest limit point (or below the lowest limit point) finite. Then, there is no completely mixed strategy equilibrium over* S.

In spite of these results, there do exist equilibria over countable sets. Given a set consisting of an increasing sequence $\{a_i\}$ with limit a and a decreasing sequence $\{b_i\}$ with limit b where $a \leqslant b$. Then it is possible to compute the mixed strategy over this set by extending the result for a finite set. The probabilities for the buyer are

$$p_{a_1} = P_1(a_1, a_2),\tag{3.9}$$

$$p_{a_k} = P_1(a_k, a_{k+1}) \prod_{i=2}^{k} P_2(a_{i-1}, a_i) \qquad \text{for} \quad k > 1,\tag{3.10}$$

$$p_{b_1} = \prod_{i=2}^{\infty} P_2(a_{i-1}, a_i) P_2(b_i, b_{i-1}),\tag{3.11}$$

and

$$p_{b_k} = \frac{b_{k-1} - b_k}{2b_k} \prod_{i=2}^{\infty} P_2(a_{i-1}, a_i) \prod_{i=k}^{\infty} P_2(b_i, b_{i-1}) \qquad \text{for} \quad k > 1,\tag{3.12}$$

and, for the seller,

$$q_{a_1} = \prod_{i=2}^{\infty} Q_1(a_{i-1}, a_i) Q_1(b_i, b_{i-1}),\tag{3.13}$$

$$q_{a_k} = \frac{a_k - a_{k-1}}{2 - 2a_k} \prod_{i=k}^{\infty} Q_1(a_{i-1}, a_i) \prod_{i=2}^{\infty} Q_1(b_i, b_{i-1}) \qquad \text{for} \quad k > 1.\tag{3.14}$$

$$q_{b_1} = Q_2(b_2, b_1),\tag{3.15}$$

and

$$q_{b_k} = Q_2(b_{k+1}, b_k) \prod_{i=1}^{k-1} Q_1(b_{i+1}, b_i) \qquad \text{for} \quad k > 1.\tag{3.16}$$

If each infinite product converges to a number in $(0, 1)$, then we have a completely mixed equilibrium.

Let

$$a_i = \tfrac{1}{2} - (\tfrac{1}{2})^{i+1},\tag{3.17}$$

and

$$b_i = \tfrac{1}{2} + (\tfrac{1}{2})^{i+1} \cdot \qquad \text{for} \quad i = 1, 2, \dots.\tag{3.18}$$

Then,

$$P_2(a_{i-1}, a_i) = Q_1(b_i, b_{i-1})$$

$$= 1 - \frac{1}{2^{i+1} - 3}$$

and

$$Q_1(a_{i-1}, a_i) = P_2(b_i, b_{i-1})$$
$$= 1 + \frac{1}{2^{i+1} + 3}.$$

It can be shown that the infinite products in Eqs. (3.9)–(3.16) converge. Thus we have a completely mixed equilibrium over a countable set.

3.4. Mixed Strategy Equilibria over Uncountable Sets

PROPOSITION 5.   *There are no absolutely continuous mixed strategy equilibria over measurable sets.*

Proof. Assume there are p and q, absolutely continuous probability density functions which are nonzero only on a measurable set $S \subset [0, 1]$, so that $\{p, q\}$ form a mixed Nash equilibrium of the split-the-difference mechanism under certainty. (Actually, there may be points in S which only the seller is playing, if they are above all such points for the buyer and vice versa.) Then, for all c in S,

$$\pi_S(c) = \int_{\substack{V \in S \\ V \geqslant c}} \left(\frac{V + c}{2} \right) p(V) \, dV = \text{constant.} \qquad (3.19)$$

Let $\bar{s} = \sup S$. Then, given $\varepsilon > 0$,

$$\pi_S(\bar{s} - \varepsilon) = \int_{\substack{V \in S \\ V \geqslant \bar{s} - \varepsilon}} \left(\frac{V + \bar{s} - \varepsilon}{2} \right) p(V) \, dV.$$

Let ε approach 0, then $\pi_S(\bar{s} - \varepsilon)$ approaches 0. Thus, $\pi_S(c) = 0$ for all $c \in S$. But, $\pi_S(c)$ equals the expected value of $(V + c)/2$, which is positive. Thus, there can be no Nash equilibrium with absolutely continuous completely mixed strategies over measurable sets.   ∎

PROPOSITION 6.   *Let p be a probability density function on $[0, 1]$ which can be decomposed into p_1, an absolutely continuous function, and p_2, a probability mass function defined on a set $\{a_i\}$ (i.e. a step function). Then, there is no equilibrium in which the buyer plays p as a mixed strategy.*

The proof of Proposition 6 is similar to the proof of Proposition 5: the seller's expected profit function is set equal to a constant and a contradiction results.

Thus, we know there are no completely mixed equilibria whose strategies have uncountable sets without singular parts. It is an open question whether or not there are equilibria which have mixed strategies (over uncountable sets) with singular parts. It seems likely that none exist and even more likely that, if they did, no player would ever think of playing such a strategy.

4. LOWER HEMI-CONTINUITY

To show that the correspondence of equilibria, given a distribution, is lower hemi-continuous at certainty, we must show that for every sequence of distributions approaching certainty, there is a corresponding sequence of equilibria approaching each equilibrium under certainty. We will say that a sequence of equilibria approaches another equilibrium if their outcomes in the buyer and seller's expected profits approach the given certainty outcome; strategies may not converge, because they differ on a set with probability zero.

We use weak convergence (defined in Appendix A) to define sequences of distributions approaching certainty, denoted by $\bar{\sigma}$. So, $\bar{\sigma}(A) = 0$ for all Borel sets $A \subset [0, 1] \times [0, 1]$ which do not contain the point where $V = 1$ and $C = 0$. Thus, $\sigma_m \Rightarrow \bar{\sigma}$ if $\sigma_m(A) \to 0$ for all closed A not containing the point $(1, 0)$. Furthermore, $\sigma_m\{V = 1, C = 0\} \to 1$.

4.1. *Pure Equilibria*

Given σ_m, a probability measure on $[0, 1] \times [0, 1]$. Then the following pair of strategies is an equilibrium:

$$\beta(V) = \begin{cases} 0 & \text{if} \quad V \in [0, a), \\ a & \text{if} \quad V \in [a, 1], \end{cases} \tag{4.1}$$

$$\gamma(C) = \begin{cases} a & \text{if} \quad C \in [0, a), \\ 1 & \text{if} \quad C \in [a, 1]. \end{cases} \tag{4.2}$$

Thus, the outcome under this equilibrium is that trade takes place whenever $C < a$ and $V \geqslant a$, and the transfer price is a. The buyer's expected profit is

$$\int_{\substack{V \in [a,1] \\ C \in [0,a)}} (V - a) \, d\sigma_m \tag{4.3}$$

which approaches $1 - a$ as $\sigma_m \Rightarrow \bar{\sigma}$, and the seller's is

$$\int_{\substack{V \in [a,1] \\ C \in [0,a)}} (a - C) \, d\sigma_m \tag{4.4}$$

which approaches a. Thus, the outcomes of these equilibria approach the pure equilibria in the certainty case. The limits of these strategies are not the same as the pure strategies under certainty; however, they differ only when $V < a$ and $C \geqslant a$ which occurs with probability zero.

4.2. Mixed Strategy Equilibria over Finite Sets

Given a set $\{a_1, ..., a_n\}$ of possible bids with $0 < a_i < a_{i+1} < 1$ for all i and a distribution σ_m. Let β_k be the following strategy for the buyer:

$$\beta_k(V) = \begin{cases} 0 & \text{if } V \in [0, a_k), \\ a_k & \text{if } V \in [a_k, 1], \end{cases} \tag{4.5}$$

and γ_k be the following seller's strategy:

$$\gamma_k(C) = \begin{cases} a_k & \text{if } C \in [0, a_k), \\ 1 & \text{if } C \in [a_k, 1]. \end{cases} \tag{4.6}$$

Then, if the buyer is playing a completely mixed strategy $(p_1(\sigma_m), ..., p_n(\sigma_m))$ over the set of strategies $\{\beta_1, ..., \beta_n\}$, the seller's best response is to play some completely mixed strategy $(q_1(\sigma_m), ..., q_n(\sigma_m))$ over the set of strategies $\{\gamma_1, ..., \gamma_n\}$, because the seller's best response to any strategy β_i is the strategy γ_i.

Thus, to find an equilibrium in this case, we must solve for a $(p_1(\sigma_m), ..., p_n(\sigma_m))$ which makes $\pi_S(\gamma_k)$ constant for all k (and similarly for the seller's strategy). We get the linear system

$$\begin{bmatrix} 1 & 1 & 1 & \cdots & 1 & 1 \\ A_{11} & -A_{12} & -A_{13} & \cdots & -A_{1,n-1} & -A_{1,n} \\ 0 & A_{22} & -A_{23} & \cdots & -A_{2,n-1} & -A_{2,n} \\ \cdot & 0 & A_{33} & & & \cdot \\ \cdot & \cdot & 0 & & & \cdot \\ \cdot & \cdot & \cdot & & & \cdot \\ \cdot & \cdot & \cdot & \cdots & -A_{n-2,n-1} & -A_{n-2,n} \\ 0 & 0 & 0 & ..0 & A_{n-1,n-1} & -A_{n-1,n} \end{bmatrix} \begin{pmatrix} p_1(\sigma_m) \\ \vdots \\ p_n(\sigma_m) \end{pmatrix} = \begin{pmatrix} 1 \\ 0 \\ \vdots \\ 0 \end{pmatrix}$$

$$\tag{4.7}$$

where

$$A_{ij} = \int_{\substack{V \in [a_j, 1] \\ C \in [0, a_i)}} \left(\frac{a_j - a_i}{2} \right) d\sigma_m + \int_{\substack{V \in [a_j, 1] \\ C \in [a_i, a_i + 1)}} (a_j - C) \, d\sigma_m. \tag{4.8}$$

By induction, it can be shown that the above matrix is nonsingular; thus, there is an equilibrium. Then, one can show that the matrix converges to the matrix from the certainty case as $\sigma_m \Rightarrow \bar{\sigma}$. If a sequence of nonsingular matrices converges to another then the sequence of their inverses converges to the inverse of their limit. Thus, the solutions $p_i(\sigma_m)$ converge to the p_i in the certainty case as $\sigma_m \Rightarrow \bar{\sigma}$. It is then simple to prove that the seller's and buyer's expected profits converge to the profits under certainty. Thus, we can prove the following theorem:

THEOREM 1. *For every equilibrium under certainty with a finite support and every sequence of distributions weakly converging to σ_m, there is a sequence of equilibria corresponding to σ_m whose outcomes converge to the equilibrium outcome under certainty.*

4.3. *Mixed Strategies over Countable Sets*

Unfortunately, it is not easy to extend the arguments of the last section in order to prove lower hemi-continuity of equilibria mixing over countable sets, because such equilibria cannot be found explicitly and not all countable sets are supports of mixed equilibria. However, there are two methods that could possibly extend the proof, though each appears to be difficult. First, one could try approaching a countable set with a sequence of finite sets, so that the sequence of sequences approaching equilibria over the finite sets approaches each countable equilibrium. Another possible method of proof is to extend the proof for finite sets using linear operator theory.

5. UPPER HEMI-CONTINUITY

In order to prove that the equilibrium correspondence is upper hemi-continuous, we need a form of the Maximum Theorem. However, Berge's Maximum Theorem requires the function being maximized to be continuous, and the profit function in our game is not continuous: with a small change in strategies, trades may appear or disappear, so that the profit function will have discontinuities.

Allowing only discrete distributions and pure strategies, we can show that the profit function is upper semi-continuous. Then, we can use a generalization of the Maximum Theorem which holds for a class of upper semi-continuous functions, those which are graph-continuous with respect to a correspondence a.

5.1. *Leininger's Generalized Maximum Theorem*

DEFINITION. Let S and T be metric spaces. The function $f: S \times T \to \mathbf{R}$ is *graph-continuous* with respect to the correspondence $\alpha: S \to T$ if, for any (x, y) with $y \in a(x)$, one can find $r(x, y) \in T$ with $r(x, y) \in \alpha(x)$ such that, given $\varepsilon > 0$, there exists $\delta > 0$ so that $d(x, x') < \delta$ implies $|f(x', r(x', y)) - f(x, y)| < \varepsilon$.

That is, a function f is graph-continuous with respect to α, if, when we change x slightly, we can find a new y with $y \in \alpha(x)$ which keeps f close to the previous level.

Now, we can state the generalized Maximum Theorem:

GENERALIZED MAXIMUM THEOREM (Leininger). *S and T are metric spaces. Given a correspondence* $\alpha: S \to T$ *which is compact-valued and continuous and a function* $f: S \times T \to \mathbf{R}$ *which is upper semi-continuous and graph-continuous with respect to* α. *Then:*

(i)   *the function* $m: S \to \mathbf{R}$ *with* $m(x) = \max\{f(x, y) \mid y \in \alpha(x)\}$ *is well defined and upper semi-continuous, and*
(ii)   *the correspondence* $\Phi: S \to T$ *with* $\Phi(x) = \{y \mid y \in \alpha(x), f(x, y) = m(x)\}$ *is nonempty-valued, compact-valued, and upper hemi-continuous.*

5.2. Properties of the Expected Profit Function

We will prove upper semi-continuity and graph-continuity of π_{B} with respect to a correspondence α_{B} for discrete distributions and pure strategies. (All derivations and proofs will be given for the buyer's expected profit function, since the seller's function is analogous.) Thus, we only allow benefits and costs from the set

$$\Omega = \left\{0, \frac{1}{n}, \frac{2}{n}, ..., \frac{n-1}{n}, 1\right\}$$

for some fixed n. Priors are all possible $n+1 \times n+1$ matrices σ_{ij}, where $\sigma_{ij} = \mathrm{Prob}\{V = i/n, C = j/n\}$. Let the space of all such matrices be Σ. The buyer and seller's pure strategies are vectors $(\beta_0, \beta_1, ..., \beta_n)$ and $(\gamma_0, \gamma_1, ..., \gamma_n)$, where β_i and γ_i are the buyer's and seller's bids, respectively, given the value i/n. We can restrict the space of strategies by allowing only those with two properties we know are characteristic of equilibrium strategies, as discussed in Section 2.5. First, we assume that strategies are nondecreasing, and, second, that $\beta(V) \leqslant V$ for all V and $\gamma(C) \geqslant C$ for all C. Then, let X_{B} be the space of the buyer's strategies: all $(n+1)$-component vectors which are nondecreasing and for which $\beta_i \leqslant i/n$ for all i. Define X_{S} for the seller analogously.

The buyer's expected profit function $\pi_{\mathrm{B}}: \Sigma \times X_{\mathrm{S}} \times X_{\mathrm{B}} \to \mathbf{R}$ is

$$\pi_{\mathrm{B}}(\sigma, \gamma, \beta) = \sum_{j=0}^{n} \sum_{i=0}^{n} I(\beta_i, \gamma_j) \left[\frac{i}{n} - \left(\frac{\beta_i + \gamma_j}{2}\right)\right] \sigma_{ij} \qquad (5.1)$$

where

$$I(\beta_i, \gamma_j) = \begin{cases} 1 & \text{if } \beta_i \geqslant \gamma_j, \\ 0 & \text{otherwise.} \end{cases} \tag{5.2}$$

We must show that $\pi_B(\sigma, \gamma, \beta)$ is upper semi-continuous in (σ, γ). Let the metric on $\Sigma \times X_S$ be

$$d((\sigma, \gamma), (\sigma', \gamma')) = \max \{ \sup_{i,j} |\sigma_{ij} - \sigma'_{ij}|, \sup_j |\gamma_j - \gamma'_j| \}, \tag{5.3}$$

and, similarly, use the supremum metric for X_B.

To prove upper semi-continuity of π_B, find a δ_{ij} for each pair (i, j) so that

$$I(\beta_i, \gamma'_j) \left[\frac{i}{n} - \left(\frac{\beta_i + \gamma'_j}{2} \right) \right] \sigma'_{ij} < I(\beta_i, \gamma_j) \left[\frac{i}{n} - \left(\frac{\beta_i + \gamma_j}{2} \right) \right] \sigma_{ij} + \frac{\varepsilon}{(n+1)^2} \tag{5.4}$$

for $d((\sigma, \gamma), (\sigma', \gamma')) < \delta_{ij}$. Since there is a finite number of pairs (i, j), $\delta = \min_{i,j} \{\delta_{ij}\}$ exists. Thus,

$$\pi_B(\sigma', \gamma', \beta) < \pi_B(\sigma, \gamma, \beta) + \varepsilon \tag{5.5}$$

for $d((\sigma, \gamma), (\sigma', \gamma')) < \delta$. This proves:

LEMMA 3. $\pi_B(\sigma, \gamma, \beta)$ *is jointly upper semi-continuous in* σ *and* γ.

In order to use the Generalized Maximum Theorem, we need a correspondence α_B and metric spaces S and T. If these are defined properly and $f = \pi_B$, Φ_B will be the buyer's best-reply correspondence. Thus, we define S to be $\Sigma \times X_S$ and T to be X_B: the buyer faces a state which gives the prior and the seller's strategy, and responds with the strategy which maximizes her expected profit. The correspondence α_B can be interpreted as a feasibility correspondence, giving all strategies which are feasible as a reply. Since we have eliminated all strategies that are not individually rational, we define $\alpha_B: \Sigma \times X_S \to X_B$ such that $\alpha_B(\sigma, \gamma) = X_B$. This correspondence is obviously continuous and compact-valued.

To prove graph continuity, we first show that if γ changes in one component and σ changes in any way, then the buyer can choose a new β to keep her expected profit "close" to the original. That is, if the seller's strategy becomes

$$\gamma' = (\gamma_0, ..., \gamma_{j-1}, \gamma_j + \delta, \gamma_{j+1}, ..., \gamma_n)$$

and σ changes so that $\sup_{i,j} |\sigma_{ij} - \sigma'_{ij}| < \delta$, then the buyer uses the strategy with components:

$$\beta'_i = \begin{cases} \gamma_j + \delta & \text{if } \gamma_j \leqslant \beta_i < \gamma_j + \delta \leqslant i/n, \\ i/n & \text{if } \gamma_j \leqslant \beta_i \leqslant i/n < \gamma_j + \delta, \\ \beta_i & \text{otherwise.} \end{cases}$$

It can be shown that β' is in $\alpha(\sigma', \gamma')$ and that the change in expected profits for the buyer is less than $\varepsilon/(n+1)$. Then, one can generalize this argument for the case of the seller changing several components of his strategy. Thus we get the following result:

LEMMA 4. $\pi_B(\sigma, \gamma, \beta)$ is graph-continuous with respect to α_B.

Using the previous two lemmas and the Generalized Maximum Theorem we get:

LEMMA 5.   *The buyer's best reply correspondence*

$$\Phi_B(\sigma, \gamma) = \{ \beta \mid \pi_B(\sigma, \gamma, \beta) = \max_\beta \{ \pi_B(\sigma, \gamma, \beta) \} \}$$

is upper hemi-continuous.

THEOREM 2.   *The Nash equilibria correspondence* $E: \Sigma \to X_B \times X_S$ *defined by*

$$E(\sigma) = \{ \text{all Nash equilibria of the bargaining game, given a distribution } \sigma \}$$

is upper hemi-continuous on Σ.

This is proved by taking the projection of Φ_B and Φ_S onto σ and showing that these are upper hemi-continuous. $E(\sigma)$ is the intersection of two upper hemi-continuous correspondences so it is upper hemi-continuous [1].

In extending the proof to include mixed strategies, it is possible to show that the expected profit function is upper semi-continuous, but proving graph continuity is more difficult. If we can prove graph continuity in that case (for discrete distributions), it can probably be extended to the space of all distributions. However, it is not clear that π_B is upper semi-continuous for this case unless we assume that β and γ are continuous, which is too restrictive. Thus, the upper hemi-continuity of equilibrium correspondences for more general distributions and strategies is an open question.

6. Conclusion

In writing this paper, I set out to prove that the correspondence which consists of all Nash equilibria of the split-the-difference game under a given distribution is continuous at certainty. This turns out to be difficult to prove for *all* distributions and *all* equilibria. Instead, I have proved that the equilibrium correspondence consisting of pure equilibria over discrete distributions is continuous at certainty.

There are several important results contained in this continuity result. First, I have made a thorough investigation of the equilibria under certainty, deriving all finite mixed strategy equilibria, showing what mixed equilibria over countable sets might look like, and proving that there are no equilibria over uncountable sets (except possibly singular sets). Second, I have shown that, if we restrict ourselves to finite mixed strategies, the correspondence is lower hemi-continuous at certainty (leaving open only the question of infinite countable supports and singular strategies). Last, I have proved that the correspondence is upper hemi-continuous when restricted to pure strategies and finite distributions. Thus, the correspondence is continuous if the priors are finite and only pure strategies are used.

There remain several open questions: Can the countable sets which are supports of mixed strategy equilibrium be found explicitly along with their equilibria? Are there equilibria over uncountable sets with singular parts? Is the correspondence upper hemi-continuous for all strategies and distributions?

APPENDIX A: Weak Convergence

Given a metric space X, let $M(X)$ be the space of all probability measures defined on all Borel sets of X. Let μ be a measure in $M(X)$. We say that a sequence of measures μ_n converges weakly to μ (written $\mu_n \Rightarrow \mu$), if

$$\lim_{n \to x} \mu_n(A) = \mu(A)$$

for every Borel set $A \subset X$ with $\mu(\partial A) = 0$, where ∂A is the boundary of A.

This definition of convergence can be shown to be equivalent to the following: $\mu_n \Rightarrow \mu$ if and only if $\int f \, d\mu_n \to \int f \, d\mu$ for all continuous, bounded, real-valued f defined on X.

Given this sense of weak convergence, we have a topology on the space $M(X)$, called the weak topology. That is, we should say that μ_n converges to μ under the weak topology.

Topsoe defined the weak topology so that $\mu_n \Rightarrow \mu$ if and only if $\int f\, d\mu_n \to \int f\, d\mu$ for all upper semi-continuous, bounded, real-valued functions on X (upper semi-continuity is defined on page 39 of [8]). This is the topology used in this paper.

Another fact we need is that X is a compact metric space, if and only if $M(X)$ is a compact metric space. This holds for both definitions of the weak topology and was proved in Parthasarathy [7].

APPENDIX B: Proofs from Section 3.3

Proof of Proposition 2. Given a^*, a limit point which is not the infimum of $\{a_n\}$. Then, for small enough $\varepsilon > 0$,

$$\sum_{a_k \geqslant a^* - \varepsilon} \left(\frac{a^* - \varepsilon + a_k}{2} \right) p_k = \sum_{a_k \geqslant a^* + \varepsilon} \left(\frac{a^* + \varepsilon + a_k}{2} \right) p_k, \qquad \text{(B.1)}$$

since the seller's profits must be constant on $\{a_n\}$. Both sides of (B.1) are positive since a^* is a limit point and there exist $a_k > a^*$, and, by the Common Support Lemma, q is nonzero on $[a^* - \varepsilon, a^* + \varepsilon]$. This implies

$$\sum_{a_k \in [a^* - \varepsilon, a^* + \varepsilon)} \left(\frac{a^* - \varepsilon + a_k}{2} \right) p_k = \sum_{a_k \geqslant a^* + \varepsilon} \varepsilon p_k \leqslant \varepsilon.$$

Let ε approach 0. Then

$$a^* p_{a^*} = 0.$$

Thus, p_{a^*} must equal zero, so q_{a^*} is also zero, by the Common Support Lemma. If $a^* = \sup_n \{a_n\}$, (B.1) still holds, though the right-hand side is zero, but q_{a^*} is not necessarily zero.

Similarly, if there are $a_k < a^*$, one can prove that $p_{a^*} = q_{a^*} = 0$, unless $a^* = \inf_n \{a_n\}$. Therefore, no limit point of a countable set can be in the support of both p and q for a Nash equilibrium. ∎

Proof of Proposition 3. Assume $\bar{a}$ is a limit point of a subsequence of S. Then,

$$\pi_S(c) = \sum_{a_k \geqslant c} \left(\frac{a_k + c}{2} \right) p_k$$

$$\leqslant \bar{a} \sum_{a_k \geqslant c} p_k.$$

Because there is an infinite number of $a_k \in [c, \bar{a})$ and $\sum p_k = 1$, given $\varepsilon > 0$, we can find a $\bar{c}$ such that

$$\sum_{a_k \geqslant \bar{c}} p_k \leqslant \varepsilon.$$

For this $\bar{c}$,

$$\pi_S(\bar{c}) \leqslant \bar{a}\varepsilon.$$

Thus, $\pi_S(c)$ goes to zero as ε approaches zero. Hence, there can be no completely mixed equilibrium on S since π_S must be constant and cannot equal zero everywhere. The case where the infimum is a limit point can be proved by looking at the buyer's expected profits. ∎

Proof of Proposition 4.   Without loss of generality, assume there is one point $a \in S$ above a subsequence $\{a_i\} \subset S$ increasing to $a^* < a$. Then,

$$\pi_S(a) = a p_a.$$

Let $c < a^*$. As in the previous proposition, we can choose c so that $\sum_{a_k \geqslant c} p_k \leqslant \varepsilon$, given $\varepsilon > 0$. Then,

$$\pi_S(c) = \left(\frac{a+c}{2}\right) p_a + \sum_{a_k \geqslant c} \left(\frac{a_k+c}{2}\right) p_k$$

$$< \left(\frac{a+a^*}{2}\right) p_a + a^* \sum_{a_k \geqslant c} p_k$$

$$\leqslant \left(\frac{a+a^*}{2}\right) p_a + a^*\varepsilon$$

$$\rightarrow \left(\frac{a+a^*}{2}\right) p_a.$$

But, this is strictly less than $a p_a$. Thus, $\pi_S(c)$ cannot be constant; there is no equilibrium. The proof is similar if there is a finite number of points below the least limit point. ∎

References

1. C. BERGE, "Topological Spaces," Oliver & Boyd, Edinburgh, 1963.
2. E. M. BROMAN, "The Bilateral Monopoly Model: Approaching Certainty under the Split-the-Difference Mechanism," Senior thesis, Princeton University, May 1986.
3. K. CHATTERJEE AND W. SAMUELSON, Bargaining under incomplete information, *Oper. Res.* **31** (1983), 835–851.

4. W. LEININGER, A generalization of the "maximum theorem," *Econ. Lett.* **15** (1984), 309–313.
5. W. LEININGER, P. B. LINHART, AND R. RADNER, The sealed-bid mechanism for bargaining with incomplete information, AT&T Bell Laboratories, January 1987.
6. R. B. MYERSON AND M. A. SATTERTHWAITE, Efficient mechanisms for bilateral trading, *J. Econ. Theory* **29** (1983), 265–281.
7. K. R. PARTHASARATHY, "Probability Measures on Metric Spaces," Academic Press, New York, 1967.
8. F. TOPSOE, "Topology and Measure," Lecture Notes in Mathematics, Vol. 133, Springer-Verlag, Berlin, 1970.

JOURNAL OF ECONOMIC THEORY **48**, 179–220 (1989)

173 – 214

1989

The Sealed-Bid Mechanism: An Experimental Study*

02 62

C 7 8

C 9 t

ROY RADNER

AT & T Bell Laboratories, 600 Mountain Road, Murray Hill, New Jersey 07974

AND

ANDREW SCHOTTER

New York University, Department of Economics, 269 Mercer Street, New York, New York 10003

Received March 11, 1987; revised September 22, 1988

This paper presents the results of a set of experiments performed to test the properties of a bargaining mechanism (called the *sealed-bid mechanism*) used to structure bargaining under incomplete information. Our results indicate that the mechanism performs quite well. When using it, experimental subjects are able to capture a large portion of the potential gains from trade. In addition, the behavior of the subjects is qualitatively consistent with one particular equilibrium of the mechanism, namely, the one with linear bidding strategies. Finally, an experiment performed allowing experienced subjects to repeat the experiment for relatively large numbers of rounds, suggests that, with enough experience, other equilibria may appear, in which the subjects use "step function" strategies. *Journal of Economic Literature* Classification Numbers: 022, 026. © 1989 Academic Press, Inc.

1. INTRODUCTION

This paper presents the results of a set of experiments performed to test the theoretical and empirical properties of a bargaining mechanism (called the *sealed-bid mechanism*) used to structure bargaining under incomplete information. The mechanism, first studied by Chatterjee and Samuelson [4], has been investigated in greater detail by Myerson and Satterthwaite [11] and more recently by Leininger *et al.* [8]. In this paper the sealed-bid

* The authors would like to thank Ken Rogoza for his valuable research assistance on this paper. The research presented in this paper was made possible by a grant from the C. V. Starr Center for Applied Economics. The views expressed here are those of the authors, and do not necessarily reflect the views of AT & T Bell Laboratories.

173

mechanism is tested by performing a set of eight different experiments. Our results indicate that the mechanism performs quite well. When using it, experimental subjects are able to capture a large portion of the potential gains from trade. In addition, the behavior of the subjects is qualitatively consistent with one particular equilibrium of the mechanism, namely, the one with linear bidding strategies. However, while experimental sellers tended, on average, to bid according to their predicted linear strategy, buyers, while bidding in a linear fashion, tended not to shave their bids by as much as the linear equilibrium bidding strategy dictates. This overbidding is partly responsible for the good performance of the mechanism. Finally, an experiment performed allowing experienced subjects to repeat the experiment for relatively large numbers of rounds suggests that, with enough experience, other equilibria may appear, in which the subjects use "step-function" strategies.

In this paper we shall proceed as follows: In Section 2, we motivate the problem by quickly reviewing the sealed-bid mechanism and the different types of equilibria it can generate. In Section 3 we present our experimental design. In Section 4 the results of our sealed-bid mechanism experiments are presented. Section 5 presents the results of our remaining experiments run to test a set of auxiliary questions about the mechanism and its robustness. Finally, in Section 6, we offer some conclusions and suggestions for further experimental work on this topic.

2. The Sealed-Bid Mechanism and Its Equilibria

A potential buyer B and a potential seller S are bargaining over the terms of a possible trade of a single object. If the object is traded, the value to B is V and the cost to S is C. (The seller incurs no cost if there is no trade.) The *sealed-bid mechanism* works as follows: B and S simultaneously choose bids, v and c, respectively. If $v \geq c$, then trade takes place, and B pays S the price $P = (v + c)/2$, i.e., the average of the two bids. If $v < c$, then no trade takes place and B pays S nothing.

Suppose that at the time of bidding, B knows V but not C, and S knows C but not V. This situation is modelled by supposing that V and C are random variables with a joint probability distribution, called the *prior*, which is known to both parties. Before the bidding takes place, B observes V but not C, and S observes C but not V. B's *strategy* is a function β that determines his bid v for each value of V, and S's strategy is a function ψ that determines his bid c for each value of C. Thus

$$v = \beta(V),$$
$$c = \psi(C) \tag{2.1}$$

The buyer's and seller's profits are, respectively,

$$\Phi_B = \begin{cases} V - (v+c)/2, & v \geqslant c, \\ 0, & v < c, \end{cases}$$

$$\Phi_S = \begin{cases} (v+c)/2 - C, & v \geqslant c, \\ 0, & v < c. \end{cases} \tag{2.2}$$

Suppose that the parties are risk-neutral, so that, for a given pair of strategies, β and ψ, the respective expected utilities are

$$\pi_B(\beta, \psi) = E\Phi_B,$$
$$\pi_S(\beta, \psi) = E\Phi_S, \tag{2.3}$$

where the expectation is taken with respect to the prior distribution of V and C. Equations (2.1)–(2.3) determine a noncooperative game. As usual, an equilibrium of the game is a pair of strategies such that neither player can increase his expected utility (expected profit) by unilaterally changing his strategy.

If V and C are uniformly distributed over the closed interval $[0, 100]$, then as Chatterjee and Samuelson [4] have demonstrated, there exists a pair of linear bidding strategies which together form an equilibrium of the game defined by the sealed-bid mechanism.

These strategies are

$$v = \begin{cases} V, & V < 25, \\ 25/3 + (2/3)\,V, & V \geqslant 25, \end{cases}$$

$$c = \begin{cases} C, & C > 75, \\ 25 + (2/3)\,C, & C \leqslant 75. \end{cases} \tag{2.4}$$

At the equilibrium, the buyer bids his value for all realizations less than 25, but underbids for all realizations above that value, while the seller bids his cost for all realizations greater than 75, and overbids for all realizations below that value.

Myerson and Satterthwaite [11] have demonstrated that this particular equilibrium has a very strong welfare property: it maximizes the ex ante gains from trade[1] that can be achieved at any Bayesian–Nash equilibrium of any individually rational bargaining mechanism employed in this environment, in which what the seller receives equals what the buyer pays. If this were the only equilibrium of the sealed-bid mechanism, a strong case could be made for its use. However, as Leininger et al. [8] have demonstrated, this mechanism has a multitude of other equilibria, some of

---

[1] That is, the expected total profits of the two players, $\pi_B + \pi_S$.

which form a two-parameter family of nonlinear differentiable bidding functions for the bargainers while others have them use discontinuous step functions. More disturbing, however, is the fact that the efficiency of these other equilibria vary from second-best efficient to practically worthless. It is this theoretical morass that furnishes the inspiration for our experiment. We ask four simple questions. Did buyers and sellers in our experiment tend to use linear strategies? If they did, did they use the ones predicted by the equilibrium? How well did the mechanism perform and what accounts for this performance? Does the bidding behavior of subjects change as the number of rounds in the experiment increases? The answers to these questions have significance for the eventual implementation of the sealed-bid mechanism. Furthermore, since the sealed-bid mechanism for two players is a special case of the double auction, our results also have relevance for that literature (see Cox *et al.* [5]). If buyers or sellers, despite the plethora of equilibria, tend either to latch on to the predicted linear equilibrium, or do someting else which turns out to be efficient, then the results of Leininger *et al.* [8] are less disturbing. If neither of these possibilities is true, we may be led to search for other mechanisms to structure bargaining in environments with incomplete information.

3. The Experiment and the Experimental Design

(i) *The Experiment*

The experiment was quite simple.[2] Student subjects were recruited from undergraduate economics courses at New York University and brought into a room in groups of about 20. The chairs were arranged so as to minimize eye contact among the subjects. Written instructions were then handed out and subjects randomly assigned the role of buyer and seller. These designations were kept throughout the entire experiment. Before reading the instructions and having questions about them answered, each seller/buyer drew 15 envelopes from a pile of 500. Each envelope contained a slip of paper with a number written on it. The numbers were generated randomly according to a commonly known probability distribution. If the subject was a buyer, then this random number indicated the value to him of the good being sold in that round. If the subject was a seller, the number represented the cost of producing the good in that round. After observing the realization in the envelope and recording it on their work sheets, subjects then wrote their bids on pieces of paper and handed them to a set of experimental administrators who collected them. When the slips of the buyers and sellers were brought to the front of the room, they were ran-

---

[2] Appendix A presents a sample of the instruction sheets used in three of the experiments.

domly sorted into pairs, each containing the bid of one buyer and one seller. These bids were then compared, and, using the rules of the sealed-bid mechanism defined in Section 2, prices and payoffs were determined. The price and trade results of these transactions were then distributed back to the subjects, and the next round began, which was conducted in an identical manner. In subsequent rounds subjects were paired against the same pair member.[3] In all experiments except one, only information about a subject's own transaction was transmitted. Despite the danger of introducing repeated-game elements into what is intended to be a test of a static theory, we felt that this design feature was necessary if the subjects were to successfully select one equilibrium from the multitude defined by the mechanism. Everything described so far was common knowledge to the subjects except, of course, for the realizations of the random numbers and the identity of a subject's pair member. All values and costs were denumerated in a fictitious currency called francs and converted into dollars at the end of the experiment, at the rate of either 1 franc = $.05 or 1 franc = $.01 depending upon the parameters of the experiment. Final payoffs in the experiment were determined by converting the cumulative franc payoffs of a subject over the 15 rounds of the experiment. Average payoffs tended to be about $13.00 for an hour and a half, with a considerable range and variance. Payoffs in the $20.00 to $25.00 range were fairly common. (In one face-to-face bargaining experiment, a subject earned $45.00.) Finally, in all experiments the subjects used were not experienced either in this experiment or in any others.

(ii) The Experimental Design

To investigate the properties of the sealed-bid mechanism, we ran eight distinct experiments with eight different groups of subjects. Each group of subjects performed one experiment with one set of parameters for 15 rounds (except for the group performing Experiment 6 who did it for 40 rounds). The experiments performed are described in Table I.

Experiment 1 was a baseline. It employed a uniform prior distribution for both buyers and sellers. Its linear equilibrium is identical to the equilibrium of Chatterjee and Samulelson [4] described in (2.4). In Experiment 2, we repeated Experiment 1 except for the fact that after each round price information concerning all pairs was written on the blackboard.[4] This extra information was provided in order to enhance learning without increasing the number of repetitions in the experiment and gave more

---

[3] These experimental procedures were used successfully in the past by Bull et al. [3] where it was observed that the equilibrium of the symmetric game performed there was insensitive to the rotation of pair members between rounds.

[4] Since subjects did not know the values and costs of others, this procedure did not violate the precept of privacy (see Smith [15] and Wilde [16].

TABLE I

Experimental Design

Exp	Trade rule	Price rule	Prior distributions	Linear equilibrium
1	Trade if $v \geqslant c$	$P = (v + c)/2$	Uniform $[0, 100]$	See (2.4)
2	Trade if $v \geqslant c$	$P = (v + c)/2$	Uniform $[0, 100]$	Same as in Experiment 1
3	Trade if $v \geqslant c + 25$	$P = (v + c + 50)/3$	Uniform $[0, 100]$	$v = V$, $c = C$
4	Trade if seller accepts	$P = v$	Uniform $[0, 100]$	$v = (1/2) V$ accept if $v \geqslant C$
5	Trade if $v \geqslant c$	$P = (v + c)/2$	Buyer: $1 - \left(\dfrac{100 - V}{100}\right)^{.04}$ Seller: $\left(\dfrac{C}{100}\right)^{.04}$	See note 7
6	Trade if $v \geqslant c$	$P = (v + c)/2$	Buyer: $1 - \left(\dfrac{100 - V}{100}\right)^{.04}$ Seller: $\left(\dfrac{C}{100}\right)^{.04}$	Same as in Experiment 5
7	Trade if agreement reached	As agreed to	Buyer: $1 - \left(\dfrac{100 - V}{100}\right)^{.04}$ Seller: $\left(\dfrac{C}{100}\right)^{.04}$	None
8	Trade if $v \geqslant c$	$P = (v + c)/2$	Uniform $[0, 100]$	Same as Experiment 1

Notes:

[1] In all experiments except Experiment 6 subjects had no prior experimental experience. Subjects in Experiment 6 were experienced in this experiment.

[2] In all experiments except Experiment 2 subjects were informed only about the results of their trade after each round. In Experiment 2 subjects received information about all prices formed in each round.

[3] In all experiments except Experiment 6 the experiment lasted for 15 round. In Experiment 6 there were 40 rounds.

[4] In all experiments except Experiment 6, 1 franc = $.05. In Experiment 6, 1 franc = $.018.

[5] In Experiment 8 we employed the Roth–Berg et al. risk neutrality inducement procedure. See the text for a description.

[6] Number of subjects: Experiment 1 = 14, Experiment 2 = 14, Experiment 3 = 10, Experiment 4 = 18, Experiment 5 = 22, Experiment 6 = 18, Experiment 7 = 24, Experiment 8 = 18.

[7] In Experiments 5 and 6 the linear equilibrium strategies are: Buyer: bid value if $V < 36$, bid $20.25 + 0.438(V)$ if $V \geqslant 36$; Seller: bid cost if $C > 64$, bid $36 + 0.438(C)$ if $C \leqslant 64$.

information about the bid and offer distributions of the other subjects. Experiment 3 tests a particular direct form of the mechanism and hence the Revelation Principle. It represents subjects with an experiment that is strategically isomorphic to the baseline experiment but has a different set of price and trade rules. In this experiment, subjects again submit bids. Here, however, the rules dictate that the buyer's bid must exceed the seller's by 25 or more in order to make a trade. If a trade is made, the price is $P = (v + c + 50)/3$.

With this set of rules, the Revelation Principle dictates that, at the linear equilibrium, each buyer bids his value and each seller bids his cost. Experiment 4 tested the robustness of the sealed-bid mechanism to changes in its price-formation rule. While in Experiment 1 price is set by the rule $P = kv + (1 - k)c$ with $k = \frac{1}{2}$, in Experiment 4, $k = 1$. This is equivalent to a mechanism in which the buyer makes a take-it-or-leave-it bid to the seller, who merely accepts it or rejects it. In actually performing the experiment, we used this sequential format and had the buyer subjects first make bids to anonymous seller subjects. The seller then either accepted or rejected the offer. This structure is more consistent with the description of the mechanism and its real world implementation.

Experiment 5 ran the baseline experiment with nonuniform but symmetric prior distributions. Here buyers and sellers chose envelopes from different envelope piles and the distributions were skewed so that the probability that a buyer has a high value was greater than the probability he had a low value, while the symmetrically opposite was true for the seller. For these prior distributions, there also exists an equilibrium with linear strategies. (The full analysis of this case is treated in Leininger et al. [8].) We ran this experiment to try to increase the probability of trade in the experiment and thereby increase the experience of the subjects without having to increase the number of rounds in the experiment. (We were concerned that not enough trades were taking place in the baseline experiment.) Experiment 6 was identical to Experiment 5 except that the experiment was run for 40 periods instead of just 15. This was done in response to Alger [1], whose results indicate that the behavior of experimental subjects may change as the number of iterations increases, and to see if learning could increase the goodness of fit between observed and the predicted linear equilibrium behavior. To explain these nonuniform distributions to the subjects we first presented a graphical representation of the cumulative distributions involved indicating the probabilities of drawing values and costs less than and above 25, 50, and 75. We then actually drew a sample of 40 envelopes from both the buyer and seller boxes and wrote them on the blackboard for all subjects to see. This sample clearly illustrated the properties of the distribution. To run these experiments we employed a battery of experimental administrators, each one assigned to run messages between two pairs of subjects seated in back-to-back semi-enclosed booths. Subjects were seated in such a way as to prevent them from seeing their pair member and strict silence was enforced. Experiment 7 involved a totally different bargaining mechanism, face-to-face bargaining. In this experiment, subjects were brought into a room two at a time, and after choosing 15 envelopes from the same boxes used in Experiments 5 and 6, were allowed to bargain freely for a maximum of five minutes. An experimental administrator was present in each room and enforced a set of simple rules, which stipulated that no bargainer could reveal his value or cost in any current or previous round of the experiment, that no threats could be made, that transactions could not be negotiated for future rounds, and finally that no side payments outside of the experiment could be negotiated. Other than that, subjects were free to bargain as they wished. If a transaction was made in any round, it was formalized by signing a contract sheet. The price of a transaction was the one negotiated. This experiment was performed in order to place our results on the sealed-bid mechanism in perspective and in order to compare them to a laboratory version of a commonly used bargaining alternative.

Finally, after conjecturing that the overbidding observed by the buyers could be due to risk aversion on their part, we ran Experiment 8 employing the Roth and Malouf [12]–Berg *et al.* [2] risk-neutrality inducement procedure. In this experiment subjects were informed that they were playing for points, which were to be transformed into probabilities of winning a fixed lottery prize. By making this conversion linear, and assuming that the Von Neumann–Morgenstern axioms apply, risk neutrality can be induced.

In presenting our results about the sealed-bid mechanism we shall concentrate on the results of Experiments 1, 2, and 5, since they are concerned with the direct test of the mechanism. Experiments 3, 4, and 8 confound the data by introducing either a different price formation and/or trade rule (Experiments 3 and 4) or a treatment for risk neutrality (Experiment 8). Experiment 6 tested learning in an extended time horizon version of the experiment, while Experiment 7 investigated an alternative mechanism. The results of these experiments will be discussed separately.

4. RESULTS

In this section we attempt to answer the four questions stated in Section 2: Did buyers and sellers in our experiment tend to use linear strategies? If they did, did they use the ones predicted by equilibrium theory? How well did the mechanism perform and what accounts for this performance? Does the bidding behavior of subjects change as the horizon of the experiment increases? Since Experiments 1, 2, and 5 constitute the purest tests of the sealed-bid mechanism, we shall tend to concentrate our discussion on them.

Linear Bidding Strategies

As a general rule one could say that the bidding strategies employed by both buyers and sellers in our experiment tended to be linear. This fact can be demonstrated several ways. In Figure 1a we present three representative bid–value relationships for buyers and sellers in Experiment 2. While these particular plots are just a small sample, the typical pattern was obviously a linear one. (In Appendix B, we present the plots of bids and values for *all* of the buyers and sellers in Experiment 2. As one can see, the linear pattern is quite pronounced for almost all subjects.)

To give a general impression of the linear nature of the bidding functions employed, Figs. 1b and 1c display the histograms of R^2 for the estimates of the linear regressions of each subject's bid against his value over the 15 rounds of the Experiments 1, 2, 3, 4, 5, and 8.[5]

As we can see, these figures add credence to the belief that bidders employed linear bidding strategies. Of the 48 buyer regressions in these experiments, over 76% has an R^2 greater than 0.7 and 88% had an R^2 greater than 0.5, while for the seller regressions 60% had an R^2 greater than 0.7 and 79% had R^2 greater than 0.5. Figures 1d and 1e present the same distribution using data only from Experiment 1, 2, and 5—our sealed-bid mechanism experiments.

To provide a more rigorous test for linearity we ran the following regressions for each buyer and seller in each of our experiments, except, of course, Experiment 7:

$$v = \alpha + \beta_1 V + \beta_2 V^2 + \beta_3 V^3 + u_b,$$
$$c = \alpha + \beta_1 C + \beta_2 C^2 + \beta_3 C^3 + u_s,$$

where the α's and β's are coefficients, v and c are the bids and asks for the buyers and sellers, respectively, and u_b and u_s are disturbance terms endowed with the usual properties. An F-test was run on the results of these regressions to test the null hypothesis that the coefficients β_2 and β_3 were both zero in each regression. Such a result would indicate that the nonlinear terms were not contributing significantly to the explanatory power of the regression.

The results of these tests strongly support the linearity hypothesis. Of the 105 F-tests for individual regressions, none demonstrated a significant difference from zero at the 99% confidence level. More precisely, of the

---

[5] A similar technique was employed previously by Cox et al. [5], who also investigated whether bidders in their sealed-bid auctions employed linear-bid strategies.

Buyer 1

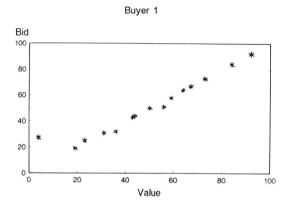

Buyer 3

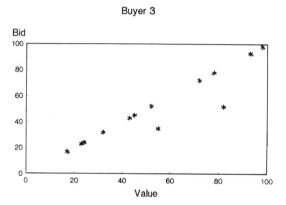

Buyer 5

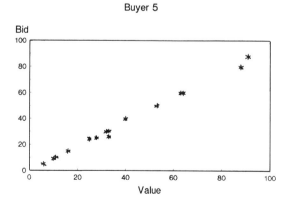

FIG. 1A. Selected bid–value relationships, Experiments 2.

Seller 2

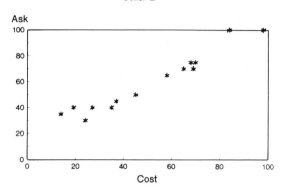

Seller 4

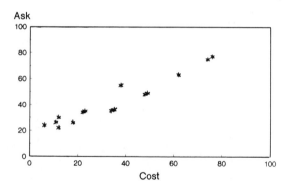

Seller 12

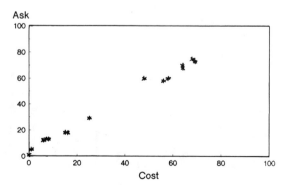

FIG. 1A—*Continued.* Selected cost–ask relationships, Experiment 2.

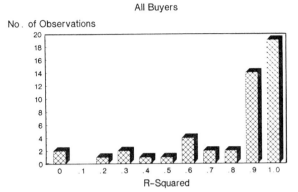

FIG. 1B.   Distribution of R-squared, Experiments 1, 2, 3, 4, 5, and 8.

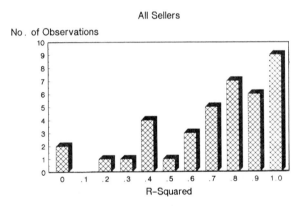

FIG. 1C.   Distribution of R-squared, Experiments 1, 2, 3, 4, 5, and 8.

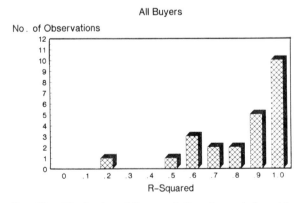

FIG. 1D.   Distribution of R-squared, Experiments 1, 2, and 5.

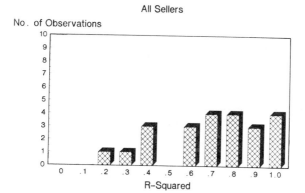

FIG. 1E.   Distribution of R-squared, Experiments 1, 2, and 5.

57 F-tests for buyer regressions, none rejected the hypothesis that the β_2 and β_3 coefficients were jointly zero. The same was true for the 48 F-tests performed for seller regressions. (The difference in the number of buyer and seller regressions is explained by the fact that in Experiment 4 sellers did not make asks but merely accepted or rejected bids made by buyers.)

While these results are supportive of the idea that, in general, subjects tended to employ linear strategies, they say nothing as to whether the strategies employed were the theoretically predicted ones or not. First, remember that the theoretically predicted bidding functions are piecewise linear; e.g., for the buyers, with a segment of slope 1 up to some critical value and then a segment with slope less than 1. Having established linearity on the part of subjects over the relevant intervals, we proceeded to test whether subjects behaved according to the predicted equilibrium bid functions by pooling the data of buyers and sellers within each experiment and running pooled regressions on the observations below and above the critical kink in the equilibrium bid function. Significant differences for these regressions would indicate different bidding behavior on either side of the critical value. The results of these regressions are presented in Table II.

This table presents the results of our pooled regressions done separately for all buyers and sellers in each experiment on a split sample of data containing observations of values and costs above and below the predicted kink-point or critical value in the equilibrium bidding functions. Under each α coefficient we present the t-test of the null hypothesis that $\alpha = 0$. Under each β coefficient for value (cost) realizations below (above) the critical value we present t-statistics for two null hypotheses; $\beta = 0$ and $\beta = 1$ (its predicted value). Finally, for value (cost) realizations above (below) the critical value we present t-statistics under three null hypotheses; $\beta = 0$, $\beta = 1$, and $\beta =$ the predicted equilibrium value.

TABLE II

Regression Coefficients and t-Tests for Buyer/Seller Regressions

	Buyer regressions					
	Coefficient for bid–value regressions for observations below critical value			Coefficients for bid–value regressions for observations above critical value		
Experiment	Degrees of freedom	α	β	Degrees of freedom	α	β
1	28	-1.2318 $(-1.26)_{\alpha=0}$	1.0006 $(15.06)_{\beta=0}$ $[-0.01]_{\beta=1}$	70	-0.8293 $(-0.29)_{\alpha=0}$	0.8488 $(19.32)_{\beta=0}$ $[4.14]_{\beta=2/3}$ $(-3.44)_{\beta=1}$
2	23	1.8289 $(0.62)_{\alpha=0}$	0.9135 $(5.49)_{\beta=0}$ $[-0.52]_{\beta=1}$	80	-5.7986 $(-1.50)_{\alpha=0}$	1.0555 $(17.83)_{\beta=0}$ $[1.28]_{\beta=2/3}$ $(0.94)_{\beta=1}$
3	20	7.4238 $(0.52)_{\alpha=0}$	0.9226 $(0.97)_{\beta=0}$ $[-0.08]_{\beta=1}$	53	5.2514 $(0.78)_{\alpha=0}$	0.7258 $(6.99)_{\beta=0}$ $[-2.64]_{\beta=1}$
4	24	1.0714 $(0.91)_{\alpha=0}$	0.5534 $(6.88)_{\beta=1}$ $[0.66]_{\beta=1/2}$	109	6.9458 $(3.00)_{\alpha=0}$	0.5799 $(16.80)_{\beta=0}$ $[2.32]_{\beta=1/2}$
5	23	0.2204 $(0.20)_{\alpha=0}$	0.7984 $(16.53)_{\beta=0}$ $[-4.17]_{\beta=1}$	140	19.7822 $(1.42)_{\alpha=0}$	0.5039 $[8.46]_{\beta=0}$ $[1.12]_{\beta=28/84}$ $[-8.33]_{\beta=1}$
6 First 20 Round	33	0.3797 $(0.14)_{\alpha=0}$	0.8491 $(7.85)_{\beta=0}$ $[-1.40]_{\beta=1}$	145	20.4149 $(3.43)_{\alpha=0}$	0.3980 $(5.68)_{\beta=0}$ $[-0.56]_{\beta=28/64}$ $(-8.58)_{\beta=1}$
6 Second 20 Rounds	26	-2.7137 $(-0.63)_{\alpha=0)}$	1.1131 $(6.86)_{\beta=0}$ $[0.70]_{\beta=1}$	153	24.5899 $(3.85)_{\alpha=0}$	0.3178 $(4.12)_{\beta=0}$ $[-1.55]_{\beta=28/64}$ $(-8.85)_{\beta=1}$
8	32	11.3338 $(0.47)_{\alpha=0}$	0.9090 $(1.43)_{\beta=0}$ $[-0.14]_{\beta=1}$	101	7.3180 $(1.93)_{\alpha=0}$	0.8037 $(13.93)_{\beta=0}$ $[6.35]_{\beta=28/64}$ $(-3.40)_{\beta=1}$

Table continued

TABLE II (*continued*)

	Seller regressions					
	Coefficient for ask–cost regressions for observations below ask cost			Coefficients for ask–cost regressions for observations above ask cost		
Experiment	Degrees of freedom	α	β	Degrees of freedom	α	β
1	80	30.7014 $(12.99)_{\alpha=0}$	0.5791 $(8.76)_{\beta=0}$ $[-1.38]_{\beta=2/3}$ $(-6.30)_{\beta=1}$	23	2.7234 $(0.89)_{\alpha=0}$	0.9675 $(9.62)_{\beta=0}$ $[-0.32]_{\beta=1}$
2	85	21.6984 $(8.86)_{\alpha=0}$	0.7413 $(12.74)_{\beta=0}$ $[1.28]_{\beta=2/3}$ $(-4.45)_{\beta=1}$	18	3.1353 $(0.07)_{\alpha=0}$	1.0711 $(2.13)_{\beta=0}$ $[0.14]_{\beta=1}$
3	57	-7.1427 $(-0.77)_{\alpha=0}$	1.0577 $(19.12)_{\beta=0}$ $[7.07]_{\beta=2/3}$ $(1.04)_{\beta=1}$	16	17.9383 $(1.08)_{\alpha=0}$	0.6748 $(1.21)_{\beta=0}$ $[-0.58]_{\beta=1}$
4	N.A.	N.A.	N.A.	N.A.	N.A.	N.A.
5	123	30.7557 $(3.28)_{\alpha=0}$	0.4821 $(9.44)_{\beta=0}$ $[0.87]_{\beta=28/64}$ $(-10.14)_{\beta=1}$	40	0.1773 $(0.095)_{\alpha=0}$	1.0377 $(16.47)_{\beta=0}$ $[0.60]_{\beta=1}$
6 First 20 rounds	152	28.0400 $(18.0)_{\alpha=0}$	0.5702 $(9.27)_{\beta=0}$ $[2.16]_{\beta=28/64}$ $(-6.99)_{\beta=1}$	26	3.6874 $(1.69)_{\alpha=0}$	0.9737 $(29.21)_{\beta=0}$ $[-0.79]_{\beta=1}$
6 Second 20 Rounds	158	26.4935 $(16.97)_{\alpha=0}$	0.5224 $(7.40)_{\beta=0}$ $[1.20]_{\beta=28/64}$ $(-6.77)_{\beta=1}$	20	6.4528 $(1.04)_{\alpha=0}$	0.9481 $(12.59)_{\beta=0}$ $[-0.69]_{\beta=1}$
8	104	24.0449 $(10.59)_{\alpha=0}$	0.7487 $(15.02)_{\beta=0}$ $[1.65]_{\beta=2/3}$ $(-5.04)_{\beta=1}$	29	2.0755 $(6.05)_{\alpha=0}$	1.0674 $(2.67)_{\beta=0}$ $[0.17]_{\beta=1}$

Our results are strongly supportive of the hypothesis that bidding behavior for both buyers and sellers is different on different sides of the equilibrium bidding function kink point. They also support the hypothesis that subjects bid (ask) their value (cost) when the linear equilibrium predicts they should. Finally, it appears that while both buyers and sellers changed their bidding behavior as they cross their critical values, sellers seemed actually to bid with a β not significantly different from the predicted level while buyers tended not to shave their bids by the amount called for by the theory and hence used a bidding function whose β was too high.

Table II supports these conclusions. The β coefficients for both buyers and sellers in the below (above) critical value regions were insignificantly different from 1 (α's were insignificantly different from 0 in all experiments). Hence, the hypothesis that in these areas of the domain of the bidding function subjects bid their value (cost) is not contradicted by the data. For regressions estimated from the remaining data, we can reject the hypothesis that either buyers or sellers where bidding their values at the 95% level of significance in all experiments (except for buyers in Experiment 2). Hence, while we cannot reject the hypothesis that buyers and sellers bid their value (cost) on the respective intervals predicted by the linear equilibrium, we can reject the hypothesis that they continued to do so on the complementary interval. Finally note that while, in general, buyer behavior to the right of the critical value was not strictly consistent with equilibrium behavior, seller behavior to the left of their critical value was consistent in the sense that in all experiments their β coefficients were not significantly different from their predicted values.

These results are particularly striking in our sealed-bid mechanism experiments (Experiments 1, 2, and 5). Figures 2a, 2b, and 2c present the mean buyer and seller regressions generated over the domain of their bidding functions above (and below) their kink points by the subjects in Experiments 1, 2, and 5, and projects them back to the lower endpoint of the value (cost) interval. It juxtaposes them against the theoretically predicted equilibrium regression lines over these same intervals. These mean regressions are defined by taking the mean of the coefficients determined by the individual buyer and seller regressions of each seller/buyer in these three experiments[6]. From these figures it appears that, on average, sellers tended to bid approximately as predicted by the linear equilibrium. In Experiment 1, the fit is especially close with a mean regression slope of 0.67 as opposed to the predicted level of 0.66 and a constant term of 24.2 instead of 25. In Experiments 2 and 5 the mean regression slopes were 0.72 and 0.47 as opposed to 0.66 and 0.44, while the constant terms were 22.5 and 31.7 instead of 25 and 36, respectively. These are remarkably close

---

[6] Appendix C presents the individual regression results for Experiments 1, 2, and 5.

Buyers

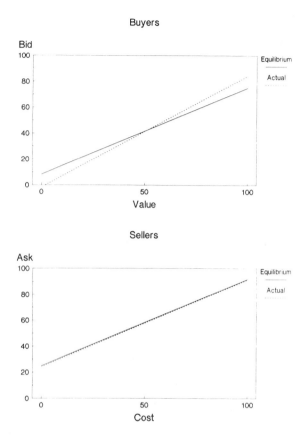

Fig. 2A. Mean regression versus linear equilibrium bidding strategy (Experiment 1).

approximations. For the buyers a different pattern was observed. While Experiments 1, 2, and 5 predict intercepts of 8.33, 8.33, and 20, the observed mean intercepts in these experiments were − 1.6, 0.17, and 16.2, respectively. The mean regression slopes were all greater than their predicted values, however, registering values of 0.86, 0.99, and 0.52 instead of the predicted values of 0.66, 0.66, and 0.44. As a result, buyers tended to overbid when they received high realizations of their random variable, which are precisely those realizations for which trade is most likely.

In summary, from our review of the data, it appears that as a general rule the assumption that subjects employed linear bidding strategies seems to organize the data quite effectively. In addition, it appears that sellers more closely approximated the behavior posited by the linear equilibrium than did buyers, who tended not to shave their bids by an amount great enough to satisfy the equilibrium prediction.

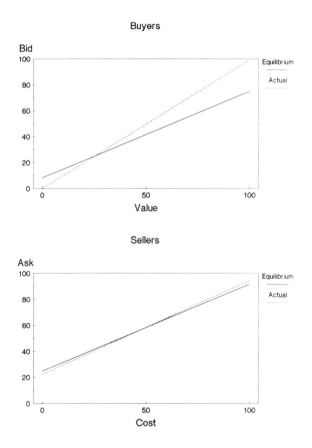

FIG. 2B.   Mean Regression versus linear equilibrium bidding strategy (Experiment 2).

Learning and Step-Function Equilibria

A step-function equilibrium is defined by a pair of step functions, one
each for the buyer and seller. The characterizing feature of such equilibria
is that the steps of the buyer and seller functions occur at identical points
in the domain of their respective bidding functions. For example, a
two-step equilibrium can be defined in Experiments 1, 2, and 5 for any
$x \in [0, 100]$ as

$$v = \begin{cases} 0, & V < x, \\ x, & V \geqslant x, \end{cases}$$

$$c = \begin{cases} x, & C < x, \\ 1, & C \geqslant x. \end{cases}$$

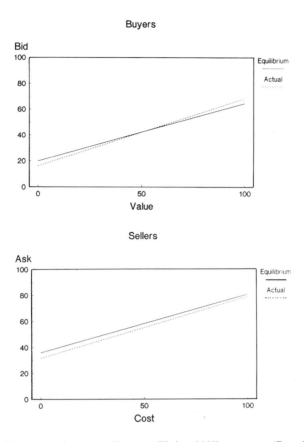

FIG. 2C. Mean regression versus linear equilibrium bidding strategy (Experiment 5).

Experiment 6 was run after we observed the general linear pattern of bids described above. It was our original conjecture that if the length of the experiment was sufficiently long, the β coefficients of both the buyer and seller regressions estimated from the data of the last 15 round of the experiment, would converge to their theoretically predicted linear equilibrium levels. What was observed was rather surprising in that there appears to be evidence that step-function-like behavior began to make its appearance. In fact, over the last 20 rounds one pair of subjects actually adhered to what was almost an exact step-function equilibrium as demonstrated in Fig. 3. Notice that this pair of subjects seemed able to coordinate their activities and employ a step-function-like equilibrium with a common step at 40. Their behavior was only approximate, however, since the buyer and seller failed to bid 0 and 1 when it was called for.

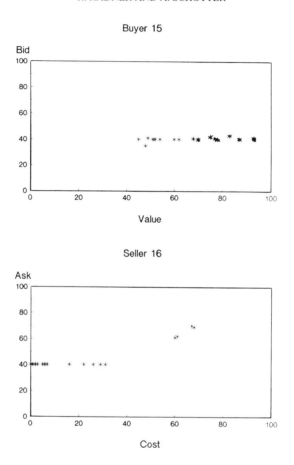

FIG. 3.   Approximate step-function equilibrium, Experiment 6 (last 20 rounds).

The more typical pattern observed in these experiments was for buyers to evolve a bidding function with an initial linear portion with positive slope and then a flat segment thereafter, while sellers evolved a strategy containing a flat segment followed by a segment with positive slope. Figures 4 and 5 present a sample of three such observed bidding functions employed by buyers and sellers, respectively, over the last 20 rounds of the experiment. This is, of course, merely a selection of the results. The important point about these figures, however, is that they clearly exhibit flat segments in the bidding functions of both buyers and sellers preceded or followed by positively sloped linear segments, and that such behavior was not visible in any systematic way in Experiments 1 and 2 (see Appendix B, for example.)

Buyer 1

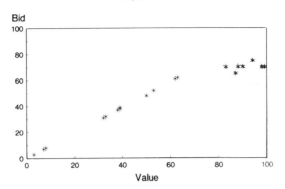

Buyer 7

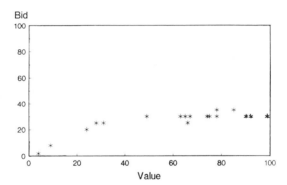

Buyer 17

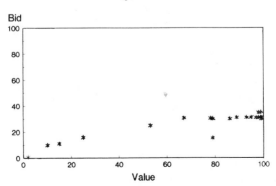

FIG. 4. Selected buyer behavior, Experiment 6 (last 20 rounds).

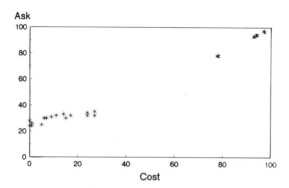

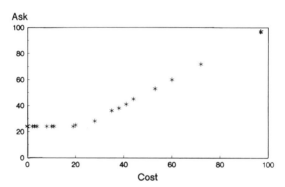

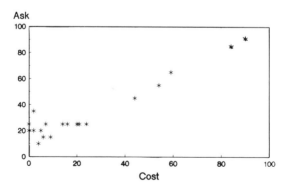

FIG. 5. Selected seller behavior, Experiment 6 (last 20 rounds).

There is some evidence that a modified version of this behavior for sellers did occur in Experiment 5, which is a 15-round experiment that employs the same probability distributions as does Experiment 6. For instance, Figures 6a–6d present the mean bid(ask)-value relationship for buyers and sellers in Experiments 5 and 6 over the beginning and ending segments of the experiment. As is clearly seen, during the last 8 rounds of Experiment 5, sellers had, on average, already developed the flat-segment bidding behavior exhibited by sellers during the last 15 rounds of Experiment 6. The pattern for buyers is less clear. What is interesting is that in both Experiment 5 and Experiment 6, the value of 40 seems to be salient, with sellers bidding about 40 for all cost realizations below that value. Above 40 they seem to bid their value. The similarity of these bidding patterns across Experiments 5 and 6 (and their nonexistence in Experiments 1 and 2 in which uniform probability distributions are used) seems to indicate that it

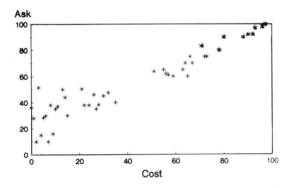

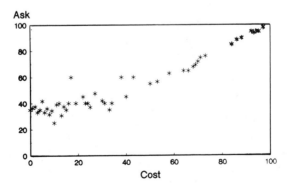

FIG. 6A.   Mean asks versus costs, Experiment 5.

Buyers: First Seven Rounds

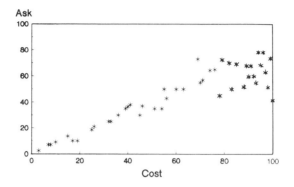

Buyers: Last Eight Rounds

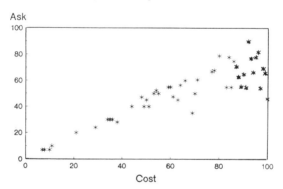

FIG. 6B.   Mean bids versus values, Experiment 5.

is the probability functions used in these experiments rather than the expanded horizon of Experiment 6 which is responsible for these results. Clearly, however, longer horizons do appear to facilitate the evolution of step-function-like behavior (see Fig. 3).

Performance in the Sealed-Bid Mechanism Experiments

The sealed-bid mechanism performed quite well. A clear pattern of performance improvement was also seen with the later rounds of experiments outperforming beginning rounds. For instance, in Experiments 1 and 2 if buyers and sellers are bidding according to the linear equilibrium bidding strategies, then trade should take place only when the buyer's value exceeds the seller's value by 25. For Experiment 5 this critical difference is 36. Over

Sellers: First 15 Rounds

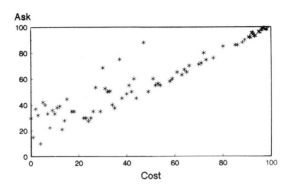

Sellers: Last 15 Rounds

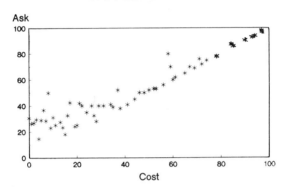

FIG. 6C. Mean asks versus costs, Experiment 6.

the last eight rounds of these experiments, subjects succeeded in making practically all of the trades dictated by the linear equilibrium (i.e., 20 out of 20 in Experiment 1, 20 out of 21 in Experiment 2, and 41 out of 42 in Experiment 5). In addition, subjects also made some trades which were mutually beneficial but would not take place if the equilibrium strategies were used. Similar patterns exist in our other experiments as well. However, as we discuss in Section 5, the performance of subjects deteriorates in Experiments 3, 4, and 8. These data are presented in Table III.

Before we present our next performance measure it is important to remind the reader that the linear equilibrium of the sealed-bid mechanism achieves second-best gains from trade when the prior distributions are

Buyers: First 15 Rounds

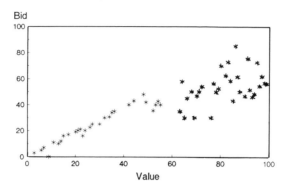

Buyers: Last 15 Rounds

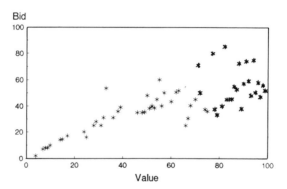

FIG. 6D.   Mean bids versus values, Experiment 6.

uniform. In Table IV we present the fractions of both the first-best and linear equilibrium gains from trade captured by our subjects. As we see, whereas subjects in Experiment 1 captured practically 90% of the gains from trade expected at the linear equilibrium and subjects in Experiment 2 captured 98%, subjects in Experiment 5 realized gains from trade greater than those predicted by the linear equilibrium. In terms of the first-best gains from trade, the subjects in these three experiments captured between 85 and 92% of the available gains. Hence, given the information-poor environment in which these experiments were conducted, the sealed-bid mechanism performed quite well.

The reason that our subjects in the sealed-bid experiment were so successful at capturing the gains from trade can be seen clearly in Figs. 2a, 2b,

TABLE III

Performance

Experiment	First 7 rounds	Last 8 rounds	Total
	Fraction of linear equilibrium predicted trades occurring		
1	0.889	1.000	0.996
2	0.733	0.952	0.861
3	0.200	0.750	0.588
4	0.889	0.880	0.884
5	0.976	0.946	0.959
6[a]	0.863	0.904	0.885
7	1.000	1.000	1.000
8	0.870	0.909	0.889
	Ratio of the total number of trades made to total number predicted by linear equilibrium		
1	1.11	1.15	1.14
2	1.13	1.14	1.14
3	0.40	0.92	0.77
4	1.11	0.96	1.02
5	1.07	1.05	1.06
6[a]	0.96	1.00	0.98
7	1.37	1.34	1.35
8	1.09	0.96	1.02
	Number of inefficient trades		
1	5[b]	0	5[b]
2	0	1	1
3	0	0	0
4	1	0	1
5	0	0	0
6[a]	1	0	1
7	1	1	1
8	2	2	4

[a] For Experiment 6 we present the results of the first 20 and last 20 rounds instead of the first 7 and last 8 rounds.

[b] These false trades were made by one buyer during the first 5 rounds of his experiment. From round 6 onward he no longer bid above his value.

and 2c. In these figures it is clear that, on average, in Experiments 1, 2, and 5, sellers employed a linear bidding strategy whose slope was approximately equal to the equilibrium strategy, while buyers tended not to shave their bids by as much as the linear equilibrium dictated. Hence, it is not surprising that we observed almost better than linear-equilibrium performance since, given the bidding behavior of sellers, the failure of buyers to sufficiently shave their bids naturally leads to a situation in which a greater than predicted number of trades are made.

TABLE IV

Fractions

Experiment	Fraction of potentially available (first-best) gains from trade captured
1	0.86[a]
2	0.85
3	0.57
4	0.86
5	0.92
6	0.86
7	0.99
8	0.62
	Fraction of linear equilibrium gains from trade captured
1	0.90[a]
2	0.98
3	0.80
4	1.09
5	1.00
6	0.94
7	1.11
8	0.90

[a] False or mistaken trades removed (see footnote b on Table III).

TABLE V

Mean Price Deviation from Linear Equilibrium Price (Actual Price-Optimal Price)[a]

Experiment	Mean	Variance	Number of observations
1	0.74	56.6	28
2	6.93	87.7	31
3	−0.74	35.2	10
4	14.4	46.2	35
5	0.48	70.4	94
6[b]	−6.108	119.98	209
7[b]	−1.541	360.9	90
8	3.969	115.1	38

[a] Only for those trades which actually were made and which should have been made had bids and asks been made optimally (actual price − optimal price).

[b] Optimal prices calculated using nonuniform distributions with $r = 0.4$ (see Table I).

In terms of price performance, the sealed-bid mechanism conformed remarkably, on average, to the price predictions of the linear equilibrium theory. Table V presents the mean deviation of our observed price from the price predicted by the linear equilibrium. From this table it would appear that, on average, in those trades predicted to occur by the linear equilibrium of the sealed-bid mechanism, the prices forthcoming are close to their predicted values.

5. Other Experiments

Three experiments were run to test the robustness of the sealed-bid mechanism.

The Revelation Principle

Experiment 3 tested a direct form of the mechanism which has value and cost revelation as a linear equilibrium. Consequently, this experiment probably presents the first experimental setting of the Revelation Principle (see, e.g., Myerson [9, 10] and Harris and Townsend [6]). In general, this test was not successful. Because the trade rule dictates that trade only takes place when $v \geq c + 25$, given the uniform distributions employed, few trades took place. For instance, while in Experiment 5 there was an average of 9.4 trades per 15 rounds, in Experiment 3 there were only 2.6 per 15 rounds. This lack of trading experience may have been responsible for the relatively poor performance of the mechanism. In fact, in this experiment, subjects were able to capture only 57% of the available gains from trade (as opposed to 92% in Experiment 5) and 80% of the linear equilibrium gains from trade (as opposed to 100% in Experiment 5). Bids also tended not to fit the linear pattern exhibited so regularly in other experiments. These results are interesting since, as in the double oral auction literature (see Smith [14]) it is also the number of trades taking place and not the number of trading rounds experienced that is important in fostering good performance.

In addition to its poor performance, Experiment 3 failed completely to support one of the key comparative-static predictions of the theory; that for random value realizations (cost realizations) greater than (less than) their critical values, the slopes of the bidding functions for buyers and sellers in Experiment 3 should be greater than the slopes of the bidding functions observed in Experiment 1. (See Appendix C for a substantiation of this point.) Two alternative hypotheses exist for the explanation of the poor performance of Experiment 3. One is that, since the direct mechanism has a more complicated set of rules, it is harder for subjects to understand. Hence performance deteriorates. The second is that, since underbidding (overasking) is a natural thing to do in such settings, subjects may need more guidance in the instructions in order to achieve truthful revelation. While we were reluctant to provide such guidance in this experiment, a new experiment in which instructions lead the subjects to the truthful revelation equilibrium and then check to see if it is self-sustaining, might certainly be an interesting one to attempt in the future.

Risk Aversion

Because we feared that the overbidding employed by buyers resulted from risk aversion on their part, Experiment 8 employed the Roth and Malouf [12]–Berg *et al.* [2] payoff conversion procedure which, in theory induces risk neutral behavior. This treatment did not seem to induce the increased bid shaving we expected from the buyers, nor did it induce sellers to increase their asks. A Wilcoxon test for the buyer and seller regressions across Experiments 1 and 8 rejects the hypothesis that there was no difference in bidding behavior across the two experiments.[7] In fact, it appears that, on average, both buyers and sellers *raised* their bids in response to the risk neutrality treatment. To illustrate this point, Figs. 7a and 7b juxtapose the mean regressions of the buyers and sellers in these two experiments. One sees that, the mean regression line for buyers in Experiment 8 is everywhere above that of Experiment 1. For the sellers the effect was more pronounced. Interestingly, the slope of the mean regression line remained the same for the sellers while the function was simply displaced upward. In summary, it appears that this treatment in Experiment 8 yielded subject behavior that was further away from the risk neutral linear equilibrium bidding strategies than the subject behavior that was observed in Experiment 1.

Take-It-or-Leave-It Bargaining

In Experiment 4 the buyers make a bid and the sellers can either accept it or reject it. Chatterjee and Samuelson [4] have shown that at the linear equilibrium of this variant of the sealed-bid mechanism, the realized gains from trade should fall, along with the seller profits. Neither prediction was substantiated by the data. A Wilcoxon test was unable to reject the hypothesis that subject pairs were equally as efficient in capturing the gains from trade available in Experiment 4 as they were in Experiment 1.[8] In addition, a Wilcoxon test run on these fractions indicates that the fractions of the potentially available gains from trade captured by sellers were not significantly different between Experiments 1 and 4.[9]

---

[7] The Wilcoxon–Mann–Whitney U statistics here were 20 and 22 for the α and β coefficients in the buyer regressions and 26 and 20 for the α and β coefficients of the seller's regressions.

[8] The Wilcoxon–Mann–Whitney U statistic here was 31.

[9] The Wilcoxon–Mann–Whitney U statistic here was 27.

Buyers

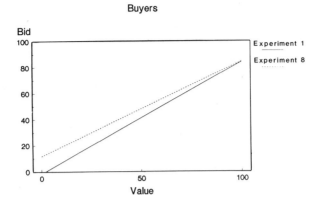

FIG. 7A. Mean Buyer Regressions, Experiments 1 and 8.

Sellers

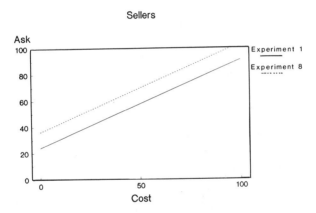

FIG. 7B. Mean seller regressions, Experiments 1 and 8.

Face-to-Face Bargaining

One of the most surprising outcomes of our experiments was the performance of the face-to-face mechanism (Experiment 7). In fact, under all performance (efficiency) measures it clearly out-performed the sealed-bid mechanism in all its variations tested. For example, over the 15 rounds of the experiment the face-to-face bargaining mechanism was able to capture over 99% of the first-best gains from trade. This compares to the 92% achieved in Experiment 5 (sealed-bid) where values and costs were generated by the same probability distributions, respectively. Of the 129 rounds in which our subjects were bargaining in situations where trade was mutually beneficial, they were able to make a transaction in 121 of them. In addition, when trade failed to occur it did so only when the gains from trade were minimal. One characteristic of the face-to-face bargaining experiment was the high variance of prices formed. This variance implies that the outcomes of such experiments were very sensitive to the bargaining personalities of the subjects. As such, while the face-to-face mechanism may exhibit high efficiency levels, it may be lacking in terms of equity.

The success of the face-to-face mechanism, if replicated, might lead to a halt in the search for better ways to structure bargaining in situations of incomplete information. It would create, however, a need for a theory of such unstructured bargaining in order to enable us to understand why the mechanism is so successful. (We know of no such finite-horizon theory at present.) These results are, of course only tentative. They leave many questions unanswered. For instance, was the weaker performance of the sealed bid-mechanism due, in part to its anonymous nature? Would our face-to-face mechanism perform less well if all interaction were engaged in anonymously through typed interactive computer messages? Or would such a protocol preserve the efficiency of the face-to-face mechanism but merely cut down on the personality-related variance of payoffs?[10] The answers to such questions will have to be pursued elsewhere.

6. CONCLUSIONS

In response to the four questions that motivated our analysis, it appears that both buyers and sellers seemed to employ (piecewise) linear bidding functions, especially when the underlying probability distributions in the experiment were uniform. When the distributions were not uniform, however, there appeared to be some evidence that step-function equilibria began to evolve. This pattern was particularly evident when the horizon of the experiment was lengthened from 15 to 40 rounds. In bidding linearly, sellers tended, on average, to employ bidding functions that conformed to the predictions of the linear equilibrium, while buyers tended not to shave their bids by as much as the equilibrium suggests. The combination of these two behaviors accounts for the good performance of the mechanism.

As is true of most experiments, this paper has raised about as many questions as it has answered. For instance, it appears that the probability distributions used in the experiments have an influence on the "type" of

---

[10] Hoffman and Spitzer [7], in a set of face-to-face experiments testing the properties of the Coase theorem, observe equally high efficiency levels, while in a series of anonymous computer protocol experiments Roth and Murnighan [13] exhibit higher instances of inefficiencies (i.e., disagreements). We do not offer these observations as proof that anonymity in bargaining is efficiency decreasing.

equilibrium observed. When nonuniform distributions were used, even with a 15-round horizon, evidence of seller step-function-like behavior began to appear during the last seven rounds of the experiment. Such behavior was not seen in experiments in which uniform distributions were used. When the horizon in such experiments was extended to 40 rounds, this behavior was more pronounced and was seen for both buyers and sellers. Since the distributions used are members of a one-parameter family, it would be interesting to see exactly how behavior is affected by a greater range of changes in the parameter: Is there a point at which linear bidding behavior gives way to step-function behavior?

Increasing the horizon of the experiment does appear to have a significant impact on the type of behavior observed. Since we repeated our experiments for at most 40 rounds, it is natural to ask what would happen if the horizon were longer. This would, of course, have to be done in conjunction with variations of the probability distributions.

In summary, one can consider this paper to be a step in the investigation of structured bargaining in environments with incomplete information. While it is obvious that further experiments will have to be done before a clear picture of how the types of bargaining mechanism studied here perform, we feel confident that the types of question raised by our experiments will be central to the final unraveling of the puzzles presented by these bargaining mechanisms.

APPENDIX A: Instructions To Experiment 1

Introduction

You are about to engage in an experiment concerning decision making. Various research institutions have provided funds for these experiments and if you make appropriate decisions you will earn a good monetary payment.

The Experiment

As you walked into the room, two things occurred. First you were randomly assigned the role of a buyer or a seller. (Look at the upper right-hand corner of your instruction sheet to see which one you are.) Second, you chose 15 envelopes from a pile 500. Each envelope has a number between 0 and 100 written on a slip of paper in it. These numbers were randomly generated by a computer such that each number between 0 and 100 has an equally likely chance of being on any slip of paper. The way the

Worksheet of Subject #_____   Type of Subject_____

	Column 1	Column 2	Column 3	Column 4	Column 5
Rounds	Random No.	Bid or ask	Did a transaction occur	Price	Payoff
1					
2					
3					
4					
5					
6					
7					
8					
9					
10					
11					
12					
13					
14					
15					

experiment works is as follows: In each round you will be given a chance to buy or sell a ficticious object depending on whether you are a buyer or a seller. In round one, you will be asked to open any one of the 15 envelopes you have chosen. If you are a buyer, the number in the envelope will represent the amount of a ficticious currency called francs we will pay you if you purchase an object during this round. It is your redemption value for the object. If you are a seller, this number will represent how much you will have to pay us in order to obtain the object for sale. It is in essence, the cost of the object to you. Note that you and only you know this random number and that you will not be told the random number of any other subject. After you observe your number, write it in column 1 of your worksheet. Also write in on one of the slips of paper provided to you along with your subject number and the number of the round of experiment. (Your subject number is written in the upper left-hand corner of your instruction sheet.) Also, write it in column 1 of your worksheet. Next, you will choose a number between 0 and 100 and record this number on the same slip of paper and in column 2 of your worksheet. If you are a buyer this number will represent the amount of francs you are bidding for the ficticious object for sale in this round. If you are a seller, it will represent the amount of francs you are asking to be paid. These francs will be converted into dollars at the end if the experiment as described below.

Payoffs

When these slips have all been filled out, we will collect them in two boxes one containing all of the buyer's bids and one containing all of the seller's asks. These boxes will then be brought to the front of the room. The slips will then be drawn out in pairs, one from the seller's and one from the buyer's box. This process will randomly match you with a subject of the oppositve type. When your slip is drawn, along with that of your pair member, the experimental administrator will look at the bid and ask made. If the buyer's bid is below the seller's ask, then no transaction will take place. If the buyer's bid is greater than or equal to the seller's ask, a transaction will be made. The price of the transaction will be the average of the buyer's bid and the seller's ask, i.e., (buyer's bid + seller's ask)/2. When such a transaction is made, the payoff to the buyer will be the difference between his value (determined randomly by his envelope draw) and the price he has to pay the seller (as described above). The seller's payoff will be the difference between the price he receives for his object and his cost. If no transaction is made, all payoffs will be zero.

After all the slips have been drawn, the experimenal administrator will compare the bids and asks, determine if a transaction is made or not, and, if so, at what price. He will then write this information on slips of paper and return it to you. If your slip is blank, it will mean that no transaction took place in that period. If a transaction did take place, the slip of paper returned to you will contain a number representing the price at which the transaction was made.

After the results of round 1 are known, write in column 3 whether or not you made a transaction by writing yes or no. If you made a transaction, place the price of the transaction in column 4 and your payoff in column 5. If you did not make a transaction, place zeros in column 4 and 5. Round 2 will now start. You will open your second envelope, get a new random number and follow the same procedures as you did in round 1. However, in each round you will be with the same subject you were paired with in round 1. There will be 15 rounds in the experiment.

To illustrate how your payoff is determined, say a buyer draws a value from an enveloppe of 75 while the seller draws a cost of 40. If the buyer bids 60 and the seller asks for 50, then a transaction will be made at a price of $55 = (60 + 50)/2$. The payoff to the buyer will then be $75 - 55 = 20$, while the payoff to the seller will then be $55 - 40 = 15$. In this example, if the buyer, in an effort to increase his/her payoff decides to lower his/her bid to 45, while the seller, with a similar motivation increases his/her ask to 57, then no transaction will take place, and all payoffs will be zero. Hence, a tradeoff exists for both the buyer and the seller. The more they try to make by lowering their bid or increasing their ask, the more likely it is that no transaction will take place. Finally, note that your payoff can be negative if you are a buyer if the price you pay is greater than your value, and it can be negative if you are a seller if the price you determine is less than your value.

When the 15 rounds of the experiment are over, your final payoff will be determined by summing up all of the francs accumulated over the 15 rounds of the experiment. These francs will be converted into dollars at the rate of 1 franc = $.01. You will also be paid $3.00 for participating. However, if by the end of the experiment your total franc payoff is negative, these losses will be subtracted from this $3.00. You will be paid when you leave.

APPENDIX B

Bid–Value Relationships, Experiment 2

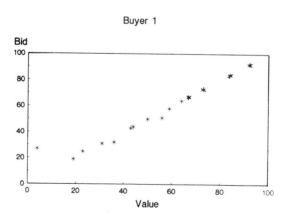

Buyer 1

Buyer 3

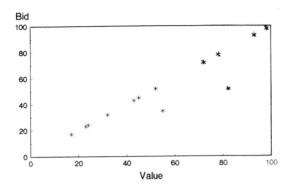

Buyer 5

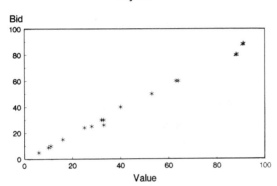

Buyer 7

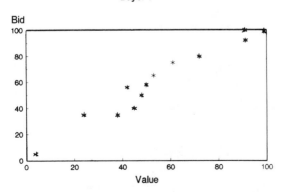

Buyer 9

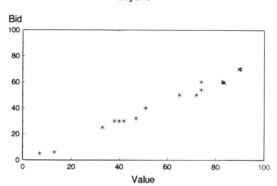

Buyer 11

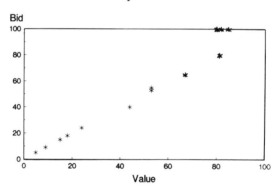

Buyer 13

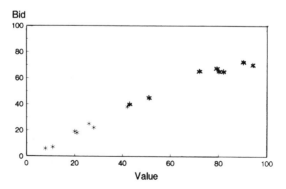

Cost–Ask Relationships, Experiment 2

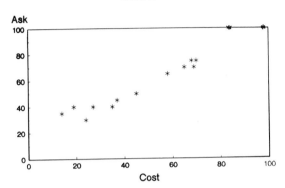

Seller 2

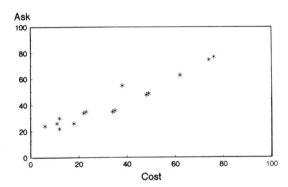

Seller 4

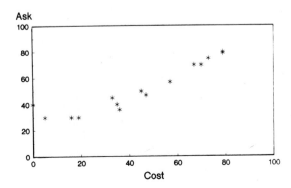

Seller 6

Seller 8

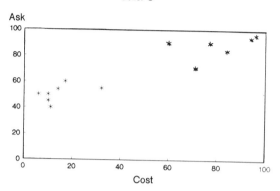

Seller 10

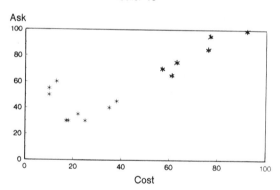

Seller 12

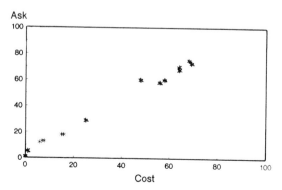

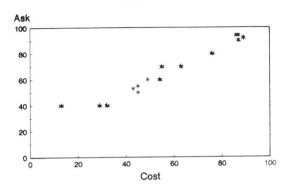

Seller 14

APPENDIX C

Table VI presents both the mean regressions and the pooled regressions run on all relevant data generated by Experiments 1 and 3.

As we see in this table, while in both the pooled and mean regressions there was a distinct rotation and steepening of the sellers' bidding function as we move from Experiment 1 to 3, the slopes of the buyers regressions appear not to have been altered by a change in the bargaining rules. A t-test used to test the hypothesis that the slopes and intercepts of the bidding functions did not change in moving from Experiment 1 to 3 was supported by the pooled buyer regressions but was rejected by the seller regression at the 5% level of significance.[11] In addition, a Wilcoxon test

TABLE VI

Bidding Function Coefficients: Experiments 1 and 3

Experiment	Buyer		Seller	
	α	β	α	β
1				
Mean regression	−1.6	0.86	24.2	0.67
pooled regression	11.2	0.74	30.7	0.57
3				
Mean regression	2.08	0.815	−4.8	0.91
pooled regression	5.25	0.72	−7.14	1.0

[11] The t-statistics here were 0.88 and 0.19 for the α and β coefficients in the buyer-pooled regressions and 13.8 and 7.8 for the α and β coefficients in the pooled sellers regressions.

run on the samples of α and β coefficients from the individual regressions generated by Experiments 1 and 3 again failed to substantiate any change in buyer behavior but did detect a statistically significant change in the seller behavior in the predicted direction.[12]

REFERENCES

1. D. ALGER, Laboratory tests of equilibrium predictions with disequilibrium data, unpublished manuscript, Bureau of Economics, Federal Trade Commission, January 1986.
2. J. BERG, L. DALEY, J. DICKHAUT, AND J. O'BRIEN, Controlling preferences for lotteries on units of experimental exchange, *Quart. J. Econ.* (1986), 281–306.
3. C. BULL, A SCHOTTER, AND K. WEIGELT, Tournaments and piece rates: An experimental study, *J. Polit. Econ.* **29** (1987), 1–34.
4. K. CHATTERJEE AND W. SAMUELSON, Bargaining under incomplete information, *Oper. Res.* **31** (1983), 835–851.
5. J. COX, V. SMITH, AND J. M. WALKER, Theory and individual behavior of first price auctions, unpublished manuscript, University of Arizona, May 1986.
6. M. HARRIS AND R. TOWNSEND, Resource allocation under asymmetric information, *Econometrica* **49** (1981), 33–64.
7. E. HOFFMAN AND M. SPITZER, The coase theorem: Some experimental tests, *J. Law Econ.* **73** (1982).
8. W. LEININGER, P. LINHART, AND R. RADNER, Equilibria of the sealed-bid mechanism for bargaining with incomplete information, *J. Econ. Theory* **48** (1989), 63–106.
9. R. MYERSON, Incentive compatibility and the bargaining problem, *Econometrica* **47** (1979), 61–73.
10. R. MYERSON, Optimal auction design, *Math. Oper. Res.* **6** (1981), 58–73.
11. R. MYERSON AND M. SATTERTHWAITE, Efficient mechanisms for bilateral trading, *J. Econ. Theory* **29** (1983), 265–281.
12. A. ROTH AND W. MALOUF, Game theory models and the role of information in bargaining, *Psy. Rev.* **86** (1979), 574–594.
13. A. ROTH AND K. MURNIGHAN, The role of information in bargaining: An experimental study, *Econometrica* **50** (1982), 1123–1143.
14. V. SMITH, Bidding and auctioning institutions: Experimental results, *in* "Bidding and Auctioning for Procurement and Allocation" (Y. Amihud, Ed.), New York Univ. Press, New York, 1976.
15. V. SMITH, Micro economic systems as an experimental science, *Amer. Econ. Rev.* **72** (1982), 923–955.
16. L. WILDE, The use of Laboratory Experiments in Economics, *in* "Philosophy and Economics" (J. C. Pitt, Ed.), Dordrecht, Reidel, 1981.

---

[12] The Wilcoxon–Mann–Whitney U statistics here were 16 and 14 for the α and β coefficients in the buyer regressions and 0 and 3 for the α and β coefficients of the sellers regressions.

JOURNAL OF ECONOMIC THEORY **48**, 152–178 (1989)

215 — 41

0262

0227

C 78

D 83

Minimax-Regret Strategies for Bargaining over Several Variables*

P. B. LINHART AND R. RADNER

AT & T Bell Laboratories, Murray Hill, New Jersey 07974

Received July 29, 1987; revised November 7, 1988

For the sealed-bid mechanism for bilateral bargaining, we explore models in which each player bids so as to minimize his maximum regret. Here *regret* is defined as the difference between the profit the player could have made with the wisdom of hindsight and the profit he actually made. We study bargaining over both price and quantity, as well as over more general sets of bargaining alternatives, with complete and incomplete information. In each case there is a minimax-regret strategy that is linear in the true value or cost, and the minimax regret is not "unacceptably" large. *Journal of Economic Literature* Classification Numbers: 022, 026.   © 1989 Academic Press, Inc.

1. INTRODUCTION

The bulk of the current theoretical literature on bargaining deals with bargaining over the price of a single object (Sutton [11]). For two-person bargaining, bids may be simultaneous (as in the sealed-bid mechanism) (Leininger *et al.* [4]) or sequential (Sutton [11]). Information may be complete or incomplete; that is, each bargainer may or may not know with certainty the value of the object to the other.

In the case of uncertainty, the current approach, following Harsanyi [3], is to model the situation as a noncooperative game with incomplete information. For example, sealed-bid bargaining over a single object would be modeled as follows: Denote by V the value of the object to the buyer and by C its cost to the seller. The players' beliefs about V and C are represented as a common joint prior probability distribution. "Nature" first chooses V and C according to this distribution, and then reveals V to the buyer and C to the seller, but not vice versa. The buyer and seller then simultaneously choose their respective bids. Trade occurs if and only if the buyer's bid is at least as large as the seller's bid, and at a price equal to the average of the two bids. The buyer's strategy is thus a function mapping V into his bid v, and the seller's strategy is a function mapping C into his bid c. One then

---

* The views expressed here are those of the authors, not necessarily those of AT & T Bell Laboratories. We are indebted to P. K. Dutta, A. Orlitsky, F. W. Sinden and S. R. Williams for helpful discussions.

215

examines the equilibria of this game: a (Bayesian–Nash) equilibrium is a pair of strategies such that neither player can increase his expected profit by unilaterally changing his own bid.

Several objections can be made to this whole model. The first concerns the single object. It is rare that bargaining—for example, in the context which particularly interests us, that of intracompany transfers—is this simple. One frequently bargains over not just price but also quantity, various parameters of quality, delivery date, penalties for late delivery, and so on indefinitely.

Other objections concern the game-theoretic description, even in the case of a single object. These are:

(a) *The common prior.* Ordinary experience seems to indicate that what makes horseraces is variation among priors. While an analysis of bargaining in which players' differing priors are common knowledge is possible in principle, we do not know of such an analysis. If even common knowledge is lacking, it is not clear to us that theory could offer any guidance to bargaining behavior. (For a discussion of consistent beliefs and common knowledge, see Myerson [6].)

(b) *The multiplicity of equilibria.* It is shown in Leininger *et al.* [4], and in Satterthwaite and Williams [9], that there is a continuum of differentiable equilibria (i.e., equilibria with differentiable strategies), as well as a continuum of discontinuous equilibria, for sealed-bid bargaining under uncertainty, even if one considers only pure strategies; moreover these equilibria may range in efficiency from zero to second best. Because of this multiplicity of equilibria, it is undetermined in the model how the players are to coordinate their strategies.

In the present paper, therefore, we explore the consequences of an entirely different behavioral assumption, namely, that each player bids in such a way as to minimize his maximum regret. Here *regret* is defined as the difference between the profit the player could have made with the wisdom of hindsight and the profit he actually made; the *maximum* is taken with respect to the opponent's possible bids.

The idea of a minimax-regret rule—although not in a bargaining context—was advocated by Savage [10], and apparently originated by Wald [12]. Minimax (-regret) strategies have been proposed for single-person decision problms in cases in which—for whatever reason—it seems inappropriate to assign probabilities (objective or personal) to the alternative events anticipated by the decision-maker. In the present case, once one of the bargainers—say the buyer—knows the true value of the object to him, those events are the alternative bids that the other bargainer might make.

If the buyer abandons Nash-equilibrium theory for resolving this uncertainty, for the reasons just noted, he must turn to some other theory or principle. For example, he might simply assign "subjective" probabilities to the alternative bids of the seller. On the other hand, many decision-makers would probably find such a procedure arbitrary, meaningless, or otherwise unattractive. Such a decision-maker might find the principle of minimizing maximum regret attractive, *especially if the minimax regret were not so high as to be "unacceptable."*

Savage offers another interpretation of the minimax-regret principle, which could be relevant to the situation of transfer pricing. Suppose that the bargainer must justify or rationalize his bid for a group of persons who have widely varying "subjective" probability distributions over the seller's prospective bids. In this case, the buyer might want to bid in such a way as to minimize the maximum "outrage" felt in the group; here "outrage" is equated to regret.

It has been objected, by Chernoff [2] among others, that the minimax-regret principle does not satisfy the condition that Arrow [1, pp. 26–28], in a social-choice context, called "independence of irrelevant alternatives." Chernoff expresses this condition as follows: "In some examples the min max regret criterion may select a strategy d_3 among the available strategies d_1, d_2, d_3, and d_4. On the other hand, if for some reason d_4 is made unavailable, the min max regret criterion will select d_2 among d_1, d_2, and d_3. The author feels that for a reasonable criterion the presence of an undesirable strategy d_4 should not have an influence on the choice among the remaining strategies."

We shall explain at the end of Section 2b why this objection does not apply with any great force to the class of sealed-bid bargaining problems considered in the present paper.

As an alternative to minimizing maximum regret, one might consider the maximization of minimum profit. In the present case, the latter rule offers the bargainer no guide to action, since the minimum profit for any bid is zero. In a more general context, Savage [10, pp. 169–171, 200–201] has described how the second rule can lead a decision-maker to ignore information that, intuitively, seems useful. Finally, it has been pointed out (Milnor [5]) that the action selected by the second rule need not be invariant under the addition to the player's payoff function of a function that depends only on the *other* player's action; on the other hand, the first rule (minimax regret) is not open to this objection.

Our attitude toward this minimax-regret principle in the present context is pragmatic. We are prepared to consider it seriously if it leads to simple and/or realistic bargaining strategies that give "adequate" protection against a wide range of bargaining behavior by the other player. In fact, in the case of the sealed-bid mechanism, there are minimax-regret bids that are linear in the player's own value (or cost). The calculation of these bids requires only minimal information about the range of values (costs) and bids of the other player. There may be other minimax-regret bids, but they have the same maximum regret.

We illustrate these ideas with the application of our main result to the case of bargaining over price and quantity, when each player is uncertain about the other player's true values (resp. costs). Let $V(q)$ denote the value to the (potential) buyer of receiving q units of a good or service, and let $C(q)$ be the corresponding cost to the (potential) seller. Assume that there is some finite set of alternative quantities, or that they lie in some (closed) interval of finite length. In the sealed-bid mecahnism, for each possible quantity q the buyer submits a bid, say $v(q)$, and the seller submits corresponding bids $c(q)$. When these (sealed) bids are simultaneously opened, a quantity, say q_1, is chosen that maximizes

$$v(q) - c(q);$$

trade then takes place at the quantity q_1 if the above difference is non-negative, at a price equal to the arithmetic mean of the two bids $v(q_1)$ and $c(q_1)$. (We require that the bid functions $v(\cdot)$ and $c(\cdot)$ be continuous.)

For each possible quantity q, let $C_{\min}(q)$ denote the minimum possible true cost $C(q)$; then, as we shall show, a (pure) minimax-regret bid function for the buyer is

$$v(q) = \tfrac{2}{3} V(q) + \tfrac{1}{3} C_{\min}(q).$$

The corresponding minimax-regret bid function for the seller is

$$c(q) = \tfrac{2}{3} C(q) + \tfrac{1}{3} V_{\max}(q).$$

In the above formulation, one can replace the characteristic "quantity" by any characteristic or vector of characteristics—such as quality, delivery time, etc.—provided that the set of alternative "objects" (individual vectors of characteristics) is compact, and the functions $V(\cdot)$ and $C(\cdot)$ are continuous.

In the remainder of this paper we study minimax-regret bids for the sealed-bid mechanism for both the case of complete information (Section 2) and the case of incomplete information (Section 3). In Section 4, we compare the minimax-regret bids with the corresponding Nash (or Harsanyi–Nash) equilibria, where the latter are known. In particular, in the case of complete information, the (many) Nash equilibria are typically inefficient, whereas the outcome of the pair of linear minimax-regret bids is efficient.

In the case of incomplete information, at least two alternative versions of the minimax-regret principle suggest themselves, according as a player does not—or does—take account of the probability distribution of the other player's true value (resp. cost). Note, however, that in neither case does a player make any assumption about the other player's *bid*. In the second version, we have studied the minimax-regret bids only in the case of bargaining over the price of a single object.

Up to this point, we have been discussing only pure, i.e., nonrandomized, bids. In Section 5 we show—for the case of a single object—that a player can reduce his maximum regret by using randomized bidding, and we derive the minimax-regret randomized bids for this case. However, an extension of this analysis to the general case of many objects appears to present significant technical difficulties. Furthermore, we are not persuaded that randomized bidding is realistic in this context.

Finally, in Section 6, we summarize our conclusions and mention some open questions.

2. MINIMAX-REGRET BIDDING WITH COMPLETE INFORMATION

a. *The General Model and the Sealed-Bid Mechanism*

A buyer (B) and a seller (S) bargain over which (if any) of a set of alternative trades to make, and what the price will be if trade does take place. The set of alternative trades is indexed by a parameter q. For example, q might denote the quantity to be traded, in which case it would be a nonnegative real number. Or q might denote the quantity to be supplied, the delivery date, and certain other specifications, in which case q would be a vector; or q might denote any subset of a finite set of candidate objects to be traded. We shall assume only that the set of alternative trades is some compact set, say Q, e.g., a closed bounded interval on the line, or a closed bounded set in Euclidean space. In particular, Q might be finite, or even have only one element. In the last case, we shall say that B and S are bargaining over the price of a single object; this is the case discussed in almost all of the recent game-theoretic literature.

The *sealed-bid mechanism* as defined here determines whether trade takes place, and if so, which object is traded and at what price. Each player submits a *bid* in the form of a (real-valued) function on Q. If B's bid is the function $v(\cdot)$, then for each q in Q, $v(q)$ is interpreted as the maximum price that B is willing to pay for object q. Similarly, if S's bid is the function $c(\cdot)$, then $c(q)$ is the minimum payment that S will accept for object q. In the general case, we shall call the elements of Q the alternative *objects*; a generic object in Q will be denoted by q. The players' bids (functions) are required to be continuous on Q.

Let $V(q)$ be the value to the buyer of obtaining the object q, and let $C(q)$

be the cost to the seller of providing q. If q is traded at *price* p, then B's profit is $V(q) - p$, and S's profit is $p - C(q)$. If no trade takes place, then each party's profit is zero. (Thus we assume that S does not make or purchase the object q unless he has a buyer for it.) Note that p is the *total* price, not the price per unit.

Given the bids $v(\cdot)$ and $c(\cdot)$, let q_1 be a value of q that maximizes $v(q) - c(q)$. The sealed-bid mechanism stipulates that:

(i)   Trade occurs if and only if $v(q_1) \geqslant c(q_1)$.

(ii)   If trade occurs, the object traded is q_1, and the price paid by B to S is

$$p_1 = \tfrac{1}{2}[v(q)_1) + c(q_1)]. \tag{2.a.1}$$

If $v(q) = c(q)$ attains a nonnegative maximum at more than one object q, then the mechanism will have to select one of them for trade. For our present purposes, it is not necessary for us to specify a particular selection rule.

If B and S bid their true value and cost (resp.), i.e., if $v = V$ and $c = C$, then the sealed-bid mechanism would choose a q that yielded the maximum total "surplus" or "gains from trade," $V(q) - C(q)$, provided the latter were nonnegative. It would also divide the gains from trade equally between the two players. In these respects it is similar, but not identical, to the "standard Walrasian market mechanism" for equating supply and demand. Thus, if the players reveal their true value and cost (resp.), then under "classical" conditions the Walrasian mechanism will select a trade that maximizes the total gains from trade, but it will typically not divide the gains equally.

To illustrate this point, suppose that q represents the number of units of a homogeneous commodity, and let ϕ denote the *price per unit* of the commodity. Faced with a fixed price ϕ, the buyer would demand a quantity q that maximized

$$V(q) - \phi q;$$

for V sufficiently regular this would be equivalent to

$$V'(q) = \phi.$$

Thus $V'(q)$ is the price (per unit) at which the buyer would demand the quantity q (sometimes called the "demand price"). Similarly, $C'(q)$ is the price ("supply price") at which the seller would supply the quantity q. Equating the two prices, we get $V'(q_1) = C'(q_1)$, or

$$V'(q_1) - C'(q_1) = 0,$$

which is the first-order condition for the maximization of total gains from trade. However, the per-unit price would be

$$\phi = V'(q_1) = C'(q_1),$$

whereas the sealed-bid mechanism yields a per-unit price of

$$\frac{V(q_1) + C(q_1)}{2q_1}.$$

It is easy to verify that these two prices are equal if and only if

$$\frac{V(q_1)}{q_1} - V'(q_1) = C'(q_1) - \frac{C(q_1)}{q_1},$$

which is a condition that would be satisfied only by accident. (Note that the left-hand side is the difference between average value (per unit) and marginal value, whereas the right-hand side is the difference between marginal cost and average cost.)

(In a slightly different specification of the model, the alternative "no trade" could be included in the set Q. We have chosen the present formulation in order to guarantee that trade never takes place at a strictly negative price. In the alternative specification, one could equivalently require that the bids for "no trade" be zero.)

We shall assume that the function $V(\cdot)$ and $C(\cdot)$ are common knowledge to both players, and that they are continuous and nonnegative. To avoid uninteresting complications, we also assume that, for all q in Q, $V(q) \geqslant C(q)$.

If B bids $v(\cdot)$ and S bids $c(\cdot)$, let q_1 as above be the selected value of q for which $v(q) - c(q)$ attains a maximum; q_1 is implicitly a function of $v(\cdot)$ and $c(\cdot)$. B's profit is

$$\Pi_B[v(\cdot), c(\cdot)] \equiv \begin{cases} V(q_1) - p_1, & \text{if } v(q_1) \geqslant c(q_1), \\ 0, & \text{otherwise,} \end{cases} \tag{2.a.2}$$

where p_1 is the price determined by (2.a.1). Given $c(\cdot)$, B's maximum profit is

$$\Pi_B^*[c(\cdot)] \equiv \begin{cases} \max_q [V(q) - c(q)], & \text{if this is } > 0, \\ 0, & \text{otherwise.} \end{cases} \tag{2.a.3}$$

Note that if B's maximum profit is strictly positive, B can attain this profit with a bid that equals $c(q)$ at every q for which $V(q) - c(q)$ is at a maximum, and is strictly less that $c(q)$ otherwise. On the other hand, a maximum profit of zero can be attained with a bid that is strictly less than $c(q)$ for every q.

It is never in B's interest to make a bid for which $v(q)$ is strictly greater than $V(q)$ for some q. For suppose to the contrary that $v(q) > V(q)$. If trade occurs at q, then there are two possibilities:

  1. $c(q) \leqslant V(q)$. In this case B's profit would have been higher if he had bid $v(q) = V(q)$.

  2. $c(q) > V(q)$. In this case the price exceeds $V(q)$ and B makes a loss; he would have been better off had he bid $v(q) = V(q)$ and there had been no trade.

If trade does not occur at q, then the outcome would have been the same if B had bid $v(q) = V(q)$. Hence in all cases, B would have been better off–or no worse off—had he bid $v(q) = V(q)$.[1] A similar argumant shows that S should never bid $c(q) < C(q)$. Therefore we henceforth consider only bids for which, for every q in Q

$$v(q) \leqslant C(q),$$
$$c(q) \geqslant C(q). \tag{2.a.4}$$

When there is no danger of confusion, we shall write v for the function $v(\cdot)$ and c for the function $c(\cdot)$.

Given the bids v and c, B's regret is

$$R_B(v, c) = \Pi_B^*(c) - \Pi_B(v, c). \tag{2.a.5}$$

A bid v^* is a *minimax-regret* bid for B if, for all bids v,

$$\sup_c R_B(v^*, c) \leqslant \sup_c R_B(v, c), \tag{2.a.6}$$

where it is understood that all bids are continuous and satisfy (2.a.4). (Note that R_B is bounded, so that the suprema in (2.a.6) are finite.)

In Section 2c we shall show that, under the conditions described above, a minimax-regret bid for B is

$$v^*(q) = (\tfrac{2}{3}) \, V(q) + (\tfrac{1}{3}) \, C(q). \tag{2.a.7}$$

The seller's regret function is defined in a corresponding way, and we shall also show that his corresponding minimax-regret bid is

$$c^*(q) = (\tfrac{2}{3}) \, C(q) + (\tfrac{1}{3}) \, V(q). \tag{2.a.8}$$

---

[1] Just as a bid for which $v(q) > V(q)$ cannot increase B's profit, so it cannot decrease his regret, since optimum profit Π_B^* is independent of B's bid.

Because the proof is somewhat complicated, although elementary, we first give a proof for the case of bargaining over the price of a single object.

b. *Minimax-Regret Bids in the Case of a Single Object*

The buyer (B) and seller (S) bargain over the price of a single object, whose value to B is V, and whose cost to S is C, where $V > C$. The numbers V and C are common knowledge. Simultaneously, B bids v, and S bids c. Trade occurs if and only if $v \geqslant c$. When trade occurs, the price is

$$p = \frac{v + c}{2}.$$ (2.b.1)

Thus B's *profit* is

$$\Pi_B = \begin{cases} V - \frac{1}{2}(v + c), & v \geqslant c, \\ 0, & v < c. \end{cases}$$ (2.b.2)

Similarly, S's profit is

$$\Pi_S = \begin{cases} \frac{1}{2}(v + c) - C, & v \geqslant c, \\ 0, & v < c. \end{cases}$$ (2.b.3)

The situations of B and S are symmetric in an obvious way. Therefore, in what follows, we shall often confine our attention to the buyer's profit.

Following (2.a.4) we shall assume that

$$v \leqslant V,$$
$$c \geqslant C.$$ (2.b.4)

Suppose that B bids v. Then his profit, *regarded as a function of c*, is given by (2.b.2). If B had acted optimally (with the wisdom of hindsight), he would have matched S's bid, and the price would have been c. Thus B's *optimum profit* is

$$\Pi_B^* = \begin{cases} V - c, & V \geqslant c, \\ 0, & V < c, \end{cases}$$ (2.b.5)

and his regret is

$$R_B \equiv \Pi_B^* - \Pi_B = \begin{cases} (v - c)/2, & c \leqslant v, \\ V - c, & v < c \leqslant V, \\ 0, & V < c. \end{cases}$$ (2.b.6)

Equation (2.b.6) implies that B's maximum regret if trade occurs is

$\frac{1}{2}(v - C)$, while the supremum of his regret if trade does not occur is $V - v$. Overall,

$$\sup_c R_B = \max\left(\frac{v - C}{2}, V - v, 0\right). \tag{2.b.7}$$

This function of v is shown in Fig. 1. It is clear that it is minimized when

$$\frac{v - C}{2} = V - v;$$

that is,

$$v = \tfrac{1}{3}C + \tfrac{2}{3}V. \tag{2.b.8}$$

Substituting (2.b.8) in (2.b.7),

$$\min_v \sup_c R_B = \frac{V - C}{3}. \tag{2.b.9}$$

Similarly, S's min sup regret is achieved at

$$c = \tfrac{2}{3}C + \tfrac{1}{3}V, \tag{2.b.10}$$

and is also

$$\min_c \sup_v R_S = \frac{V - C}{3}. \tag{2.b.11}$$

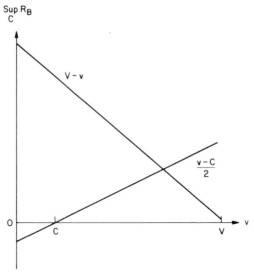

FIG. 1. Maximum regret, for the case of a single object, complete information [Eq. (2.b.7)].

Note that by the bid (2.b.8) the buyer has reduced his regret by two thirds, with respect to the worst (maximax) case. (In the worst case for the buyer, the seller makes a small bid, $c = C + \varepsilon$, while the buyer makes a still smaller one, $v = C + \varepsilon'$, where $\varepsilon' < \varepsilon$. There is no trade, so $\Pi_B = 0$. But $\Pi_B^* = V - C - \varepsilon$. Thus the buyer's regret can be as great as $V - C - \varepsilon$ for every $\varepsilon > 0$.) A similar remark is applicable to the seller. We shall see in Section 5 that the buyer can do even better by randomizing his bid.

If *both* B and S make minimax-regret bids, the price is $p = \frac{1}{2}(V + C)$, and each has regret $\frac{1}{6}(V - C)$, and profit $\frac{1}{2}(V - C)$. Thus the outcome is efficient, i.e., total gains from trade are maximized.

With regard to independence of irrelevant alternatives, the following remarks are easily verified for the problem treated in this section:

1. If one deletes from the range of allowed bids by the buyer any set of bids lying entirely below C, the buyer's minimax regret bid is still given by (2.b.8), and is thus independent of the presence or absence of these irrelevant alternatives.

2. If, on the other hand, one prohibits the buyer from making bids below x, where $C < x \leqslant (\frac{2}{3})V + (\frac{1}{3})C$, then his minimax regret bid becomes

$$v = (\tfrac{2}{3})V + (\tfrac{1}{3})x.$$

Thus, if x is lowered, the buyer's bid will change, even though his new bid will not lie in the newly accessible region. In short, the condition of independence of irrelevant alternatives is not satisfied in this case.

It seems to us, however, that the imposed constraint, $v \geqslant x \geqslant C$, is not a natural one in the present context.

c. *Minimax-Regret Bids for the General Case*

We now return to the general case, and a derivation of the minimax-regret bids (2.a.7) and (2.a.8). For the reader's convenience, we recall here our assumptions and requirements:

1. The set Q of alternative objects of trade is compact.

2. The true value function $V(\cdot)$ and cost function $C(\cdot)$ are continuous on Q.

3. All bids $v(\cdot)$ and $c(\cdot)$ are required to be continuous on Q.

4. All bids $v(\cdot)$ and $c(\cdot)$ are assumed to satisfy (2.a.4), namely, for each q,

$$v(q) \leqslant V(q),$$
$$c(q) \geqslant C(q). \tag{2.c.1}$$

5. For all q in Q, $V(q) \geqslant C(q)$.

Note that 1, 2, 4, 5 are assumptions, whereas 3 is a requirement of the sealed-bid mechanism.

Recall that, given the bids $v(\cdot)$ and $c(\cdot)$, the mechanism selects a q_1 that maximizes $v(q) - c(q)$. The mechanism then stipulates that trade occurs if and only if

$$v(q_1) \geqslant c(q_1), \tag{2.c.2}$$

and if trade does occur, object q_1 is traded at (total) price

$$p = (\tfrac{1}{2})[v(q_1) + c(q_1)]. \tag{2.c.3}$$

Because of the symmetry of the situation, we shall derive only the linear minimax-regret bid of the buyer, namely,

$$v^*(q) = (\tfrac{2}{3})\, V(q) + (\tfrac{1}{3})\, C(q). \tag{2.c.4}$$

We begin the derivation by calculating a lower bound on the supremum of B's regret. We then show that there is a bid for B that attains this lower bound.

Let $v(\cdot)$ be a bid by B, and let q_2 maximize $V(q) - v(q)$. Let ε be a positive number, and let $c(\cdot)$ be a bid by S such that

(i) $c(q_2) = v(q_2) + \varepsilon,$
(ii) $c(q) > v(q) + \varepsilon,$ for every $q \neq q_2$.

No trade occurs, so $\Pi_{\mathrm{B}} = 0$. Now B's best response to $c(\cdot)$ (the situation is like that in Fig. 3, with q^* replaced by q_2) would lead to trade of amount q_2 at price $c(q_2)$, resulting in a profit of

$$\Pi_{\mathrm{B}}^* = V(q_2) - v(q_2) - \varepsilon, \tag{2.c.5}$$

which is also the regret. Thus we have a lower bound for the supremum regret:

$$\sup_{c(\cdot)} R_{\mathrm{B}}(v(\cdot)) \geqslant V(q_2) - v(q_2) = \max_v [V(q) - v(q)]. \tag{2.c.6}$$

Now, for the same $v(\cdot)$, consider a seller's bid $c(\cdot)$ such that

(i) $c(q_3) = C(q_3)$,

(ii) $c(q) > C(q)$ for every $q \neq q_3$,

where q_3 maximizes $v(q) - C(q)$. Trade occurs at price $p = \frac{1}{2}[v(q_3) + C(q_3)]$, leading to a profit of

$$\Pi_B = V(q_3) - \tfrac{1}{2}[v(q_3) + C(q_3)]. \tag{2.c.7}$$

The buyer's best response to this $c(\cdot)$ would result in trade of the quantity q_3 at price $C(q_3)$, leading to a profit of

$$\Pi_B^* = V(q_3) - C(q_3), \tag{2.c.8}$$

and a regret

$$R_B = \tfrac{1}{2}[v(q_3) - C(q_3)]. \tag{2.c.9}$$

This is another lower bound for B's supremum regret:

$$\sup_{c(\cdot)} R_B \geq \tfrac{1}{2}[v(q_3) - C(q_3)]. \tag{2.c.10}$$

From (2.c.6) and (2.c.10)

$$\sup_{c(\cdot)} R_B \geq \max\{V(q_2) - v(q_2), \tfrac{1}{2}[v(q_3) - C(q_3)]\}. \tag{2.c.11}$$

Now let q_4 maximize $V(q) - C(q)$; then

$$\begin{aligned} V(q_2) - v(q_2) &\geq V(q_4) - v(q_4), \\ v(q_3) - C(q_3) &\geq v(q_4) - C(q_4). \end{aligned} \tag{2.c.12}$$

From (2.c.11) and (2.c.12),

$$\sup_{c(\cdot)} R_B \geq \max\{V(q_4) - v(q_4), \tfrac{1}{2}[v(q_4) - C(q_4)]\}. \tag{2.c.13}$$

Hence

$$\min_{v(\cdot)}\sup_{c(\cdot)} R_B \geq \min_{v(\cdot)} \max\{V(q_4) - v(q_4), \tfrac{1}{2}[v(q_4) - C(q_4)]\}. \tag{2.c.14}$$

For a bid v that minimizes the maximum on the right-hand side of (2.c.14),

$$V(q_4) - v(q_4) = \tfrac{1}{2}[v(q_4) - C(q_4)];$$

otherwise we could decrease the maximum by varying $v(q_4)$. Solving for $v(q_4)$, it follows that

$$\min_{v(\cdot)} \sup_{c(\cdot)} R_B \geq \tfrac{1}{3}[V(q_4) - C(q_4)]. \tag{2.c.15}$$

Next consider the particular bid function

$$v^*(q) = \tfrac{1}{3}C(q) + \tfrac{2}{3}V(q). \tag{2.c.16}$$

For $v^*(\cdot)$, it is clear that

$$q_2 = q_3 = q_4; \tag{2.c.17}$$

let us denote thus common value by q_0. What is the supremum of the regret for $v^*(\cdot)$?

If trade does not occur, that is, if $v(q) < c(q)$ for all q, then B's regret is Π_B^*, his optimal-response profit. This cannot be greater than, but can be arbitrarily close to, the maximum of $V(\cdot) - v(\cdot)$, that is, $V(q_2) - v(q_2)$. Thus, for no trade, it follows from (2.c.16) and (2.c.17) that

$$\sup_{c(\cdot)} R_B = \tfrac{1}{3}[V(q_0) - C(q_0)]. \tag{2.c.18}$$

If trade does occur, we claim that the maximum regret is also given by (2.c.18). This is the value attained if $v(\cdot)$ is given by (2.c.16) and

(i) $c(q_0) = C(q_0)$,
(ii) $c(q) > C(q)$ for all $q \neq q_0$.

(See Fig. 2.) Thus it remains to show that, for $v(\cdot)$ given by (2.c.16), B's regret cannot exceed the right-hand side of (2.c.18).

Let q_5 maximize $V(\cdot) - c(\cdot)$; then for any bid $c(\cdot)$,

$$\Pi_B = V(q_1) - \tfrac{1}{2}[v(q_1) + c(q_1)], \tag{2.c.19}$$

and

$$\Pi_B^* = V(q_5) - c(q_5). \tag{2.c.20}$$

(Recall that q_1 maximizes $v(q) - c(q)$.) Hence B's regret is

$$R_B = V(q_5) - c(q_5) - V(q_1) + \tfrac{1}{2}[v(q_1) + c(q_1)]. \tag{2.c.21}$$

Now, using (2.c.16), let us substitute in (2.c.21):

$$V(q_5) = \tfrac{1}{3}[V(q_5) - C(q_5)] + v(q_5),$$
$$V(q_1) = \tfrac{3}{2}v(q_1) - \tfrac{1}{2}C(q_1). \tag{2.c.22}$$

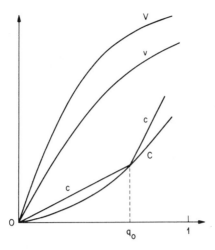

FIG. 2. Seller's bid function achieving maximum regret (Section 4b).

Then

$$R_{\mathrm{B}} = \tfrac{1}{3}[V(q_5) - C(q_5)] + v(q_5) - c(q_5) - \left[v(q_1) - \frac{c(q_1) + C(q_1)}{2}\right]. \quad (2.\mathrm{c}.23)$$

Using (2.c.1), and the definition of q_1, we have

$$R_{\mathrm{B}} \leqslant \tfrac{1}{3}[V(q_5) - c(q_5)] \leqslant \tfrac{1}{3}[V(q_0) - C(q_0)], \quad (2.\mathrm{c}.24)$$

by the definition of q_4, and using (2.c.17).

If B plays this strategy, and S plays the corresponding linear minimax regret strategy,

$$c^*(q) = \tfrac{1}{3}V(q) + \tfrac{2}{3}C(q), \quad (2.\mathrm{c}.25)$$

then trade occurs at q_4, which maximizes $V(\cdot) - C(\cdot)$, and hence the outcome is efficient.

3. Minimax-Regret Bidding with Incomplete Information

a. First Version

Several definitions of minimax-regret bidding with incomplete information are plausible. In the first version that we consider, each player makes minimal assumptions about the range of possible bids that he may face. Specifically, for each object q in Q, the buyer knows a lower bound, say

$C_{\min}(q)$, on the seller's cost, and the seller knows an upper bound, say $V_{\max}(q)$, on the buyer's value. We assume that $C_{\min}(\cdot)$ and $V_{\max}(\cdot)$ are continuous, and, for every q in Q, $V_{\max}(q) \geqslant C_{\min}(q)$. It follows from (2.a.4) that

$$v(q) \leqslant V_{\max}(q),$$
$$c(q) \geqslant C_{\min}(q). \tag{3.a.1}$$

(The first line of (3.a.1) is of interest to the seller, the second to be buyer.) A bid for the buyer (seller) is a continuous function on Q that satisfies (3.1). Accordingly, the buyer chooses a bid that minimizes

$$\sup_{c(\cdot)} R_B[v(\cdot), c(\cdot)], \tag{3.a.2}$$

where the supremum in (3.a.2) is over all seller's bids $c(\cdot)$ with the above properties. It is straightforward to adapt the argument of Section 2c to prove that a buyer's minimax-regret bid is given by

$$v^*(q) = (\tfrac{2}{3}) V(q) + (\tfrac{1}{3}) C_{\min}(q). \tag{3.a.3a}$$

Similarly, a seller's minimax-regret bid is

$$c^*(q) = (\tfrac{2}{3}) C(q) + (\tfrac{1}{3}) V_{\max}(q). \tag{3.a.3b}$$

From (2.b.12) and (2.b.14), the minimax-regrets of B and S are

$$\min_{v} \sup_{c} R_B = \frac{V - C_{\min}}{3}, \qquad \min_{c} \sup_{v} R_S = \frac{V_{\max} - C}{3}. \tag{3.a.4}$$

If both players use these minimax-regret bids, the outcome need not be efficient; in this respect the case of incomplete information differs from that of complete information. For example, if there is only a single object, trade will take place if and only if $v - c \geqslant 0$. From (3.a.3) and (3.a.4)

$$v - c = (\tfrac{2}{3})(V - C) - \tfrac{1}{3}(V_{\max} - C_{\min});$$

hence trade takes place if and only if

$$V - C \geqslant (\tfrac{1}{2})(V_{\max} - C_{\min}). \tag{3.a.5a}$$

For efficiency, trade should take place if and only if

$$V - C \geqslant 0; \tag{3.a.5b}$$

It is clear that, if V can be strictly less than $V_{\max}$ and /or C can be strictly greater than C_{min}, then (3.a.5a) and (3.a.5b) are not equivalent. (We shall return to this point in Section 3b.)

b. *Second Version*

In the Harsanyi–Nash equilibrium theory of the sealed-bid mechanism (see Section 4), it is assumed that there is a prior probability distribution of V and C, which is common knowledge to the players B and S. Before B and S submit their bids, the actual realizations of V and C are revealed to B and S, respectively, but not vice versa. We shall propose a second version of minimax-regret bidding, in which the players make use of their knowledge about the prior probability distribution of V and C. Thus far we have been able to characterize in this second version minimax-regret bids only for the case of a single object.

Suppose that, a priori, V has cumulative probability distribution function (cdf) M, C has cdf N, and V and C are independently distributed. For simplicity, assume that the support of both M and N is the unit interval, $[0, 1]$, and that M and N are strictly increasing there.

Given B's bid v and his true value V, the supremum of B's regret will also depend on C, since S's bid c will be at least C. Denote this by $R_B(v \mid V, C)$, i.e.,

$$R_B(v \mid V, C) = \sup_{c \geqslant C} R_B(v, c), \qquad (3.b.1)$$

where $R_B(v, c)$ is given by (2.b.6). We now suppose that B chooses v to maximize the *expected value* of $R_B(v \mid V, C)$, given V, i.e.,

$$\bar{R}_B(v \mid V) \equiv \int_0^1 R_B(v \mid V, C) \, dN(C). \qquad (3.b.2)$$

In the present case, B is ignorant of the true cost C, and hence may bid below it. Thus, instead of (2.b.7), we have

$$R_B(v \mid V, C) = \begin{cases} 0, & C > V \\ \max\left\{V - v, \dfrac{v - C}{2}\right\}, & V \geqslant v \geqslant C \\ V - C, & V \geqslant C > v. \end{cases} \qquad (3.b.3)$$

Note that

$$\frac{v - C}{2} \geqslant V - v \qquad \text{iff} \quad C \leqslant 3v - 2V. \qquad (3.b.4)$$

Therefore,

$$\bar{R}(v, V) = \int_0^{3v-2V} \frac{v-C}{2}\, dN(C) + \int_{3v-2V}^{v} (V-v)\, dN(C) + \int_v^V (V-C)\, dN(C).$$

$$(3.b.5)$$

If, however, $v < \frac{2}{3}V$, then the first term in (3.b.5) is missing, and we have instead

$$\bar{R}(v, V) = \int_0^v (V-v)\, dN(C) + \int_v^V (V-C)\, dN(C). \qquad (3.b.6)$$

Using integration by parts, we have from (3.b.5) and (3.b.6),

$$\bar{R}(v \mid V) = \begin{cases} \dfrac{1}{2}\displaystyle\int_0^{3v-2V} N(C)\, dC + \int_v^V N(C)\, dC, & \frac{2}{3}V \leqslant v \leqslant V, \\[2ex] \displaystyle\int_v^V N(C)\, dC, & 0 \leqslant v \leqslant \frac{2}{3}V. \end{cases} \quad (3.b.7)$$

We seek the v that minimizes (3.b.7). Differentiating,

$$\frac{d}{dv}\,\bar{R}_B(v \mid V) = \begin{cases} \frac{3}{2}N(3v-2V) - N(v), & \frac{2}{3}V \leqslant v \leqslant V, \\ -N(v), & 0 \leqslant v \leqslant \frac{2}{3}V. \end{cases} \qquad (3.b.8)$$

This derivative is continuous, and is decreasing in v on $[0, \frac{2}{3}V]$. Hence, the minima, if any, of $\bar{R}_B(v \mid V)$ lie on $[\frac{2}{3}V, V]$. In fact, on this interval, the derivative is negative at $v = \frac{2}{3}V$, and positive at $v = V$. Hence the equation

$$\tfrac{3}{2}N(3v - 2V) - N(v) = 0$$

has a root in the interior of the interval $[\frac{2}{3}V, V]$.

As an example, we use a class of priors analyzed in Leininger et al. [4]:

$$N(C) = C^r,$$
$$M(V) = 1 - (1-V)^r, \qquad (3.b.9)$$

where $0 \leqslant r \leqslant \infty$. Define $k(r)$ by

$$v = k(r)V. \qquad (3.b.10)$$

Then (3.b.8) gives

$$k(r) = 2/[3 - (\tfrac{2}{3})^{1/r}]. \qquad (3.b.11)$$

If $r = 0$, we have the certainty case, treated in Section 2, and (3.b.11) implies $v = \frac{2}{3}V$, as before (where $V = 1$ with probability 1). If $r = 1$, we have uniform priors, and the min sup bid is

$$v = \tfrac{6}{7}V. \tag{3.b.12}$$

From (3.b.6), this bid yields an expected maximum regret of $\frac{3}{14}V^2$. However, in the worst case in the sense of (3.a.2) ($C = 0$, $c = 0$), it yields a regret of $\frac{3}{7}V$. This is greater than the $\frac{1}{3}V$ of the previous, more conservative, strategy, as one would expect.

Now suppose both buyer and seller use this strategy. We write (to display the symmetry)

$$
\begin{aligned}
v &= V - \tfrac{1}{7}(V - 0) = \tfrac{6}{7}V, \\
c &= C + \tfrac{1}{7}(1 - C) = \tfrac{6}{7}C + \tfrac{1}{7}.
\end{aligned}
\tag{3.b.13}
$$

Then trade occurs if and only if

$$V \geq C + \tfrac{1}{6}. \tag{3.b.14}$$

4. Comparisons with Equilibrium Strategies

In this section we compare minimax-regret bids with the strategies in Nash equilibria of the noncooperative game defined by the sealed-bid mechanism. In the case of complete information, we shall see that there is an infinity of Nash equilibria, and—except in the case of a single object—"most" of them are inefficient.

In the case of incomplete information, previous research has characterized the Harsanyi–Nash equilibria for the special case of a single object, and we shall confine our discussion to this case. Here again the multiplicity of equilibria is dramatic.

a. *Complete Information*

We return now to the model of Section 2.a, in which B's value function, V, and S's cost function, C, are common knowledge. Recall that a *Nash equilibrium* is a pair of bids, (v, c), such that neither player can increase his profit by *unilaterally* changing his bid.

The case of a single object is particularly simple, and well known. In fact, any pair of *equal* bids between C and V is an equilibrium (we suppose that $C < V$):

$$C \leq c = v \leq V. \tag{4.a.1}$$

For if B increases his bid above c, he will raise the price and lower his profit. If he lowers his bid below c, trade will not occur and his profit will drop from $V - c$ to zero.

Note that all these equilibria are efficient, that is,

$$\Pi_B + \Pi_B = (V - p) + (p - C) = V - C; \qquad (4.a.2)$$

all possible gains from trade are realized.

Note also that there is no mechanism (within the model) for the players to coordinate their bids.

There also exists a "perverse" equilibrium of this game, namely,

$$\begin{aligned} v &= C, \\ c &= V. \end{aligned} \qquad (4.a.3)$$

Here the profit of each player is zero, and neither can improve it by unilaterally changing his bid. The efficiency of this equilibrium (i.e., the fraction of possible gains from trade realized) is zero.

We turn now to the general case of more than one object. Without loss of generality, we may assume that, for every q in Q, $V(q) \geq C(q)$.

Let q^* be any such q and let p be any number such that

$$C(q^*) < p^* < V(q^*). \qquad (4.a.4)$$

Then any $v(\cdot)$ and $c(\cdot)$ are in equilibrium if they satisfy the following conditions:

(i) $v(q^*) = c(q^*) = p^*$,

(ii) $V(q) - c(q) \leq V(q^*) - c(q^*)$ for all $q \neq q^*$,
       $v(q) - C(q) \leq v(q^*) - C(q^*)$ for all $q \neq q^*$,

(iii) $v(q) < c(q)$ for all $q \neq q^*$.

This situation is shown schematically in Fig. 3. In general, there will be no difficulty in constructing functions $v(\cdot)$ and $c(\cdot)$ that satisfy these conditions. Such functions are in equilibrium because:

Given $c(\cdot)$, if B lowers $v(q^*)$ then trade will not occur, and he will lose the profit $V(q^*) - p^* > 0$.

If B raises $v(q^*)$ then trade will still occur, but at a higher price, hence at a lower profit.

If B changes $v(\cdot)$ so that trade occurs at some $q \neq q^*$, then he cannot make a higher profit, since q^* maximizes $V(\cdot) - c(\cdot)$.

Similar reasoning applies to S.

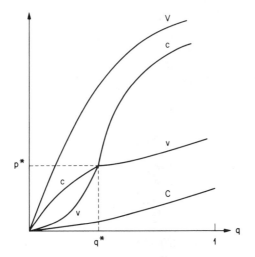

FIG. 3. An equilibrium, for the case of bargaining over price and quantity, complete information (Section 4a).

Thus there is a (two-parameter) continuum of equilibria. In contrast to the situation with a single object, even with complete information *almost all of these equilibria are inefficient.* They are efficient, in fact, only when we choose q^* to maximize $V(q) - C(q)$.

b. *Incomplete Information*

We confine our discussion of incomplete information to the case of a single object, since Harsanyi–Nash equilibria have been characterized only for this case. As noted in the Introduction, there is a very large set of equilibria, which typically cover a wide range of efficiency.

For example, in the model of Section 3b, suppose that C and V are independently and uniformly distributed on the unit interval. First-best efficiency would be attained if each player bid his true value (cost), i.e., $v = V$ and $c = C$, because trade would then occur if and only if $V \geqslant C$; in this case the expected total gains from trade are

$$J = \tfrac{1}{6}. \tag{4.b.1}$$

Of the many equilibria, the one with the maximum expected gains from trade uses the following strategies[2]:

---

[2] Actually this equilibrium is not unique, in the following trivial sense: in the range in which trade does not occur, $0 \leqslant V \leqslant \tfrac{1}{4}$, any function v lying between 0 and V (inclusive) could form part of such an equilibrium. Similarly for $\tfrac{3}{4} \leqslant C \leqslant 1$, any function c lying between C and 1 would do.

$$v = \begin{cases} (\frac{2}{3})V + \frac{1}{12}, & \frac{1}{4} \leqslant V \leqslant 1, \\ V, & 0 \leqslant V \leqslant \frac{1}{4}, \end{cases}$$

$$c = \begin{cases} (\frac{2}{3})C + \frac{1}{4}, & 0 \leqslant C \leqslant \frac{3}{4}, \\ C, & \frac{3}{4} \leqslant C \leqslant 1 \end{cases} .$$

(4.b.2)

In this equilibrium, the expected gains from trade are

$$K = 0.14063.$$

(4.b.3)

The efficiency of the equilibrium is

$$\eta \equiv \frac{K}{J} = 0.844$$

(4.b.4)

(see Leininger *et al.* [4]). (In fact, it has been shown that for this model (with the uniform prior distributions on [0, 1]) there is no other bargaining mechanism with "reasonable" properties that has an equilibrium with larger expected gains from trade; see Myerson and Satterthwaite [7]. In the terminology of the theory, this equilibrium of this mechanism is "second best.")

By comparison, if *both* players use their respective *version-one* minimax-regret bids, then the expected gains from trade are

$$K = \frac{1}{12},$$

(4.b.5)

which gives an efficiency

$$\eta = \frac{1}{2}.$$

(4.b.6)

(To calculate the expected gains from trade, first note that they are equal to

$$K \equiv E(\Pi_{\mathrm{B}} + \Pi_{\mathrm{S}})$$

$$= \int_0^1 \int_0^1 \underset{v \geqslant c}{(V - C)} \, dV \, dC.$$

(4.b.7)

From (3.a.3ab) we see that $v \geqslant c$ (trade takes place) if and only if $V \geqslant C + \frac{1}{2}$; from this and (4.b.7) an elementary calculation yields (4.b.5).)

On the other hand, if both players use their respective *version-two* minimax-regret bids, (3.b.13), then a corresponding calculation shows that the expected gains from trade are

$$K = \frac{50}{324} = 0.1543,$$

so that the corresponding efficiency is

$$\eta = \frac{0.1543}{0.1667} = 0.9256.$$

Of course, this does not contradict the fact that (4.b.2) constitutes a second-best equilibrium, since the pair of minimax-regret strategies (3.b.13) does *not* constitute an equilibrium.

5. RANDOMIZED BIDDING

It is well known that the use of randomized behavior in a game can often lead to a lower value of minimax-regret than would be possible with non-randomized behavior alone. In this section we show that this is in fact the case for the sealed-bid mechanism.

One may question whether randomization is behaviorally "plausible" or "realistic" in the context of the sealed-bid mechanism. Radomization is of course familiar in the theory of equilibria of games, and plays a particularly important role in the theory of equilibria of two-person zero-sum games. Bluffing in card games such as poker (where bidding occurs!) has been interpreted as randomized behavior. In statistical decision theory, randomization is important in the design of sampling and other experiments.

A complete analysis of minimax-regret randomized bidding is beyond the scope of the present paper, and we are content here to provide the solution for bargaining over the price of a single object, with complete information about the value and cost of the object. We consider, therefore, the model of Section 2b, and without loss of generality we adopt the convention that $V = 1$ and $C = 0$.

Recall that, from (2.b.4), bids will satisfy $v \leqslant 1$ and $c \geqslant 0$. It follows from this that we need only consider bids that satisfy $v \geqslant 0$ and $c \leqslant 1$. Therefore, a *randomized bid* is a probability distribution on the unit interval, which will be characterized by its cumulative distribution function.

Let F and G denote randomized bids of B and S, respectively. By a slight abuse of notation, define B's regret function by

$$R_B(F, G) = \int_0^1 \int_0^1 R_B(v, c)\, dF(v)\, dG(c), \tag{5.1}$$

where $R_B(v, c)$ is given by (2.b.6):

$$R_B(v, c) = \begin{cases} (v - c)/2, & c \leqslant v, \\ 1 - c, & c > v. \end{cases} \tag{5.2}$$

To make the notation more acceptable, we may think of a nonrandomized bid v as a special case of a randomized bid in which all of the probability is concentrated at the point v. With this interpretation, the meaning of $R_B(F, c)$ and $R_B(v, G)$ is also clear.

The main result of this section is

$$\min_{F} \max_{c} R_B(F, c) = \min_{F} \max_{G} R_B(F, G) = \tfrac{1}{4}. \tag{5.3}$$

(Notice that in (5.3) it does not matter whether one takes the "max" over randomized or nonrandomized bids by the seller.) Equation (5.3) should be compared with (2.b.9), which in the present context, with $V = 1$ and $C = 0$, yields

$$\min_{v} \sup_{c} R_B(v, c) = \tfrac{1}{3}. \tag{5.4}$$

Thus B can actually reduce his minimax (expected) regret by randomizing his bid.

We prove (5.3) with a standard technique (see, e.g., Savage [10, Ch. 12, p. 186, Th. 31], by exhibiting randomized bids F^* and G^* such that $R_B(F^*, G^*) = \tfrac{1}{4}$, and for all randomized bids F and G

$$R_B(F^*, G) \leqslant R_B(F^*, G^*) \leqslant R_B(F, G^*). \tag{5.5}$$

The bids F^* and G^* are given by

$$F^*(v) = \begin{cases} (1/\sqrt{1-v}) - 1, & 0 \leqslant v \leqslant \tfrac{3}{4}, \\ 1, & \tfrac{3}{4} \leqslant v \leqslant 1; \end{cases} \tag{5.6}$$

$$G^*(c) = \begin{cases} 1/2 \sqrt{1-c}, & 0 \leqslant c \leqslant \tfrac{3}{4}, \\ 1, & \tfrac{3}{4} \leqslant c \leqslant 1. \end{cases} \tag{5.7}$$

Note that $F^*(0) = 0$, and F^* is absolutely continuous on $[0, 1]$, with density

$$f^*(v) = \begin{cases} (\tfrac{1}{2})(1-v)^{-3/2}, & 0 \leqslant v \leqslant \tfrac{3}{4}, \\ 0, & \tfrac{3}{4} \leqslant v \leqslant 1. \end{cases} \tag{5.8}$$

On the other hand, although the support of G^* is also $[0, \tfrac{3}{4}]$, $G^*(0) = \tfrac{1}{2}$, so that G^* assigns probability $\tfrac{1}{2}$ to the bid 0, and has a density $g^*(x) = (\tfrac{1}{2}) f^*(x)$ on the interval $(0, \tfrac{3}{4}]$.

It is straightforward to verify from (5.2), (5.6), and (5.7) that

$$R_B(F^*, c) = \begin{cases} \tfrac{1}{4}, & 0 \leqslant c \leqslant \tfrac{3}{4}, \\ 1 - c, & \tfrac{3}{4} \leqslant c \leqslant 1, \end{cases} \tag{5.9}$$

$$R_B(v, G^*) = \begin{cases} \tfrac{1}{4}, & 0 \leqslant v \leqslant \tfrac{3}{4}, \\ (\tfrac{1}{2})(v - \tfrac{1}{4}), & \tfrac{3}{4} \leqslant v \leqslant 1. \end{cases} \tag{5.10}$$

Condition (5.5) now follows directly from (5.9) and (5.10), as does the fact that $R_B(F^*, G^*) = \frac{1}{4}$, which completes the proof of (5.3).

6. CONCLUSIONS AND UNFINISHED BUSINESS

(a) We have seen that, in the application to sealed-bid bargaining, the instruction "Bid so as to minimize your maximum regret" has several advantages over the instruction "Bid the best response to your opponent's bid."

There is, in this application, a continuum of Nash equilibria, even for bargaining over the price of a single object; in the case of incomplete information, the efficiency of these equilibria ranges down to zero. The theory is silent on how to select one of these equilibria, i.e., on how a bargainer is to coordinate his bidding strategy with that of his opponent. Thus the instruction to bid the best response cannot be obeyed.

On the other hand, the non-uniqueness of the minimax-regret bid is not as serious an issue. Even if there are several bids that minimize the maximum regret, the player is indifferent among them.

(Moreover, with complete information in the case of a single object, the best pure bid succeeds in reducing the bidder's maximum regret by two thirds (with respect to the maximax), while the best randomized bid reduces this maximum regret by three-quarters. This is a point in favor of the use of minimax regret bidding in this case.)

We also note that in the case of complete information, players who have as their *primary* objective the minimization of maximum regret (in pure strategies) can in addition obtain an efficient outcome by both using the linear minimax-regret strategies. We find this an interesting, if not compelling, reason for using these strategies.

Minimax regret behavior with incomplete information does not require common priors, or even that priors be common knowledge. In the case of Nash equilibrium, on the other hand, if there are not common priors the players do not know (using existing theory) how to figure out what the equilibria are, much less how to coordinate on one. If there is not even common knowledge, theory seems to have no guidance to offer the bargainer.

Despite all this, we want to make it clear that we are *not* claiming that the minimax-regret decision rule works well in all cases.

(b) There is another version of the bargaining problem with incomplete information; we might call it the *ex ante* version. Let $\pi_B(\beta, \gamma)$ denote the buyer's expected profit if he uses the bidding strategy β and the seller uses the bidding strategy γ. For example, in the case of bargaining over the price of a single object, with incomplete information, the buyer's bid is $v = \beta(V)$ and the seller's bid is $c = \gamma(C)$. Let $\pi_B^*(\gamma)$ denote the maximum (or supremum) of the buyer's expected profit, with respect to his own strategy, given that the seller uses the strategy γ. The buyer's regret function is defined by

$$R_B(\beta, \gamma) = \pi_B^*(\gamma) - \pi_B(\beta, \gamma).$$

With this definition of the buyer's regret, we can now define his minimax-regret strategy in the usual way. One can show that the buyer's minimax regret in this version will not exceed (and will typically be less than) the expected minimax regret in the second version above. However, we have not succeeded in actually calculating the minimax-regret strategies for this version, even in the case of a single object. To our knowledge, the only treatment of this problem is by Welch [13] for a single object; there, however, the strategies β and γ are restricted to be linear, for mathematical tractability.

(c) Considered as a hypothesis about behavior, the minimax-regret rule should be subject to empirical testing. An experimental study of sealed-bid bargaining has been conducted (its earlier stages are reported in Radner and Schotter [8]). A statistical test of the minimax-regret hypothesis using these data may be possible.

(d) In another class of models, one can retain the Nash equilibrium concept while applying it to payoff functions other than expected profit (to be maximized), for example, to maximum regret (to be minimized). That is, each bargainer

(i) knows the other's strategy, but is uncertain about the value of the object to the other (the reverse of the "complete information" situation in the present paper);

(ii) knows the value of the object to himself;

(iii) bids in such a way as to minimize the expectation (taken over his prior as to the other's value) of his own maximum regret.

It is interesting that there is a unique equilibrium of this type for sealed-bid bargaining over a single object, that it is the familiar linear "second-best" equilibrium, and that it is independent of priors. But that is another subject.

REFERENCES

1. K. J. ARROW, "Social Choice and Individual Values," 2nd ed., Yale Univ. Press, New Haven, CT, 1951.
2. H. CHERNOFF, Rational selection of decision functions, *Econometrica* **22** (1954), 422–443.

3. J. G. HARSANYI, Games with incomplete information played by Bayesian players *Management Sci.* **14** (1967, 68), 159–182, 320–334, 486–502.

4. W. LEININGER, P. B. LINHART, AND R. RADNER, Equilibria of the sealed-bid mechanism for bargaining with incomplete information, *J. Econ. Theory* **48** (1989), 63–106.

5. J. MILNOR, Games against nature, *in* "Decision Processes" R. M. Thrall, C. H. Coombs and R. L. Davis, Eds.), pp. 49–59, Wiley, New York, 1954.

6. R. B. MEYERSON, Bayesian equilibrium and incentive compatibility: An introduction, *in* "Social Goals and Social Organization; Essays in Memory of Elisha Pazner" (L. Hurwicz. D. Schmeidler, and H. Sonnenschein, Eds.) pp. 229–259, Cambridge Univ. Press, Cambridge, 1985.

7. R. B. MYERSON AND M. A. SATTERTHWAITE, Efficient mechanisms for bilateral trading, *J. Econ. Theory* **29** (1983), 265–281.

8. R. RADNER AND A. SCHOTTER, The sealed-bid mechanism: An experimental study, *J. Econ. Theory* **48** (1989), 179–220.

9. M. A. SATTERWAITE AND S. R. WILLIAMS, Bilateral trade with the sealed-bid double auction: Existence and efficiency, *J. Econ. Theory* **48** (1989), 107–133.

10. L. J. SAVAGE, "The Foundations of Statistics," Wiley, New York, 1954.

11. J. SUTTON, Non-cooperative bargaining theory, *Rev. Econ. Stud.* **53** (1986), 709–724.

12. A. WALD, "Statistical Decision Functions," New York, Wiley, New York, 1950.

13. C. WELCH, The minimax regret strategy in bargaining with incomplete information, AT & T Bell Laboratories, 1986.

C 78
D 83

242 - 63
0260

Econometrica, Vol. 53, No. 5 (September 1985)

A BARGAINING MODEL WITH INCOMPLETE INFORMATION ABOUT TIME PREFERENCES

By Ariel Rubinstein[1]

The paper studies a strategic sequential bargaining game with incomplete information: Two players have to reach an agreement on the partition of a pie. Each player, in turn, has to make a proposal on how the pie should be divided. After one player has made an offer, the other must decide either to accept it or to reject it and continue the bargaining. Player 2 is one of two types, and player 1 does not know what type player 2 actually is.

A class of sequential equilibria (called bargaining sequential equilibria) is characterized for this game. The main theorem proves the (typical) uniqueness of the bargaining sequential equilibrium. It specifies a clear connection between the equilibrium and player 1's initial belief about his opponent's type.

1. INTRODUCTION

ONE OF THE MOST BASIC HUMAN SITUATIONS is one in which two individuals have to reach an agreement, chosen from among several possibilities. Traditional bargaining theory seeks to indicate one of the agreements as the expected (or desired) outcome on the sole basis of the set of possible agreements and on the point of non-agreement. Usually, the solution is characterized by a set of axioms. (For a survey of the axiomatic models of bargaining, see Roth [13].)

Much of the recent work on bargaining aims at explaining the outcome of a bargaining situation using additional information about the time preference of the parties and the bargaining procedure. Such models are associated with the strategic approach. The players' negotiating maneuvers are moves in a noncooperative game that describes the procedure of the bargaining; noncooperative solutions to the game are explored.

The strategic approach also seeks to combine axiomatic cooperative solutions and noncooperative solutions. Roger Myerson recently named this task the "Nash Program." Though Nash is usually associated with the axiomatic approach, he was the first to suggest that this approach must be complemented by a noncooperative game (see Nash [10]).

In a previous paper [14], I analyzed the following bargaining model, using the strategic approach. Two players have to reach an agreement on the partition of a pie of size 1. Each player in turn has to make a proposal on the division of the pie. After one player has made an offer, the other must decide either to accept it or to reject it and continue the bargaining. The players have preference relations which are defined on the set of ordered pairs (s, t), which is interpreted as agreement on partition s at time t. Several properties are assumed: "pie" is

[1] This research began when I was a research fellow at Nuffield College, Oxford. It was continued at Bell Laboratories and at the Institute for Advanced Studies of the Hebrew University. I am grateful to these three institutions for their hospitality.

I owe thanks to many friends with whom I have discussed this subject during the past five years. Specifically I would like to thank Asher Wolinsky, Leo Simon and Ed Green for many valuable remarks; Avner Shaked, whose idea helped me simplify the proof of the main theorem; and an associated editor and referee of this journal for their extraordinarily helpful remarks.

deairable, "time" is valuable, the preference is continuous and stationary, and the larger the portion of the pie the more "compensation" a player needs to consider a delay of one period immaterial.

The set of outcomes of Nash equilibria for this game includes almost every possible agreement, and the bargaining in a Nash equilibrium may last beyond the first round of negotiations. The Nash equilibria are protected by threats, such as responding to a deviation by insisting on receiving the whole pie. It is very useful to apply the concept of (subgame) perfect equilibrium (see Selten [16]) which requires that the players' strategies induce an equilibrium in any subgame. This usually leads to a single solution, which is characterized by a pair of partitions, P_1 and P_2, that satisfies (i) Player 1 is indifferent between "P_2 today" and "P_1 tomorrow," and (ii) Player 2 is indifferent between "P_1 today" and "P_2 tomorrow." When a unique pair of P_1 and P_2 satisfies the above statements, the only perfect equilibrium partition is P_1 when 1 starts the bargaining and P_2 when 2 starts the bargaining. The structure of the unique perfect equilibrium is as follows: Player 1 (2) always suggests P_1 (P_2) and Player 2 (1) accepts any offer which is better for him than P_1 (P_2). For example, when each player has a fixed discounting factor δ, the perfect equilibrium outcome gives player 1 $1/(1+\delta)$ if he starts the negotiation, and $\delta/(1+\delta)$ if 2 starts. Both partitions tend to the equal partition when δ tends to 1. It is clear that the method demonstrated by this model is useful for analyzing other bargaining procedures and other properties of time preferences. Additional properties of the model are studied by Binmore [1].

A critical assumption of the model is that each player has complete information about the other's preference. This assumption makes it less surprising that, typically, the bargaining in perfect equilibrium ends in the first period, although it could continue endlessly.

When incomplete information exists, new elements appear; a player may try to conclude from the other player's moves who his opponent really is; the other player may try to cheat him by leading him to believe that he is tougher than he actually is. In general terms, the incomplete information model enables us to address the issues of "reputation building," signalling, and self-selection mechanisms. Here continuation of bargaining beyond the first period becomes more likely.

A number of works have appeared on bargaining with incomplete information. For example, Harsanyi and Selten [7] present a generalized Nash solution for two-person bargaining games with incomplete information. Myerson [9] presents another generalization. Both solutions are characterized by sets of axioms. Finite-horizon bargaining games with incomplete information are treated by Fudenberg and Tirole [5], Sobel and Takahashi [17], and Ordover and Rubinstein [11]. In addition, Cramton [2], Perry [12], and Fudenberg, Levine, and Tirole [4] analyze seller–buyer infinite-horizon bargaining games in which reservation prices are uncertain, but time preferences are known.

The present article attempts to explain bargaining with incomplete information by investigating the model introduced in [14], with one additional element: Player

2 may be one of two types: 2_w (weak) or 2_s (strong). The types differ in their time-preferences (for example, higher or lower discounting factors). Player 1 adopts an initial belief regarding the identity of Player 2.

The difficulties of extending the notion of perfect equilibrium to games with incomplete information have been discussed extensively in the last few years (see Kreps and Wilson [8]). Generally speaking, the problem is that in order to check the optimality of 1's strategy after a given sequence of moves, we must verify his beliefs. Therefore, the notion of sequential equilibrium includes player 1's beliefs both on and off the equilibrium path.

The set of sequential equilibria for this game is very large. The freedom to choose new conjectures off the equilibrium path enables the players to establish credibility for "too many" threats and thus to support "too many" equilibria. I suggest that many of the sequential equilibria are unreasonable. These can be eliminated by making additional requirements on beliefs and on equilibrium behavior. Indeed, as Kreps–Wilson claims, "...the formation [of sequential equilibria] in terms of players' beliefs gives the analyst a tool for choosing among sequential equilibria" [8, p. 884].

The quite reasonable, additional requirements are described in Section 5. The key requirement $(B-1)$ makes it possible for type 2_s to screen himself: if player 2 rejects an offer made by player 1 and makes a counteroffer which is worse than 1's offer for the weak type but better for the strong type, then 1 concludes that player 2 is strong (2_s).

The main theorem of this paper specifies a clear connection between the unique bargaining sequential equilibrium and 1's initial belief that 2 is 2_w, denoted by ω_0. The theorem states that there exists a cut-off point ω^* such that if ω_0 is strictly below ω^*, player 1 gives up: he offers the partition he would have offered if he thought he was playing against 2_s, and player 2, whatever his type, accepts it. If ω_0 is strictly above ω^*, some continuation of the bargaining is possible. In equilibrium, player 1 offers P_1, 2_w would accept it, and 2_s would reject it and offer P_2, which is accepted by 1. The partitions P_1 and P_2 are the only ones satisfying: (i) Player 1 is indifferent between "P_2 today" and the lottery of "P_1 tomorrow" with probability ω_0 and "P_2 after tomorrow" with probability $1 - \omega_0$; (ii) Player 2_w is indifferent between "P_1 today" and "P_2 tomorrow".

2. THE BARGAINING MODEL

Two players, 1 and 2, are bargaining on the partition of a pie. The pie will be partitioned only after the players reach an agreement. Each player in turn makes an offer and his opponent may agree to the offer, "Y", or reject it, "N". Acceptance of an offer ends the bargaining. After rejection, the rejecting player has to make a counteroffer and so on without any given limit. There are no rules which bind the players to previous offers they have made.

Formally, let $S = [0, 1]$. A partition of the pie is identified with a number s in S by interpreting s as the proportion of the pie that 1 receives (2 receives $1 - s$).

A strategy specifies the offer that a player makes whenever it is his turn to make an offer, and his reaction to any offer made by his opponent. A strategy includes the player's plans even after a series of moves that are inconsistent with the strategy itself.

Let F denote the set of all strategies available to the player who starts the bargaining. Formally, F is the set of all sequences of functions $f = \{f^t\}_{t=0}^{\infty}$, when for t even, $f^t: S^{t-1} \to S$ and for t odd, $f^t: S^t \to \{Y, N\}$, where S^t is the set of all sequences of length t of elements of S. (For example, $f^2(s^0, s^1)$ is a player's offer at time 2 assuming that he offered s^0, his opponent rejected it and made the offer s^1, which was rejected by the other player.) Similarly, G is the set of all strategies for a player whose first move is a response to the other player's offer. Note that mixed strategies are not allowed.

A typical outcome of the game is a pair (s, t), which is interpreted as agreement on the partition s in period t. Perpetual disagreement is denoted by $(0, \infty)$.

The outcome function of the game $P(f, g)$, then, takes the value (s, t) if two players who adopt strategies f and g reach an agreement s at period t, and the value $(0, \infty)$ if they do not reach an agreement.

The players have preference relations $\geqslant_1$ and $\geqslant_2$ on the set of pairs $S \times T = [0, 1] \times \{0, 1, 2, \ldots\}$. It is assumed that $\geqslant_1$ satisfies the following assumptions (analogous assumptions are assumed about $\geqslant_2$; recall that according to our notation, player 2 receives the fraction $1 - x$ in the partition x):

ASSUMPTION (A-0): *The relation is complete, reflexive, and transitive.*

ASSUMPTION (A-1): *"Pie" is desirable: If $x > y$, then $(x, t) >_1 (y, t)$.*

ASSUMPTION (A-2): *"Time" is valuable: If $x > 0$ and $t_2 > t_1$, then $(x, t_1) >_1 (x, t_2)$.*

ASSUMPTION (A-3): *Continuity: The graph of $\geqslant_1$ is closed in $(S \times T) \times (S \times T)$.*

ASSUMPTION (A-4): *Stationarity: $(x, t) \geqslant_1 (y, t+1)$ iff $(x, 0) \geqslant_1 (y, 1)$.*

ASSUMPTION (A-5): *The increasing compensation property: If*

$$(x, 0) \sim_1 (x + \varepsilon(x), 1),$$

then ε is strictly increasing.

For the sake of simplicity I make the following assumption:

ASSUMPTION (A-6): *For every x there is $d(x) \in [0, 1]$, such that $(x, 1) \sim_1 (d(x), 0)$.*

This implies that $(0, t) \sim_1 (0, 0)$ for all t and I assume further that $(0, \infty) \sim_1 (0, 0)$.

The present value of (x, t) is the t-fold composition of d with itself. Notice that by (A-1)–(A-3) and (A-6) the function d is increasing, continuous, and satisfies $d(0) = 0$ and $d(x) < x$ for $x > 0$. By Assumption (A-5), $x - d(x)$ is an increasing function and by Assumption (A-4) the function d gives us all the information about the relation $\succeq_1$.

The most important family of relations satisfying the above assumptions are those induced by a utility function $x\delta^t$. The number $0 < \delta < 1$ is interpreted as the fixed discounting factor.

It is shown in Fishburn and Rubinstein [3] that time preferences satisfying (A-0)–(A-4) and (A-6) can be represented by a utility function of the form $u(x)\delta^t$. A sufficient (but not necessary) condition for the preference to satisfy Assumption (A-5) is that it be representable by $u(x)\delta^t$ where u is concave. The fixed bargaining costs preference (induced from a utility function $x - ct$) does not satisfy Assumptions (A-5) and (A-6).

In the current paper player 1's preference must be extended to refer to the lotteries of elements in $S \times T$. (The symbol $\omega 0_1 \oplus (1 - \omega) 0_2$ stands for the lottery which provides the outcome 0_1 with probability ω, and outcome 0_2 with probability $(1 - \omega)$.)

ASSUMPTION (A-7): *Player maximizes the expectation of $u(x)\delta^t$ for some concave function $u(x)$ and some δ.*

The new element in this paper is the extension of the analysis to situations of incomplete information. Player 1's preference is known by player 2, but player 2 may possess one of the preferences $\succeq_w$ (weak) or $\succeq_s$ (strong). If 2 holds $\succeq_w$ ($\succeq_s$) it is said that he is of type 2_w (2_s).

It is assumed that 2_w is more impatient than 2_s, that is:

ASSUMPTION (C-1): *If $x \neq 1$ and $(y, 1) \sim_w (x, 0)$, then $(y, 1) >_s (x, 0)$.*

With fixed discounting factors δ_w and δ_s, this assumption means that $\delta_s > \delta_w$. In [14] a full characterization of the perfect equilibrium outcomes of this game with complete information is presented. We summarize these results here.

Under the current assumptions about the time preferences there is a unique $(x^*, y^*) \in S^2$ satisfying

$$(x^*, 1) \sim_1 (y^*, 0) \quad \text{and} \quad (y^*, 1) \sim_2 (x^*, 0).$$

Denote the pair (x^*, y^*) by $\Delta(\succeq_1, \succeq_2)$. It was proved in [14] that the only perfect equilibrium partition is x^* when 1 starts the bargaining, and y^* when 2 starts the bargaining and in any case the negotiation ends in the first period. Denote

$$\Delta(\succeq_1, \succeq_w) = (V_w, \hat{V}_w),$$

$$\Delta(\succeq_1, \succeq_s) = (V_s, \hat{V}_s).$$

Since 2_w is more impatient than 2_s, $V_w > V_s$ and $\hat{V}_w > \hat{V}_s$.

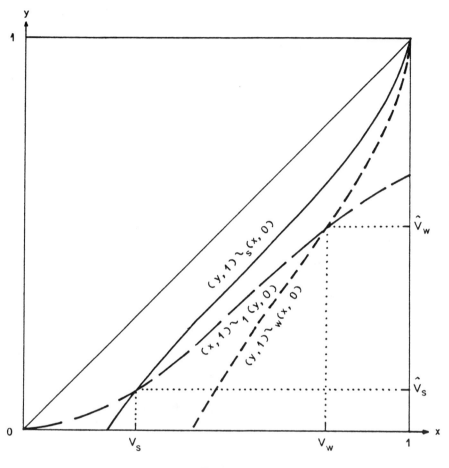

FIGURE 1

Figure 1 is useful at several subsequent points. The curve which includes the origin represents the present value to player 1 of the partition x tomorrow, that is, it includes all the pairs (x, y) such that $(x, 1) \sim_1 (y, 0)$. The other two curves represent the present value to player 2 of y tomorrow, depending on whether he is weak or strong. That is, they include the pairs (x, y) such that $(y, 1) \sim_s (x, 0)$ and $(y, 1) \sim_w (x, 0)$. The intersections of those curves with player 1's present value curve are $(V_s, \hat{V}_s)$ and $(V_w, \hat{V}_w)$.

EXAMPLE: When the players have fixed discounting factors δ_1 and δ_2,

$$\Delta = \left(\frac{1 - \delta_2}{1 - \delta_1 \delta_2}, \, \delta_1 \frac{1 - \delta_2}{1 - \delta_1 \delta_2} \right).$$

Binmore [1] shows that where the δ_i are derived from the continuous discounting formula $x(e^{-r_i\tau})^t$ (τ is the length of one period of bargaining), then

$$\lim_{\tau \to 0} \Delta = \left(\frac{r_2}{r_1 + r_2}, \frac{r_2}{r_1 + r_2} \right).$$

In other words, when the time interval tends to 0, player 1 gets $r_2/r_1 + r_2$, regardless of whether he is the first or the second player to make an offer. In particular, if the players have identical time preferences, the solution coincides with the equal partition.

The last assumption about the time preferences is the following:

ASSUMPTION (C-2): $(\hat{V}_w, 0) <_w (V_s, 1)$.

By (C-1), $(\hat{V}_w, 0) <_w (\hat{V}_s, 0)$. Here it is further assumed that type 2_w prefers the complete information partition between 1 and 2, even if player 1 starts the bargaining, and there is a delay of one period in the agreement. Assumption (C-2) excludes the possibility that in equilibrium 2_w sorts himself by making an offer z satisfying $(z, 0) \succcurlyeq_1 (V_w, 1)$ (and thus $(z, 0) \preccurlyeq_w (\hat{V}_w, 0)$) and $(z, 0) \succcurlyeq_w (V_s, 1)$ (see Proposition 4). Notice that if the players have discounting factors $\delta_i = e^{-r_i\tau}$ (see the previous example), then Assumption (C-2) is satisfied whenever $r_w > r_s$ and τ is small enough.

3. NASH EQUILIBRIA

Section 2 defines a game with incomplete information. The usual solution concept for such games is Harsanyi's Bayesian Nash equilibrium (see [6]). Let (f, g, h) be a triple of strategies for 1, 2_w, and 2_s, respectively. The outcome of the play of (f, g, h) is

$$P(f, g, h) = \langle P(f, g), P(f, h) \rangle.$$

This means that the outcome of the game is a pair of outcomes, one each for the cases that 2 is actually 2_w or 2_s.

DEFINITION: A triple $(\hat{f}, \hat{g}, \hat{h}) \in F \times G \times G$ is a Nash equilibrium if there is no $f \in F$ such that

$$\omega_0 P(f, \hat{g}) \oplus (1 - \omega_0) P(f, \hat{h}) >_1 \omega_0 P(\hat{f}, \hat{g}) \oplus (1 - \omega_0) P(\hat{f}, \hat{h}),$$

and there is no $g \in G$ or $h \in G$ such that

$$P(\hat{f}, g) >_w P(\hat{f}, \hat{g}) \quad \text{or} \quad P(\hat{f}, h) >_s P(\hat{f}, \hat{h}).$$

(A similar definition is suitable for $(\hat{f}, \hat{g}, \hat{h}) \in G \times F \times F$.)

In other words, 1's strategy has to be a best response against 2_w's and 2_s's plans, "weighted" by ω_0 and $1 - \omega_0$, respectively, and $\hat{g}$ and $\hat{h}$ have to be best responses in the usual sense.

As in the complete information case, the set of Nash equilibria in this model is very large. Proposition 1 provides a complete characterization of the set of Nash equilibrium outcomes in this model. In particular, Proposition 1 implies that, for every partition P, $\langle (P, 0), (P, 0) \rangle$ is a Nash equilibrium outcome.

PROPOSITION 1: $\langle (P_w, t_w), (P_s, t_s) \rangle = \langle 0_w, 0_s \rangle$ is a Nash equilibrium outcome if and only if

$$0_w \geqslant_w 0_s, \quad and \quad 0_s \geqslant_s 0_w.$$

PROOF: If $\langle 0_w, 0_s \rangle$ satisfies the conditions, then the following is a description of a Nash equilibrium: both players demand the entire pie and reject every offer except at periods t_w and t_s when players 1 and 2_w, and 1 and 2_s, offer and accept P_w and P_s, respectively.

Obviously the conditions $0_w \geqslant_w 0_s$ and $0_s \geqslant_s 0_w$ are necessary.   Q.E.D.

4. SEQUENTIAL EQUILIBRIUM

The basic idea of sequential equilibrium is similar to the idea of perfect equilibrium: the players' strategies are best responses not only at the starting point, but at any decision node. For player 1, the test whether a strategy is the best response depends on 1's belief that 2 is 2_w. Therefore, a sequential equilibrium includes the method of updating 1's belief that 2 is 2_w.

Define a belief system to be a sequence $\omega = (\omega^t)_{t=-1,1,3,...}$, such that $\omega^{-1} = \omega_0$ and, for $t \geqslant 1$, $\omega^t: S^t \to [0, 1]$. $\omega^t(s^1, \ldots, s^t)$ is 2's belief that 2 is 2_w, after the sequence of rejected offers $s^1, \ldots, s^{t-1}$ and after 2 made offer s^t.

The formal definition of (f, g, h, ω) being a sequential equilibrium is messy but intuitively straightforward. The belief system must be consistent with the Bayesian formula. Moreover, after unexpected behavior by player 2, player 1 makes a new conjecture regarding 2's type; the equilibrium behavior of player 1 must be consistent with the new conjecture as long as no new deviation is observed. Player 1 does not change his belief about player 2 as a result of any deviation of his own.

For formal definition, let us use the notation $s^t = (s^0 \cdots s^t)$ and the brief notation $\omega^t = \omega^t(s^t)$, $f^t = f^t(s^t)$, or $f^t(s^{t-1})$ according to the evenness of t, and similarly define g^t and h^t.

The Bayesian requirements are:

(i) If $g^{T-1} = h^{T-1} = N$ and $g^T = h^T = s^T$, then $\omega^T = \omega^{T-2}$.

(ii) If $0 < \omega^{T-2} < 1$, $g^{T-1} = N$ and $g^T = s^T$, and either $h^{T-1} = Y$ or $h^T \neq s^T$, then $\omega^T = 1$.

(iii) If $0 < \omega^{T-2} < 1$, $h^{T-1} = N$, $h^T = s^T$ and either $g^{T-1} = Y$ or $g^T \neq s^T$, then $\omega^T = 0$.

Finally I add to the definition of sequential equilibrium another constraint which does not follow from Kreps–Wilson's definition. If 1 concludes with probability 1 that player 2 is of a certain type, he continues to hold this belief whatever occurs after he comes to this conclusion; in other words, if he concludes that $\omega' = 0$ or $\omega' = 1$, he continues to play the game as if it were a game with complete information against 2_s or 2_w respectively.

Formally, if $\omega^{T-2} = 1$, then $\omega^T = 1$, and if $\omega^{T-2} = 0$, then $\omega^T = 0$.

The next proposition can be proved using the arguments presented in [14].

PROPOSITION 2: *Let* (f, g, h, ω) *be a sequential equilibrium in the game when* 1 *starts; then* $P(f, h) \geqslant_1 (V_s, 0)$ *and* $P(f, g) \leqslant_1 (V_w, 0)$; *and if* 2 *starts,* $P(f, h) \geqslant_1 (\hat{V}_s, 0)$ *and* $P(f, g) \leqslant_1 (\hat{V}_w, 0)$.

Thus, a sequential equilibrium outcome cannot be better (worse) for player 1 than the perfect equilibrium outcome in the complete information bargaining game with 2_w (2_s).

The next proposition demonstrates that the set of sequential equilibrium outcomes is very large.

The sequential equilibrium, which is constructed in the proof, is supported by player 1's belief that a deviation must be of type 2_w. Whenever there is a deviation from the equilibrium path, player 1 concludes that he is playing against 2_w. Such conjectures serve as threats against player 2. The definition of sequential equilibrium that was suggested to exclude noncredible threats does not exclude threatening by beliefs.

PROPOSITION 3: *For every* ω_0, *and for all* x^* *satisfying* $(\hat{V}_s, 1) \geqslant_w (x^*, 0)$ *and* $(x^*, 0) \geqslant_s (\hat{V}_w, 1)$, *either* $\langle (x^*, 0), (x^*, 0) \rangle$ *or* $\langle (x^*, 0), (y^*, 1) \rangle$ *(where* $(y^*, 1) \sim_w (x^*, 0)$) *is a sequential equilibrium outcome.*

PROOF: Let x^* satisfy $(\hat{V}_s, 1) \geqslant_w (x^*, 0)$ and $(x^*, 0) \geqslant_s (\hat{V}_w, 1)$. Let y^* and z^* satisfy $(y^*, 1) \sim_w (x^*, 0)$ and $(z^*, 0) \sim_s (y^*, 1)$. Let $\bar{y}$ and $\bar{z}$ satisfy $(\bar{y}, 0) \sim_1 (x^*, 1)$ and $(\bar{z}, 0) \sim_w (\bar{y}, 1)$. Let us distinguish between the following two comprehensive (and nonexclusive) cases:

CASE I: $\omega_0(x^*, 0) \oplus (1 - \omega_0)(y^*, 1) \geqslant_1 (z^*, 0)$.

CASE II: $\omega_0(\bar{z}, 0) \oplus (1 - \omega_0)(\bar{y}, 1) \leqslant_1 (x^*, 0)$.

By Proposition 7, at least one of the following inequalities is true:

$$\omega_0(x^*, 1) \oplus (1 - \omega_0)(y^*, 2) \geqslant_1 (y^*, 0),$$

$$(\bar{y}, 0) \geqslant_1 \omega_0(\bar{z}, 1) \oplus (1 - \omega_0)(\bar{y}, 2).$$

Combining $(y^*, 0) \geqslant_1 (z^*, 1)$ and $(x^*, 1) \sim_1 (\bar{y}, 0)$ with the stationarity of $\geqslant_1$, we get that for all ω_0 either Case I or Case II must be true.

The following is a description of a sequential equilibrium for Case I with the outcome $\langle (x^*, 0), (y^*, 1) \rangle$:

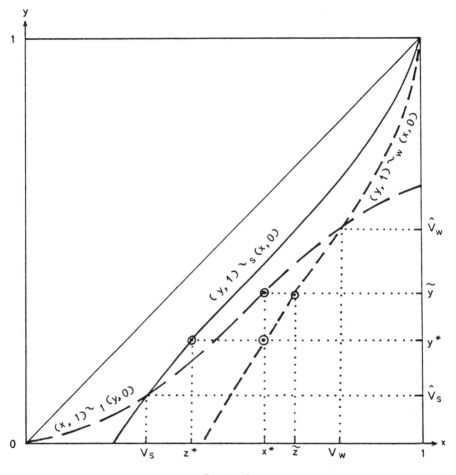

FIGURE 2

Unless 1 changes his belief, he always demands x^* and agrees at most to y^*; type 2_w accepts only any offer below x^* and demands y^*; type 2_s accepts offer x satisfying $(x, 0) \succcurlyeq_s (y^*, 1)$ and always offers y^*. On condition that 2 made a move unplanned by any of the types, 1 changes ω' to 1 and the continuation is as in the complete information game between 1 and 2_w. Clearly the only change for a profitable deviation of 1 would be to make a lower demand like z^* which would be accepted by both types. But since $\omega_0(x^*, 0) \oplus (1 - \omega_0)(y^*, 1) \succcurlyeq_1 (z^*, 0)$, this is not profitable. Checking the other conditions of the sequential equilibrium condition is straightforward.

The following is a description of a sequential equilibrium for case II with the outcome $\langle (x^*, 0), (x^*, 0) \rangle$:

Unless 1 changes his belief, he always offers x^* and accepts y only if $(y, 0) \succcurlyeq_1 (x^*, 1)$, $(y \geq \tilde{y})$. Both 2_w and 2_s agree to settle for x only if $(x, 0)$ is preferable (according to $\geqslant_w$ and $\geqslant_s$ respectively) to $(\bar{y}, 1)$. They always offer $\bar{y}$. After 2 made a move unexpected from both types, 1 changes ω' to 1 and the continuation is as in the complete information game between 1 and 2_w.

Notice that if 1 demands $x > x^*$, 2_s rejects it because $(\bar{y}, 1) >_s (x^*, 0)$. Thus the most that 1 can achieve by deviating is that 2_w would agree to $\bar{z}$ and 2_s would offer $\bar{y}$. However since $\omega_0(\bar{z}, 0) \oplus (1 - \omega_0)(\bar{y}, 1) \leqslant_1 (x^*, 0)$, this is not profitable. The requirement that $(x^*, 0) \geqslant_s (\hat{V}_w, 1)$ is important to assure that 2_s will not gain by rejecting x^*.   Q.E.D.

5. BARGAINING SEQUENTIAL EQUILIBRIUM

Section 4 shows that it might be desirable to place additional requirements on the belief systems in a sequential equilibrium (f, g, h, ω).

In order to demonstrate the first Assumption, (B-1), imagine that 1 makes an offer x and 2 rejects it and offers y which satisfies that $(y, 1) \geqslant_s (x, 0)$ and $(x, 0) >_w (y, 1)$. That is, 2 presents a counteroffer which is better for 2_s and worse for 2_w than the original offer x. Then, we assume, 1 concludes that he is playing against 2_s.

This assumption is related to an element which is missing from most studies in Game Theory: we tend to conclude facts from other people's behavior even when the unexpected occurs. (B-1) is this type of inference. The effect of (B-1) is to exclude sequential equilibria like those constructed in the proof of Proposition 3.

ASSUMPTION (B-1): ω is such that if $\omega^{t-2}(s^{t-2}) \neq 1$, $(s^t, 1) \geqslant_s (s^{t-1}, 0)$, and $(s^{t-1}, 0) >_w (s^t, 1)$, then $\omega^t(s^1 \cdots s^{t-1}, s^t) = 0$.

The next assumption states that 2's insistence cannot be an indication that 2 is more likely to be 2_w. Assume that 2 rejects an offer x and suggests an offer y, such that

$$(y, 1) \geqslant_w (x, 0) \quad \text{and} \quad (y, 1) \geqslant_s (x, 0).$$

Then when 1 updates his belief, his subjective probability that he is playing against 2_w does not increase.

ASSUMPTION (B-2): If $(s^t, 1) \geqslant_s (s^{t-1}, 0)$ and $(s^t, 1) \geqslant_w (s^{t-1}, 0)$, then $\omega^t(s^t) \leqslant \omega^{t-2}(s^{t-2})$.

The next two assumptions place direct restrictions on the players' equilibrium behavior, rather than describing their beliefs or preferences.

Assumption (B-3) is a "tie-breaking" assumption. If player 1 has been offered a partition x and after rejecting it he expects to reach an agreement whereby he is indifferent to x, then 1 accepts x.

ASSUMPTION (B-3): *If* $\langle P(f_{|s^1\cdots s^t}, g_{|s^1\cdots s^t}, h_{|s^1\cdots s^t}), 1 \rangle \sim_1 (s^t, 0),$ *then* $f(s^i) = Y.$
($f_{|s^1\cdots s^t}$ *is the residual strategy of f after the history* $s^1 \cdots s^t.$)

The last assumption is that player 2 never makes an offer lower than $\hat{V}_s$.

ASSUMPTION (B-4): *Whenever it is 2's turn to make an offer,*

$$g^t \geq \hat{V}_s \quad and \quad h^t \geq \hat{V}_s.$$

Notice that by Proposition 2, player 2 rejects any offer which is lower than $\hat{V}_s$. Still, the players could use such offers as a communication method. Assumption (B-4) excludes this possibility.

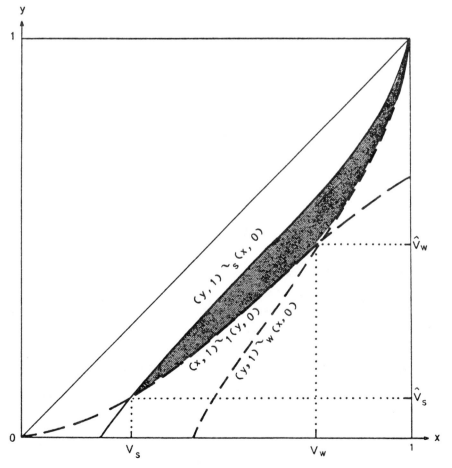

FIGURE 3

I would also like to mention the associate editor's suggestion that Assumption (B-4) can be replaced by a requirement on the beliefs that if 2_w is supposed to accept an offer and 2_s is supposed to reject it, then whatever is 2's offer, 1 concludes from 2's rejection that he is playing against 2_r. The reader can verify that the alternative assumption plays the same role as Assumption (B-4) in the only place it is used (the Proof of Proposition 6).

DEFINITION: (f, g, h, ω) is a *bargaining sequential equilibrium* if it is a sequential equilibrium and satisfies (B-1)–(B-4).

For the following examination of some of the properties of bargaining sequential equilibrium, let (f, g, h, ω) be a bargaining sequential equilibrium:

PROPOSITION 4: *Whenever it is 2's turn to make an offer, 2_w and 2_s make the same offer.*

PROOF: Assume that there is a history after which 2_w and 2_s make the offers y and z, respectively, and that $y \neq z$. If 1 accepts both y and z, then the type making the higher offer will deviate to the lower offer.

If 1 rejects both y and z, then in the next period he believes he knows which type 2 is, and he offers V_w or V_s accordingly. Then type 2_w will gain by offering z.

If 1 accepts only z, then the outcome against 2_w will be V_w in the next period. By definition of sequential equilibrium, $(z, 0) \geqslant_s (V_w, 1)$. By Assumption (C-1), $(z, 0) >_w (V_w, 1)$. Thus, 2_w can deviate and gain by offering z.

If 1 accepts y and rejects z, it must be that $(y, 0) \geqslant_1 (V_w, 1)$ and $(y, 0) \geqslant_w (V_s, 1)$, in contradiction to Assumption (C-2).   Q.E.D.

PROPOSITION 5: *If both 2_w and 2_s accept an offer x, then $x \leqslant V_s$.*

PROOF: If $x > V_s$, then 2_s may deviate, say "N" and suggest y at the next period, where $(y, 1) >_s (x, 0)$, $(y, 1) <_w (x, 0)$, and $(y, 0) >_1 (V_s, 1)$.

Any y that satisfies that (x, y) is in the shaded area in Figure 3 will do. By Assumption (B-1), player 1 concludes that 2 is 2_s, and since $(y, 0) >_1 (V_s, 1)$, he accepts the offer y; since $(y, 1) >_s (x, 0)$, 2_s gains by the deviation. When $x = 1$ there is no (x, y) in the shaded area of the figure. However, $(\hat{V}_w, 1) >_s (1, 0)$ and 2_s could gain by offering and accepting $\hat{V}_w$.   Q.E.D.

PROPOSITION 6: *If 2_w accepts offer x and 2_s rejects it, then 2_s makes an offer y such that $(y, 1) \sim_w (x, 0)$, and player 1 accepts it.*

PROOF: If 1 rejects y then he offers V_s in the next period. Therefore, $(V_s, 1) \succcurlyeq_1 (y, 0)$, and by Assumption (B-3) $(V_s, 1) \succ_1 (y, 0)$ which means $y < \hat{V}_s$, contradicting (B-4). Thus, 1 accepts y, which implies $(y, 0) \succcurlyeq_1 (V_s, 1)$. It must be that $(x, 0) \succcurlyeq_w (y, 1)$. If $(x, 0) \succ_w (y, 1)$ and $y > \hat{V}_s$, then 2_s gains by decreasing the offer to $y - \varepsilon$ (for $\varepsilon > 0$ small enough). This lower offer persuades 1 that 2 is 2_s and 1 accepts it because $(y - \varepsilon, 0) \succ_1 (V_s, 1)$.

If $(x, 0) \succ_w (y, 1)$ and $y = \hat{V}_s$, then 1 may deviate and demand $x + \varepsilon$. Type 2_w will accept the offer if ε is small enough to satisfy $(x + \varepsilon) \succ_w (y, 1)$, and 2_s will reject it and will offer $\hat{V}_s$, the same offer he intended to make before the deviation. Thus 1 gains by the deviation. $\qquad$ Q.E.D.

REMARK: Unless we assume (B-3) and (B-4) we can get additional equilibria, where 1 offers x, 2_w accepts x, 2_s rejects it and offers y $(y < \hat{V}_s)$, which 1 rejects in favor of the agreement V_s in the next period.

From Propositions 4, 5, and 6 we may conclude that a bargaining sequential equilibrium must end with one of the following:

(T-1): 1 *offers* x, 2_w *accepts it and* 2_s *rejects it*; 2_s *offers* y *at the next period and* 1 *accepts it. The offer* y *satisfies*

$$(x, 0) \sim_w (y, 1),$$

$$(y, 0) \succcurlyeq_1 (V_s, 1) \quad (i.e., \ y \geqslant \hat{V}_s),$$

and $\qquad \omega_0(x, 0) \oplus (1 - \omega_0)(y, 1) \succcurlyeq_1 (V_s, 0).$

(T-2): 1 *offers* V_s *and* 2 *accepts it.*

(T-3): 2_w *and* 2_s *offer* y *and* 1 *accepts it.*

6. THE POINT (x^ω, y^ω)

Let $z(x)$ be the z satisfying $(x, 0) \sim_w (z, 1)$ if such a z exists. Define for every $0 \leqslant \omega \leqslant 1$,

$$d^\omega(x) = y \quad \text{where} \quad (y, 0) \sim_1 \omega(x, 1) \oplus (1 - \omega)(z(x), 2).$$

Thus, $d^\omega(x)$ is the minimum that 1 would now agree to accept from 2 if he expects a bargaining sequential equilibrium in the subgame starting the next period, where his agreement with 2_w is x, and his agreement with 2_s is $z(x)$ one period later.

The function d^ω has several straightforward properties. It is continuous, it is strictly increasing, it satisfies $d^\omega(x) < d_1(x) < x$ for $x \geqslant V_s$, where $(d_1(x), 0) \sim_1 (x, 1)$. It satisfies $d^{\omega_1}(x) \geqslant d^{\omega_2}(x)$ if $\omega_1 > \omega_2$.

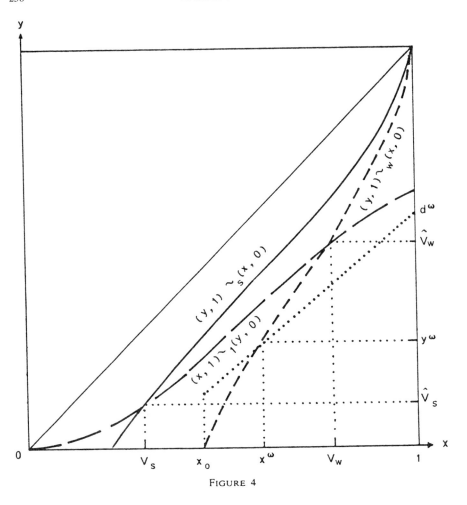

Let d_w be the graph of the present value function for 2_w (i.e., $(d_w(y), 0) \sim_w (y, 1)$). For x_0 satisfying $(x_0, 0) \sim_w (0, 1)$, $d^\omega(x_0) = \omega d_1(x_0) + (1 - \omega_0) \cdot 0 \geq 0$ and therefore d^ω and d_w must have a nonempty intersection.

The next proposition states that the intersection of d^ω and d_w consists of a single point (x^ω, y^ω). This point plays an important role in the main theorem:

PROPOSITION 7: *There is a unique point (x, y) such that $(x, 0) \sim_w (y, 1)$ and* $y = d^\omega(x)$.

PROOF: Assume that both (x_1, y_1) and (x_2, y_2) satisfy the two equations and $x_1 < x_2$. By definition,

$$(y_i, 0) \sim_1 \omega(x_i, 1) \oplus (1 - \omega)(y_i, 2) \quad \text{for} \quad i = 1, 2.$$

By (A-7), $(1-\omega)(u(y_i)-\delta^2 u(y_i)) = \omega(\delta u(x_i)-u(y_i))$. Therefore $y_2 > y_1$ implies that $\delta u(x_2) - u(y_2) > \delta u(x_1) - u(y_1)$ and $u(x_2) - u(x_1) > u(y_2) - u(y_1)$. The function u is concave and $x_i > y_i$. Therefore, $y_2 - y_1 > x_2 - x_1$, contradicting (A-5) as to $\geqslant_w$.   Q.E.D.

7. THE MAIN RESULT

THEOREM: *For a game starting with player 1's offer*: (i): *If ω_0 is high enough such that $y^{\omega_0} > \hat{V}_s$, then the only bargaining sequential equilibrium outcome is* $\langle (x^{\omega_0}, 0), (y^{\omega_0}, 1) \rangle$. (ii): *If ω_0 is low enough such that $y^{\omega_0} < \hat{V}_s$, then the only bargaining sequential equilibrium outcome is* $\langle (V_s, 0), (V_s, 0) \rangle$.

In the first case, player 1 offers x^{ω_0}, 2_w accepts this offer, and 2_s rejects it and offers y^{ω_0}, which is accepted. 2_w is indifferent between $(x^{\omega_0}, 0)$ and $(y^{\omega_0}, 1)$. In the second case, 1 offers V_s and both types 2_w and 2_s accept it. In the boundary between the two zones more than one bargaining sequential equilibrium outcome is possible.

Let us contrast the equilibrium determined in the Theorem with that derived with complete information: the weak player is better off whereas the strong player suffers a disadvantage in the incomplete information game. It is not clear whether player 1 would benefit from having the information about player 2's type. Delays can occur but only if they result in some information transmission.

EXAMPLE: Assume that 1, 2_w, and 2_s have discounting factors δ, δ_w, and δ_s, respectively. Then

$$V_s = \frac{1-\delta_s}{1-\delta\delta_s}, \quad V_w = \frac{1-\delta_w}{1-\delta\delta_w},$$

$$\hat{V}_s = \delta V_s, \quad \text{and} \quad \hat{V}_w = \delta V_w.$$

Here, if

$$\omega_0 > \frac{V_s - \delta^2 V_s}{1 - \delta_w + \delta V_s(\delta_w - \delta)} = \omega^*$$

we are in case (i) of the theorem and

$$x^\omega = \frac{(1-\delta_w)(1-\delta^2(1-\omega))}{1-\delta^2(1-\omega) - \delta\delta_w\omega}.$$

Notice that $1 \geqslant \omega^*$ if and only if $V_w \geqslant V_s$.

Where the discounting factors are derived from the continuous discounting formula we get the following limit result when we tend the length of a period to zero: If $\omega_0 > 2r_s/(r_s + r_w)$, the outcome is $\omega_0 r_w/(\omega_0 r_w + (2 - \omega_0)r)$, and if $\omega_0 < 2r_s/(r_s + r_w)$, the outcome is $r_s/(r + r_s)$.

The main difficulty here is to prove the uniqueness of the bargaining sequential equilibrium outcome. However, for a better insight of the result, I begin by describing a bargaining sequential equilibrium which induces the outcome $\langle(x^{\omega_0}, 0), (y^{\omega_0}, 1)\rangle$ if $y^{\omega_0} > \hat{V}_s$ and induces the outcome $\langle(V_s, 0), (V_s, 0)\rangle$ if $y^{\omega_0} < \hat{V}_s$.

1's *beliefs*: Player 1 does not change his initial belief unless player 2 has rejected an offer s'^{-1} and offers s' such that $(s'^{-1}, 0) \succcurlyeq_w (s', 1)$; then he changes his belief to $\omega'(s') = 0$. (This belief system certainly satisfies (B-1)-(B-2).)

1's *strategy*: Let s' be the "empty" history or a history that ends with 2's offer s'. Let $\omega = \omega'(s')$. If $y^{\omega} \leq \hat{V}_s$ (this case includes the possibility that $\omega = 0$), then 1 accepts s' if and only if $s' \geq \hat{V}_s$; otherwise he accepts s' only if $s' \geq y^{\omega}$. If 1 rejects s' (or s' is the empty history), then he makes the offer x^{ω} if $y^{\omega} > \hat{V}_s$ and the offer V_s if $y^{\omega} \leq \hat{V}_s$.

2_w's *strategy*: Let s' be a history that ends with 1's offer s'. If $y^{\omega} \leq \hat{V}_s$ then 2_w accepts s' if and only if $(s', 0) \succcurlyeq_w (\hat{V}_s, 1)$. If $y^{\omega} > \hat{V}_s$ then 2_w accepts s' only if $s' \leq x^{\omega}$. In case 2_w rejects s' he offers $\hat{V}_s$ if $y^{\omega} \leq \hat{V}_s$ and if $y^{\omega} > \hat{V}_s$ then he offers the lowest number from among y^{ω} and the y satisfying $(s', 0) \succcurlyeq_w (y, 1)$ and $y \geq \hat{V}_s$.

2_s's *strategy*: Player 2_s always makes the same offer that 2_w does. He accepts only V_s or less.

Whenever $\omega'(s') = 0$ or $\omega'(s') = 1$, player 1 follows the perfect equilibrium strategy described in [14] for games with complete information between 1 and 2_s, or between 1 and 2_w. If $\omega' = 0$, 2_s follows the perfect equilibrium strategy and 2_w chooses a perfect best-response strategy to 1's strategy (and similarly for the case $\omega' = 1$).

8. PROOF OF THE UNIQUENESS OF THE BARGAINING SEQUENTIAL EQUILIBRIUM

Assume that $y^{\omega_0} > \hat{V}_s$; in what follows it is proved that the only bargaining sequential equilibrium outcome is $\langle(x^{\omega_0}, 0), (y^{\omega_0}, 1)\rangle$. The proof for the case that $y^{\omega_0} < \hat{V}_s$ is very similar.

Let BSE_1 be a short notation for a bargaining sequential equilibrium in the game where 1 starts the bargaining, and let BSE_2 be a short notation for a bargaining sequential equilibrium in a subgame in which 2 starts the bargaining, if an offer of 1 exists such that 2's reply "N" and continuation according to the BSE_2 is a bargaining sequential equilibrium in the subgame starting after 1's offer. Given a number $0 \leq \omega \leq 1$, define:

$$A^{\omega} = \{u \mid (u, 0) \sim_w 0_w \text{ where } \langle 0_w, 0_s\rangle \text{ is a } BSE_1 \text{ outcome}\},$$

$$B^{\omega} = \{v \mid (v, 0) \sim_w 0_w \text{ where } \langle 0_w, 0_s\rangle \text{ is a } BSE_2 \text{ outcome}\}.$$

In Section 7 it was proved that $x^{\omega_0} \in A^{\omega_0}$ and $y^{\omega_0} \in B^{\omega_0}$.

LEMMA 1: $\langle(V_s, 0)(V_s, 0)\rangle$ *is not a* BSE_1 *outcome and* $\langle(\hat{V}_s, 0)(\hat{V}_s, 0)\rangle$ *is not a* BSE_2 *outcome.*

PROOF: In any of these cases, player 1 would be able to deviate and offer a partition x such that $(x, 0) \sim_w (\hat{V}_s, 1)$. Type 2_w must accept it. Since $y^\omega > \hat{V}_s$, $\omega_0(x, 1) \oplus (1 - \omega_0)(\hat{V}_s, 2) >_1 (\hat{V}_s, 0) \sim_1 (V_s, 1)$; thus $\omega_0(x, 0) \oplus (1 - \omega_0)(\hat{V}_s, 1) >_1 (V_s, 0)$, and 1 gains by the deviation.

LEMMA 2: *If $v \in B^\omega$ there exists a $u \in A^\omega$ such that $(u, 0) \sim_w (v, 1)$.*

PROOF: Define the following BSE_1: Player 1 offers u, 2_w accepts it, 2_s rejects it and offers v at the next period. Type 2_w rejects any offer higher than u and 2_s rejects any offer higher than V_s. In the case that 1's offer is rejected, the continuation is like the original BSE_2 without a change in 1's belief.

Notice that $\omega_0(u, 1) \oplus (1 - \omega_0)(v, 2) >_1 (\hat{V}_s, 0) \sim_1 (V_s, 1)$; thus $\omega_0(u, 1) \oplus (1 - \omega_0)(v, 1) >_1 (V_s, 0)$ and 1 cannot gain by offering V_s.

LEMMA 3: *Define $m_1 = \inf A^{\omega_0}$, $m_2 = \inf B^{\omega_0}$; then $(m_1, 0) \sim_w (m_2, 1)$.*

PROOF: By Lemma 2, $(m_1, 0) \geqslant_w (m_2, 1)$. Assume $(m_1, 0) >_w (m_2, 1)$. Notice that $t_w = 0$ in every BSE_1 outcome $\langle 0_w, 0_s \rangle$ such that $0_w = (s_w, t_w)$ is $\geqslant_w$ close enough to $(m_1, 0)$; otherwise $(s_w, t_w - 1) \sim_w (v, 0)$ for $v < m_2$, and $(s_w, t_w - 1)$ is a BSE_2 outcome and thus $v \in B^{\omega_0}$. If 1 deviates from the BSE_1 which yields the outcome $\langle 0_w, 0_s \rangle$, and demands x such that $(x, 0) \sim_w (m_2, 1)$, 2_w agrees and 1 gains since $x > m_1$ and, by Lemma 1, the BSE_1 must be of type $(T - 1)$. Thus $(m_1, 0) \sim_w (m_2, 1)$.

LEMMA 4: $\omega_0(m_1, 1) \oplus (1 - \omega_0)(z(m_1), 2) \sim_1 (m_2, 0)$. *(Recall that $(x, 0) \sim_w (z(x), 1)$.)*

PROOF: The existence of bargaining sequential equilibrium described in Section 5 implies that $m_1 \leqslant x^{\omega_0}$ and $m_2 \leqslant y^{\omega_0}$. Therefore by Lemma 3

$$\omega_0(m_1, 1) \oplus (1 - \omega_0)(z(m_1), 2) \geqslant_1 (m_2, 0).$$

Assume that we have a strict inequality. A BSE_2 with an outcome $\langle 0_w, 0_s \rangle$ where 2_w is indifferent between $0_w = (s_w, t_w)$ and an outcome in which he receives a partition whose present value is quite close to m_2, satisfies that $t_w = 0$ (otherwise it contradicts Lemma 3). Thus the BSE_2 has to be of type (T-3). Player 1 can deviate profitably by demanding m_1, accepting it from 2_w, and accepting $z(m_1)$ from 2_s.

LEMMA 5: $m_1 = x^{\omega_0}$ and $m_2 = y^{\omega_0}$.

PROOF: Use Lemmas 3 and 4.

LEMMA 6: *Define $M_1 = \sup_{\omega \leqslant \omega_0} A^\omega$ and $M_2 = \sup_{\omega \leqslant \omega_0} B^\omega$; then $(M_1, 0) \leqslant_w (M_2, 1)$.*

PROOF: Similar to the proof of Lemma 2.

LEMMA 7: $(M_1, 0) \sim_w (M_w, 1)$.

PROOF: This is clear if $M_1 = x^{w_0}$. Assume $M_1 > x^{w_0}$ and $(M_1, 0) <_w (M_2, 1)$. Let $x > x^{w_0}$ be close enough to M_1 and $\varepsilon > 0$ small enough such that $x \in A^w$ for some $w \leq w^0$, $z(x) - \varepsilon > M_2$, and $(z(x) - \varepsilon, 0) >_1 w_0(M_1, 1) + (1 - w_0)(z(M_1), 2)$. There exists a BSE_1 such that 1 offers x and 2_w accepts it (otherwise it contradicts the definition of M_2). Assume 2 deviates and offers $z(x) - \varepsilon$. Player 1 must reject it.

Let $\bar{w} \leq w_0$ be 1's belief that 2 is 2_w after the offer $z(x) - \varepsilon$. Then

$$(z(x) - \varepsilon, 0) >_1 \bar{w}(M_1, 1) \oplus (1 - \bar{w})(z(M_1), 2).$$

When rejecting $z(x) - \varepsilon$, 1 must expect an outcome better than $z(x) - \varepsilon$ of a bargaining sequential equilibrium in the subgame after the rejection. The last inequality with Lemma 1 implies that this bargaining sequential equilibrium must be of type (T-3). Therefore there is $y \in B^{\bar{w}}$ such that $(y, 2) >_1 (z(x) - \varepsilon, 0)$. Since $z(x) - \varepsilon > M_2$, this contradicts M_2's definition.

LEMMA 8: $w_0(M_1, 1) \oplus (1 - w_0)(M_2, 2) \sim_1 (M_2, 0)$.

PROOF: By Lemma 7 and $M_1 \geq x^{w_0}$,

$$w_0(M_1, 1) \oplus (1 - w_0)(M_2, 2) \leq_1 (M_2, 0).$$

Assume $w_0(M_1, 1) + (1 - w_0)(M_2, 2) <_1 (M_2, 0)$. Let $y < v < M_2$ satisfying that v is the 2_w's present value of a BSE_2, $w_0(M_1, 1) \oplus (1 - w_0)(M_2, 2) <_1 (y, 0)$, and $(M_2, 2) <_1 (y, 0)$.

By the definition of BSE_2 there exists an offer of player 1, x, such that 2's reply "N" and continuation according to the BSE_2 is a bargaining sequential equilibrium in the subgame starting with 1's offer. Then if player 2 deviates by refusing x and offering y then player 1 must reject y; otherwise it would be a profitable deviation. This contradicts the fact that by the choice of y, and since 1's belief that 2 is of type 2_w after 2's deviation is lower than w_0, it is optimal for 1 to accept y.

LEMMA 9: $M_1 = x^{w_0}$ and $M_2 = y^{w_0}$.

PROOF: A conclusion of Lemmas 7 and 8.

9. FINAL REMARKS

The Length of Negotiation

There is a significant difference between the bargaining sequential equilibria in the two cases where $y^{w_0} > \hat{V}_s$ and $y^{w_0} < \hat{V}_s$. When $y^{w_0} < \hat{V}_s$ the bargaining ends at the first period and there is no screening of player 2's type. If $y^{\omega_0} > \hat{V}_s$, then the bargaining in equilibrium might continue into the second period. Further research is needed for clarifying the direction for the generalization of the current result.

The Choice of Conjectures

In [15] I study the set of sequential equilibrium outcomes under several other assumptions about the choice of conjectures in the bargaining game with fixed bargaining costs. Specifically, I study the "optimistic conjectures" according to which a deviation of player 2 always convinces player 1 that 2 is of type 2_w. The optimistic conjectures are very often used in the incomplete information bargaining literature since they serve as the best deterring conjectures.

The Game Starts with Player 2's Proposal

In the main theorem the bargaining sequential equilibria are characterized for the case that player 1 opens the game. If player 2 starts the bargaining and if $y^{\omega_0} > \hat{V}_s$, then $\langle (y^{\omega_0}, 0), (y^{\omega_0}, 0) \rangle$ is a BSE outcome and if $y^{\omega_0} < \hat{V}_s$, then $\langle (\hat{V}_s, 0), (\hat{V}_s, 0) \rangle$ is a BSE outcome. This can be verified from the construction of a BSE in the Theorem while noticing that the strategies, after 1 has demanded the whole pie and has been refused, are BSE in a subgame starting with player 2's proposal and initial belief ω_0. However, this is not the only BSE since (B-1)-(B-2) are not effective as restrictions on 1's belief after 2's first offer. By Proposition 4, 2_w and 2_s make the same offer at the first period. We may extend (B-2) so that we require that if 2 was supposed to make the offer y and his offer s^0 was less than y, then $\omega^1(s^0) \leq \omega_0$. With the extension of (B-2) we get that if $y^{\omega_0} < \hat{V}_s$, then $\langle (\hat{V}_s, 0), (\hat{V}_s, 0) \rangle$ is the only BSE outcome. If $y^{\omega_0} > \hat{V}_s$, we get one additional BSE outcome $\langle (y^{\omega_0}, 1), (x^{\omega_0}, 2) \rangle$: player 2 starts with the offer $\hat{V}_s$, which is rejected by player 1 who continues as if he had started the game; if 2 makes an offer $s_0 > \hat{V}_s$, 1 concludes that 2 is 2_w and demands V_w.

Fixed Bargaining Costs

Assume that player 1's utility is $s - ct$ while the utilities of types 2_w and 2_s are $(1-s) - c_w t$ and $(1-s) - c_s t$. The preferences which are represented by these utilities do not satisfy Assumptions (A-5), (A-6) but the same techniques which are used to prove the main theorem are useful to calculate the bargaining sequential equilibrium here:

(i) If

$$\omega_0 > \frac{2c}{c + c_w},$$

the only bargaining sequential equilibrium outcome is $\langle (1, 0), (1 - c_w, 1) \rangle$.

(ii) If

$$\frac{2c}{c + c_w} > \omega_0 > \frac{c + c_s}{c + c_w},$$

the only bargaining sequential equilibrium outcome is $\langle (c_w, 0), (0, 1) \rangle$.
(iii) If

$$\frac{c + c_s}{c + c_w} > \omega_0,$$

the only bargaining sequential equilibrium outcome is $\langle (c_s, 0), (c_s, 0) \rangle$. (The appearance of the intermediate zone (2) is due to the fact that here $(V_s, 1) <_1 (\hat{V}_s, 0)$ and not $(V_s, 1) \sim_1 (\hat{V}_s, 0)$, as in the previous case.)

The Hebrew University of Jerusalem

Manuscript received August, 1983; final revision received October, 1984.

REFERENCES

[1] BINMORE, K. G.: "Perfect Equilibria in Bargaining Models," International Centre for Economics and Related Disciplines, London School of Economics, Discussion Paper 82/58, 1982.
[2] CRAMTON, P. C.: "Bargaining with Incomplete Information: An Infinite Horizon Model with Continuous Uncertainty," *Review of Economic Studies*, 51(1984), 579–593.
[3] FISHBURN, P. C., AND A. RUBINSTEIN: "Time Preference," *International Economic Review*, 23(1982), 719–736.
[4] FUDENBERG, D., D. LEVINE, AND J. TIROLE: "Infinite-Horizon Models of Bargaining with One-Sided Incomplete Information," forthcoming in *Game Theoretic Models of Bargaining*, edited by Alvin Roth. Cambridge: University of Cambridge Press, 1985.
[5] FUDENBERG, D., AND J. TIROLE: "Sequential Bargaining with Incomplete Information," *Review of Economic Studies*, 50(1983), 221–247.
[6] HARSANYI, J. C.: "Games with Incomplete Information Played by 'Bayesian Players'," *Management Science*, 14(1967), 159–182, 320–334, and 486–502.
[7] HARSANYI, J. C., AND R. SELTEN: "A Generalized Nash Solution for Two-Person Bargaining Games with Incomplete Information," *Management Science*, 18(1972), 80–106.
[8] KREPS, D. M., AND R. WILSON: "Sequential Equilibria," *Econometrica*, 50(1982), 863–894.
[9] MYERSON, R. B.: "Two-Person Bargaining Problems with Incomplete Information," *Econometrica*, 52(1984), 461–488.
[10] NASH, J. F.: "Two-Person Cooperative Games," *Econometrica*, 21(1953), 128–140.
[11] ORDOVER, J., AND A. RUBINSTEIN: "On Bargaining, Settling and Litigating: A Problem in Multistage Games with Incomplete Information," mimeo, New York University, November, 1982.
[12] PERRY, M.: "A Theory of Price Formation in Bilateral Situations," *Econometrica* forthcoming.
[13] ROTH, A. E.: "Axiomatic Models of Bargaining," Lecture Notes in Economics and Mathematical Systems No. 170. Berlin: Springer-Verlag, 1979.

[14] RUBINSTEIN, A.: "Perfect Equilibrium in a Bargaining Model," *Econometrica*, 50(1982), 97–109.
[15] ———: "The Choice of Conjectures in a Bargaining Game with Incomplete Information," forthcoming in *Game Theoretic Models of Bargaining*, edited by Alvin Roth. Cambridge: University of Cambridge Press, 1985.
[16] SELTEN, R.: "Speiltheoretische Behandlung eines Oligopolmodels mit Nachfragetragheit," *Zeitschrift fur die Gesamte Staatswissenschaft*, 12(1965), 301–324 and 667–689.
[17] SOBEL, J., AND I. TAKAHASHI: "A Multi State Model of Bargaining," *Review of Economic Studies*, 50(1983), 411–426.

JOURNAL OF ECONOMIC THEORY **39**, 155–190 (1986)

Foundations of Dynamic Monopoly and the Coase Conjecture*

FARUK GUL

University of Pennsylvania, Philadelphia, Pennsylvania 19104

HUGO SONNENSCHEIN

Princeton University, Princeton, New Jersey 08544

AND

ROBERT WILSON

Stanford University, Stanford, California 94305

Received June 2, 1985; revised January 15, 1986

Subgame-perfect equilibria are characterized for a market in which the seller quotes a price each period. Assume zero costs, positive interest rate, continuum of buyers, and some technical conditions. If buyers' valuations are positive then equilibrium is unique, buyers' strategies are stationary, and the price sequence is determinant along the equilibrium path but possibly randomized elsewhere. Otherwise a continuum of stationary equilibria can exist, but at most one with analytic strategies. Coase's conjecture is verified for stationary strategies: reducing the period length drives all prices to zero or the least valuation. Connections to bargaining models are described. *Journal of Economic Literature* Classification Number: 022. © 1986 Academic Press, Inc.

INTRODUCTION

A dynamic theory of monopoly must take into account the fact that a monopolist cannot normally sign contracts to guarantee that the future prices of his output will be above some minimal level. Thus, in a dynamic theory the time path of prices will generally not be the one which, if a com-

* This paper was prepared during Gul and Sonnenschein's visit for a year at the Stanford Business School, which they acknowledge with appreciation. Gul and Sonnenschein acknowledge research support from National Science Foundation grant SES 8510135 to Princeton University; and Wilson, from NSF Grant SES 8308723 and ONR contract N00014-79-C0685 to Stanford University.

264

mitment to future prices were possible, would bring forth demands that maximize the discounted stream of revenues minus costs. Let p_1^c, p_2^c,... be a maximizing price plan if commitment is possible. Without commitment, after the first price in such a plan, it will almost never be in the monopolist's interest to announce p_2^c. But consumers know this, and so we can expect that they will not anticipate the later prices in the plan when the first price is announced. Thus, even if consumers individually have no market power, they will not purchase in the first period as if the subsequent prices p_2^c, p_3^c,... where given. As a consequence, in a dynamic theory it is not in the monopolist's interest to announce p_1^c in the first period. In order for a plan to be dynamically consistent it must be the case that:

(a)   Consumers correctly anticipate prices, and

(b)   At *every* point in time the monopolist can not increase the expected present value of his remaining profit by deviating from the price path that is expected by consumers.

In other words, a dynamic theory of monopoly is an equilibrium theory, and it seems natural that an equilibrium perspective is necessary for analyzing the problem.

To clarify further the necessity for an equilibrium perspective, consider the determination of the first price in a market in which the monopolist announces prices in quick succession: think of a supplier of mineral water standing at his source; assume that he is able to pump at any rate at zero cost and to change his price at will.[1] Assume also that there are consumers with every valuation less than some arbitrary positive value. On the one hand, one might argue that the monopolist will be able to discriminate perfectly, since the time he needs to make his way down the demand curve will be very short. On the other hand, one might argue to the contrary that the monopolist will make negligible rents: each consumer knows that the monopolist intends to sell eventually to the lowest-valuation consumer, and since the time between offers is short, he believes that the amount of time until the minimal valuation is reached is also short, and thus he will not buy until the price is close to that minimal valuation. The interplay of these factors is the main theme in the recent literature on durable goods monopoly of Bulow [1], Kahn [7], and Stokey [11]. A major result of this paper is to affirm a conjecture of Coase [2] that states that the market will open at a price close to zero. In summary, without repeat purchases monopoly rents must depend substantially on a monopolist's ability to commit to prices or quantities offered in the future.

A second purpose of the paper is to extend Rubinstein's analysis of the

---

[1] The spirit of the model is best captured by assuming that the water is medicinal, and that only one glass is desired in a lifetime.

bilateral monopoly bargaining problem with alternating offers to the case that a seller makes repeated offers to many consumers. The striking conclusion of Rubinstein's analysis is that with discounting the bilateral monopoly has a unique subgame-perfect equilibrium in pure strategies, even when there is no *a priori* restriction on how long the bargaining might continue. In fact, Rubinstein shows that a bargain is reached immediately, with the division of the gains from trade uniquely determined by the parties' rates of discount. That is, discounting is sufficient to render the bargaining problem determinate.

In contrast, we show that the situation in which a monopolist makes repeated offers to a continuum of consumers is considerably more complicated. If the minimum valuation of the consumers exceeds the monopolist's (constant) unit cost, as in Rubinstein's formulation, then again there is generically a unique subgame-perfect equilibrium determined by the distribution of the consumers' valuations, the unit cost, and the discount factor.[2] This equilibrium predicts a decreasing sequence of prices with sales made in every period until the market is exhausted after a finite number of periods at a final price equal to the least valuation. Off the equilibrium path, however, the monopolist may employ a randomized strategy. In the alternative case that the minimum valuation does not exceed the unit cost, the market remains open forever, and there may be many distinct equilibria. The simple case of a uniform distribution of valuations (i.e., a linear demand function) produces both one equilibrium that involves no randomization off the equilibrium path, and a continuum of equilibria requiring such randomization—and all of these equilibria have different price paths and profits for the monopolist. A substantial regularity assumption, requiring a smooth variation of the consumers' strategies as their valuations vary, is shown to restore the generic uniqueness of the equilibrium. Absent some such assumption, nevertheless, we conclude that in monopolized markets discounting is insufficient in itself to determine the division of the gains from trade. The same lack of uniqueness occurs if the seller makes repeated offers to a single buyer with private information about his valuation.[3] This suggests a qualitative discontinuity in the equilibria of bargaining problems formulated à la Rubinstein.

The paper is organized as follows: In Section 1 we define the preferences and strategies of the players and explain the notion of equilibrium. In Section 2 we consider a particular example of a market with zero costs of production, and describe its unique equilibrium. The equilibrium exhibits properties that are important in the analysis. First, it requires no randomization along the equilibrium path: prices are determinant and

---

[2] We assume that the monopolist and the consumers all have the same discount factor.

[3] Assume that the seller's cost is interior to the support of the buyer's valuation.

decrease over time. Second, randomization is required off the equilibrium path. Third, the strategies of consumers satisfy a stationarity property; namely, the distribution of consumers left in the market after any price (that is lower than all preceding prices) is independent of the prior price history in the market. Section 3 states the main existence and uniqueness results for the case that the minimum valuation among the consumers is greater than the unit cost of production, and Section 4 presents the theory for the case that this hypothesis does not hold. Section 5 states the Coase conjecture for arbitrary market demand. Section 6 is composed of a variety of notes, several of which relate our results to existing literature. Among these is the observation that our notion of equilibrium provides foundations for the equilibrium concept used in the theory of durable goods monopoly and that all our theorems apply to that theory. Also, we observe that our existence and uniqueness theorems both generalize and strengthen the work of Sobel and Takahashi [10], Cramton [3], and Fudenberg, Levine, and Tirole [4] on equilibrium for bargaining models in which a seller with known valuation makes price offers to a single consumer whose valuation is a random variable (the value of which is known only to the consumer); such bargaining models have a formal equivalence to the models studied here. The proofs are presented in an Appendix.

1. SPECIFICATION OF THE MODEL

The monopolist faces a unit (Lebesgue) measure of non-atomic consumers indexed by $q \in [0, 1]$. Each consumer is in the market to buy one unit of the monopolist's product, and can buy that unit at any time $i = 0, 1, 2, \ldots$. The preferences of consumers are defined by specifying a non-increasing left-continuous function $f: [0, 1] \to \Re_+$ and a discount factor δ. Specifically, if consumer $q \in [0, 1]$ buys the product at time i at price p, then his utility is $[f(q) - p] \delta^i$.[4] Assume without loss of generality that $f(q)$ is positive for all $q < 1$. At various times, the following two conditions are imposed:

(B) $f(1)$ is positive.

(L) f satisfies a Lipschitz condition at 1.

The discount factor δ is positive and less than one; all of the consumers and the monopolist have the same discount factor.[5] The monopolist's unit costs are constant and zero.[6] Each consumer maximizes his expected

---

[4] See **6.7** in Section 6 for the interpretation of the utility function.

[5] Only the coincidence of the consumers' discount factors is necessary for the analysis.

[6] To see that the analysis with zero costs captures the case of a general constant cost c, reinterpret prices and consumers' valuations as net of the cost.

utility, and the monopolist maximizes the expected present value of his revenue stream.[7]

In each period, first the monopolist specifies a price and then those consumers who have not previously purchased simultaneously choose whether to accept or to reject this price. A consumer who rejects continues as an active player until he eventually accepts some price; his utility is zero if he never accepts an offered price. At any time all players have perfect recall of the previous history of the game.

A strategy for the monopolist specifies at each time a price to charge as a function of the history of the game.[8] A strategy for a consumer specifies at each time and after each history in which he has not previously purchased whether to accept or to reject the monopolist's offered price; equivalently, it specifies the set of prices the consumer will accept. We seek a subgame-perfect Nash equilibrium of this game.

There are some subtle issues involved in defining the game that naturally arise from the above description; for example, technical restrictions are necessary to insure that at each stage the set of consumers accepting an offer is measurable so that the monopolist's revenue can be evaluated. We also argue that in order to characterize the subgame-perfect equilibrium paths of a sensible version of the above game, it is sufficient to consider strategies depending only on the past history of prices.

First, we observe that in this extensive-form game, if the players' strategies prescribe behavior that is optimal for each player for all histories that result from no *simultaneous* deviations, then the equilibrium path prescribed is the equilibrium path of a subgame-perfect equilibrium. To see this replace that portion of the strategies in any subgame that follows simultaneous deviations by equilibrium behavior in the subgame: this does not change the equilibrium path. Next we *assume* that the equilibrium actions of each agent are constant on histories in which prices are the same and the sets of agents accepting at each point in time differ at most by sets of measure zero. To some extent this represents a natural regularity requirement; however, the assumption has substantial force and it affects the set of equilibria. It is a *maintained hypothesis* in the analysis.[9] With this assumption, unilateral deviations by non-atomic consumers can change neither the actions of the remaining consumers nor the actions of the monopolist. Thus, only unilateral deviations of the monopolist can affect the course of the game. From the observation that simultaneous deviations

---

[7] If m_i is the measure of the consumers purchasing in response to the price p_i in period i then the monopolist's present value is $\sum_0^\infty p_i m_i \delta^i$. We adopt the convention that the initial period is $i = 0$.

[8] We shall show that the game in which the monopolist chooses quantities is a special case allowing somewhat simpler specification of the off-the-equilibrium-path strategies.

[9] See note **6.1** in Section 6.

from the equilibrium path are unimportant in checking for subgame perfection, it follows that in order to show that a path is associated with a subgame-perfect equilibrium it is necessary and sufficient to specify actions for each agent as functions of the monopolist's previous plays (that is, price histories), so that (a) these functions generate the given path, and (b) after each price history the prescribed actions are optimal.

2. A SIMPLE EXAMPLE

In this example only, the consumers are uniformly distributed on the interval $[0, 2]$ with total measure 2. The monopolist initially holds at least measure 2 of the commodity or can produce at zero cost. Those consumers $q \in [0, 1]$ have the valuation 3 and those in $(1, 2]$ have the valuation 1. The discount factor is $\delta = 1/2$.

There is a unique "perfect foresight" equilibrium, as considered by Bulow [1], Stokey [11], and Kahn [7] for this example. It is given by the price sequence $p_0 = 2$, $p_1 = 1$, and the sale quantities $m_0 = m_1 = 1$. These prices and quantities also occur along the equilibrium path in the subgame-perfect equilibrium. However, there is *no pure strategy* equilibrium for the game as specified with the monopolist offering prices.

To see this, first observe that in any equilibrium the prices must be 2 and 1 in the last two periods before sales cease. If sufficiently few high-valuation consumers remain (less than half as we shall see below), then the monopolist prefers to offer the price 1 and clear the market, so the final price is 1. If the initial price is 1 or the penultimate price exceeds 2, then all the high-valuation consumers will buy at the final price of 1 (they prefer a price of 1 tomorrow to any price exceeding 2 today); this is not optimal for the monopolist since he can make some sales at a penultimate price not exceeding 2 and do better (as we shall see in more detail below). This price can not be less than 2, however, since if it were then all of the high-valuation consumers would buy (they prefer any price less than 2 to a price of 1 later) and therefore the monopolist prefers to increase any price less than 2: no price between 1 and 2 can be optimal for the monopolist. Thus, the final prices are 2 and then 1. These can not be the prices in a subgame-perfect pure-strategy equilibrium, however. If the monopolist deviates from the prescribed price of 2 and offers a slightly higher price, then either all, some, or none of the high-valuation consumers will purchase. If all, then the next price is expected to be 1, so their behavior is not optimal.[10] If some, then the next price is expected to be between 1 and 2, so that the

---

[10] We ignore here the possibility that a single consumer's choice of whether or not to buy affects the next price charged; see note **6.1** in Section 6.

high-valuation consumers are indifferent about purchasing now rather than waiting; but we have seen that such a price is never optimal for the monopolist. If none, then the next price is expected to be 2, in which case they should accept the slightly higher price offered now. Thus, there can not be a subgame-perfect equilibrium in pure strategies.

A subgame-perfect equilibrium for this example requires that the monopolist employs a mixed strategy off the equilibrium path. Half of the high-valuation consumers purchase if the price offered does not exceed $2\frac{1}{2}$, and the other half buy when it does not exceed 2; the low-valuation consumers buy when the price does not exceed 1. If the monopolist charges any price exceeding $2\frac{1}{2}$, then none of the consumers accept: they expect him to charge 2 next period. If he charges any prices in $(2, 2\frac{1}{2}]$, then half of the high-valuation consumers accept: they are indifferent about accepting since they expect that next period he will randomize between the prices 2 and 1 (with probabilities that substantiate their indifference). If he charges any price not exceeding 2, then all the high-valuation consumers accept. The monopolist's strategy is to charge 2 if at least half the high-valuation consumers remain, and 1 otherwise—unless he previously deviated by charging a price in $(2, 2\frac{1}{2})$, in which case he randomizes between 2 and 1 if precisely half of the high-valuation consumers remain. Note that the randomization following a deviation is optimal for the monopolist since with half of the high-valuation consumers remaining he is indifferent whether to charge 2 now (and 1 next period), or to clear the market by charging 1: both yield a present value of $1\frac{1}{2}$.

In this example there is no randomization on the equilibrium path, the strategies of consumers are stationary, the equilibrium specifies a determinant decreasing sequence of prices, and the market closes after a finite number of periods. Theorem 1 and its corollary show that we have identified the unique equilibrium for this example, and that the form of the equilibrium is general for markets in which the minimum of the consumers' valuations exceeds the constant unit cost of production.

3. Markets with Consumers' Valuations Bounded Away From Zero

Theorem 1. *If f satisfies* (B) *and* (L) *then there exist* $A \subset [0, 1]$, $t: [0, 1] \to [0, 1]$, *and* $P: [0, 1] \to \Re_{++}$ *such that* $\{q_i, p_i\}_{i=0}^{\infty}$ *is an equilibrium path if and only if* $q_0 = 0$, $q_1 \in A$, $(\forall i \geq 1)\, q_{i+1} = t(q_i)$, *and* $(\forall i \geq 0)\, p_i = P(q_{i+1})$.[11]

---

[11] Fudenberg, Levine, and Tirole prove a related result in the context of a bargaining model in which a seller with known valuation makes offers to a consumer whose valuation is a ran-

Explanation:

• q_1 is the initial quantity sold in response to the monopolist's initial offer p_0.

• t determines subsequent quantities sold along the equilibrium path, in terms of the market penetration achieved.

• P defines equilibrium prices as a function of the market penetration achieved.

Let $\Sigma(f, \delta)$ denote the set of equilibria for the market (f, δ) and let $\Sigma^s(f, \delta)$ denote the subset of equilibria which satisfy the condition that the state of the market, after any price that is lower than all preceding prices, is independent of the earlier price history in the market. Equilibria in $\Sigma^s(f, \delta)$ are said to be stationary for the consumers, since the sets of those accepting and those rejecting depend only on the current price. The following is an immediate consequence of Theorem 1.

COROLLARY. *Generic markets satisfying* (B) *and* (L) *have a unique equilibrium path and this path leads to a determinate sequence of price offers and acceptances. Furthermore, the path is associated with an equilibrium that is stationary for the consumers, prices are decreasing along the equilibrium path, and all consumers are served after a finite number of offers.*[12]

4. MARKETS WITH VALUATIONS ARBITRARILY CLOSE TO ZERO

Theorem 1 and its corollary are concerned with markets in which the valuations of consumers are bounded away from zero; that is, assumption (B) is satisfied. For such markets we establish that all equilibria are associated with stationary strategies on the part of the consumers; that is, $\Sigma^s(f, \delta) = \Sigma(f, \delta)$. Furthermore, we prove that an equilibrium generically defines a unique decreasing sequence of price offers and acceptances. For markets in which the valuations of consumers are not bounded away from zero, the theory is not nearly so orderly. Before entering into a discussion of these markets, we would like to make clear why they represent the relevant case.

---

dom variable. We learned a great deal from their analysis; in particular, our proof of Theorem 1 makes substantial use of their ideas. Our hypotheses are weaker since we do not assume that f is differentiable with differentiable inverse. Also, our conclusion substantially strengthens the characterization of equilibrium prices. See note **6.2** in Section 6.

[12] All equilibria are equivalent in the sense that they specify (a) the same equilibrium path, (b) the same strategy for the monopolist, and (c) up to closure, the same acceptance sets for consumers.

So far discussion has ignored costs of production. This was done because we have in mind stationary constant unit costs, and as we have mentioned (see footnote 6) such costs can be subsumed into the definition of demand (replace f by $f - c$). With this formulation prices are interpreted as net of unit cost, and the net valuation of consumers can be negative. Indeed, in a monopolized market, without the possibility for commitment past the current period, the commodity will eventually be sold to all consumers with a net positive valuation. The case in which $f(1) > 0$ corresponds to a situation in which there is no "marginal" consumer. When $f(1) \leq 0$, the market remains open for an infinite number of periods, and the marginal consumer is identified. Since consumers with negative net valuations are never served, one can consider, without loss of generality, the case $f(1) = 0$.

Even when one confines attention to equilibria in $\Sigma^s(f, \delta)$, without the assumption (B) that $f(1) > 0$ it is not the case that there is a unique equilibrium. In fact, even for the case of linear demand there is a continuum of disjoint equilibrium paths. In Examples 1 and 2 two distinct equilibria are exhibited. In Example 3 it is shown how Example 2 can be altered to produce a continuum of equilibria.

EXAMPLE 1.   We consider the example with a linear demand function $f(q) = 1 - q$. Stokey [11] studies this example in a Cournot formulation in which the monopolist offers quantities rather than prices. In the equilibrium she derives, in period i after any history that results in sales to the q_i consumers with valuations exceeding $1 - q_i$, the monopolist offers a quantity $\alpha[1 - q_i]$ that receives the price $p_i = \beta[1 - q_i]$, where α and β are two parameters to be determined. One can determine α and β from symmetry conditions, since along the equilibrium path successive markets are related to each other by a scaling transformation. Thus, if the price is $p_i = p(q_i)$ when q_i consumers have been served then $p(q) = [1 - q] p(0)$ and the monopolist's present value of remaining profits is $R(q) = \frac{1}{2}[1 - q]^2 p(0)$, where the initial price is $p(0) = \beta$ and the initial quantity is α. Optimality of the monopolist's strategy requires that $\bar{q} = t(q) \equiv q + \alpha[1 - q]$ is the choice that achieves the maximum in the monopolist's associated dynamic programming problem

$$R(q) = \max_{\bar{q} \geq q} P(\bar{q})[\bar{q} - q] + \delta R(\bar{q}),$$

where $P(\bar{q})$ is the highest price that will induce all consumers with valuations exceeding $f(\bar{q})$ to accept. Utility maximization by the consumers implies that

$$f(\bar{q}) - P(\bar{q}) = [f(\bar{q}) - P(t(\bar{q}))] \delta,$$

so that consumer $\bar{q}$ is indifferent between accepting or waiting another period. By hypothesis,

$$t(\bar{q}) = \bar{q} + \alpha[1 - \bar{q}],$$

$$P(t(\bar{q})) = p(\bar{q}) = \beta[1 - \bar{q}];$$

hence,

$$P(\bar{q}) = [1 - \delta] f(\bar{q}) + \delta\beta[1 - \bar{q}]$$

$$\equiv \gamma[1 - \bar{q}],$$

where $\gamma \equiv 1 - \delta + \delta\beta$. The unique values that satisfy these relationships are

$$\alpha = \beta = \bar{\delta}/(1 + \bar{\delta}),$$

where $\bar{\delta} \equiv \sqrt{1 - \delta}$. One can further verify using the methods developed later that with these values a subgame-perfect equilibrium is in fact obtained. The Coase conjecture is verified in this example by noting that as $\delta \to 1$ the initial price $p(0) = \beta \to 0$, the initial quantity $\alpha \to 0$, and the monopolist's present value $R(0) \to 0$. Also, if one interprets the increase in the discount factor as due to a shortening of the duration of a period, say $\delta \equiv e^{-r\Delta}$ and $\Delta \to 0$, then the limiting value of each consumer's expected utility is his valuation; that is, trades occur early.

EXAMPLE 2. In this example we assume the same linear demand function $f(q) = 1 - q$ as in Example 1, but we require that the discount factor is sufficiently large. We construct an equilibrium with strikingly different properties, although the equilibrium path has a superficial resemblance to the equilibrium path of Example 1 and it enjoys the same asymptotic properties as $\delta \to 1$. In each period i after serving q_i consumers the monopolist charges the price $p_i = \beta[1 - q_i]$ and sells the quantity $\alpha[1 - q_i]$; thus, $\beta = p_0/[1 - q_0]$ and $\alpha = [q_1 - q_0]/[1 - q_0]$, or starting from $q_0 = 0$ the initial price is $p_0 = \beta$ and the initial quantity is $q_1 = \alpha$. Similarly,

$$t(q_i) = q_i + \alpha[1 - q_i],$$

$$p_i = [1 - \alpha]^i p_0,$$

$$P(q_i) = [1 - \delta][1 - q_i] + \delta p_i,$$

along the equilibrium path, precisely as along the equilibrium path of Example 1. The resemblance ends here, however, since the equilibrium values of α and β are different, and the strategies off the equilibrium path are quite different.

The key to the construction of this equilibrium is the specification of the strategies off the equilibrium path. The form of the equilibrium strategies is the following: In any period (not necessarily period i), if those consumers previously served are those with valuations exceeding $1-q$ and $q \in (q_{i-1}, q_i)$, then the monopolist charges p_i. He does the same if $q = q_i$ unless in the previous period he deviated and charged a price $p \in (\hat{p}_i, p_{i-1})$, where $\hat{p}_{i-1} \equiv [1-\delta][1-q_{i-1}] + \delta p_i$, in which case he randomizes between the prices p_i and p_{i+1} with probabilities determined so as to make the consumer with valuation $1-q_i$ indifferent whether to accept the price p in the previous period or to wait for the subsequent lottery between the next two prices. The consumers' responses have essentially the simple form derived in Example 1: one with the valuation $1-q$ accepts any price $p \leqslant P(q)$, where if $q \in (q_{i-1}, q_i]$ then

$$P(q) = [1-\delta][1-q] + \delta p_i;$$

note, however, that unlike Example 1 in this case the consumers' reservation price strategy is represented by the piecewise-linear left-continuous decreasing function P with downward jumps at q_i of magnitude $\delta[p_i - p_{i+1}]$.

An equilibrium of this form entails the following relationships: First, the present value of the monopolist's subsequent revenues after serving the q consumers with valuations exceeding $1-q$ is piecewise-linear and continuous of the form $R(q) = R_i + p_i[q_i - q]$ if $q \in (q_{i-1}, q_i]$ and $R_i \equiv R(q_i)$. In addition,

$$p_i = [1-\delta][1-q_{i+1}] + \delta p_{i+1}, \tag{1}$$

$$R_i = p_i[q_{i+1} - q_i] + \delta R_{i+1}, \tag{2}$$

$$R_i = R_{i+1} + p_{i+1}[q_{i+1} - q_i]; \tag{3}$$

which express respectively the consumers' behavior, the recursion for the monopolist's present value, and the continuity of the monopolist's present value function, all along the equilibrium path. An immediate consequence of (2) and (3) is that

$$R_i = p_{i+1}[q_{i+2} - q_i] + \delta R_{i+2}, \tag{4}$$

which with (2) assures that the monopolist is in fact willing to randomize at q_i between the prices p_i and p_{i+1} when required after a previous deviant price $p \in (\hat{p}_i, p_{i-1})$. The conditions (1), (2), and (3) have a solution

$$p_i = \bar{\alpha}^i p_0, \qquad R_i = \bar{\alpha}^{2i} R_0, \qquad 1 - q_i = \bar{\alpha}^i[1 - q_0],$$

where

$$p_0 = [1 - q_0] \frac{\bar{\alpha} - \delta\bar{\alpha}}{1 - \delta\bar{\alpha}}, \qquad R_0 = p_0 [1 - q_0] \frac{\bar{\alpha}}{1 + \bar{\alpha}},$$

and $\bar{\alpha}$ is determined as the solution in $(0, 1)$ of the equation [13]

$$\bar{\alpha} = \frac{1 - \bar{\alpha}^2}{1 - \delta\bar{\alpha}^2}.$$

One can show that $\bar{\alpha} \to 1$ as $\delta \to 1$; indeed, as a function of δ, $\bar{\alpha}$ is convex and increasing with an infinite rate of increase at 1. In terms of the specification above,

$$\alpha = 1 - \bar{\alpha} \qquad \text{and} \qquad \beta = \frac{\bar{\alpha} - \delta\bar{\alpha}}{1 - \delta\bar{\alpha}},$$

which both tend to 0 as $\delta \to 1$.

The verification that this specification yields an equilibrium can be accomplished in two parts. For the first part we can apply the following lemma, which is a consequence of repeated applications of (2) and (3): If $j \geq i + 2$ then $R_i > p_j[q_{j+1} - q_i] + \delta R_{j+1}$. Along the equilibrium path this assures that the monopolist prefers to name the price p_i at q_i rather than any price $p_j < p_{i+1} < p_i$. For the second part we must verify that at any $q \in (q_{i-1}, q_i]$ the monopolist prefers the price p_i to any other $p \neq p_i$ (except p_{i+1} if $q = q_i$). We omit the lengthy derivation of this result except to remark that the proof depends on the assumption that $\bar{\alpha}^2 > \frac{1}{2}$, which is assured if $\delta > 2 - \sqrt{2}$. Thus if the discount factor is sufficiently large then the specification yields an equilibrium.

EXAMPLE 3. We now turn to the demonstration that the equilibrium derived in Example 2 can be generalized to generate a continuum of equilibria. The key observation is to note that in the construction of Example 2 the specification of q_0 is a free parameter. For each sufficiently small negative value of q_0 there exists an additional equilibrium in which the play of the game proceeds as follows: The monopolist begins with $q = 0$ which lies in one of the intervals $(q_{j-1}, q_j]$ generated by the choice of q_0. Interpret this situation as the initiation of a subgame imbedded in the larger game corresponding to the choice of q_0; that is, imagine that the measure 1 of consumers present is the residual after a portion $|q_0|$ of a larger population of measure $1 - q_0$ has been served. Then, the equilibrium prescribes that the monopolist opens with the initial offer p_j, and that the consumers

---

[13] A typical example with $q_0 = 0$ and $\delta = 0{,}9$ yields $\bar{\alpha} = 0.8247$, $p_0 = 0.3199$ and $R_0 = 0.1446$.

with valuations no less than $1 - q_{j+1}$ accept. Similarly, if the monopolist deviates and opens with any offer $p \in (p_j, p_{j-1}]$ then those consumers with valuations no less than $1 - q_j$ accept, and in particular if $p \in (\hat{p}_j, p_{j-1})$ then they expect that next time he will randomize between the prices p_j and p_{j+1}. And, if he opens with a price exceeding p_{j-1} then no consumers accept. All these behaviors are simply the subgame-perfect equilibrium strategies in the subgame of the game in which the 'real' game is interpreted as imbedded. After these opening moves, the play continues precisely in the same fashion, using the critical values q_k and p_k for $k \geqslant j$ generated from the choice of q_0.

From this construction, therefore, we see that the market with a linear demand function and a discount factor sufficiently large has a continuum of equilibria. All of these equilibria have entirely disjoint equilibrium paths, though they share many features in common such as described above: in each case the monopolist's prices in successive periods have a constant ratio, and after the first period a constant percentage of the unserved consumers accept each period (these constants differ between Example 1 and Examples 2 and 3).

The possibility of a continuum of equilibria presents serious difficulties for the theory. The striking feature of Rubinstein's [8] seminal paper on the bargaining problem is that it demonstrates that even with an infinite horizon, impatience is sufficient to give a determinant solution to the bargaining problem. Theorem 1 tells us that this conclusion remains true with one-sided offers and many consumers when the valuation of the monopolist is not a member of the set of valuations of the consumers. The preceding examples tell us that when one leaves such a regime, one loses the determinacy of the solution. In a noncooperative game with a continuum of players and a continuum of equilibria, it is difficult to invoke an argument to select among the equilibria, to judge any one more likely than another, or even to rest assured that the players' expectations will enable any equilibrium to be realized. Thus, whether or not the valuation of the monopolist is disjoint from the set of consumers' valuations represents a critical distinction for the theory.

Observe that among the many equilibria for the linear demand case there is only one (Example 1) for which P, the function specifying the consumers' strategies, is continuous. This suggests the following conjecture: if the demand function f is continuous then there exists a unique equilibrium $\sigma \in \Sigma^s(f, \delta)$ such that the associated function P is continuous in some neighborhood of 1. We argue that such an equilibrium is a salient predictor of market behavior, for two reasons. First, where P is continuous the equilibrium specifies a pure strategy for the seller off the equilibrium path (as well as on the path). Second, general considerations of continuity indicate that this class of equilibrium selections is the only plausible candidate that could ensure that small changes in the data of the problem (e.g., variations in f) induce correspondingly small changes in the agents' strategies. Unfortunately we have not been able to establish this conjecture in the strong form mentioned; instead, we establish uniqueness of the equilibrium for which P is analytic in a neighborhood of 1, using the following construction. Suppose that P and P^* specify equilibrium strategies for the consumers in the market (f, δ), where f has an nth order derivative at 1. We show that if the derivatives of nth order at 1 also exist for P and P^*, then these derivatives are identical. This is then shown to imply that if f has continuous derivatives of all orders at 1, and P and P^* are analytic at 1, then P and P^* are identical functions. For instance, this result confirms that in the case of linear demand the equilibrium path constructed by Stokey [11], as in Example 1, is the only one sustained by an analytic strategy for the consumers.

THEOREM 2. *Assume that $f(1) = 0$, $n \geqslant 1$, $f \in C^n(1)$, and $f'(1) \neq 0$. Consider two equilibria, σ_P, $\sigma_Q \in \Sigma^s(f, \delta)$ for which P, Q: $[0, 1] \to \Re_+$ specify the stationary strategies of the consumers, and for $k \leqslant n$ let P^k and Q^k denote their kth order derivatives. Then, if $P^k(1)$ and $Q^k(1)$ exist they are equal. Moreover, if $(\forall n) f \in C^n(1)$, and P and Q are analytic in a neighborhood of 1, then $(\forall q \in (0, 1]) P(q) = Q(q)$.*

Note. It is easy to show that if P is analytic in a neighborhood of 1, then for any δ and any n there exists a demand function $f \in C^n(1)$ so that P defines an equilibrium of the market (f, δ). The equilibrium so defined will be in $\Sigma^s(f, \delta)$. This is one way to see that the analyticity assumption does not render the problem vacuous.

5. THE COASE CONJECTURE

Finally, we resolve the Coase conjecture [2] with a general result that requires only that the consumers' strategies are stationary.[14]

THEOREM 3 (Coase conjecture). *For each $\varepsilon > 0$ there exists $\delta < 1$ such that for all $\delta > \bar{\delta}$ and for all equilibria $\sigma \in \Sigma^s(f, \delta)$, the first price prescribed by σ is less than ε.*

---

[14] The theorem is stated for the case that $f(1) = 0$. If $f(1) \neq 0$, then the statement need not include the hypothesis that $\sigma \in \Sigma^s(f, \delta)$ and the first price prescribed by σ will be less than $f(1) + \varepsilon$. The proof of this case is less difficult and follows the ideas in the first half of the proof of Theorem 3.

Since each consumer has the option of accepting the first price offered, we obtain the following corollary:

COROLLARY. *For each $\varepsilon > 0$ there exists $\bar{\delta} < 1$ such that for all $\delta > \bar{\delta}$ and for all equilibria $\sigma \in \Sigma^s(f, \delta)$, a consumer q with the valuation $f(q)$ obtains an equilibrium payoff not less than $f(q) - \varepsilon$.*

The proof of Theorem 3 in the Appendix is rather complicated, so here we sketch a more intuitive line of argument, although it is incomplete in several respects. The key consideration is that, since the consumers' *equilibrium* strategies are stationary, the monopolist has the option at any time to accelerate the process by offering tomorrow's price today and thereby advancing the acceptance dates of subsequent consumers. The cost of doing this is the foregone higher profit on those consumers accepting today, whereas the benefit is the interest on the monopolist's present value of continuation, which is thereby made to arrive a day earlier. Since an equilibrium requires that exercising this option must be disadvantageous for the monopolist, we know that the cost must exceed the benefit. But the cost is approximately the price cut times the number of consumers who accept today's price, and the benefit is the daily interest on the continuation value. Consequently, the daily interest on the continuation value is bounded by approximately the day-to-day price drop times the number accepting per day. Fix the interest rate per unit time to be 100%, and divide this inequality through *twice* by the length of a day: then the continuation value divided by the length of a day is bounded by the product of the rates (per unit time) at which prices decline and consumers accept. As the length of a day shrinks, the rate of price decline must be bounded or consumers would prefer to wait rather than accept the current price. If the rate of acceptance is also bounded, then as the length of a day shrinks the continuation value must also shrink to zero—if opportunities remain for the monopolist to reduce his price. If the continuation value shrinks to zero then the monopolist's later prices must all be converging to his unit cost, and therefore his present prices too: otherwise, if the day is sufficiently short then the consumers all prefer to delay purchasing. If no opportunities for further price reductions remain then the price must already be at its minimum, which is the minimal valuation among the consumers. The remaining case, therefore, is that the rate of acceptances is unbounded. But in this case also the prices offered by the monopolist must all be converging downward to his unit cost (or the consumers' least valuation), since this is the only way that a positive fraction of the consumers will accept in each of several days when their interest cost of delay is small; that is, the sequence of prices must become flat in the limit, yet the sequence is tied down at the end. In outline, this is one interpretation of the arguments supporting the Coase conjecture.

6. NOTES

6.1. We demonstrate that a genuine restriction is imposed by the assumption that agents treat as equivalent those histories that differ only by the actions of sets of consumers of measure zero. We do so by showing that for a slightly altered version of the example in Section 2, there is an equilibrium in which the monopolist distinguishes among "equivalent" histories and that has a different equilibrium path than obtains if he can not make such distinctions.

Alter the example in Section 2 so that the consumers with the valuation 3 have measure 2 (rather than 1). It remains true that there is an equilibrium in which the sequence of prices is first 2 and then 1. A second equilibrium that distinguishes among equivalent histories has a different equilibrium path, as follows: Consider the consumers' strategies specified by the function

$$P(q) = \begin{cases} 2\frac{1}{2} & \text{if} \quad q \in [0, \frac{3}{2}], \\ 2 & \text{if} \quad q \in (\frac{3}{2}, 2], \\ 1 & \text{if} \quad q \in (2, 3]. \end{cases}$$

Suppose that the monopolist charges $2\frac{1}{2}$ first and then charges 1 provided that *all* consumers $q \leqslant \frac{3}{2}$ accept the first offer. If one or more of these consumers to not accept the first offer, and no other agent does accept, then the monopolist next charges 2 followed by the final offer of 1. Observe that the consumers $q \leqslant \frac{3}{2}$ can do no better than to accept the first offer of $2\frac{1}{2}$ since their expectations of the subsequent price depend on whether or not each one accepts. Thus, with an off-the-equilibrium-path strategy for the monopolist specified similarly to the original example, this provides an alternative equilibrium with a different equilibrium path.

6.2. The formalism of Theorems 1–3 and their corollaries accommodates the case of bilateral bargaining in which a seller with a known valuation repeatedly makes offers to a single buyer with a privately known valuation whose probability distribution is common knowledge. If F is the cumulative distribution function (assumed invertible for simplicity), then the buyer of type q has the valuation $f(q) = F^{-1}(1-q)$; that is, the right-cumulative distribution functions is interpreted as the inverse demand function. The appropriate criterion for the bargaining problem is a sequential equilibrium. For a subgame-perfect equilibrium of the monopoly problem, given any price history the residual demand in the monopoly market defines the seller's posterior distribution of the buyer's type in the corresponding sequential equilibrium of the bargaining problem after the same price history. It is for this reason that analyses of bargaining models with repeated offers by the uninformed party have produced results formally identical to those obtained in analyses of durable goods monopoly; see for example Fudenberg, Levine, and Tirole [4] on the one hand and (for the case of linear demand) Stokey [11] on the other. This equivalence is surprising, since the histories in the monopoly market include the particular sets of consumers who have purchased at each price, whereas in the bargaining problem the buyer says only "*no*" until he accepts and the game terminates. In fact, our previous note indicates that these two games are not formally identical in the absence of our maintained hypothesis that agents do not distinguish among histories differing only by the actions of consumers (or types of the buyer) of measure zero. In particular, the alternative equilibrium described in **6.1** is not a sequential equilibrium for the corresponding bargaining model in which a single seller with valuation 0 makes offers to a buyer who is twice as likely to have the valuation 3 as 1 and both parties use the discount factor $\delta = \frac{1}{2}$. Only with the hypothesis that agents can not distinguish among equivalent histories do the two models become formally identical.

With the formalism of this paper interpreted as applying to the bargaining problem, Theorem 1 and its corollary strengthen a theorem of Fudenberg, Levine, and Tirole [4] in two ways. First, we dispense with their assumption that the cumulative distribution function of the buyer's valuation is differentiable and has a differentiable inverse. More significantly, we show that there is no randomization along the equilibrium path, so that (generically) there is a determinate sequence of price offers.[15]

Section 4 can also be interpreted as applying to the bargaining problem, with the added possibility that the buyer's valuation may be no more than the seller's. In this case exchange may never occur if there are no gains from trade. Previous analysis of this problem did not discover the equilibria in Examples 2 and 3.[16] The existence of multiple equilibria suggests a qualitative discontinuity as the supports of the buyer's and the seller's valuations intersect; this discontinuity is also likely to appear in bargaining with alternating offers.[17]

For the case that assumption (B) is satisfied, Theorem 1 proves both existence and uniqueness of equilibrium. Fudenberg, Levine, and Tirole [4] provide an existence theorem for markets in which the demand function does not satisfy assumption (B). The idea of their proof is to consider the limit of a sequence of equilibria for markets satisfying (B), with demand functions $f(\cdot) + b$ as b decreases to zero. The proof that a limit

---

[15] Fudenberg, Levine, and Tirole [4] allow a random path of price offers, with each price depending on the realizations of earlier price randomizations.

[16] See, for example, Sobel and Takahashi [10] and Cramton [3].

[17] See, for example, Rubinstein [9], Cramton [3], and Grossman and Perry [5].

exists and is an equilibrium at $b = 0$ is rather intricate and we have not verified that it would apply to the more general class of demand functions that we admit. Combined with Theorem 1, however, application of their method may lead to a generalization of their existence theorem.

6.3. Stokey [11] analyzes a model of durable-good monopoly with perfect secondary markets using a rational expectations formulation. The monopolist chooses a profit maximizing sequence of cumulative quantities offered. Deviations from the profit-maximizing plan are important in her analysis (hence, her use of the term "perfection"), but her model is not game-theoretic since neither the preferences nor the actions of the consumers are modeled explicitly. Nevertheless, her model and ours specify the same equilibrium path. In addition to providing game-theoretic foundations for her specification, our results can be interpreted as clarifying the general problem of existence and uniqueness of equilibria for her model. Stokey focuses on the Coase conjecture and the case of linear demand. She verifies the conjecture for the special case of the equilibrium presented in Example 1.

6.4. One can define an analog of our model in which the monopolist chooses quantities rather than prices, and which leads to the same equilibrium path of quantities and prices as in our model. To do so in a complete game-theoretic formulation requires a specification of how prices are determined when a sequence of quantities is offered on the market. This is accomplished by adopting an auction procedure. This formulation leads to rather complicated strategies for the buyers, however: stationarity is lost since each consumer's bids change over time.

6.5. Kahn [7] introduces quadratic production costs into Stokey's model with linear demand and considers the case that, as the period length shrinks, the cost functions converges to the continuous-time total cost function

$$\gamma[Q(\cdot)] = c \int_0^x [Q'(t)]^2 e^{-rt} dt,$$

where Q is a path of cumulative production. For the discrete-time model he identifies an equilibrium similar to Example 1 (that is, the monopolist serves a fraction of the remaining consumers that is invariant with respect to the history). For this equilibrium, he observes that as the period length shrinks the monopolist's production path does not converge to the efficient path; and in fact yields positive profit, thus excluding an analog of the Coase conjecture. Kahn's result reinforces our theme that monopoly rents depend on the monopolist's ability to commit to future prices or sales for some duration. Increasing costs, and hence the necessity of spreading production over time, enable the monopolist to commit credibly to constrain the rate of supply offered in the near future. Kenneth Arrow has suggested to us that decreasing costs may also provide means for credible commitments.

6.6. Gul [6] studies the problem of dynamic oligopoly. He proves that with two or more firms the perfection requirement on the seller's strategies (a strategy must be profit maximizing after every history) imposes no restriction on the total profits that can be earned in equilibrium. This refutes the analog of the Coase conjecture for oligopolistic markets; moreover, he shows that there is no tendency towards the perfectly competitive outcome as the number of firms is increased or the period length shrinks.

6.7. We offer two interpretations of the utility functions of the consumers. In the first, a consumer q receives $f(q)$ "utiles" at the instant he consumes the product, and he has use for at most one unit. Utiles are measured so that at any time \$1 provides a flow of utility having a present value of 1 utile. Thus, if consumer q purchases in period i at the price p_i then he obtains the utility $f(q) \delta^i$ and gives up $p_i \delta^i$. The consumer maximizes utility by timing his purchase to make the expectation of $[f(q) - p_i] \delta^i$ as large as possible. In the second interpretation he obtains $[1 - \delta] f(q)$ utiles per period in each period after purchase, whereas one unit of the numeraire commodity (money) gives each consumer $1 - \delta$ utiles each period. Note that the value of one dollar held for one period is $[1 - \delta]/\delta$ tomorrow or $\delta[(1 - \delta)/\delta] = 1 - \delta$ today. Thus, a consumer who in period i trades p_i of the numeraire for a unit of the durable commodity changes his utility according to the value of the stream

$$[1 - \delta]\{0, 0,..., f(q) - p_i, f(q) - p_i,...\},$$

where the first nonzero element is in period i. The value of this stream is $[f(q) - p_i] \delta^i$ and this accounts for the form of the utility function.

The absence of infusions of new demand into the market is central to our analysis. However, the model does not require that consumers purchase only one unit. The demand function can just as well be viewed as the integral of the demand functions of consumers. As a very special case, each consumer could have the same demand function f; in this situation the mean demand is also f.

Finally we observe that none of our results depend substantially on the assumption that the monopolist has the same time preferences as the consumers. On the other hand, our methods do not apply to the case that consumers' discount factors differ.

6.8. For the case that $f(1) = 0$, the possibility of non-stationary equilibria follows from the existence of multiple stationary equilibria such as we exhibited in Example 3. Let σ and σ' be two equilibria in $\Sigma^s(f, \delta)$, using P and P' to define the stationary strategies of the consumers in the two equilibria. Assume that $P \neq P'$ and that the monopolist's profit is not less in σ than in σ'. Let p_0 be the monopolist's initial offer using σ, and consider the following strategy: If the monopolist charges p_0 initially then σ is followed thereafter; otherwise σ' is followed; finally specify that the monopolist does charge p_0 initially. Clearly this is an equilibrium strategy but is not a member of $\Sigma^s(f, \delta)$, since each consumer's strategy depends on the initial price offered. Recalling from Example 3 that a continuum of equilibria is possible, it is evident that this approach enables the construction of highly nonstationary equilibria in which at every time the selection of the continuation depends on the entire history of prices.

APPENDIX: PROOFS

Note. In all of the following "equilibrium" means "subgame-perfect equilibrium." Assumptions (B) and (L) are assumed in Theorem 1 and its preceding lemmas.

LEMMA 1. *In any equilibrium σ and after any history, if the state in period i is q_i, then the present value of the monopolist's expected profit is at least $[1 - q_i] f(1)$; that is*

$$R^\sigma(q_i) \geq [1 - q_i] f(1),$$

and the monopolist's price prescribed by σ is at least $f(1)$.

Proof. It is sufficient to observe that in equilibrium all of the consumers accept the price $f(1)$. Suppose this were not so, and for any selected equilibrium let $c \leq f(1)$ be the supremum of the prices that will be accepted by all consumers (except possibly for a set of measure zero) after any history. If $c = f(1)$ and a positive measure of consumers reject c then no optimal strategy exists for the monopolist, so assume that $c < f(1)$. An optimal strategy for the monopolist can not specify an offer less than c, since any such offer is less than an offer that is sure to be accepted by all remaining consumers. Consider the offer $p = [1 - \delta] f(1) + \delta c$. By construction, each consumer prefers the offer $p - \varepsilon$ now to an anticipated offer c later. But notice that $p - \varepsilon > c$ for small $\varepsilon > 0$ since $c < f(1)$. Therefore, $p - \varepsilon$ will be accepted now by every consumer. Since this is true for every date and history, the definition of c as a supremum is contradicted. Thus we conclude that $c \geq f(1)$. ∎

LEMMA 2. *There exists $q < 1$ such that in any equilibrium and in any period i after any history, if the state is $q_i \geqslant q$ and the next period's state is q_{i+1} when the actions prescribed by the equilibrium strategies are taken, then $q_{i+1} = 1$.*

Proof. Since the function f is Lipschitzian at 1, there exists $q^* < 1$ and k such that if $\bar{q} > q^*$ then

$$f(\bar{q}) \leqslant f(1) + k[1 - \bar{q}]. \tag{1}$$

Given any equilibrium σ and any history, if q_i is the state and p_i is the price prescribed by σ, then the state q_{i+1} in the next period will satisfy $q_i \leqslant q_{i+1} \leqslant 1$, and since f is left-continuous and consumer q does not purchase at price p_i if $p_i > f(q)$,

$$f(q_{i+1}) \geqslant p_i. \tag{2}$$

Since every consumer remaining in the market in period $i + 1$ at state q_{i+1} has a valuation not exceeding $f(q_{i+1})$, we obtain

$$R^\sigma(q_i) \leqslant [q_{i+1} - q_i] \, p_i + \delta[1 - q_{i+1}] f(q_{i+1}). \tag{3}$$

By Lemma 1 and Eqs. (3), (2), and then (1) above, if $1 \geqslant q_{i+1} \geqslant q_i > q^*$ then

$$
\begin{aligned}
0 &\geqslant [1 - q_i] f(1) - R^\sigma(q_i) \\
&\geqslant [1 - q_i] f(1) - [q_{i+1} - q_i] f(q_{i+1}) - \delta[1 - q_{i+1}] f(q_{i+1}) \\
&\geqslant [1 - q_i] f(1) - [q_{i+1} - q_i]\{f(1) + k[1 - q_{i+1}]\} \\
&\quad - \delta[1 - q_{i+1}]\{f(1) + k[1 - q_{i+1}]\} \\
&\geqslant [1 - \delta][1 - q_{i+1}] f(1) - [q_{i+1} - q_i][1 - q_{i+1}] k - \delta[1 - q_{i+1}]^2 k \\
&\geqslant [1 - q_{i+1}]\{[1 - \delta] f(1) - [1 - q_i] k - \delta[1 - q_i] k\}.
\end{aligned}
$$

The term in the last bracket is positive for all sufficiently small values of $1 - q_i$. Therefore, there exists $q < 1$ such that $q_i \geqslant q$ implies that $1 - q_{i+1} = 0$. ∎

DEFINITION. A pair (q, P) is a *reservation price strategy* if it satisfies the following three properties:

(i) $0 \leqslant q < 1$, and $P: [q, 1] \to \Re_{++}$ is non-increasing and left-continuous.

In any equilibrium and in any period i after any history, if q_i is the state and $\bar{q} > q$, and if the monopolist offers any price p in period i, then

(ii) if $p < P(\bar{q})$ then $q_{i+1} \geqslant \bar{q}$, and

(iii) if $p > P(\bar{q})$ then $q_{i+1} < \bar{q}$.

LEMMA 3. *There exists a reservation price strategy pair (q, P).*

Proof. Define $P(\bar{q}) \equiv [1 - \delta] f(\bar{q}) + \delta f(1)$ for all $\bar{q} \in [q, 1]$, where q is defined as in the statement of Lemma 2. Obviously P satisfies (i). Assume that $p_i < P(\bar{q})$ and $q_{i+1} < \bar{q}$; then consumer $\bar{q}$ does not buy in period i. The greatest utility that $\bar{q}$ can obtain is bounded by

$$[f(\bar{q}) - f(1)] \delta^{i+1} = [f(\bar{q}) - (1 - \delta) f(\bar{q}) - \delta f(1)] \delta^i$$
$$= [f(\bar{q}) - P(\bar{q})] \delta^i$$
$$< [f(\bar{q}) - p_i] \delta^i;$$

hence, $\bar{q}$ should purchase the good in period i, which contradicts utility maximization. Similarly, if $p_i > P(\bar{q})$ and $q_{i+1} \geqslant \bar{q}$ then from the fact that $q_{i+1} \geqslant \bar{q} > q$ and from Lemma 2, we know that $q_{i+1} = 1$. Thus, p_{i+1} will be $f(1)$. As before,

$$[f(\bar{q}) - f(1)] \delta^{i+1} = [f(\bar{q}) - P(\bar{q})] \delta^i,$$

so

$$[f(\bar{q}) - p_i] \delta^i < [f(\bar{q}) - f(1)] \delta^{i+1}.$$

Since f is left-continuous, the above inequality also holds for some $q' < \bar{q}$, and so by utility maximization the consumer q' must not buy in period i. This contradicts the fact that $q_{i+1} \geqslant \bar{q}$. ∎

DEFINITION. Fix a reservation price strategy pair (r, P) and define

$$L(\bar{Q}, \{Q_j, \pi_j\}_{j=0}^{\infty}) \equiv \sum_{j=0}^{\infty} \pi_j [Q_{j+1} - Q_j] \delta^j,$$

and specify the constrained maximization problem:

$$Z(\bar{Q}) \equiv \max_{\mathscr{C}} L(\bar{Q}, \{Q_j, \pi_j\}_{j=0}^{\infty}), \tag{A}$$

where $\mathscr{C}$ is the set of sequences $\{Q_j, \pi_j\}_{j=0}^{\infty}$ satisfying the constraints

$$Q_0 = \bar{Q}, \quad r \leqslant Q_1, \quad Q_j \leqslant Q_{j+1} \leqslant 1, \quad \pi_j \leqslant P(Q_{j+1}). \tag{C}$$

Also, define

$$M(\bar{Q}) \equiv \{Q \mid P(Q)[Q - \bar{Q}] + \delta Z(Q) = Z(\bar{Q})\}.$$

LEMMA 4. *For any reservation price strategy pair (r, P) the constrained maximization problem $[(A)$ subject to $(C)]$ has a solution and any solution has the property that $(\forall j)\, \pi_j = P(Q_{j+1})$ and $Q_{j+1} > Q_j$ (or $Q_j = Q_{j+1} = 1$). Further, there exists $r' < r$ (or $r' = r = 0$) such that in any equilibrium and in any state $q_i \geqslant r'$ in any period i after any history,*

$$R^\sigma(q_i) = Z(q_i). \tag{i}$$

The set of solutions has the properties that

$$\inf M(\bar{Q}) \in M(\bar{Q}) \quad and \quad Q' > Q \in M(\bar{Q}) \Rightarrow P(Q') < P(Q). \tag{ii}$$

If $q_i = \bar{Q} \geqslant r'$ then the next state is $q_{i+1} \in M(\bar{Q})$. The function

$$\hat{P}(\bar{Q}) \equiv P(\inf M(\bar{Q}))$$

is non-increasing and left-continuous; in particular, if $Q > \bar{Q}$ then

$$p^1 \in P(M(\bar{Q})) \quad and \quad p^2 \in P(M(Q)) \Rightarrow p^1 \geqslant p^2. \tag{iii}$$

Proof. That (A) has a solution follows from the fact that P is left-continuous and non-increasing. That $\pi_j = P(Q_{j+1})$ and (if $Q_j < 1$) that $Q_{j+1} > Q_j$ are obvious.

We first establish (i). Let $\{Q_j, \pi_j\}_{j=0}^{\infty}$ be a solution to (A) for $\bar{Q} = q_i$. Suppose that $R^\sigma(q_i) = Z(q_i) - \varepsilon$ for some $\varepsilon > 0$, and set $p_{i+j} = \pi_j - \varepsilon/2$. If the monopolist follows the strategy $\{p_{i+j}\}_{j=0}^{\infty}$ after period i, then the present value of his profit is at least

$$\sum_{j=0}^{\infty} p_{i+j}[Q_{j+1} - Q_j]\,\delta^j = Z(q_i) - [1 - q_i]\varepsilon/2 > R^\sigma(q_i),$$

which contradicts the optimality of the monopolist's plan. Hence, $R^\sigma(q_i) \geqslant Z(q_i)$ for all $q_i \in [0, 1]$. On the other hand, if $q_i \geqslant r$ then the p's and q's specified by the equilibrium strategy σ are feasible for (A); hence, also $R^\sigma(q_i) \leqslant Z(q_i)$. We will now use the fact that if $q_i < r$ and $q_{i+1} < r$ then

$$R^\sigma(q_i) < [r - q_i]f(0) + \delta Z(r).$$

For q_i sufficiently close to r,

$$[r - q_i]\,f(0) + \delta Z(r) < Z(r),$$

so

$$R^\sigma(q_i) < Z(r) \leqslant Z(q_i),$$

which is a contradiction. Thus, if q_i is sufficiently close to r then $q_{i+1} \geqslant r$; and hence, once again the p's and q's specified by σ are feasible for (A), implying that $R^\sigma(q_i) \leqslant Z(q_i)$, which proves the desired result.

To show that $m \equiv \inf M(\bar{Q}) \in M(\bar{Q})$, we begin with the observation that $M(\bar{Q})$ is bounded and that $m \geqslant r$. Let $\{x_t\}_{t=0}^\infty \subset M(\bar{Q})$ be a decreasing sequence converging to m. Since P is left-continuous and non-increasing, $p^* \equiv \lim P(x_t) \leqslant P(m)$. From the definition of M,

$$Z(\bar{Q}) = P(x_t)[x_t - \bar{Q}] + \delta Z(x_t),$$

for all t. Since Z is continuous,

$$Z(\bar{Q}) = p^*[m - \bar{Q}] + \delta Z(m).$$

If $p^* < P(m)$ then

$$Z(\bar{Q}) < P(m)[m - \bar{Q}] + \delta Z(m),$$

which contradicts the definition of $Z(\bar{Q})$ and the principle of optimality of dynamic programming. Hence $P(m) = p^*$, implying that $m \in M(\bar{Q})$.

If $Q' > Q \in M(\bar{Q})$ then it is obvious that $P(Q) > P(Q')$. Furthermore, note that $\bar{Q} = q_i > r'$ implies that $q_{i+1} \in M(\bar{Q})$, using $R^\sigma(q_i) = Z(q_i)$ as established earlier and the principle of optimality.

Finally, we establish (iii). If $p^1 \in P(M(\bar{Q}))$, $p^2 \in P(M(Q))$, $Q > \bar{Q}$, and $p^1 < p^2$, then there exist $x_1 \in M(\bar{Q})$ and $x_2 \in M(Q)$ such that $P(x_1) < P(x_2)$. (Since P is non-increasing this implies that $x_1 > x_2$.) Therefore,

$$\begin{aligned}
Z(\bar{Q}) &\geqslant P(x_2)[x_2 - \bar{Q}] + \delta Z(x_2) \\
&= P(x_2)[Q - \bar{Q}] + P(x_2)[x_2 - Q] + \delta Z(x_2) \\
&= P(x_2)[Q - \bar{Q}] + \delta Z(Q),
\end{aligned}$$

Similarly,

$$Z(Q) \geqslant -P(x_1)[Q - \bar{Q}] + \delta Z(\bar{Q}),$$

so

$$0 \geqslant [P(x_2) - P(x_1)][Q - \bar{Q}],$$

hence

$$P(x_1) \geqslant P(x_2),$$

which is a contradiction. Thus we have established that $p^1 \in P(M(\bar{Q}))$, $p^2 \in P(M(Q))$, and $Q > \bar{Q}$ imply that $p^1 \geqslant p^2$. Since $\inf M(\bar{Q}) \in M(\bar{Q})$ and $\inf M(Q) \in M(Q)$ we have $\hat{P}(\bar{Q}) \in P(M(\bar{Q}))$ and $\hat{P}(Q) \in P(M(Q))$. Using the result stated in the previous sentence, $Q > \bar{Q}$ implies $\hat{P}(\bar{Q}) \geqslant \hat{P}(Q)$; that is, $\hat{P}$ is non-increasing.

Now let $\{x_t\}_{t=0}^{\infty}$ be an increasing sequence converging to $\bar{Q}$ and define

$$p^* \equiv \lim_{t \to \infty} \hat{P}(x_t).$$

The limit exists since $\hat{P}$ is non-increasing. Define $y_t \equiv \inf M(x_t)$ for all t. Then $\{y_t\}$ has a convergent subsequence and without loss of generality assume that $\{y_t\}$ converges to y. Since $\hat{P}$ is non-increasing we have $p^* \leqslant P(\bar{Q})$; also,

$$Z(x_t) = P(y_t)[y_t - \bar{Q}] + \delta Z(y_t),$$

for all t. Since Z is continuous,

$$Z(\bar{Q}) = p^*[y - \bar{Q}] + \delta Z(y).$$

Since P is non-increasing and left-continuous we have $p^* \leqslant P(y)$. If $p^* < P(y)$ then substituting $P(y)$ into the preceding equality contradicts the defining property of Z, so $p^* = P(y)$. Thus, $y \in M(\bar{Q})$ and therefore $\hat{P}(\bar{Q}) \leqslant P(y) = p^*$, proving that $p^* = \hat{P}(\bar{Q})$ and establishing the left-continuity of $\hat{P}$. ∎

Notation. In the following we let $\hat{P}(\cdot; (r, P))$ and $M(\cdot; (r, P))$ be the functions $\hat{P}$ and M as defined in Lemma 4 using (r, P) as the reservation price strategy pair.

LEMMA 5. *If (q, P) is a reservation price strategy pair satisfying the consumer-equilibrium property*[18]

$$(\forall \bar{q} \geqslant q) \qquad P(\bar{q}) = [1 - \delta] f(\bar{q}) + \delta \hat{P}(\bar{q}; (q, P)) \qquad \text{(CE)}$$

and $q > 0$, then there exists a reservation price strategy pair (q', P') with $q' < q$ that also satisfies (CF) for which $P'(\bar{q}) = P(\bar{q})$ for all $\bar{q} \geqslant q$.

Proof. For all $\bar{q} \in [0, 1]$ define

$$P'(\bar{q}) \equiv [1 - \delta] f(\bar{q}) + \delta \hat{P}(\bar{q}; (q, P)).$$

Note that P' is left-continuous and non-increasing. Furthermore, since (q, P) satisfies (CE) we know that $P'(\bar{q}) = P(\bar{q})$ whenever $\bar{q} \geqslant q$.

---

[18] See the definition that follows Lemma 2.

We now show that there exists $q' < q$ such that (q', P') satisfies (CE). Fact (ii) of Lemma 4 establishes the existence of $q' < q$ such that in any equilibrium σ and after any history, if the state $q_i \geqslant q'$ and $q_i = \bar{q}$ then $q_{i+1} \in M(\bar{q}; (q, P))$, where q_{i+1} is the state in period $i + 1$. Observe that the argument used in proving this result establishes that $M(\bar{q}; (q, P)) = M(\bar{q}; (q', P'))$ for all $\bar{q} \geqslant q'$, so also

$$\inf M(\bar{q}; (q, P)) = \inf M(\bar{q}; (q', P'))$$

for all $\bar{q} \geqslant q'$. By definition, $\inf M(\bar{q}; (q, P)) \geqslant q$; hence,

$$\hat{P}(\bar{q}; (q', P')) = P'(\inf M(\bar{q}; (q', P')))$$
$$= P(\inf M(\bar{q}; (q, P))) = \hat{P}(\bar{q}; (q, P)),$$

and so

$$P'(\bar{q}) = [1 - \delta] f(\bar{q}) + \delta \hat{P}(\bar{q}; (q', P'))$$

for all $\bar{q} \geqslant q'$. Therefore (q', P') satisfies (CE).

Next we prove that (q', P') satisfies (ii) of Lemma 3; that is, we show that $q_i < \bar{q}$, $\bar{q} \geqslant q'$, and $p_i < P'(\bar{q})$ imply that $q_{i+1} \geqslant \bar{q}$. If $\bar{q} \geqslant q$ then, since $P'(\bar{q}) = P(\bar{q})$, the fact that (q, P) satisfies (ii) implies that also (q', P') satisfies (ii). Now suppose that $\bar{q} < q$. By the definition of q', if $q_{i+1} \geqslant q'$ then $q_{i+2} \in M(q_{i-1}; (q, P))$ and hence $q_{i+2} \geqslant q > q$. If $\bar{q} > q_{i+1}$ then $q_{i+2} > \bar{q} > q_{i+1}$; that is, consumer $\bar{q}$ buys in period $i + 1$. But, if σ prescribes p_{i+1} then by Lemma 4,

$$p_{i+1} = P(q_{i+2}) \in P(M(q_{i+1}); (q, P)).$$

Recall that $\hat{P}(\bar{q}; (q, P)) \in P(M(\bar{q}); (q, P))$ and $\bar{q} > q_{i+1}$ so by (iii) of Lemma 4, $p_{i+1} \geqslant \hat{P}(\bar{q}; (q, P))$. However by the definition of P',

$$[f(\bar{q}) - P'(\bar{q})] \delta^i = [f(\bar{q}) - \hat{P}(\bar{q}; (q, P))] \delta^{i+1},$$

so

$$[f(\bar{q}) - p_i] \delta^i > [f(\bar{q}) - p_{i+1}] \delta^{i+1}.$$

Thus, consumer q prefers buying in period i to buying in period $i + 1$, contradicting utility maximization. (For the case that $\bar{q} < q$ and $q_{i+1} < q'$, (ii) is established by considering p_k, where $q_k < \bar{q}$ and $q_{k+1} \geqslant \bar{q}$.)

Finally, we show that (q', P') satisfies (iii) of Lemma 4. Assume that $q_i < \bar{q}$, $\bar{q} > q'$, $p_i > P(\bar{q})$, and $q_{i+1} \geqslant q'$. If $\bar{q} \geqslant q$ then, since $P'(\bar{q}) = P(\bar{q})$, the fact that (q, P) satisfies (iii) yields the result that (q', P') also satisfies (iii).

Suppose, therefore, that $\bar{q} < q$ and thus $q_{i+1} \geqslant \bar{q} > q_i$. Reasoning as above we obtain

$$[f(\bar{q}) - p_i] \delta^i < [f(\bar{q}) - p_{i+1}] \delta^{i+1}.$$

Since f is left-continuous we can find $q^* \in (q_i, \bar{q})$ for which the above inequality also holds: that is consumer q^* would rather buy in period $i+1$ than in period i. But $q_i < q^* < q_{i+1}$ means that q^* buys in period i, contradicting utility maximization. ∎

THEOREM 1. *If f satisfies* (B) *and* (L) *then there exist* $A \subset [0, 1]$, $t: [0, 1] \to [0, 1]$, *and* $P: [0, 1] \to \Re_{++}$ *such that* $\{q_i, p_i\}_{i=0}^{\infty}$ *is an equilibrium path if and only if* $q_0 = 0$, $q_1 \in A$, $(\forall i \geqslant 1)$ $q_{i+1} = t(q_i)$, *and* $(\forall i \geqslant 0)$ $p_i = P(q_{i+1})$.

Proof. First note that Lemma 3 assures the existence of a reservation price strategy pair (q, P). Lemma 5 establishes that any such pair can be extended to a larger interval domain (smaller q) and retain the same properties, including condition (CE); furthermore, it is clear that the lower limit of such domains is not bounded away from zero. Hence, one such pair has $q = 0$ and satisfies (CE). Any other reservation price strategy pair $(0, P')$ has $P'(\bar{q}) = P(\bar{q})$ for all $\bar{q} \in (0, 1)$. Set $A \equiv M(0)$ and $(\forall \bar{q} \in [0, 1])$ $t(\bar{q}) \equiv \inf M(\bar{q})$. We claim that (A, t, P) has the properties required by Theorem 1.

First we prove the "only if" part of the statement. Let σ be any equilibrium. By (i) in Lemma 4, $R^\sigma(0) = Z(0)$, and so $q_1 \in M(0) = A$. Also by Lemma 4, $p_0 = P(q_1)$. We next show that $p_{i+1} = P(t(q_{i+1}))$ for all $i \geqslant 0$. By Lemma 4 we have $R^\sigma(q_i) = Z(q_i)$, $q_{i+1} \in M(q_i)$, $p_i = P(q_{i+1})$, and $q_{i+1} > q_i$ (or $q_i = 1$) for all $i \geqslant 0$. Since $(0, P)$ satisfies (CE) we have

$$[f(q_{i+1}) - p_i] \delta^i = [f(q_{i+1}) - \hat{P}(q_{i+1})] \delta^{i+1},$$

and since an interval of consumers purchase in each period, the left continuity of f and utility maximization by the consumers imply that $p_{i+1} \geqslant \hat{P}(q_{i+1})$—otherwise some consumer $\bar{q}$ would not purchase in period i. But $\hat{P}(q_{i+1}) = P(\inf M(q_{i+1}))$ and P is non-increasing, so $\hat{P}(q_{i+1})$ is the largest optimal price in period $i+1$. Thus, $p_{i+1} \leqslant \hat{P}(q_{i+1})$,, which proves that $p_{i+1} = \hat{P}(q_{i+1}) = P(t(q_{i+1}))$.

Finally, observe that if $x = \inf M(q_{i+1}) \in M(q_{i+1})$ then $q_{i+2} \geqslant x$, since $q_{i+2} \in M(q_{i+1})$. But

$$P(x) = P(t(q_{i+1})) = p_{i+1} = P(q_{i+2}).$$

Hence, if $q_{i+2} > x$ then

$$x \in M(q_{i+1}), \qquad q_{i+2} > x, \qquad \text{and} \qquad P(q_{i+2}) = P(x),$$

which contradicts (ii) of Lemma 4. Therefore

$$q_{i+2} = x = \inf M(q_{i+1}) = t(q_{i+1}),$$

which completes the proof of the "only if" part of the statement.

To prove the "if" part of the statement, choose $q_1 \in M(0)$ and $p_0 = P(q_1)$, and define strategies σ as follows:

The consumers. After any history, if the state is q_i then consumer $\bar{q} \in (q_i, 1]$ buys if and only if $p_i \leq P(\bar{q})$.

The monopolist. After any history, if the state is q_i then $p_i = P(t(q_i))$ if $p_{i-1} \geq P(q_i)$, and otherwise p_i is chosen randomly to be either $\hat{P}(q_i)$ with probability β or p_l with probability $1 - \beta$ where

$$p_l = \lim_{q \downarrow q_i} \hat{P}(q),$$

$$x = \lim_{q \downarrow q_i} f(q),$$

$$\beta = \begin{cases} 1 & \text{if } x - p_{i-1} \leq [x - \hat{P}(q_i)]\delta \\ \beta(p_{i-1}) & \text{otherwise,} \end{cases}$$

and $\beta(p)$ is the solution to

$$x - p = \beta[x - \hat{P}(q_i)]\delta + (1 - \beta)[x - p_l]\delta.$$

First we note that $\beta \in [0, 1]$. If $\beta \neq 1$ then

$$x - p_{i-1} \geq [x - \hat{P}(q_i)]\delta;$$

hence it suffices to show that

$$x - p_{i-1} \leq [x - p_l]\delta.$$

Recall that, for all q,

$$f(q) - P(q) = [f(q) - \hat{P}(q)]\delta,$$

and therefore,

$$\lim_{q \downarrow q_i} [f(q) - P(q)] = \lim_{q \downarrow q_i} [f(q) - \hat{P}(q)]\delta$$

and

$$x - \lim_{q \downarrow q_i} P(q) = [x - p_l]\delta.$$

But $p_{i-1} \geq \lim_{q \downarrow q_i} P(q)$, so we have established the desired result.

Next we observe that after any history resulting in a state q_i in period i, the monopolist charges either $\hat{P}(q_i)$, p_l, or a mixture of the two. The optimality of $\hat{P}(q_i)$ follows from its definition and Lemma 4. To prove the optimality of p_l we first note that $\inf M(q)$ is a non-decreasing function—using the argument made in proving that $\hat{P}$ is non-increasing. Let $\{x_t\}$ be a decreasing sequence converging q_i and define $y_t \equiv \inf M(x_t)$ and $y = \lim y_t$. Then

$$p_l = \lim P(y_t) \leqslant P(y),$$

and

$$Z(x_t) = P(y_t)[y_t - x_t] + \delta Z(y_t),$$

which, since Z is continuous, implies that

$$Z(q_i) = p_l[y - q_i] + \delta Z(y).$$

Thus $P(y) \leqslant p_l$, proving that $P(y) = p_l$. This shows that p_l is an optimal price in state q_i. Since $\hat{P}(q_i)$ and p_l are optimal, every randomization between them is also optimal. This establishes that the specified strategy for the monopolist is optimal.

To prove optimality of the consumers' strategy we first show that the consumers never regret not purchasing when their strategy prescribes not to purchase. Consider any history resulting in a state q_i in period i, and a price p_i offered by the monopolist. If $p_i > P(\bar{q})$ for some $\bar{q} \in (q_i, 1]$ then $q_{i+1} < \bar{q}$ and the (possibly random) price $\tilde{p}_{i+1}$ that will follow is such that it makes consumer q_{i+1} indifferent between buying in period i or period $i+1$. Hence,

$$[f(q_{i+1}) - p_i]\delta^i = \mathbf{E}\{f(q_{i+1}) - \tilde{p}_{i+1}\}\delta^{i+1};$$

so

$$[f(q_{i+1}) - p_i]\delta^i = [f(q_{i+1}) - \mathbf{E}\{\tilde{p}_{i+1}\}]\delta^{i+1};$$

implying

$$[f(\bar{q}) - p_i]\delta^i = [f(\bar{q}) - \mathbf{E}\{\tilde{p}_{i+1}\}]\delta^{i+1}.$$

Thus consumer $\bar{q}$ does not regret not buying in period i, since he can do at least as well by waiting an additional period.

Finally we prove that consumers do not regret purchasing whenever the strategy σ prescribes that they purchase. After any history resulting in state q_i in period i the strategy σ prescribes that consumer $\bar{q} \in (q_i, 1]$ buys if and only if the offered price p_i satisfies $p_i \leqslant P(\bar{q})$. Assume for the moment that, according to σ, p_i is followed by a sequence of non-random prices p_j and states q_j, $j > i$. In this case,

$$[f(q_{j+1}) - p_j]\, \delta^j = [f(q_{j+1}) - p_{j+1}]\, \delta^{j+1},$$

for all $j \geq i$. Since $q_{j+1} \geq \bar{q}$ for all $j \geq i$,

$$f(\bar{q}) - p_i \geq [f(\bar{q}) - p_{j+1}]\, \delta \qquad (\forall j \geq i).$$

It follows that

$$[f(\bar{q}) - p_i]\, \delta^i \geq [f(\bar{q}) - p_{j+1}]\, \delta^{j+1} \qquad (\forall j \geq i),$$

which establishes the required result. On the other hand, if p_i is followed by a nondegenerate random variable $\tilde{p}_{i+1}$, then

$$[f(q_{i+1}) - p_i]\, \delta^i = [f(q_{i+1}) - \mathbf{E}\{\tilde{p}_{i+1}\}]\, \delta^{i+1},$$

and $q_{i+1} \geq \bar{q}$. Hence, consumer $\bar{q}$ likes buying in period i at least as much as waiting for the next period; and repeating the reasoning above he weakly prefers any outcome of the randomization to any price that follows. This establishes the optimality of buying in period i for consumer $\bar{q}$ and completes the proof. ∎

THEOREM 2. *Assume that $f(1) = 0$, $n \geq 1$, $f \in C^n(1)$, and $f'(1) \neq 0$. Consider two equilibria σ_P, $\sigma_Q \in \Sigma^s(f, \delta)$ for which P, $Q: [0, 1] \to \mathfrak{R}_+$ specify the stationary strategies of the consumers, and for $k \leq n$ let P^k and Q^k denote their kth order derivatives. Then, if $P^k(1)$ and $Q^k(1)$ exist they are equal. Moreover, if $(\forall n)\, f \in C^n(1)$, and P and Q are analytic in a neighborhood of 1, then $(\forall q \in (0, 1])\, P(q) = Q(q)$.*

Proof. Recall that $f(q) \geq P(q) \geq [1 - \delta]\, f(q)$ and $f(1) = 0$; consequently $P(1) = 0$, and since $f'(1) \neq 0$, $P'(1) \neq 0$. Choose $\varepsilon > 0$ such that $P \in C^n([1 - \varepsilon, 1])$. Define $Z(q)$ for $q \in [1 - \varepsilon, 1]$ as in Lemma 4 of Theorem 1, and define

$$\bar{Z}(t_0, q) = P(t_0)[t_0 - q] + \delta Z(t_0)$$

for all $q \in [1 - \varepsilon, 1]$ and $t_0 \in [q, 1]$. Since P is continuously differentiable and $P'(1) \neq 0$, for q sufficiently close to 1, $\bar{Z}$ is strictly concave in t_0. Hence the function

$$t(q) = \arg \max_{t_0 \in [q,1]} \bar{Z}(t_0, q)$$

is well defined and $Z'(q) = -P(t(q))$ by a standard result in dynamic programming. The argument used in proving Lemma 4 of Theorem 1 establishes that after any i-period history resulting in state q_i, if q_i is sufficiently close to 1 then the price in period i will be $P(t(q_i))$. Hence, t defines the strategy of the monopolist for states sufficiently close to 1. Therefore, for such q we have by consumer optimality

$$P(q) = [1 - \delta] f(q) + \delta P(t(q)). \tag{1}$$

Since $P \in C^1(1)$, profit maximization implies that

$$d\bar{Z}/dt_0 \equiv P'(t(q))[t(q) - q] + P(t(q)) + \delta Z'(t(q)) = 0$$

for q close to 1. Substituting expressions from above yields

$$P'(t(q))[t(q) - q] + [1 - \delta] f(t(q)) = 0. \tag{2}$$

Since $P'(1) \neq 0$, applying the implicit function theorem to Eq. (1) yields that t has the same order of differentiability as P; that is, $t \in C^n(1)$. Hence Eq. (2) implies, using l'Hôpital's rule, that

$$P'(1) = -\frac{[1 - \delta] f'(1) t'(1)}{t'(1) - 1}. \tag{3}$$

Differentiating Eq. (1) implicitly, evaluating it at $q = 1$, and using Eq. (3) yields

$$t'(1) = (1 - \sqrt{1 - \delta})/\delta \qquad \text{and} \qquad P'(1) = f'(1) \sqrt{1 - \delta}.$$

Repeating the argument for Q and the corresponding s associated with Q yields the same conclusion; therefore $P'(1) = Q'(1)$ and $t'(1) = s'(1)$. To complete the proof of the first part of the theorem it suffices to show that $P^k(1) = Q^k(1)$ and $t^k(1) = s^k(1)$ for all $k \leqslant n - 1$ implies that $P^n(1) = Q^n(1)$ and $t^n(1) = s^n(1)$. Observe that Eq. (2) implies, for q close to 1, that

$$P'(t(q))[t(q) - q] + [1 - \delta] f(t(q)) - Q'(s(q))[s(q) - q]$$
$$- [1 - \delta] f(s(q)) = 0. \tag{4}$$

Differentiating Eq. (4) $n - 1$ times, dividing the result by $t(q) - q$, and taking the limit as $q \to 1$, one obtains a linear equation in the variables $[Q^n(1) - P^n(1)]$ and $[s^n(1) - t^n(1)]$. Also, from Eq. (1) we have

$$P(q) - \delta P(t(q)) - Q(q) + \delta Q(s(q)) = 0. \tag{5}$$

Differentiating Eq. (5) n times and evaluating the result at 1 we obtain a second linear equation. This pair of equations forms a homogeneous linear system, and the determinant of the matrix of coefficients depends only on the first derivatives of f, P, at 1, and is nonzero for all n. This implies that $P''(1) = Q''(1)$ and $t''(1) = s''(1)$, as desired to complete the induction.

To prove the second part of the theorem, observe that if $f'(1) \neq 0$ and $f \in C^n(1)$ for all n then by the previous argument all derivatives of P and Q at 1 are equal. If P and Q are analytic in some neighborhood of 1 then, for some $\varepsilon > 0$, $P(q) = Q(q)$ for all $q \in [1 - \varepsilon, 1]$. Following the result from Theorem 1 that P can be extended uniquely from such an interval to the interval $(0, 1]$ yields that $P(q) = Q(q)$ for all $q \in (0, 1]$, as required. $\blacksquare$

THEOREM 3 (Coase conjecture). *For each $\varepsilon > 0$ there exists $\bar{\delta} < 1$ such that for all $\delta > \bar{\delta}$ and for all equilibria $\sigma \in \Sigma^s(f, \delta)$, the first price prescribed by σ is less than ε.*

Proof. Let $0, r_1, r_2, \ldots$ be an ordering of the rational $\mathcal{Q}$ in the interval $[0, 1]$. If the theorem is false then there exists $\varepsilon > 0$ such that for all $\bar{\Delta} > 0$ there exists $\Delta < \bar{\Delta}$ and P_Δ such that $P_\Delta(0) > \varepsilon$. Here, P_Δ is the P-function associated with an equilibrium in $\Sigma^s(f, \delta)$. Consider any sequence $\Delta_n \to 0$ such that $P_{\Delta_n}(0) > \varepsilon$ for all $n = 1, 2, \ldots$. Select a convergent subsequence $\{P_{\Delta_j}(0)\}$ and define $P(0) \equiv \lim_{j \to \infty} P_{\Delta_j}(0)$. Now from the sequence $\{P_{\Delta_j}(r_1)\}$ select a convergent subsequence with a limit defined to be $\bar{P}(r_1)$. Continue in this fashion to define $\bar{P}$ on all the rationals $\mathcal{Q}$ in $[0, 1]$. Extend $\bar{P}$ to the entire interval by imposing left-continuity. Note that from the procedure used to construct $\bar{P}$ and the fact that P_{Δ_n} is non-increasing for each n, it follows that also $\bar{P}$ is non-increasing. In the following, let $\delta = e^{-r\Delta}$.

We first show that assuming the function $\bar{P}$ so constructed is continuous yields a contradiction. Thus, suppose that $\bar{P}$ is continuous. Then there exist x_1 and $x_2 > x_1$ such that

$$\bar{P}(0) > \bar{P}(x_1) \geqslant \bar{P}(x_2) > 0,$$

and consequently there exist $0 < a < b < c$ such that

$$\bar{P}(0) > c > b > \bar{P}(x_1) \geqslant \bar{P}(x_2) > a > 0.$$

By the nature of the construction of $\bar{P}$, there exists a subsequence $\{\Delta_i\}$ and an integer N such that, for all $i > N$,

$$P_{\Delta_i}(0) > c \quad \text{and} \quad P_{\Delta_i}(x_1), P_{\Delta_i}(x_2) \in (a, b).$$

If the monopolist initially charges the price c then, for $i > N$ consumer 0 accepts in the equilibrium associated with Δ_i. From the utility maximization of consumer 0, at least t units of time must pass before the price falls to b, where t is defined by

$$c = [1 - e^{-rt}] f(0) + e^{-rt} b.$$

Since at least t units of time must pass between prices c and b after c is charged, the profit left in the market for the monopolist facing P_{A_i}, $i > N$, when he follows the equilibrium strategy, is at most

$$\int_{q^i(c)}^{x_1} P_{A_i} + e^{-rt} R^i(x_1), \qquad (\mathrm{I})$$

where $q^i(c)$ is the state of the market after c is charged, and $R^i(x_1)$ is the present value of the monopolist's profits beginning from state x_1—both according to the equilibrium associated with A_i.

We next observe that there exist $\hat{t} < t/2$ and an integer $I > N$ such that

$$\left| e^{-r\hat{t}} \sum_{j=1}^{K} P_{A_I}(h_j)\mu - \int_{q^i(c)}^{x_1} P_{A_I} \right| < a[x_2 - x_1][e^{-rt/2} - e^{-rt}], \qquad (\mathrm{II})$$

where K is the largest integer that does not exceed $\hat{t}/A_i$, $h_0 = q^i(c)$, $h_K = x_1$, the h_j's are equally spaced, and $\mu = [x_1 - q^i(c)]/K$. (This is little more than the statement that the integral of the uniformly bounded, left-continuous function P_{A_I} can be approximated uniformly by Riemann sums; for, the right side of (II) is independent of $\hat{t}$ and i, $e^{-r\hat{t}}$ is close to 1 for $\hat{t}$ small, and K is large for $\hat{t}$ fixed and i large.)

We are now able to construct a plan that yields the monopolist more profit than he obtains from the prescribed bahavior in the equilibrium associated with A_I after c is charged, and thereby obtain a contradiction. This is achieved by having the monopolist spend $\hat{t}$ units of time getting from $q^I(c)$ to x_1 and then following the strategy prescribed in the equilibrium associated with A_I. According to (II), his profit will then be at least

$$\int_{q^I(c)}^{x_1} P_{A_I} - a[x_2 - x_1][e^{-rt/2} - e^{-rt}] + e^{-r\hat{t}} R^I(x_1).$$

But since $\hat{t} < t/2$ and $R^I(x_1) \geq a[x_2 - x_1]$, the profit from this plan will exceed the bound on the profit given in (I) for the hypothesized equilibrium strategy.

To get a contradiction for the case that $\bar{P}$ is discontinuous, observe first that $\bar{P}$ is continuous at 1, so if x is a point of discontinuity then $x < 1$.[19] Now choose α so that $p_h > p_l$, where

$$p_h = \lim_{q \uparrow x} \bar{P}(q) - \alpha \qquad \text{and} \qquad p_l = \lim_{q \downarrow x} \bar{P}(q) + \alpha.$$

---

[19] The continuity of $\bar{P}$ at 1 follows from the fact that f is left-continuous, $\bar{P}(1) = f(1)$ and $\bar{P}(q) \leq f(q)$ for all $q \in \mathcal{Q} \subset [0, 1]$.

The existence of such an α is guaranteed by the fact that $\bar{P}$ is non-increasing and x is a point of discontinuity. Observe that since $\bar{P}(q) \leqslant f(q)$ for all $q \in \mathcal{Q}$ and f is left-continuous, there exists $\eta > 0$ such that $x + \eta/2 < 1$ and $p_h < f(x - \eta)$. Hence, there exists $t > 0$ that solves

$$f(x - \eta) - p_h = [f(x - \eta) - p_l] e^{-rt}.$$

By utility maximization of consumers, in any equilibrium if a consumer with a valuation no greater than $f(x - \eta)$ purchases at price p_h, then at least a duration t must pass before the price falls to p_l.

For all $\varepsilon \in (0, \eta)$ choose $q_\varepsilon^h \in (x - \varepsilon/2, x) \cap \mathcal{Q}$ and $q_\varepsilon^l \in (x, x + \varepsilon/2) \cap \mathcal{Q}$. Let $\{\Delta_{\varepsilon j}\}_{j=0}^\infty$ be a subsequence of $\{\Delta_i\}_{i=0}^\infty$ such that

$$\lim_{j \to \infty} P_{\Delta_{\varepsilon j}}(q_\varepsilon^h) = \bar{P}(q_\varepsilon^h),$$

$$\lim_{j \to \infty} P_{\Delta_{\varepsilon j}}(q_\varepsilon^l) = \bar{P}(q_\varepsilon^l).$$

The existence of such a sequence is guaranteed by the construction of $\bar{P}$. Pick n such that

$$P_{\Delta_{\varepsilon n}}(q_\varepsilon^h) > p_h \qquad \text{and} \qquad P_{\Delta_{\varepsilon n}}(q_\varepsilon^l) > p_l.$$

Suppose that p_h is charged in the initial period. Since $P_{\Delta_{\varepsilon n}}(q_\varepsilon^h) > p_h$, by the fashion in which $P_{\Delta_{\varepsilon n}}$ defines the strategies of consumers, all consumers $q \leqslant q_\varepsilon^h$ buy at this price. Observe that $q_\varepsilon^h > x - \eta$ when $\varepsilon > \eta$; hence, if price p_h is charged in the initial period then there will be consumers with valuations no greater than $f(x - \eta)$ that buy, and therefore at least a duration t must elapse before the price falls below p_l. In other words, there will be at least $t/\Delta_{\varepsilon n}$ price offers before a price below p_l can be charged. Let $p_1, p_2, ..., p_m$ be the prices above p_l that follow p_h according to the equilibrium. Define

$$a_0 = p_h$$

$$a_i = p_h - i \frac{2\Delta_{\varepsilon n}}{t} [p_h - p_l], \qquad i = 1, ..., \frac{t}{2\Delta_{\varepsilon n}}.$$

Define the sequence $p_1', ..., p_m'$ by $p_1' = a_{k_1}$, where

$$k_1 = \inf\{r \geqslant 1 \mid \exists p_j \in [a_r, a_{r-1}]\},$$

and $p_i' = a_{k_i}$, where

$$k_i = \inf\{r \geqslant k_{i-1} + 1 \mid \exists p_j \in [a_r, a_{r-1}]\}$$

if the inf is over a nonempty set and $k_i = t/2\Delta_{\varepsilon n}$ otherwise.[20] We observe the following points:

First, $m \leqslant t/2\Delta_{\varepsilon n}$. Hence if the time interval between offers is $\Delta_{\varepsilon n}$ then the m offers $p'_1,..., p'_m$ can be made in $t/2$ amount of time.

Second, after an initial period in which the price p_n is charged, if the monopolist charges the sequence of prices $p'_1,..., p'_m$ rather than the sequence $p_1,..., p_{\bar{m}}$ then any consumer $q \in [x - \varepsilon/2, x + \varepsilon/2]$ that is willing to buy at some price p_i is also willing to buy at some price p'_j, where $j \leqslant i$ and $p'_j \geqslant p_i - 2\Delta_{\varepsilon n}/t$. Hence the monopolist charging the sequence of prices $p'_1,..., p'_m$ rather than $p_1,..., p_{\bar{m}}$ does not lose time and loses at most $[p_h - p_l]2\Delta_{\varepsilon n}/t$ on each sale.

Third, if R^ε_1 is the return to the monopolist from the strategy that has him charging $p_h, p_1,..., p_{\bar{m}}$ in the first $\bar{m}$ periods and playing optimally thereafter, and if R^ε_2 is the return to the monopolist charging $p_h, p'_1,..., p'_m$ in the first m periods and then continuing optimally, then since $\bar{m}\Delta_{\varepsilon n} \geqslant t$ and $m\Delta_{\varepsilon n} \leqslant t/2$ we have

$$R^\varepsilon_2 - R^\varepsilon_1 \geqslant [e^{-rt/2} - e^{-rt}]\, R^\varepsilon(x + \varepsilon/2) - \frac{2\Delta_{\varepsilon n}}{t}\, \varepsilon(p_h - p_l),$$

where $R^\varepsilon(x + \varepsilon/2)$ is the monopolist's maximal return after state $x + \varepsilon/2$ in the equilibrium associated with $P_{\Delta_{\varepsilon n}}$. Hence,

$$R^\varepsilon_2 - R^\varepsilon_1 \geqslant [e^{-rt/2} - e^{-rt}][1 - e^{-r\Delta_{\varepsilon n}}]\, M - (2\Delta_{\varepsilon n}/t)\, \varepsilon[p_h - p_l],$$

where

$$M = \max_y f(y)[y - x - \eta/2],$$

using the fact that

$$P_{\Delta_{\varepsilon n}} \geqslant [1 - e^{-r\Delta_{\varepsilon n}}]f \qquad \text{and} \qquad \varepsilon < \eta.$$

Let

$$A = [e^{-rt/2} - e^{-rt}]\, M,$$

$$B = 2[p_h - p_l]/t.$$

Then $A, B > 0$ and A and B are independent of ε and $\Delta_{\varepsilon n}$; furthermore,

$$R^\varepsilon_2 - R^\varepsilon_1 \geqslant [1 - e^{-r\Delta_{\varepsilon n}}]\left[A - B\varepsilon\, \frac{\Delta_{\varepsilon n}}{1 - e^{-r\Delta_{\varepsilon n}}} \right].$$

[20] An obvious adjustment is required if $t/2\Delta_{\varepsilon n}$ is not an integer.

Since $1 - e^{-r\Delta_{en}} > 0$ and the function $g(\Delta) \equiv \Delta/[1 - e^{-r\Delta}]$ is bounded on the interval $(0, \Delta_1]$ for sufficiently small $\varepsilon > 0$, we have $R_2^\varepsilon - R_1^\varepsilon > 0$. But this contradicts the fact that the sequence of prices $p_1, ..., p_{\bar{m}}$ were optimal for the monopolist after charging the price p_h in the initial period. ∎

REFERENCES

1. J. I. BULOW, Durable-goods monopolists, *J. Polit. Econ.* **90** (1982), 314–332.
2. R. H. COASE, Durability and monopoly, *J. Law Econ.* **15** (1972), 143–149.
3. P. C. CRAMTON, "The Role of Time and Information in Bargaining," Ph.D. dissertation, Stanford University, 1984.
4. D. FUDENBERG, D. LEVINE, AND J. TIROLE, Infinite horizon models of bargaining with one-sided incomplete information, *in* "Bargaining with Incomplete Information" (Alvin Roth, Ed.), London/New York, Cambridge Univ. Press, pp.73–98, 1985.
5. S. J. GROSSMAN AND M. PERRY, Sequential bargaining under asymmetric information, working paper, University of Chicago, December 1984.
6. F. GUL, "Two Essays on the Bargaining Foundations of Value Theory," Ph.D. dissertation, Princeton University, 1986.
7. CHARLES KAHN, The durable goods monopolist and consistency with increasing costs. *Econometrica* **54** (1986), 275–294.
8. A. RUBINSTEIN, Perfect equilibrium in a bargaining model, *Econometrica* **50** (1982), 97–110.
9. A. RUBINSTEIN, A bargaining model with incomplete information about preferences, *Econometrica* **53** (1985), 1151–1172.
10. J. SOBEL AND I. TAKAHASHI, A multi-stage model of bargaining, *Rev. Econ. Stud.* **50** (1983), 411–426.
11. N. L. STOKEY, Rational expectations and durable goods pricing, *Bell J. Econ.* **12** (1982), 112–128.

Econometrica, Vol. 57, No. 3 (May, 1989), 511–531

REPUTATION IN BARGAINING AND DURABLE GOODS MONOPOLY

By Lawrence M. Ausubel and Raymond J. Deneckere[1]

This paper analyzes durable goods monopoly in an infinite-horizon, discrete-time game. We prove that, as the time interval between successive offers approaches zero, all seller payoffs between zero and static monopoly profits are supported by subgame perfect equilibria. This reverses a well-known conjecture of Coase. Alternatively, one can interpret the model as a sequential bargaining game with one-sided incomplete information in which an uninformed seller makes all the offers. Our folk theorem for seller payoffs equally applies to the set of sequential equilibria of this bargaining game.

Keywords: Durable goods monopoly, bargaining, Coase conjecture, reputation, folk theorem.

1. INTRODUCTION

Assume that a single firm controls the supply of an infinitely durable good. In a classic paper, Ronald Coase (1972) asked what sales plan this monopolist would adopt to maximize her profits. Coase provided a partial answer by observing that the naive policy of forever offering the good at a static monopoly price is not credible. To paraphrase Martin Hellwig (1975), the monopolist who announces such a policy cannot "keep a straight face"—she has an irresistable temptation to cut the price at future dates, to generate additional sales and profits. Coase supplemented his answer by conjecturing that, with rational consumer expectations, "the competitive outcome may be achieved even if there is but a single supplier." Several subsequent authors have produced models possessing subgame perfect equilibria which support Coase's conjecture.

Nevertheless, Coase's original puzzle concerning the optimal monopoly pricing rule remains essentially unsolved. In this paper, we propose an answer: the firm introduces the durable good at approximately the static monopoly price. She then follows the slowest rate of price descent that enables her to maintain her credibility. As the time interval between successive periods of the game approaches zero, the rate of descent can be made arbitrarily slow while preserving subgame perfection. This enables the supplier to earn nearly static monopoly

[1] The authors' work was supported in part by National Science Foundation Grants SES-85-69701 and IST-86-09129, by the Kellogg School's Paget Research Fund and Esmark Research Chair, and by National Science Foundation Grant SES-83-20464 at the Institute for Mathematical Studies in the Social Sciences, Stanford University, Stanford, California. The appendices make substantial use of ideas and analysis contained in the papers of Fudenberg, Levine, and Tirole (1985) and Gul, Sonnenschein, and Wilson (1986). We learned a great deal from these authors, and we are glad to be able to acknowledge our intellectual debt here. We would also like to thank Varadarajan Chari, Kenneth Judd, David Kreps, and Roger Myerson for helpful suggestions and stimulating discussions, and two anonymous referees for comments which greatly improved the exposition of this paper. The usual disclaimer applies.

profits. Thus it is possible, even in a durable goods market, that a monopoly *is* a monopoly.[2]

The identical reasoning carries over to bargaining games with incomplete information, since essentially the same mathematical model may depict either a continuum of actual consumers with different valuations or a single buyer with a continuum of possible valuations. Thus, in an infinite-horizon bargaining game where the seller makes repeated offers to a buyer whose valuation she does not know, we prove that there exist sequential equilibria where the seller extracts essentially monopoly surplus.

In contrast, the Coase conjecture predicts that the monopolist's initial offer inexorably descends toward marginal cost (and her profits approach zero) as the time interval between periods shrinks to zero. The intuition behind the conjecture is that, once any initial quantity of the good has been sold, the monopolist is always tempted to sell additional output, until the competitive level is reached. But if consumers expect the monopolist to flood the market "in the twinkling of an eye" (Coase (1972)), they will decline to purchase at prices much above marginal cost.

Bulow (1982) analyzed Coase's reasoning in a finite-horizon model. By backward induction, Bulow calculated the monopolist's best action in each period before the last and showed that it is always to charge unambiguously less than the static monopoly price. Stokey (1981) studied the monopolist who lacks commitment powers in an infinite-horizon model. She constructed an equilibrium which is the limit of the unique equilibria of finite-horizon versions of the same model, and demonstrated that it satisfies the Coase conjecture. Gul, Sonnenschein, and Wilson (1986) discovered a continuum of additional subgame perfect equilibria in the infinite-horizon game. However, they proved that these weak-Markov equilibria (subgame perfect equilibria in which buyers use "stationary" strategies) behave qualitatively like the backward induction equilibrium —the initial price converges to marginal cost.[3]

The noncooperative bargaining literature developed in parallel to the study of durable goods monopoly.[4] To escape from Rubinstein's (1982) complete information result that all bargaining is concluded in the first round, this literature introduced incomplete information into the bargaining process. Incomplete information often added a continuum of sequential equilibria (e.g., Fudenberg and Tirole (1983)). One modeling technique, however, offered apparent promise for

---

[2] This provides an answer to Coase's puzzle by identifying the equilibrium which (subject to credibility) is most favorable to the firm. Given that the firm is a monopolist and has the sole ability to make offers, this equilibrium certainly seems quite sensible. However, we show in Theorem 6.4 that there exists a continuum of other equilibria, in which the monopolist may earn substantially lower profits.

[3] Bond and Samuelson (1984) examined a durable good subject to depreciation. The prospect of replacement sales reduces the monopolist's tendency to cut prices, when the time interval between periods is positive; however, Coase's limiting result continues to hold. Kahn (1986) considered the case of increasing marginal cost and showed that this provides the durable goods monopolist with some incentive not to flood the market instantaneously. Consequently, initial price does not converge to marginal cost.

[4] For a thorough review of this literature, see Rubinstein (1987).

yielding results with greater predictive value: restricting the game to one-sided offers with one-sided uncertainty. When the uninformed party makes all the offers (the informed party only responding with "yes" or "no"), the complications of strategic communication largely disappear. One may have (unjustifiably and, we will show, incorrectly) conjectured from this literature that the multiplicity of equilibrium outcomes vanished as well.

Sobel and Takahashi (1983) wrote the first paper to explore this approach. Their results mirror those obtained by Bulow (1982) and Stokey (1981) in the durable goods monopoly context. Fudenberg, Levine, and Tirole (1985) analyzed two distinct cases in the infinite-horizon game. In the case where the buyer's valuation is known discretely to exceed the seller's, they proved that the model generically has a unique sequential equilibrium and that there is a finite time by which all negotiations conclude. In the second (and, we think, more reasonable) case where there is no gap between the lowest buyer valuation and the seller's valuation, they demonstrated the existence of a backward induction equilibrium. All of the equilibria they constructed are weak-Markov and can be shown to satisfy the Coase conjecture.

The main result of our paper is a folk theorem for seller payoffs, for the "no gap" case. As the time interval between successive periods approaches zero in durable goods monopoly (bargaining), the set of monopolist (seller) payoffs associated with subgame perfect (sequential) equilibria expands to the entire interval from zero to static monopoly profits.

We prove our Folk Theorem by constructing "reputational equilibria" consisting of a main price path and a punishment path. The main path starts with an arbitrary initial price and follows with an arbitrarily-slow (but positive) real-time rate of sales. The punishment path is taken from a weak-Markov equilibrium. As the time interval between periods approaches zero, adherence to the main path becomes subgame perfect, because (by the Coase conjecture) the punishment becomes increasingly severe. Continuously varying the initial price and the subsequent rate of sales yields all levels of profit.

Let us provide an interpretation of these equilibria. Initially, consumers believe they are facing a strong monopolist who will continue to adhere to the main price path specified in the equilibrium. However, the moment a deviation from the main price path occurs, consumers decide they are dealing with a weak monopolist who has read the Coase (1972) paper (and believes its message). The prospect of ruining her reputation thus deters the monopolist from ever deviating.

Observe that the vast multiplicity of equilibria in the current game is not due to the presence of incomplete information. "Reputation," in our equilibria, does not involve the seller's type[5]—buyers have no beliefs to be updated when off-equilibrium behavior is observed. Indeed, the durable goods monopoly model is a game of complete information. In the bargaining interpretation of the model, the only (observable) off-equilibrium buyer behavior which continues the game is

---

[5] One can also introduce reputation effects by adding buyer uncertainty about the monopolist's marginal cost.

rejection of a nonpositive offer, and so there is little or no scope for the seller to make alternative inferences about the buyer's type. Hence, an equilibrium refinement which acts only to constrain off-equilibrium beliefs about type would have no effect on the set of equilibrium payoffs. Alternatively, one can limit the set of outcomes by restricting attention to weak-Markov equilibria. We do not find this restriction completely natural and, in any case, it is interesting to see what equilibria arise when the Markovian assumption is relaxed.

We extend and use two types of results (which seemingly endorse the Coase conjecture) to prove our folk theorem (which reverses the Coase conjecture). After describing the model (Section 2) and presenting a linear example (Section 3), we first demonstrate a general existence result on weak-Markov equilibria (Section 4). We then show that price paths associated with weak-Markov equilibria are uniformly low compared to the demand curve (Section 5). In Section 6, we proceed to establish the folk theorem for seller payoffs, under very general conditions. We conclude with Section 7.

2. THE MODEL

We consider a market for a good which is infinitely durable, and which is demanded only in quantity zero or one. There is a continuum of infinitely-lived consumers, indexed by $q \in I = [0,1]$. The preferences of these consumers are completely specified by a monotone nonincreasing function $f: [0,1] \rightarrow \mathbb{R}_+$ satisfying $f(q) > 0$ for $q \in [0,1)$, where $f(q)$ denotes the reservation value of customer q, and by a common discount rate r. More precisely, if individual q purchases the good at time t for the price p_t, he derives a net surplus of $e^{-rt}[f(q) - p_t]$. Consumers seek to maximize their net surplus. The monopolist, meanwhile, faces a constant marginal cost of production, which we assume (without loss of generality) to equal zero. Her objective is to maximize the net present value of profits, using the same discount rate as consumers.

The monopolist offers the durable good for sale at discrete moments in time, spaced equally apart. The symbol z will denote the time interval between successive offers, and so sales occur at times $t = 0, z, 2z, \ldots, nz, \ldots$. We will sometimes refer to the "period" n rather than to the "time" t $(= nz)$. Within each period, the timing of moves is as follows: first, the monopolist names a price; then, consumers who have not previously purchased decide whether or not to buy. After a time interval z elapses, play repeats.

A strategy for the monopolist specifies the price she will charge in each period, as a function of the history of prices charged in previous periods and the history of purchases by consumers. A strategy for a consumer specifies, in each period, whether or not to buy in that period, given the current price charged and the history of past prices and purchases. Formally, let $G(z, r)$ denote the above game when the time interval between successive sales is z and payoffs are discounted at the rate r. Let σ be a *pure* strategy for the monopolist. Then σ is a sequence of functions $\{\sigma^n\}_{n=0}^{\infty}$. The function σ^n at date nz determines the monopolist's price in period n as a function of the prices she charged in previous periods and the actions chosen by consumers in the past. We impose measurability restrictions on joint consumer strategies below which imply that the set of consumer acceptances in period n, Q_n, will be a measurable set, i.e., $Q_n \in \Omega$, where Ω is the Borel σ-algebra on I. Then $\sigma^n\colon Y^n \times \Omega^n \to Y$, with $Y = [0, f(0)]$ and Y^n and Ω^n the n-fold Cartesian products of Y and Ω. A strategy combination for consumers is a sequence of functions $\{\tau^n\}_{n=0}^{\infty}$ where $\tau^n\colon Y^{n+1} \times \Omega^n \times I \to \{0,1\}$ is such that for each $y^{n+1} \in Y^{n+1}$ and each $B^n \in \Omega^n$, $\tau^n(y^{n+1}, B^n, \cdot)$ is measurable. Decision "0" is to be interpreted as a decision not to buy in the current period; decision "1" indicates that a sale takes place in the current period. Obviously, we require that $\tau^n(y^{n+1}, B^n, q) = 0$ for all $q \in \bigcup_{j=0}^{n-1} Q_j$.[6]

Let Σ be the pure strategy space for the monopolist, and T be the set of pure strategy combinations for consumers. The strategy profile $\{\sigma, \tau\}$, with $\tau = \{\tau^n\}_{n=0}^{\infty}$, generates a path of prices and sales which can be computed recursively. The pattern of prices and sales over time in turn determines the payoffs to the players. Let $\pi(\sigma, \tau)$ be the net present value of profits generated by the strategy profile $\{\sigma, \tau\}$, and let $u_q(\sigma, \tau)$ be the discounted net surplus derived by consumer q. The profile $\{\sigma, \tau\}$ is a Nash equilibrium if and only if

$$\pi(\sigma, \tau) \geqslant \pi(\sigma', \tau), \qquad \forall \sigma' \in \Sigma, \qquad \text{and}$$

$$u_q(\sigma, \tau_q, \tau_{-q}) \geqslant u_q(\sigma, \tau_q', \tau_{-q}), \qquad \forall \tau_q' \in T_q, \; q\text{-a.e.},$$

where τ_q is the projection of τ onto the qth component (and similarly for T_q). An n-period history of the game is a sequence of prices in periods $0, \ldots, (n-1)$ and a specification of the set of consumers who bought in each period prior to n. We denote such a history by the symbol H_n. Thus, $H_n \in Y^n \times \Omega^n$. The symbol H_n' refers to H_n followed by a price announced by the monopolist in period n. Thus, $H_n' \in Y^{n+1} \times \Omega^n$. The strategy profile (σ, τ) induces strategy profiles $(\sigma|_{H_n}, \tau|_{H_n})$ and $(\sigma|_{H_n'}, \tau|_{H_n'})$, after the histories H_n and H_n', respectively. The strategy pair (σ, τ) is a *subgame perfect* equilibrium if and only if $(\sigma|_{H_n}, \tau|_{H_n})$ is a Nash equilibrium in the game remaining after the history H_n, for all n and all H_n, and similarly after any history H_n'. In order to ensure the existence of an equilibrium, we will have to allow the monopolist to mix at any stage of the game. $\hat{\Sigma}$ will denote her set of behavioral strategies. It should be clear to the reader how to extend the above definitions when behavioral strategies are allowed. We will henceforth restrict attention to equilibria in which deviations by sets of measure zero of consumers change neither the actions of the remaining consumers nor those of the monopolist. This requirement reflects our quest for equilibria in which consumers act as price takers.[7] Since $f(\cdot)$ is monotone, and given the measure-zero restriction, there is no further loss of generality in assuming that $f(\cdot)$ is left-continuous.

---

[6] For notational simplicity, we chose to indicate the domain of definition of σ^n to be $Y^n \times \Omega^n$ and the domain of definition of τ^n to be $Y^{n+1} \times \Omega^n \times I$. However, only elements of Ω^n consistent with the restriction that a consumer can accept at most one offer by the monopolist can occur. One should restrict the domain of definition of σ^n and τ^n accordingly.

[7] This restriction may affect the equilibrium set, as demonstrated in Gul, Sonnenschein, and Wilson (1986, p. 170).

Let $q_n = m(\bigcup_{j=0}^{n-1} Q_j)$ be the (Lebesgue) measure of customers who have purchased. The next lemma, whose proof is given in Fudenberg, Levine, and Tirole (1985, Lemma 1), will imply that, along any equilibrium path, the remaining buyer valuations are a truncated sample of the original ones. Consequently, the single number q_n (incompletely) summarizes prior consumer actions.

LEMMA 2.1: *In any subgame perfect equilibrium, after any history H_n, and for any current price p, there exists a cutoff valuation $\beta(p, H_n)$ such that every consumer with valuation exceeding $\beta(p, H_n)$ accepts the monopolist's offer of p and every consumer with valuation less than $\beta(p, H_n)$ rejects.*

In general, a buyer's accept/reject decision may depend not only on the current price, p, but also on the history, H_n. We define a *weak-Markov equilibrium* to be a subgame perfect equilibrium in which (after histories that contain no simultaneous buyer deviations of positive measure; see footnote 9, below) the accept/reject decisions of all (remaining) buyers depend only on the current price. The set of all weak-Markov equilibria is denoted by the symbol $E^{wm}(f, z)$.

The buyer's strategy in a weak-Markov equilibrium can be described by an acceptance function $P(\cdot)$, where consumer q accepts a price p if and only if $p \leq P(q)$. When $f(\cdot)$ is strictly monotone, Lemma 2.1 implies that $P(\cdot)$ is nonincreasing. When $f(\cdot)$ has flat sections, $P(\cdot)$ may be nonmonotone. However, any consumers who violate monotonicity for $P(\cdot)$ have identical valuations, so by permuting them, we may (without loss of generality) assume that $P(\cdot)$ is monotone. Since deviations by sets of measure zero of consumers do not affect the equilibrium, we further assume (still without loss of generality) that $P(\cdot)$ is a left-continuous, nonincreasing function. Thus (after histories that contain no buyer deviations), the set of remaining buyers is an interval $(q, 1]$, where $0 \leq q \leq 1$.

For a given weak-Markov equilibrium, consider the net present value of profits to the monopolist after any history for which the set of remaining buyers (except for sets of measure zero) equals $(q, 1]$. Since buyer acceptances depend only on the prices which the monopolist will henceforth charge, this value is a function $R(\cdot)$ of q only, and must satisfy the dynamic programming equation:

$$(2.1) \qquad R(q) = \max_{y \in [q, 1]} \{ P(y)(y - q) + \delta R(y) \},$$

where $\delta \equiv e^{-rz}$. Observe that $P(y) > 0$, for $y \in [0, 1)$, and hence that $R(y) > 0$ on the same domain.[8] Consequently, (2.1) implies that there are sales in every period in any weak-Markov equilibrium, until consumers are exhausted. Moreover, in the case of "no gap" (i.e., $f(1) = 0$), sales necessarily occur over infinite

---

[8] In any subgame perfect equilibrium, the monopolist only charges nonnegative prices (Fudenberg, Levine, and Tirole (1985, Lemma 2)). Thus, a rational consumer y will always accept a price of $(1 - \delta)f(y)$, as $f(y) - (1 - \delta)f(y) \geq \delta^k \{ f(y) - p \}$, for all $p \geq 0$ and $k \geq 1$. Since $f(y) > 0$ for all $y \in [0, 1)$, this establishes $P(y) \geq (1 - \delta)f(y) > 0$.

time. This is because only nonpositive prices can clear the market entirely and because it is suboptimal for the monopolist to ever charge a nonpositive price (since $P(y) > 0$ for $y \in [0,1)$).

Let $T(q)$ be the argmax correspondence in (2.1) and let $t(q) = \inf\{T(q)\}$. Then the monopolist's equilibrium action when customers $(q,1]$ remain is always to charge a price of $P(y)$, for some $y \in T(q)$. Since $T(\cdot)$ is monotone, it is single-valued except at possibly a countable set of q. Excluding this set, the monopolist's action depends only on the summary statistic q, and in fact is to charge the price $S(q) \equiv P(t(q))$. Meanwhile, suppose that the set of remaining customers was brought to $(q,1]$ by an offer of $P(q)$, where q has the property that $T(q)$ is single-valued. Buyer optimization requires that consumer q was indifferent between the price $P(q)$ and the deferred offer $S(q)$. Consequently:

$$(2.2) \qquad f(q) - P(q) = \delta[f(q) - S(q)].$$

When $T(q)$ is multiple-valued, the monopolist may now mix among prices in the set $P(T(q)) \equiv \{P(y): y \in T(q)\}$. A variant of (2.2) still holds, where $S(q)$ is replaced by an element of the convex hull of $P(T(q))$ which has the interpretation of expected price. If p_{-1} was the price charged in the previous period, the monopolist should now play a (possibly) mixed strategy such that the expected price, $\bar{p}$, satisfies:

$$(2.3) \qquad \begin{aligned} f(q) - p_{-1} &\geqslant \delta[f(q) - \bar{p}], \qquad \text{but} \\ f(q') - p_{-1} &\leqslant \delta[f(q') - \bar{p}], \qquad \text{for all } q' \in (q,1]. \end{aligned}$$

Such a mixed strategy justifies the decision of q to purchase in the previous period and of all $q' \in (q,1]$ to reject. Proposition 4.3 will demonstrate that randomization cannot occur along the equilibrium path except, possibly, in the initial period.

Equation (2.2) and inequality (2.3) establish that it is sufficient for a monopolist, in optimizing against consumers who use an acceptance function $P(q)$, to utilize a strategy which only depends on q and the previous price p_{-1}. It is convenient to restrict attention to equilibria which have this property. We will henceforth consider this restriction part of the definition of weak-Markov equilibrium. Note, via Proposition 4.3, that requiring the monopolist to condition only on q and p_{-1} does not affect the players' equilibrium payoffs attainable in weak-Markov equilibria.

Perhaps a more natural Markovian restriction would be to limit the monopolist to condition her strategy on the payoff-relevant part of the history, namely q, only. Unfortunately, such equilibria (termed strong-Markov equilibria) do not, in general, exist (see Fudenberg, Levine, and Tirole (1985)). In fact, if (P, R) is associated with a weak-Markov equilibrium and $P(\cdot)$ is discontinuous, it is possible to show that randomization is (generically) necessary whenever p_{-1} lies in a discontinuity of the range of $P(\cdot)$.

One final remark: for expositional ease, all of our subsequent definitions, theorems and proofs will be phrased in the language of durable goods monopoly.

However, all of our results also hold for the bargaining game, provided one substitutes "sequential equilibrium" whenever the phrase "subgame perfect equilibrium" appears. It should then be understood that if $F(v)$ denotes the (commonly known) distribution function of buyer valuations, $F(v) = 1 - y$, where $y = \inf\{q: f(q) = v\}$. Furthermore, q_n then corresponds to the seller's point of truncation, after history H_n, of her prior distribution on the buyer's valuation.

3. A LINEAR EXAMPLE

Consider a linear demand example with unit slope and unit intercept, i.e., $f(q) = 1 - q$. Let z be the time interval between periods. For this case, Stokey (1981) and Sobel and Takahashi (1983) proved the existence of a strong-Markov equilibrium in which the monopolist charges a price equalling $\alpha_z(1 - q)$ after any history in which all consumers $(q, 1]$ remain, and earns a corresponding profit of $R(q) = (\alpha_z/2)(1 - q)^2$. These authors also showed that $\lim_{z \downarrow 0} \alpha_z = 0$, thereby confirming the Coase conjecture.

We will now indicate how to construct reputational equilibria which yield the monopolist, for sufficiently small z, essentially any payoff between zero and static monopoly profits. Consider a strategy in which the monopolist follows an exponentially descending price path $p(t) = p_0 e^{-\eta t}$ (confined to the grid of times $\{0, z, 2z, \ldots\}$), as long as no deviation from this rule has occurred in the past, and reverts to the strong-Markov equilibrium described above, otherwise. Consumers adopt strategies which are optimal given this behavior.

Fix the real-time rate of descent $\eta > 0$ to be sufficiently slow that, independently of z, the sales in the initial period are bounded away from zero. For any time interval $z > 0$, let the (equilibrium path) price in period n be $p_n \equiv p(nz)$. Then, by consumer indifference, the set of consumers remaining after period n equals $(q_{n+1}, 1]$, where q_{n+1} satisfies: $f(q_{n+1}) - p_n = \delta[f(q_{n+1}) - p_{n+1}]$. Hence, $f(q_{n+1}) = p_n[(1 - \delta e^{-\eta z})/(1 - \delta)]$. Since demand is linear, this establishes that sales exponentially descend at the same rate η, and that the price and sales in every period are constant multiples of $(1 - q_n)$. Consequently, along the equilibrium path, the continuation profits evaluated in any period $n \geq 1$ are a constant multiple, λ_z, of $(1 - q_n)^2$. Observe that as the interval z approaches zero, consumers purchase at arbitrarily close to the times that they would against a continuous-time price path $p_0 e^{-\eta t}$. Thus, $\lambda_z \to \lambda > 0$, where λ is the constant derived from a profit calculation along a continuous time path.

In every period, the monopolist must weigh continuation profits against the payoff from optimally deviating. Any deviation causes the consumers to instantly adopt the acceptance function from the strong-Markov equilibrium. Hence, the optimal derivation when customers $(q_n, 1]$ remain yields profits of exactly $R(q_n) = (\alpha_z/2)(1 - q_n)^2$. Observe that there exists $z_1 > 0$ such that whenever the time interval satisfies $0 < z < z_1$, we have $\alpha_z/2 < \lambda_z$, deterring deviations from the continuation path in all periods $n \geq 1$. Meanwhile, let $\pi_0(\eta, z)$ denote the seller's equilibrium profits evaluated in period zero. Since $\lim_{z \downarrow 0} \pi_0(\eta, z) > 0$, there exists z_2 $(0 < z_2 < z_1)$ such that whenever the time interval satisfies $0 < z < z_2$, we have $\alpha_z/2 < \pi_0(\eta, z)$, deterring deviations in period zero as well.

Finally, note that $\lim_{z \downarrow 0} \pi_0(\eta, z) = p_0(1 - p_0)$ and that static monopoly profits equal $1/4$. We conclude that by continuously varying the initial price p_0 and the rate of descent η, and by making z sufficiently small, *every* level of profits in $(0, 1/4)$ can be sustained.

4. EXISTENCE OF WEAK-MARKOV EQUILIBRIA

In order to extend the reasoning of the previous section to general demand curves, we need to demonstrate two facts which were demonstrated by formula for the linear case. We lay this groundwork here and in the next section. First, we show the existence of weak-Markov equilibria for general demand curves (see also Appendix A). This gives us well-defined secondary paths, reverted to in case of deviation from the proposed equilibrium path. Then, in Section 5, we demonstrate that these secondary paths become uniformly low (compared to the highest valuation remaining) as z approaches zero, enabling them to be effective deterrents.

We begin by defining general demand curves.

DEFINITION 4.1: An (inverse) *demand curve* f is a nonnegative-valued, left-continuous, nonincreasing function on $[0, 1]$ which, without loss of generality, we normalize so that $f(0) = 1$ and $f(q) > 0$ whenever $0 \leqslant q < 1$.

Using this terminology, we prove the following theorem in Appendix A:[9]

THEOREM 4.2 (Existence of Weak-Markov Equilibria): *Let f be any (inverse) demand curve. Then for every $r > 0$ and every $z > 0$, there exists a weak-Markov equilibrium.*

This theorem strengthens results by Fudenberg-Levine-Tirole (1985), who prove existence for differentiable demand curves with derivative bounded below and above, and Gul-Sonnenschein-Wilson (1986), who prove existence for demand curves with $f(1) > 0$ that satisfy a Lipschitz condition at 1. For example, Theorem 4.2 extends existence to nondifferentiable and possibly discontinuous curves with $f(1) = 0$. It also contains the case where $f(1) > 0$ but $f'(1)$ is infinite. The proof of Theorem 4.2 may be of some general interest, since it uses a version

---

[9] We follow the tradition of Gul, Sonnenschein, and Wilson (1986, pp. 159–160) of not specifying equilibrium behavior following *simultaneous* deviations by consumers. This is formally correct in the case of a durable goods monopoly since any such deviation will lead to a rescaled (see Definition 5.2) demand curve satisfying the conditions of Theorem 4.2. We can thus specify a subgame perfect equilibrium which is played from that node onward. Note, however, that neither of the prior existence theorems would guarantee existence of equilibria following (off-equilibrium) nonmonotone purchase behavior by consumers. Notice also that in the bargaining interpretation of the model, simultaneous deviations are unobservable and, hence, are not an issue.

of the maximum theorem which does not require objective functions to be continuous. In Appendix A, we also establish the following theorem:

PROPOSITION 4.3: *Along any weak-Markov equilibrium path, the monopolist does not randomize, except (possibly) in the initial period.*

5. THE UNIFORM COASE CONJECTURE

In this section, we strengthen the "Coase conjecture" by presenting a theorem that guarantees *uniformly* low prices for all weak-Markov equilibria of *families* of demand curves.

While the uniform Coase conjecture is of independent interest, we require it here as an intermediate step for use in the main result of the paper: the folk theorem of Section 6. It should be observed that there is a straightforward reason why we did not need to examine families of demand curves to treat the linear case in Section 3: given linear demand, every derived residual demand curve is linear as well.[10] For generic demand curves, however, the residual demand curves are no longer rescaled versions of the original one. Thus, considerations of subgame perfection lead us naturally to study families of demand curves. We will demonstrate, for all residual demand curves arising from a demand curve f, that all price paths derived from weak-Markov equilibria are uniformly low compared to the highest remaining consumer valuation. This establishes that weak-Markov price paths may be used to deter deviation from the main price paths of reputational equilibria.

Define $\mathscr{F}_{L, M, \alpha}$ to be the family of demand curves which are enveloped by scalar multiples of demand curves $(1 - q)^{\alpha}$, for some positive α. To be precise, we have the following definition:

DEFINITION 5.1: For $0 < M \leqslant 1 \leqslant L < \infty$ and $\alpha > 0$, $\mathscr{F}_{L, M, \alpha}$ is the set of all (inverse) demand curves $f(\cdot)$ such that $M(1 - x)^{\alpha} \leqslant f(x) \leqslant L(1 - x)^{\alpha}$, for all $x \in [0, 1]$.

The only significant restriction implicit in the definition of $\mathscr{F}_{L, M, \alpha}$ is that $f(1) = 0$. Otherwise, the family is very general. It allows, for example, differentiable demand curves with derivatives bounded above and bounded away from zero, demand curves which are not Lipschitz-continuous at 1, and demand curves which are severely discontinuous.

Let us also define a rescaled residual demand curve as a normalized version of the demand that remains after any proportion of customers have purchased:

---

[10] Identical reasoning applies to the case where $f(q) = (1 - q)^{\alpha}$, considered by Sobel and Takahashi (1983). Furthermore, this is the only family that is closed under the joint operation of truncation and rescaling (see Definition 5.2).

DEFINITION 5.2: Let f be any demand curve. We define f_q to be the *rescaled residual (inverse) demand curve of f at q* $(0 \leqslant q < 1)$ by:

$$f_q(x) = \frac{f[q + (1-q)x]}{f(q)}, \qquad \text{for all } x \in [0,1].$$

LEMMA 5.3: *If $f \in \mathscr{F}_{L,M,\alpha}$, then for every q $(0 \leqslant q < 1)$, $f_q \in \mathscr{F}_{L/M, M/L, \alpha}$.*

PROOF: Observe that

$$f(q + (1-q)x) = f(1 - (1-q)(1-x))$$
$$\leqslant L(1-q)^\alpha (1-x)^\alpha$$

and

$$f(q + (1-q)x) \geqslant M(1-q)^\alpha (1-x)^\alpha.$$

Also,

$$M(1-q)^\alpha \leqslant f(q) \leqslant L(1-q)^\alpha,$$

so

$$\frac{M}{L}(1-x)^\alpha \leqslant \frac{f[q+(1-q)x]}{f(q)} \leqslant \frac{L}{M}(1-x)^\alpha,$$

proving the desired result.   Q.E.D.

Let $L = L'/M'$ and $M = M'/L'$. Lemma 5.3 demonstrates that if $f \in \mathscr{F}_{L', M', \alpha}$ then all residual demand curves arising from f are elements of $\mathscr{F}_{L, M, \alpha}$. Hence, if we can show that the *initial price* is uniformly low for all demand curves in the family $\mathscr{F}_{L, M, \alpha}$, then we will also have established that all price paths arising from weak-Markov equilibria are uniformly low (compared to residual demand). We prove this fact in the following theorem:

THEOREM 5.4 (The Uniform Coase Conjecture): *For every $L \geqslant 1$, $0 < M \leqslant 1$, $0 < \alpha < \infty$ and $\varepsilon > 0$, there exists $\bar{z}(L, M, \alpha, \varepsilon)$ such that for every $f \in \mathscr{F}_{L, M, \alpha}$, for every z satisfying $0 < z < \bar{z}(L, M, \alpha, \varepsilon)$, and for every weak-Markov equilibrium $(P, R) \in E^{wm}(f, z)$, the monopolist charges an initial price less than or equal to ε (and earns profits less than ε).*

PROOF: See Appendix B.

A uniform Coase conjecture also holds when $f(1) > 0$. Consider the family of demand curves satisfying $f(1) \leqslant c$ and $M(1-x)^\alpha \leqslant f(x) - f(1) \leqslant L(1-x)^\alpha$, for all $x \in [0,1]$. Then an analogous result to Theorem 5.4 holds for this family, provided one substitutes "$f(1) + \varepsilon$" for the bound on the initial price and profits.

6. THE FOLK THEOREM FOR SELLER PAYOFFS

In this section, we prove Theorem 6.4, the main result of the paper. First, let $SE(f, r, z)$ denote, for the durable goods monopoly model, the set of all monopolist payoffs arising from subgame perfect equilibria when the demand curve is f, the interest rate is r, and the time interval between periods is z. For the bargaining game with one-sided incomplete information, the same expression denotes the set of all seller payoffs arising from sequential equilibria. Theorem 6.4 will establish that $SE(f, r, z)$ expands to the entire interval from zero to static monopoly profits, as the time interval z approaches zero. Its proof utilizes the fact that $f \in \mathscr{F}_{L, M, \alpha}$ has the uniform Coase property, which we now define:

DEFINITION 6.1: We will say that f has the *uniform Coase property* if, for some $z_1 > 0$:

(6.1)   there exists a subgame perfect equilibrium (σ_z, τ_z) for all games with time interval z between periods, where $0 < z < z_1$, and,

(6.2)   for every $\varepsilon > 0$, there exists $\bar{z}(\varepsilon)$ $(0 < \bar{z}(\varepsilon) < z_1)$ such that $S_z(q)/f(q) \leqslant \varepsilon$, for all z $(0 < z < \bar{z}(\varepsilon))$ and all q $(0 \leqslant q < 1)$,

where $S_z(q)$ denotes the supremum of all prices that the monopolist charges using strategy σ_z when the current state equals q (the supremum is taken over all possible price histories).

LEMMA 6.2: *If* $f \in \mathscr{F}_{L, M, \alpha}$, *then f has the uniform Coase property.*

PROOF: Suppose $f \in \mathscr{F}_{L, M, \alpha}$. Then by Theorem 4.2 there exists $(\sigma_z, \tau_z) \in E^{wm}(f, z)$ for all $z > 0$. We wish to show that $\{\sigma_z, \tau_z\}_{z > 0}$ satisfies (6.2). Observe, for any z, that (σ_z, τ_z) induces a weak-Markov equilibrium for any residual demand curve arising from f. Define $(\sigma_{z, q}, \tau_{z, q})$ by multiplying all prices in (σ_z, τ_z) by $f(q)$; observe that $(\sigma_{z, q}, \tau_{z, q})$ is a weak-Markov equilibrium for the rescaled residual demand curve f_q, for all $0 \leqslant q < 1$. (See Definition 5.2.)

Using the notation in Definition 6.1, observe that $S_z(q) = f(q)S_{z, q}(0)$. Further observe, by Lemma 5.3, that $f_q \in \mathscr{F}_{L', M', \alpha}$, where $L' \equiv L/M$ and $M' \equiv M/L$. By the uniform Coase conjecture (Theorem 5.4), for every $\varepsilon > 0$, there exists $\bar{z}(\varepsilon)$ such that the initial price in any weak-Markov equilibrium is less than ε, for any z $(0 < z < \bar{z})$ and any demand curve in $\mathscr{F}_{L', M', \alpha}$. We conclude that (6.2) holds.
                                                                    Q.E.D.

Fudenberg, Levine, and Tirole (1985) have shown that $S_z(q) \geqslant f(1)$, for all $q \in [0, 1)$, in any subgame perfect equilibrium. Hence, in the case of a "gap" (i.e., $f(1) > 0$), the uniform Coase property cannot hold. Indeed, these authors and Gul, Sonnenschein, and Wilson (1986) demonstrated that when $f(1) > 0$ and $f(q) - f(1) \leqslant L(1 - q)$, for some $L < \infty$, there exists a (generically) unique subgame perfect equilibrium. Obviously, if $f \in \mathscr{F}_{L, M, \alpha}$, there is no gap, and hence there is scope for a folk theorem.

Let p^i denote the price actually charged in period i $(0 \leqslant i \leqslant n - 1)$.

DEFINITION 6.3: For any $\vec{p} = \{p_n\}_{n=0}^{\infty}$, any $\vec{q} = \{q_n\}_{n=0}^{\infty}$, and any monopolist strategy σ, define the *reputational price strategy* $(\vec{p}, \vec{q}, \sigma)$ by:

$$p^n = \begin{cases} p_n, & \text{if } p^i = p_i \text{ and } Q_i = [q_i, q_{i+1}] \text{ for all } i \ (0 \leqslant i \leqslant n - 1), \\ \sigma^n, & \text{otherwise,} \end{cases}$$

where the set equality is up to sets of measure zero.

We will further call $(\vec{p}, \vec{q}, \sigma)$ a *reputational equilibrium* if this reputational price strategy, in conjunction with optimal consumer behavior, forms a subgame perfect equilibrium.

Observe that the definition of reputational equilibrium requires that strategy σ, by itself, be associated with a subgame perfect equilibrium. A reputational equilibrium is defined analogously for the bargaining game; note that "$\vec{q}$" is then omitted. We can now state and prove the main result.

THEOREM 6.4 (The Folk Theorem for Seller Payoffs): *Let f belong to $\mathcal{F}_{L,M,\alpha}$ and let π^* denote static monopoly profits. Then for every real interest rate $r > 0$ and for every $\varepsilon > 0$, there exists a $\bar{z} > 0$ such that whenever the time interval between successive offers satisfies $0 < z < \bar{z}$:*

$$(6.3) \qquad [\varepsilon, \pi^* - \varepsilon] \subset SE(f, r, z).$$

PROOF: By Lemma 6.2, f has the uniform Coase property. Let $\{\sigma_z, \tau_z\}_{0 < z < z_1}$ be the family of subgame perfect equilibria guaranteed by (6.1), and let $\{S_z\}_{0 < z < z_1}$ be defined as in Definition 6.1. Define the function $g(z) = \sup\{S_x(q)/f(q): 0 < x \leqslant z \text{ and } 0 \leqslant q < 1\}$. Observe that $g(z)$ is well defined for $0 < z < z_1$, since S_z is defined and $S_z(q)/f(q)$ is uniformly bounded above by 1. Further observe, by (6.2), that $\lim_{z \to 0} g(z) = 0$. By definition, $q_0 = 0$. Choose arbitrary sales q_1 in period zero ($0 \leqslant q_1 < 1$). Let us define an exponential rate of subsequent sales by:

$$(6.4) \qquad 1 - q_{n+1} = e^{-naz(rz + g(z))}(1 - q_1), \qquad \text{for any } a > 0 \text{ and all } n \geqslant 0.$$

Our first step is to construct a price sequence $\{p_n\}_{n=0}^{\infty}$ which yields sales of $(q_{n+1} - q_n)$ in period n (for all $n \geqslant 0$). Observe that if $0 < q_1 < 1$, then (6.4) implies sales in all periods. To make consumer q_{n+1} indifferent between purchasing at price p_n in period n and at price p_{n+1} one period later, we must have:

$$(6.5) \qquad f(q_{n+1}) - p_n = \delta[f(q_{n+1}) - p_{n+1}], \qquad \text{for all } n \geqslant 0,$$

where $\delta = e^{-rz}$. Solving for p_n and telescoping the resulting summation yields:

$$(6.6) \qquad p_n = (1 - \delta) \sum_{k=0}^{\infty} \delta^k f(q_{n+1+k}), \qquad n \geqslant 0.$$

Furthermore, the price sequence $\vec{p} \equiv \{p_n\}_{n=0}^{\infty}$ implied by (6.4) and (6.6) satisfies $f(q_{n+1}) \geqslant p_n$ (for all $n \geqslant 0$) and equation (6.5), proving that consumers optimize along the sales path $\vec{q} \equiv \{q_n\}_{n=1}^{\infty}$.

CLAIM 1: For any q_1 ($0 \leqslant q_1 < 1$), there exists $a > 0$ and $\bar{z} > 0$ such that $(\vec{p}, \vec{q}, \sigma_z)$ defined by (6.4) and (6.6) is a reputational equilibrium for all z satisfying $0 < z < \bar{z} < z_1$.

PROOF OF CLAIM 1: Let π_n denote profits starting from period n if the price path $\vec{p}$ is followed in all periods. Define m to be the least integer greater than

$1/z$. Certainly $\pi_n \geqslant \delta^{m-1}[q_{n+m} - q_n]p_{n+m}$. Observe that $\delta^{m-1} \equiv e^{-(m-1)rz} \geqslant e^{-r}$ and, by (6.4), $q_{n+m} - q_n = (1 - q_n) - (1 - q_{n+m}) \geqslant (1 - q_n)(1 - e^{-a(rz+g(z))})$, for all $n \geqslant 1$. Meanwhile, by (6.6), $p_{n+m} \geqslant (1 - \delta)\sum_{k=0}^{m-1} \delta^k f(q_{n+m+1+k}) \geqslant f(q_{n+2m})$ $(1 - \delta)\sum_{k=0}^{m-1} \delta^k \geqslant (1 - e^{-r})f(q_{n+2m})$. Hence:

$$(6.7) \qquad \pi_n \geqslant e^{-r}(1 - q_n)(1 - e^{-a(rz+g(z))})(1 - e^{-r})f(q_{n+2m}), \qquad n \geqslant 1,$$

and by similar reasoning,

$$(6.8) \qquad \pi_0 \geqslant q_1 p_0 \geqslant q_1(1 - e^{-r})f(q_m).$$

Now, let π_n^z denote profits starting from period n if (σ_z, τ_z) is followed. Let q $(0 \leqslant q < 1)$ denote a customer and let p_q denote the price at which customer q purchases, according to (σ_z, τ_z). Let p_q' denote the next (expected) price charged after p_q, following σ_z. Observe by the definition of $g(z)$ that $p_q' \leqslant g(z)f(q)$. By consumer optimization, $f(q) - p_q \geqslant \delta[f(q) - p_q']$. Together these inequalities imply $p_q \leqslant [1 - \delta + \delta g(z)]f(q)$, for all q $(0 \leqslant q < 1)$, and so:

$$(6.9) \qquad \pi_n^z \leqslant [1 - \delta + \delta g(z)] \int_{q_n}^1 f(q) \, dq, \qquad \text{for all } n \geqslant 0.$$

Observe that the bound of (6.9) is a consequence of the uniform Coase property, but does not follow from the ordinary Coase conjecture.

Let $a = (8L/M)[e^{-r}(1 - e^{-r})]^{-1}$. To prove subgame perfection, we must show that $\pi_n \geqslant \pi_n^z$, for all $n \geqslant 0$. Observe that there exists z_2 such that for all z $(0 < z < z_2)$: $1 - e^{-a[g(z)+rz]} > (a/2)[g(z) + rz]$. Hence, (6.7) implies that $\pi_n > 4(L/M)(g(z) + rz)(1 - q_n)f(q_{n+2m})$ for all $n \geqslant 1$ and $0 < z < z_2$. Since $q_n < q_{n+2m} < 1$ and f is monotone nonincreasing:

$$\int_{q_n}^1 f(q) \, dq \leqslant (q_{n+2m} - q_n)f(q_n) + (1 - q_{n+2m})f(q_{n+2m}).$$

Observe that $f \in \mathcal{F}_{L,M,\alpha}$ implies $f(q) \leqslant (L/M)\beta^{-\alpha}f(q')$ whenever $(1 - q')/(1 - q) = \beta$. By (6.4), $(1 - q_{n+2m})/(1 - q_n) = \beta(z)$, for all n, where $\lim_{z \to 0} \beta(z) = 1$. Consequently, there exists $z_3 > 0$ such that $f(q_n) \leqslant (2L/M)f(q_{n+2m})$, and hence $\int_{q_n}^1 f(q) \, dq \leqslant (2L/M)(1 - q_n)f(q_{n+2m})$, for all $n \geqslant 1$ and for all z $(0 < z < z_3)$. Finally, there exists $z_4 > 0$ such that $[1 - \delta + \delta g(z)] \leqslant 2[g(z) + rz]$ for all z $(0 < z < z_4)$. Hence, for all z satisfying $0 < z < \min\{z_1, z_2, z_3, z_4\}$ and for all $n \geqslant 1$, we have by (6.9) that $\pi_n \geqslant \pi_n^z$. It can easily be shown that we may set $\bar{z}$ so that $\pi_0 \geqslant \pi_0^z$ for all z $(0 < z < \bar{z})$ as well.

CLAIM 2: For any q $(0 < q < 1)$ and any λ $(0 < \lambda < 1)$, there exists $\bar{z} > 0$ such that for every z $(0 < z < \bar{z})$, there is a reputational equilibrium with profits at least $\lambda q f(q)$.

PROOF OF CLAIM 2: Set $q_1 = \sqrt{\lambda} q$. Define m to be the least integer greater than $-\log(1 - \sqrt{\lambda})/rz$. (Observe that $e^{-rmz} \approx 1 - \sqrt{\lambda}$.) Now define $\{q_n\}_{n=2}^\infty$ by (6.4). Then for arbitrary $a > 0$, there exists z_5 such that for every z $(0 < z < z_5)$, $q_m < q$. By (6.6), $p_0 > (1 - \delta)\sum_{k=0}^{m-1} \delta^k f(q_{k+1}) \geqslant (1 - \delta^m)f(q_m)$ $\geqslant [1 - (1 - \sqrt{\lambda})]f(q) = \sqrt{\lambda}f(q)$, whenever $0 < z < z_5$. Hence, $\pi_0 \geqslant p_0 q_1 \geqslant \lambda q f(q)$.

Using Claim 1, there exists $\bar{z} > 0$ such that $(\vec{p}, \vec{q}, \sigma_z)$ defined using $q_1 = \sqrt{\lambda}\,q$, (6.4) and (6.6) is a reputational equilibrium, for all z $(0 < z < \bar{z})$, proving Claim 2.

REMAINDER OF PROOF OF THEOREM 6.4: Given any q_1, let the quantity path $\vec{q}$ be defined by (6.4), let the price path $\vec{p}$ be defined by (6.6), and let $\pi(q_1, z)$ denote the profits associated with $\vec{q}$ and $\vec{p}$. Then:

$$(6.10) \quad \pi(q_1, z) = \sum_{k=0}^{\infty} e^{-krz}(q_{k+1} - q_k)p_k = q_1 p_0 + \sum_{k=1}^{\infty} \delta^k(q_{k+1} - q_k)p_k.$$

Suppose $q_1' > q_1$, and define $\vec{q}'$ and $\vec{p}'$ analogously. Observe, by (6.4), that $q_{k+1}' - q_k' < q_{k+1} - q_k$ for all $k \geq 1$, and by (6.6), that $p_k' \leq p_k$ for all $k \geq 0$. Hence, using (6.10), $\pi(q_1', z) \leq \pi(q_1, z) + |q_1' - q_1|$. Define $\tilde{\pi}(q_1, z) = \sup\{\pi(q, z): 0 \leq q \leq q_1\}$. Observe that $\tilde{\pi}$ is monotone nondecreasing in q_1 and also satisfies $\tilde{\pi}(q_1', z) \leq \tilde{\pi}(q_1, z) + |q_1' - q_1|$. Thus, $\tilde{\pi}$ is continuous in q_1, for any $z > 0$.

Let $\pi^* = \sup_{0 \leq q \leq 1} qf(q)$ and choose q^* so that $\pi^* = q^* f(q^*)$. Given ε $(0 < \varepsilon < \pi^*)$, define $\lambda = [\pi^* - \varepsilon]/\pi^*$. By Claim 2, there exists $z_6 > 0$ such that there exists a reputational equilibrium with profits at least $\lambda \pi^* = \pi^* - \varepsilon$ whenever $0 < z < z_6$. Also, using (6.10), observe that $\lim_{z \to 0} \pi(0, z) = 0$, and so there exists $z_7 > 0$ such that $\pi(0, z) < \varepsilon$ whenever $0 < z < z_7$. Finally, by Claim 1, there exists $z_8 > 0$ such that $(\vec{p}, \vec{q}, \sigma_z)$ defined from $q_1 = 0$ is a reputational equilibrium whenever $0 < z < z_8$.

Define $\bar{z} = \min\{z_6, z_7, z_8\}$. Then for any z satisfying $0 < z < \bar{z}$, $\pi(0, z) < \varepsilon$ and $\pi(\sqrt{\lambda}\,q^*, z) > \pi^* - \varepsilon$. Furthermore, we have already shown that $\pi_n \geq \pi_n^z$ for $0 < z < \bar{z}$ and $n \geq 1$, so $(\vec{p}, \vec{q}, \sigma_z)$ is a reputational equilibrium for all q_1 that yield $\pi_0 \geq \pi(0, z)$. Finally, since $\tilde{\pi}(q_1, z)$ is continuous in q_1, the set $\{\pi(q_1, z): 0 \leq q_1 \leq \sqrt{\lambda}\,q^*$ and $\pi(q_1, z) \geq \pi(0, z)\}$ is an interval. Since ε and $\pi^* - \varepsilon$ are both contained in that interval, we have established (6.3).   Q.E.D.

7. CONCLUSION

Consider the outcome of durable goods monopoly (or bargaining) when the time interval between successive periods approaches *infinity*. In this situation, the monopolist (seller) has close to unlimited commitment power, and thus her maximum equilibrium payoff approaches static monopoly profits. Meanwhile, as we demonstrated in the Folk Theorem, the same outcome is attainable in the limit as the time interval between periods approaches zero. We conclude that the "maximum possible seller surplus" is minimized at some intermediate time interval—let us call this the *time interval of least commitment*.

We explain this phenomenon as the result of two countervailing forces. When the time interval between periods is short, reputational effects may be devastatingly effective in preserving monopoly power. When the time interval between periods is long, reputational effects are superfluous. The most adverse circumstance for the monopolist may be when the time interval is just long enough to preclude reputational equilibria (but still sufficiently short that the inability to commit is a problem).

Let us also explain the somewhat unexpected discontinuity in the equilibrium set, based on whether or not there is separation between seller and buyer valuations. Fudenberg, Levine, and Tirole (1985) demonstrated that in the case of a "gap" between seller and buyer valuations (and subject to some regularity conditions) there is a uniform finite bound to the number of periods in which sales can occur in any subgame perfect equilibrium. Backward induction then forces subgame perfect equilibria to be Markovian, and the Coase conjecture drives the initial price near the lowest buyer valuation. However, in the case of "no gap" treated here, sales necessarily occur over infinite time. There is no last period from which to apply backward induction, and reputation supports equilibria which approximate static monopoly pricing.

We can also draw an interesting comparison between the present monopoly model and the analogous oligopoly model (Ausubel and Deneckere (1987) and Gul (1987)). Folk theorems for joint profits hold in the durable goods oligopoly, even when there is a "gap," because oligopolists can extend sales over infinite time. This defeats monopoly results driven by backward induction. Moreover, the oligopolists' joint profits may exceed the monopolist's theoretical maximum (when the time interval between periods is short), since Bertrand competition is a more severe "punishment" than Coase pricing.

A limitation of the present analysis is that our Folk Theorem is only stated in terms of *seller* payoffs, and that we examine a model where only the *uninformed* party makes offers. We extend our results to buyer payoffs and to other extensive forms in a sequel (Ausubel and Deneckere (1989)). In particular, there is a folk theorem for seller payoffs in the alternating-offer game if and only if the (lowest) monopoly price does not exceed one-half the highest buyer valuation.

Department of Managerial Economics & Decision Sciences, J. L. Kellogg Graduate School of Management, Northwestern University, Evanston, IL 60208, U.S.A.

Manuscript received July, 1986; final revision received August, 1988.

APPENDIX A

Existence of Weak-Markov Equilibria

DEFINITION A.1: Let $P(\cdot)$ and $R(\cdot)$ be left-continuous functions on $[\bar{q}, 1]$, where $0 \leqslant \bar{q} < 1$, and let $P(\cdot)$ be nonincreasing and nonnegative. We will say that (P, R) *supports* a weak-Markov equilibrium on $[\bar{q}, 1]$ for (inverse) demand curve $f(\cdot)$ if equations (2.1) and (2.2) are satisfied for every $q \in [\bar{q}, 1)$.

We have already argued in Section 2 that if (P, R) is associated with a weak-Markov equilibrium, then (2.1) holds for all $q \in [0, 1]$ and (2.2) is satisfied at all continuity points of $t(\cdot)$ in $[0, 1]$. The left-continuity of $f(\cdot)$, $P(\cdot)$, and $t(\cdot)$, and the monotonicity of $T(\cdot)$, imply that (2.2) must hold everywhere. Conversely, suppose (2.1) and (2.2) are satisfied for all elements of $[\bar{q}, 1)$. Then if the state $q \in [\bar{q}, 1)$ and if the previous price, p_{-1}, was in the range of $P(\cdot)$, we specify a weak-Markov equilibrium by requiring that all consumers y accept if and only if $P(y) \geqslant p_{-1}$ and that the monopolist charge $S(q')$ in the next period, where $q' = \sup\{y \in [q,1): P(y) \geqslant p_{-1}\}$. If p_{-1} was not in the range of $P(\cdot)$, consumers accept using the same rule, but the monopolist randomizes in the next period between $\sup P(T(q))$ and $\inf P(T(q))$ in such a way that the expected price, $\bar{p}$, satisfies (2.3). That such a randomization is possible can be demonstrated using (2.2).

LEMMA A.2: *Suppose that (P, R) supports a weak-Markov equilibrium on $[\bar{q}, 1]$. Then $R(\cdot)$ is decreasing and Lipschitz continuous, satisfying: $0 < R(q_1) - R(q_2) \leqslant q_2 - q_1$, whenever $\bar{q} \leqslant q_1 < q_2 \leqslant 1$.*

PROOF: Observe that $R(q_1) \geqslant [t(q_2) - q_1]P(t(q_2)) + \delta R(t(q_2)) > [t(q_2) - q_2]P(t(q_2)) + \delta R(t(q_2)) = R(q_2)$, since $P(x) \geqslant (1-\delta)f(x) > 0$ for all $x \in [\bar{q}, 1)$. Meanwhile, define $t^1(q_1) = t(q_1)$, $t^2(q_1) = t(t(q_1))$, etc. Then the monopolist, starting from q_2, has the option of selecting a sales path equal to $\max\{q_2, t^k(q_1)\}$, for $k = 1, 2, 3, \ldots$. This assures $R(q_2) \geqslant R(q_1) - (q_2 - q_1)$.   Q.E.D.

LEMMA A.3:[11] *Suppose that $(P_{\bar{q}}, R_{\bar{q}})$ supports a weak-Markov equilibrium on $[\bar{q}, 1]$, where $0 < \bar{q} < 1$. Then there exists (P, R) which supports a weak-Markov equilibrium on $[0,1]$, with the property that $P(q) = P_{\bar{q}}(q)$ and $R(q) = R_{\bar{q}}(q)$ for all $q \in [\bar{q}, 1]$.*

PROOF: We proceed constructively. Let $\bar{q}' = \max\{0, \bar{q} - (1-\delta)R_{\bar{q}}(\bar{q})/2\}$. Observe that $\bar{q} < 1$ implies $R(\bar{q}) > 0$ and so $\bar{q}' < \bar{q}$. Let us extend $R_{\bar{q}}(\cdot)$ to $R_{\bar{q}'}(\cdot)$ defined on $[\bar{q}', 1]$ by:

$$\text{(A.1)} \qquad R_{\bar{q}'}(q) = \max_{y \in [q,1] \cap [\bar{q},1]} \{[y - q]P_{\bar{q}}(y) + \delta R_{\bar{q}}(y)\},$$

and define $t_{\bar{q}'}(q)$ to be the infimum of the argmax correspondence of (A.1). Also extend $P_{\bar{q}}(\cdot)$ to $P_{\bar{q}'}(\cdot)$ defined on $[\bar{q}', 1]$ by:

$$\text{(A.2)} \qquad P_{\bar{q}'}(q) = (1-\delta)f(q) + \delta P_{\bar{q}}(t_{\bar{q}'}(q)).$$

It should now be observed that $(P_{\bar{q}'}, R_{\bar{q}'})$ satisfy:

$$\text{(A.3)} \qquad R_{\bar{q}'}(q) = \max_{y \in [q,1]} \{[y - q]P_{\bar{q}'}(y) + \delta R_{\bar{q}'}(y)\}, \qquad \text{for all} \quad q \in [\bar{q}', 1],$$

using (A.1) and the fact that, for $v \in [q, \bar{q}]$, $[v - q]P_{\bar{q}'}(v) + \delta R_{\bar{q}'}(v) \leqslant (1/2)(1-\delta)R_{\bar{q}}(\bar{q}) + \delta R_{\bar{q}'}(v) \leqslant (1/2)(1-\delta)R_{\bar{q}'}(q) + \delta R_{\bar{q}'}(q) < R_{\bar{q}'}(q)$. Thus, $(P_{\bar{q}'}, R_{\bar{q}'})$ supports a weak-Markov equilibrium on $[\bar{q}', 1]$. A finite number of repetitions of the above argument extends $(P_{\bar{q}}, R_{\bar{q}})$ to the entire unit interval.   Q.E.D.

We will now introduce some notation and state a result which we use in proving Theorem 4.2. Let X and Y be compact, nonempty subsets of $\mathbf{R}$. Let J_n $(n = 1, 2, \ldots)$ and $J: X \to Y$ be upper semicontinuous functions. Define $R(J_n) = \max\{J_n(x): x \in X\}$, and $T(J_n) = \{x \in X: J_n(x) = R(J_n)\}$, and similarly for $R(J)$ and $T(J)$. Also define: $\bar{J}_n(x) = \text{conv}\{y: y = \lim_{i \to \infty} J_n(x_i)$, for some $\langle x_i \rangle_{i=1}^{\infty} \subset X$ such that $x_i \to x\}$; $G(J_n) = $ graph of J_n; and $B_\varepsilon(J_n) = \{(x', y') \in X \times Y: \|(x', y') - (x, y)\| < \varepsilon$ for some $(x, y) \in G(\bar{J}_n)\}$. Finally, define:

$$\text{(A.4)} \qquad \rho(J, J_n) = \inf\{\varepsilon > 0: G(J) \subset B_\varepsilon(J_n) \text{ and } G(J_n) \subset B_\varepsilon(J)\}.$$

We may now state a generalization of the theorem of the maximum which does not require continuity of the objective. A proof may be found in Ausubel and Deneckere (1988):

THEOREM OF THE MAXIMUM: *Suppose $J_n(\cdot)$ and $J(\cdot)$ are upper semicontinuous functions from X into Y, and suppose $\lim_{n \to \infty} \rho(J, J_n) = 0$. Then $\lim_{n \to \infty} R(J_n) = R(J)$ and any cluster point from $\{T(J_n)\}_{n=1}^{\infty}$ is an element of $T(J)$.*

We are now ready to prove the following theorem:

---

[11] This lemma builds on Fudenberg, Levine, and Tirole (1985, Lemma 3) and Gul, Sonnenschein, and Wilson (1986, Lemma 5).

THEOREM 4.2 (Existence of Weak-Markov Equilibria): *Let f be any (inverse) demand curve satisfying Definition 4.1. Then for every $r > 0$ and every $z > 0$, there exists a weak-Markov equilibrium.*

PROOF: Consider the sequence of demand curves:

$$f_n(q) = \begin{cases} f(q), & \text{if } 0 \leqslant q \leqslant (n-1)/n, \\ (n-nq)f((n-1)/n) + (1-n+nq)f(1), & \text{if } (n-1)/n < q \leqslant 1. \end{cases}$$

Observe that f_n and f differ only on $((n-1)/n, 1]$ and that, for every n, f_n is linear on the latter interval. Hence, one can explicitly calculate a linear-quadratic pair $(\tilde{P}_n, \tilde{R}_n)$ which supports a strong-Markov equilibrium on $[(n-1)/n, 1]$ for f_n. (See Section 3.) By Lemma A.3, this pair can be extended to (P_n, R_n) which supports an equilibrium on the entire unit interval.

Without loss of generality, we may assume that $\{P_n\}_{n-1}^{\infty}$ converges pointwise for all rationals in $[0,1]$. (This can be assured by taking successive subsequences and applying a diagonal argument.) For every rational $r \in [0,1]$, let $\Phi(r) = \lim_{n \to \infty} P_n(r)$. Define $P(0) = \Phi(0)$ and, for every $x \in (0,1]$, define $P(x) = \lim_{k \to \infty} \Phi(r_k)$, where each r_k is rational and $r_k \uparrow x$. Observe that $P(\cdot)$ is well-defined, nonincreasing, and left continuous. Without loss of generality, we may also assume that $\{R_n\}_{n-1}^{\infty}$ converges uniformly to a continuous function, which we denote by $R(\cdot)$. (This is made possible by Lemma A.2, which implies that $\{R_n\}_{n-1}^{\infty}$ is an equicontinuous family which thus has a uniformly convergent subsequence.) The remainder of the proof will establish that the constructed (P, R) supports a weak-Markov equilibrium on $[0,1]$ for the (limit) demand curve f.

Define $J_n(q, y) = [y - q]P_n(y) + \delta R_n(y)$ and $J(q, y) = [y - q]P(y) + \delta R(y)$. Also define $T_n(q) = \operatorname{argmax}\{J_n(q, y): y \in [q, 1]\}$ and $T(q)$ analogously. Finally, let $t_n(q) = \inf T_n(q)$ and $t(q) = \inf T(q)$. We will now argue that $\rho(J(q, \cdot), J_n(q, \cdot)) \to 0$. The theorem of the maximum is then applicable, establishing that (2.1) is satisfied, for all $q \in [0,1]$.

Select arbitrary $\varepsilon > 0$. Cover the closure of $G(P)$ with $\varepsilon/5$-balls. Take a finite subcover, denoting the centers $(x_i, P(x_i))_{i \in I}$, where $x_i < x_{i+1}$ for all $i \in I$. By the definition of $P(\cdot)$, there exist rationals $\{y_i\}_{i \in I}$ such that $|y_i - x_i| < \varepsilon/5$ and $|\Phi(y_i) - P(x_i)| < \varepsilon/5$. Furthermore, there exists N_1 such that for all $n \geqslant N_1$, and all $i \in I$, $|P_n(y_i) - \Phi(y_i)| < \varepsilon/5$. Hence, the distance from $(y_i, P_n(y_i))$ to $(x_i, P(x_i))$ is less than $3\varepsilon/5$, and so the ε-ball centered at $(y_i, P_n(y_i))$ contains the $\varepsilon/5$-ball centered at $(x_i, P(x_i))$, for all $i \in I$. Consequently, $B_\varepsilon(P_n) \supset G(P)$, for all $n \geqslant N_1$.

Consider any consecutive x_i, x_{i+1}. Note that $0 \leqslant x_{i+1} - x_i < 2\varepsilon/5$, and:

(A.5)
$$P_n(y_i) < P(x_i) + 2\varepsilon/5, \quad \text{and}$$
$$P_n(y_{i+1}) > P(x_{i+1}) - 2\varepsilon/5.$$

Let us observe that for every $v \in [P(x_{i+1}), P(x_i)]$, there exists $w(v) \in [x_i, x_{i+1}]$ such that $v \in \bar{P}(w(v))$. Consequently, the union of all ε-balls around the points $\{(w(v), v): v \in [P(x_{i+1}), P(x_i)]\}$ covers the rectangle $D \equiv \{(y, v): x_i - \varepsilon/5 \leqslant y \leqslant x_{i+1} + \varepsilon/5 \text{ and } P(x_{i+1}) - 2\varepsilon/5 \leqslant v \leqslant P(x_i) + 2\varepsilon/5\}$. Using (A.5), note that $(y_i, P_n(y_i)) \in D$ and $(y_{i+1}, P_n(y_{i+1})) \in D$. By the monotonicity of $P_n(\cdot)$, it follows that $G(P_n) \subset B_\varepsilon(P)$, demonstrating that $\rho(P, P_n) < \varepsilon$ for all $n \geqslant N_1$.

Since $R_n \to R$ uniformly, there also exists N_2 such that for all $n \geqslant N_2$, $\rho(R, R_n) < \varepsilon$. Using the fact that $|y - q| \leqslant 1$, we conclude that $\rho(J(q, \cdot), J_n(q, \cdot)) < 2\varepsilon$, for $n \geqslant \max\{N_1, N_2\}$. Consequently, the hypothesis of the theorem of the maximum is satisfied, so (2.1) holds for all $q \in [0,1]$.

It remains to be argued that (2.2) is also satisfied. Consider any $q \in [0,1]$ where $t(\cdot)$, $P(\cdot)$, and $P(t(\cdot))$ are continuous. Observe that each of these functions is monotone: hence this restriction excludes at most countably many points. First, the theorem of the maximum implies that every cluster point of $\{t_n(q)\}_{n-1}^{\infty}$ is an element of $T(q)$. Now $T(\cdot)$ is single-valued at q since $t(\cdot)$ is continuous: hence $\lim_{n \to \infty} t_n(q) = t(q)$. Second, observe from the definition of $P(\cdot)$ that $P(\cdot)$ is continuous at q if and only if $\Phi(\cdot)$ is continuous at q. Let p be any accumulation point of $\{P_n(q)\}_{n-1}^{\infty}$ and let $r_k \uparrow q$ and $s_k \downarrow q$ be sequences of rationals. Then, for all k, $P_n(r_k) \geqslant P_n(q) \geqslant P_n(s_k)$, and hence $\Phi(r_k) \geqslant p \geqslant \Phi(s_k)$. The continuity of $\Phi(\cdot)$ implies p is unique and $p = \lim_{k \to \infty} \Phi(r_k) \equiv P(q)$, demonstrating that $\lim_{n \to \infty} P_n(q) = P(q)$. Third, since $t(\cdot)$ and $P(t(\cdot))$ are continuous at q, $P(\cdot)$ is continuous at $t(q)$ and, hence, $\Phi(\cdot)$ is continuous at $t(q)$. Let p' be any accumulation point of $\{P_n(t_n(q))\}_{n-1}^{\infty}$ and let $r_k' \uparrow t(q)$ and $s_k' \downarrow t(q)$ be sequences of rationals. Observe that for every $k > 0$, there exists $N(k)$ such that $t_n(q) \in (r_k', s_k')$ for all $n \geqslant N(k)$. Consequently, $P_n(r_k') \geqslant P_n(t_n(q)) \geqslant P_n(s_k')$, for all $n \geqslant N(k)$, and $\Phi(r_k') \geqslant p' \geqslant \Phi(s_k')$, for all k. As before, we can conclude $\lim_{n \to \infty} P_n(t_n(q)) = P(t(q))$. Finally, by our construction of $f_n(\cdot)$, $f_n \to f$ uniformly, and so $\lim_{n \to \infty} f_n(q) = f(q)$. Observe now that since (P_n, R_n) supports a weak-Markov equilibrium for f_n, we have for each n:

$$(A.6) \qquad f_n(q) - P_n(q) = \delta[f_n(q) - P_n(t_n(q))].$$

By taking limits as $n \to \infty$, we see that (2.2) is satisfied for all but (possibly) countably many q.

Now consider any of the (at most countably many) excluded $q \in (0,1]$. Select a sequence of nonexcluded q_k such that $q_k \uparrow q$. Since (2.2) is satisfied for all q_k, and since $f_n(\cdot)$, $P_n(\cdot)$, and $P_n(t_n(\cdot))$ are left-continuous, we conclude that (2.2) is satisfied for q as well. This completes the proof of the theorem. $Q.E.D.$

Finally, we obtain the following proposition:.

PROPOSITION 4.3: *Along any weak-Markov equilibrium path, the monopolist does not randomize, except (possibly) in the initial period.*

PROOF: Suppose otherwise. Then there exists a history after which the state is q and the monopolist randomizes among elements of $P(T(q))$ to yield an expected price $p^2 < p^1 \equiv \sup P(T(q))$. Define $\hat{p}^i$ by $f(q) - \hat{p}^i = \delta[f(q) - p^i]$, $i = 1, 2$. By (2.2) the price in the previous period must have been $\hat{p}^2$. We now claim that $P(q) \geqslant \hat{p}^1$, showing that the monopolist could have profited by setting $\hat{p}^1$ instead. To see this, first observe that $T(\cdot)$ is a monotone increasing correspondence and so $P(T(\cdot))$ is a nonincreasing correspondence. Next, let q_n be such that $q_n \uparrow q$ and $P(T(q_n))$ is single-valued. Then, using (2.2): $P(q) = \lim_{n \to \infty} P(q_n) = \lim_{n \to \infty} [(1 - \delta)f(q_n) + \delta S(q_n)] \geqslant (1 - \delta)f(q) + \delta p^1 = \hat{p}^1$, establishing the proposition. $Q.E.D.$

APPENDIX B

THE UNIFORM COASE CONJECTURE

PROOF OF THEOREM 5.4: Suppose not. Then there exist $\varepsilon > 0$, a sequence $\{f_n\}_{n-1}^{\infty} \subset \mathscr{F}_{L, M, \alpha}$, a sequence of positive numbers $\{z_n\}_{n-1}^{\infty} \to 0$, and a sequence of weak-Markov equilibria $\{P_n, R_n\}_{n-1}^{\infty}$ such that the initial price $S_n(0) \geqslant \varepsilon$ for all $n \geqslant 1$. Construct (P, R) as in the proof of Theorem 4.2. Let $y = \inf\{r: P(r) < \varepsilon\}$. By left continuity, $P(y) \geqslant \varepsilon$, but $P(r) < \varepsilon$ for every $r > y$. Recall that any weak-Markov equilibrium has sales in every period; hence $S_n(0) \geqslant \varepsilon$ implies $P_n(0) \geqslant \varepsilon$ for all n. But since P_n is monotone and $f_n(q) \leqslant L(1 - q)^\alpha$, we have $P_n(1 - (\varepsilon/2L)^{1/\alpha}) \leqslant f_n(1 - (\varepsilon/2L)^{1/\alpha}) \leqslant \varepsilon/2$, for all $n \geqslant 1$, implying that $0 \leqslant y < 1$.

Case I: Suppose $R(y) > 0$.

Since $R_n \to R$ uniformly, there exists a rational q $(y < q < 1)$ and an integer $\bar{n}_1$ such that $R_n(q) > R(y)/2$, for all $n \geqslant \bar{n}_1$. Since $q > y$, $P(q) < \varepsilon$, so there exists $\omega > 0$ and integer $\bar{n}_2$ such that $P_n(q) < \varepsilon - \omega$ for all $n \geqslant \bar{n}_2$. We will establish a lower bound on the real time t before which the price can drop by ω, in equilibrium, and hence before which consumer q purchases. Consumer 0 prefers to purchase at the initial equilibrium price, which is at least ε, to buying at a price below $\varepsilon - \omega$ at time t, so $1 - \varepsilon \geqslant e^{-rt}[1 - (\varepsilon - \omega)]$, or $e^{-rt} \leqslant 1 - \omega/(1 - \varepsilon + \omega)$. This gives an upper bound on the profits attainable by the monopolist:

$$(B.1) \qquad R_n(0) \leqslant \int_0^q P_n(x)\,dx + e^{-rt} R_n(q), \qquad \text{for all} \qquad n \geqslant \bar{n}_2.$$

Choose any integer m. Then for any consumer reservation price function P_n, the monopolist may charge prices $(m - 1)/m, (m - 2)/m, \ldots, 1/m$, respectively, in the first $(m - 1)$ periods. This earns the monopolist within $1/m$ of all "available surplus," within a factor $e^{-(m-2)z}$ of discounting. Hence $R_n(0) \geqslant e^{-r(m-2)z}\{\int_0^1 P_n(x)\,dx - 1/m\}$. Since $z_n \to 0$, there exists $\bar{n}_3(m)$ such that $rz_n \leqslant 1/m^2$ for all $n \geqslant \bar{n}_3(m)$, and so:

$$(B.2) \qquad R_n(0) \geqslant e^{-1/m}\left\{\int_0^1 P_n(x)\,dx - 1/m\right\}, \qquad \text{for all} \qquad n \geqslant \bar{n}_3(m).$$

Since $0 < R(y)/2 < R_n(q)$ for all $n \geqslant \bar{n}_1$, there exists an integer m such that (B.1) and (B.2) are contradictory for $n \geqslant \max\{\bar{n}_1, \bar{n}_2, \bar{n}_3(m)\}$.

Case II: Suppose $R(y) = 0$.

By hypothesis, (P_n, R_n) is a subgame perfect equilibrium for all n. Suppose that, in the initial period, the monopolist chooses to deviate by charging a price of $\varepsilon/2$. This defines a subgame. We will show that, for sufficiently large n, the posited behavior under (P_n, R_n) in this subgame cannot be optimal for both the monopolist and consumers.

Observe that any weak-Markov equilibrium has sales in every period; hence $P_n(0) \geqslant \varepsilon$ for all n. Customer 0 is optimizing when he purchases at price $\varepsilon/2$, so he must believe that the price will not drop rapidly thereafter. In particular, let t_n be the first (real) time in which the price will drop below $\varepsilon/4$. Then $1 - \varepsilon/2 \geqslant e^{-rt_n}[1 - \varepsilon/4]$. Letting $e^{-rt} = (1 - \varepsilon/2)/(1 - \varepsilon/4)$, we have $t_n \leqslant t$ for all n. Thus a price less than or equal to $\varepsilon/4$ is not charged until at least time t.

Recall that y has been defined so that $P(y) \geqslant \varepsilon$. Therefore, there exists a sequence of rationals $y_n \uparrow y$ such that $P_n(y_n) \geqslant \varepsilon/2$ for all n. For arbitrarily chosen $z > 0$, there exists $\bar{n}_1$ such that $z_n < z$ for all $n \geqslant \bar{n}_1$. Since $R(y) = 0$, $R_n \to R$ uniformly, and $y_n \to y$, there also exists $\bar{n}_2$ such that $R_n(y_n) < (1/4)\varepsilon z e^{-rt}$ for all $n \geqslant \bar{n}_2$. Write n for max $\{\bar{n}_1, \bar{n}_2\}$. Meanwhile, let m be the greatest even integer less than t/z. Let $p_1, \ldots, p_m$ denote the first m prices charged by the monopolist along a subgame arising after the monopolist charges an initial price $p_0 = \varepsilon/2$. (When a mixed strategy is called for in period 1, let p_1 be the largest price which the monopolist randomizes over.) Observe that $p_m > \varepsilon/4$. Following Gul-Sonnenschein-Wilson (1986), let $a_i = \varepsilon/2 - (2i/m)[\varepsilon/2 - p_m]$ for $0 \leqslant i \leqslant m/2$. Define an alternative sequence $p_0', \ldots, p_{m/2}'$ by $p_i' = \min\{a_i, p_i\}$ (for $0 \leqslant i \leqslant m/2$). Observe that, by following $p_0', \ldots, p_{m/2}'$, the monopolist "does not lose time" on any sale and loses at most $2(p_0 - p_m)/m$ on each sale. Furthermore, since $R_n(y_n) < (1/4)\varepsilon z e^{-rt}$ and since each sale before time t is at a price greater than $\varepsilon/4$, the total number of customers sold to at $p_1, \ldots, p_m$ is less than z.

Let V_n denote the net present value of profits from following the equilibrium price path $p_1, p_2, p_3, \ldots$ after a price $p_0 = \varepsilon/2$ was charged. Let V_n' denote the value from following $p_1', \ldots, p_{m/2}'$ in the first $m/2$ periods and then continuing optimally. Let V_n'' denote the value to the monopolist of playing optimally, beginning in the period after a price p_m is charged. Then:

$$V_n' - V_n \geqslant [e^{-rt/2} - e^{-rt}]V_n'' - (2/m)(p_0 - p_m)z.$$

We now place a lower bound on V_n''. Observe that, in the period after p_m is charged, customer $1 - (\varepsilon/4L)^{1/\alpha}$ remains in the market, since by the upper bound on f_n: $P_n(1 - (\varepsilon/4L)^{1/\alpha}) \leqslant f_n(1 - (\varepsilon/4L)^{1/\alpha}) \leqslant \varepsilon/4$. Meanwhile, customer $1 - (\varepsilon/4L)^{1/\alpha}/2$ prefers to purchase at a price of $[1 - e^{-rt}]f_n(1 - (\varepsilon/4L)^{1/\alpha}/2)$ this period to purchasing at a price of zero next period. By Definition 5.1, $f_n(1 - (\varepsilon/4L)^{1/\alpha}/2) \geqslant M[1 - (1 - (\varepsilon/4L)^{1/\alpha}/2)]^\alpha = M(\varepsilon/4L)2^{-\alpha}$. Hence, a price of $(M/2^\alpha)(\varepsilon/4L)(1 - e^{-rt})$ induces all customers in the interval $[1 - (\varepsilon/4L)^{1/\alpha}, 1 - (\varepsilon/4L)^{1/\alpha}/2]$ to purchase, so $V_n'' \geqslant [1 - e^{-rt}](M/2^{1+\alpha})(\varepsilon/4L)^{1 + (1/\alpha)}$.

Recall that $(p_0 - p_m) \leqslant \varepsilon/4$ and $m \approx t/z$. Hence, for sufficiently small z (and the implied n):

$$V_n' - V_n \geqslant (e^{-rt/2} - e^{-rt})(1 - e^{-rz})(M/2^{1+\alpha})(\varepsilon/4L)^{1 + (1/\alpha)} - (\varepsilon/3t)z^2$$

$$\geqslant (1 - e^{-rz})\left\{(e^{-rt/2} - e^{-rt})(M/2^{1+\alpha})(\varepsilon/4L)^{1 + (1/\alpha)}\right.$$

$$\left. - (\varepsilon/3t)(z^2/(1 - e^{-rz}))\right\}.$$

Since $\lim_{z \to 0}(z^2/(1 - e^{-rz})) = 0$, $V_n' - V_n > 0$ for sufficiently small choice of z. This contradicts our hypothesis that, for all n, (S_n, P_n) is a subgame perfect equilibrium. $\qquad$ *Q.E.D.*

REFERENCES

AUSUBEL, L., AND R. DENECKERE (1987): "One is Almost Enough for Monopoly," *The Rand Journal of Economics*, 18, 255–274.

———— (1988): "A Generalization of the Theorem of the Maximum," manuscript, Northwestern University.

———— (1989): "A Direct Mechanism Characterization of Sequential Bargaining with One-Sided Incomplete Information," *Journal of Economic Theory*, forthcoming.

BOND, E., AND L. SAMUELSON (1984): "Durable Good Monopolies with Rational Expectations and Replacement Sales," *The Rand Journal of Economics*, 15, 336–345.

BULOW, J. (1982): "Durable Goods Monopolists," *Journal of Political Economy*, 90, 314–332.

COASE, R. (1972): "Durability and Monopoly," *Journal of Law and Economics*, 15, 143–149.

FUDENBERG, D., AND J. TIROLE (1983): "Sequential Bargaining with Incomplete Information," *Review of Economic Studies*, 50, 221–247.

FUDENBERG, D., D. LEVINE, AND J. TIROLE (1985): "Infinite Horizon Models of Bargaining with One-Sided Incomplete Information," in *Game Theoretic Models of Bargaining*, ed. by A. Roth. Cambridge: Cambridge University Press.

GUL, F. (1987): "Foundations of Dynamic Oligopoly," *The Rand Journal of Economics*, 18, 248–254.

GUL, F., H. SONNENSCHEIN, AND R. WILSON (1986): "Foundations of Dynamic Monopoly and the Coase Conjecture," *Journal of Economic Theory*, 39, 155–190.

HELLWIG, M. (1975): "Monopolistic Discrimination Over Time: Remarks on Periodization in Economic Models," Economic Research Program, Research Memorandum No. 174, Princeton University.

KAHN, C. (1986): "The Durable Goods Monopolist and Consistency with Increasing Costs," *Econometrica*, 54, 275–294.

RUBINSTEIN, A. (1982): "Perfect Equilibrium in a Bargaining Model," *Econometrica*, 50, 97–109.

——— (1987): "A Sequential Strategic Theory of Bargaining," in *Advances in Economic Theory*, ed. by T. Bewley. Cambridge: Cambridge University Press.

SOBEL, J., AND I. TAKAHASHI (1983): "A Multi-Stage Model of Bargaining," *Review of Economic Studies*, 50, 411–426.

STOKEY, N. (1981): "Rational Expectations and Durable Goods Pricing," *Bell Journal of Economics*, 12, 112–128.

Review of Economic Studies (1987) LIV, 345-364
© 1987 The Society for Economic Analysis Limited

Strategic Delay in Bargaining

ANAT R. ADMATI
Stanford University

and

MOTTY PERRY
Hebrew University, Jerusalem

First version received April 1986; final version accepted January 1987 (eds.)

This paper analyses a bargaining model with incomplete information in which the time between offers is an endogenous strategic variable. We find equilibria involving a delay to agreement that is due to the use of strategic time delay by bargainers to signal their relative strength. Under some specifications of the parameters, delay is present in the unique sequential equilibrium whose beliefs satisfy one intuitive restriction. This delay does not vanish as the minimal time between offers becomes small.

1. INTRODUCTION

In this paper we analyse a bargaining game with incomplete information where the time between offers is a strategic variable. We find equilibria involving a delay to agreement that is due to the use of time delay to signal a bargainer's strength. This delay does not vanish as the minimal time between offers becomes small.

The large recent literature on bargaining, starting with the seminal work of Rubinstein (1982), has focused on non-cooperative sequential games. In the basic game, players make (alternating) offers sequentially, *one offer per time unit*, until an agreement is reached about how the gains from trade should be divided. Rubinstein (1982) showed that the alternating offers game with complete information has a unique subgame perfect equilibrium. In this equilibrium the first offer is accepted, i.e. agreement is reached within one time period. More recent papers have analysed bargaining games with incomplete information, where at least one of the player's preferences are private information (unknown to the other).[1] These papers show that incomplete information may cause agreement to be delayed. Recently, Gul, Sonnenschein and Wilson (1986) and Gul and Sonnenschein (1985) have shown that for a large class of equilibria, such delay essentially disappears as the time between offers becomes arbitrarily small. In their words, ... "delay to agreement can only be explained by the time between offers" (Gul and Sonnenschein (1985, p. 5)).

In the standard bargaining game, a fixed time between offers is specified exogenously. In real bargaining situations, however, bargainers may employ a number of strategies to affect the length of time between offers. For example, if the bargainers do not face each other throughout the bargaining process (communication takes place by telephone, etc.), then a player can "disappear" for some time or close communication channels when it is his turn to make, receive or respond to an offer. In view of this, it is interesting to see what happens if we relax the assumption that the designated player *must* make or respond to an offer at a specified time. With incomplete information, actions taken to delay making or receiving an offer may then serve as a signalling device, used by bargainers to communicate their relative strength.

In this paper we study a simple variation on the standard alternating offers bargaining model. We capture with this model the idea that endogenous time between offers can be an important strategic variable in bargaining with incomplete information. The game we analyse is similar to the one in Rubinstein (1985), except that each player, when it is his turn to respond to an offer, can delay his response for as long as he wishes (beyond an exogenously fixed minimum time unit). We assume that until an offer has been made by the relevant player, the other player must remain passive and cannot revise previous offers. (This is a strong assumption. See, however, Section 8.5, where we show how it can be relaxed.) We characterize the equilibrium outcomes of the game and show that endogenous time between offers will be used in equilibrium by players to signal their relative strength, which may then cause delay in reaching agreement. This delay does *not* vanish as the minimal time between offers becomes arbitrarily small. We conclude that the suggestion that one-sided incomplete information does not cause delay is sensitive to the assumption that players cannot affect the time between offers. Our results also support the casual observation that, in many bargaining situations, some delay between offers exists, although the technology permits the time between offers to be small.

It is well known that games with incomplete information in which the informed player makes a move (particularly signalling and bargaining games) tend to have many sequential equilibria. We will analyse sequential equilibria of our game that satisfy one additional requirement pertaining to out of equilibrium beliefs. This requirement is in the spirit of the criteria developed by Banks and Sobel (1987), Cho and Kreps (1987), and Cho (1987). (We can replace it by an assumption similar to (B-1) in Rubinstein (1985) without changing the results.) It is important to note, however, that our assumptions are weaker than those used by Rubinstein (1985) to define what he calls a Bargaining Sequential Equilibrium. (In particular, we do not make his assumption (B-2); we permit optimistic beliefs.)

A summary of our main results follows. Suppose the bargainers are a seller, whose valuation of the object that he sells is common knowledge, and a buyer, who may have either a high or a low valuation for the object. Suppose that the seller makes the first offer. If the initial probability that the buyer has the high valuation is sufficiently large, then there exists a unique equilibrium path. On this path, the high valuation buyer accepts an offer that is identical to the perfect equilibrium offer in the complete information game between him and the seller. The low valuation buyer does not accept the seller's first offer, and instead counteroffers the perfect equilibrium offer that he would make in the complete information game between himself and the seller. However, the offer by the low valuation buyer is (typically) delayed strategically, *in order for the buyer to communicate his* (relatively strong) *type to the seller.* In other words, *time delay* acts as a screen.[2]

If the initial probability that the buyer has the high valuation is sufficiently low, then the unique equilibrium path is identical to the perfect equilibrium path in the game where it is common knowledge that the buyer has the low valuation. This occurs because separation is too costly to the seller in this case; in order to extract extra surplus from the high valuation buyer, the seller must run the risk (in these cases considerable) of having a delay to agreement, as the (low valuation) buyer uses delay as a signal. The seller, therefore, prefers to forego the surplus he might get from the high valuation buyer; agreement is reached immediately at terms appropriate for the low valuation buyer. In addition to the two cases mentioned above, there is an intermediate range of parameters, where both of the equilibrium paths described above, as well as some others, are possible. We characterize these equilibria and provide, among other things, conditions and bounds on the possible equilibrium offers and on the length of time before agreement is reached.

Two related contributions should be noted. In the context of games with complete information, McLennan (1986) provides a general analysis of bargaining games with finite horizon in which the time between offers can be endogenous. (In many of his results, however, it is assumed that the time between moves vanishes.) With perfect and complete information, delay to agreement does not arise. Herrero (1986) analyses a model with complete but imperfect information, in which information pertaining to the gains from trade arrives while an offer is outstanding. Because offers remain open for a length of time while information is received, delay to agreement can occur.

The paper is organized as follows. In the next section we describe the model and the equilibrium concept that we use. We also state some preliminary results. Section 3 derives some key results that characterize the potential equilibrium strategies and paths. In Section 4 we discuss the separating equilibrium described above. Conditions under which this equilibrium exists and under which it yields the unique equilibrium paths are derived. A similar analysis is performed in Section 5 with regard to the pooling equilibrium. Section 6 discusses the case where both these equilibria, and some others as well, are possible. In Section 7 it is shown that the time delay may be bounded below even as the minimal time between offers becomes small. Section 8 provides a set of concluding remarks and extenions.

2. MODEL AND PRELIMINARY RESULTS

There are two players, one seller, denoted S, who owns an indivisible object, and one buyer, denoted B. The value of the object to S is commonly known to be s, while its value b to the buyer is the buyer's private information. (In Section 8.3 we comment on the case where both valuations are private information.) Except in Section 8.2, it is assumed that the seller's prior assessment of the value of b is that it is either l (low) or h (high), where $s < l < h$.[3] We use π^0 to denote the seller's prior assessment that $b = h$. (This assessment is common knowledge.) We make the normalization $s = 0$, so that b is the surplus to be divided in the bargaining process. We denote the buyer with low valuation B_l and the buyer with high valuation B_h. Note that B_l is, intuitively, in a stronger bargaining position vis a vis S than is B_h.

The bargaining game starts at time zero, when it is S's turn to make an offer. (The game in which B makes the first offer is discussed in Section 8.1.) Subsequently, players make alternating offers until they reach an agreement, namely a price at which the buyer purchases the object from the seller. A response to an offer involves either an acceptance or a counteroffer, and it is made within no shorter than a given length of time (since the time in which the last offer was made), which we normalize to one. However, the response can be made *at any time later*. The opponent is assumed to remain passive until an acceptance or a counteroffer has been announced—he cannot revise the original offer after it has been made and before the other player has responded. The first offer in the game can be made at any time $t \geq 0$.

We use Δ to denote what we will term *delay*, i.e. the length of the time *above the minimal time of one* at which the relevant player either accepts an existing offer or makes a counteroffer. We allow Δ to be any nonnegative number; Δ is not constrained to be an integer. Since the acceptance of an offer terminates the game, a relevant *history* for the game is a sequence of unacceptable offers and a sequence of times between offers. Formally, if $N \in \{1, 2, \ldots, \infty\}$ is the number of rounds (offers), then a history of the N

rounds is denoted by $H^N = (P^n, \Delta^n)_{n=1}^N$. Note that Δ^N denotes the time delay in round N *beyond* the minimum of one since offer P^{N-1} was made; this history corresponds to the passage of $t = N + \sum_{n=1}^N \Delta^n$ "real" time units.

A *strategy* for a player is a function that specifies for each history after which it is the player's turn to move, the length of the time delay Δ until the player responds, whether the latest offer is accepted (if such an offer exists) and, if not accepted, a counteroffer. We denote the strategies of S, B_l and B_h by σ_s, σ_l, and σ_h, respectively. We consider only pure strategies.

An outcome of the game is a pair (P, t), with the interpretation that, at time t, the buyer pays P to the seller and obtains the object. The players' payoffs in a game whose outcome is (P, t) are $\delta^{t-1}P$ for the seller and $\delta^{t-1}(b - P)$ for the buyer with valuation b. For example, if the first offer of P is made at time zero and it is accepted at time $t = 1$ then the seller obtains a payoff of P and the buyer with valuation b obtains a payoff of $b - P$.[4] With these preferences, B_h is more impatient than is B_l. (Note that, as players are assumed to use pure strategies, for any triple $\sigma = (\sigma_s, \sigma_l, \sigma_h)$ of strategies, there correspond two possible outcomes—one if $b = l$ and the other if $b = h$. Of course, from the seller's point of view the outcome is random.) The preference relations of S, B_l and B_h over pairs (P, t) are extended to lotteries over such pairs by taking the expected value; these preferences are denoted by $>_s$, $>_l$, and $>_h$, respectively.

A simple observation is that, if B's valuation is common knowledge, then our game has a unique subgame perfect equilibrium. (This can be shown using arguments as in Rubinstein (1982). See also Lemma 2.2 below.) Let P_l and P_h denote the perfect equilibrium offers by S in a game of complete information against B_l and B_h, respectively. Then, since $s = 0$,

$$P_l = \frac{l}{1 + \delta}, \quad \text{and} \quad P_h = \frac{h}{1 + \delta}. \tag{2.1}$$

Also from Rubinstein (1982), δP_l (respectively, δP_h) is B_l's (respectively, B_h's) perfect equilibrium offer in the game of complete information.

The equilibrium concept we use is sequential equilibrium. In a sequential equilibrium, one specifies the strategies σ and also the *beliefs* of S (i.e. the probability he assesses to the event $b = h$) for every history H^N. We use $\pi(H^N)$ to denote S's belief at H^N that $b = h$, and we use π to denote the entire system of beliefs. With this, the usual definition of a sequential equilibrium is used; see Kreps and Wilson (1982), or, in the bargaining context, Rubinstein (1985).

The following simple lemma is our first preliminary result. Parts (i)-(vi) can be proved using arguments similar to those in Lemmas 3.1 and 3.2 in Grossman and Perry (1985). Part (vii) is straightforward.

Lemma 2.1. *In any sequential equilibrium:*
  (i) *S never accepts an offer P if $P < \delta P_l$.*
  (ii) *S always accepts an offer P if $P \geq \delta P_h$.*
  (iii) *B never accepts an offer P if $P > P_h$.*
  (iv) *B always accepts an offer P if $P \leq P_l$.*
  (v) *B_h always accepts an offer P if $P \leq \bar{P}$, where $(\bar{P}, 0) \sim_h (\delta P_l, 1)$. (Note that $\bar{P} > P_l$.)*
  (vi) *Let (P', t') be the equilibrium outcome for B_h and (P'', t'') be the equilibrium outcome for B_l. Then $t' \leq t''$ and $P' \geq P''$.*
  (vii) *An acceptance of an offer occurs with no delay, i.e. exactly one time period after the offer is received.*

The set of sequential equilibria for our game is very large. This set includes, in particular, all the sequential equilibria in the game considered in Rubinstein (1985), where the time between offers is fixed. For a partial characterization of these equilibria see Proposition 3 in Rubinstein (1985). As in Rubinstein (1985), a large number of equilibria can be supported by "optimistic beliefs" off the equilibrium path, i.e., any deviation by B is followed by the belief that $b = h$ with probability 1. We will impose two restrictions on our equilibria. The first is a tie breaking assumption that pertains to the strategy choice of the players.

Assumption (A1). If a player can obtain the same payoff by making fewer offers, then he makes fewer offers.

The second restriction we impose pertains to beliefs off the equilibrium path. It is in the spirit of the forward induction equilibrium concept discussed in Cho (1987). Basically, the restriction is that, if possible, the belief should put zero weight on a type for whom the deviation is an "unreasonable" action relative to the equilibrium strategy.

Let $\sigma = (\sigma_s, \sigma_l, \sigma_h)$ be a profile of sequential equilibrium strategies for the players in the game. Consider a history $H^N = (P^n, \Delta^n)_{n=1}^N$ that ends in an offer by S. For $b \in \{h, l\}$, let $U_b^*(\sigma, H^N)$ be B_b's payoff in the continuation game from H^N given strategies σ. Suppose the last offer P^N is rejected by the buyer, and the buyer offers P^{N+1} after delaying the offer for Δ^{N-1}. For $b \in \{h, l\}$, let $\{V_b(\pi, (H^N, P^{N+1}, \Delta^{N+1}))\}$ be the set of sequential equilibrium payoffs of B_b for the continuation game where the seller believes that $b = h$ with probability π. Finally, let $V_b^*(H^N, P^{N+1}, \Delta^{N+1}) \equiv \sup \bigcup_\pi \{V_b(\pi, (H^N, P^{N+1}, \Delta^{N+1}))\}$. That is, $V_b^*(H^N, P^{N+1}, \Delta^{N+1})$ is the best sequential equilibrium outcome for B_b in any continuation game (i.e., for any possible initial beliefs π).

Now fix a history H^N and a sequential equilibrium strategies profile σ. A deviation (P^{N+1}, Δ^{N+1}) is called *bad* for type b if $U_b^*(\sigma, H^N) > V_b^*(H^N, P^{N+1}, \Delta^{N+1})$. Intuitively, a deviation is bad for a type if this type would prefer to play according to σ and obtain the equilibrium payoff rather than to deviate to (P^{N+1}, Δ^{N+1}) and obtain the payoff of some continuation game. We will restrict our attention to sequential equilibria (σ, π) where:

Assumption (A2). Suppose a deviation (P^{N+1}, Δ^{N+1}) is bad for type b' given history H^N and equilibrium strategies σ, and it is not bad for type b. Then the belief after history $H^{N+1} = (H^N, P^{N+1}, \Delta^{N+1})$ puts zero probability on b'.

It is worthwhile noting that, in the context of our bargaining game, the above assumption can be replaced by the following simpler (but somewhat stronger) assumption without changing the results. Suppose that, according to the equilibrium strategies, either (i) at time t, S accepts an offer P made by B, or (ii) at time t, B_h accepts an offer P made by S. Suppose (P', Δ) satisfies $(P, t) >_h (P', t + \Delta + 1)$ and $(P, t) <_l (P', t + \Delta + 1)$. If B offers P' at time $t + \Delta$, then the belief of S upon getting this offer must be that $b = l$ with probability one, i.e. $\pi = 0$. (This assumption, which is in the spirit of assumption (B-1) in Rubinstein (1985), compares the equilibrium payoff with that obtained if the "deviant" offer is accepted rather than with the best continuation game payoff.) We also note that our restriction is stronger than that in Cho (1987), in that in the definition of a bad deviation, Cho compares the equilibrium payoff to a larger set of possible continuation payoffs than the set of sequential equilibrium continuation payoffs.

For the rest of the paper, the term equilibrium refers to a sequential equilibrium that satisfies (A1) and (A2).

We close this section with a very useful result, which also indicates the power of Assumption (A2) in our model.

Lemma 2.2.   *Consider a history H^N which ends with an offer of P by B. Then in any equilibrium,*
   (i) *If $\pi(H^N) = 0$, then S accepts P if and only if $P \geq \delta P_l$.*
   (ii) *If $\pi(H^N) = 1$, then S accepts P if and only if $P \geq \delta P_h$.*

Remark.   In many analyses of bargaining with incomplete information, e.g. Bikhchandani (1985), Grossman and Perry (1985), and Rubinstein (1985), it is assumed that if, after some history, the beliefs put zero probability on a type of player, then the beliefs do not put positive probability on that type ever after. This assumption, which is not a requirement of a sequential equilibrium, facilitates, among other things, the application of the analysis of the complete information game in the context of the game with incomplete information. Lemma 2.2 shows that assumption (A2) accomplishes this task in our model, by providing the means by which the results of the complete information game can be applied. In fact, the requirement that beliefs stay fixed at zero once they become zero is inconsistent with assumption (A2), which suggests that it may be an undesirable restriction on beliefs.

Proof.   Let (σ, π) be an equilibrium. The "only if" part of (i) follows immediately from Lemma 2.1(i). To prove the "if" part, it is sufficient to show that under the conditions of the lemma, according to σ, the best outcome for S in the continuation game if S does not accept P, is P_l. Define $\hat{P} \equiv \sup\{P | \text{after some history } H^N \text{ which ends with an offer by } B \text{ which is not accepted by } S \text{ and such that } \pi(H^N) = 0, \text{ there exists an equilibrium continuation whose outcome if } b = l \text{ is } (P, t) \text{ for some } t\}$. Assume by way of contradiction that $\hat{P} > P_l$. Then there exists a continuation game after history H^N as in Part (i), whose outcome if $b = l$, according to σ, is (P', t') and $P' > P_l$. Suppose that, in this equilibrium, S made the last offer P' at time $t' - 1$. (The case where B makes the last offer is similar.) Since $h > l$ and $\hat{P} > P_l$, we can take P' close enough to $\hat{P}$ so that there exists P'' which satisfies

$$(P'', 1) >_l (P', 0), \tag{2.2}$$

$$(P'', 1) <_h (P', 0), \tag{2.3}$$

and

$$(P'', 0) >_s (\hat{P}, 1). \tag{2.4}$$

Now suppose that, instead of accepting P' at time t', B_l counteroffers P'' at time t'. Using assumption (A2), S's beliefs after such a deviation must put zero weight on the event $b = h$. Moreover, it must be that, according to σ, S does not accept the offer of P'', otherwise B_l would prefer to make it. From equation (2.4) it follows that for S to reject P'' there must be an equilibrium outcome (P, t) when $b = l$ where $P > \hat{P}$, contradicting the definition of $\hat{P}$.

The "if" part of (ii) follows from Lemma 2.1(ii). The proof of the "only if" part involves an argument similar to the above, but it does not require the application of assumption (A2). ‖

3. CHARACTERIZATION RESULTS

In this section we develop some necessary conditions for the set of possible equilibrium strategies and outcomes. These conditions are independent of the initial probability π^0.

Most importantly, we show that the equilibrium outcome for B_l, the stronger type of buyer, must involve the perfect equilibrium offers made in the complete information game between S and B_l. We also show that at most two offers are made in every equilibrium. The length of the delay until agreement is reached between S and B_l depends on the equilibrium strategies of S and B_h—unless S offers P_l, B_l does not accept his offer and delays making the counteroffer long enough to separate himself from B_h, thereby convincing S to accept δP_l.

The following definition is useful.

Definition. For a given offer P, let $\Gamma^*(P)$ be the solution to the equation

$$(P, 0) \sim_h (\delta P_l, \Gamma^*(P)). \tag{3.1}$$

That is, B_h is indifferent between paying P at time zero and paying δP_l at time $\Gamma^*(P)$. As we show below, separation between B_l and B_h takes the form of time delay. If in equilibrium B_h pays P and B_l pays δP_l, then B_l's settlement must occur at least $\Gamma^*(P)$ time units after B_h's settlement in order to prevent B_h from imitating B_l. Note that $\Gamma^*(P)$ is increasing in P. Also, $\Gamma^*(\bar{P}) = 1$, where $\bar{P}$ was defined in Lemma 2.1 Part (v). Thus, $\Gamma^*(\bar{P}) \geq 1$ if and only if $P \geq \bar{P}$.

We now state the main characterization result of this section, which is proved by a series of lemmas.

Proposition 3.1. *Suppose along an equilibrium path the first offer by S, which is made at time t, is P. Then,*

(i) $P \geq P_l$.

(ii) *If $P = P_l$, then the equilibrium outcome is $(P_l, 1)$ whether $b = h$ or $b = l$.*

(iii) *If $P > P_l$, then*

    (iiia) *If B_h accepts P, then along the equilibrium path B_l offers δP_l at time $t' = \max\{t+1, t+\Gamma^*(P)\}$, which S accepts.*

    (iiib) *If B_h does not accept P, then along the equilibrium path B_h offers δP_h at time $t+1$, which S accepts, and B_l offers δP_l at time $t+1+\Gamma^*(\delta P_h)$, which S accepts.*

Parts (i) and (ii) follow immediately from Lemma 2.1. Part (ii) describes the only possible pooling equilibrium, in which S offers P_l at time zero, and both types of buyer accept. (Clearly, if S's first offer is P_l, then he must offer it at time zero, since, by Lemma 2.1, this offer is accepted with probability one.) Part (iii), which discusses the possible separating equilibrium outcomes, is proved in the rest of the section.

To analyse the separating equilibria, the following definition is useful.

Definition. For an offer P^0, let $F(P^0)$ be the set of pairs (P, Γ) such that

(i) $(P^0, 0) >_h (P, \Gamma)$,

(ii) $(P^0, 0) <_l (P, \Gamma)$,

and

(iii) $P \geq \delta P_l$.

To interpret $F(P^0)$, suppose S offers $P^0 > \bar{P}$ at time t^0, and let $(P, \Gamma) \in F(P^0)$ be such that $\Gamma \geq 1$. Now assume that B counteroffers P at time $t^0 + \Gamma$. Then, assuming S accepts the counteroffer, B_h strictly prefers to accept P^0 rather than to make this counteroffer. The reverse is true for B_l. Moreover, if upon receiving the counteroffer S believes that it is made by B_l with probability one, then (by Lemma 2.2) he accepts it. The set $F(P^0)$, therefore, represents a potential "no imitation" region. The graphical representation is given in Figure 1 below; the indifference curves of B_h and B_l that pass through (P^0, t^0) are shown, which delimit the set $F(P^0)$. Simple algebra shows that the indifference curve of B_h is steeper than that of B_l, and so these curves intersect just at (P^0, t^0).

The next lemma, which can easily be seen in Figure 1, shows that the most efficient way for B_l to distinguish himself is by waiting just long enough so that he can make the lowest potentially acceptable offer δP_l.

Lemma 3.1. $(\delta P_l, \Gamma^*(P^0)) >_l (P, \Gamma)$ *for every* $(P, \Gamma) \in F(P^0)$.

Proof. Assume first that $(\delta P_l, \Gamma) \in F(P^0)$, but $\Gamma \neq \Gamma^*(P^0)$. Then from the definition of $F(P^0)$, $\Gamma > \Gamma^*(P^0)$. It is easy to see that for $\Gamma' = 0 \cdot 5(\Gamma + \Gamma^*(P^0))$, we have $(\delta P_l, \Gamma') \in F(P^0)$ and $(\delta P_l, \Gamma') >_l (\delta P_l, \Gamma)$. Next assume that $P > \delta P_l$ and $(P, \Gamma) \in F(P^0)$. Let Γ' be such that $(P, \Gamma) \sim_h (\delta P_l, \Gamma')$. Since $h > l$, it follows that $(\delta P_l, \Gamma') \in F(P^0)$, and $(\delta P_l, \Gamma') >_l (P, \Gamma)$. ‖

The following lemma is central to our analysis.

Lemma 3.2.   *In any equilibrium, the following hold:*
(i) *Suppose it is B's turn to move, and B_h offers $P^0 > \delta P_l$ at time t^0, which S accepts. Then, B_l offers δP_l at time $t^0 + \Gamma^*(P^0)$, which S accepts. Moreover, no other offers are made by B_l.*

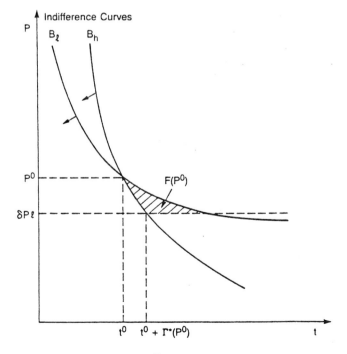

FIGURE 1

(ii) *Suppose it is S's turn to move. If B_h accepts an offer $P^0 > P_l$, which is made at time t^0, then B_l does not accept, and B_l counteroffers δP_l at time $t = \max \{t^0 + 1, t^0 + \Gamma^*(P^0)\}$, which S accepts. Moreover, no other offers are made by B_l.*

Proof. We first prove Part (i). Suppose B_h offers P^0 at time t^0, which S accepts (at time $t^0 + 1$), and suppose that the equilibrium outcome if $b = l$ is (P, t). Let $\Gamma = t - (t^0 + 1)$. Then we must have $(P, \Gamma) \in \text{Closure}(F(P^0))$. To see this, suppose $(P, \Gamma) \notin \text{Closure}(F(P^0))$. Then either $(P, t) >_h (P^0, t^0 + 1)$, contradicting the fact that $(P^0; t^0 + 1)$ is the equilibrium outcome if $b = h$, or $(P, t) >_l (P^0, t^0 + 1)$, contradicting the fact that (P, t) is the equilibrium outcome if $b = l$. (See Figure 1.) Next assume, by way of contradiction, that $(P, \Gamma) \neq (\delta P_l, \Gamma^*(P^0))$. Then by Lemma 3.1 and the continuity of the preferences, there exists $(P', \Gamma') \in F(P^0)$ such that $(P', \Gamma') >_l (P, \Gamma)$ and such that making an offer P' at time $t^0 + \Gamma'$ is a bad deviation for B_h but not for B_l. Thus, from (A2), S should, upon obtaining this offer, assess that $b = l$ with probability one. By Lemma 2.2, S should accept the offer. This contradiction, together with assumption (A1), completes the proof.

The proof of Part (ii) is similar. However, in this case B_l cannot make his offer before one time unit has elapsed. If $P^0 < \bar{P}$, then $\Gamma^*(P^0) < 1$. In this case, if B_h accepts an offer of P^0 made at time t^0, then B_l offers δP_l at time $t^0 + 1$, which S accepts. For $P^0 \geq \bar{P}$, the counteroffer of B_l is made at time $t^0 + \Gamma^*(P^0) - 1$. ‖

The above lemma proves Part (iiia) of Proposition 3.1. It also implies that in any equilibrium, if B_l makes an offer P that S accepts, then $P = \delta P_l$, and if S makes an offer P that B_l accepts, then $P = P_l$. In other words, the equilibrium outcome if $b = l$ must involve the perfect equilibrium offers in the complete information game. The lemma also specifies the length of the strategic delay necessary for separation relative to the time at which agreement is reached between S and B_h. As for the equilibrium outcome when $b = h$, Lemma 3.2 implies that, if in equilibrium B_h makes an offer P that S accepts, then $P \in \{\delta P_l, \delta P_h\}$, as any offer by B that is not δP_l reveals that it is made by B_h. The next two lemmas are concerned with the set of possible equilibrium paths.

Lemma 3.3. *If, along an equilibrium path, S's first offer is $P \neq P_l$, then the equilibrium outcome must be different for B_l and B_h.*

Proof. From Part (i) of Proposition 3.1, S's first offer P must satisfy $P \geq P_l$. Now, if $P > P_l$ and the equilibrium outcome is the same for B_l and B_h, then, by Lemma 3.2, this outcome must involve δP_l at some time $t \geq 2$. But in this case S would prefer to offer P_l at time zero. ‖

Lemma 3.4. *If, along an equilibrium path, B_h does not accept S's first offer, which is made at time t, then along the path B_h offers δP_h at time $t + 1$, which S accepts.*

Proof. If, along the equilibrium path, B_h rejects S's offer of P, then it must be that $P > P_l$. Thus, by Lemma 3.3, the equilibrium outcome is different for B_l and B_h. Moreover, by Lemma 3.2, B_l counteroffers δP_l at some time t', which S accepts. Since, by the above, B_h does not also offer δP_l at the same time t', B_h's next offer must reveal his type. It follows from Lemma 2.2 that B_h cannot do better than offering δP_h with no delay. ‖

Since Part (iiib) of Proposition 3.1 follows from Lemma 3.4, the proof of the proposition is now complete.

Proposition 3.1 greatly restricts the set of potential equilibrium paths, but does not pin it down precisely. While the set of possible equilibrium paths can be restricted still further (see Lemma 4.2), the form and number of equilibria generally depend on the value of π^0. In the following sections we show that an equilibrium always exists, and that it is unique in two of three subsets of values of π^0. Specifically, the next section focuses on a particular separating equilibrium. Section 5 focuses on the pooling equilibrium. We establish that the separating equilibrium exists for a range of initial conditions $\pi^0 \in [\pi^*, 1]$ (π^* will be defined shortly), and that it yields the unique equilibrium outcome if $\pi^0 \in (l/h, 1]$, where $\pi^* < l/h$. The pooling equilibrium exists if $\pi^0 \in [0, l/h]$, and it yields the unique equilibrium outcome if $\pi^0 \in [0, \pi^*)$. If $\pi^0 \in [\pi^*, l/h]$, then both equilibria, as well as others, exist. This case is discussed in Section 6.

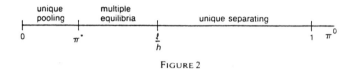

FIGURE 2

4. EXISTENCE AND UNIQUENESS OF THE SEPARATING EQUILIBRIUM

In this section, we focus on a separating equilibrium that takes the following form. S offers P_h at time zero, which B_h accepts at time $t = 1$. B_l counteroffers δP_l at time $\Gamma^*(P_h)$, which S accepts. (Note that $\Gamma^*(P_h) > 1$, since $P_h > \bar{P}$.) In this equilibrium, the path if $b = h$ is identical to that in the perfect equilibrium of the complete information game between S and B_h (in which S makes the first offer). Thus, the relatively weak buyer B_h does not benefit from the incomplete information; he pays exactly what he would if his type was known. The outcome if $b = l$ is that B_l does not accept S's offer, and makes the perfect equilibrium offer in the complete information game between S and B_l. This offer, however, is delayed by $\Gamma^*(P_h)$ in order for B_l to separate himself from B_h.

For the rest of the paper, it is useful to define the following function.

$$W(P; \pi) \equiv \pi P + (1 - \pi)\delta^{\Gamma^*(P)}\delta P_l. \tag{4.1}$$

To interpret $W(P; \pi)$, recall first from Lemma 2.1 (Part (v)), that $\bar{P} \equiv h - \delta(h - \delta P_l)$ is an offer that is accepted by B_h in any equilibrium. Suppose S's prior belief is that $b = h$ with probability π, and that S offers $P \in [\bar{P}, P_h]$ at time zero, which B_h accepts at time $t = 1$. Then from Proposition 3.1, $W(P; \pi)$ is the expected payoff of S. Note that if S offers $P \in (P_l, \bar{P})$ at time zero, which B_h accepts at time $t = 1$, then from Proposition 3.1, B_l counteroffers δP_l at time $t = 1$. In this case S's payoff is

$$\hat{W}(P; \pi) \equiv \pi P + (1 - \pi)\delta^2 P_l \tag{4.2}$$

The following lemma provides some properties of the functions $W(P; \pi)$ and $\hat{W}(P; \pi)$.

Lemma 4.1.
  (i) For $P > P_l$, $W(P; \pi)$ is a linear function of P, and it is strictly increasing in P if and only if $\pi > \delta P_l/h = \delta l/h(1+\delta)$.
  (ii) For every π, $W(\bar{P}; \pi) = \hat{W}(\bar{P}; \pi)$, and for $P_l < P < \bar{P}$, $\hat{W}(P; \pi) < W(P; \pi)$.

Proof. Using the definition of $\Gamma^*(P)$ (equation (3.1)), we can rewrite $W(P; \pi)$ as

$$W(P; \pi) = \pi P + (1 - \pi)\frac{(h - P)}{(h - \delta P_l)}\delta P_l. \tag{4.3}$$

Part (i) is immediate. For (ii), we use the definition of $\bar{P}$ and rearrange. ‖

Lemma 4.1 can be used to sharpen the characterization of the possible equilibrium paths provided in Proposition 3.1. The next result shows, in particular, that the first offer of S in any equilibrium is either P_l or it is not smaller than $\bar{P}$. Thus, if S's first offer of P, which is made at time t, is accepted by B_h and $P > P_l$, then along the equilibrium path B_l offers δP_l at time $t + \Gamma^*(P) \geq t + 1$, which S accepts.

Lemma 4.2. *Suppose the equilibrium outcome if $b = h$ is (P', t) where $P' > P_l$. Then $P' \geq \bar{P}$. Moreover, S's payoff in this equilibrium is $\delta^{t-1}W(P'; \pi^0)$.*

Proof. From Lemmas 2.1 and 3.2 it follows that S's equilibrium payoff is bounded below by $\max\{P_l, W(\bar{P}; \pi^0)\}$. Under the assumption of the proposition, it must be that $W(\bar{P}, \pi^0) > P_l$. Thus, from Lemma 4.1, $W(P; \pi^0)$ is strictly increasing in P. Moreover, for every $P \in [P_l, \bar{P}]$, $\hat{W}(P; \pi^0) \leq W(\bar{P}; \pi^0)$. Thus, offering $P < \bar{P}$ at any time is dominated for S by offering $\bar{P}$ at time zero. The rest follows from Proposition 3.1 and the definition of $W(P; \pi)$. ‖

Simple algebra shows that $W(P_h; \pi) < P_l$ if and only if $\pi < \pi^*$, where

$$\pi^* = \frac{l}{h}\left(\frac{h + \delta(h - l) - h\delta^2}{h + \delta(h - l) - l\delta^2}\right). \tag{4.4}$$

We are now ready to analyse the separating equilibrium.

Proposition 4.1. *If $\pi^0 \geq \pi^*$ then there exists an equilibrium in which S offers P_h at time zero, B_h accepts, and B_l counteroffers δP_l at time $\Gamma^*(P_h)$, which S accepts. If $\pi^0 < \pi^*$ then such an equilibrium does not exist.*

Proof. Suppose first that $\pi^0 < \pi^*$. Then $W(P_h; \pi^0) \leq P_l$. Offering P_h at time zero cannot be an equilibrium strategy of S, since S strictly prefers to offer P_l, which (by Lemma 2.1) will be accepted with probability one.

Now suppose $\pi^0 \geq \pi^*$. Then the following is an equilibrium.

- *S's beliefs*: Suppose in response to the last offer of P by S, B offered P' after an additional delay (beyond one) of Δ. (i) Suppose $P \leq P_h$. If $(P, 0) \geq_h (P', 1 + \Delta)$ then $\pi = 0$. Otherwise $\pi = 1$. (ii) Suppose $P > P_h$. If $(\delta P_h, 0) \geq_h (P', \Delta)$, then $\pi = 0$. Otherwise, $\pi = 1$.
- *S's strategy*: Offer P_h at time zero. If in response to an offer P of S, B makes a counteroffer P' after an additional delay of Δ, and S's belief at this node is that $b = h$ with probability π, then:
  - (i) If $\pi = 1$, then accept P if $P \geq \delta P_h$, otherwise counteroffer P_h with no delay ($\Delta = 0$).
  - (ii) If $\pi = 0$, then accept P if $P \geq \delta P_l$, otherwise counteroffer P_l with no delay ($\Delta = 0$).
- *B_h's strategy*: At any point, if S makes an offer P, accept if $P \leq P_h$; otherwise, counteroffer δP_h with no delay ($\Delta = 0$).

- B_l's strategy: At any point, if S offers P, accept if $P \leqq P_l$; otherwise, (i) If $P_h \geqq P > P_l$, counteroffer δP_l after an additional delay of $\Delta = \max \{0, \Gamma^*(P) - 1\}$; (ii) If $P > P_h$ counteroffer δP_l after a delay of $\Delta = \Gamma^*(\delta P_h) = \Gamma^*(P_h) - 1$.

To verify this equilibrium note first that S would not offer $P > P_h$, since given B's strategy this leads to a lower payoff than would offering P_h. Since $\pi^0 \geqq \pi^* > \delta l / h (1 + \delta)$, $W(P; \pi^0)$ is increasing in P, and $W(P_h; \pi^0) > P_l$. Thus, from Lemma 4.1, offering P_h is optimal for S. The rest of the verification is straightforward. Note that the beliefs above satisfy (A2); whenever a deviation is bad for B_h, $\pi = 0$. ∥

By Lemmas 2.1 and 3.2, the seller can guarantee himself an expected payoff of $W(\bar{P}; \pi^0)$ by offering $\bar{P}$ at time zero. On the other hand, by offering P_l at time zero, the seller can obtain a payoff of P_l. The comparison between $W(\bar{P}; \pi^0)$ and P_l is key in determining the uniqueness of the separating equilibrium.

It is easy to verify that $W(\bar{P}; \pi^0) > P_l$ if and only if $\pi^0 > l / h > \pi^*$. Thus, from Lemma 4.1 and Proposition 4.1, if $W(\bar{P}; \pi^0) > P_l$, then (i) $W(P; \pi^0)$ is increasing in P, and (ii) the separating equilibrium of Proposition 4.1 exists. The rest of this section is devoted to showing that if $\pi^0 > l / h$, then the equilibrium of Proposition 4.1 yields the unique equilibrium path. We start by showing that if $\pi^0 > l / h$, then there cannot be a pooling equilibrium.

Lemma 4.3. *Suppose $\pi^0 > l / h$. Then along any equilibrium path*
(i) *If S makes an offer P which B_h accepts, then $P > P_l$.*
(ii) *If B_h makes an offer P which S accepts, then $P > \delta P_l$.*

Proof. To prove Part (i) suppose, by way of contradiction, that along an equilibrium path S offers P_l and B_h accepts this offer. Consider the deviation by S of offering $\bar{P}$ instead. From Lemma 2.1, B_h would accept $\bar{P}$; from Lemma 3.2, B_l would counteroffer δP_l with no delay (since $\Gamma^*(\bar{P}) = 1$), which S accepts. Since $W(\bar{P}; \pi^0) > P_l$, S obtains a higher payoff than he gets from offering P_l. Part (ii) is proved similarly. ∥

Next we show that if $\pi^0 > l / h$ then the equilibrium outcome if $b = h$ must involve the perfect equilibrium offers in the complete information game between S and B_h.

Lemma 4.4. *Suppose $\pi^0 > l / h$. Then along any equilibrium path,*
(i) *If B_h makes an offer P which S accepts then $P = \delta P_h$.*
(ii) *If S makes an offer P which B_h accepts, then $P = P_h$.*

Proof. Recall that by Proposition 3.1, the outcome of the game if $b = l$ must involve either P_l or δP_l, depending on who makes the last offer. Lemma 4.3 implies that if $\pi^0 > l / h$, then any equilibrium outcome must be different for B_h and B_l. Applying again Proposition 3.1, this proves Part (i).

To prove Part (ii), let $\hat{P} = \inf \{P | \text{there exists an equilibrium in which } B_h \text{ accepts an offer } P \text{ by } S, \text{ and } S\text{'s initial belief is } \pi^0 > l / h\}$. From Lemmas 4.2 and 4.3, we must have $\hat{P} \geqq \bar{P}$. Suppose, by way of contradiction, that $\hat{P} < P_h$. Let $\check{P} = \min \{P_h, \alpha\}$, where $(\alpha, 0) \sim_h (\hat{P}, 2)$. Note that $\check{P} > \hat{P}$. From the definition of $\hat{P}$, there exists $P' < \check{P} \leqq P_h$, and an equilibrium (σ, π), such that in this equilibrium S offers P' at some time t' and B_h accepts.

We claim that according to σ_h, B_h never accepts any offer $P > P'$ made at time t' or earlier. If B_h accepted an offer $P > P'$, then, by Lemmas 3.2 and 4.2, S gets a payoff of at least $\delta' W(P; \pi^0)$ instead of $\delta' W(P'; \pi^0)$. Since for $\pi^0 > l/h$, $W(P; \pi^0)$ is strictly increasing in P, S would then prefer to offer P rather than P'. In particular, for every $\varepsilon > 0$, B_h rejects $P' + \varepsilon$ (according to σ_h). Let ε be small so that $P' + \varepsilon < P_h$, and consider the continuation game after B_h rejects the offer $P' + \varepsilon$ made by S at time zero. Denote the outcome of this game if $b = h$ and players use (continuation) strategies σ by (P'', t''). Since $P' + \varepsilon < P_h$, it follows that $P'' < \delta P_h$. Thus, from Part (i), the game cannot end with an offer from B_h that S accepts. In particular, it must be that B's first counteroffer is rejected by S and that S's beliefs if $b = h$ after the counteroffer is made are $\pi^1 > l/h$. Therefore, P'' is an offer that is accepted by B_h in an equilibrium in which S's initial beliefs are $\pi^0 > l/h$. Now, because at least two more offers must be made, we have $t'' \geq 3$. Since the equilibrium outcome must be preferred by B_h to accepting $P' + \varepsilon$ at time 1, it must be that

$$(P' + \varepsilon, 0) <_h (P'', 2).$$

Since $P' < \check{P} \leq \alpha$, for ε small enough,

$$(P' + \varepsilon, 0) >_h (\alpha, 0) \sim_h (\hat{P}, 2).$$

It follows that for ε small enough,

$$(P'', 2) >_h (P' + \varepsilon, 0) >_h (\hat{P}, 2).$$

This implies $P'' < \hat{P}$. But this is a contradiction to the definition of $\hat{P}$. ‖

To summarize, we have

Proposition 4.2. *If $\pi^0 > l/h$, then the unique equilibrium path is that S offers P_h at time zero, B_h accepts, and B_l counteroffers δP_l at time $\Gamma^*(P_h)$, which S accepts.*

Proof. From Lemma 4.4, the best outcome that B_h can obtain in equilibrium is $(P_h, 1)$. This implies that in equilibrium B_h cannot reject an offer $P \leq P_h$ at any time. From Lemma 3.2 and the assumption that $\pi^0 > l/h$, the highest payoff S can obtain is $W(P_h; \pi^0)$. Moreover, this payoff can be obtained if S offers P_h at time zero. Thus, the proposed path is the only candidate for an equilibrium path. The existence of an equilibrium that supports this path was established in Proposition 4.1. ‖

5. EXISTENCE AND UNIQUENESS OF THE POOLING EQUILIBRIUM

In this section we analyse the pooling equilibrium, in which S offers P_l and both types of buyer accept. As in the previous section, we first discuss the existence and then the uniqueness of the pooling equilibrium outcome.

Proposition 5.1. *If $\pi^0 \leq l/h$ then there exists an equilibrium in which S offers P_l and both types accept. If $\pi^0 > l/h$ then such an equilibrium does not exist.*

Proof. If $\pi^0 > l/h$ then, by Proposition 4.2, there is no pooling equilibrium. Suppose $\pi^0 \leq l/h$. Then the following describes an equilibrium assessment that gives rise to the proposed equilibrium path:

- *S's beliefs*: Suppose in response to the latest offer of P by S, B offered P' after a delay of Δ. (i) Suppose $P \leq P_h$. If $(P, 0) \geq_h (P', \Delta)$ then $\pi = 0$. Otherwise, $\pi = \pi^0$. (ii) Suppose $P > P_h$. If $(\delta P_h, 1) \geq_h (P', \Delta)$, then $\pi = 0$. Otherwise, $\pi = \pi^0$.
- *S's strategy*: Offer P_l at time zero. If in response to S's offer of P, B made a counteroffer P' after an additional delay of Δ, and the belief of S at this node put probability π on the event $b = h$, then accept the offer if $P' \geq \delta P_l$; otherwise, counteroffer P_l with no delay ($\Delta = 0$).
- B_h's strategy: Accept P if $P \leq \bar{P}$; otherwise, counteroffer δP_l with no delay ($\Delta = 0$).
- B_l's strategy: Accept P if $P \leq P_l$; otherwise, counteroffer δP_l with no delay ($\Delta = 0$).

Note that in the above, B_h does not accept any offer higher than $\bar{P}$. It is easy to see that, given the strategies of B_l and B_h, and S's prior beliefs, the best response of S is to offer P_l at time zero, which would be accepted. This follows since $W(\bar{P}; \pi^0)$, which is strictly smaller than P_l, is (by Lemmas 4.1 and 4.2) the highest payoff S can obtain by making any other offer. The optimality of B's strategies is obvious. ‖

Consider now the case $\pi^0 < \pi^*$, i.e. $W(P_h; \pi^0) < P_l$. The next proposition shows that no separating equilibria exist in this case. It follows that the only candidate for equilibrium in this range of parameters is the pooling equilibrium described above.

Proposition 5.2. *If $\pi^0 < \pi^*$, then the unique equilibrium path is that S offers P_l at time zero and both types accept.*

Proof. By Proposition 3.1 and Lemma 4.2, if in equilibrium B_h accepts an offer $P > P_l$, then S's payoff is bounded above by $W(P; \pi^0)$. Under the assumed condition, $W(P_h; \pi^0) < P_l$. Thus, S's payoff if his offer in equilibrium is different from P_l and it is accepted by B_h is strictly smaller than P_l. If the game ends with an offer by B_h that is accepted by S, then S's payoff is bounded above by $\delta \max \{\delta P_l, W(\delta P_h; \pi^0)\} < P_l$. The result follows from the fact that S can guarantee himself P_l by offering P_l at time zero. ‖

6. THE INTERMEDIATE PARAMETERS

We now discuss the case $\pi^0 \in [\pi^*, l/h]$, i.e. $W(\bar{P}; \pi^0) \leq P_l \leq W(P_h; \pi^0)$. It was proved above that there are at least two equilibrium paths in this case, as both Propositions 4.1 and 5.1 apply. Note that S prefers the separating equilibrium outcome to the pooling equilibrium outcome, while the reverse is true for B. It is not surprising, therefore, that when both equilibria exist, other equilibrium paths can also be supported. These additional equilibria are characterized below.

We know that, since S makes the first offer, his payoff in any equilibrium is bounded below by P_l. The following set characterizes the potential equilibrium outcomes of the game if $b = h$. For a given prior probability π, let

$$G(\pi) \equiv \{(P, t) \mid P \in [\bar{P}, P_h], t \geq 1, \text{ and } \delta^{t-1} W(P; \pi) \geq P_l\}. \tag{6.1}$$

Let $(P, t) \in G(\pi^0)$ and suppose S offers P at time $t - 1$ and B_h accepts (at time t). We know that, since $P \geq \bar{P} > P_l$, B_l counteroffers δP_l at time $t - 1 + \Gamma^*(P)$, which S accepts. (Note also that if $(P, t) \in G(\pi)$ than $\Gamma^*(P) \geq 1$.) Thus, S's expected payoff if he believes that $b = h$ with probability π^0 is $\delta^{t-1} W(P; \pi^0)$, which is at least as large as his payoff in the pooling equilibrium, namely P_l. It turns out that if $(P, t) \in G(\pi^0)$ then there exists an equilibrium whose outcome is (P, t) if $b = h$, in which B_h accepts the offer of P made by S at time $t - 1$. Note that the larger is π, the larger is the set $G(\pi)$. For example, for every $P \in [\bar{P}, P_h]$, $(P, 1) \in G(l/h)$, while $G(\pi^*) = \{(P_h, 1)\}$. In the latter case, if in equilibrium S offers P at time $t - 1$ and B_h accepts at time t, then it must be that $P \in \{P_l, P_h\}$ and $t = 1$. (This follows since $\delta^{t-1} W(P; \pi^0) < P_l$ for every $P < P_h$ and $t \geqq 1$.)

To see how additional equilibrium outcomes are supported, and to gain intuition, take some $(P', t') \in G(\pi^0)$, and suppose each player's strategy after S has made the first offer is as follows: If S's first offer is $P \leqq P'$, and it is made at time $t \geqq t' - 1$, then use the separating equilibrium strategy in the proof of Proposition 4.1 (with B_h accepting the initial offer of P). Otherwise, use the pooling equilibrium strategy described in the proof of Proposition 5.1. That is, S's first offer determines which equilibrium is played.[5] In this case, a best response of S is to offer P' at time $t' - 1$, which B_h accepts, B_l rejects, and counteroffers δP_l at time $t' - 1 + \Gamma^*(P')$, which S accepts. The reader can verify that this can indeed be supported as an equilibrium. Note that this equilibrium has the same form as the separating equilibrium of Section 4, except that the first offer by S may be lower than P_h. Still, S prefers this outcome to that of the pooling equilibrium. The reason that B_h can pay less than the highest offer P_h in a separating equilibrium is, intuitively, that the "threat" to use the pooling equilibrium strategy if S's first offer is "too high" is credible in this range of parameters.

In all the equilibria discussed so far, B_h accepts the seller's first offer. However, for π^0 in the intermediate range, this need not be true. Suppose there exists $(\delta P_h, t') \in G(\pi^0)$, with $t' \geqq 2$. Let the players' strategies after S made his first offer be as follows. If S's first offer is $P \leqq P_h$, or it is made at time $t \leqq t' - 2$, then use the pooling equilibrium strategies of Proposition 5.1. Otherwise, use the separating equilibrium strategies of Proposition 4.1. In this case, a best response of S's is to offer $P > P_h$ at time $t' - 2$. The equilibrium path in this case is that S's first offer is not accepted by B, and then B_h counteroffers δP_h at time $t' - 1$, and B_l counteroffers δP_l at time $t' - 1 + \Gamma^*(\delta P_h)$, and in both cases S accepts the offer. One might describe this equilibrium as follows. If the seller makes a sufficiently high initial offer, the buyers are "scared" into playing the separating equilibrium; B_h, in particular, makes the high counteroffer of δP_h with no delay. But if the initial offer by S is "weak", then the buyer insists on the pooling equilibrium, where the seller accepts the low offer of δP_l. The seller, given this choice, begins with a sufficiently high offer.

The above discussion, together with Proposition 3.1 yields the following characterization result.

Proposition 6.2. *If $\pi^* \leqq \pi^0 \leqq l/h$, then every equilibrium path is given by one of the following:*

(i) *S offers P_l at time zero and both types accept;*

(ii) *For some $(P', t') \in G(\pi^0)$, S makes his first offer of P' at time $t' - 1$, B_h accepts and B_l counteroffers δP_l at time $t + \Gamma^*(P')$, which S accepts;*

(iii) *For some $P' > P_h$, and $t' \geqq 2$ such that $(\delta P_h, t') \in G(\pi^0)$, S offers P' time $t' - 2$, B_h counteroffers δP_h at time $t' - 1$, which S accepts, and B_l counteroffers δP_l at time $t' - 1 + \Gamma^*(\delta P_h)$, which S accepts.*

7. LETTING THE MINIMAL TIME BETWEEN OFFERS BECOME SMALL

We now show that when equilibrium involves delay (i.e. when more than one offer is made in equilibrium), then this delay does not vanish as the minimal time between offers becomes arbitrarily small. It will be shown that the delay converges to the time needed to make B_h indifferent between paying $h/2$ at time zero and $l/2$ later.

Up to now, the minimal time between offers has been fixed at one. Now we let θ denote this time. In terms of a "real time" per period rate of interest ρ, the discount factor per period of length θ is

$$\delta(\theta) = \exp(-\rho\theta). \tag{7.1}$$

Note that $\delta(\theta) \to 1$ as $\theta \to 0$, and $\delta(\theta) \to 0$ as $\theta \to \infty$.

Recall that the separating equilibrium of Section 4 exists if $\pi^0 \in [\pi^*, 1]$, where π^* is defined in equation (4.4). With the appropriate substitutions to allow for minimal time of θ between offers, it is easy to verify that $\pi^* \to l/2$ as $\theta \to 0$, and $\pi^* \to l/h$ as $\theta \to \infty$. Thus, as $\theta \to 0$, the set of parameters for which the separating equilibrium exists (which always includes any $\pi^0 \in [l/h, 1]$) becomes larger.

In the separating equilibrium of Section 4, there is a positive probability $(1 - \pi^0)$ that the time until agreement is reached is $2\theta + \Gamma^*(P_h)$. Using the definition of $\Gamma^*(P)$, we get

$$\delta^{\Gamma^*(P_h)} = \frac{h - P_h}{h - \delta P_l} = \frac{h\delta}{h + (h-l)\delta}. \tag{7.2}$$

In our new notation, we have

$$\exp(-\rho\theta\Gamma^*(P_h)) = \frac{h \exp(-\rho\theta)}{h + (h-l)\exp(-\rho\theta)}. \tag{7.3}$$

As $\theta \to 0$, $\exp(-\rho\theta\Gamma^*(P_h)) \to h/(2h-l)$. Thus

$$\lim_{\theta \to 0} \Gamma^*(P_h) = \frac{1}{\rho} \log\left(\frac{2h-l}{h}\right). \tag{7.4}$$

Thus, the possible delay is bounded below by the right-hand side expression above, which is a positive number.

To gain some intuition, note that the difference between P_h, which is the price paid by B_h in the separating equilibrium, and δP_l, the price paid by l in this equilibrium, is bounded below by $(h-l)/2$. The time delay used by B_l to separate himself from B_h is therefore bounded below by the time needed to make B_h indifferent between $h/2$ at time zero and $l/2$ later. This is independent of the length of time between offers.

8. EXTENSIONS AND CONCLUDING REMARKS

8.1. *The game in which the buyer makes the first offer*

Consider the game in which at time zero it is B's turn to make an offer. (To adapt our notation so far to this case, assume that, at time -1, S offers ∞, i.e. $H^0 = (\infty, 0)$.) First, it can be shown, using similar arguments to those used in the previous sections, that along the equilibrium path, B_l only offers δP_l, and B_h offers either δP_l or δP_h. With the obvious modifications, it is easy to see that the strategies and belief system used in the proof of Proposition 4.1 describe a separating equilibrium for the game in which B makes the first offer. In this equilibrium, B_h offers δP_h at time zero, which S accepts, and B_l offers δP_l at time $\Gamma^*(\delta P_h)$, which S accepts. Unlike the case where S makes the first offer, this describes an equilibrium for every value of π^0. Lemmas 4.3 and 4.4 imply that if $\pi^0 > l/h$, then it yields the unique equilibrium path.

Again, with the obvious modifications to the strategies and beliefs described in Proposition 5.1, we see that, if $\pi^0 \leqq l/h$, then there exists a pooling equilibrium, in which both types of buyer offer δP_l at time zero and S accepts. Moreover, if $\pi^0 \leqq \pi^*$, then B_h makes his first offer at time zero, so that there are exactly two equilibrium outcomes. In the .ntermediate range, $\pi^0 \in [\pi^*, l/h]$, either B_h offers δP_h at time zero (and B_l offers δP_l at $\Gamma^*(\delta P_h)$), or both B_l and B_h offer δP_l at some time t, where $0 \leqq t \leqq \Gamma^*(\delta P_h)$. The possibility of a delay is due to the multiplicity of equilibria in the game in which S makes the first offer.

8.2. More than two types of buyer

It is conceptually straightforward to extend our analysis to the case of more than two types of buyer. Consider again the game in which S makes the first offer. As in the case of two types, the set of equilibrium outcomes depends on the distribution of buyer's valuation. The important properties that characterize the set of equilibria in the two type case continue to hold here as well. For example, no type of buyer pays more than he would in the perfect equilibrium of the relevant complete information game. Also, no more than two offers are made along any equilibrium path.

There is one profile of strategies that yields an equilibrium for all possible distributions. For a buyer B_b, denote by P_b and δP_b the perfect equilibrium offers in the relevant complete information game. Suppose according to B_b's strategy, B_b accepts an offer $P \leqq P_b$, and in response to an offer $P > P_b$, B_b counteroffers δP_b after waiting just enough to distinguish himself from the buyer with valuation immediately above b. (Note that this recursively defines B_b's strategy for every b.) Then the first offer by S determines a set of types who accept the offer. The rest of the buyer's types separate themselves over time, each making the relevant offer of δP_b, which S accepts. The seller's choice of the first offer can be formulated as a simple optimization problem, in which S chooses the cutoff point between the set of buyers who accept his first offer and those who do not accept it. It is easy to find a belief system satisfying our restrictions which supports such an equilibrium path. If there is a continuous distribution of possible valuations, then the equilibrium is characterized by a differential equation. [See Cramton (1984b).]

8.3. Two-sided uncertainty

In the model analysed above, the seller's valuation is assumed to be common knowledge, while the buyer's valuation is private information. The analysis can easily be applied to symmetrical situations in which the buyer's valuation is common knowledge but the seller's valuation is private information. An interesting extension of the model above is to the case of two-sided uncertainty, where both players' valuations are private information. Following the ideas of this paper, Cramton (1986) provides an analysis of the game with two-sided uncertainty and a continuum of types. With further assumptions on beliefs, he obtains a unique equilibrium path in which at most two offers are made. Our assumptions, however, allow for equilibria in the game with two-sided uncertainty in which more than two offers may be made along the equilibrium path.

To see this, suppose the buyer's valuation (which is the buyer's private information) is h_b with probability π_b^0 and l_b with probability $1 - \pi_b^0$. Similarly, suppose the seller's valuation (which is the seller's private information) is h_s with probability π_s^0 and l_s with probability $1 - \pi_s^0$, with $l_s < h_s < l_b < h_b$. Suppose the parameters are such that if it is common knowledge that the seller's valuation is h_s, then the unique equilibrium outcome (in the game where S makes the first offer) is the separating equilibrium of Section 4, while if it is common knowledge that the seller's valuation is l_s, then the unique equilibrium outcome if the seller makes the first offer is the pooling equilibrium of Section 5. In addition, suppose the seller whose valuation is l_s prefers the pooling equilibrium outcome in the game between himself and the buyer with unknown type to the separating equilibrium outcome in the game between the other type of seller and the buyer with unknown type. (It is always possible to find parameters such that the above holds.) The reader can verify that if π_s^0 is small enough then the following is an equilibrium path of the game in which the buyer makes the first offer: both types of buyer make the pooling offer as if they are playing against the seller with valuation l_s (namely the perfect equilibrium offer in the game of complete information in which the buyer's valuation is l_b and the seller's valuation is l_s). If the seller's valuation is l_s he accepts. Otherwise, he rejects and the game proceeds as in the one-sided uncertainty game between the seller with valuation h_s and the buyer with unknown valuation. Such an equilibrium can be supported by beliefs that satisfy an assumption analogous to (A2). Note that if the seller's valuation is h_s and the buyer's valuation is l_b (i.e. if both sides are relatively strong), three offers are made along the equilibrium path.

8.4. A connection with related literature

It is critical to our model that, once a player makes an offer, he cannot revise it until the other player has responded, and that the other player is allowed to delay for as long as he wishes (beyond the minimal time between offers). To see why, consider a discrete version of the model, in which the time between offers must be an integer. Suppose, for example, that in the separating equilibrium of this game, B_l delays making his offer for, say, 13 periods beyond the time in which B_h accepts S's offer. One may wonder whether such an equilibrium can be supported in the standard bargaining game, by having S and B_l make a series of non-serious offers until the settlement time has arrived. This is impossible: After the first non-serious offer by B is made, when it is S's turn to move, S knows that $b = l$ with probability one. Perfection (Lemma 2.2) requires that he offers P_l, which B_l accepts. This clearly upsets the equilibrium. Note that a similar phenomenon can arise in the context of the Spence (1974) job market signaling model if we let employers make offers to workers while they are still being educated.[6]

8.5. Letting both players move between offers

From the previous paragraph we see that one cannot allow the seller to revise continually his offer while the buyer is delaying his response and keep our separating equilibrium outcome. However, by modifying the game somewhat, we can allow the seller to try. This is done by explicitly allowing players to refuse to receive offers from their opponents. The idea is that before making an offer, a player has to "call", i.e. to invite the other player to receive the offer. Such an invitation may be turned down.

Consider the following game. Assume that at time $t \geq 0$, one player, say S, calls to make an offer. The other player, B, has to decide whether to receive the offer (i.e. accept the call) or not. If B agrees to receive the offer, then S makes an offer at time t. Otherwise, no offer is made. In any case, the game proceeds at time $t + 1$. Starting at time $t + 1$, *and at any time later*, B can either accept an offer if one was made, or both players can call to make new offers. If both players call simultaneously, then, in the spirit of alternating moves, only B's call is effective, and it is S's turn to decide whether to receive B's offer.

(After this, if the game continues, S's call takes precedence, until S makes a call, and so on.)[7] At time zero, it is, say, S's turn to call.

A *history* in this game specifies, in addition to actual offers and strategic time delays, times at which calls were made and whether the calls were accepted. It is easy to adapt the assumptions made in Section 2 to this game.

If the minimal time between calls is small enough, then the set of equilibrium outcomes of this game is only slightly different from that of our original game. In particular, if π^0 is large enough, there exists a separating equilibrium outcome which is $(P_h, 1)$ if $b = h$ and (P_l, t^*) if $b = l$, where t^* satisfies $(P_h, 1) \sim_h (P_l, t^*)$. For $t \in [1, t^*]$, B_l refuses to receive calls from S made at time t, hence S might as well not call. B_l refuses to receive calls earlier than t^*, because (in the equilibrium) such an action would be interpreted as an indication that $b = h$. Thus, strategic delay to agreement still emerges in equilibrium.

Acknowledgement. We are grateful to Milton Harris, Ed Lazear, Bob Wilson, Asher Wolinsky, Mark Wolfson, two anonymous referees, and especially David Kreps and Ariel Rubinstein for very helpful discussions and comments.

NOTES

1. See, for example, Bikhchandani (1985), Cramton (1984*a,b*), Fudenberg and Tirole (1983), Fudenberg, Levine and Tirole (1985), Grossman and Perry (1985), Rubinstein (1985), Sobel and Takahashi (1983), and Wilson (1985).

2. This separating equilibrium outcome shares many of the intuitive features of the equilibria found by Cramton (1984*b*) for a different game. The chosen equilibrium in his model, however, is only one of a continuum of possible equilibria.

3. Note that with one-sided uncertainty, the fact that the gains from trade are positive with probability one follows from individual rationality.

4. For an extension of our model to the case where the seller's payoff is $\delta^{t-1} U(P)$, where $U(\cdot)$ is concave see Bower (1986).

5. See Rubinstein (1982) for a similar phenomenon in the complete information game where players incur equal fixed costs per period.

6. The argument goes as follows. Once a high ability worker has gone to school long enough to distinguish himself from a worker of a lower ability, the firms would offer wages appropriate to high ability worker *before* enough time has elapsed to present an effective screen.

7. An alternative formulation, in the spirit of Binmore (1982), is one where if both players call simultaneously, then the actual caller is selected randomly. The results are qualitatively the same.

REFERENCES

BANKS, J. and SOBEL, J. (1987), "Equilibrium Selection in Signalling Games" *Econometrica* (forthcoming).

BIKHCHANDANI, S. (1985), "A Bargaining Model with Incomplete Information" (Working Paper, Graduate School of Management, UCLA).

BOWER, T. (1986), "Risk Aversion in a Bargaining Model with Delay" (Working Paper, Graduate School of Business, Stanford University).

BINMORE, K. G. (1982), "Perfect-Equilibria in Bargaining Models" (Working Paper, International Center for Economics and Related Disciplines, London School of Economics).

CHO, I.-K. (1987), "A Refinement of the Sequential Equilibrium Concept" *Econometrica* (forthcoming).

CHO, I-K. and KREPS, D. M. (1987), "Signaling Games and Stable Equilibria", *Quarterly Journal of Economics* (Forthcoming).

CRAMTON, P. C. (1984*a*), "Bargaining with Incomplete Information: An Infinite Horizon Model with Two-Sided Uncertainty", *Review of Economic Studies*, 51, 579-593.

CRAMTON, P. C. (1984*b*) *The Role of Time and Information in Bargaining* (Stanford: Stanford University).

CRAMTON, P. C. (1986), "Strategic Delay in Bargaining with Two-Sided Uncertainty" (Working Paper, Yale University).

FUDENBERG, D., LEVINE, D. and TIROLE, J. (1985), "Infinite Horizon Models of Bargaining with One-Sided Incomplete Information", in Roth A. *Bargaining with Incomplete Information* (Cambridge University Press).

FUDENBERG, D. and TIROLE, J. (1983), "Sequential Bargaining with Incomplete Information", *Review of Economic Studies*, 50, 221-247.

GROSSMAN, S. and PERRY, M. (1985), "Sequential Bargaining Under Asymmetric Information", *Journal of Economic Theory*, **39**, 120-154.

GUL, F. and SONNENSCHEIN, H. (1985), "Bargaining with One-Sided Uncertainty" (Working Paper, Stanford University, Graduate School of Business).

GUL, F., SONNENSCHEIN, H. and WILSON, R. (1986), "Foundations of Dynamic Monopoly and the Coase Conjecture", *Journal of Economic Theory*, **39**, 155-190.

HERRERO, M. J. (1986), "Delays in Good Faith Bargaining" (Working Paper, GSIA, Carnegie-Mellon University).

KREPS, D. M. and WILSON, R. (1982), "Sequential Equilibria", *Econometrica*, **50**, 863-894.

McLENNAN, A. (1986), "Bargaining Between Two Symmetrically Informed Agents" (Working Paper, Department of Economics, Cornell University).

RUBINSTEIN, A. (1982), "Perfect Equilibrium in a Bargaining Model", *Econometrica*, **50**, 97-110.

RUBINSTEIN, A. (1985), "A Bargaining Model with Incomplete Information about Preferences", *Econometrica*, **50**, 1151-1172.

SOBEL, J. and TAKAHASHI, I. (1983), "A Multi-Stage Model of Bargaining", *Review of Economic Studies*, **50**, 411-426.

SPENCE, A. M. (1974) *Market Signalling* (Cambridge: Harvard University Press).

WILSON, R. B. (1985), "Game-Theoretic Analyses of Trading Processes", in Bewley, T. (ed.) *Advances in Economic Theory* (Proceedings of the Fifth World Congress).

JOURNAL OF ECONOMIC THEORY **48**, 18-46 (1989)

$341-69$

0262

0210

0220

A Direct Mechanism Characterization
of Sequential Bargaining
with One-Sided Incomplete Information*

LAWRENCE M. AUSUBEL AND RAYMOND J. DENECKERE

*Department of Managerial Economics and Decision Sciences,
J. L. Kellogg Graduate School of Management,
Northwestern University, Evanston, Illinois 60208*

Received May 19, 1987; revised February 25, 1988

We characterize the sequential equilibria of a class of infinite-horizon bargaining games with one-sided incomplete information. When the seller (the uninformed party) makes all the offers, we prove a folk theorem: *every* incentive compatible, individually rational, direct bargaining mechanism is implementable by sequential equilibria. Introducing buyer counteroffers eliminates outcomes which are unfavorable to that party. As the proportion of buyer offers increases, the set of implementable mechanisms shrinks continuously; when the proportion reaches one, only the single outcome most favorable to the buyer remains. Thus, depending on the offer structure, sequentiality may (or may not) impose restrictions beyond static incentive compatibility. *Journal of Economic Literature* Classification Numbers: 021, 022, 026. © 1989 Academic Press, Inc.

1. INTRODUCTION

Much recent work has sought to clarify our understanding of the bargaining process by analyzing noncooperative, sequential, explicitly game-theoretic models of bilateral trade. Rubinstein [20] found a unique subgame perfect equilibrium in the alternating-offer bargaining game with complete information; subsequent authors have searched for related equilibrium concepts in games with similar extensive forms but containing incomplete information. In particular, considerable effort has been devoted

* This research was supported by National Science Foundation Grants IST-86-09129 and SES-86-19012, and by the Kellogg School's Paget Research Fund. We would like to acknowledge very helpful discussions with Peter Cramton, Herman Quirmbach, and, especially, Roger Myerson. Our work also benefited from the comments of two anonymous referees, an associate editor, and seminar participants at Queens University and the University of Chicago. The usual disclaimer applies.

341

to the study of infinite-horizon, discrete-time bargaining models where the seller's valuation s is common knowledge, the buyer's valuation b is private information (but its distribution function over the interval $[\underline{b}, \bar{b}]$ is common knowledge), and time enters agents' utility functions through discounting.

It will be the purpose of this paper to provide an essentially complete description of the sequential equilibria of this bargaining game with one-sided incomplete information, when $\underline{b} = s$ and when the time interval z between successive offers is allowed to tend to zero. We examine sequential bargaining for a class of extensive forms which allow the seller to make k offers and then the buyer to make l counteroffers, after which the game repeats. This includes the three extensive forms that are commonly analyzed in the literature: (a) the seller makes all the offers; (b) the seller and buyer alternate in making offers; and (c) the buyer makes all the offers. In every case, we find the entire set of sequential equilibria, in terms of (static) direct mechanisms, as z approaches zero.

A substantial number of authors have analyzed the extensive form where the uninformed party makes all the offers, and the related problem of durable goods monopoly. A line of papers which includes Coase [9], Bulow [4], Stokey [23], Sobel and Takahashi [22], Fudenberg et al. [12], and Gul et al. [15] has developed three valuable insights. First, there exist sequential equilibria—some of which form limits of equilibria of finite-horizon games—which satisfy a weak-Markov restriction on strategies. Second, in the case that $\underline{b} > s$, this sequential equilibrium is generically unique. Third, whenever $\underline{b} \geqslant s$, and the time interval between successive offers is short, the weak-Markov equilibria satisfy the "Coase Conjecture" property that the initial offer is close to $\underline{b}$. Previous work by the present authors (Ausubel and Deneckere [2]) amended this understanding by considering non-Markovian equilibria in the case where $\underline{b} = s$. There we reversed the Coase Conjecture by demonstrating the existence of "reputational equilibria" which mimic static monopoly pricing but are nevertheless sequential.

Some authors have also analyzed sequential bargaining with one-sided incomplete information where the two parties alternate in making offers.[1] Grossman and Perry [13] showed that there exists at most one so-called "perfect sequential equilibrium," under the assumption $\underline{b} > s$. Gul and Sonnenschein [14] proved that with certain stationary assumptions and $\underline{b} > s$, trade occurs arbitrarily quickly as the time interval between offers approaches zero. Admati and Perry [1] obtained delay by modifying the rules of the game. A thorough survey of this sequential bargaining

---

[1] Two-sided incomplete information is not considered here. For some recent treatments, see Cramton [10] and Chatterjee-Samuelson [6, 7].

literature, as well as a treatment of the extensive form where the informed party makes all the offers, is contained in Wilson [25].

In characterizing the set of sequential equilibria of these games, we make use of a second line of work which is often seen as at odds with the sequential bargaining approach. The mechanism design literature (see Myerson [16–18]), Chatterjee and Samuelson [8], Myerson and Satterthwaite [19], and Williams [24]) analyzes the bargaining problem by utilizing the revelation principle: *any* equilibrium of *any* static bargaining game may be rewritten as a direct mechanism for which truth telling must be a Nash equilibrium. The reason for the tension between the two lines of literature is that the mechanism approach is explicitly one-shot, while the sequential approach allows infinitely many opportunities for the parties to reach agreement. If a sequential equilibrium in these infinite-horizon games has trade occurring in finite time, the finiteness is endogenously generated; whereas the finite time in a direct mechanism is assumed.

Nevertheless, we find the two strands of literature complementary. First, static mechanisms give us a compact language for describing the set of sequential equilibria. Any conceivable equilibrium is payoff equivalent to an element of the set of all individually rational, incentive compatible bargaining mechanisms; our main theorems tell us which elements of this set are implementable by sequential equilibria of the class of infinite-horizon bargaining games analyzed in this paper. Second, the fact that certain direct mechanisms are implementable by sequential equilibria provides a justification for studying direct mechanisms. The "Nash program," in general, asks if there is a noncooperative justification for various solution concepts in cooperative game theory. The most conspicuous success along these lines is the work associated with Binmore [3] and Rubinstein [20]: take the alternating-offer, complete information bargaining game and let the time interval z between offers approach zero. With equal discount factors, the unique sequential equilibrium converges (in payoff terms) to split-the-difference; with unequal discount factors, one obtains the asymmetric Nash bargaining solution. Similarly, here, mechanisms have a cooperative flavor, as players are assumed to be able to commit to them. Mechanisms also have an axiomatic development—see, for example, Myerson [17]. Our folk theorem for seller-offer, sequential bargaining games provides a noncooperative justification.

Throughout this paper, we will be assuming that $\underline{b} = s$, which many authors have considered to be the most "relevant" case (e.g., Gul *et al.* [15, p. 162]) because demand is then not perfectly inelastic at the seller's valuation. This explicitly leaves open the case $\underline{b} > s$ for alternating-offer games. (Fudenberg *et al.* [12] and Gul *et al.* [15] solve the seller-offer game when $\underline{b} > s$; in Theorem 4 below, we solve the buyer-offer game, including the case $\underline{b} > s$.) We will *not* impose any "refinements," but rather we will seek to find the full set of sequential equilibria. As in Coase Conjecture studies and in Binmore [3], we perform the limiting exercise of letting the time interval between offers approach zero.

In Section 2, we discuss direct mechanisms. Section 3 formulates the sequential model and defines "implementable by sequential equilibria." Section 4 reviews some earlier results on sequential bargaining games. In Section 5, we prove the Folk Theorem for sequential bargaining where the uninformed seller makes all the offers: *every* individually rational, incentive compatible bargaining mechanism is implementable by sequential equilibria. In Section 6, we analyze alternating-offer bargaining with the same information structure and find that the equilibrium set is *distinctly smaller* than in the previous case: a bargaining mechanism must satisfy an additional individual-rationality-like constraint to be implementable by alternating-offer equilibria. In Section 7, we consider the case of buyer offers and show that the equilibrium set shrinks dramatically—to a single point. In Section 8, we complete the analysis of the class of alternating-offer games where k seller offers are followed by l buyer counteroffers. We conclude in Section 9.

2. STATIC MECHANISMS

Consider a trading situation in which one individual (henceforth referred to as the seller) owns an object he would like to sell to another individual (referred to as the buyer). Let the seller's valuation s for the object be common knowledge, and let the buyer's valuation b be distributed according to the (common knowledge) distribution function $F(\cdot)$. The support of $F(\cdot)$ is a subset of $[\underline{b}, \bar{b}]$ containing $\underline{b}$ and $\bar{b}$. For most of what follows, we will consider the case $\underline{b} = s$ and, without loss of generality, we thus set $s = \underline{b} = 0$.

Define a *bargaining mechanism* to be a game in which the buyer reports his private information b to a mediator, who then determines whether the good is transferred from the seller to the buyer and how much the buyer must pay the seller. A bargaining mechanism is characterized by two outcome functions: $p(b)$ which denotes the probability of trade, and $x(b)$ which denotes the expected transfer payment. A bargaining mechanism is *incentive compatible* if honest reporting forms a Bayesian Nash equilibrium, i.e.,

$$bp(b) - x(b) \geqslant bp(b') - x(b'), \qquad \forall b, b' \in \text{supp } F. \qquad (1)$$

A bargaining mechanism is (ex post) *individually rational* iff:

$$bp(b) - x(b) \geqslant 0, \qquad \text{and} \qquad x(b) \geqslant 0, \qquad \forall b \in \text{supp } F. \qquad (2)$$

Mechanisms satisfying both the individual rationality and the incentive constraints will be referred to as *incentive compatible bargaining mechanisms* (ICBMs). Let $U(\cdot)$ and V defined by

$$U(b) = bp(b) - x(b) \quad \text{and} \quad V = \int_0^{\bar{b}} x(b) \, dF(b), \tag{3}$$

be the buyer's and seller's (expected) utilities, respectively. Then we may define the set of *incentive feasible points* M as

$$M = \{(U(\cdot), V): U(\cdot) \text{ and } V \text{ satisfy (3) for some ICBM } (p, x)\}.$$

If the support of the distribution function $F(\cdot)$ is the entire interval $[0, \bar{b}]$ (note that this is *not* assumed for subsequent results), the following theorem provides a complete characterization of the set of ICBMs and incentive feasible points:

THEOREM 1. *Let $F(\cdot)$ be any strictly monotone distribution function. Then $\{p, x\}$ is an ICBM if and only if $p: [0, \bar{b}] \to [0, 1]$ is (weakly) increasing and x is given by the Stieltjes integral*

$$x(b) = \int_0^b r \, dp(r).$$

Furthermore, $U(0) = 0$ and, for all $0 \leqslant b \leqslant \bar{b}$:

$$U(b) = \int_0^b p(r) \, dr.$$

Proof. An adaption of Myerson and Satterthwaite [19]. The analogue to Myerson and Satterthwaite's inequality (2) holds for all (weakly) increasing functions p. Ex post individual rationality implies $U(0) = 0$. ∎

Consider a static bargaining game in which the seller makes a single take-it-or-leave-it offer. After the buyer's decision whether or not to accept the offer, the game concludes. All equilibria of this game have the seller offer a price q_*, where $q_* \in \arg\max_r\{r[1 - F(r)]\}$; the buyer accepts if and only if his valuation is greater than or equal to q_* (see Example 2 for the associated bargaining mechanism). While such an outcome seems perfectly reasonable in a static context, it may appear much less so in a dynamic world, because of the associated ex-post inefficiency: if $0 < b < q_*$, traders do not transact even though gains from trade exist.

Indeed, Cramton [11] and others (e.g., Chatterjee and Samuelson [6, 7], Chatterjee [5], and Fudenberg *et al.* [12]) have criticized the static ICBM approach on account that it "implicitly assumes that the players are able to commit to walking away [from the bargaining table] without trad-

ing, after it has been revealed that substantial gains from trade exist"
(Cramton [11, p. 150]). In fact, these authors take the position that any
bargaining game that is modeled as having an exogenously given, finite
number of stages violates a broad interpretation of sequential rationality:
commitments not to reopen or continue the bargaining process after the
prescribed number of stages has passed are not credible. Thus, "a useful
bargaining game must allow the number of potential stages to be infinite,
with the actual length of bargaining determined endogenously by the
bargaining process" (Chatterjee and Samuelson [6, p. 5]).

In this paper, we will follow these authors' implicit suggestions, and
study the set of sequential equilibria of infinite-horizon bargaining games.

3. SEQUENTIAL GAMES AND SEQUENTIAL MECHANISMS

In our study of infinite-horizon bargaining games, we examine "offer/
counteroffer" extensive forms,[2] in particular:

Seller offers: the seller makes all the offers, and the buyer waits to
accept an appropriate price.

Alternating offers: the seller and buyer alternate in making offers until
one of the parties accepts the other's offer.

Buyer offers: the buyer makes all the offers, and the seller waits to
accept an appropriate price.

With every trading rule, price offers will be assumed to occur at discrete
moments in time, spaced equally apart. Let z $(z > 0)$ denote the time interval between successive offers. Then bids are made at times $t = 0, z, 2z, 3z, ...$
Both players exhibit impatience,[3] which is specified by a common discount
rate r $(r > 0)$. Hence, if the good is traded at time t for the price p, the seller
obtains surplus of $e^{-rt}p$ and the buyer derives surplus of $e^{-rt}(b - p)$.

Corresponding to any equilibrium of the infinite-horizon bargaining
games, there exists a *direct revelation sequential bargaining mechanism*.[4]
Such a mechanism specifies a pair of outcome functions $t(\cdot)$ and $x(\cdot)$,
where $t(b)$ is the time that the good will be transferred to the buyer, and
$x(b)$ is the discounted expected transfer to the seller, given that the buyer
reports b. The incentive compatibility constraints now become

$$U(b) = be^{-rt(b)} - x(b) \geqslant be^{-rt(b')} - x(b'), \qquad \forall b, b' \in \text{supp } F, \qquad (4)$$

---

[2] We do not study simultaneous-move trading rules, since even in the one-shot complete
information case these rules permit every division of the pie as an equilibrium.

[3] This assumption is what makes the game form dynamic: not only do the probabilities of
trade and the expected payment matter, but also the time at which the trade is concluded!

[4] The terminology here is from Cramton [11].

and the (ex post) individual rationality constraints are

$$be^{-rt(b)} - x(b) \geq 0 \quad \text{and} \quad x(b) \geq 0, \quad \forall b \in \text{supp } F. \quad (5)$$

Observe the close resemblance between (4)–(5) and (1)–(2). In fact, if we make the transformation $p(b) = e^{-rt(b)}$, the conditions for the sequential mechanism match up exactly with those for the static mechanism. Thus, every sequential equilibrium of the infinite-horizon bargaining games induces, through the above transformation, a static bargaining mechanism which is incentive compatible.

The next lemma shows that with one-sided incomplete information every sequential equilibrium must also be ex post rational. This explains why we chose to impose ex post individual rationality in our definition of an ICBM, rather than the more common (see, e.g., Myerson and Satterthwaite [19]) interim rationality.

LEMMA 1. *Let the discount factor between periods be bounded away from one. Then every sequential equilibrium of the infinite-horizon bargaining game with one sided incomplete information is ex post individually rational in any offer/counteroffer extensive form.*[5]

Proof. If the extensive form permits the seller to make offers, let q denote the infimum of all prices offered with positive probability by the seller in *any* sequential equilibrium and after *any* history. We claim that $q \geq 0$. For suppose not. Define δ to be the supremum of discount factors between successive periods. Then there exists a sequential equilibrium σ and a history h such that the seller offers a price q_h with positive probability where $q_h < \delta q < 0$. Observe that *all* buyers must accept this offer, since even the zero type prefers trade at q_h in the current period to trade at q in the next period. But, then, the seller benefits by deviating from the equilibrium and offering a price of zero forever. We conclude $q \geq 0$.

We have just shown that the seller never offers the good to the buyer at a negative price. Clearly, the seller also never accepts a buyer's counteroffer to purchase at a negative price, since rejection dominates. Thus, the seller's utility is nonnegative in all states of the world.

Finally, we will show that $U(0) = 0$. (This immediately implies that $U(b) \geq 0$ for all b.) We argued above that the seller never offers or accepts a negative price. Consequently, the buyer of type zero can have no reason to counteroffer a positive price which has positive probability of acceptance; nor to accept a positive price. We conclude $U(0) = 0$. ∎

We have just observed that *every* sequential equilibrium of an infinite-

---

[5] Fudenberg *et al.*'s [12] Lemma 2 implies this result for the seller-offer game.

horizon bargaining game may be represented as a static ICBM. The
interesting question which remains to be asked is: When can we go the
other direction? When can a static ICBM be implemented as a sequential
equilibrium of an infinite-horizon bargaining game?

Before answering this question we need to make precise what we mean
by "implementation as a sequential equilibrium." Suppose, given a
mechanism $\{p, x\}$ and a positive number z, we can find an equilibrium σ
such that: (a) σ is a sequential equilibrium of the infinite-horizon bargaining game; and (b) σ, written in mechanism terms, yields $\{p, x\}$. Then we
could certainly say that "$\{p, x\}$ is implemented by σ in the game with time
interval z." There are two related reasons why we will adopt a somewhat
different definition of implementation. First, we are working in a discrete-
time model and, under the proposed definition, changing the time interval
z between periods is likely to change which mechanisms are implementable
and which are not. We would prefer a criterion for implementability which
is essentially independent of z. Second, our discrete-time game is meant to
model a situation where there is basically no constraint on the rate at
which parties can make successive offers. The meaningful question to ask
is then: What can we say about equilibrium behavior as the time interval
between successive offers approaches zero?

These considerations motivate the following definitions:

DEFINITION 1.   Let σ be a sequential equilibrium in pure strategies of an
infinite-horizon bargaining game. Suppose that, in equilibrium, the buyer
of type b trades at time $t(b)$ and at price $q(b)$. Then we define the ICBM
corresponding to σ by

$$p_\sigma(b) = e^{-rt(b)}$$

and

$$x_\sigma(b) = q(b) e^{-rt(b)}. \tag{6}$$

DEFINITION 2.   Let $\{p, x\}$ be any (static) direct mechanism, not
necessarily IR or IC. For any offer rule (e.g., seller-offer, buyer-offer, or
alternating-offer), we will say that the bargaining mechanism $\{p, x\}$ is
implementable by sequential equilibria of the infinite-horizon bargaining
game if $p(0) \leqslant \lim_{b \downarrow 0} p(b)$,[6] and if there exists a sequence $\{\sigma_n, z_n\}_{n=1}^{\infty}$ such
that

---

[6] Without the condition $p(0) \leqslant \lim_{b \downarrow 0} p(b)$, our definition would impose no restrictions on
the behavior of $p(\cdot)$ at 0, due to the asymmetric treatment of $b = 0$ in (7) and (8) below.
Observe that any *incentive compatible* bargaining mechanism necessarily satisfies the condition.

(i) $z_n \downarrow 0$ and, for every $n \geqslant 1$, σ_n is a sequential equilibrium of the infinite-horizon bargaining game where z_n is the time interval between successive offers; and

(ii) the ICBMs $\{p_n, x_n\}$ corresponding to σ_n converge to $\{p, x\}$, in the following sense: for every $\varepsilon > 0$, there exists $\bar{n}(\varepsilon)$ such that

$$|p_n(b) - p(b)| < \varepsilon, \qquad \forall n \geqslant \bar{n}(\varepsilon) \quad \text{and} \quad \forall b \in \text{supp } F \text{ s.t. } b > \varepsilon, \qquad (7)$$

and

$$|x_n(b) - x(b)| < \varepsilon, \qquad \forall n \geqslant \bar{n}(\varepsilon) \quad \text{and} \quad \forall b \in \text{supp } F. \qquad (8)$$

The asymmetric treatment of $b = 0$ in the above definition deserves some comment. A symmetric treatment would have required that $\{p_n, x_n\}$ converge uniformly to $\{p, x\}$.[7] While such a definition would be satisfactory in the sense that it also implies uniform convergence of buyer and seller utilities, it is too harsh in that it would preclude implementation of mechanisms in which all trade occurs in finite "time," i.e., those for which $\lim_{b \downarrow 0} p(b) > 0$ (see Example 3, below). This is because any sequential equilibrium in the seller-offer or alternating-offer game has the property that sales occur over infinite time.[8] Hence, if p_n is derived from such a sequential equilibrium, we must have $\lim_{b \downarrow 0} p_n(b) = 0$.

Our definition of "implementation" is a very strong one: (7) and (8) together immediately imply *uniform convergence of buyer and seller utilities*, i.e., $\forall n \geqslant \bar{n}(\varepsilon)$ and $\forall b \in \text{supp } F$:

$$|[bp_n(b) - x_n(b)] - [bp(b) - x(b)]| < (\bar{b} + 1) \varepsilon,$$

and

$$\left| \int_0^b x_n(b) \, dF(b) - \int_0^b x(b) \, dF(b) \right| < \varepsilon.$$

In fact, if every ICBM is implementable, every incentive feasible point can be arbitrarily closely approximated, and we will say that the Folk Theorem holds. More precisely:

FOLK THEOREM. *For every $m = (U(\cdot), V) \in M$, there exist sequences $\{\varepsilon_n, \sigma_n, z_n\}_{n=1}^{\infty}$ with $\varepsilon_n, z_n \downarrow 0$, such that σ_n is a sequential equilibrium for*

---

[7] Our definition of implementation is equivalent to uniform convergence if and only if $\lim_{b \downarrow 0} p(b) = 0$.

[8] In fact, the same is true with any offer structure which allows the seller to make offers infinitely often, whenever $s = \underline{b}$.

the infinite-horizon bargaining game when z_n is the time interval between successive offers,

$$|[bp_n(b) - x_n(b)] - U(b)| < \varepsilon_n, \qquad \forall b \in \text{supp } F,$$

and

$$\left| \int_0^b x_n(b) \, dF(b) - V \right| < \varepsilon_n, \tag{9}$$

where each $\{p_n, x_n\}$ is the ICBM corresponding to σ_n.

4. Preliminaries to the Main Results

This section collects some existing results on the seller-offer game, which will be useful in our subsequent analysis. For more formal statements of these definitions and theorems, and for complete proofs, we urge the reader to consult the references mentioned. The following assumption will henceforth be made on the distribution function $F(\cdot)$ of buyer valuations:

> There exist $L \geqslant M > 0$ such that $Mb \leqslant F(b) \leqslant Lb$ for all $b \in [0, \bar{b}]$. (10)

For example, if F has density in a neighborhood of 0, and this density is bounded above and below by positive numbers, then it satisfies the above conditions. Observe, however, that (10) also allows mass points and gaps in the support. It is helpful to define,[9] for fixed L and M ($L \geqslant M > 0$), the family $\mathscr{F}_{L,M} = \{F : F$ is a distribution function and $Mb \leqslant F(b) \leqslant Lb$ for all $b \in [0, \bar{b}]\}$.

Many of the results in the literature concern sequential equilibria in which the buyer's strategy is history-independent. To be more precise:

WEAK-MARKOV EQUILIBRIUM. *Let σ_s be a strategy for the seller and σ_b be a strategy for the buyer. (σ_s, σ_b) is a weak-Markov equilibrium if (σ_s, σ_b) is a sequential equilibrium and σ_b depends only on the seller's most recent offer.*

---

[9] We depart here slightly from the notation in [2]. The distribution function $F(b)$ here is related to the indirect demand function $f(q)$ in [2] through the transformation $F(b) = 1 - f^{-1}(b)$. Thus, $\mathscr{F}_{L,M}$ in the present paper corresponds to $\mathscr{F}_{1/M, 1/L, 1}$ in [2].

One of the principal reasons to be interested in these equilibria is that the celebrated Coase Conjecture [9] holds: the seller is forced to offer the good at an introductory price barely above his valuation. This was first proven for a linear demand example by Stokey [23] and was subsequently generalized to the whole class of weak-Markov equilibria by Gul *et al.* [15, Theorem 3]. Here, we will need a somewhat stronger version of this theorem.

UNIFORM COASE CONJECTURE [2, Theorem 5.4]. *For every* L $(L \geqslant 1/\bar{b})$, *every* M $(0 < M \leqslant 1/\bar{b})$, *and every* ε $(\varepsilon > 0)$, *there exists* $\bar{z}(L, M, \varepsilon)$ *such that for every* $F \in \mathscr{F}_{L,M}$, *for every* z *satisfying* $0 < z < \bar{z}(L, M, \varepsilon)$, *and for every weak-Markov equilibrium in the seller-offer game where the distribution function of buyers is F and the time interval between periods is z, the seller's initial offer is less than* ε.

In fact, the above theorem is not vacuous, as one may also prove that the set of weak-Markov equilibria is nonempty. The first such existence theorem is due to Fudenberg *et al.* [12, Proposition 2]; we use a somewhat stronger version here:

EXISTENCE OF WEAK-MARKOV EQUILIBRIA [2, Theorem 4.2]. *Let F be any distribution function. Then for any time interval z between periods, there exists a weak-Markov equilibrium of the seller-offer game.*

The weak-Markov equilibria are decidedly unfavorable to the seller. However, relaxing the weak-Markov restriction drastically enlarges the equilibrium set:

THE FOLK THEOREM FOR SELLER PAYOFFS [2, Theorem 6.4]. *Assume F satisfies* (10). *Define* $\pi^* = \sup_b \{b[1 - F(b)]\}$. *Then for every* $\varepsilon > 0$ *and every* $\pi \in [\varepsilon, \pi^* - \varepsilon]$, *there exists* $\bar{z}(\varepsilon) > 0$ *such that whenever the time interval z satisfies* $0 < z < \bar{z}(\varepsilon)$, *there exists a sequential equilibrium of the seller-offer game which yields the seller an expected surplus of* π.

Let us explore the intuition for this result. A constant price path over time, such as charging the static monopoly price q_* forever, is not time-consistent by Coase's original critique. Instead, we utilize the exponentially descending price path[10] $q(t) = q_* e^{-\eta t}$ (confined to the grid of times $\{0, z, 2z, ...\}$). Observe first that if η and z are small positive numbers, then this price path becomes an excellent approximation to charging the monopoly price forever, in the sense of yielding almost the same expected

---

[10] The proof in [2] literally uses an exponential quantity path in order to establish the result in full generality.

seller surplus. Second, this price path generates sales over infinite time, since (10) implies that the expected net present value of seller surplus, evaluated at every time, remains positive. Third, using the Uniform Coase Conjecture, it can be shown that for sufficiently small z, the net present value of expected seller surplus along any weak-Markov equilibrium price path is uniformly (at all times) lower than along the price path $q_* e^{-\eta t}$.

Consider now a strategy in which the seller follows the proposed exponential price path unless he has deviated from it in the past, in which case a reversion to a weak-Markov equilibrium is triggered. Our reasoning above guarantees that this strategy, coupled with corresponding buyer acceptance behavior, forms a sequential equilibrium for sufficiently small z. Thus, $\pi^* - \varepsilon$ is attainable by such reputational equilibria. Continuously varying the initial price makes possible all other seller surpluses between ε and $\pi^* - \varepsilon$.

Observe that the above theorem says nothing about buyer payoffs, and deals only with the seller-offer game. In the next section, we will prove the Folk Theorem (as defined in Section 3) for the seller-offer game; in subsequent sections we analyze alternating-offer and buyer-offer games.

5. THE SELLER-OFFER GAME

Consider any incentive compatible bargaining mechanism $\{p(\cdot), x(\cdot)\}$. In Definition 1, we wrote p and x as functions of t (the time of trade) and q (the price of trade). We may invert the transformation (6) to obtain

$$t(b) = -(1/r) \log p(b),$$
$$q(b) = x(b)/p(b). \tag{11}$$

Define $\mathscr{A} = \{t(b): 0 \leqslant b \leqslant \bar{b}\}$, i.e., $\mathscr{A}$ is the range of $t(\cdot)$ in (11). Observe that (11) parametrically defines q in terms of T for all $T \in \mathscr{A}$; call this function $Q(T)$. This may be extended to a function of all $t \geqslant 0$ by letting $T(t) = \sup\{t': t' \in \mathscr{A} \text{ and } t' \leqslant t\}$ and defining

$$q(t) = \begin{cases} Q(T(t)), & \text{if } t \geqslant \inf \mathscr{A}, \\ \bar{b}, & \text{otherwise.} \end{cases} \tag{12}$$

The function $q(t)$ in Eq. (12) will be called the *price path associated with* $\{p, x\}$. It is consistent with the parametric representation (11) at all times belonging to $\mathscr{A}$, and it defines a "flat" price path at all other times. Roughly speaking, we will implement the ICBM $\{p, x\}$ in the seller-offer game by constructing sequential equilibria whose main price paths approximate $q(t)$. The following examples will both illustrate the basic procedure and demonstrate some of the difficulties that must be overcome.

EXAMPLE 1. *Exponentially descending price path; uniform distribution.* Consider the direct mechanism

$$p^1(b) = \begin{cases} 1, \\ \left[\dfrac{rb}{(r+\eta)\,q_0}\right]^{r/\eta}, \end{cases} \quad x^1(b) = \begin{cases} q_0, & b \geq \dfrac{r+\eta}{r}\,q_0, \\ & \text{if} \\ \left[\dfrac{rb}{(r+\eta)}\right]^{1+(r/\eta)} q_0^{-(r/\eta)}, & b < \dfrac{r+\eta}{r}\,q_0, \end{cases}$$

where $0 < q_0 < 1$, $\eta > 0$, and buyer valuations are distributed according to the uniform distribution $F(b) = b$ $(0 \leq b \leq 1)$. Observe, using Theorem 1, that $\{p^1, x^1\}$ is an ICBM. By (11) and (12), the price path associated with $\{p^1, x^1\}$ is $q^1(t) = q_0 e^{-\eta t}$, for all $t \geq 0$.

Using our previous paper (Ausubel and Deneckere [2]), Example 1 is straightforward to handle. As observed in the next-to-last paragraph of Section 4, grid approximations to the price path $q^1(t)$ can be supported as the main equilibrium paths of sequential equilibria, for sufficiently short time intervals between offers. Furthermore, since $q^1(t)$ is continuous and because every buyer type has a single most-preferred purchase time, it is relatively easy to show that the purchase probabilities and expected transfers (associated with these sequential equilibria) converge uniformly to $p^1(\cdot)$ and $x^1(\cdot)$, respectively.

EXAMPLE 2. *Take-it-or-leave-it offer; uniform distribution.* Consider the direct mechanism

$$p^2(b) = \begin{cases} 1, \\ 0, \end{cases} \quad x^2(b) = \begin{cases} q_0, \\ 0, \end{cases} \quad \text{if} \quad \begin{matrix} b \geq q_0, \\ \text{otherwise}, \end{matrix}$$

where $0 < q_0 < 1$. Observe that $\{p^2, x^2\}$ is an ICBM and that the associated price path is $q^2(t) = q_0$, for all $t \geq 0$.

It is worth noting, given a sequence $\eta_m \downarrow 0$, that the sequence of mechanisms $\{p_m^1, x_m^1\}$ (defined by using $\eta = \eta_m$ in Example 1) does not converge uniformly to $\{p^2, x^2\}$ in neighborhoods of q_0. Thus, a diagonal argument is not sufficient to establish that $\{p^2, x^2\}$ is implementable.

Similarly, a "naive approach" to constructing sequential equilibrium price paths will fail to establish implementability. Let T_n denote the time which players discount to $1/n$, i.e., $e^{-rT_n} = 1/n$. We might propose a sequence of equilibria σ_n in which, along the equilibrium path, the seller follows a grid approximation to the price path $q^2(t)$ until time T_n and then follows an exponentially descending price path $q_0 e^{-\eta(t - T_n)}$. For sufficiently small z_n, we can show that σ_n are sequential equilibria.[11] Let b_n denote the lowest buyer type who purchases at time zero in σ_n. Then σ_n, expressed as an ICBM $\{\pi_n^2, \psi_n^2\}$, satisfies: $\pi_n^2(b) = 1$, if $b \geqslant b_n$; and $\pi_n^2(b) < 1/n$, if $b < b_n$. However, observe that $b_n > q_0$ for all n, and so $\pi_n^2(q_0) < 1/n$ for all n, implying that $\{\pi_n^2\}$ does *not* converge to p^2 at q_0.

We prove implementability by a more sophisticated argument. Let $\mu(n)$ denote the time of buyer q_0's most-preferred offer after time T_n. That is, let $\mu(n) \equiv \arg \max_{kz} \{e^{-rkz}[q_0 - q_0 e^{-\eta(kz - T_n)}] : kz \geqslant T_n$ and k is an integer$\}$ and let $\phi(n)$ denote the price offered at $\mu(n)$. Also define $s_{n,z}$ by

$$q_0 - s_{n,z} = e^{-r\mu(n)}[q_0 - \phi(n)]. \tag{13}$$

Consider now a price path for σ_n given by $q_n^2(t) = s_{n,z}$, if $0 \leqslant t < T_n$; and $q_n^2(t) = e^{-\eta(t - T_n)}$, if $t \geqslant T_n$. As before, this price path yields a sequential equilibrium when z is sufficiently small. Observe, however, that type q_0 is now *exactly indifferent* between purchasing at times 0 and $\mu(n)$, by (13), so our equilibrium can specify that type q_0 purchase at either time (or randomize between the two). In particular, we may impose that he purchase at time 0. Letting $\{p_n^2, x_n^2\}$ be the associated ICBM: $p_n^2(b) = 1$, if $b \geqslant q_0$; and $p_n^2(b) < 1/n$, if $b < q_0$. This converges uniformly to p^2.

The failure to converge at a single point q_0 may have seemed fairly innocuous in Example 2. But modify that example by assuming a mass point in the distribution at q_0. Then the seller's expected surplus V_n^2, computed using ICBMs $\{\pi_n^2, \psi_n^2\}$, fails to converge to V^2, computed from $\{p^2, x^2\}$. Thus, the "naive approach" fails to establish a folk theorem.

Example 2 has also illustrated how our general proof handles discontinuities in the function $p(\cdot)$. If p is discontinuous at $\hat{b}$, then for sufficiently large n, σ_n makes $\hat{b}$ exactly indifferent between purchasing at times approximately corresponding to $\lim_{b \uparrow \hat{b}} p(b)$ and $\lim_{b \downarrow \hat{b}} p(b)$.

EXAMPLE 3. *Two-step price path; uniform distribution.* Consider the direct mechanism

$$p^3(b) = \begin{cases} 1, \\ \frac{1}{2}, \end{cases} \qquad x^3(b) = \begin{cases} \frac{1}{4}, & \text{if } b \geqslant \frac{1}{2}, \\ 0, & \text{if } b < \frac{1}{2}. \end{cases}$$

Observe that $\{p^3, x^3\}$ is an ICBM and that the associated price path is $q^3(t) = \frac{1}{4}$, if $\frac{1}{2} < e^{-rt} \leqslant 1$; and $q^3(t) = 0$, if $e^{-rt} \leqslant \frac{1}{2}$. This price path is more

---

[11] For sufficiently small z_n', the "endgame" is supported as a sequential equilibrium. For sufficiently small z_n'', expected surplus in the endgame (discounted to the beginning of the game) exceeds expected surplus along the punishment path. Let $z_n = \min(z_n', z_n'')$.

difficult to implement because it drops to zero in finite time, whereas in any sequential equilibrium, price stays forever positive.

Define $T^z \equiv \inf\{kz: e^{-rkz} \leqslant \frac{1}{2}$, for some integer $k\}$. Since we cannot set a zero price at time T^z, we instead set a price of $1/n$ at time T^z in the nth equilibrium price path. Analogous to (13), define $s_{n,z}$ such that $\frac{1}{2} - s_{n,z} = e^{-rT^z}[\frac{1}{2} - 1/n]$. We then specify a price path $q_n^3(t) = s_{n,z}$, if $0 \leqslant t < T^z$; and $q_n^3(t) = (1/n) e^{-\eta(t-T^z)}$, if $t \geqslant T^z$. As usual, $q_n^3(t)$ yields a sequential equilibrium when z is sufficiently small. Now, however, type $1/2$ is exactly indifferent between purchasing at times 0 and T^z. Moreover, $p_n^3(b) = 1$ for $b \geqslant \frac{1}{2}$, and $p_n^3(b) \approx \frac{1}{2}$ for $b < \frac{1}{2}$, except for b close to zero. We thus obtain uniform convergence to $p^3(\cdot)$ except in neighborhoods of zero, proving implementability.

Analogous arguments allow us to construct equilibrium price paths which mimic arbitrarily complicated ICBMs, so we have:

THEOREM 2. *A direct bargaining mechanism $\{p, x\}$ is implementable by sequential equilibria of the seller-offer game if and only if it is an* ICBM.

Proof. See the Appendix.

6. THE ALTERNATING-OFFER GAME

In the previous section, we studied a very restricted infinite-horizon bargaining game: only the uninformed party was permitted to make offers. We will now consider a richer game form: the seller and buyer alternate, in consecutive periods, making offers and counteroffers. This would seem to open up a wealth of new possibilities for equilibrium behavior,[12] as the informed party is now allowed a much larger vocabulary (the interval $[0, b]$, instead of just $\{Y, N\}$).[13] Indeed, appearances have been that an assumption of one-sided offers artificially restricts the equilibrium set.

Of course, one should immediately observe that the addition of buyer counteroffers to the infinite-horizon bargaining game *cannot possibly expand* our set of sequential equilibrium outcomes: we already have a folk theorem for the seller-offer game.

More surprisingly, the introduction of buyer counteroffers actually *reduces* the equilibrium set of payoffs. The richer extensive form enables us

---

[12] If the seller makes all the offers and if trade occurs over infinite time, there is *no* (observable) out-of-equilibrium behavior for the informed player.

[13] For example, Grossman and Perry [13] state in footnote 2, "We do not analyze a concession game, i.e., a game where only one party can make offers and the other only accepts or rejects, because the party that is unable to make counteroffers is artificially restricted."

to exclude some outcomes, because when the buyer has the opportunity to make counteroffers, he can observably deviate by making an unexpected demand. The most adverse inference which the seller can form is the ("optimistic") conjecture that the buyer's type is $\bar{b}$. But, in that event, the high-valuation buyer must earn at least what he obtains in the complete information, alternating-offer game (see Grossman and Perry's [13] Lemma 3.1). When the time interval between offers shrinks to zero, this amount converges to one-half of total surplus. We have:

THEOREM 3. *A direct bargaining mechanism* $\{p, x\}$ *is implementable by sequential equilibria of the alternating-offer game if and only if* $\{p, x\}$ *is an* ICBM *and*

$$\bar{b}p(\bar{b}) - x(\bar{b}) \geqslant \bar{b}/2. \tag{14}$$

Proof. We first prove the "only if" part. Suppose $\{p, x\}$ is not IC or IR. Then we obtain the same contradiction as in the proof of Theorem 2. Now, suppose $\bar{b}p(\bar{b}) - x(\bar{b}) < \bar{b}/2$. We will show that there exists a positive measure of buyer types who can break the alleged equilibria σ_n, for sufficiently large n. Observe that there exists $\varepsilon > 0$ and $N \geqslant 1$ such that

$$bp(\sigma_n; b) - x(\sigma_n; b) < b/2,$$

$$\text{for all} \quad n \geqslant N \quad \text{and} \quad b \in [\bar{b} - \varepsilon, \bar{b}] \cap \text{supp } F. \tag{15}$$

Note that, by definition, $F(\bar{b}) - F(\bar{b} - \varepsilon) > 0$ for all $\varepsilon > 0$.

Let $\delta_n = e^{-r z_n}$, the discount factor between successive periods in the equilibrium σ_n. By Lemma 3.1(ii) of Grossman and Perry [13],[14] after any history in any sequential equilibrium, the seller will accept any buyer counteroffer greater than or equal to $\delta_n \bar{b}/(1 + \delta_n)$ (the price offered by buyer $\bar{b}$ in the Rubinstein [20] game). Hence, the buyer with valuation b has the option of rejecting the seller's initial offer in equilibrium σ_n, instead counteroffering $\delta_n \bar{b}/(1 + \delta_n)$. Discounting to the beginning of the game, this assures the buyer with valuation b a payoff of $\delta_n\{b - \delta_n \bar{b}/(1 + \delta_n)\}$. Hence, buyer b can break an alleged equilibrium σ_n unless

$$bp(\sigma_n; b) - x(\sigma_n; b) \geqslant \delta_n\{b - \delta_n \bar{b}/(1 + \delta_n)\}. \tag{16}$$

It is easy to see that (15) leads to a contradiction of (16) for appropriate choice of ε and N, for all $b \in [\bar{b} - \varepsilon, \bar{b}] \cap \text{supp } F$ and all $n \geqslant N$, since $\lim_{n \to \infty} \delta_n = 1$. This establishes the "only if" part of the theorem.

---

[14] We specifically make use of the assumption in the definition of sequential equilibrium that the support of the seller's (updated) beliefs about the buyer's valuation never moves outside supp F.

We now prove the "if" part of the theorem, by "embedding" the seller-offer equilibria (with time interval $2z$) of Theorem 2 into the alternating-offer game (with time interval z).[15] If $\delta = e^{-rz}$, define the following candidate equilibrium:

If there have been no prior buyer deviations:
In even periods $(t = 0, 2z, 4z, ...)$:
   Seller offers $q_{n,2z}(t)$ as defined in the proof of Theorem 2, if there have been no prior seller deviations.
   Seller offers the price from a weak-Markov equilibrium (with time interval $2z$), if there have been prior seller deviations.
   Buyer responses and seller beliefs also correspond exactly to the seller-offer equilibrium (with time interval $2z$).
In odd periods $(t = z, 3z, 5z, ...)$:
   Buyer counteroffers zero.
   Seller rejects.

If the buyer has ever counteroffered a positive price:
   The seller updates his beliefs to:

$$\hat{F}(b) = \begin{cases} 1, & \text{if } b = \bar{b}, \\ 0, & \text{if } b < \bar{b}, \end{cases}$$

   and never changes his beliefs again.
In even periods:
   Seller offers $\bar{b}/(1 + \delta)$.
   Buyer of type b accepts any offer $\leqslant \min\{\bar{b}/(1 + \delta), b\}$.
In odd periods:
   Buyer of type b offers $\min\{\delta\bar{b}/(1 + \delta), b\}$.
   Seller accepts any price $\geqslant \delta\bar{b}/(1 + \delta)$.

Observe that, in the case of no prior buyer deviations, the seller follows the equilibrium by the same argument as in the proof of Theorem 2. The buyer of type b follows the equilibrium in period zero if and only if (16) is satisfied, since the left side gives the buyer's utility from following the equilibrium path and the right side gives profits from optimally deviating. Suppose that (14) is satisfied with strict inequality. Then there exists $\alpha > 0$ such that

$$\bar{b}p(\bar{b}) - x(\bar{b}) > \bar{b}/2 + \alpha. \tag{17}$$

---

[15] Fudenberg *et al.* [12, Section 5.4] used a similar technique. See also Section 4 of Gul and Sonnenschein [14].

The incentive compatibility of $\{p, x\}$ implies, for all $b < \bar{b}$,[16] that $bp(b) - x(b) \geqslant bp(\bar{b}) - x(\bar{b})$. Subtracting $\bar{b}p(\bar{b}) - x(\bar{b})$ from each side yields

$$[bp(b) - x(b)] - [\bar{b}p(\bar{b}) - x(\bar{b})] \geqslant [b - \bar{b}] p(\bar{b}) \geqslant b - \bar{b}, \qquad (18)$$

since $p(\bar{b}) \leqslant 1$ and $[b - \bar{b}]$ is negative. But adding (17) and (18) yields

$$bp(b) - x(b) \geqslant b - \bar{b}/2 + \alpha, \qquad \text{for all} \quad b \leqslant \bar{b}. \qquad (19)$$

As in Theorem 2, $[bp(\sigma_n; b) - x(\sigma_n; b)]$ converges uniformly to $[bp(b) - x(b)]$, implying (16) for all $b \leqslant \bar{b}$ and for sufficiently large N. Thus, no buyer type deviates from the equilibrium σ_n, for $n \geqslant N$.

Now suppose that (14) is only satisfied with equality. Observe that there exists a sequence of ICBMs $\{p^m, x^m\}_{m=1}^{\infty}$, uniformly converging to $\{p, x\}$, such that $\bar{b}p^m(\bar{b}) - x^m(\bar{b}) > \bar{b}/2$ for every m. For every m there exists $\{\sigma_n^m\}_{n=1}^{\infty}$ and $N(m)$ such that no buyer type deviates from σ_n^m whenever $n \geqslant N(m)$. We conclude that the sequence $\{\sigma_{N(m)}^m\}_{m=1}^{\infty}$ has the desired properties.

Finally, suppose that the buyer has ever counteroffered a positive price. The prescribed strategies are a minor adaptation of the Rubinstein [20] (complete information) strategies, and can be shown to form a sequential equilibrium by a similar argument. ∎

7. THE BUYER-OFFER GAME

We have just seen that in the alternating-offer and seller-offer games, sequential equilibria implement a rather large set of ICBMs, including both relatively efficient and inefficient mechanisms. It may thus come as a surprise that in the buyer-offer game, the inefficiency as well as the multiplicity necessarily disappear. In Theorem 4, we prove that the unique sequential equilibrium has the buyer offer zero, and the seller accept:

THEOREM 4. *A direct bargaining mechanism* $\{p, x\}$ *is implementable by sequential equilibria of the buyer-offer game if and only if*

$$p(b) = 1 \quad and \quad x(b) = 0, \qquad for \ all \quad b \in \text{supp } F.$$

Proof. Let $\bar{Q}$ denote the supremum of all prices (offered by buyers) which are ever rejected with positive probability (by the seller), in *any* equilibrium after *any* history. We will first prove the "only if" part of the theorem by showing that $\bar{Q} = 0$; recall, by Lemma 1, that the buyer never offers $q < 0$.

---

[16] This technique owes to Myerson and Satterthwaite [19, Section 2].

Suppose to the contrary, that $\bar{Q} > 0$. Observe that for every $\alpha > 0$ there exists a price q, greater than $\bar{Q} - \alpha$, and a history such that if the buyer offers q after this history, the seller will reject with positive probability. In particular, we may pick $\alpha = (1 - \delta) \bar{Q}$, where $\delta = e^{-rz}$. For the seller to reject the price $q > \delta \bar{Q}$ in equilibrium, it must be that he expects a (higher) price q' with positive probability in the future. Since q' is offered at least one period later, it must be that $\delta q' > q$. But then $\delta q' > \delta \bar{Q}$, and $q' > \bar{Q}$. However, no rational buyer will ever offer such a price, since the offer $(q' + \bar{Q})/2$ would be accepted with probability one. We conclude that $\bar{Q} = 0$.

To prove the "if" part of the theorem, observe that for *any* $z > 0$, it is an equilibrium for the buyer always to offer zero, and the seller to accept any price that is at least zero.[17] Thus $p(b) \equiv 1$ and $x(b) \equiv 0$ on supp F is implementable. ∎

Observe that the proof of Theorem 4 depends in no way on the assumption that $\underline{b} = s$.

8. THE (k, l)-ALTERNATING-OFFER GAME

The sequential bargaining literature has primarily considered the three extensive forms in which the proportion of offers made by the buyer equals zero, one-half, or one. We demonstrated in the preceding sections that as the fraction of buyer offers was increased, the buyer's bargaining power in effect also increased and the equilibrium set shrank. It is interesting to consider whether this proposition holds in full generality. We analyze this question by defining a class of sequential bargaining games which allows us to continuously vary the proportion of buyer offers from zero to one.

Consider the sequential bargaining game in which the seller and buyer alternate by making k and l successive offers, respectively. To be precise, if $n \equiv i \pmod{(k + l)}$, then the seller (buyer) makes an offer at time $t = nz$ if $0 \leqslant i \leqslant k - 1$ $(k \leqslant i \leqslant k + l - 1)$. We denote this the (k, l)-*alternating-offer game*, where k and l are permitted to be any positive integers. We first analyze the complete-information version of this game where $s = 0$ and $b = \bar{b}$.

THEOREM 5. *The complete-information, (k, l)-alternating-offer game has a unique subgame perfect equilibrium. Players' strategies are stationary in the following sense: if $n \equiv i \pmod{(k + l)}$, $0 \leqslant i \leqslant k - 1$, the seller offers* $p_i = \bar{b}\{1 - \delta^{k-i}(1 - \delta^l)/(1 - \delta^{k+l})\}$ *in period n; the buyer accepts any price*

---

[17] See Wilson [25, pp. 43–44 and 66–67].

$\leqslant p_i$ and rejects otherwise. If $n \equiv j \pmod{k+l}$, $k \leqslant j \leqslant k+l-1$, the buyer offers $p_j = \bar{b} \delta^{k+l-j}(1-\delta^k)/(1-\delta^{k+l})$ in period n; the seller accepts any price $\geqslant p_j$ and rejects otherwise.

Proof. An adaptation of Shaked and Sutton [21].

Thus, as in the complete-information, $(1, 1)$-alternating-offer game, trade occurs in the initial period, but the division of surplus depends on k and l. We now turn to the game with one-sided incomplete information where, as usual, $\underline{b} = s$. In fact, the results in Section 6 generalize directly to arbitrary integers (k, l):

THEOREM 6. *A direct bargaining mechanism $\{p, x\}$ is implementable by sequential equilibria of the (k, l)-alternating-offer game if and only if $\{p, x\}$ is an* ICBM *and*

$$\bar{b} p(\bar{b}) - x(\bar{b}) \geqslant (l/(k+l))\, \bar{b}. \tag{20}$$

Proof. We first treat the "only if" part. Let m be any period when the buyer makes offers, i.e., $m \equiv j \pmod{k+l}$, where $k \leqslant j \leqslant k+l-1$. It is possible to generalize Grossman and Perry's [13] Lemma 3.1(ii): in period m, in any sequential equilibrium, after any history, the seller will accept any buyer offer at least equal to $\delta^{k+l-j}((1-\delta^k)/(1-\delta^{k+l}))\, \bar{b}$. Hence, the buyer has the option of rejecting the k initial seller offers and counteroffering $\delta^l((1-\delta^k)/(1-\delta^{k+l}))\, \bar{b}$ in period k. This assures the buyer of valuation b a payoff of $\delta^k\{b - \delta^l((1-\delta^k)/(1-\delta^{k+l}))\, \bar{b}\}$, which when evaluated at $b = \bar{b}$ yields $(l/(k+l))\, \bar{b}$ as z approaches zero.

We prove the "if" part by embedding the seller-offer equilibria (with time interval $(k+l)z$) of Theorem 2 into the (k, l)-alternating-offer game (with time interval z). For any $\{p, x\}$ satisfying inequality (20), along the equilibrium path, the seller offers $q_{n,(k+l)z}(t)$ at times $t = 0$, $(k+l)z$, $2(k+l)z, \ldots$. At all other periods in the cycle, nonserious offers are made: the seller offers $\bar{b}$; the buyer offers 0. If there has been a seller deviation (and no buyer deviation), play reverts to a cyclical weak-Markov equilibrium, described in the next paragraph. After any buyer deviation, the seller updates his beliefs to $b = \bar{b}$, and an adaptation of the complete-information, (k, l)-alternating-offer equilibrium is played (the strategies of Theorem 5, modified as in the proof of Theorem 3).

Consider a version of the (k, l)-alternating-offer game in which the buyer is constrained to only make counteroffers of zero (i.e., the seller makes k successive offers, followed by l periods of inactivity). We define a *cyclical weak-Markov equilibrium* to be a sequential equilibrium in which the buyer's strategy σ_b depends only on the seller's most recent offer *and* the period modulo $(k+l)$. Two theorems can be proven concerning cyclical weak-Markov equilibria, under the same distributional assumptions as in Section 4. First, for any time interval $z > 0$ between periods, such an equilibrium exists. Second, a modified version of the Uniform Coase Conjecture holds: there exists $\bar{z}$ such that whenever $0 < z < \bar{z}$, a price less than ε is charged *in the initial cycle* (of k offers).

These two theorems imply the existence of punishments sufficiently severe to deter the seller from ever deviating from the equilibrium path in the game where buyer moves are suppressed. Finally, the cyclical weak-Markov equilibria can be embedded in the actual (k, l)-alternating-offer game, by specifying strategies in which the buyer is "expected" (instead of "required") to offer zero, and the seller updates his beliefs to be $b = \bar{b}$ if the buyer ever offers a positive price.

As in the proof of Theorem 3, it can be proven that the strategies specified above form a sequential equilibrium for each n, and that the sequence of equilibria implements $\{p, x\}$. ∎

9. CONCLUSION

In this paper, we examined incomplete information bargaining games which, while sequential and infinite-horizon, were not literally "repeated" games. We have proven, in the seller-offer game, that a folk theorem *literally* holds, as the time interval between successive offers approaches zero. In alternating-offer games, there is also a continuum of sequential equilibria, but *not* a folk theorem: only a strict subset of all ICBMs is implementable. Finally, in the buyer-offer game, we are much further distanced from the realm of folk theorems: there exists one unique sequential equilibrium.

We have found, in offer/counteroffer bargaining games, that the right to make offers confers bargaining power. Recall the set M of incentive feasible points, defined in section 2. The set of sequential equilibria of the seller-offer game is quite large, yielding all the payoffs in M. Addition of buyer counteroffers to the seller-offer game has two effects. First, if we let $\lambda = l/(k + l)$ and $\hat{p}(\lambda) = (1 - \lambda)\bar{b}$, then all elements in M violating $U(b) \geqslant b - \hat{p}(\lambda)$ are eliminated as possible payoffs of the game where the proportion of buyer offers equals λ. Second, if $\hat{p}(\lambda)$ is less than the lowest monopoly price of $F(\cdot)$, then all payoffs in M violating $V \leqslant \sup_{0 \leqslant p \leqslant \hat{p}(\lambda)} \{p[1 - F(p)]\}$ are eliminated. Thus, as λ is increased, outcomes most one-sidedly unfavorable to the buyer and outcomes most one-sidedly favorable to the seller are removed. Consequently, increasing λ also eliminates the most inefficient equilibria, and $\lambda = 1$ guarantees that all possible gains from trade are realized.

In our model, information also confers bargaining power. When the buyer makes all the offers, trade occurs at the same terms as in the unique subgame perfect equilibrium of the complete-information, buyer-offer game. Thus, when the informed party has the exclusive right to make offers, he is assured of his most preferred outcome in M. However, when the uninformed party has the exclusive right to make offers, the same is not necessarily true—any payoff in M may ensue.

An interesting question that remains is whether the right to make offers confers bargaining power in sequential bargaining games with two-sided incomplete information, or whether the Folk Theorem holds. We will address these issues in a future paper.

APPENDIX

Proof of Theorem 2

If $\{p, x\}$ is implementable, then there exists a sequence $z_n \downarrow 0$ and a sequence of sequential equilibria inducing, for each n, an ICBM $\{p_n, x_n\}$ such that $\lim_{n \to \infty} (p_n(b), x_n(b)) = (p(b), x(b))$ for all $b > 0$. Observe that ICBMs satisfy (1) and (2). Since these inequalities are preserved by the limiting operation, $U(b \mid b') \leq U(b)$ for all $b, b' \neq 0$, where $U(b \mid b')$ is the utility to b posing as type b'. Obviously, $U(b \mid b') \leq U(b)$ at $b = 0$. Finally, observe that $U(b \mid 0) \leq \lim_{b' \downarrow 0} U(b \mid b') \leq U(b)$, since $p(0) \leq \lim_{b' \downarrow 0} p(b')$. Thus $\{p, x\}$ is incentive compatible. Lemma 1 implies that it is also (ex post) individually rational.

Conversely, consider any ICBM $\{p, x\}$. We will show the existence of a sequence $z_n \downarrow 0$, and a sequence of sequential equilibria σ_n (corresponding to a time interval between offers of z_n), with the property that for all $\varepsilon > 0$, there exists $\bar{n}(\varepsilon)$ such that for all $n \geq \bar{n}(\varepsilon)$: $|p_n(b) - p(b)| < \varepsilon$ for all $b \in \text{supp } F$ such that $b > \varepsilon$; and $|x_n(b) - x(b)| < \varepsilon$ for all $b \in \text{supp } F$.

We first need the following definitions:

$$\mathscr{P} = \text{closure}\{p(b): b \in \text{supp } F \text{ and } b > 0\},$$

and

$$R_{k,n} = \min\{\pi \in \mathscr{P}: \pi \geq k/n\} \cup \max\{\pi \in \mathscr{P} \cap [1/n, 1]: \pi \leq k/n\},$$

where n is a positive integer, and $\min(\cdot)$ and $\max(\cdot)$ are taken to be the empty set if their arguments are empty. Also let $\hat{\mathscr{P}}_n = \bigcup_{k=1}^{n} R_{k,n}$. Observe that $\hat{\mathscr{P}}_n$ has at most $2n$ elements. Furthermore, if there is a "gap" in $\mathscr{P}$ with length at least $1/n$, then both endpoints of that gap are contained in $\hat{\mathscr{P}}_n$. Also define $b(\pi) = \{b \in [0, \bar{b}]: p(b) = \pi\}$, for all π in the range of $p(\cdot)$, and

$b(\pi) = \lim_{n \to \infty} b(\pi_n)$, for those π that are limits of $\pi_n \in \mathscr{P}$, but are not contained in the range of $p(\cdot)$. Observe that $b(\pi)$ is set-valued.

Let $b^1(\pi) = \sup b(\pi)$ and $b^2(\pi) = \inf b(\pi)$. Define: $\mathscr{P}_n = \{\pi \in \hat{\mathscr{P}}_n : U(b^2(\pi)) > b^2(\pi)/n$ and $x(b^2(\pi))/p(b^2(\pi)) > 1/n\}$; and $\mathscr{B}_n = \{\beta : \beta = b^1(\pi)$ or $\beta = b^2(\pi)$, for some $\pi \in \mathscr{P}_n\}$. For any $z > 0$ and $\pi \in \mathscr{P}_n$, let $t_z^1(\pi) = \sup\{kz : e^{-rkz} \geq \pi$, for integer $k\}$ and $t_z^2(\pi) = t_z^1(\pi) + z$. Also, for all $\pi \in \mathscr{P}_n$ and $i = 1, 2$, define $s_z^i(\pi)$ by

$$U(b^i(\pi)) = e^{-rt_z^i(\pi)} [b^i(\pi) - s_z^i(\pi)]. \tag{21}$$

Select $\bar{z}_n^1 > 0$ such that for all z $(0 < z < \bar{z}_n^1)$: $|t_z^1(\pi) - t_z^1(\pi')| > 2z$ for all $\pi \neq \pi'$ $(\pi, \pi' \in \mathscr{P}_n)$; $s_z^i(\pi) > 1/n$ for all $\pi \in \mathscr{P}_n$ and $i = 1, 2$; and $1 - e^{-rz} < 1/n$. Define $\tilde{\pi}_n = \min \mathscr{P}_n$, if $\mathscr{P}_n \neq \varnothing$, and $\tilde{\pi}_n = 1/n$ otherwise. Also let $\tilde{b}_n = \min \mathscr{B}_n$, if $\mathscr{B}_n \neq \varnothing$, and $\tilde{b}_n = 0$ otherwise. Furthermore, let $T_{n,z} = \inf\{kz : e^{-rkz} \leq 1/n$, for some integer $k\} + t_z^2(\tilde{\pi}_n)$.

We now construct a sequence of offers which the seller is supposed to make at times t, where $t \in \{0, z, 2z, 3z, \ldots\}$:

$$q_{n,z}(t) = \begin{cases} s_z^i(\pi), & \text{if } t = t_z^i(\pi) \text{ and } \pi \in \mathscr{P}_n, \text{ for } i = 1, 2, \\ (1 - e^{-rz}) \sum_{k=0}^{\infty} e^{-rkz} F^{-1}[e^{-(m+k)z} F(1/n)], \\ & \text{if } t = T_{n,z} + mz, \text{ for some nonnegative integer } m, \\ \tilde{b}, & \text{otherwise,} \end{cases}$$

where $F^{-1}(y) \equiv \inf\{b : F(b) \geq y\}$.

Consider a strategy for the seller in which he charges $q_{n,z}(t)$ if he has not deviated from that path in any prior period, and in which he reverts to a weak-Markov equilibrium otherwise. Buyers optimize given their predictions derived from the seller's strategy and, in case of indifference, choose the purchase time closest to what the mechanism $\{p, x\}$ prescribes. To be precise, let $Y(n, z; \beta) = \arg \max_t \{e^{-rt}(\beta - q_{n,z}(t))\}$, for $\beta \in (0, \tilde{b}] \cap \operatorname{supp} F$, and $Y(n, z; \beta) = +\infty$ for $\beta = 0$. For β such that $Y(n, z; \beta)$ is single-valued define the purchase time $\tau(n, z; \beta) = Y(n, z; \beta)$, and for β such that $Y(n, z; \beta)$ is multiple-valued mix between the lowest and highest members of Y, to yield a purchase probability as close to $p(\beta)$ as possible. Concretely, choose $\theta \in [0, 1]$ such that $|\theta e^{-rc} + (1 - \theta) e^{-rd} - p(\beta)|$ is minimal, where c and d are the lowest and highest element in $Y(n, z; \beta)$, respectively.[18] By Ausubel and Deneckere [2], there exists $\bar{z}_n^2 > 0$ such that for all

---

[18] Mixed strategies along the equilibrium path could be avoided by introducing extra prices offered between c and d, but only at considerable notational expense.

$0 < z \leqslant \bar{z}_n^2$, $q_{n,z}(t)$ is a sequential equilibrium price path for all periods starting at time $T_{n,z}$. Let Π be the seller's expected profits along the sequential equilibrium starting at $T_{n,z}$, discounted back to period zero. Observe that $\Pi > 0$. By the Coase Conjecture there exists $\bar{z}_n^3 > 0$ such that for all $0 < z \leqslant \bar{z}_n^3$, and for every weak-Markov equilibrium of the seller-offer game (in which all potential buyers are still present), the seller's expected profits in the initial period are less than Π. Hence the seller has no incentive to deviate from $q_{n,z}(t)$ in any period t provided z is no larger than min $(\bar{z}_n^1, \bar{z}_n^2, \bar{z}_n^3, \bar{z}_n^4)$, where $\bar{z}_n^4 > 0$ will be defined below.

Next, we show that for every $\varepsilon > 0$ there exists $\bar{n}(\varepsilon)$ such that for every $n \geqslant \bar{n}(\varepsilon)$, $|p_n(b) - p(b)| < \varepsilon$ if $b \geqslant \varepsilon$. In other words, we show that $p_n(\cdot)$ converges uniformly to $p(\cdot)$ on $[\varepsilon, \bar{b}]$, and this for every $\varepsilon > 0$. Recall, however, that any sequential equilibrium has the property that sales occur over infinite time, and thus that the graph of $p_n(\cdot)$ is anchored at the origin. Define $\tilde{b} = \inf\{b \in \operatorname{supp} F: p(b) > 0\}$, and observe that $\tilde{b}_n \to \tilde{b}$. If $\lim_{b \downarrow \tilde{b}} p(b) = 0$, no special problems are encountered in obtaining $p_n(\cdot)$'s which have the right convergence properties, since the graph of the limiting $p(\cdot)$ is also anchored at the origin (this is Case 1). In Case 2, however, there is a discontinuity in $p(b)$ at the point $\tilde{b} > 0$. In order to obtain uniform convergence, then, we must construct equilibria which ensure that all $b < \tilde{b}$ have a small probability of trade, whereas all $b > \tilde{b}$ must have a large probability of trade. We accomplish this by making $\tilde{b}$ indifferent between an offer at a time approximately corresponding to $\tilde{p}$, and the next price accepted. In Case 3, a somewhat similar problem arises since there is (essentially) a discontinuity in $p(b)$ at the origin. The previous approach no longer works, however, since $\tilde{b}$ cannot be made to accept any positive offers. We circumvent this difficulty by letting a type $\hat{b}_n$ be the indifferent type, where $\hat{b}_n \to 0$ as $n \to \infty$. We now consider the three cases in sequence.

Case 1. Suppose $\lim_{b \downarrow \tilde{b}} p(b) = 0$.

Observe that if $b \in \mathscr{B}_n$, then b can attain $U(b)$ by purchasing at one of the prices offered before $T_{n,z}$. Indeed, *every* price offered before $T_{n,z}$ gives some type $b \in \mathscr{B}_n$ the utility he achieves under the mechanism $\{p, x\}$. Furthermore, since $U(b) > b/n$, type b does better purchasing before $T_{n,z}$ than after, for all z, i.e., $\tau(n, z; b) < T_{n,z}$.

Suppressing z, define $p_n(\beta) = e^{-r\tau(n,z;\beta)}$. We will now prove the following claim: there exists $\bar{z}_n^4 > 0$ s.t. for all z $(0 < z < \bar{z}_n^4)$ and for all $\beta \in \operatorname{supp} F \cap [\tilde{b}_n, \bar{b}]$, we have $|p_n(\beta) - p(\beta)| < 3/n$. First, we will demonstrate the claim for all $\beta \in \mathscr{B}_n$.

Let $U(\beta \,|\, t)$ denote the payoff to β of purchasing at time t. We need to show that if $\pi \in \mathscr{P}_n$ and $|\pi - p(\beta)| > 1/n$, then

$$U(\beta \,|\, t_z^i(\pi)) \leqslant \max_{j=1,2} \{U[\beta \,|\, t_z^j(p(\beta))]\}. \tag{22}$$

Observe that the right side equals $U(\beta)$, since $\beta \in \mathcal{B}_n$, and that the left side converges to $\pi\beta - x(b^i(\pi))$, as $z \to 0$.

(i) Suppose $\pi\beta - x(b^i(\pi)) < U(\beta)$. Then there exists $\bar{z}(\beta, \pi)$ such that for all z $(0 < z < \bar{z}(\beta, \pi))$, (22) is satisfied with strict inequality.

(ii) Suppose $\pi\beta - x(b^i(\pi)) = U(\beta)$, and $|\pi - p(\beta)| > 1/n$. Without loss of generality, let $\pi > p(\beta)$. Observe that $b^2(\pi) = \beta = b^1(p(\beta))$, since any $b > \beta$ prefers π over $p(\beta)$ and any $b < \beta$ prefers $p(\beta)$ over π. By construction, β is indifferent between purchasing at $t_z^2(\pi)$ and $t_z^1(p(\beta))$, since both give $U(\beta)$. It is also fairly straightforward to show that β does strictly worse by purchasing at $t_z^1(\pi)$. We conclude that $U(\beta \mid t_z^i(\pi)) \leqslant U(\beta \mid t_z^1(p(\beta)))$, for $i = 1, 2$, and (22) follows.

(iii) The case $\pi\beta - x(b^i(\pi)) > U(\beta)$ is vacuous.

Finally, observe that $\Lambda \equiv \{(\beta, \pi): \beta \in \mathcal{B}_n, \pi \in \mathcal{P}_n \text{ and } \pi\beta - x < U(\beta)\}$ is finite. Define $\bar{z}_n^4 = \min\{\bar{z}(\beta, \pi): (\beta, \pi) \in \Lambda\}$. We have just shown that β purchases at a time which corresponds to a probability in the mechanism within $1/n$ of $p(\beta)$. We previously assumed that z is such that $(1 - e^{-rz}) \leqslant 1/n$. We may conclude that $|p_n(\beta) - p(\beta)| \leqslant 2/n$, for $\beta \in \mathcal{B}_n$, and $0 < z \leqslant \bar{z}_n^4$.

Second, we will demonstrate the claim for all $\beta \in \text{supp } F \cap [\underline{b}_n, \bar{b}]$. Let $\beta' = \max\{b \in \mathcal{B}_n \text{ s.t. } b \leqslant \beta\}$ and $\beta'' = \min\{b \in \mathcal{B}_n \text{ s.t. } b \geqslant \beta\}$. By Fudenberg et al.'s [12] Lemma 1, β purchases no later than β' and no earlier than β'' in *any* sequential equilibrium. We have already shown that β' purchases no later than a time yielding a purchase probability of $p(\beta') - 2/n$, and β'' purchases no earlier than a time associated with a probability of $p(\beta'') + 2/n$. Observe also that since $p(\beta) \in \mathcal{P}$, and by the definition of $\mathcal{P}_n$, we must have $p(\beta') > p(\beta) - 1/n$ and $p(\beta'') < p(\beta) + 1/n$. We conclude that the time at which β purchases in the sequential equilibrium translates to a probability between $p(\beta) - 3/n$ and $p(\beta) + 3/n$.

Finally, choose arbitrary $\varepsilon > 0$. We may pick $\bar{n}(\varepsilon)$ such that $3/n < \varepsilon$ and $p(\underline{b}_n) < \varepsilon$ for all $n \geqslant \bar{n}(\varepsilon)$. Every equilibrium constructed above satisfies $|p_n(b) - p(b)| \leqslant \varepsilon$, for all $b \in \text{supp } F$ and $n \geqslant \bar{n}(\varepsilon)$. This concludes Case 1.

Case 2. Suppose $\bar{b} > 0$ and $\tilde{p} \equiv \lim_{b \downarrow \bar{b}} p(b) > 0$.

Restrict attention to n such that $1/n < \min(\tilde{p}, \bar{b})$. Repeat the construction of the previous price path, *except* define $s_z^2(\tilde{\pi}_n)$ by

$$e^{-rt_z^2(\tilde{\pi}_n)}[\bar{b} - s_z^2(\tilde{\pi}_n)] = e^{-rT_{n,z}}[\bar{b} - q_{n,z}(T_{n,z})].$$

First, we claim that the buyer of type $\bar{b}$ is indifferent between purchasing at $t_z^2(\tilde{\pi}_n)$ and $T_{n,z}$, and for sufficiently small z, strictly prefers these two times to all others. Observe

(i) $\bar{b}$ gets positive surplus buying either at $T_{n,z}$ or $t_z^2(\tilde{\pi}_n)$, and is indifferent between them, by construction.

(ii) $\bar{b}$ strictly prefers $T_{n,z}$ to all later times. This follows from our construction of the endgame which makes the buyer of type $1/n$ purchase at either $T_{n,z}$ or $T_{n,z}+z$ (he is indifferent between them). By hypothesis, $\bar{b} > 1/n$, so type $\bar{b}$ strictly prefers $T_{n,z}$ to $T_{n,z}+z$ and later times.

(iii) $\bar{b}$ strictly prefers $t_z^2(\tilde{\pi}_n)$ to all earlier times, for sufficiently small z. Observe that prices charged at all times before $t_z^2(\tilde{\pi}_n)$ are defined to give some type b $(b \geqslant \bar{b})$ the payoff he receives in the mechanism $\{p, x\}$. Also note that all prices in the mechanism associated with positive purchase probabilities are greater than or equal to $\bar{b}$. Hence, for any $\varepsilon > 0$, there exists $\bar{z}_\varepsilon > 0$ such that for all z $(0 < z < \bar{z}_\varepsilon)$, the prices charged in the price path are greater than $\bar{b} - \varepsilon$, yielding $\bar{b}$ surplus less than ε. Meanwhile, the price charged at $t_z^2(\tilde{p})$ has been chosen to give $\bar{b}$ the same surplus he would receive as by purchasing at $T_{n,z}$ (at a price less than $1/n$, since type $1/n$ purchases at $T_{n,z}$). Note that $T_{n,z}$ is uniformly bounded in z, so purchasing at $t_z^2(\tilde{p})$ gives $\bar{b}$ surplus which is bounded away from zero. We conclude that for sufficiently small ε (and $\bar{z}_\varepsilon$), $\bar{b}$ strictly prefers to purchase at $t_z^2(\tilde{p})$ to earlier. This concludes the proof of the claim.

The claim establishes that for all n, all types $\beta < \bar{b}$ prefer to purchase at time $T_{n,z}$ or later. Note that agents discount time $T_{n,z}$ by a factor of $1/n$, so $|p_n(\beta)| < 1/n$, for all $\beta < \bar{b}$, i.e., $|p_n(\beta) - p(\beta)| < 1/n$, for all $\beta < \bar{b}$. The claim also establishes that all types $\beta > \bar{b}$ prefer to purchase at time $t_z^2(\tilde{\pi})$ or earlier.

Define $\hat{b}_n = \sup\{b: t_z^2(\tilde{\pi}_n) = \tau(n, z; b)\}$. Observe that $\hat{b}_n$ converges to $b^1(\tilde{p})$, as $n \to \infty$. Choose arbitrary $\varepsilon > 0$. There exists $\bar{n}_1(\varepsilon)$ such that $|\tilde{\pi}_n - \tilde{p}| < \varepsilon/2$, and $|p(\hat{b}_n) - \tilde{p}| < \varepsilon/2$, for all $n \geqslant \bar{n}_1(\varepsilon)$. Hence $|p_n(b) - p(b)| = |\tilde{\pi}_n - p(b)| \leqslant |\tilde{\pi}_n - \tilde{p}| + |\tilde{p} - p(b)| < \varepsilon$ for all $b \in (\bar{b}, \hat{b}_n]$.

By reasoning identical to Case 1, there exists $\bar{z}$ sufficiently small such that $|p_n(b) - p(b)| < 3/n$, for $b \in (\hat{b}_n, \bar{b}]$, and $0 < z < \bar{z}$. Finally, note that $\bar{b}$ can be made to purchase with probability near $p(\bar{b})$ by mixing between purchasing at $t_z^2(\tilde{\pi}_n)$ and $T_{n,z}$, since $0 \leqslant p(\bar{b}) \leqslant \tilde{p}$. We may thus conclude that there exists $\bar{z}_n^4 > 0$ such that for all z $(0 < z < \bar{z}_n^4)$ and for all $\beta \in \text{supp } F \cap [[0, \bar{b}] \cup (\hat{b}_n, \bar{b}]]$, $|p_n(\beta) - p(\beta)| < 3/n$. Finally, let $\varepsilon > 0$ be arbitrary. Pick $n \geqslant \bar{n}(\varepsilon)$ such that $3/n \leqslant \varepsilon$. We then have constructed equilibria that satisfy, for $n \geqslant \bar{n}(\varepsilon)$ and $0 < z \leqslant \bar{z}_{n(\varepsilon)}^4$, $|p_n(\beta) - p(\beta)| < \varepsilon$, for all $\beta \in \text{supp } F$. This concludes Case 2.

Case 3. Suppose $\bar{b} = 0$ and $\tilde{p} \equiv \lim_{b \downarrow \bar{b}} p(b) > 0$.

We restrict attention to the case where $b^1(\tilde{p}) > 0$, i.e., there is a mass point of people buying at a zero price (if $b^1(\tilde{p}) = 0$, the proof proceeds just as in Case 1). Let n be sufficiently large that $b^1(\tilde{p}) > 1/n$, and $U(b^1(\tilde{p})) > b^1(\tilde{p})/n$. In what follows, assume that $\mathscr{P}_n \neq \varnothing$ for some $n < \infty$.[19]

Let $t^* = \min\{kz: e^{-rkz}[b^1(\tilde{p}) - 1/n] < U(b^1(\tilde{p}))$, for some nonnegative integer $k\}$, and define $q(t^*)$ such that $U(b^1(\tilde{p})) = e^{-rt^*}[b^1(\tilde{p}) - q(t^*)]$. Note that $q(t^*) < 1/n$, but very close to $1/n$ when z is small. Also, let $T_{n,z} = \inf\{kz: e^{-rkz} \leqslant 1/n$, for some integer $k\} + t^*$. Then, for sufficiently large n, $\mathscr{B}_n \neq \varnothing$, and $\tilde{b}_n > b^1(\tilde{p})$. Observe now that:

(i) If $\beta < b^1(\tilde{p})$, β purchases at time t^* or later, provided z is sufficiently small. Indeed, for such z, t^* is an optimal purchase time for $b^1(\tilde{p})$. Purchasing at t^* yields $U(b^1(\tilde{p}))$. Purchasing after t^* yields a surplus of at most $b^1(\tilde{p})/n$, which is less than $U(b^1(\tilde{p}))$. Finally, all earlier prices either yield exactly $U(b^1(\tilde{p}))$, or approximately $U(b^1(\tilde{p})|b)$ for some $b \in \mathscr{B}_n$. By incentive compatibility of the mechanism, the latter options yield $b^1(\tilde{p})$ strictly lower utility, for sufficiently small z. Hence, if $\beta < b^1(\tilde{p})$, β strictly prefers to buy at t^* or later.

(ii) If $\beta > \tilde{b}_n$, β purchases at a time corresponding to $\tilde{\pi}_n$ or earlier, by similar reasoning as in (i).

Consequently, if $(\tilde{b} + 1)/n < \beta < b^1(\tilde{p})$, β purchases at t^*. Indeed, since the price at t^* is less than $1/n$, buying at t^* gives a surplus of at least: $e^{-rt^*}[\beta - 1/n] > e^{-rt^*}(\tilde{b}/n)$. The next price after t^* is not offered until $T_{n,z}$, and thus, buying after t^* yields surplus of at most $e^{-rt^*}(\beta/n) < e^{-rt^*}(\tilde{b}/n)$. Also, if $\beta > \tilde{b}_n$, we obtain $|p_n(\beta) - p(\beta)| < 3/n$, by reasoning similar to that of Case 1.

Finally, consider $\beta \in [b^1(\tilde{p}), \tilde{b}_n]$. First, we treat the case where $\lim_{b \downarrow b^1(\tilde{p})} p(b) = \tilde{p}$. Then, for any $\varepsilon > 0$, there exists $\bar{n}(\varepsilon)$ such that for all $n \geqslant \bar{n}(\varepsilon)$, $|p(\tilde{b}_n) - \tilde{p}| < \varepsilon/2$ and $2/n < \varepsilon/2$. Since β purchases at either t^* or a time corresponding to $p(\tilde{b}_n)$, we obtain $|p_n(\beta) - p(\beta)| < \varepsilon$.

Second, consider $\beta \in [b^1(\tilde{p}), \tilde{b}_n]$, and assume $\lim_{b \downarrow b^1(\tilde{p})} p(b) \equiv \hat{p} > \tilde{p}$. By incentive compatibility of the mechanism, $b^1(\tilde{p}) \, \tilde{p} \geqslant b^1(\tilde{p}) \, \hat{p} - \hat{x}$, where $\hat{x}$ is the discounted price associated with $\hat{p}$, and 0 is associated with $\tilde{p}$. Thus, $\hat{x} \geqslant b^1(\tilde{p})[\hat{p} - \tilde{p}] > 0$, and the price $\hat{x}/\hat{p}$ is bounded away from zero. Hence, for sufficiently large n, $\hat{p} \in \mathscr{P}_n$ and so $\tilde{b}_n = b^2(\hat{p})$. Our argument above has treated all $\beta \in [(\tilde{b} + 1)/n, \tilde{b}] \cap \text{supp } F$, except possibly $b^1(\tilde{p})$ and $b^2(\hat{p})$. If $b^1(\tilde{p}) = b^2(\hat{p})$, observe that for sufficiently large n, $b^1(\tilde{p})$ attains the same payoff at t^* as at $t^2_z(\hat{p})$, and via mixed strategies, can be made to buy with any probability p satisfying $\tilde{p} \leqslant p \leqslant \hat{p}$. If $b^1(\tilde{p}) < b^2(\hat{p})$, then by definition, $b^1(\tilde{p})$ strictly prefers $\tilde{p}$ to $\hat{p}$ in the mechanism, and the reverse for $b^2(\hat{p})$. Since the constructed sequential equilibrium approximates the mechanism, the same strict preference relationship will hold here, for sufficiently large n. This concludes the proof of Case 3, as we have shown that for arbitrary

---

[19] If $\mathscr{P}_n = \varnothing$ for all n, use the construction below, with $q(t^*) = 1/n$.

$\varepsilon > 0$ there exists sufficiently large $\bar{n}(\varepsilon)$ such that $|p_n(b) - p(b)| < \varepsilon$, for all $n \geq \bar{n}(\varepsilon)$ and all $b \in [(\bar{b} + 1)/n, \bar{b}] \cap \operatorname{supp} F$.

Note that n can be chosen sufficiently large that $(\bar{b} + 1)/n < \varepsilon$. Hence, we conclude that for every $\varepsilon > 0$, there exists $\bar{n}_1(\varepsilon)$ such that for all $n \geq \bar{n}_1(\varepsilon)$ and for all $b \in \operatorname{supp} F$ satisfying $b > \varepsilon$, $|p_n(b) - p(b)| < \varepsilon$. Lemma 2 below then implies there exists $\bar{n}_2(\varepsilon)$ such that for all $n \geq \bar{n}_2(\varepsilon)$ and all $b \in \operatorname{supp} F$, $|x_n(b) - x(b)| < \varepsilon$. This ends the proof of Theorem 2. ∎

LEMMA 2. *Suppose* $|p_n(b) - p(b)| < \varepsilon$, *for all* $b \in \operatorname{supp} F$ *such that* $b > \varepsilon$, *and* $bp_n(b) - x_n(b) = U(b)$ *for all* $b \in \mathcal{B}_n$. *Then*

$$|x_n(b) - x(b)| < \bar{b}(3\varepsilon + 2/n), \qquad \text{for all} \quad b \in \operatorname{supp} F.$$

Proof. First observe that for all $b \leq \varepsilon$, $|x_n(b) - x(b)| \leq \varepsilon$, since both $x_n(b)$ and $x(b)$ are in the interval $[0, b]$. Second, for $b \in \mathcal{B}_n$, $U(b) - bp_n(b) + x_n(b) = b(p(b) - p_n(b)) - (x(b) - x_n(b)) = 0$, implying $|x_n(b) - x(b)| = b|p_n(b) - p(b)| \leq \bar{b}\varepsilon$. Third, by incentive compatibility of the sequential equilibrium, for any b and $b' \in \operatorname{supp} F$: $bp_n(b) - x_n(b) \geq bp_n(b') - x_n(b')$; and $b'p_n(b') - x_n(b') \geq b'p_n(b) - x_n(b)$. These two inequalities imply that $|x_n(b) - x_n(b')| \leq \bar{b}|p_n(b) - p_n(b')|$.

Finally, consider any $b \in \operatorname{supp} F$ such that $b > \varepsilon$. Observe that there exists $\beta \in \mathcal{B}_n$ such that $|p(b) - p(\beta)| < 1/n$. Note that $|x_n(b) - x(b)| \leq |x_n(b) - x_n(\beta)| + |x_n(\beta) - x(\beta)| + |x(\beta) - x(b)|$. The first term on the right side is bounded by $\bar{b}|p_n(b) - p_n(\beta)|$, which in turn is bounded above by $\bar{b}(2\varepsilon + 1/n)$. The second term is bounded above by $\bar{b}\varepsilon$, and the last by $\bar{b}/n$. Thus, $|x_n(b) - x(b)| \leq \bar{b}(3\varepsilon + 2/n)$. ∎

REFERENCES

1. A. ADMATI AND M. PERRY, Strategic delay in bargaining, *Rev. Econ. Stud.* **54** (1987), 345–364.
2. L. AUSUBEL AND R. DENECKERE, Reputation in bargaining and durable goods monopoly, *Econometrica* (1989), forthcoming.
3. K. BINMORE, "Nash Bargaining Theory I, II, and III," ICERD Discussion Papers Nos. 9, 14, and 15, London School of Economics, 1980.
4. J. BULOW, Durable-goods monopolists, *J. Polit. Econ.* **90** (1982), 314–332.
5. K. CHATTERJEE, Disagreement in bargaining: Models with incomplete information, *in* "Game Theoretic Models of Bargaining" (A. Roth, Ed.), pp. 9–26, Cambridge Univ. Press, New York, 1985.
6. K. CHATTERJEE AND L. SAMUELSON, Bargaining with two-sided incomplete information: An infinite horizon model with alternating offers, Pennsylvania State University, mimeo, 1984.
7. K. CHATTERJEE AND L. SAMUELSON, Bargaining under incomplete information: The unrestricted offers case, Pennsylvania State University, mimeo, 1986.

8. K. CHATTERJEE AND W. SAMUELSON, Bargaining under incomplete information, *Oper. Res.* **31** (1983), 835–851.

9. R. COASE, Durability and monopoly, *J. Law. Econ.* **15** (1972), 143–149.

10. P. CRAMTON, Bargaining with incomplete information: an infinite-horizon model with continuous uncertainty, *Rev. Econ. Stud.* **51** (1984), 579–593.

11. P. CRAMTON, Sequential bargaining mechanisms, *in* "Game Theoretic Models of Bargaining" (A. Roth, Ed.), pp. 149–180, Cambridge Univ. Press, New York, 1985.

12. D. FUDENBERG, D. LEVINE, AND J. TIROLE, Infinite horizon models of bargaining with one-sided incomplete information, *in* "Game Theoretic Models of Bargaining" (A. Roth, Ed.), pp. 73–98, Cambridge Univ. Press, New York, 1985.

13. S. GROSSMAN AND M. PERRY, Sequential bargaining under asymmetric information, *J. Econ. Theory* **39** (1986), 119–154.

14. F. GUL AND H. SONNENSCHEIN, One-sided uncertainty does not cause delay, Stanford University, mimeo, 1986.

15. F. GUL, H. SONNENSCHEIN, AND R. WILSON, Foundation of dynamic monopoly and the Coase conjecture, *J. Econ. Theory* **39** (1986), 155–190.

16. R. MYERSON, Incentive compatibility and the bargaining problem, *Econometrica* **47** (1979), 61–73.

17. R. MYERSON, Two-person bargaining problems with incomplete information, *Econometrica* **52** (1984), 461–487.

18. R. MYERSON, Analysis of two bargaining problems with incomplete information, *in* "Game Theoretic Models of Bargaining" (A. Roth, Ed.), pp. 115–147, Cambridge Univ. Press, New York, 1985.

19. R. MYERSON AND M. SATTERTHWAITE, Efficient mechanisms for bilateral trading, *J. Econ. Theory* **28** (1983), 265–281.

20. A. RUBINSTEIN, Perfect equilibrium in a bargaining model, *Econometrica* **50** (1982), 97–109.

21. A. SHAKED AND J. SUTTON, Involuntary unemployment as a perfect equilibrium in a bargaining model, *Econometrica* **52** (1984), 1351–1364.

22. J. SOBEL AND I. TAKAHASHI, A multi-stage model of bargaining, *Rev. Econ. Stud.* **50** (1983), 411–426.

23. N. STOKEY, Rational expectations and durable goods pricing, *Bell J. Econ.* **12** (1981), 112–128.

24. S. WILLIAMS, Efficient performance in two agent bargaining, *J. Econ. Theory* **41** (1987), 154–172.

25. R. WILSON, Game-theoretic analyses of trading processes, *in* "Advances in Economic Theory" (T. Bewley, Ed.), pp. 33–70, Cambridge Univ. Press, New York, 1987.

JOURNAL OF ECONOMIC THEORY **48**, 47–62 (1989)

Bargaining with Common Values*

DANIEL R. VINCENT

The Kellogg Graduate School of Management,
Northwestern University, Evanston, Illinois 60208

Received January 16, 1987; revised March 28, 1988

This paper examines a bargaining model with asymmetric information in which the private valuations of the two bargaining agents are correlated. It shows that equilibria in such models typically exhibit a significant probability of a significant delay to agreement. The paper characterizes the unique perfect Bayesian equilibrium to the game in which an uninformed buyer makes offers to a privately informed seller. It also shows, by example, that in this framework bargainers may rationally break off negotiations even in the presence of commonly known gains from trade. *Journal of Economic Literature* Classification Numbers: 022, 026. © 1989 Academic Press, Inc.

Since Rubinstein's paper in 1982, an important area of research in microeconomic theory has centred on strategic bargaining games. Recent work has focussed on bargaining games in which there is either one-sided or two-sided uncertainty about the preferences of the opponents who are bargaining. Although this is a natural extension, it is surprising to realize how restrictive these models are. Much of the current research on bargaining with incomplete information shares a common feature—each agent has perfect information about his own valuation of the object to be traded and, so, the models say little, for example, about behaviour when there is asymmetric information about the quality of the good to be traded. This paper takes the view that a more general specification of uncertainty is the appropriate method of modelling these games and shows that extending the models in this way alters some important conclusions of previous research. In particular, it is shown that allowing a more general form of private information re-establishes the possibility of significant delay to agreement even when bargaining offers can be made arbitrarily quickly. In addition, a common values model provides an explanation for the

* I am grateful to Professors Sanford Grossman and Hugo Sonnenschein for advice and encouragement in conducting this research. The comments of referees of this Journal are also appreciated. I would like to thank Princeton University, the Sloan Foundation, and the Social Sciences and Humanities Research Council of Canada for financial support.

breakdown of negotiations even in the presence of commonly known gains from trade.

In previous models of bargaining under uncertainty an agent's valuation of a good is assumed to be independent of his opponent's valuation. Borrowing a term from the theory of auctions, these models might be called private values models. A common values model of bargaining incorporates the private values model as a special case but also allows the study of cases where values are correlated. If a player enjoys private information in this game, such information could include information which is relevant for his opponent's valuation as well. For example, one agent might have private information about the quality of the good to be traded. This feature of the information structure is recognizable in many well-known economic problems such as the market for lemons, job-market signalling, or credit-rationing models. It is a natural environment in which to set incomplete information bargaining games.[1]

The bulk of the paper restricts attention to games where only the uninformed agent makes offers. This is a strong restriction. Solutions to the more complicated alternating offer games, however, still pose significant problems even in the private values models. The one-sided offer game has been examined in the private values case by Fudenburg, Levine, and Tirole [6] (henceforth FLT), and Gul, Sonnenschein, and Wilson [9] (henceforth GSW).[2] The first theorem of this paper shows that with slightly stronger assumptions on the parameters of the game (including the requirement that the uninformed agent be at least as patient as the informed agent), the uniqueness results of FLT and GSW carry over to the case of common values. That is, for a broad class of one-sided offer, one-sided uncertainty common values bargaining games there exists a unique perfect Bayesian equilibrium. The equilibrium is characterized and is shown to be similar to that of the FLT and GSW models.

A branch of the recent literature on bargaining with incomplete information has been concerned with the relationship between uncertainty and delay to agreement. In Rubinstein's [10] game of complete information, the unique subgame perfect equilibrium involved agreement in the first period of bargaining. However, the expectation was that in models with private information there would be realizations of the bargaining game where significant delay to agreement resulted as agents delay to communicate their private information. Recent studies have suggested that this expectation was not justified. Work by GSW and Gul and Sonnenschein [8] on games with one-sided uncertainty showed that significant delay to agree-

---

[1] For an early treatment of bargaining models with common values, see Samuelson [12]. As this paper went to press, I was made aware of a closely related paper by R. Evans [5]. The interested reader is urged to consult this paper.

[2] This game has also been examined in Sobel and Takahashi [13] and Cramton [3].

ment occurred only as a result of the inability to make offers quickly. Delay was generated by the technology of the game not by uncertainty. This paper shows that the conclusions of GSW and Gul and Sonnenschein depend on the formulation of uncertainty. A simple and natural generalization of the asymmetric information bargaining game to allow for correlated values re-establishes the possibility of delay no matter how quickly bargaining may occur. Delay results because when the buyer does not know his own valuation the possibility arises that the buyer may pay more for the good than it is worth to him. Suppose that the probability that the good is worth little to him is relatively high. Unless the buyer can ensure that he will pay a correspondingly lower price for the bad quality object he may suffer a net loss in the game. There is thus an additional incentive to keep prices paid to sellers of goods of different qualities far enough apart. In this game form, the only way trading prices can differ while maintaining self-selection constraints is if real time elapses in the bargaining process to induce low quality sellers to deal at significantly lower prices. This effect generates delay.

It would be desirable to examine what happens when players are allowed to alternate offers. Solutions to these more general games are typically plagued by the problems of multiple equilibria. It is known that bargaining games with two-sided uncertainty can exhibit delay. Section 4 shows that in many common values models with one-sided uncertainty delay also occurs independent of the extensive form bargaining game and the time between offers.

Another result of the paper shows that equilibrium behaviour can involve no trade even when it is common knowledge that there are gains from trade. The characterization of the equilibrium in the game where the uninformed agent makes all the offers requires that the buyer be at least as patient as the seller. If this condition is violated, there are games with a perfect Bayesian equilibrium which involves the buyer making an offer which would extract all the surplus from a low quality seller. If the offer is rejected, the buyer breaks off negotiations. The model thus may suggest why breakdowns in bargaining processes occur even in the apparent presence of gains from trade.

1. THE MODEL

A seller of a single, indivisible good and a buyer seek to agree on a price at which to trade. In standard formulations of bargaining games, outcomes are characterized by a pair (p, t), where t is the period in which trade occurs, if ever, and p is the price agreed upon. For a game to be specified, then, preferences must be defined over the (p, t) space. It is assumed that preferences can be represented by the functions $b'(v(q) - p)$, for the buyer and $s'(p - f(q))$ for the seller. b and s are the buyer's and the seller's discount factors and lie in the open interval $(0, 1)$. The random variable q is determined by nature and distributed uniformly over the unit interval. In the paper, q will be interpreted as an index of the quality of the good or, more generally, an index of the "type" of the seller. It is assumed that only one agent (here, the seller) observes the true value of q while the other agent knows only its prior distribution. The functions $v(\cdot)$ and $f(\cdot)$ represent the valuations of the object for the buyer and the seller in money terms, $f(\cdot)$ is assumed to be a nondecreasing, left-continuous function of q. The buyer's valuation function $v(\cdot)$ may also be a function of q. It is restricted to be nondecreasing and it will be required that $v(q) > f(q)$ for all q, that is there are always gains from trade to be realized. Agents maximize expected utility. All these features of the model are common knowledge. Note that since the seller observes q, he still enjoys full information about the relevant details of the model. The buyer, though, may be uncertain not only about the seller's valuation but about his own valuation as well.

Note that this model can incorporate a broad range of distributions concerning the seller's and buyer's types. For example, setting $f(q) = q$ yields the special case for which the seller's valuation is distributed uniformly on the unit interval. Setting $f(q) = 0$ for $q \leqslant \frac{1}{2}$ and $f(q) = 4$ otherwise yields the special case for which the seller's valuation has a discrete distribution taking the values 0 and 4 each with probability one half. Assuming that $v(q)$ is a constant $v \geqslant f(1)$ yields the private values models usually studied—a seller has private information about his valuation of the object but the buyer's valuation is common knowledge. For the purposes of this paper, of course, we are interested in cases in which $v(\cdot)$ is a nontrivial function of q.

Given this common values specification it remains to describe an extensive form game which characterizes the process of coming to agreement. The canonical extensive form bargaining game is that described by Ståhl [14] and Rubinstein [9] in which players alternate making and responding to offers sequentially. The game ends when an offer made by one agent is accepted by the other. It is well known that with models of incomplete information such games yield a multiplicity of perfect and perfect Bayesian equilibria.[3]

Restricting attention to games where only the uninformed agent makes offers avoids this problem. FLT showed that in the one-sided offer, one-

---

[3] Perfect Bayesian equilibrium is a slightly weaker concept than sequential equilibrium. It requires that beliefs and strategies be specified for all histories of the game, that strategies be optimal given the specified beliefs and that, wherever possible, beliefs are defined by Bayes' rule and the equilibrium strategies. The first definition of it that I am aware of is given in FLT.

sided uncertainty bargaining game, as long as the seller's valuation is bounded away from the buyer's, there exists a unique perfect Bayesian equilibrium in mixed strategies and that bargaining ends in a finite number of periods. GSW strengthened this result to allow for more general types of distributions for the seller. They also showed that along the equilibrium path, the buyer follows a strategy of determinate offers—that is, equilibrium behaviour involved no mixing on the part of the uninformed agent.

In view of these results the paper restricts attention to the one-sided offer bargaining game. The next section characterizes the perfect Bayesian equilibria to the extensive form game in which the uninformed buyer makes successive offers to an informed seller. The first theorem of the paper shows that this equilibrium is generically unique and that, with some modifications, the FLT–GSW results carry over.[4]

2. Perfect Bayesian Equilibria of
the One-sided Offer Bargaining Game

Impose the following further restrictions on the model of Section 1:

(1) f satisfies a Lipschitz condition at $q = 1$;

(2) b, the discount factor of the buyer is not less than that of the seller—$s \leqslant b$;

(3)   There is an $\varepsilon > 0$ such that for all q, $v(q) - f(q) \geqslant \varepsilon$.[5]

---

[4] Note one final aspect of this game. In general, a seller can follow a strategy of mixing responses. In what follows, sellers with the same valuation will be said to be of the same type. Thus the seller who observes q is the same type as the seller who observes q' if and only if $f(q) = f(q')$. When sellers of a certain type have probability measure zero, the effect of their mixing has no consequence for expected payoffs and so can be ignored. This is not so for sellers whose type have positive probability. Since mixed strategies can, in fact, form part of an equilibrium profile, it is not desirable to keep them from following such strategies by fiat. However, such strategies complicate the analysis considerably. The approach of this paper is to disallow mixed strategies on the part of individual sellers. When mixing is called for by sellers of types of positive measure, different sellers within that type group will be assumed to follow different pure strategies so that the final consequence will be as if a mixed strategy was followed. For example, when $f(q) = f$ for q in $[\frac{1}{2}, \frac{2}{3}]$, and a mixed strategy of accept price p with probability $\frac{1}{2}$ is called for, it will be interpreted as the strategy:

accept for q in $[\frac{1}{2}, \frac{7}{12}]$;   and   reject for q in $(\frac{7}{12}, \frac{2}{3}]$.

Thus, when the seller has valuation f, one-half of the time he is of the type that accepts and one-half of the time he is of the type that rejects.

[5] Let $f(q) = q$ and $v(q) = 1.5q$, $q \in [0, 1]$, buyer and seller have equal discount factors so (3) is violated. Samuelson [11] shows that the best possible mechanism for trade for the buyer is that for which the time of transfer and price of transfer is 0. That is, the only seller to trade if at all is the seller $q = 0$ at price $p = 0$. The proof of this is a simple generalization of the Samuelson static model.

Condition (2) is problematic. It requires that the buyer be at least as patient as the seller. An example in Appendix 2 shows that if the condition does not hold, then the equilibrium proposed by the theorem involves strategies which are dominated. Furthermore, an equilibrium is derived in which bargaining breaks off in the presence of known gains from trade. This condition is explored further in Section 5.

Given these conditions, Theorem 1 shows that there is a unique perfect Bayesian equilibrium.

THEOREM 1 (similar to that of GSW). *Let conditions* (1)–(3) *along with those of Section* 1 *be satisfied. In the game in which the uninformed agent makes all the offers there is a "generically" unique perfect Bayesian equilibrium.*[6] *The equilibrium strategies of the seller are stationary and the equilibrium path of the buyer involves a determinate, monotonic sequence of price offers. Furthermore, bargaining ends after a finite number of periods.*

Proof. The proof of this theorem is provided in an earlier version of this paper and is available from the author on request [15].

The determinate nature of the buyer's equilibrium behaviour enables us to characterize the equilibrium path by backward programming for many specifications of the game. Furthermore, the fact that there is a unique equilibrium allows us to analyze how payoffs and behaviour change with changes in the parameters of the game.

Consider the following simple example of the bargaining game. With probability $\frac{3}{4}$, the seller has an object which is of good quality and is worth 4 to him and 5 to the buyer. Otherwise the object is of bad quality and is worth 0 to the seller and 1 to the buyer. Discount factors are equal and set at $\frac{1}{2}$. The highest (and final) price offered in equilibrium by the buyer is $p = 4$. If there is a period before the final period, the price must be such that the low quality seller is indifferent between accepting and waiting for the higher price next period. With the discount rate at $\frac{1}{2}$, this price is 2. Similarly, the price before that if there is an earlier period is 1, before that, $\frac{1}{2}$, and so on. In fact, the equilibrium strategies for this game call for only two periods of offers. The equilibrium strategies are:

---

[6] "Generically unique" is meant in the following sense. Let the lower end of the support of q be q_0 not necessarily zero. Define a class of games by fixing a pair of valuation functions. $(f(\cdot), v(\cdot))$, a pair of discount factors, (b, s), any $\varepsilon > 0$, and any continuous probability density function over the support $[0, \varepsilon]$, $g(q_0)$. A game in this class is parametrized by the lower end of the initial support of q, q_0. Therefore we can define a measure over this class of games by $g(q_0)$. The event that games in this class have more than one *pBe* occurs with probability zero.

For the seller: In every period,

if $q \leqslant \frac{1}{16}$ accept all price offers $p \geqslant 1$;

if $q \leqslant \frac{1}{4}$ accept all price offers $p \geqslant 2$;

if $q > \frac{1}{4}$ accept all price offers $p \geqslant 4$.

For the buyer: Given beliefs on q such that

if $q \in (\frac{1}{4}, 1]$ offer $p = 4$;

if $q \in (\frac{1}{16}, 1]$ offer $p = 4$ with probability β

$\qquad\qquad\qquad\qquad = 2$ with probability $1 - \beta$

where, if last period price was p', β satisfies

$p' = \frac{1}{2}(\beta 4 + (1 - \beta)2)$;

if $q \in [0, 1]$ offer $p = 2$.

(Note that $q \in [a, b]$ should be read as the distribution of q conditional on q in the interval $[a, b]$, etc. See Appendix 1 for a description of how the strategies are computed.) The equilibrium path involves an offer of 2 in the first period and if that is rejected an offer of 4 in the second. All sellers will have accepted by the end of the second period. The buyer's expected payoff from playing the game is $\frac{1}{4}(-1) + \frac{1}{2}(\frac{3}{4})(1) = \frac{1}{8}$.

Notice that there may be periods where the buyer makes offers which he knows will be accepted only by the low-quality seller. In the example above, the offer of 2 attracts only sellers of a good that is worth 1 to the buyer. If the buyer hears an acceptance, he would like to withdraw his offer. It is important to emphasize, then, the fact that an offer implies a true commitment on the part of the buyer. The reason the buyer is willing to make such offers is that if he hears a rejection, he knows that he can go after the owner of the high-quality object and extract the maximum surplus. The buyer is taking a gamble in order to acquire information that is of some positive value.[7]

Notice, also, the role of mixing in the example. Along the equilibrium path, the behaviour of both the buyer and seller involves only pure strategies. While this is true in general for the buyer it is not always the case for the seller. As observed in note 3, mixed strategies by the seller are to be interpreted as pure strategies of sellers who have the same valuation but observe different values of q. Off the equilibrium path, both the buyer and the seller may, in general, mix. In the example, a seller of "type" 0 mixes his acceptance of nonequilibrium price offers between 1 and 2 with probability $\frac{1}{4}$. If this offer is rejected, then the buyer is indifferent between

---

[7] Of course, the buyer would also like to renegotiate in the private values game as well. In that game, however, the buyer is always sure of gaining some nonnegative surplus.

offering 2 or 4 and mixes between the two in such a way as to justify the indifference of the seller.

The next section uses our ability to characterize equilibria to show what happens when it becomes possible to make offers arbitrarily quickly.

3. BARGAINING WITH ONE-SIDED UNCERTAINTY CAUSES DELAY

Typically, in economic contexts where there is incomplete information, it is necessary to use up resources to enable trade. This is because a cost of transaction is screening. In bargaining games, this cost should be represented by delay to agreement. In view of this conventional wisdom, the GSW and Gul and Sonnenschein results were striking. When the degree of commitment is insignificant, in the models they examine, practically no surplus is consumed by the trading process. If the time between offers is very small, the probability that bargaining will continue past any given time becomes arbitrarily small as well. The belief that asymmetries of information impose social costs was not borne out in their models.

It should be noted that other researchers have shown the existence of bargaining games which exhibit delay. Admati and Perry [1] show that if the informed agent can delay his response to the move of an uninformed agent there exist specifications of private values games which have equilibria with significant delay to agreement. Ausubel and Deneckere [2] also show that delay may occur as the outcome of some perfect Bayesian equilibrium if the restriction that the buyer's valuation be strictly greater than the seller's valuation is relaxed. In this case, there also exist equilibria in which there is no delay. The possibility of delay to agreement, independent of the speed of offers is present in a common values game as well and in a stronger form. For many specifications of a common values bargaining model *all* equilibria must exhibit delay to agreement.

In order to analyze the effects of shorter time between offers it is helpful to respecify the earlier model. Let the preferences over time be generated by a continuous discounting process of the form $e^{-rDt}(v-p)$ for the buyer where the discount factor b comes from the loss from waiting for the length of period D discounted at the continuous rate r. That is,

$$b = e^{-rD}.$$

A similar representation holds for the seller where σ is the seller's continuous time discounting factor. With this specification, it is now possible to parametrize equilibria by the length of time between offers, D.

The result in Section 2 showed that for any given bargaining game, bargaining ended within a finite number of periods. For some game with length of period D let the maximum number of periods in equilibrium be $n(D)+1$. As D goes to zero, one might expect two opposing effects to occur. A shorter time between offers allows the buyer to screen finely at a lower delay cost and so the number $n(D)$ may become very large. On the other hand, D itself becomes very small so the effects on total bargaining time, $Dn(D)$ may also be very small. In the private values case, this is in fact what happens. D goes to zero faster than n grows so we get the result that, if the extensive form game allows arbitrarily fast offers, bargaining ends arbitrarily quickly. This result was first shown by GSW and was later extended by Gul and Sonnenschein [8] to many of the sequential equilibria of two-sided offer games as well.

A simple example shows that a similar conclusion does not hold for the general common values game. Consider why we might expect it not to hold. If the total time between the first and last offers in the bargaining game is short, then the incentive compatibility constraints which induce low valuation sellers to accept early will force the initial price offers to be close to the final price offers. In the case of the private values models where the buyer's valuation is always greater than the seller's, this rise in the first price offer has the effect of reducing the buyer's ability to extract surplus from the low valuation sellers. In a common values model, though, it is possible for a buyer to pay more than the object is worth to him and, so, there is a further incentive to extend bargaining over a period of time; that is, to keep from having to pay higher prices for goods of lower value. This effect leads to a lower bound on the maximum bargaining time for some specifications of the bargaining game.

The following example illustrates this point. Adapt the example in Section 2 so that

$$\text{for} \quad q \in [0, \tfrac{1}{2}], \qquad f(q) = 0 \quad \text{and} \quad v(q) = 1,$$
$$\text{and for} \quad q \in (\tfrac{1}{2}, 1], \qquad f(q) = 4 \quad \text{and} \quad v(q) = 5.^8$$

Set the discount factors equal so that $s = b = e^{-Dr} = \delta$. For a fixed period between offers, D, there exists a unique perfect Bayesian equilibrium with a maximum time to agreement, $n(D) + 1$. The theorem in Section 2 enables us to describe the path of offers in the equilibrium. It is of the form

$$(\delta^n 4, \delta^{(n-1)}4, ..., \delta 4, 4).$$

Since the buyer can always offer a price of 0, the expected value of follow-

---

[8] To correspond to the GSW framework, $v(q)$ would be set to 5 for all q. Since this falls within the class of models they examine, their Theorem 3 shows that no delay would result if the time between offers was arbitrarily small.

ing the equilibrium path must be nonnegative. The value of the game to the buyer is easily calculated to be

$$0 \leqslant u = [(1 - \delta^n 4) m_1 + \delta(1 - \delta^{n-1} 4) m_2 + \cdots$$
$$+ \delta^{n-1}(1 - \delta 4) m_n]/2 + \delta^n(\tfrac{1}{2})$$

where m_i is the probability a seller accepts an offer $\delta^{n-i+1} 4$ given that the seller is of low valuation. Therefore,

$$m_1 + m_2 + \cdots + m_n = 1, \qquad m_i \geqslant 0,$$

and

$$u \leqslant (\tfrac{1}{2})[(1 - \delta^n 4) + \delta^n].$$

This yields

$$1 - 3\delta^n \geqslant 0$$

or

$$\tfrac{1}{3} \geqslant \delta^n = e^{-rDn}$$
$$-\log 3 \geqslant -r\, Dn$$

or

$$(\log 3)/r \leqslant Dn(D).$$

With $r > 0$, this then gives us a lower bound on $n(D)D$, the total elapsed time until the final possible offer of 4 is made. An equilibrium offer of 4 is made whenever the seller is of a good type, so, ex ante, with probability $\tfrac{1}{2}$ bargaining lasts for at least $(\log 3)/r$ time units.

4. Variations on the Extensive Form

While the one-sided offer game generates pleasingly concrete results, it is a very restrictive characterization of a bargaining process. One would like to extend the analysis to games where both parties are able to make offers. It is well known, however, that in the private value, two-sided offer game, one-sided uncertainty leads to many sequential equilibria.[9] To conduct analyses of these games it is usually necessary to refine out this multiplicity.

[9] The same is also true of the common values game in which only the informed agent makes offers.

This is the approach used in Grossman and Perry [7] and Rubinstein [11]. That approach is beyond the scope of this paper but it is an area where further research could be fruitful. It is possible, though, to extend the result of the previous section to include these more complicated games. This section shows that, for a broad class of extensive form games and a broad class of specifications of valuations, equilibrium behaviour requires delay to agreement.

To see this result, use the technique employed by Samuelson [12] for static trading mechanisms with common values. Consider any static mechanism which generates outcomes represented by a pair $(m(f), P(f))$ where $m(f)$ is the expected payment given that a seller reports f and $P(f)$ is the probability that trade occurs. Samuelson shows that the incentive compatibility (IC) and individual rationality (IR) constraints of any equilibrium require that the $P(\cdot)$ function satisfy the restriction

$$\int_0^g (v(f) - f - G(f)/g(f)) \, P(f) \, df \geq 0 \qquad (1)$$

where $G(f)$ is the continuous distribution function of the seller's type f, and $g(f)$ is its strictly positive density function on the range $[0, g]$. For simplicity let the buyer's valuation $v = f + 1$ and set $G(f) = f/g$—the seller's type varies uniformly over the interval $[0, g]$. Equation (1) becomes

$$\int_0^g (1 - f) \, P(f) \, df \geq 0. \qquad (2)$$

In this case, any Pareto optimal mechanism should always ensure trade since $v - f = 1$. However, it is clear that as g becomes large, setting $P(f) = 1$ for all f violates the constraints implied in (2). Some expected gains from trade must be used up to enable trade.

Now use the insight of Cramton [3, 4] which extends the static analysis to sequential mechanisms. For any f, a sequential mechanism generates a probability distribution T_f over the price and time of trade. If we restrict discount factors to be equal, the IC and IR constraints of a sequential mechanism can also be expressed as Eq. (2) where, now, the $P(\cdot)$ function represents the discounted probability of trade. That is,

$$P(f) = \int_0^\infty \delta^t \, dT_f(t).$$

Here, loss is generated not by the probability of no trade but by the probability of having to wait some period of time for trade.

Equation (2) tells us that if an equilibrium exists then, typically, delay must occur. A mechanism in which the probability of significant delay is arbitrarily small is one for which the $P(\cdot)$ function is arbitrarily close to one for all but an arbitrarily small set of f. For g large enough, however, any such $P(\cdot)$ function violates the constraints implied by IC and IR. Alternatively speaking, any mechanism which satisfies IC and IR given the specification of this model and given a large g, must use up surplus by imposing a significant probability of significant delay.

Notice that the argument applies to a broad class of examples. Let the seller's valuation range uniformly from 0 to g and the buyer's valuation always be one more than the seller. Give each identical rates of time preference. The theorem in Section 2 shows that in the one-sided offer game, for given discount factors, there exists a unique perfect Bayesian equilibrium and that trade always occurs. The above argument shows that when g is large the equilibrium must exhibit a significant probability of significant delay to agreement.

Observe how general this result is in terms of game forms as well. As long as the trading mechanism of the game form yields equilibrium outcomes in price–time space and has an exit option (and discount factors are equal), the incentive compatibility constraints of any equilibrium to this mechanism imply the need for delay. Since the alternating offers game as well as the altered version of the game form described by Admati and Perry [1] fit into this framework, these games will often exhibit delay to agreement in common values models.

5. The Endogeneity of Take It or Leave It Offers

It might seem reasonable to expect that as long as there are known gains from trade, if bargainers do not have the power to commit to breaking off negotiations, bargaining will continue until these gains are realized. Indeed, one reason for examining infinite horizon games was to study what occurs when neither agent can credibly threaten to stop bargaining before a trade is consummated. However, it is important to recognize that a net gain from trade must include the costs of trading as well—these include the costs of delay and, in these models, the risk of purchasing a poor quality object. When these costs are too high, the benefits from trade may not be great enough to induce an agent to continue bargaining. This section illustrates that the consideration of infinite horizon bargaining games does not ensure that trade occurs even in the presence of a known positive surplus.

The equilibrium characterized in Section 2 required that the buyer be at least as patient as the seller—that is, $b \geqslant s$. If this condition holds, the value of the bargaining game to the buyer is always strictly positive and the buyer can never credibly threaten to leave the game before trade occurs. When the condition does not hold, when the seller is more patient than the buyer, there are specifications of the model such that the buyer has an expected value of zero in the game. Equilibrium behaviour, therefore, can involve breaking off negotiations.

The example in Appendix 2 illustrates this phenomenon. It is a variation of the example of Section 2. With probability $\frac{5}{16}$ the object is worth 0 to the seller and 1 to the buyer and with probability $\frac{11}{16}$ it is worth 4 to the seller and 5 to the buyer. Both the buyer and the seller know that there are gains from trade of 1 in the game. However, when the buyer's discount factor is $\frac{1}{2}$ and the seller's is $\frac{3}{4}$ the game exhibits an equilibrium in which the buyer makes an offer of 0 throughout the game. If trade takes place, it must occur in the first period.

When the seller's discount factor is relatively high, the price a buyer must offer to ensure that low-type sellers are not in the continuation game is correspondingly higher. When, in addition, the buyer's discount factor is low, the value of any continuation game is low. The expected cost of eliminating low valuation sellers may exceed the expected value of the continuation game and buyers would then prefer to end negotiations as occurs in this example.

Note that an equivalent type of behaviour would be for the buyer to offer a price of zero in the first period and, if he is rejected, then to break off negotiations. The example suggests how we might explain failure to come to agreement even in the apparent presence of gains from trade. The buyer breaks off bargaining because the cost of acquiring further information needed to obtain a positive payoff is too high. It is clear that a slight modification of this example could provided cases where a number of offers are made before bargaining ends in disagreement.

6. CONCLUSION

The paper examines a natural extension of one-sided uncertainty bargaining games to include common values and shows that, for the one-sided offer game there is a unique perfect Bayesian equilibrium. It uses the characterization of equilibrium to show that such games typically exhibit delay to agreement as sellers of different types use time to signal their information. This result remains true when more general extensive form bargaining games are considered. The paper also provides an example of a one-sided offer bargaining game in which equilibrium behaviour may involve breaking off negotiations in the presence of gains from trade. It thus shows that the Akerlof lemons problem may persist in infinite horizon bargaining games and despite the common knowledge that there are gains from trade.

APPENDIX 1

The equilibrium strategies in the example in Section 2 are calculated in the following way. Let the mass of good quality sellers be fixed at $\frac{3}{4}$ and let m be the mass of bad quality sellers. Determine, first, the point m_1 at which a buyer is indifferent between offering a price of 4 immediately and gaining acceptance by any seller type or offering 2 (accepted by low quality sellers) and then a price of 4. At $m_1 = \frac{3}{16}$, or if the relative weights are 1:4 the buyer is just indifferent. (This would correspond to the state $q \in [\frac{1}{16}, 1]$.) At $m_2 = \frac{9}{32}$, or $q \in [-\frac{1}{32}, 1]$, the buyer is indifferent between the two-period game and a three-period game consisting of a price offer of 1, then 2, and then 4. For states $[x, 1]$ with $x \in (0, \frac{1}{16})$, the buyer strictly prefers the two-period game. If sellers in $[0, \frac{1}{16})$ reject a price p in a given period and are expected to reject p they can expect a price of 2 in the next period which is worth 1 to them now. Thus $p < 1$ and any price greater than 1 is acceptable to them immediately. Similarly, if sellers in $(\frac{1}{16}, \frac{1}{4})$ reject a price $p' > 1$ in the current period and are expected to do so, they can get a price of 4 in the next period. Therefore, $p' < 2$. For $x = \frac{1}{16}$, the buyer is indifferent between offering prices of 2 and 4 and his ex post mixing justifies the behaviour of the low quality sellers with the appropriate definition of β. This reasoning shows that an offer of 2 in the first period, acceptance for sure by low-quality sellers and an offer of 4 in the second period is an equilibrium profile. By the theorem, this path is generically unique.

APPENDIX 2

One of the conditions required to prove the theorem in the paper is that the buyer's discount factor be no less than the seller's or that the buyer be at least as patient as the seller. An example in this section illustrates what may happen when the condition is not met and helps to explain the role of the requirement.

Consider, the example described in Section 2 modified as follows:

$$\text{for} \quad q \in [0, \tfrac{5}{16}], \qquad f(q) = 0, \quad v(q) = 1;$$

$$\text{for} \quad q \in (\tfrac{5}{16}, 1], \qquad f(q) = 4, \quad v(q) = 5.$$

Let the discount factors be $b = \frac{1}{2}$ for the buyer and $s = \frac{3}{4}$ for the seller.

If m is the measure of low valuation sellers left in the game, note that $m^* = \frac{11}{48}$ yields the buyer an expected utility of 0 if he offers a price equal to 4 and buys the good for sure. Any equilibrium of the form described in the theorem must end with an offer of 3 and then 4 if bargaining is to take more than one period. However, if $m < m^*$, the buyer will always prefer to offer 4 rather than to screen out some sellers by offering $p = 3$. Furthermore, if $m > \frac{11}{48}$, for any strategy of the low-valuation seller, an offer of 3 and then 4 yields a strictly negative expected utility. At $m^* = \frac{11}{48}$, if any low valuation seller accepts $p = 3$, the buyer would receive an expected utility of less than zero. Therefore, the only way the path described in the theorem could be an equilibrium path is if low-valuation sellers follow a strategy of always rejecting $p = 3$. If this is an equilibrium strategy, note that it is dominated for the buyer by offering either 4 or 0. Any tremble on the part of the seller would yield a negative payoff.

It is not known whether the path of the theorem can be supported as an equilibrium. However, it is possible to describe another, quite different, equilibrium. The following strategies form an equilibrium to the game above.

Equilibrium Strategies

For the buyer: $p_0 = 0$, if $p_{i-1} = 0$ offer $p_i = 0$;
   if $p_{i-1} \in (0, 3)$, offer 4 with probability β
        or 0 with probability $1 - \beta$
          where $p_{i-1} = s4\beta$;
   if $p_{i-1} \geqslant 3$, offer $p_i = 4$.

For the seller: if $q \leqslant \frac{4}{48}$, accept $p \geqslant 0$;
   if $q \in (\frac{4}{48}, \frac{5}{16}]$, accept $p \geqslant 3$;
   if $q \geqslant \frac{5}{16}$, accept $p \geqslant 4$.

In this equilibrium, a buyer extracts all of the surplus from the low-valuation seller $\frac{4}{11}$ of the time and none $\frac{7}{11}$ of the time. He never trades with a high-valuation seller. If he tries to attract more low-valuation sellers by offering a little higher price, the expectation of his future mixing between 4 and 0 prevents this. Note that his strategy, here, is undominated.

REFERENCES

1. A. R. ADMATI AND M. PERRY, "Strategic Delay in Bargaining," Research Paper No. 874, Graduate School of Business, Stanford University, 1986.
2. L. AUSUBEL AND R. DENECKERE, "Reputation in Bargaining and Durable Goods Monopoly," Discussion Paper No. 695, The Center for Mathematical Studies in Economics and Management Science, Northwestern University, 1986.
3. P. CRAMTON, "The Role of Time and Information in Bargaining," Ph.D. thesis, Stanford University, 1984.
4. P. CRAMTON, Sequential bargaining mechanisms, *in* "Game Theoretic Models of Bargaining" (A. Roth, Ed.), pp. 149–179, Cambridge University Press, Cambridge, 1986.
5. R. EVANS, Sequential bargaining with correlated values, Cambridge University, mimeo, 1988.

6. D. FUDENBERG, D. LEVINE, AND J. TIROLE, Infinite horizon models of bargaining with incomplete information, *in* "Game Theoretic Models of Bargaining" (A. Roth, Ed.), pp. 73–98, Cambridge Univ. Press, Cambridge, 1986.

7. S. GROSSMAN AND M. PERRY, Sequential bargaining under asymmetric information, *J. Econ. Theory* **39** (1986), 120–154.

8. F. GUL AND H. SONNENSCHEIN, Bargaining with one-sided uncertainty does not cause delay, Princeton University, mimeo, 1985.

9. F. GUL, H. SONNENSCHEIN, AND R. WILSON, Foundations of dynamic monopoly and the Coase conjecture, *J. Econ. Theory* **39** (1986), 155–190.

10. A. RUBINSTEIN, Perfect equilibria in bargaining models, *Econometrica* **50** (1982), 97–109.

11. A. RUBINSTEIN, A bargaining model with incomplete information, *Econometrica* **53** (1985), 1151–1172.

12. W. SAMUELSON, Bargaining with asymmetric information, *Econometrica* **53** (1984), 995–1005.

13. J. SOBEL AND I. TAKAHASHI, A multi-stage model of bargaining. *Rev. Econ. Stud.* **50** (1983), 411–426.

14. I. STÅHL, "Bargaining Theory," Stockholm School of Economics, 1972.

15. D. VINCENT, Bargaining with common values, mimeo, Princeton University, 1986.

JOURNAL OF ECONOMIC THEORY **48**, 221–237 (1989)

Cheap Talk Can Matter in Bargaining*

JOSEPH FARRELL

*Department of Economics, University of California,
Berkeley, California 94720*

AND

ROBERT GIBBONS

*Department of Economics, Massachusetts Institute of Technology,
Cambridge, Massachusetts 02139*

Received July 18, 1987; revised April 13, 1988

This paper describes an intuitive way in which cheap talk can matter in a two-stage bargaining game in which talk may be followed by serious negotiation. The intuition that all buyers would claim to have low reservation prices is incorrect in our model. Instead, if good-faith participation is endogenously determined then the parties can use talk to trade off bargaining position against the probability of continued negotiation. Our cheap-talk equilibrium features bargaining behavior that could not be equilibrium behavior in the absence of talk. *Journal of Economic Literature* Classification Numbers: 026, 022.   © 1989 Academic Press, Inc.

1. INTRODUCTION

Since the seminal work of Spence [17], economists have understood how an informed agent's choices may reveal private information if they affect him differently depending on what he knows. This idea of costly signaling has been extremely influential in recent economic theory, underlying analyses of everything from education to entry deterrence. But perhaps its greatest influence has been in the noncooperative theory of bargaining: a large and growing literature, beginning with Fudenberg and Tirole [7] and Sobel and Takahashi [16], analyzes how bargainers can improve their

* We thank Peter Cramton, Steven Matthews, William Samuelson, two referees, and seminar audiences at Berkeley, Chicago, Duke, MIT, the 1987 NSF Decentralization Conference, and Stanford for helpful comments. Research support through NSF grants IRI-8712238 and IST-8609691 is gratefully acknowledged.

terms of trade by undertaking costly actions (notably delay) meant to convince their "opponent" that their interest in trade is at best lukewarm.

While such communication through costly signals is undoubtedly important, much communication also occurs through costless words, or *cheap talk*. Talk is ubiquitous and is often listened to, even where no real penalty attaches to lying, and where claims do not directly affects payoffs. Crawford and Sobel [2] showed formally that such cheap talk can be credible in equilibrium if the parties have at least some interests in common.

Despite Crawford and Sobel's result, one might expect that cheap talk could not matter in bargaining, because each side has an obvious incentive to seem unenthusiastic: we think of a bazaar, where the buyer sneers at the seller's goods, which the latter declares are so precious as to be scarcely for sale. Yet casual observation reveals much cheap talk of the opposite kind: people often claim to be "seriously interested" in trading. Unless this is mere meaningless noise, something is missing in the theory.

One possibility is that these claims—or confessions—of urgent desire to trade are meant to encourage the other side to participate in more detailed negotiation. As we show below, if saying that one is "keen" makes one's partner more likely to negotiate, then it is the keenest types (high-value buyers, low-value sellers) who are most willing to say so, damaging as it is to their terms of trade if trade occurs.

The following story illustrates the element of common interest that drives our analysis: cheap talk can affect whether negotiation ensues. Imagine that one Saturday evening, two corporate moguls have a chance encounter at their country club. One mogul's company owns a division that the other mogul's firm may wish to buy. Serious negotiation, involving binding offers and hordes of lawyers, can take place on Monday morning; all that can happen Saturday night is talk. If, based on this talk, the moguls conclude that there is sufficient prospect of gains from trade, then they will send their lawyers into the fray on Monday morning. Otherwise, Saturday evening will be the end of it. Therefore, each mogul has an incentive not to sneer too much, lest the other choose not to try to do business with one who seems uninterested. The strategy (common in bazaars) of sneering and then returning for serious bargaining is less attractive to the moguls because a sneer may end negotiations.

In this paper, we turn this basic intuition into a precise equilibrium statement in a particular bargaining model, the sealed-bid double auction studied by Chatterjee and Samuelson [1]. We analyze a two-stage game: talk comes first, then formal (binding) negotiation. Not only is information conveyed by cheap talk in equilibrium, but the equilibrium mapping from the buyer's and seller's reservation values to outcomes (whether trade occurs and if so at what price) differs from any that could occur in an equilibrium without talk. Further, some outcomes of the "talk" stage lead to second-stage bidding strategies that could not be equilibrium strategies absent the changes in beliefs that the talk causes.

To complete this Introduction, we describe the differences between our cheap-talk equilibrium and the literatures on bargaining and on mechanism design. As described above, in most game-theoretic analyses of bargaining, communication takes place only through actions that can directly affect payoffs, and that therefore can be costly signals. Typically, such an action either directly imposes costs of delay, or directly affects payoffs by constituting an offer that is binding if the other player accepts it, or both. Cheap talk does neither of these things. Of course, *in equilibrium,* different types have incentives to choose different cheap-talk messages, but no part of these incentives consists of *exogenous* costs or benefits. This distinguishes cheap talk from signaling, and distinguishes our analysis from a standard bargaining game.

Cheap talk also differs from a mechanism (in the sense of Myerson and Satterthwaite [13]). In a mechanism, messages without direct costs are used, but a mediator controls the communication and is committed to enforcing a given outcome as a function of the messages. In cheap-talk equilibrium, by contrast, no agent can commit to a choice of outcome as a function of messages; rather, the outcome must be a perfect Bayesian equilibrium given the information conveyed by the messages. Moreover, these messages become common knowledge, whereas a Myerson–Satterthwaite mediator can, and typically does, limit the information he passes on to the players. Of course, every cheap-talk equilibrium can be implemented as a mechanism, but in general the converse is not true. Matthews and Postlewaite [11] explore the extent to which this converse holds in a double auction. We discuss their work in more detail in Section 2.

2. A CHEAP-TALK EQUILIBRIUM

This section analyzes cheap talk in a well-known model of bargaining under incomplete information. In terms of our story of the two corporate moguls, if the parties do meet on Monday, they play the following sealed-bid double auction. Buyer and seller name prices p_b and p_s, respectively, and trade takes place at price $(p_b + p_s)/2$ if $p_b \geq p_s$; otherwise, there is no trade.[1]

---

[1] For those who miss the lawyers, consider the commitment necessary to play even this simple game: what, for instance, stops one party from reneging on his offer in order to capitalize on the information conveyed by the other party's offer?

Before the double-auction stage of our two-stage game there is a cheap-talk stage. (On Saturday the moguls can engage in cheap talk.) We consider the simplest possible language: each party can claim either to be "keen" or to be "not keen." We assume that these claims are made simultaneously. We emphasize that these claims do not directly affect payoffs: they work *only* by affecting the other player's beliefs. In particular, they are not commitments nor are they verifiable.

To summarize, the extensive form is as follows. First, the parties simultaneously announce whether they are "keen" or "not keen"; these announcements do not directly affect either party's payoff. After observing the pair of announcements, the parties play the double auction described above. If trade takes place at price p, then a buyer with valuation v_b achieves payoff $v_b - p$ and a seller with valuation v_s achieves payoff $p - v_s$; if trade does not occur then payoffs are zero.

The extensive form of our formal model differs slightly from our informal story about the corporate moguls: in the formal model, the double auction is played after any pair of cheap-talk announcements, whereas in the informal story, Saturday evening could be the end of it. Intuitively, we think that a player who is made sufficiently pessimistic about the likely gains from trade will not bother to participate in bargaining. This is, of course, because there are *costs* to such participation: both disbursements (on lawyers, etc.) and opportunity costs (notably alternative negotiations foregone). We do not model these costs, since doing so would complicate the model and obscure the basic tradeoff. Even so, we could simply posit that insufficiently encouraged traders do not show up to bargain on Monday: although (absent costs) this choice is weakly dominated, it is still an equilibrium for neither side to show up (since trade cannot happen unless both sides appear). Alternatively, we can think of the parties playing the following "no-trade" equilibrium in the second stage after a discouraging conversation: the buyer bids $p_b = 0$, and the seller bids $p_s = 1$. Whichever choice the reader prefers, there is no trade in such a subgame.[2]

Chatterjee and Samuelson [1] analyze a class of equilibria of the double auction without cheap talk. They show that bounded, strictly monotone, and differentiable equilibrium strategies must satisfy a linked pair of differential equations. In the standard case in which v_s and v_b are independently and uniformly distributed on $[0, 1]$, these differential equations have a solution in which both the buyer and the seller play linear strategies. We

---

[2] A third rationale for there being no trade after both players say "not keen" is that they need to coordinate on when and where to meet on Monday, and an attempt to arrange a meeting belies a party's claim that he is "not keen." Note that this is *not* the same as saying that talk determines whether the parties *can* meet; such talk would not be cheap talk. Here the set of times and places available for a meeting is independent of the talk, but is large enough and sufficiently lacking in focal points that meeting without agreement is unlikely.

call this the Chatterjee–Samuelson equilibrium and we use it to define equilibrium behavior whenever possible. There are, however, many other equilibria in a double auction in the absence of cheap talk (including the "no-trade" equilibrium above), only some of which satisfy the conditions that Chatterjee and Samuelson assumed. Leininger *et al.* [9] and Satterthwaite and Williams [14] explore some of these alternative equilibria, and we use one in our model when it is not possible to use the Chatterjee–Samuelson equilibrium.

In our game, as in every cheap-talk game, there is an uncommunicative (or "babbling") equilibrium: if cheap talk is taken to be meaningless, then parties are willing to randomize uninformatively over the possible messages. But there are also two more interesting equilibria in which cheap talk is meaningful. In one, serious bargaining takes place only if both parties claim to be "keen"; in the other, a single such claim suffices. In both of these equilibria, serious bargaining does not occur if neither party claims to be "keen".

In the first of these equilibria with meaningful cheap talk, the Chatterjee–Samuelson equilibrium reappears: everyone claims to be "keen" except those types who are sure not to trade.[3] In this equilibrium, cheap talk is credible, but does not affect the equilibrium outcome: the mapping from type-pairs to bids and probability of trade is the same as in the Chatterjee–Samuelson equilibrium, which has no cheap talk.

In the other equilibrium, however, cheap talk matters in an important way: low-value buyers and high-value sellers are willing to jeopardize continued negotiation so as to improve their bargaining position; those who have more at stake cannot afford this risk. We focus on this equilibrium because it involves second-stage bidding strategies that could not be equilibrium strategies in the absence of talk.

We analyze our equilibrium in the standard case in which v_s and v_b are independently and uniformly distributed on $[0, 1]$. We show in the Appendix that the following strategies for the cheap-talk stage are part of a perfect Bayesian equilibrium. Buyers above the critical type

$$y = \frac{22 + 12\sqrt{2}}{49} = 0.795$$

say "keen" while those below say "not keen." Sellers below $(1 - y)$ say "keen," while those above say "not keen."

If both parties say "not keen" then the negotiation effectively ends, as

---

[3] In the standard case in which v_b and v_s are independently and uniformly distributed on $[0, 1]$, all buyers with $v_b > \frac{1}{4}$ and all sellers with $v_s < \frac{3}{4}$ claim to be "keen." Strictly, the other types of buyers and sellers, who will not trade, may say anything. But if there are any costs of serious bargaining, then they must say "not keen."

discussed above. If at least one says "keen" then bargaining continues with a (possibly asymmetric) sealed-bid double auction. If, for instance, the seller says "not keen" and the buyer says "keen" then it becomes common knowledge that the buyer believes that the seller's type is above $1 - y$ and that the seller believes that the buyer's type is above y, and negotiation proceeds on that basis. Similarly, if the seller says "keen" and the buyer says "not keen" then it becomes common knowledge that the buyer believes that the seller's type is below $1 - y$ and that the seller believes that the buyer's type is below y. In both of these cases, we use the Chatterjee–Samuelson equilibrium to solve the resulting bargaining game. Finally, if the buyer and the seller both say "keen" then it becomes common knowledge that the buyer believes that the seller's type is below $1 - y$ and that the seller believes that the buyer's type is above y. In this case, the linear Chatterjee–Samuelson equilibrium breaks down because gains from trade are guaranteed ($y > \frac{5}{8}$). Because of this, and because the subgame is symmetric, we focus on the equilibrium in which trade occurs with certainty at a price of $\frac{1}{2}$. Formally, this is a "one-step" equilibrium (see Leininger *et al.* [9]): the buyer bids $\frac{1}{2}$ if his value is above $\frac{1}{2}$ but otherwise bids 0, and the seller follows an analogous strategy. In the Appendix we state and prove Lemma 1, which describes in more detail the cheap-talk and bargaining behavior in our cheap-talk equilibrium.

Propositions 1 and 2 show that cheap-talk really matters in our equilibrium. (Proofs of these results are given in the Appendix.) Proposition 1 shows that the equilibrium mapping from pairs of types (v_b, v_s) to outcomes (whether trade occurs, and if so at what price) differs from any that could occur in a no-talk equilibrium, because talk achieves some correlation of bids.

PROPOSITION 1. *The equilibrium mapping from types to outcomes in our cheap-talk equilibrium cannot arise in an equilibrium without talk.*

Proposition 2 shows that cheap talk matters in our equilibrium in a more fundamental way: in the {"not keen," "keen"} and {"keen," "not keen"} subgames, the bidding stategies we specify form an equilibrium only because talk changes each party's belief about the other's type.

PROPOSITION 2. *There does not exist an equilibrium without cheap talk in which sellers $v_s \in [1 - y, 1]$ and buyers $v_b \in [y, 1]$ name the prices that they name in the {"not keen," "keen"} subgame of our cheap-talk equilibrium.*

We close this section by discussing the related work of Matthews and Postlewaite, who also analyze cheap talk preceding a double auction. They characterize the equilibrium outcomes that can be obtained through both mediated communication (as in mechanism design) and unmediated communication (as in our definition of cheap talk). Their constructive proofs of these characterization results restrict attention to a simple form of unmediated-communication equilibrium: talk simply coordinates different types on different equilibria, each of which is an equilibrium without talk. This kind of coordination is impossible in an equilibrium without talk.

Proposition 1 summarizes the role of this Matthews–Postlewaite-style coordination in our cheap-talk equilibrium. Proposition 2 makes precise our claim that in our equilibrium cheap talk is credible because it allows players to trade off bargaining position against the probability of continued negotiation. Different types view this tradeoff differently, and credible talk results from these differences. This intuition is not brought out in the Matthews–Postlewaite analysis, although their characterization does include our equilibrium.

3. Welfare

This section compares the payoffs in our cheap-talk equilibrium to those in the Chatterjee–Samuelson equilibrium. Calculation shows that our cheap-talk equilibrium yields buyer-type v_b an interim payoff, evaluated before the cheap-talk phase, of

$$
W_b(v_b) = \begin{cases}
0 & \text{if } v_b \leq \tfrac{1}{4}y, \\
\tfrac{1}{2}(v_b - \tfrac{1}{4})^2 & \text{if } \tfrac{1}{4}y < v_b \leq 1 - \tfrac{3}{4}y, \\
(1 - y)(v_b - \tfrac{1}{2} + \tfrac{1}{4}y) & \text{if } 1 - \tfrac{3}{4}y < v_b \leq y, \\
\tfrac{1}{2}(v_b - \tfrac{1}{4}y)^2 - \tfrac{1}{2}(\tfrac{7}{4}y - 1)^2 & \text{if } v_b > y.
\end{cases}
$$

An immediate consequence is that if $\tfrac{1}{4}y = 0.199 < v_b \leq \tfrac{1}{4}$, then buyer-type v_b is strictly better off than in the Chatterjee–Samuelson equilibrium. In fact, many other types are better off in our equilibrium than in Chatterjee–Samuelson. Equating our $W_b(v_b)$ to the Chatterjee–Samuelson equivalent $W_b^{CS}(v_b) \equiv \tfrac{1}{2}(v_b - \tfrac{1}{2})^2$ yields a unique crossover point, which lies in the range $1 - \tfrac{3}{4}y < v_b < y$, given by the solution v_b to

$$
(1 - y)(v_b - \tfrac{1}{2} + \tfrac{1}{4}y) = \tfrac{1}{2}(v_b - \tfrac{1}{4})^2,
$$

which is approximately equal to 0.599. Thus, all buyer types in (0.199, 0.599), and similarly all seller types in (0.401, 0.801), are better off with cheap talk. In fact, exactly as many types strictly prefer our equilibrium as strictly prefer Chatterjee–Samuelson. (Types who never trade are of course indifferent.)

The pairs (v_b, v_s) who trade in our equilibrium are illustrated in Fig. 1, which also shows the corresponding region for the Chatterjee–Samuelson equilibrium. The (ex-ante) probability that (v_b, v_s) falls in the trading region for our equilibrium is $\tfrac{3}{2}y(1 - y)$, or approximately 0.244, somewhat

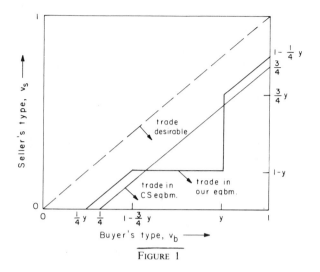

$$\text{FIGURE 1}$$

less than the corresponding probability (0.281) for the Chatterjee–Samuelson equilibrium: our equilibrium involves less trade. Similarly, the ex-ante expected total gains from trade in our equilibrium[4] are approximately 0.124, less than the Chatterjee–Samuelson figure of 0.140.

Both of these comparisons are special cases of Myerson and Satterthwaite's general result that the Chatterjee–Samuelson equilibrium maximizes both the ex-ante probability of trade and the ex-ante gains from trade (for the independent, uniform case we have analyzed). Myerson [12], however, convincingly argues that such ex-ante efficiency is often irrelevant, because there is seldom an opportunity to make binding arrangements ex-ante (i.e., before either player knows his "type"). Myerson gives an example of an incentive-compatible mechanism (for the independent, uniform case) in which even high-value sellers (and low-value buyers) trade with positive probability, and therefore are better off than in the Chatterjee–Samuelson equilibrium. Our cheap-talk equilibrium is in the same spirit, but is derived from an extensive-form game in which talk takes place without a mediator.[5]

---

[4] The ex-ante expected total gains from trade in our equilibrium are given by

$$(1-y)^2 \cdot \frac{8-11y}{12} + \left(1 - \frac{1}{4}y\right)^2 \cdot \frac{2+y}{12} - \frac{1}{3}\left(\frac{3}{4}y\right)^3 + \frac{1}{2}(1-y)\left[y^2 - \left(1 - \frac{3}{4}y\right)^2\right].$$

[5] Of course, the subsequent sealed-bid double auction does require a mediator, both to accept simultaneous reports and to force the parties to walk away if trade is not prescribed (even if trade would be efficient). But such a game is hardly central to the tradeoff between bargaining position and the probability of continued negotiation that allows cheap talk to be credible in our analysis.

4. CONCLUSION

We believe that the economic importance of costless, nonverifiable, informal communication is much greater than its role in the literature suggests. The seminal work by Crawford and Sobel is justly famous, but applications have only recently begun to appear.

This paper introduces cheap talk to bargaining games. We emphasize that cheap talk can matter in bargaining when participation is endogenous, because the parties can then use talk to trade off bargaining position against the probability of continued negotiation. This talk can matter in an essential way: the cheap-talk equilibrium we analyze features bargaining outcomes that could not be equilibrium behavior in the absence of talk. Not surprisingly, this intuition does not require anything as specific as a sealed-bid double auction. See Farrell and Gibbons [4] for a more general discussion of these issues.

Cheap talk is important in many other economic settings as well. Farrell [3], for instance, studies cheap talk between potential entrants in a natural monopoly, Farrell and Saloner [5] consider cheap talk between potential adopters of a new technology, Forges [6] analyzes cheap talk in a hiring and job-assignment game, Gibbons [8] models interest arbitration as a cheap-talk game, Matthews [10] describes presidential rhetoric as a cheap-talk veto threat in the budgetary process, and Sobel [15] develops a theory of credibility in finitely repeated relationships. The fundamental insight that cheap talk can be credible in variable-sum games, combined with the ubiquity of such talk, suggests that a rich collection of other applications lies ahead.

APPENDIX

In this Appendix we adapt the Chatterjee–Samuelson analysis to suit our purposes, and then use the results to derive the equilibrium value of y. We give a formal statement (and proof) of the equilibrium cheap talk and bargaining behavior in Lemma 1. We also prove Propositions 1 and 2.

Consider a sealed-bid double auction in which it is common knowledge that the seller-type v_s is uniformly distributed on $[\underline{v}_s, \bar{v}_s]$ and buyer-type v_b is independently and uniformly distributed on $[\underline{v}_b, \bar{v}_b]$. Both parties name prices, p_s and p_b, and trade occurs at the average of the two prices if the buyer's price exceeds the seller's.

As Chatterjee and Samuelson show, an essential part of a bounded, monotone, and differentiable equilibrium is the solution of a linked pair of differential equations, and one solution (on which we and they focus) is linear:

$$\tilde{p}_s(v_s) = \tfrac{2}{3}v_s + \tfrac{1}{4}\bar{v}_b + \tfrac{1}{12}\underline{v}_s,$$

$$\tilde{p}_b(v_b) = \tfrac{2}{3}v_b + \tfrac{1}{4}\underline{v}_s + \tfrac{1}{12}\bar{v}_b. \tag{1}$$

Three cases must be considered. First, if the use of these strategies would imply that no type of either party is sure to trade (i.e., $\tilde{p}_b(\bar{v}_b) \leqslant \tilde{p}_s(\bar{v}_s)$ and $\tilde{p}_s(\underline{v}_s) \geqslant \tilde{p}_b(\underline{v}_b)$), then the equilibrium strategies are $p_s(v_s) = \tilde{p}_s(v_s)$ and $p_b(v_b) = \tilde{p}_b(v_b)$. Second, if the use of these strategies would make some types of at least one party sure to trade, but would not make all types of both parties sure to trade, then the buyer-type v_b names the price $p_b(v_b) = \min(\tilde{p}_b(v_b), \tilde{p}_s(\bar{v}_s))$ and the seller-type v_s names the price $p_s(v_s) = \max(\tilde{p}_s(v_s), \tilde{p}_b(\underline{v}_b))$. Third, if the use of these strategies would make all types of both players sure to trade, then the Chatterjee–Samuelson equilibrium breaks down. A continuum of equilibria still exist, but these equilibria are unrelated to the bidding strategies described in (1). In some of these equilibria, all types of both parties name a given price in the interval $[\bar{v}_s, \underline{v}_b]$ and trade occurs with certainty. We deal with this case below.

When no seller type is sure to trade, calculation shows that the buyer's interim payoff is

$$U_b(v_b; [\underline{v}_s, \bar{v}_s], [\underline{v}_b, \bar{v}_b]) = \begin{cases} 0 & \text{if } v_b \leqslant \underline{\beta}, \\[2ex] \dfrac{(v_b - \underline{\beta})^2}{2(\bar{v}_s - \underline{v}_s)} & \text{if } \underline{\beta} < v_b \leqslant \bar{\beta}, \quad (2) \\[2ex] v_b - \bar{\beta} + \dfrac{\bar{v}_s - \underline{v}_s}{2} & \text{if } v_b > \bar{\beta}, \end{cases}$$

where $\Delta = (\bar{v}_b - \underline{v}_s)/4$, $\underline{\beta} = \underline{v}_s + \Delta$, and $\bar{\beta} = \bar{v}_s + \Delta$. (In this notation, no seller type is sure to trade when $\underline{v}_b < \bar{\beta}$.) The three cases in (2) correspond to the cases in which the buyer, given v_b and the supports of the players' types, is sure not to trade, might trade, or is sure to trade, respectively.

When some but not all seller types are sure to trade (i.e., $\underline{\beta} < \underline{v}_b < \bar{\beta}$), an interval of seller types trade with the lowest buyer type. The interim payoff to $\underline{v}_b$ is then

$$\underline{U}_b \equiv U_b(\underline{v}_b; [\underline{v}_s, \bar{v}_s], [\underline{v}_b, \bar{v}_b]) = \frac{(\underline{v}_b - \underline{v}_s - \Delta)^2}{3(\bar{v}_s - \underline{v}_s)}, \tag{3}$$

and the interim payoff for other buyer types is

$$
U_b(v_b; [\underline{v}_s, \bar{v}_s], [\underline{v}_b, \bar{v}_b]) =
\begin{cases}
\dfrac{(v_b - \underline{v}_s - \Delta)^2}{2(\bar{v}_s - \underline{v}_s)} - \tfrac{1}{2}U_b & \text{if } v_b \leqslant \beta, \\[4mm]
v_b - \beta - \tfrac{1}{2}U_b + \dfrac{\bar{v}_s - \underline{v}_s}{2} & \text{if } v_b > \beta.
\end{cases}
\tag{4}
$$

Finally, when all seller types are sure to trade ($\beta < \underline{v}_b$), then all buyer types also are sure to trade, and the Chatterjee–Samuelson equilibrium breaks dows: the bids given by (1) are irrelevant, and the strategies $p_b(v_b) = \tilde{p}_s(\bar{v}_s)$ and $p_s(v_s) = \tilde{p}_b(\underline{v}_b)$ are *not* an equilibrium. Without proposing a general theory for this problem, we note that the subgame $\{v_s \in [0, 1-y], v_b \in [y, 1]\}$ is symmetric about $\tfrac{1}{2}$ and so (when $y > \tfrac{1}{2}$) it is natural to assume that trade will occur with certainty at a price of $\tfrac{1}{2}$. Then a buyer-type $v_b \geqslant \tfrac{1}{2}$ gets a payoff ($v_b - \tfrac{1}{2}$). As noted in the text, a "one-step" equilibrium at price $\tfrac{1}{2}$ formalizes this outcome.

As described in the text, an equilibrium value of y must satisfy the necessary condition

$$
(1 - y)\,U_b(y; [0, 1 - y], [y, 1]) + y U_b(y; [1 - y, 1], [y, 1])
$$

$$
= (1 - y)\,U_b(y; [0, 1 - y], [0, y]),
\tag{5}
$$

since the left-hand side represents buyer-type y's expected payoff if he says "keen" and the right-hand side represents his expected payoff if he says "not keen."

The first term on the left-hand side of (5) is strictly less than the right-hand side, because the only difference is that in the first term the seller is more optimistic about the buyer's type. Therefore the second term on the left-hand side is strictly positive, so the buyer-type y trades at least sometimes in that subgame ($y > \underline{\beta} = 1 - \tfrac{3}{4}y$, or $y > \tfrac{4}{7}$), and some seller types trade for sure. On the other hand, since in this subgame $\bar{\beta} > 1$, not all seller types trade for sure. Thus (3) applies in the second term of (5).

On the right-hand side of (5), which involves the subgame $\{v_s \in [0, 1 - y], v_b \in [0, y]\}$, the critical type $\bar{\beta}$ is equal to $1 - \tfrac{3}{4}y$, so y trades for sure in that subgame, since $y > \tfrac{4}{7}$ implies $y > \bar{\beta}$. But $\underline{v}_b = 0 < \underline{\beta} = \tfrac{1}{4}y$, so no seller type is sure to trade and the bottom case of (2) applies.

Finally, in the first term on the left-hand side of (5), involving the subgame $\{v_s \in [0, 1 - y], v_b \in [y, 1]\}$ (in which both players are keen), $\beta = \tfrac{5}{4} - y$. So if $y > \tfrac{5}{4} - y$, or $y > \tfrac{5}{8}$, then y trades for sure when both agents are keen. This means that all types of both agents trade for sure, and the Chatterjee–Samuelson analysis breaks down; as discussed in the text, we consider the one-step equilirium in which trade occurs with certainty at price $\frac{1}{2}$.

Substituting all this into (5) yields

$$(1 - y)(y - \tfrac{1}{2}) + \tfrac{1}{3}y(\tfrac{7}{4}y - 1)^2 = (1 - y)(\tfrac{5}{4}y - \tfrac{1}{2}),$$

which has solutions

$$y = \{22 \pm 12\sqrt{2}\}/49 = 0.103 \text{ or } 0.795.$$

Since the analysis of the second term of (5) proved that $y > \frac{4}{7}$, the solution is $y = 0.795$, which exceeds $\frac{5}{8}$, confirming that the Chatterjee–Samuelson equilibrium indeed breaks down when both parties say "keen."

This completes our derivation of the equilibrium value of y. We next state and prove Lemma 1, which describes our equilibrium. Finally, we prove Propositions 1 and 2.

LEMMA 1. *The following behavior defines the equilibrium path of a perfect Bayesian equilibrium in our two-stage bargaining game.* (Our proof does not require explicit descriptions of the optimal bids following deviations in the cheap-talk phase, so we omit these bids from the description of equilibrium.)

Buyer. (A) If $v_b < y$ then

(i) say "not keen" in the first stage, and

(ii) if the seller says "not keen" in the first stage then bid $p_b = 0$ in the second stage, but if the seller says "keen" in the first stage then bid

$$p_b = \min\{\tfrac{2}{3}v_b + \tfrac{1}{12}y, \tfrac{2}{3} - \tfrac{5}{12}y\}$$

in the second stage.

(B) If $v_b \geq y$ then

(i) say "keen" in the first stage, and

(ii) if the seller says "keen" in the first stage then bid $p_b = \frac{1}{2}$ in the second stage, but if the seller says "not keen" in the first stage then bid

$$p_b = \tfrac{2}{3}v_b + \tfrac{1}{4}(1 - y) + \tfrac{1}{12}$$

in the second stage.

Seller. (A) If $v_s > 1 - y$ then

(i) say "not keen" in the first stage, and

(ii)   if the buyer says "not keen" in the first stage then bid $p_s = 1$ in the second stage, but if the buyer says "keen" in the first stage then bid

$$p_s = \max\{\tfrac{2}{3}v_s + \tfrac{1}{4} + \tfrac{1}{12}(1 - y), \tfrac{1}{3} + \tfrac{5}{12}y\}$$

in the second stage.
        (B) If $v_s \leqslant 1 - y$ then

(i)   say "keen" in the first stage, and

(ii)   if the buyer says "keen" in the first stage then bid $p_s = \tfrac{1}{2}$ in the second stage, but if the buyer says "not keen" in the first stage then bid

$$p_s = \tfrac{2}{3}v_s + \tfrac{1}{4}y$$

in the second stage.

Proof.   The equilibrium bidding strategies in the {"keen," "not keen"} and {"not keen," "keen"} subgames follow from the analysis in the first part of this Appendix. This means that the bidding strategies specified in the lemma are sequentially rational. It therefore suffices to show that the necessary condition (5) is also sufficient. This is a direct result of the fact that higher buyer types are more concerned with the probability of trade than are lower buyer types.

Formally, define the difference between the payoffs from saying "keen" and saying "not keen," given subsequent optimal behavior for a buyer of type v_b, as

$$\begin{aligned}
D(v_b) &\equiv (1 - y)\, W_b(v_b; [0, 1 - y], [y, 1]) \\
&\quad + y W_b(v_b; [1 - y, 1], [y, 1]) \\
&\quad - (1 - y)\, W_b(v_b; [0, 1 - y], [0, y]),
\end{aligned}$$

where $W_b(v_b; [\underline{v}_s, \bar{v}_s], [\underline{v}_b, \bar{v}_b])$ is the expected payoff to buyer-type v_b from making the optimal bid when the seller's type is uniformly distributed on $[\underline{v}_s, \bar{v}_s]$ and the seller *believes* that the buyer's type is independently and uniformly distributed on $[\underline{v}_b, \bar{v}_b]$. Note that W_b is defined even if v_b falls outside the interval $[\underline{v}_b, \bar{v}_b]$ that the seller believes contains the buyer's type, as will occur off the equilibrium path. If $v_b \in [\underline{v}_b, \bar{v}_b]$, however, then

$$W_b(v_b; [\underline{v}_s, \bar{v}_s], [\underline{v}_b, \bar{v}_b]) = U_b(v_b; [\underline{v}_s, \bar{v}_s], [\underline{v}_b, \bar{v}_b]),$$

as will occur in equilibrium.

We must show that $D(v_b) \geqslant 0$ for $v_b \geqslant y$ and that $D(v_b) \leqslant 0$ for $v_b \leqslant y$. This will show that our proposed equilibrium is indeed an equilibrium— that is, that no buyer can gain by deviating in the cheap-talk stage and then submitting an unexpected bid. (A similar proof works for the seller.) We do this by showing that

(i) for $v_b \leqslant \frac{1}{2}$, $D(v_b) \leqslant 0$,

(ii) for $v_b > \frac{1}{2}$, $D'(v_b) \geqslant 0$.

Since $y > \frac{1}{2}$ and since $D(y) = 0$, (i) and (ii) prove our proposition. Note that the arguments below do not require explicit descriptions of optimal bids following deviations in the cheap-talk phase.

Consider first $v_b \leqslant \frac{1}{2}$. Since the seller bids $\frac{1}{2}$ after {"keen," "keen"}, the first term of $D(v_b)$ vanishes. Moreover, the seller's minimum bid after {"not keen," "keen"} is

$$p_s(1-y) = \max\{\tilde{p}_s(1-y), \tilde{p}_b(y)\} = \tilde{p}_b(y) = \frac{1}{3} + \frac{5}{12}y,$$

and since $\frac{1}{3} + \frac{5}{12}y > \frac{1}{2}$, the second term of $D(v_b)$ also vanishes. Hence, it is immediate that $D(v_b) \leqslant 0$ for $v_b \leqslant \frac{1}{2}$.

Now consider the derivative $D'(v_b)$, for $v_b \geqslant \frac{1}{2}$. Note that the derivative of the interim payoff is equal to the probability of trade (by the envelope theorem), *even off the equilibrium path.* Since buyer types $v_b \geqslant \frac{1}{2}$ trade for sure in the {"keen," "keen"} subgame (since the seller bids $\frac{1}{2}$ for sure), the derivative of the first term of $D(v_b)$ is $(1-y)$. The derivative of the third (negative) term is $[-(1-y)]$ times a probability. So, for $v_b \geqslant \frac{1}{2}$,

$$D'(v_b) \geqslant \frac{d}{dv_b}\{yW_b(v_b; [1-y, 1], [y, 1])\} \geqslant 0. \quad \text{Q.E.D.}$$

PROPOSITION 1. *The equilibrium mapping from types to outcomes in our cheap-talk equilibrium cannot arise in an equilibrium without talk.*

Proof. Consider a buyer of type $v_b > y$. In equilibrium he sometimes bids $\frac{1}{2}$ (following "keen" from the seller) and sometimes bids

$$\tilde{p}_b(v_b; [1-y, 1], [y, 1]) = \frac{2}{3}v_b + \frac{1}{4}(1-y) + \frac{1}{12} = \frac{1}{3} + \frac{2}{3}v_b - \frac{1}{4}y$$

(following "not keen" from the seller). Note that the latter bid exceeds $\frac{1}{2}$. Dividing his bids into the two classes, "bids $= \frac{1}{2}$" and "bids $> \frac{1}{2}$," we see that the frequency of the first class is $(1-y)$ (i.e., the probability that the seller says "keen"). We notice also that the seller facing this buyer sometimes bids $\frac{1}{2}$ and sometimes bids

$$p_s(v_s) = \max\{\tilde{p}_s(v_s; [1-y, 1], [y, 1]), \tilde{p}_b(y; [1-y, 1], [y, 1])\}$$

$$\geqslant \tilde{p}_b(y; [1-, 1], [y, 1])$$

$$= \frac{1}{3} + (\frac{2}{3} - \frac{1}{4})y = \frac{1}{3} + \frac{5}{12}y > \frac{1}{2}.$$

Given knowledge only of the buyer's type $v_b > y$, therefore, we see a joint distribution of buyer's and seller's bids as

		p_s	
		$\frac{1}{2}$	$> \frac{1}{2}$
	$\frac{1}{2}$	$(1 - y)$	0
p_b			
	$> \frac{1}{2}$	0	y

But such correlation in bids would be unattainable in a Nash equilibrium without cheap talk. This shows that the equilibrium *strategies* (maps from types to bids) could not arise without talk.

We now extend this argument to show that the equilibrium mapping from types to outcomes (whether trade occurs and if so at what price) is unattainable in a Nash equilibrium without cheap talk. Consider the buyer types $v_b \in [y, 1]$, who say "keen" in the talk phase. If the seller says "not keen" then trade occurs with positive probability, and if trade occurs then (by Lemma 1) the price moves in v_b. If the seller says "keen," however, then trade occurs with probability one at price $\frac{1}{2}$, which is independent of v_b. Thus, the price at which trade occurs either does or does not depend on v_b according to the value of v_s. Clearly, the equilibrium map from types to outcomes in a double auction without talk cannot behave in this way.   Q.E.D.

LEMMA 2. *In any equilibrium without talk, the seller's bid p_s is a weakly increasing function of his type v_s.*

Proof. Given any seller's bid p_s, the distribution $F_b(\cdot)$ of the buyer's bid p_b determines a probability of trade, $\pi = 1 - F_b(p_s)$, and an expected price conditional on trade,

$$e = E_{p_b}\{(p_b + p_s)/2 \mid p_b \geq p_s\}.$$

Thus in choosing a bid p_s the seller is choosing a point in (e, π) space. The relationship between p_s and e is strictly monotone, moreover.

In terms of (e, π), the seller's expected payoff is just $\pi(e - v_s)$. Therefore sellers with higher v_s have steeper indifference curves in (e, π) space. This means that for $e' < e$, if v_s prefers (e, π) to (e', π') then so does $v_s' > v_s$.

Let $e^*(v_s)$ be the optimal choice of e on the available locus for seller-type v_s. Then our observation concerning the slopes of the indifference curves for different types implies that e^* is (weakly) increasing in v_s. Consequently, so is the bid p_s.   Q.E.D.

PROPOSITION 2. *There does not exist an equilibrium without cheap talk in which sellers* $v_s \in [1 - y, 1]$ *and buyers* $v_b \in [y, 1]$ *name the prices that they name in the* {*"not keen," "keen"*} *subgame of our cheap-talk equilibrium.*

Proof. Suppose the buyer believes that the seller's bid is distributed as $F(p_s)$. Define $Z(v_b, p_b, F)$ to be the expected payoff to buyer-type v_b from bidding p_b when p_s is distributed as F. This buyer-type's optimal bid, $p_b(v_b; F)$, maximizes $Z(v_b, p_b, F)$.

Let F be the buyer's belief about p_s in the {"not keen," "keen"} subgame of our cheap-talk equilibrium. Then from Lemma 1 we have that

$$p_b(v_b; F) = \tfrac{2}{3}v_b + \tfrac{1}{4}(1 - y) + \tfrac{1}{12}$$

and that for $v_b \in (y, 1)$ the derivative

$$\left. \frac{\partial Z(v_b, p_b, F)}{\partial p_b} \right|_{p_b(v_b;F)}$$

exists and equals zero.

Now let G be any distribution with support bounded above by $p_s(1 - y)$, the lowest seller bid in our {"not keen," "keen"} subgame. A simple computation shows that $p_b(v_b; F)$ can be rewritten as

$$p_b(v_b; F) = p_s(1 - y) + (\tfrac{2}{3})(v_b - y),$$

which exceeds $p_s(1 - y)$ for $v_b > y$. Since $\tilde{G}[p_s(1 - y)] = 1$ and $p_s(1 - y) < p_b(v_b; F)$,

$$\left. \frac{\partial Z(v_b, p_b, G)}{\partial p_b} \right|_{p_b(v_b;F)}$$

exists and is strictly negative, for $v_b > y$.

Finally, suppose that there were an equilibrium without talk in which the relevant buyers and sellers name the required prices. Then by Lemma 2, the prices named by sellers $v_s \in [0, 1 - y]$ cannot exceed $p_s(1 - y)$. The buyer's belief about p_s in such an equilibrium can be described by the distribution

$$H = \lambda F + (1 - \lambda)G$$

for some $\lambda \in (0, 1)$ and distributions F and G as described above. Note that

$$Z(v_b, p_b, H) = \lambda Z(v_b, p_b, F) + (1 - \lambda) Z(v_b, p_b, G).$$

Hence,

$$\left.\frac{\partial Z(v_b, p_b, H)}{\partial p_b}\right|_{p_b(v_b;F)} < 0,$$

so $p_b(v_b; F)$ is no longer an equilibrium bid for buyer-type $v_b > y$.   Q.E.D.

REFERENCES

1. K. CHATTERJEE AND W. SAMUELSON, Bargaining under incomplete information, *Oper. Res.* **31** (1983), 835–851.
2. V. CRAWFORD AND J. SOBEL, Strategic information transmission, *Econometrica* **50** (1982), 1431–1452.
3. J. FARRELL, Cheap talk, coordination, and entry, *Rand J. Econ.* **18** (1987), 34–39.
4. J. FARRELL AND R. GIBBONS, "Cheap Talk in Bargaining Games," MIT Working Paper No. 422, June 1986.
5. J. FARRELL AND G. SALONER, Standardization, compatibility, and innovation, *Rand J. Econ.* **16** (1985), 70–83.
6. F. FORGES, "Negotiation without a Deadline: A Job Market Example," CORE Discussion Paper No. 8639, 1986.
7. D. FUDENBERG AND J. TIROLE, Sequential bargaining with incomplete information, *Rev. Econ. Stud.* **50** (1983), 221–247.
8. R. GIBBONS, Learning in equilibrium models of arbitration, *Amer. Econ. Rev.* **78** (1988), 896–912.
9. W. LEININGER, P. LINHART, AND R. RADNER, Equilibria of the sealed-bid mechanism for bargaining with incomplete information, *J. Econ. Theory* **48** (1989), 63–106.
10. S. MATTHEWS, Veto threats: Rhetoric in a bargaining game, *Quart. J, Econom.* **104** (1989), in press.
11. S. MATTHEWS AND A. POSTLEWAITE, Pre-play communication in two-person sealed-bid double auctions, *J. Econ. Theory* **48** (1989), 238–263.
12. R. MYERSON, Analysis of two bargaining problems with incomplete information, in "Game-Theoretic Models of Bargaining" (A. Roth, Ed.), Cambridge Univ. Press, Cambridge, 1985.
13. R. MYERSON AND M. SATTERTHWAITE, Efficient mechanisms for bilateral trading, *J. Econ. Theory* **29** (1983), 265–281.
14. M. SATTERTHWAITE AND S. WILLIAMS, Bilateral trade with the sealed bid double auction: Existence and efficiency, *J. Econ. Theory* **48** (1989), 107–133.
15. J. SOBEL, A theory of credibility, *Rev. Econ. Stud.* **52** (1985), 557–573.
16. J. SOBEL AND I. TAKAHASHI, A multistage model of bargaining, *Rev. Econ. Stud.* **50** (1983), 411–426.
17. A. M. SPENCE, "Market Signaling," Harvard Univ. Press, Cambridge, MA, 1974.

JOURNAL OF ECONOMIC THEORY **48**, 238–263 (1989)

Pre-play Communication in Two-Person Sealed-Bid Double Auctions*

STEVEN A. MATTHEWS

Northwestern University, Evanston, Illionois 60208

AND

ANDREW POSTLEWAITE

*University of Pennsylvania,
Philadelphia, Pennsylvania 19104*

Received June 17, 1987; revised March 21, 1988

Allowing unmediated communication in a two-person double auction dramatically enlarges the set of equilibrium outcomes. It then consists of all allocation rules that are equilibrium outcomes of games in which all traders have the power at the end to veto proposed trades. All the allocation rules so characterized are equilibrium outcomes of a single game in which the traders exchange messages once before bidding in a double auction. These outcomes are all obtained by equilibria in which the traders truthfully tell each other their values. Adding a mediator achieves no further outcomes. *Journal of Economic Literature* Classification Numbers: 026, 021, 022. © 1989 Academic Press, Inc.

1. INTRODUCTION

The currently predominant approach to the study of bargaining and trading institutions is rooted in Nash [20] and exposited in Wilson [27, 28]. Its basic tenet is that institutions can be evaluated by studying the noncooperative games that reflect their relevant features. It is often acknowledged that this approach can fail if the game does not represent all the real-world actions allowed to traders, and also if the game has multiple equilibria. Yet, we maintain that in environments with incomplete informa-

* This research was partially supported by grants from the National Science Foundation. We thank Bob Gibbons, George Mailath, and Steve Williams for useful conversations, as well as two referees and an associate editor for useful comments. We especially thank Françoise Forges, who alerted us to a critical error in a previous version. This work was begun when S. Matthews was a visitor at the University of Pennsylvania.

403

tion, these two problems are more severe than is generally recognized. The real-world actions that we are concerned with, and which have almost never been formally considered, are pre-trade communications among the traders. It is our claim that following the Nash program to the point of strategically modelling communication can greatly exacerbate the multiplicity problem.

To establish this claim, we consider the sealed-bid double auctions studied initially by Chatterjee and Samuelson [3]. The environment is standard: a risk neutral seller initially owns an indivisible item that a risk neutral buyer may wish to purchase, and their evaluations of the item are privately known. Given a number $k \in [0, 1]$, the rules of a k-double auction require that both traders submit bids, that trade occurs if the bid of the buyer exceeds that of the seller, and that the price when trade occurs is a weighted average of the bids, with the weight on the buyer's bid being k. Double auctions have served as noncooperative models of bargaining when commitment is possible [3, 17, 19], and of markets when generalized to many buyers and sellers [26, 27]. They have also been the subject of considerable experimental scrutiny [21, 24].

Attention is usually restricted to a particularly tractable equilibrium of a double auction, e.g., the linear equilibria found by Chatterjee and Samuelson in the uniform case. Even without considering pre-play communication, selecting this equilibrium may be questionable in view of the significant multiplicities of equilibria uncovered by Leininger et al. [13] and Satterthwaite and Williams [23]. One's confidence in this selection should be further eroded by our main result: pre-play communication dramatically enlarges the set of equilibrium outcomes of a double auction.

A corollary of our results is that allowing for communication renders the set of equilibrium outcomes invariant with respect to the double auction's parameter k. Thus, the real-world outcome of a k-double auction may not only be far off what is predicted from a model that neglects communication possibilities, but it may not even depend upon what is supposedly a design parameter of the auction.

The largest caveat to our results, in our opinion, is that they rely on simultaneous message exchange, i.e., on both players talking at the same time. Most (but not all!) real-world conversations are sequential, with only one person talking at a time. (This issue is discussed further in the concluding section.)

We have mentioned here only a sampling of the results. Broadly speaking, we obtain a complete characterization of the equilibrium outcomes allowed by mediated and unmediated communication in double auctions—the concluding remarks in Section 5 give a thorough summary. In Section 2 the model is presented. In Section 3, as an introductory special case, the monopoly and monopsony allocations are shown to be equilibrium outcomes of any two-person double auction in which the traders can communicate. Section 4 contains statements and discussions of the theorems, and the Appendix contains their proofs. Section 5 contains remarks on the results, possible extensions, and the literature.

2. THE MODEL

The seller's *value* (*type*) for the item is v_1 and the buyer's is v_2. Each trader knows only his own value. It is common knowledge that trader $j \neq i$ believes that v_i is the realization of a random variable $\tilde{v}_i$ that has a distribution F_i on an interval $T_i = [a_i, b_i]$. Trade is assumed to be possibly beneficial: $a_1 < b_2$. No further assumptions are made about the distributions F_i—they need not be continuous, for example.

An *allocation* is a pair of numbers, a probability of trade and an expected payment of money from the buyer to the seller. If the item is traded with probability p and the expected payment is x, the buyer's expected utility is $v_2 p - x$ and the seller's expected utility is $x - v_1 p$.

What has been defined so far is a particular *Bayesian collective choice environment* (a slight paraphrase of Myerson's [18] term). An *allocation rule* for this environment is a mapping (p, x) that determines a trade probability $p(v_1, v_2) \in [0, 1]$ and an expected payment $x(v_1, v_2) \in \Re$ for each pair (v_1, v_2) of trader types.

Given an allocation rule (p, x), define functions $U_i: T_i^2 \to \Re$ by

$$U_1(r_1, v_1) \equiv E[x(r_1, \tilde{v}_2) - v_1 p(r_1, \tilde{v}_2)] \quad \text{and}$$
$$U_2(r_2, v_2) \equiv E[v_2 p(\tilde{v}_1, r_2) - x(\tilde{v}_1, r_2)]. \tag{1}$$

The allocation rule is *incentive compatible* if

$$U_i(v_i, v_i) \geqslant U_i(r_i, v_i) \quad \text{for all} \quad r_i, v_i \in T_i \quad \text{and} \quad i = 1, 2. \tag{IC}$$

An allocation rule satisfies IC if and only if it is an equilibrium outcome of a Bayesian game defined by adding a "mechanism" to the environment, where a *mechanism* (for this environment) is a set of actions for each player and a mapping that takes pairs of actions into allocations. (An *equilibrium outcome* of a Bayesian game, in this paper, is the allocation rule induced by an equilibrium.) Given a (p, x) satisfying IC, one game in which it is an equilibrium outcome is formed from the revelation mechanism based on (p, x). In this mechanism, each player i reports that this type is r_i, whereupon the mechanism specifies that trade occurs with probability $p(r_1, r_2)$ and that the payment is $x(r_1, r_2)$. The incentive compatibility of (p, x) ensures that truth-telling is an equilibrium of the game defined by adding this mechanism to the Bayesian collective choice environment. (For more on this "revelation principle" argument, see the Myerson [18] survey.)

Often, a mechanism designer is constrained to allow each player to choose whether to participate. In this case, the mechanism must give each type of each player an expected utility no less than what that type of player gets by not participating. In our environment this means that the resulting allocation rule must be *interim individually rational* in the following sense:

$$U_i(v_i, v_i) \geqslant 0 \qquad \text{for all} \quad v_i \in T_i \quad \text{and} \quad i = 1, 2. \qquad \text{(INTIR)}$$

The feasible set of allocation rules, the characterization of which is the main accomplishment of Myerson and Satterthwaite [19], is then

$$A \equiv \{(p, x) \,|\, \text{IC and INTER are satisfied}\}. \qquad (2)$$

A *k-double auction*, where $k \in [0, 1]$, is a particular mechanism that resembles various real-world trading and bargaining institutions. The seller and buyer in this mechanism simultaneously submit bids, β_1 and β_2. Trade occurs if and only if the higher bid is the buyer's: $\beta_2 \geqslant \beta_1$. A nonzero payment is made by the buyer to the seller if and only if trade occurs, in which case the payment is $k\beta_2 + (1 - k)\beta_1$. We denote by $D(k)$ the Bayesian game defined by adding this mechanism to our Bayesian environment. This is the game studied, for example, in [3, 13, 23].

The games studied in this paper are *communication–bidding games*. Such a game is defined by adding a "communication mechanism" to a *k*-double auction game $D(k)$, where a *communication mechanism* (for a double auction) is a device through which the buyer and seller can communicate before they submit their bids. A communication mechanism receives messages from the traders and transmits messages to the traders; in general, there may be several rounds of message exchange, and neither trader may see the messages of the other. We denote by $\mu(k)$ a Bayesian game defined by adding a communication mechanism to a *k*-double auction game $D(k)$.

A particular kind of communication mechanism is a *revelation–suggestion mechanism* which can be described as a mechanical "mediator" to whom the traders confidentially reveal their types and who, subsequently, confidentially suggests to each trader a particular bid to make. The "general revelation principle" (Myerson [16, 18], Forges [7]) states that there is no loss of generality in restricting attention to revelation–suggestion mechanisms in which one equilibrium of the resulting game consists of the traders honestly revealing their types and obediently submitting the suggested bids. More precisely, this principle states that if (p, x) is an equilibrium outcome of a communication–bidding game $\mu(k)$, then another communication–bidding game $\mu'(k)$ exists in which the communication mechanism is a revelation-suggestion mechanism, honest and obedient behavior constitutes an equilibrium, and (p, x) is the corresponding equilibrium outcome.

We are especially interested in another kind of communication–bidding game, an *unmediated* communication–bidding game. In such a game the communication is meant to be face-to-face, taking place without a mediator. The formal description in terms of a communication mechanism requires the mechanism merely to relay, accurately, each player's messages to the other. Explicit reference to a mechanism is therefore unnecessary; it is simpler to assume that each trader's messages are directly received by the other player. Accordingly, we consider *unmediated communication–bidding games* as having two stages, a *message stage* in which the players exchange messages, followed by a *bidding stage* in which they play a k-double auction. The message stages in the particular games we shall study consist of a single round of simultaneous message exchange.

An unmediated communication–bidding game of this sort was first studied by Farrell and Gibbons [6]; we defer until later a discussion of their results. Similar economic games which differ in that the second stage is other than a double auction are studied, for example, in [4, 8, 14]. Issues that arise in general with unmediated communication are considered by Farrell [5], Barany [2], and Forges [9]; the latter two papers are discussed below.

Thus far we have used the term "equilibrium of a Bayesian game" with the usual, unrefined definition in mind (see, e.g., the Myerson [18] survey). But it is convenient to refine the definition in a small way. Henceforth, an *equilibrium* of a communication–bidding game is an equilibrium in which, in the bidding stage, the seller never bids less than his value and the buyer never bids more than this value. Throwing out such strategies can be justified by the observation that they are dominated. For example, a strategy for the seller that prescribes that he bid below his value when his value is v_1 is dominated by a strategy that differs only by having this type of seller bid v_1. Thus, the seller would submit a bid less than this value in an equilibrium only if that bid and every higher bid almost surely results in no trade. Altering an equilibrium strategy in the way just described will result in another equilibrium that gives all types of both traders the same (interim) expected utilities. This refinement, therefore, does not eliminate any equilibrium that differs in an economically interesting way from an equilibrium that is not eliminated.

Before beginning our analysis of communication–bidding games, we first observe that communication can only expand a double auction's set of equilibrium outcomes. That is, an equilibrium outcome (p, x) of a double auction game $D(k)$ is also an equilibrium outcome of any communication–

bidding game $\mu(k)$ based on $D(k)$. One equilibrium of $\mu(k)$ that has (p, x) as an outcome is the following: the traders send messages to the mechanism according to probability distributions that are independent of their types, and they submit bids according to the given equilibrium of $D(k)$, regardless of any of the messages. (Such *babbling equilibria* are discussed, e.g., in [5, 14].)

If the equilibrium outcomes of $D(k)$ were to be the only equilibrium outcomes of the unmediated communication–bidding games $\mu(k)$, an economist could justifiably study double auctions without taking account of communication. Unfortunately, this is not the case.

3. THE BUYER'S AND SELLER'S BEST ALLOCATION RULES

As an introduction to the general results, we now indicate how unmediated communication in any k-double auction can achieve three particularly interesting allocation rules: the buyer's best allocation rule, the seller's best allocation rule, and a convex combination of the two.

The argument relies on a particular class of double auction equilibria. Define, for any $z \in \Re$ and $(v_1, v_2) \in T_1 \times T_2$, the bidding strategies

$$\beta_1^z(v_1) = \begin{cases} z & \text{if } v_1 \leqslant z, \\ b_2 & \text{otherwise,} \end{cases}$$

$$\beta_2^z(v_2) = \begin{cases} z & \text{if } v_2 \geqslant z, \\ a_1 & \text{otherwise.} \end{cases} \tag{3}$$

Trade occurs according to these strategies only at the price z, and precisely when both traders can profit by trading at this price. It is easy to show that these strategies constitute a perfect Bayesian equilibrium of $D(k)$ for any $k \in [0, 1]$, regardless of the beliefs F_1 and F_2. Discussed originally by Leininger *et al.* [13], we refer to such an equilibrium as a *single-price equilibrium*.

Consider first the buyer's best allocation rule in A, the set of IC and INTIR allocation rules. The most preferred such allocation rule of a type v_2 buyer—given his beliefs F_1 about the seller's value—would be achieved if he were to quote a take-it-or-leave-it price z that maximizes $(v_2 - z) F_1(z)$, and the seller were to accept this price precisely when it exceeded his value (see [17, 22, 2]). That is, the buyer's best allocation rule in A is

$$p^2(v_1, v_2) = \begin{cases} 1 & \text{if } v_1 \leqslant z^2(v_2), \\ 0 & \text{otherwise,} \end{cases}$$

$$x^2(v_1, v_2) = \begin{cases} z^2(v_2) & \text{if } v_1 \leqslant z^2(v_2), \\ 0 & \text{otherwise,} \end{cases} \tag{4}$$

where, for all $v_2 \in T_2$, $z^2(v_2)$ is the type v_2 buyer's *optimal price*:

$$z^2(v_2) \in \underset{z}{\text{argmax}} \ (v_2 - z) F_1(z). \tag{5}$$

This best allocation rule for the buyer is an equilibrium outcome of $D(1)$, the $k = 1$ double auction: as the price in this auction is determined entirely by the buyer's bid, the seller's dominant strategy is to bid his true value, and the buyer's best response is to bid his optimal price. However, if $k < 1$, then (p^2, x^2) is not an equilibrium outcome of $D(k)$. [*Proof*: if $k < 1$, a type v_1 seller who trades with positive probability should, for some $\varepsilon > 0$, never submit a bid in the interval $[v_1, v_1 + \varepsilon)$. For, increasing such a bid to $v_1 + \varepsilon$ results in a second order loss (a first order loss in probability of trade times a first order profit then foregone), but a first order gain (a first order gain in profit when trade occurs times a positive probability of trade. Thus, this seller never trades with a type v_2 buyer for whom $z^2(v_2) \in [v_1, v_1 + \varepsilon)$, as (p^2, x^2) would require.] Similarly, if we let (p^1, x^1) denote the seller's best allocation rule in A, then (p^1, x^1) is an equilibrium outcome of the double auction $D(k)$ if and only if $k = 0$.

We now show that unmediated communication in any k-double auction can achieve (p^2, x^2), even if $k = 0$. The simplest unmediated communication–bidding game which does this allows the buyer to suggest a price to the seller before they submit their bids. Consider the strategies for this game according to which the buyer suggests the optimal price for his type, $z = z^2(v_2)$, and he and the seller then play the single-price bidding strategies (β_1^z, β_2^z). The resulting outcome is obviously (p^2, x^2). Since this allocation rule is best for the buyer, his strategy is a best reply to that of the seller. And since (β_1^z, β_2^z) is an equilibrium of $D(k)$ regardless of the value of z and regardless of how the beliefs have been updated, this strategy pair is an equilibrium.

In this equilibrium, the price suggested by the buyer is "cheap talk" as opposed to a true take-it-or-leave-it offer, since he cannot commit himself to later bidding the price he had suggested. Nevertheless, his suggested price has the effect of a take-it-or-leave-it offer by its selection of a single-price equilibrium for the double auction.

Communication can also achieve convex combinations of the buyer's and the seller's best allocation rules. Take, for example, $(\bar{p}, \bar{x}) \equiv (\frac{1}{2})(p^1, x^1) + (\frac{1}{2})(p^2, x^2)$. It can be easily obtained with mediated communication. Note first that it is a *correlated* equilibrium outcome of any communication–bidding game in which both traders can suggest prices before they bid. In the correlated equilibrium, play begins with the operation of a 50–50 randomization device which selects one of their suggested prices to be the price in the single-price double auction equilibrium that they will play. By our definitions, this randomization device is a communication mechanism (it transmits but does not receive messages). Thus, its addition to the game results in a mediated communication–bidding game $\mu(k)$ that has $(\bar{p}, \bar{x})$ as an equilibrium outcome.

The allocation rule $(\bar{p}, \bar{x})$ can also be obtained from an unmediated communication–bidding game. In this game, each trader i suggests a price *and* announces a number, $y_i \in \{0, 1\}$. An equilibrium consists of each trader i suggesting his own optimal price, $z^i(v_i)$, announcing $y_i = 0$ with probability $\frac{1}{2}$ and $y_i = 1$ with probability $\frac{1}{2}$, and then bidding according to the single-price strategy β_i^z, where $z = z^1(v_1)$ if $y_1 = y_2$ and $z = z^2(v_2)$ if $y_1 \neq y_2$. According to these strategies, there is a one-half chance that each trader's optimal price will be the price in the single-price equilibrium played in the bidding stage. Thus, the outcome is $(\bar{p}, \bar{x})$. These strategies do form an equilibrium: neither player can unilaterally alter the probability distribution over single-price equilibria to be played in the bidding stage, and neither player will want to deviate from suggesting his own optimal price.

[This equilibrium produces the correlation as a result of the players using independent mixed strategies instead of an exogenous randomization device. Such "jointly controlled lotteries," which result in mixtures of Nash equilibria, were first discussed by Aumann *et al.* [1]. (See also [5, 11].)]

4. The Theorems

Before continuing our study of unmediated communication, it is useful to consider general communication–bidding games. In particular, it is useful to derive two conditions necessarily satisfied by the equilibrium outcomes of any communication–bidding game.

Given an allocation rule (p, x), define functions $U_i^*: T_i^2 \to \Re$ by

$$U_1^*(r_1, v_1) \equiv E[\max\{0, x(r_1, \tilde{v}_2) - v_1 p(r_1, \tilde{v}_2)\}],$$
$$U_2^*(r_2, v_2) \equiv E[\max\{0, v_2 p(\tilde{v}_1, r_2) - x(\tilde{v}_1, r_2)\}]. \tag{6}$$

The two necessary conditions are defined in terms of these functions. Say that (p, x) satisfies *incentive compatibility starred* if

$$U_i^*(v_i, v_i) \geqslant U_i^*(r_i, v_i) \qquad \text{for all} \quad r_i, v_i \in T_i \quad \text{and} \quad i = 1, 2, \quad \text{(IC*)}$$

and that it is *ex post individually rational* if

$$x(v_1, v_2) - v_1 p(v_1, v_2) \geqslant 0 \quad \text{and} \quad v_2 p(v_1, v_2) - x(v_1, v_2) \geqslant 0 \quad \text{for all } (v_1, v_2). \tag{EXPIR}$$

Any allocation rule that satisfies both IC* and EXPIR satisfies IC and INTIR. As the converse is false (see Example 1 below), the set defined by

$$A^* \equiv \{(p, x) | \text{IC}^* \text{ and EXPIR are satisfied}\} \qquad (7)$$

is a subset of the feasible set A defined in (2). (For nondegenerate type distributions, A^* is a proper subset of A; see Example 1 below.)

Conditions IC* and EXPIR have a natural interpretation. Recall the Bayesian collective choice environment defined in Section 2. Suppose that a mechanism designer is constrained to choose a mechanism that first publicly proposes an allocation $(\hat{p}, \hat{x}) \in [0, 1] \times \Re$ in response to actions taken by the traders, and then allows each trader to choose, as a final action, whether or not to reject $(\hat{p}, \hat{x})$. If either player rejects, no trade occurs and no payment is made. An allocation rule is an equilibrium outcome achieved by such a mechanism if and only if the allocation rule satisfies IC* and EXPIR. Thus, A^* is the feasible set of allocations when the traders have final rights of refusal.

Our first theorem indicates that A^* is also the relevant set of allocation rules when considering communication–bidding games. It states that only allocation rules in A^* are equilibrium outcomes of communication–bidding games:

THEOREM 1. *A^* contains all equilibrium outcomes of any communication–bidding game $\mu(k)$, for any $k \in [0, 1]$.*

Notes on the Proof (full proofs are in the Appendix). Much of the proof is similar to the argument mentioned above for why any mechanism in our environment that allows the traders final rights of refusal can yield only allocation rules satisfying IC* and EXPIR. This is because a double auction, when combined with any communication mechanism, is a mechanism that in essence gives the traders final rights of refusal. The seller, for example, can ensure that he never receives a negative profit, regardless of what messages he has sent or received, by simply refusing to never bid below his value. Thus, if the mechanism is a revelation–suggestion mechanism for which honest and obedient behavior is an equilibrium, a type v_1 seller receives an expected utility no less than $U_1^*(r_1, v_1)$ by reporting that he is of type r_1 and then bidding either v_1 or the bid suggested by the mechanism, whichever is larger. His equilibrium expected utility therefore exceeds $U_1^*(r_1, v_1)$, which proves IC*.

We now return to unmediated communication. In general games, fewer outcomes can be achieved with unmediated than with mediated communication [2, 7, 9, 18]. For example, when all messages are transmitted through a mediator, the information one player receives about another's type need not be independent of his own type. Or, as another example, some correlated equilibria of some two-person games can only be implemented by a mediator (see [2]). However, when the game to be played is a double auction, our next theorem indicates that unmediated communication achieves any outcome that mediated communication does.

We consider a specific unmediated communication–bidding game, although it will be clear that many others have the same equilibrium outcomes. The one we consider has a single round of simultaneous message exchange. That there is only one round of message exchange is not important. But it is important that the messages are sent simultaneously rather than sequentially. These issues are discussed later, in Remark 5 in Section 5. It is also important that the traders have rich enough message sets; we assume they are given, for the seller and buyer respectively, by

$$M_1 \equiv T_1 \times [0, 1] \quad \text{and} \quad M_2 \equiv T_2 \times [0, 1]. \tag{8}$$

The unmediated communication–bidding game in which messages from these sets are exchanged simultaneously before bids are submitted in a k-double auction is denoted $\Gamma(k)$.

Theorem 2 concerns the "full communication equilibria" of $\Gamma(k)$. A *full communication equilibrium* is an equilibrium in which no two types of a player ever send the same message. Each trader can then infer the other's type from the message he sends. (The equilibria discussed in Section 3 were of this form.)

THEOREM 2. *A^* is the set of full communication equilibrium outcomes of the unmediated communication–bidding game $\Gamma(k)$, for any $k \in [0, 1]$.*

Notes on the Proof. The proof is based on the ideas introduced in Section 3, relying on single-price equilibria (3) and jointly controlled lotteries. To obtain a given allocation in A^*, an equilibrium is constructed in which the players honestly tell each other their types, and afterwards they play the single-price equilibrium of the double auction that gives them the allocation specified by the allocation rule. They each also announce a number, drawn independently from a uniform distribution on $[0, 1]$. These two random numbers are used to realize a joint lottery if the putative allocation has a nondegenerate probability of trade. The joint lottery determines whether they will play a single-price equilibrium in which they trade or one in which they do not.

Probably the most important implication of Theorems 1 and 2 is that allowing unmediated communication in a double auction enlarges the set of equilibrium outcomes as much as possible, so that it coincides with the entire set of outcomes that could have been obtained by instead adding various types of mediators to the auction. (Other implications are discussed in the concluding section.) In our opinion, this is an unfortunate implication for mechanism designers. Consider, for example, the problem of a designer who must choose the parameter k of a double auction. The usual approach to such a problem is to choose k on the basis of the welfare properties of the equilibrium outcomes of the double auction $D(k)$. This approach requires a good equilibrium selection argument, as double auctions have large sets of equilibria [13, 23]. Our results imply that if, as is likely, the traders can converse with each other before they submit bids, the required selection argument must be much stronger. For then, the set of equilibrium outcomes does not even depend on the parameter k. Furthermore, given that the set A^* is vast, the outcomes of a double auction in the real-world (with real-world communication possibilities) may be far different from any equilibrium outcome of any formal double auction game.

It remains to show that A^* actually is vast. The following example shows that it is not the full set A of allocation rules satisfying IC and INTIR.

EXAMPLE 1. The seller has value $v_1 = 0$ or $v_1 = 2$, each with probability one-half. The buyer has value $v_2 = 1$ or $v_2 = 4$, each with probability one-half. The allocation rule (p, x) is shown in Fig. 1. [To make this allocation rule conform to our definitions, we must extend it to a domain that is a cross-product of intervals. Any allocation rule defined and incentive compatible at a finite number of points (v_1, v_2) can be extended to an incentive compatible rule defined on a cross-product of intervals. To do this here, define (p, x) on $[0, 2] \times [1, 4]$ by $(p, x) = (1, 3)$ if $v_1 < 2$ and $v_2 = 4$, $(p, x) = (1, 2)$ if $v_1 = 2$ and $v_2 = 4$, $(p, x) = (1, 1)$ if $v_1 < 2$ and $v_2 < 4$, and $(p, x) = (0, 0)$ if $v_1 = 2$ and $v_2 < 4$.] This allocation rule is easily verified to satisfy EXPIR and IC, so that it is in A. It is not in A^* because it does not satisfy IC*: if the seller is able to enforce unilaterally the no-trade allocation once he has seen the putative allocation, then, when his value is $v_1 = 2$, he will report that his value is $r_1 = 0$, and, subsequently, refuse to trade whenever the putative allocation turns out to be $(p, x) = (1, 1)$ (the

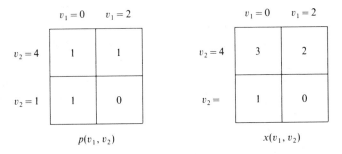

$$p(v_1, v_2) \qquad\qquad x(v_1, v_2)$$

FIGURE 1

price, 1, does not cover his cost, 2). This strategy gives him expected utility $(0.5)(3-2)+(0.5)(0)=0.5$, whereas reporting his type truthfully gives him only $(0.5)(2-2)+(0.5)(0)=0$.

We now show that A^* contains a large set of allocation rules defined by two conditions that are economically intuitive. To our knowledge, every allocation rule that has been considered in the literature for this environment satisfies these two conditions; any equilibrium outcome of a double auction certainly does [13, 23], as does any allocation rule that is ex ante efficient [25].

The first condition is that the allocation rule be almost always deterministic. This condition requires that $p(v_1, v_2)$ almost always takes on only the values 0 or 1, so that trade surely occurs or surely does not occur. More precisely, the *deterministic* condition is

$$\text{for all } v_1, \quad \{0, 1\} \supseteq p(v_1, v_2) \quad \text{for almost all } (F_2) \, v_2,$$
$$\text{for all } v_2, \quad \{0, 1\} \supseteq p(v_1, v_2) \quad \text{for almost all } (F_1) \, v_1. \qquad \text{(DET)}$$

The second condition is monotonicity. It requires, first, that the probability of trade be weakly increasing in the buyer's type (value) and weakly decreasing in the seller's type (cost). (This is almost a consequence of IC: as Myerson and Satterthwaite [19] show, the two *marginal* probability-of-trade functions have these monotonicity characteristics.) Second, monotonicity requires that the buyer's payment be an increasing function of both players' types on the set of type pairs that trade. Formally, the *monotonicity* condition is

For all $(v_1, v_2), (u_1, u_2) \in T_1 \times T_2$:

    (i) $p(v_1, v_2) \leqslant p(u_1, u_2)$ if $v_1 \geqslant u_1$ and $v_2 \leqslant u_2$,

    (ii) $x(v_1, v_2) \leqslant x(u_1, u_2)$ if $(v_1, v_2) \leqslant (u_1, u_2)$

  and $p(v_1, v_2) = p(u_1, u_2) = 1.$ (MON)

Define a set of allocation rules by

$$A^{**} \equiv \text{convex hull}(\{(p, x) \,|\, \text{IC, EXPIR, DET, and MON are satisfied}\}). \tag{9}$$

THEOREM 3. $A^* \supset A^{**}$, *so that any allocation rule in* A^{**} *is a full communication equilibrium outcome of the unmediated communication–bidding game* $\Gamma(k)$, *for any* $k \in [0, 1]$.

Notes on the Proof.   The first step is to show that a convex combination of allocation rules in A^* is also in A^*. The proof is then completed by showing that IC* is implied by IC, EXPIR, DET, and MON. Given an allocation rule (p, x), consider a two-stage mechanism in which the traders report their values (r_1, r_2) and learn of the putative allocation $(p(r_1, r_2), x(r_1, r_2))$ in the first stage, and then they each decide whether to veto this proposed allocation, thereby enacting the no-trade allocation, in the second stage. The resulting game has an equilibrium in which the traders truthfully report their values if and only if (p, x) satisfies IC*, and (p, x) is an equilibrium outcome if and only if it satisfies IC* and EXPIR. In this game there are two reasons why the seller, for example, might want to misreport his value. First, as in Example 1, misreporting may give him a chance of receiving a higher price. It is easy to show, from IC and EXPIR, that the seller will not want to over-report his value. Because of MON, however, under-reporting can only lower the price he receives from those types of buyer he would have traded with anyway. It remains only to rule out the second reason he might have for misreporting, which is that by so doing he may enlarge the set of buyer types with whom he can profitably trade. The difficult part of the proof is to show that the seller, if he under-reports his value, will not gain enough from the buyer types with whom he would not otherwise have traded to compensate for the lower price he obtains from the buyer types with whom he would have traded anyway.

The following simple example shows that the containment proved in Theorem 3 may be proper. In particular, it shows that allocation rules in A^* need not have monotonic payment functions.

EXAMPLE 2. The seller has value $v_1 = 0$ or $v_1 = 1$, each with probability one-half. The buyer has value $v_2 = 4$ or $v_2 = 5$, each with probability one-half. The allocation rule is (p, x), the important part of which is given by Fig. 2. This allocation rule does not satisfy MON(ii). Yet it trivially satisfies EXPIR and IC*, and so is an equilibrium outcome of the unmediated communication–bidding game $\Gamma(k)$.

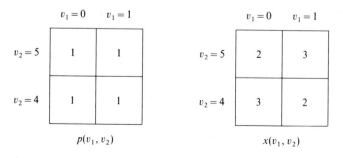

FIGURE 2

5. Concluding Remarks

1. Our results are usefully recapped by breaking them into five propositions:

(a) *the allocation rules that are outcomes of (mediated) communication–bidding games are the ones satisfying* IC* *and* EXPIR;

(b) *any outcome of any (mediated) communication–bidding game is also an outcome of an unmediated communication–bidding game;*

(c) *all such allocation rules are equilibrium outcomes of a single unmediated communication–bidding game,* $\Gamma(k)$ *(recall that* $\Gamma(k)$ *is the game in which a k-double auction is played after a simultaneously exchange of messages);*

(d) *all of these allocation rules are outcomes of full communication equilibria of* $\Gamma(k)$; *and*

(e) *the set of these allocation rules is very large, containing all convex combinations of rules satisfying* IC, EXPIR, DET, *and* MON.

We have stressed (e), as it has the most severe consequences for mechanism designers, both those who ignore the opportunities that real-world players have for conversing among themselves, and those who do not have a good equilibrium selection argument to back up their predictions. (We know of no good selection argument for this framework—see Remark 4 below.)

2. Of the results listed in Remark 1, (b) and (c) are similar to ones obtained by Forges [9] and Barany [2] for more general games.

Forges [9] shows that a "mechanism design" problem can, in a particular sense, be converted into an "equilibrium selection" problem. She considers a specific communication scheme consisting of two rounds of sequential, public announcements of messages. Her theorem states that when this scheme is used prior to the playing of any (finite) Bayesian game with at least three players, the set of correlated equilibrium outcomes of the resulting two-stage game contains all the equilibrium outcomes that could be obtained by adding any other communication mechanism.

It is not known whether Forges' theorem extends to general games with two players. Suppose it did apply to two-person k-double auctions. We could then conclude that the set of *correlated* equilibrium outcomes of an unmediated communication–bidding game $\Gamma_r(k)$ defined by adding two rounds of *sequential* message exchange would contain the equilibrium outcomes of all other communication–bidding games $\mu(k)$. Instead, we proved that the set of *Bayesian–Nash* equilibrium outcomes of the unmediated communication–bidding game $\Gamma(k)$ defined by adding one round of *simultaneous* message exchange contains the equilibrium outcomes of all other communication–bidding games $\mu(k)$. Our result is stronger in so far as it does not rely on correlated equilibria (the set of correlated equilibrium outcomes of $\Gamma(k)$ contains its Bayesian–Nash equilibrium outcomes). (In our terminology, a correlated equilibrium is not "unmediated" because it is obtained by adding a communication mechanism that transmits, but does not receive, confidential messages—a "deaf mediator.") However, as our result relies on simultaneous rather than sequential message exchange, it does not imply that Forges' result holds for the sequential communication–bidding game $\Gamma_F(k)$. (See Remark 5 below for a discussion of sequential versus simultaneous communication.)

Another related result is that of Barany [2]. Subject to some technical qualifications, this result is that any correlated equilibrium outcome of a normal form game is a Nash equilibrium outcome of a game obtained by adding a communication scheme involving "plain conversation." If the theorems of Forges and Barany both applied to our framework, the combination of his scheme with hers would be a communication mechanism that results in an unmediated communication–bidding game whose set of equilibrium outcomes contains those of all other communication–bidding games. That is, it would imply (b) and (c) above. (Barany's theorem does not actually apply to our framework. It specifically does not apply to games with only two or three players. And, it only concerns correlated equilibria in which the probabilities are rational-valued.)

3. Farrell and Gibbons [6] were the first to consider communication in a double auction. Their game is a special case of ours: each player is allowed in the message stage just two messages, "keen" and "not keen;" the value of each player is distributed uniformly on [0, 1]; and only the symmetric $k = \frac{1}{2}$ double auction is considered. Most attention is devoted to the following equilibrium. Let $y = (22 + 12\sqrt{2})/49$, which is approximately 0.795. The equilibrium strategies are for the buyer to say "keen" if his value exceeds y, and "not keen" otherwise. The seller speaks simultaneously, saying "keen" if his value is below $1 - y$ and "not keen" otherwise. If they both say "not keen," they play the no-trade equilibrium in the double auction. (In this equilibrium, the buyer surely bids a_1 and the seller surely bids b_2.) If the buyer says "keen" and the seller says "not keen," they bid according to the linear Chatterjee and Samuelson [3] strategies that are an equilibrium when their values are uniformly distributed on the intervals $[y, 1]$ and $[1 - y, 1]$, respectively. Similarly, if the buyer says "not keen" and the seller says "keen," they bid according to the linear equilibrium given that their values are uniformly distributed on $[0, y]$ and $[0, 1 - y]$. Finally, if they both say "keen," they both bid $\frac{1}{2}$, which is the average of

the highest possible value for the seller, $1 - y$, and the lowest possible value for the buyer when they have both said "keen" (as $y > 1 - y$, trade surely occurs in this case).

The Farrell–Gibbons equilibrium is a true communication equilibrium in the following sense: the bidding strategies played after at least some messages have been sent are a double auction equilibrium *only* because the messages have caused the traders to appropriately revise their beliefs about each other's type. (For example, the linear strategies played after the buyer says "keen" and the seller says "not keen" are a double auction equilibrium at that point only because the traders have revised their beliefs to be uniform distributions on $[y, 1]$ and $[1 - y, 1]$.) Thus, communication in their equilibrium serves to *transmit essential information*.

On the other hand, the single-price strategies we use to prove Theorem 2 are double auction equilibria regardless of the traders' beliefs. The fact that they do revise their priors is irrelevant. Communication in our equilibria serves merely to ensure that the traders will play the same equilibrium of the double auction; which equilibrium they play depends upon their types. Thus, communication in our equilibria plays only a *coordination role*. (Of course, communication also plays a coordination role in the Farrell–Gibbons equilibrium, e.g., the message pair (not keen, not keen) guides the traders to the no-trade bidding strategies, which form an equilibrium to the double auction regardless of the beliefs of the traders.)

4. Single-price double auction equilibria, which are the bidding components of the equilibrium strategies of the communication–bidding game $\Gamma(k)$ used to prove Theorem 2, may seem strange. They are discontinuous (but can be approximated by differentiable double auction equilibria—see [23]), and the submitting of outrageously optimistic bids, a_1 for the buyer and b_2 for the seller, may seem unreasonable (although, as long as $a_1 \leqslant a_2$ and $b_1 \leqslant b_2$, these bids are not dominated). However, there are reasons to favor single-price equilibria. First, they are easy to calculate, since they are step functions with only two steps, and do not depend upon the traders' beliefs. Second, experimental subjects experienced in the play of double auctions seem to play single-price equilibria (Radner and Schotter [21]). Third, a single-price double auction equilibrium resembles a classical Walrasian equilibrium, since in both all realized trades occur at a single price that does not depend upon the actual reservation values of the traders (assuming they are inframarginal). Fourth, if the bids in a single-price equilibrium do not induce trade, a price at which trade would be mutually beneficial is never common knowledge, so that the commitment to not renegotiate is not as severely tested as it is in, e.g., any equilibrium with invertable bidding strategies.

Of course, this last property is not true of the complete equilibrium strategies of the communication–bidding game $\Gamma(k)$ used to prove Theorem 2. Since those strategies constitute a full communication equilibrium, the traders know each other's values when they play the double auction. If the specified double auction equilibrium is the no-trade equilibrium but the buyer's value is greater than the seller's, the traders will know, at the time they submit their bids, that they could do better by switching to another equilibrium in which they do trade. Nevertheless, the equilibria of $\Gamma(k)$ used to prove Theorem 2 are reasonable in currently accepted senses: they do not entail the use of dominated strategies, and they are sequentially rational and sequentially perfect (Grossman and Perry [10]).

5. We do not feel that unmediated communication is appropriately modelled as a one-shot, simultaneous exchange of messages. In most oral, face-to-face situations, communication is sequential, i.e., only one player talks at a time. Furthermore, communication usually entails multiple rounds of message exchange. Typically, when a communication process occurs before the play of a mechanism, the set of equilibrium outcomes depends on whether the communication process has multiple rounds and on whether message exchange is simultaneous (see [8] or [15] for examples).

Altering the unmediated communication-bidding game $\Gamma(k)$ by adding more rounds of *simultaneous* message exchange would not change any results. No new equilibrium outcomes would be added, since the original $\Gamma(k)$ already has the largest set of equilibrium outcomes, A^*, that could possibly be achieved by adding any communication mechanism to a k-double auction. And no equilibrium outcomes would be subtracted by adding more rounds, since any equilibrium of the original game is equivalent to an equilibrium in the game with multiple rounds in which all types of both traders send babbling messages (which are ignored) after the first round.

On the other hand, making the message exchange sequential in $\Gamma(k)$ would change the results: no longer would every allocation rule in A^* be an equilibrium outcome. Such an allocation rule is that in Example 2. According to it, trade always occurs—only the price is determined by the traders' types. Suppose, to be concrete, that the buyer is designated as the first to send a message, and that the seller's return message is the last message sent. Assume, by way of contradiction, that the allocation rule (p, x) of Example 2 is an equilibrium outcome. The seller's equilibrium strategy, regardless of his type, must be to respond to any message of the buyer's with a message guaranteeing that the ensuing double auction equilibrium is that which yields the highest possible expected price given the buyers message (the seller cares only about the price because, by assumption, trade surely occurs regardless of the messages). The expected price therefore cannot depend upon the seller's type, contrary to the specification of (p, x).

Thus, we feel that the largest caveat to our results is that the assumption of simultaneous message exchange is not as realistic as sequential message exchange, and that the latter eliminates some of the outcomes achieved by the former. The characterization of the set of equilibrium outcomes of an unmediated, sequential communication–bidding game is an open problem. (We note, however, that the buyer's best allocation rule will remain an equilibrium outcome. Recall that only the buyer sends a message in the equilibrium that generates it, as described in Section 3. This equilibrium can be duplicated in a game with sequential communication by having all messages except for the buyer's first message be babbling messages that are ignored by their receiver. Naturally, the seller's best allocation rule can be similarly obtained.)

6. Another open question concerns the *welfare* comparison of A to A^*. That is, how does the set of outcomes obtained from arbitrary (voluntary) mechanisms compare, in utility terms, to the set of outcomes obtained when (simultaneous) communication is added to a double auction? Because distinct allocation rules can yield the same pair of interim utility functions, $U_1(v_1, v_1)$ and $U_2(v_2, v_2)$, a pair of interim utility functions generated by an allocation rule in A, but not A^*, may also be generated by a rule in A^*. It would be quite interesting to characterize the class of rules in A for which rules in A^* exist that yield the same interim utility functions. It would be most interesting if the efficient allocation rules in A were in this class. For then, we would know that a double auction with unmediated communication can, in some of its equilibria, achieve all the same levels of welfare as can general (voluntary) mechanisms.

We know an answer to this last question when both values are uniformly distributed on $[0, 1]$. Satterthwaite and Williams [23] establish the following result for this case: given any utility pair on the frontier of the ex ante utility possibility set generated by A, a number $k' \in [0, 1]$ exists such that the linear equilibrium of the double auction $D(k')$ gives the traders those ex ante utility levels. (This does not hold for generic distributions, as Satterthwaite and Williams also show.) Since the equilibrium outcomes of double auctions satisfy IC, EXPIR, DET, and MON, they are in A^* by Theorem 3. Hence, for any *fixed* $k \in [0, 1]$, *every* ex ante efficient allocation rule in A is an equilibrium outcome of the unmediated communication–bidding game $\Gamma(k)$.

7. We conclude by remarking that the properties of allocation rules that we have been concerned with, IC* and EXPIR, should be of interest in more general contexts. Recall that an allocation rule satisfies these

properties if it is an equilibrium outcome of some multistage game in which, in the last stage, each trader learns of the proposed allocation and has the ability to enact instead the no-trade allocation. Such ex post veto power is not uncommon. For example, it is often impossible, and known to be impossible, to specify in a contract all contingencies so completely as to prevent a party from essentially reneging on the contract whenever not reneging would lead to a loss [12]. In this case, credible contractual agreements must satisfy appropriate generalizations of IC* and EXPIR.

Appendix

This Appendix contains the formal proofs. They make use of the indicator function $1_{\{c \leqslant d\}}$, which takes the value 1 if $c \leqslant d$ and 0 otherwise.

THEOREM 1. *A* contains all equilibrium outcomes of any communication–bidding game $\mu(k)$, for any $k \in [0, 1]$.*

Proof. Let (p, x) be an equilibrium outcome of a communication–bidding game $\mu(k)$. By the general revelation principle, we can assume the mechanism is a revelation–suggestion mechanism in which honest reporting and obedient bidding is an equilibrium. Formally, this mechanism is a function $\delta(\cdot | \cdot)$, where $\delta(\cdot | r_1, r_2)$ is a distribution on suggested bids (β_1, β_2) for each pair $(r_1, r_2) \in T_1 \times T_2$ of reported types. Let $\tilde{\beta}_i$ and $\tilde{r}_i$ be the random bids and reported types in the obedient and honest equilibrium. Thus, $\tilde{r}_1 = \tilde{v}_1$, $\tilde{r}_2 = \tilde{v}_2$, and $\delta(\cdot | r_1, r_2)$ is the distribution of $(\tilde{\beta}_1, \tilde{\beta}_2)$ conditional on $(\tilde{r}_1, \tilde{r}_2) = (r_1, r_2)$.

We now prove that (p, x) satisfies EXPIR for the seller (EXPIR for the buyer is proved similarly). Recall from Section 2 that in our definition of an equilibrium, no seller type submits a bid less than his value. Hence, $\tilde{\beta}_1 \geqslant v_1$ always. This implies EXPIR: for any (v_1, v_2),

$$
\begin{aligned}
x(v_1, v_2) &- v_1 p(v_1, v_2) \\
&= E[[k\tilde{\beta}_2 + (1-k)\tilde{\beta}_1 - v_1] 1_{\{\tilde{\beta}_1 \leqslant \tilde{\beta}_2\}} | \tilde{r}_1 = v_1, \tilde{r}_2 = v_2] \\
&\geqslant E[[k\tilde{\beta}_2 + (1-k)v_1 - v_1] 1_{\{\tilde{\beta}_1 \leqslant \tilde{\beta}_2\}} | \tilde{r}_1 = v_1, \tilde{r}_2 = v_2] \\
&\geqslant 0.
\end{aligned}
$$

We now prove that (p, x) satisfies IC* for the seller (a similar proof works for the buyer). Suppose a type v_1 seller reports dishonestly that he is of type r_1, but then bids obediently as long as the suggested bid is no less than v_1, in which case he bids v_1. His expected utility from following this strategy is no greater than his equilibrium expected utility, $U_1(v_1, v_1)$. Hence,

$$U_1(v_1, v_1) \geqslant E[[k\tilde{\beta}_2 + (1 - k) \max(v_1, \tilde{\beta}_1) - v_1]$$
$$\times 1_{\{\max(v_1, \beta_1) \leqslant \beta_2\}} | \tilde{r}_1 = r_1]$$
$$= E\{E[[k\tilde{\beta}_2 + (1 - k) \max(v_1, \tilde{\beta}_1) - v_1]$$
$$\times 1_{\{\max(v_1, \beta_1) \leqslant \beta_2\}} | \tilde{r}_2, \tilde{r}_1 = r_1] | \tilde{r}_1 = r_1\}. \tag{10}$$

For each $\tilde{r}_2$,

$$E[[k\tilde{\beta}_2 + (1 - k) \max(v_1, \tilde{\beta}_1) - v_1] 1_{\{\max(v_1, \beta_1) \leqslant \beta_2\}} | \tilde{r}_2, \tilde{r}_1 = r_1]$$
$$\geqslant E[[k\tilde{\beta}_2 + (1 - k) \tilde{\beta}_1 - v_1] 1_{\{\beta_1 \leqslant \beta_2\}} | \tilde{r}_2, \tilde{r}_1 = r_1]$$
$$= x(r_1, \tilde{r}_2) - v_1 p(r_1, \tilde{r}_2)$$
$$= x(r_1, \tilde{v}_2) - v_1 p(r_1, \tilde{v}_2). \tag{11}$$

Also,

$$E[[k\tilde{\beta}_2 + (1 - k) \max(v_1, \tilde{\beta}_1) - v_1] 1_{\{\max(v_1, \beta_1) \leqslant \beta_2\}} | \tilde{r}_2, \tilde{r}_1 = r_1] \geqslant 0. \tag{12}$$

Putting (11) and (12) into (10) yields

$$U_1(v_1, v_1) \geqslant E\{\max\{0, x(r_1, \tilde{v}_2) - v_1 p(r_1, \tilde{v}_2)\} | \tilde{r}_1 = r_1\}$$
$$= E\{\max\{0, x(r_1, \tilde{v}_2) - v_1 p(r_1, \tilde{v}_2)\}\}$$
$$= U_1^*(r_1, v_1).$$

Thus, (p, x) satisfies IC* (as $U_1^*(v_1, v_1) = U_1(v_1, v_1)$, by EXPIR). So $(p, x) \in A^*$.   Q.E.D.

THEOREM 2. *A^* is the set of full communication equilibrium outcomes of the unmediated communication–bidding game $\Gamma(k)$, for any $k \in [0, 1]$.*

Proof. From Theorem 1, all full communication equilibrium outcomes of $\Gamma(k)$ are in A^*. So let $(p, x) \in A^*$. We construct an equilibrium with outcome (p, x).

As a preliminary, define the *binary matching function* $\varphi: [0, 1]^2 \to [0, 1]$ in the following way. Given two numbers y_1 and y_2 in $[0, 1]$, let $\varphi(y_1, y_2)$ be the number whose binary expansion has a "1" in the nth position if and only if the binary expansion of y_1 has the same digit in its nth position as does the binary expansion of y_2. Note that if y_1 and y_2 are independent random variables on $[0, 1]$, and one of them has a uniform distribution, then $\varphi(y_1, y_2)$ is also a uniformly distributed random variable on $[0, 1]$.

The equilibrium strategy pair that achieves (p, x) is as follows. The behavioral strategy of trader i in the message stage is to announce truthfully his type, and to announce the realization y_i of a number he has drawn at random from a uniform distribution on $[0, 1]$. In the bidding stage, if $\varphi(y_1, y_2) < p(v_1, v_2)$ or $p(v_1, v_2) = 1$ (these v_i's and y_i's are the announcements made in the message stage), the buyer and seller play the single-price equilibrium (β_1^z, β_2^z) of the double auction game $D(k)$, with the price z given by $z = x(v_1, v_2)/p(v_1, v_2)$. If $\varphi(y_1, y_2) \geqslant p(v_1, v_2)$ or $p(v_1, v_2) = 0$, then the *no-trade equilibrium* of $D(k)$ is played, which is defined by all types of buyer bidding a_1 and all types of seller bidding b_2. (The random drawings of y_1 and y_2 in the message stage can be dispensed with if $p(v_1, v_2) \in \{0, 1\}$ for all (v_1, v_2).)

We now show that (p, x) is the outcome of these strategies. For a given realization of values (v_1, v_2), the constructed strategies lead to the no-trade equilibrium of $D(k)$ with probability $1 - p(v_1, v_2)$, and to a single-price equilibrium with probability $p(v_1, v_2)$. If trade always occurs in this single-price equilibrium, then, as the price in it is $z = x(v_1, v_2)/p(v_1, v_2)$, the resulting allocation will be $(p(v_1, v_2), x(v_1, v_2))$. Trade does always occur in this single-price equilibrium: EXPIR implies that $v_1 \leqslant z \leqslant v_2$, so that both traders will submit the bid z. Thus, (p, x) is the outcome.

We now show that these strategies are a (perfect Bayesian) equilibrium of $\Gamma(k)$. Since the single-price strategies and the no-trade strategies are equilibria of any double auction regardless of the beliefs of the traders about each other's value, the traders' strategies are a best reply to each other in the bidding stage. In the message stage, trader i is content to draw his y_i from a uniform distribution because, given that the other trader is drawing from a uniform distribution, his choice of y_i cannot influence the distribution of $\varphi(y_1, y_2)$. So, it remains only to show that the traders are content to truthfully announce their values. Consider the seller (the argument for the buyer is similar.) Suppose he reports r_1 when his type is v_1, and that he learns the buyer's type is $\tilde{v}_2$ in the message stage. Then, depending upon the realization of $\varphi(y_1, y_2)$, in the bidding stage he will play the no-trade equilibrium with probability $1 - p(r_1, \tilde{v}_2)$, and the $\tilde{z} = x(r_1, \tilde{v}_2)/p(r_1, \tilde{v}_2)$ single-price equilibrium with probability $p(r_1, \tilde{v}_2)$. The best he can do in the no-trade equilibrium gains him zero utility. The best he can do in the single-price equilbrium is either to bid $\tilde{z}$ and so trade at the price $\tilde{z}$, or to submit a higher bid to ensure no-trade and gain zero utility. Thus, his expected utility conditional on $\tilde{v}_2$ if he claims his type is r_1 is

$$p(r_1, \tilde{v}_2)[\max\{0, \tilde{z} - v_1\}] + (1 - p(r_1, \tilde{v}_2))[0]$$

$$= \max\{0, x(r_1, \tilde{v}_2) - v_1 p(r_1, \tilde{v}_2)\}.$$

Thus, IC* implies that reporting truthfully, $r_1 = v_1$, is optimal for him.

Q.E.D.

The proof of Theorem 3 requires two lemmas.

LEMMA 1. *The set A^* is convex.*

Proof. Let $(p', x') \in A^*$ and $(p'', x'') \in A^*$, so that both satisfy IC* and EXPIR. Let $(p, x) = \lambda(p', x') + (1 - \lambda)(p'', x'')$, where $\lambda \in [0, 1]$. As EXPIR is a set of linear inequalities, (p, x) satisfies EXPIR. Thus, for any $v_1 \in T_1$ and $r_1 \in T_1$,

$$E[\max\{0, x(v_1, \tilde{v}_2) - v_1 p(v_1, \tilde{v}_2)\}]$$

$$= E[x(v_1, \tilde{v}_2) - v_1 p(v_1, \tilde{v}_2)]$$

$$= \lambda E[x'(v_1, \tilde{v}_2) - v_1 p'(v_1, \tilde{v}_2)]$$

$$+ (1 - \lambda) E[x''(v_1, \tilde{v}_2) - v_1 p''(v_1, \tilde{v}_2)]$$

$$= \lambda E[\max\{0, x'(v_1, \tilde{v}_2) - v_1 p'(v_1, \tilde{v}_2)\}]$$

$$+ (1 - \lambda) E[\max\{0, x''(v_1, \tilde{v}_2) - v_1 p''(v_1, \tilde{v}_2)\}]$$

$$\geqslant \lambda E[\max\{0, x'(r_1, \tilde{v}_2) - v_1 p'(r_1, \tilde{v}_2)\}]$$

$$+ (1 - \lambda) E[\max\{0, x''(r_1, \tilde{v}_2) - v_1 p''(r_1, \tilde{v}_2)\}]$$

$$\geqslant E[\max\{0, x(r_1, \tilde{v}_2) - v_1 p(r_1, \tilde{v}_2)\}].$$

So IC* holds for the seller; the proof is similar for the buyer. Hence, $(p, x) \in A^*$.

Q.E.D.

The following lemma, and the proof of Theorem 3 to come, are put only in terms of the seller—as usual, symmetric arguments hold for the buyer. To simplify notation, we henceforth drop the subscript "1" on the type variable of the seller. Further notation is also needed. Given an allocation rule (p, x), the expected allocation meant for any type $v \in T_1$ is $(p_1(v), x_1(v))$, where p_1 and x_2 are the marginal probability-of-trade and payment functions:

$$p_1(v) \equiv E[p(v, \tilde{v}_2)] \qquad \text{and} \qquad x_1(v) \equiv E[x(v, \tilde{v}_2)]. \qquad (13)$$

Also for the given allocation rule, define two functions on $T_1 \times T_1$ by

$$\hat{p}(r, v) \equiv E[p(r, \tilde{v}_2) 1_{\{x(r, \tilde{v}_2) > vp(r, \tilde{v}_2)\}}],$$
$$\hat{x}(r, v) \equiv E[x(r, \tilde{v}_2) 1_{\{x(r, \tilde{v}_2) > vp(r, \tilde{v}_2)\}}]. \qquad (14)$$

Then $U_1^*(r, v)$, the expected utility of type v when he reports that his type is r and he can reject any allocation that gives him nonpositive utility ex post, is given by

$$U_1^*(r, v) = E[\max\{0, x(r, \tilde{v}_2) - vp(r, \tilde{v}_2)\}]$$
$$= E[[x(r, \tilde{v}_2) - vp(r, \tilde{v}_2)] \, 1_{\{x(r, \tilde{v}_2) > vp(r, \tilde{v}_2)\}}]$$
$$= \hat{x}(r, v) - v\hat{p}(r, v). \tag{15}$$

That is, $(\hat{p}(r, v), \hat{x}(r, v))$ is the best (expected) allocation that type v can receive by reporting that his type is r.

LEMMA 2. *If (p, x) is an allocation rule satisfying* IC *and* EXPIR, *but not* IC* *(for the seller), then types $r < v < \hat{v}$ in T_1 exist such that*

$$\text{(i)} \quad U_1(v, v) < \hat{x}(r, \hat{v}) - v\hat{p}(r, \hat{v}),$$

$$\text{(ii)} \quad \hat{p}(r, \hat{v}) < p_1(v).$$

Proof. Let $\hat{v}$ be a seller type for whom IC* is violated. Hence, for some $r \neq \hat{v}$, $U_1^*(r, \hat{v}) > U_1^*(\hat{v}, \hat{v})$. Thus $U_1^*(r, \hat{v}) > U_1(\hat{v}, \hat{v})$, since EXPIR implies $U_1^*(\hat{v}, \hat{v}) = U_1(\hat{v}, \hat{v})$. Define $\hat{p} \equiv \hat{p}(r, \hat{v})$ and $\hat{x} \equiv \hat{x}(r, \hat{v})$. From (15), $\hat{x} - \hat{v}\hat{p} > U_1(\hat{v}, \hat{v})$. Hence, defining a function Δ on T_1 by

$$\Delta(v) \equiv \hat{x} - v\hat{p} - U_1(v, v), \tag{16}$$

we have $\Delta(\hat{v}) > 0$.

From IC, $U_1(\hat{v}, \hat{v}) \geqslant U_1(r, \hat{v})$, which gives $U_1^*(r, \hat{v}) > U_1(r, \hat{v})$. Some v_2 therefore exists such that $x(r, v_2) - \hat{v}p(r, v_2) < 0$ (otherwise, $U_1^*(r, \hat{v}) = U_1(r, \hat{v})$). Combining this with EXPIR, we get

$$\hat{v}p(r, v_2) > x(r, v_2) \geqslant rp(r, v_2).$$

Hence, $\hat{v} > r$.

Consider the behavior of Δ on $[r, \hat{v}]$. We know that $\Delta(\hat{v}) > 0$. From EXPIR,

$$\Delta(r) = \hat{x} - r\hat{p} - U_1(r, r)$$
$$= E[[x(r, \tilde{v}_2) - rp(r, \tilde{v}_2)] \, 1_{\{x(r, \tilde{v}_2) > \hat{v}p(r, \tilde{v}_2)\}}] - E[[x(r, \tilde{v}_2) - rp(r, \tilde{v}_2)]]$$
$$\leqslant 0.$$

Now, IC implies that $U_1(v, v)$ is continuous in v (see, e.g., [19]; the proof holds even for discontinuous distributions F_1 and F_2, since the allocation rule can always be defined, in an IC way, on a cross-product of intervals.) Hence, Δ is continuous. Therefore, as $\Delta(r) \leqslant 0 < \Delta(\hat{v})$, we conclude that for some $v \in (r, \hat{v})$, $0 < \Delta(v) < \Delta(\hat{v})$.

Part (i) of the lemma is a restatement of $0 < \Delta(v)$. Writing out $\Delta(v) < \Delta(\hat{v})$ gives

$$(\hat{x} - v\hat{p}) - (x_1(v) - vp_1(v)) < (\hat{x} - \hat{v}\hat{p}) - (x_1(\hat{v}) - \hat{v}p_1(\hat{v})),$$

which, rearranging, is

$$(\hat{v} - v)\,\hat{p} < x_1(v) - x_1(\hat{v}) - vp_1(v) + \hat{v}p_1(\hat{v}). \tag{17}$$

From IC, $U_1(\hat{v}, \hat{v}) \geqslant U_1(v, \hat{v})$, so that $x_1(v) - x_1(\hat{v}) \leqslant \hat{v}p_1(v) - \hat{v}p_1(\hat{v})$. Substituting this into (17) and using $v < \hat{v}$ yields part (ii) of the lemma. Q.E.D.

THEOREM 3. $A^* \supset A^{**}$, *i.e.*, *IC* is satisfied by any convex combination of allocation rules that each satisfy IC, EXPIR, DET, and MON.*

Proof. In view of Lemma 1, we need show only that a given allocation rule (p, x) satisfying IC, EXPIR, DET, and MON also satisfies IC*. As usual, we only show that (p, x) satisfies IC* for the seller. To save on notation, we continue to drop the subscript "1" on the type variable of the seller.

Assume (p, x) violates IC* for the seller. Then, seller types $r < v < \hat{v}$ exist satisfying Lemma 2. Observe that

$$\begin{aligned} U_1(v, v) &= E[\,[x(v, \tilde{v}_2) - v]\,1_{\{p(v, \tilde{v}_2) = 1\}}] \\ &\geqslant E[\,[x(v, \tilde{v}_2) - v]\,1_{\{p(v, \tilde{v}_2) = 1\}} \\ &\qquad \times 1_{\{p(r, \tilde{v}_2) = 1\}}\,1_{\{x(r, \tilde{v}_2) > \hat{v}p(r, \tilde{v}_2)\}}] \\ &\geqslant E[\,[x(r, \tilde{v}_2) - v]\,1_{\{p(v, \tilde{v}_2) = 1\}} \\ &\qquad \times 1_{\{p(r, \tilde{v}_2) = 1\}}\,1_{\{x(r, \tilde{v}_2) > \hat{v}p(r, \tilde{v}_2)\}}], \end{aligned} \tag{18}$$

where the equality follows from DET and EXPIR (EXPIR implies that $x(v, \tilde{v}_2) = 0$ if $p(v, \tilde{v}_2) = 0$); the first inequality follows from EXPIR; and the second inequality follows from MON(ii) (using $r < v$). Because EXPIR implies that $x = 0$ if $p = 0$,

$$\{v_2 \in T_2 \mid p(r, v_2) = 1\} \supseteq \{v_2 \in T_2 \mid x(r, v_2) > \hat{v}p(r, v_2)\}. \tag{19}$$

Now we show the following inclusion:

$$\{v_2 \in T_2 \mid p(v, v_2) = 1\} \supseteq \{v_2 \in T_2 \mid x(r, v_2) > \hat{v}p(r, v_2)\}. \tag{20}$$

If (20) is false, then $\hat{v}_2 \in T_2$ exists such that $x(r, \hat{v}_2) > \hat{v}p(r, \hat{v}_2)$ and $p(v, \hat{v}_2) \neq 1$. Because $x(r, \hat{v}_2) > \hat{v}p(r, \hat{v}_2)$, EXPIR and DET imply that

$p(r, \hat{v}_2) = 1$. Thus, from MON(ii), $x(r, v_2) > \hat{v}p(r, v_2)$ for all $v_2 \geqslant \hat{v}_2$. Because $p(v, \hat{v}_2) \neq 1$, MON(i) implies that $p(v, v_2) \neq 1$ for all $v_2 \leqslant \hat{v}_2$. Hence,

$$\hat{p}(r, \hat{v}) = E[p(r, \tilde{v}_2) \, 1_{\{x(r,\tilde{v}_2) > \hat{v}p(r,\tilde{v}_2)\}}]$$
$$= E[1_{\{x(r,\tilde{v}_2) > \hat{v}p(r,\tilde{v}_2)\}}]$$
$$\geqslant E[1_{\{\tilde{v}_2 \geqslant \hat{v}_2\}}]$$
$$\geqslant E[1_{\{p(v,\tilde{v}_2) = 1\}}] = p_1(v),$$

contrary to Lemma 2(ii). So (20) is true.

Inclusions (19) and (20) imply that

$$1_{\{p(v,\tilde{v}_2) = 1\}} 1_{\{p(r,\tilde{v}_2) = 1\}} 1_{\{x(r,\tilde{v}_2) > \hat{v}p(r,\tilde{v}_2)\}} = 1_{\{x(r,\tilde{v}_2) > \hat{v}p(r,\tilde{v}_2)\}} \qquad (21)$$

for all $\tilde{v}_2 \in T_2$. Substituting (21) into (18) yields

$$U_1(v, v) \geqslant E[[x(r, \tilde{v}_2) - v] 1_{\{x(r,\tilde{v}_2) > \hat{v}p(r,\tilde{v}_2)\}}]$$
$$= E[[x(r, \tilde{v}_2) - vp(r, \tilde{v}_2)] 1_{\{x(r,\tilde{v}_2) > \hat{v}p(r,\tilde{v}_2)\}}]$$
$$= \hat{x}(r, \hat{v}) - v\hat{p}(r, \hat{v}), \qquad (22)$$

where the first equality follows from DET and EXPIR (the latter because it implies that $x = 0$ if $p = 0$), and the second equality follows from definition (14). Observe that (22) contradicts Lemma 2(i). Hence, (p, x) must satisfy IC*.　　　　　　　　　　　　　　　　　　　　　Q.E.D.

REFERENCES

1. R. J. AUMANN, M. MASCHLER, AND R. E. STEARNS, "Repeated Games of Incomplete Information: An Approach to the Non-Zero-Sum Case," Report to the U.S. Arms Control and Disarmament Agency, Contract S.T. 143, prepared by Mathematica Inc., Princeton, NJ, 1968.
2. I. BARANY, "Fair Distribution Protocols or How the Players Replace Fortune," CORE Discussion Paper No. 8718, 1987.
3. K. CHATTERJEE AND W. SAMUELSON, Bargaining under incomplete information, *Oper. Res.* **31** (1983), 835–851.
4. V. CRAWFORD AND J. SOBEL, Strategic information transmission, *Econometrica* **50** (1982), 1431–1452.
5. J. FARRELL, "Credible Neologisms in Games of Communication," MIT Working Paper No. 386, 1985.
6. J. FARRELL AND R. GIBBONS, Cheap talk can matter in bargaining, *J. Econ. Theory* **48** (1989), 221–237.
7. F. FORGES, An approach to communication equilibria, *Econometrica* **54** (1986), 1375–1386.
8. F. FORGES, "Equilibria with Communication in a Job Market Example," CORE Discussion Paper No. 8703, 1987.

9. F. Forges, "Universal Mechanisms," CORE Discussion Paper No. 8704, 1987.

10. S. Grossman and M. Perry, Perfect sequential equilibrium, *J. Econ. Theory* **39** (1986), 97–119.

11. S. Hart, Non-zero-sum two-person repeated games with incomplete information, *Math. of Oper. Res.* **10** (1985), 117–153.

12. O. Hart and B. Holmstrom, The theory of constracts, *in* "Advances in Economic Theory" (T. Bewley, Ed.), Cambridge Univ. Press, Cambridge, 1986.

13. W. Leininger, P. Linhart, and R. Radner, Equilibria of the sealed-bid mechanism for bargaining with incomplete information, *J. Econ. Theory* **48** (1989), 63–106.

14. S. Matthews, Veto threats: Rhetoric in a bargaining game, *Quart. J. Econ.* **104** (1989).

15. S. Matthews, M. Okuno-Fujiwara, and A. Postlewaite, Communication in Bayesian Games: Issues and Problems, Northwestern, mimeo, 1988.

16. R. Myerson, Optimal coordination mechanisms in principal-agent problems, *J. Math. Econ.* **10** (1982), 67–81.

17. R. Myerson, Analysis of two bargaining problems with incomplete information, *in* "Game-Theoretic Models of Bargaining" (A. Roth, Ed.), Cambridge Univ. Press, Cambridge, 1985.

18. R. Myerson, Bayesian equilibrium and incentive-compatibility: An introduction, *in* "Social Goals and Organization" (L. Hurwicz, D. Schmeidler, and H. Sonnenschein, Eds.), Cambridge Univ. Press, Cambridge, 1985.

19. R. Myerson and M. Satterthwaite, Efficient mechanisms for bilateral trading, *J. Econ. Theory* **29** (1983), 265–281.

20. J. F. Nash, Non-cooperative games, *Ann. of Math.* **54** (1951), 286–295.

21. R. Radner and A. Schotter, The sealed bid mechanism: An experimental study, *J. Econ. Theory* **48** (1989), 179–220.

22. J. Riley and R. Zeckhauser, Optimal selling strategies: when to haggle, when to hold firm, *Quart. J. Econ.* **98** (1983), 267–287.

23. M. Satterthwaite and S. Williams, Bilateral trade with the sealed-bid *k*-double auction: Existence and efficiency, *J. Econ. Theory* **48** (1989), 107–133.

24. V. Smith, A. Williams, K. Bratton, and V. Vannoni, Competitive market institutions: double auctions vs. sealed bid-offer auctions, *Amer. Econ. Rev.* **72** (1982), 58–77.

25. S. Williams, Efficient performance in two agent bargaining, *J. Econ. Theory* **41** (1987), 154–172.

26. R. Wilson, Incentive efficiency of double auctions, *Econometrica* **53** (1985), 1101–1115.

27. R. Wilson, Efficient trading, *in* "Issues in Contemporary Microeconomics and Welfare," (G. Feiwel, Ed.), Macmillan, New York, 1985.

28. R. Wilson, Game-theoretic analyses of trading processes, *in* "Advances in Economic Theory" (T. Bewley, Ed.), Cambridge Univ. Press, Cambridge, 1987.

JOURNAL OF ECONOMIC THEORY **48**, 264–303 (1989)

Credible Negotiation Statements and Coherent Plans*

ROGER B. MYERSON

J. L. Kellogg Graduate School of Management,
Northwestern University,
Evanston, Illinois 60208

Received December 13, 1986; revised September 2, 1987

Criteria are developed to determine which negotiation statements are credible with respect to a reference payoff allocation for the negotiator's possible types. An attractive reference allocation is any limit of reference allocations that admit no credible statements. A coherent plan is a negotiation statement that all types can make with likelihood one that is credible with respect to an attractive reference allocation. Coherent plans are shown to exist. Semicoherent plans are also defined, without reference allocations. Sequentially coherent plans are defined for multistage games with no simultaneous moves. Other negotiation structures are considered, including mechanism design by an informed principal. *Journal of Economic Literature* Classification Number: 026. © 1989 Academic Press, Inc.

1. INTRODUCTION

Nash [18] argued that bargaining and cooperation in games should be studied using the methodology of noncooperative game theory, by modelling the bargaining process itself as a noncooperative game and analyzing its equilibria. Although this research program has generated a number of remarkable results and insights, there has been a growing sense that its power is limited by the fact many natural bargaining-game models have very large sets of Nash equilibria.

The advantage of Nash's program is that the derivation of behavior from rational decision-making by individuals has traditionally been much clearer in noncooperative game theory than in cooperative game theory. However, what seems to be missing from noncooperative models is the essential assumption that people listen and understand each other when they communicate to coordinate their decisions.

* The author is indebted to Sanford Grossman for long and helpful discussions on this subject, without which this paper would not have been written. Support for this research by an Alfred P. Sloan Foundation fellowship and by NSF grant SES–8605619 is gratefully ackowledged.

429

The goal of this paper is to try to provide new foundations for cooperative game theory by developing a theory of coherent decision-making by individual negotiators. To clarify the individualistic foundations of the analysis, most of the paper focuses on the determination of a single negotiation statement by one individual. We assume that this individual negotiator has an ability to make himself understood by other individuals which goes beyond what is assumed in noncooperative game theory and which gives the model its "cooperative" nature.

In general, *negotiation* may be defined as any communication process in which individuals try to determine or influence the effective equilibrium that they will play thereafter in some game. In many economic situations, it seems reasonable to believe that individuals will be able to coordinate effectively with each other and implement an equilibrium that is (at least) Pareto-undominated within the set of equilibria (given some appropriate refinement of the equilibria concept). Such a belief may be derived from an assumption that they can negotiate, in this sense.

However, the theory of noncooperative games with signalling and communication (based largely Aumann's [1] concept of *correlated equilibrium* and Kreps and Wilson's [10] concept of *sequential equilibrium*) derives the meaning of all statements and signals from the equilibrium in which they are used. Thus, noncooperative game theory does not permit us to suppose that communication can determine the effective equilibrium that is actually played, because the meanings of all statements are supposed to be determined by the effective equilibrium itself. In fact, if the mere act of saying something does not directly affect any payoffs then there is always a "babling" equilibrium, in which every player randomizes over the set of his possible statements independently of his information and his payoff-relevant actions, and in which all other players ignore his meaningless statements. Such analysis suggests that communication can only increase the set of equilibria (as, indeed, the correlated equilibria include all Nash equilibria), and cannot provide a way to select among equilibria.

To escape from this conclusion, we must drop the assumption that statements have no absolute meanings beyond what is endogenously determined by the equilibrium in which they are used. Instead, we must introduce an assumption that negotiation statements have literal meanings that are exogenously defined, at least under certain circumstances, as statements in a rich language like English which every player undestands. For example, the message "let's meet at the train station tomorrow at noon" has a given literal meaning in any conversation between two English-speaking individuals who are residents of a town with one train station and who both want to meet again soon. We may suppose that negotiations to determine equilibrium behavior in the game are conducted in such a language in which statements have exogenous literal meanings. Then, using the assumption that such literal meanings are understood by the players in negotiations, a negotiation structure may indeed determine a set of "coherent" equilibria that is narrower than the set of equilibria of the corresponding game without negotiations, instead of enlarging the set of equilibria as a general communication system does.

Rigorously describing the role of literal meanings in such negotiations can be a subtle problem, however, because rational individuals cannot be expected to believe every possible statement. That is, some statements have literal meanings that simply are not credible. For example, if a stranger approached you on the street and said "let me hold your wallet for a minute and I will give it back to you with twice as much money," you would understand what he is trying to say, but you would probably not believe him or do as he asks. In a society where many people would accept and believe such a statement, others would have an incentive to abuse their trust by using this statement with a different effective meaning, so that it would become effectively synonymous with "give me your wallet and watch how fast I can run away with it."

Thus, we need to develop general criteria to determine which statements cannot be credibly used according to their literal meanings. To be true to our assumption that literal meanings of statements are understood by all players in negotiations, we should make such criteria as narrow as possible and assume that individuals will accept the literal meaning of each others' statements unless there is a strong logical reason to distrust them.

The literal meaning of any negotiator's statement may be analyzed into three components: an *allegation* that describes some private information which may be known by the negotiator; a *promise* that describes how the negotiator may plan to choose his own future actions and messages; and a *request* (or *suggestion*) that describes strategies for the other players which the negotiator may want or expect them to use hereafter. After hearing a statement by some negotiator, the other players may ask themselves whether the following three conditions are satisfied.

> If all other players believe the negotiator's allegations and promises, then it should be rational for them all to obey his requests. (1.1)

> If the negotiator expects all other players to obey his requests, then it should be rational for him to fulfill his promises. (1.2)

> The information that the negotiator alleges should be consistent with the information that could be inferred about him from the fact that he wants other players to use the strategies that he has requested, rather than some other strategies that they might have otherwise been willing to use. (1.3)

If (1.1) is satisfied, then we say that the statement (or the request in it) is
tenable. If (1.2) is satisfied, then we say that the statement (or the promise
in it) is *reliable.* If (1.3) is satisfied, then we say that the statement (or the
allegation in it) is *plausible.* If a statement is tenable, reliable, and plausible,
then we say that is *credible.*

Our key assumption is that, if a statement is credible in this sense, so
that conditions (1.1)–(1.3) are all satisfied, then the other players will believe
what the negotiator alleges and promises about his own information and
strategy, and they will all obey his requests. On the other hand, if any of
these conditions are not satisfied, then the literal meaning of the statement
is not credible, and so the inferences and responses that the other players
make to this statement (i.e., the *effective meaning* of the statement) can be
arbitrarily determined in any way permitted by Kreps and Wilson's [10]
concept of sequential equilibrium, without further regard for the literal
meaning of the statement.

Of these three conditions, plausibility (1.3) has been the hardest to
formulate in a rigorous mathematical model, because it implicitly relies
on some notion of what the negotiator could have achieved by making
some other negotiation statement. Following common game-theoretic
terminology, we may refer to the private information that a player has at
the time that he makes a negotiation statement as his *type.* Then the formal
definition of plausibility requires us to determine *reference payoffs* that
represent a conjecture about what each type of the negotiator could have
gotten "otherwise." Once such reference payoffs are specified, one might
infer from a request that the negotiator's actual type is unlikely to be in the
set of types that would get less than their reference payoffs if this request
were obeyed.

As we seek to develop a solution concept to predict the outcome of
negotiations, we can assume without loss of generality that all statements
that are actually used with positive probability in our solution are used
consistently with their literal meanings. If this assumption were violated
then we could make it true by simply redefining the way that literal
meanings are assigned to statements in the language that negotiators use.

The assumption that literal meanings are understood by all players has
analytical force only when it is applied to a rich language of statements
that are supposed to get zero probability in our solutions. Farrell [5] calls
such statements that are not used in the predicted solution *neologisms.* The
assumption that the literal meaning of these neologisms would be understood by all players may constrain the response that such neologisms
would elicit if they were used, so that they might become profitable alternatives that tempt negotiators away from the predicted solution. Thus, as
Farrell has argued, our solutions must be defined so that there are no
neologisms that a negotiator could more profitably use. That is, we want

our analysis ultimately to predict the negotiation statements and equilibrium strategies that would be used by the each player in a given game with a negotiation structure; but to make such predictions, we must be able to show that no player would be able to find any other credible negotiation statements that would be more profitable for him than the predicted outcome. To guarantee this, most neologisms should not be credible in our solutions.

This observation is the key to determining the reference payoffs that are required to formalize the concept of credibility. A negotiator's reference payoffs must be determined in a way that narrows his range of credible statements down sufficiently so that a specific coherent plan can be predicted. This idea is used in Section 5 to derive our fundamental definition of coherent plans. That is, a coherent plan is defined to be a plan that is credible with respect to a standard of credibility that admits essentially no other credible statements.

This paper may be viewed as a part of the growing literature on ways of selecting among equilibria of games with signalling or communication. (See also Kalai and Samet [7], Kohlberg and Mertens [8], McLennan [13], Kreps [9], Banks and Sobel [2], and Cho and Kreps [3], for other recent contributions in this area.) Kumar's [11] investigation of sequential selection of mechanisms is also closely related to the subject of this paper. This paper builds most directly on the papers of Farrell [5], Grossman and Perry [6], and Myerson [16]. In each of these three papers, credible statements and signals can play a role in selecting among equilibria, because of the constraint that they should be interpreted according to their literal or natural meanings. Farrell [5] has most clearly articulated the focal role of credible literal meanings in such analysis. The dynamic models studied in this paper are adapted from the work of Grossman and Perry [6]. (See also Okuno–Fujiwara and Postlewaite [19] for other interesting modifications of Grossman and Perry's solution concept.) The fundamental solution concept used in this paper is a generalization of the solution concept developed by Myerson [16].

The plan of this paper is as follows. A basic model of the negotiation problem faced by one player in one stage of a game is developed in Sections 2 and 3. In Section 4, we define a generalization of this negotiation model which contains all the mathematical structures needed in Section 5. Section 5 develops the formal definition of a coherent plan and the general existence theorem, and also introduces a related but weaker concept of semicoherent plans. Section 6 contains two simple examples that illustrate the properties of coherent plans. In Section 7, we show how the model of Sections 2 and 3 may be embedded in a multistage game in which players move one at a time, to define the sequentially coherent plans of such a game. Section 8 discusses some other negotiation structures, and, using the general negotiation model of Section 4, shows that the concept of coherent plans generalizes the concept of neutral optima that was defined by Myerson [16] for the problem of mechanism design by an informed principal. Section 9 contains the proofs of all theorems.

Readers in need of illustrative examples may find it helpful to skip ahead and look at Section 6 before reading the more technical Sections 2–5 in detail.

2. A Basic Model of Negotiation Statements

In this and the next two sections, we develop a series of models of negotiation statements and of the environment confronting a negotiator. Before developing our first model of a negotiation move, however, a brief digression on mathematical notation is necessary. In general, for any finite set X, we will let $\Delta(X)$ denote the set of all probability distributions over X, so that

$$\Delta(X) = \left\{ p: X \to \mathbb{R} \,\middle|\, \sum_{x \in X} p(x) = 1, \quad \text{and} \quad p(y) \geq 0 \; \forall y \in X \right\}.$$

For any finite set X, we let $\Lambda(X)$ denote the set of *subprobability distributions* on X, where a subprobability distribution differs from a probability distribution in that the sum of the weights may be less than or equal to one, instead of only equal to one. That is,

$$\Lambda(X) = \left\{ p: X \to \mathbb{R} \,\middle|\, \sum_{x \in X} p(x) \leq 1, \quad \text{and} \quad p(y) \geq 0 \; \forall y \in X \right\}.$$

As usual, $[0, 1]$ denotes the interval from 0 to 1, including both endpoints; and $(0, 1]$ denotes the half-open interval from 0 to 1, including 1 but excluding 0. For any set Y and any finite set Z, we let Y^Z denote the set of all functions from Z into Y.

Let us now consider the problem faced by one player, whom we may refer to as *the negotiator*, when he has an opportunity to make a negotiation statement to the other players in a game. When the negotiator makes his statement, he may have some private information, which we refer to as his *type*, and he may have a range of payoff-relevant *actions* available to him. We let T denote the set of possible types for the negotiator, and we let C denote the set of possible actions that the negotiator must choose among. We let S denote the set of all possible combinations of pure strategies which will be available to the other players jointly in the game after the negotiator makes his negotiation statement. For any (c, s, t) in $C \times S \times T$, we let $U(c, s, t)$ denote the expected utility payoff to the negotiator if his type is t, he chooses action c, and the other players subsequently choose s. We assume that T, C, and S are nonempty finite sets.

Let us now assume that the negotiator is selecting a statement that will be his final statement to the other players. (In the next section, we will drop this assumption and allow the negotiator to follow his negotiation statement by subsequent messages.) In this statement, the negotiator may offer information about his type and the way that his action will depend on his type, and he may make a request as to how the other players should choose their strategies (possibly with randomization).

The information that the negotiator alleges about his type can be characterized by a vector of likelihoods in $[0, 1]^T$, such that every other player should update his beliefs (in $\Delta(T)$) about the negotiator's type using Bayes' formula with this vector of likelihoods. That is, if the negotiator announces some likelihood vector $\lambda = (\lambda(t))_{t \in T}$ in $[0, 1]^T$, then he is alleging that, for any t in T, any player who had prior beliefs p in $\Delta(T)$ before the statement should, after the statement, assign posterior probability $p(t) \lambda(t) / \sum_{r \in T} p(r) \lambda(r)$ to the event that t is the negotiator's actual type. The likelihood $\lambda(t)$ is interpreted as the conditional probability that this statement would be made if t were the negotiator's actual type.

The way that the negotiator promises to choose his actions can be described by a randomized strategy in $\Delta(C)^T$. That is, if the negotiator announces some strategy $\gamma = (\gamma(c \mid t))_{c \in C, t \in T}$ in $\Delta(C)^T$, then he is promising to use action c with probability $\gamma(c \mid t)$ if his type is t.

The request that the negotiator makes on the other players can always be described by some jointly randomized strategy $\sigma = (\sigma(s))_{s \in S}$ in $\Delta(S)$, in which $\sigma(s)$ denotes the probability that the others should use their joint pure strategy s.

Thus, the set of possible final statements that the negotiator could make may be identified with the set $[0, 1]^T \times \Delta(C)^T \times \Delta(S)$. When we represent a statement this way, the likelihood vector in $[0, 1]^T$ is the negotiator's *allegation*, the strategy in $\Delta(C)^T$ is the negotiator's *promise*, and the strategy in $\Delta(S)$ is the negotiator's *request*.

To complete our basic model of the negotiator's problem, we need some way to specify or determine what strategies in $\Delta(S)$ may be rational for the players who will move after the negotiator in the game. (The utility function $U(*)$ is the basic determinant of rational behavior for the negotiator in this model.) So let us assume that we are given some correspondence $F: [0, 1]^T \times \Delta(C)^T \to\to \Delta(S)$ that characterizes the tenable requests that could be made on the players other than i, for any allegation and promise that the negotiator might make. That is, for any (λ, γ) in $[0, 1]^T \times \Delta(C)^T$, $F(\lambda, \gamma)$ represents the set of all correlated strategies in $\Delta(S)$ that could be rationally implemented by the players in the subgame that will follow the negotiator's current move, if everyone believed the negotiator's allegation λ

and promise γ. Thus, $\sigma \in F(\lambda, \gamma)$ if and only if the statement $(\lambda, \gamma, \sigma)$ is tenable in the sense of (1.1). We may refer to this correspondence F as the *tenability correspondence*. The actual construction of this correspondence $F(*)$ must ultimately depend on our developing a theory of rational behavior in such subgames, but we defer such questions until Section 7 and assume for now that this correspondence is given.

We assume that this correspondence F satisfies three basic properties:

$$F(\lambda, \gamma) \neq \varnothing, \qquad \forall \lambda \in [0, 1]^T, \quad \forall \gamma \in \Delta(C)^T; \tag{2.1}$$

$$F(\alpha\lambda, \gamma) = F(\lambda, \gamma), \qquad \forall \alpha \in (0, 1], \quad \forall \lambda \in [0, 1]^T, \quad \forall \gamma \in \Delta(C)^T; \tag{2.2}$$

$$F(\cdot) \text{ is upper-semicontinuous.} \tag{2.3}$$

Condition (2.1) asserts that, whatever information is given about the negotiator's type and strategy, there must be some strategy combination for the other players thereafter that constitutes rational behavior for them. Condition (2.2) is a homogeneity condition that follows from Bayes' formula. Multiplying a vector of likelihoods by a positive scalar α does not affect the posterior probabilities in $\Delta(T)$ that any observer would calculate, and so the set of tenable requests should remain the same. Condition (2.3) is a topological regularity condition, asserting that the graph of F is a closed subset of $[0, 1]^T \times \Delta(C)^T \times \Delta(S)$.

3. NEGOTIATION STATEMENTS WITH SUBSEQUENT MESSAGES

A negotiation statement may include a promise to communicate additional information, by transmitting further messages through some communication channel. That is, we may think of communication by a player as a two-stage process, consisting of an introductory negotiation statement and subsequent messages. The player's negotiation statement advocates some equilibrium of the subsequent game with communication, and his subsequent messages form a part of this communication equilibrium. Since the intended interpretation of the subsequent messages is defined by the negotiation statement that precedes them, our analysis should focus on the negotiation statement itself. However, the possibility of such postnegotiation communication has important implications for our analysis of negotiation statements.

With such possibilities for further communication after his negotiation statement, a negotiator can make a statement of the form "I am about to transmit to you, through some suitable communication channel, either the statement μ_1 or the statement μ_2." We may refer to such a statement as the *introductory sum* of statements μ_1 and μ_2. For any two possible negotiation statements μ_1 and μ_2, if the sum of their alleged likelihoods is never greater than one then the introductory sum of μ_1 and μ_2 should also be a possible negotiation statement. The model developed in the preceding section ignores the possibility of postnegotiation messages, and the representation of negotiation statements as vectors in $[0, 1]^T \times \Delta(C)^T \times \Delta(S))$ does not include all such introductory sums. To include all such introductory sums in our set of possible negotiation statements, we must redefine the set of negotiation statements to be some larger set Ω, into which the statements in $[0, 1]^T \times \Delta(C)^T \times \Delta(S)$ can be naturally embedded. We now show how this can be accomplished by letting $\Omega = \Lambda(C \times S)^T$.

In our notation, $\Lambda(C \times S)^T$ denotes the set of all functions from the set T into the set of all subprobability distributions on $C \times S$, so

$$\Lambda(C \times S)^T =$$

$$\left\{ \mu = (\mu(c, s \mid t))_{c \in C, s \in S, t \in T} \;\middle|\; \begin{array}{l} \mu(c, s \mid t) \geqslant 0 \; \forall c \in C, \; \forall s \in S, \; \forall t \in T; \\[2mm] \text{and} \quad \sum_{c \in C} \sum_{s \in S} \mu(c, s \mid t) \leqslant 1, \; \forall t \in T \end{array} \right\}.$$

For any μ in $\Lambda(C \times S)^T$ and any t in T, we define

$$L(\mu \mid t) = \sum_{c \in C} \sum_{s \in S} \mu(c, s \mid t).$$

That is, $L(\mu \mid t)$ is the sum of the subprobabilities in the distribution on $C \times S$ that is designated for t by μ.

For any triple $(\lambda, \gamma, \sigma)$ in $[0, 1]^T \times \Delta(C)^T \times \Delta(S)$, let $\lambda * \gamma * \sigma$ be defined so that $\mu = \lambda * \gamma * \sigma$ iff

$$\mu(c, s \mid t) = \lambda(t) \, \gamma(c \mid t) \, \sigma(s), \qquad \forall c \in C, \quad \forall s \in S, \quad \forall t \in T.$$

Notice that the vector μ determined by such a star product will be in the set $\Lambda(C \times S)^T$. Furthermore, given $\mu = \lambda * \gamma * \sigma$, we can reconstruct λ from μ by the formula

$$\lambda(t) = L(\mu \mid t),$$

and, whenever $\lambda(t) \neq 0$, we can reconstruct γ and σ from μ by the formulas

$$\gamma(c \mid t) = \sum_{s \in S} \mu(c, s \mid t) / \lambda(t),$$

$$\sigma(s) = \mu(c, s \mid t) / (\gamma(c \mid t) \, \lambda(t)).$$

Thus, the negotiator's allegation, promise, and request can all be essentially reconstructed from their star product in $\Lambda(C \times S)^T$. The only terms that are lost in this representation are the strategic promises and requests that would be made by types that are alleged to have zero probability of making this statement. So any negotiation statement that can be represented by a triple in $[0, 1]^T \times \Delta(C)^T \times \Delta(S)$ can also be represented by a vector in $\Delta(C \times S)^T$, by taking this star product of the three vectors in $[0, 1]^T$, $\Delta(C)^T$, and $\Delta(S)$; and this representation in $\Delta(C \times S)^T$ does not suppress any relevant information about the negotiator's allegations, promises, and requests. This representation may seem unintuitive at first, but it will greatly improve both the simplicity and power of our notation to henceforth use this representation. The literal interpretation of a negotiation statement μ in $\Delta(C \times S)^T$ is that, for each (c, s, t) in $C \times S \times T$, if the negotiator's type were t then $\mu(c, s \mid t)$ would be the probability that the negotiator would make this negotiation statement, would choose his action c, and would have the other players after him use their pure joint strategy s.

The tenability correspondence F from Section 2 can be represented in $\Delta(C \times S)^T$ by the set $\hat{G}$ defined as

$$\hat{G} = \{\mu \mid \exists \lambda \in [0, 1]^T, \exists \gamma \in \Delta(C)^T, \text{ and } \exists \sigma \in F(\lambda, \gamma) \text{ such that } \mu = \lambda * \gamma * \sigma\}.$$

That is, if $\mu \in \hat{G}$ then the request in μ is tenable, so that the other players would be willing to obey it if they believed the negotiator's allegations and promises.

Representing negotiation statements as vectors in $\Delta(C \times S)^T$ has an important advantage over the representation in $[0, 1]^T \times \Delta(C)^T \times \Delta(S)$, because sums of vectors in $\Delta(C \times S)^T$ can be interpreted as representing introductory sums of statements. That is, if $\mu = \mu_1 + \mu_2$ in $\Delta(C \times S)^T$, then μ can be interpreted as the statement "I am about to announce either the statement μ_1 or μ_2." If the negotiator would make this introductory statement before announcing either μ_1 or μ_2, then indeed $\mu_1(c, s \mid t) + \mu_2(c, s \mid t)$ would be the conditional probability that he would make this statement and subsequently use action c and have the other players use their joint strategy s if his type were t. Not every vector in $\Delta(C \times S)^T$ can be expressed as a star pruduct of three vectors in $[0, 1]^T$, $\Delta(C)^T$, and $\Delta(S)$; but every vector in $\Delta(C \times S)^T$ can be expressed as a sum of such star products. Thus, we can identify $\Delta(C \times S)^T$ with the set of all possible introductory sums of statements that the negotiator could make in $[0, 1]^T \times \Delta(C)^T \times \Delta(S)$. In this sense, $\Delta(C \times S)^T$ represents the set of all possible negotiation statements, when subsequent messages are allowed.

We let G denote the set of all vectors in $\Delta(C \times S)^T$ that can be expressed as sums of vectors in $\hat{G}$. That is, $\mu \in G$ iff $\mu \in \Delta(C \times S)^T$ and there exists some finite set $\{\mu_1, ..., \mu_k\}$ such that $\{\mu_1, ..., \mu_k\} \subseteq \hat{G}$ and $\mu_1 + \cdots + \mu_k = \mu$. Thus, any vector in G represents the introductory sum of a set of final statements, each of which expresses a tenable request. We may therefore refer to G as the set of *tenable* statements in $\Lambda(C \times S)^T$. Condition (2.2) implies that G is convex. Convexity, condition (2.3), and Caratheodory's Theorem (see [20, Section 17]) imply that G is also a closed subset of $\Lambda(C \times S)^T$.

A negotiator may choose to transmit messages through some mediator or communication channel. We may think of such a mediator as being an agent of the negotiator who filters and transforms messages from the negotiator according to some random rule that is has been selected by the negotiator himself. We now show how such a mediator could help the negotiator to implement the terms of any statement in G.

For any μ in G, suppose that $\mu = \sum_{j=1}^{k} \mu_j$, where each $\mu_j = \lambda_j * \gamma_j * \sigma_j \in \hat{G}$ and $\sigma_j \in F(\lambda_j, \gamma_j)$. A mediator could help the negotiator to implement the terms of μ by the following scheme. After the negotiation statement μ is announced, the negotiator should report his type to the mediator. (Since the mediator is going to filter the information anyway, there is no loss of generality in assuming that the negotiator is asked to report all of his information to the mediator.) Then the mediator should select (but not yet reveal) his final message from the set $\{\mu_1, ..., \mu_k\}$. If the negotiator reported type t to the mediator then the probability of the mediator selecting μ_j should be $\lambda_j(t)/L(\mu | t)$. Next, the mediator should confidentially recommend an action to the negotiator, recommending action c with probability $\gamma_j(c | t)$ if t was reported and final announcement μ_j was selected. Finally, after the negotiator has chosen his action in C, the mediator should publicly announce the μ_j that he has selected and should request that the other players select their strategies according to the corresponding σ_j, so that each pure strategy s is recommended with probability $\sigma_j(s)$. Suppose that, for each type t, $L(\mu | t)$ is the probability that this paticular mediation scheme would have been selected by the negotiator when his type is t. Then the statement that that this mediation scheme is to be used can be represented by the given vector μ.

To verify this representation, notice that, if the negotiator's type is t, then the conditional probability that this mediation scheme would be selected and that c and s would ultimately be implemented, assuming that everyone would be honest and obedient to the mediator, is

$$L(\mu | t) \sum_{j=1}^{k} (\lambda_j(t)/L(\mu | t)) \gamma_j(c | t) \sigma_j(s) = \sum_{j=1}^{k} \mu_j(c, s | t) = \mu(c, s | t).$$

Furthermore, the mediator's final announcement of μ_j is also being used consistently with its literal meaning, because, when the negotiator's type is t, then the probability that the mediator will select μ_j using this scheme and c and s will be implemented is

$$L(\mu | t)(\lambda_j(t)/L(\mu | t)) \gamma_j(c | t) \sigma_j(s) = \mu_j(c, s | t),$$

assuming that everyone will be honest and obedient to the mediator. Notice that, since $\mu_j = \lambda_j * \gamma_j * \sigma_j \in \hat{G}$, the request σ_j in μ_j is tenable.

In this context, we can now begin to formulate the question of reliability of such a statement μ. If the negotiator is honest and all players are obedient to the mediator under the mediation scheme described above, then the expected payoff to type t of the negotiator when he selects this scheme is

$$\sum_{c \in C} \sum_{s \in S} (\mu(c, s \mid t)/L(\mu \mid t)) \, U(c, s, t),$$

because, under this scheme, given the reported type t, the probability of any (c, s) being ultimately recommended by the mediator is

$$\sum_{j=1}^{k} (\lambda_j(t)/L(\mu \mid t)) \, \gamma_j(c \mid t) \, \sigma_j(s) = \mu(c, s \mid t)/L(\mu \mid t).$$

On the other hand, suppose that the negotiator plans to lie to the mediator, claiming that his type is r when it is really t, and suppose that he plans to disobey the mediator according to some function $\delta : C \to C$, so that he will choose action $\delta(c)$ if the mediator recommends c. (We need to consider manipulative strategies for disobedience that are functions from C into C, because the negotiator's optimal disobedience may be a function of the action recommended to him, when this recommended action is correlated with the mediator's subsequent requests to the other players. We are assuming here that the negotiator will choose his action in C before the mediator's final announcement.) Then the expected payoff to type t of the negotiator from manipulating this mediation scheme in this way is

$$\sum_{c \in C} \sum_{s \in S} (\mu(c, s \mid r)/L(\mu \mid r)) \, U(\delta(c), s, t).$$

Let D denote the set of all functions from C into C, that is,

$$D = C^C.$$

For any types t and r in T, and any function δ in D, we let

$$V(\mu \mid t) = \sum_{c \in C} \sum_{s \in S} \mu(c, s \mid t) \, U(c, s, t),$$

and

$$\hat{V}(\mu, \delta, r \mid t) = \sum_{c \in C} \sum_{s \in S} \mu(c, s \mid r) \, U(\delta(c), s, t).$$

Then to guarantee that the negotiator would not want to disobey and lie to his mediator, as is required for reliability, we need that

$$V(\mu \mid t)/L(\mu \mid t) \geqslant \hat{V}(\mu, \delta, r \mid t)/L(\mu \mid r), \qquad \forall t \in T, \quad \forall r \in T, \quad \forall \delta \in D. \qquad (3.1)$$

Thus, the statement μ may be considered reliable, in the sense of (1.2), if condition (3.1) is satisfied.

These functions $V(\mu \mid t)$ and $\hat{V}(\mu, \delta, r \mid t)$ may be called *discounted-payoff functions*, because they are equal to the product of the negotiator's expected payoff (under honesty and manipulation, respectively) from μ multiplied by the likelihood of the statement μ for the reported type ($L(\mu \mid t)$ or $L(\mu \mid r)$). Notices that $V(\mu \mid t)$, $\hat{V}(\mu, \delta, r \mid t)$, and $L(\mu \mid t)$ are all linear functions of μ, for any given t, r, and δ. This linearity makes the discounted-payoff functions more convenient to work with than the corresponding expected payoffs.

Condition (3.1) does not address the question of whether the initial information supposedly conveyed by the statement μ is plausible in the sense of (1.3). That is, (3.1) cannot confirm that the probability of the negotiator announcing μ would, as claimed, be $L(\mu \mid t)$ if his type is t. Criteria to determine whether these likelihoods are plausible are developed in Section 5. Before that, in Section 4, we develop a more abstract model of negotiation statements, to generalize further the model just developed and to bring its essential structures into better focus.

4. ABSTRACT NEGOTIATION PROBLEMS

To summarize the mathematical properties of the model derived above, we define one further mathematical model of a negotiation problem.

An abstract *negotiation problem* is any $(\Omega, G, T, D, L, V, \hat{V})$ such that Ω is a closed convex subset of some topological vector space, G is a compact subset of Ω, T and D are nonempty finite sets, L is a function mapping $G \times T$ into the interval $[0, 1]$, V is a function mapping $G \times T$ into the real numbers $\mathbb{R}$, $\hat{V}$ is a function mapping $G \times D \times T \times T$ into $\mathbb{R}$, and the following properties are satisfied:

$L(\mu \mid t)$, $V(\mu \mid t)$, and $\hat{V}(\mu, \delta, r \mid t)$ are continuous linear functions
of μ in Ω, $\forall t \in T$, $\forall r \in T$, $\forall \delta \in D$;   (4.1)

$\alpha\mu \in G$, $\forall \mu \in G$, $\forall \alpha \in (0, 1]$;   (4.2)

if $L(\mu_1 \mid t) + L(\mu_2 \mid t) \leqslant 1$ $\forall t \in T$, then $\mu_1 + \mu_2 \in G$, $\forall \mu_1 \in G$,
$\forall \mu_2 \in G$;   (4.3)

$V(\mu \mid t)/L(\mu \mid t)$ and $\hat{V}(\mu, \delta, t \mid r)/L(\mu \mid t)$ are bounded functions on
$\{\mu \in G \mid L(\mu \mid t) > 0\}$, $\forall t \in T$, $\forall r \in T$, $\forall \delta \in D$;   (4.4)

$\forall \lambda \in (0, 1]^T$, $\exists \mu \in G$ such that $\forall t \in T$, $\forall r \in T$, $\forall \delta \in D$,

$$L(\mu|t) = \lambda(t) \text{ and } V(\mu|t)/L(\mu|t) \geqslant \hat{V}(\mu, \delta, r|t)/L(\mu|r); \tag{4.5}$$

$\forall \lambda \in [0, 1]^T$, $\forall \mu \in \Omega$, $\exists (\lambda * \mu) \in \Omega$ such that $\forall t \in T$, $\forall r \in T$, $\forall \delta \in D$,

$$V(\lambda * \mu|t) = \lambda(t)\, V(\mu|t),$$

$$V(\lambda * \mu, \delta, r|t) = \lambda(r)\, V(\mu, \delta, r|t),$$

$$L(\lambda * \mu|t) = \lambda(t)\, L(\mu|t). \tag{4.6}$$

In the interpretation of this abstract model, Ω is the set of possible negotiation statements. G is the set of tenable statements in Ω: that is, G is the set of statements that include requests that the other players would be willing to obey if they believed the negotiator's allegations and promises. T is the set of possible types for the negotiator, and D is the set of possible manipulative strategies that the negotiator could use if he chose to disobey his own strategic promise.

$L(\mu|t)$ is the likelihood of type t making statement μ, according to the literal meaning of μ. For any vector μ in G and any scalar α between 0 and 1, the vector $\alpha\mu$ can be interpreted as the statement "after observing an extraneous event that had probability α, I have decided to make the statement μ." Condition (4.2) asserts that such a statement is tenable if μ is tenable. The sum of two vectors μ_1 and μ_2 in G can be interpreted as the statement, "I am about to make either the statement μ_1 or μ_2." Condition (4.3) asserts that this introductory sum is a tenable statement if each of the individual statements is tenable and the sum of their likelihoods never exceeds one.

The functions V and $\hat{V}$ are discounted-payoff functions. They are defined so that, if the requests in μ are obeyed by all other players, then

$$V(\mu|t)/L(\mu|t)$$

is the negotiator's expected payoff from μ when his type is t and he is honest and obedient to the terms of μ, and

$$\hat{V}(\mu, \delta, r|t)/L(\mu|r)$$

is his expected payoff when his type is t but he pretends that his type is r and then disobeys the terms of μ in choosing his actions according to the manipulative strategy δ. The functions V and $\hat{V}$ are linear in μ, by condition (4.1), and they must be divided by the corresponding likelihoods to compute his expected utility payoffs. Condition (4.4) asserts that expected utility payoffs are bounded. Condition (4.5) asserts that, given any vector of positive likelihoods λ, there exists some tenable statement that is consistent with the allegation λ and that gives the negotiator no incentive to lie or disobey his own promise.

Condition (4.6) asserts that we can define a star product between allegations in $[0, 1]^T$ and statements in Ω. The star product $\lambda * \mu$ represents the statement that is derived from μ by appending the further allegation that all players should reupdate their posterior beliefs after μ using the likelihoods in λ. In the model of Section 3, where $\Omega = \Lambda(C \times S)^T$, this star product is defined by

$$(\lambda * \mu)(c, s \mid t) = \lambda(t) \, \mu(c, s \mid t), \qquad \forall c \in C, \quad \forall s \in S, \quad \forall t \in T.$$

This statement $\lambda * \mu$ is not necessarily tenable, even if μ is, since the additional information conveyed by λ may disturb the other players' incentives to obey the requests in μ.

LEMMA 1. *The model constructed in Section 3 satisfies all the properties of an abstract negotiation problem defined in this section.*

Proof. See Section 9.

5. REFERENCE PAYOFFS AND COHERENT PLANS

In our model, a statement is tenable (in the sense of (1.1)) if it is in the set G. Condition (3.1) is a formalization of reliability (1.2). However, we have not yet considered the third component of credibility, the plausibility (1.3) of a statement. That is, we still need to develop criteria to answer the question of whether the types that would want to make this statement are the types that the negotiator is alleging that his actual type is among. The answer to this question depends on what each type of the negotiator could have gotten if he had made some other statement instead. Thus, to assess the plausibility of a statement, we need some *reference payoff allocation* $w = (w(t))_{t \in T}$ in $\mathbb{R}^T$, where the reference payoff $w(t)$ may be interpreted as the expected payoff that type t of the negotiator could have safely gotten by making some other statement. Once such a reference allocation w has been specified, one might suppose that a statement μ is plausible if, for every type t in T,

$$\text{if} \quad L(\mu \mid t) > 0 \qquad \text{then} \quad V(\mu \mid t)/L(\mu \mid t) \geqslant w(t), \qquad (5.1)$$

and

$$\text{if} \quad V(\mu \mid t)/L(\mu \mid t) > w(t) \qquad \text{then} \quad L(\mu \mid t) = 1. \qquad (5.2)$$

Condition (5.1) asserts that any type that could possibly make the statement μ should not get less from μ than the reference payoff. Condition (5.2) asserts that any type that would get strictly more from μ than the reference payoff should surely make the statement μ.

Conditions (3.1) and (5.2) are difficult to work with. Notice first that, if $L(\mu \mid t) = 0$ or $L(\mu \mid r) = 0$ then the ratios in these inequalities are not well defined. Conditions (4.1) and (4.4) guarantee that the numerator on either side of (3.1) must equal zero whenever the denominator does, but this still leaves us the problem of dividing zero by zero. Furthermore, even when the denominators are nonzero, the nonlinearity of these conditions (3.1) and (5.2) makes them difficult to work with. (Actually, there are ways to try to resolve the problem of dividing zero by zero here. One way is to arbitrarily pick some sequence of statements $\{\mu_k\}_{k=1}^{\infty}$ such that $\mu_k \to \mu$ as $k \to \infty$, and all ratios $V(\mu_k \mid t)/L(\mu_k \mid t)$ and $\hat{V}(\mu_k, \delta, r \mid t)/L(\mu_k \mid r)$ are well defined and convergent as $k \to \infty$. Then we may define $V(\mu \mid t)/L(\mu \mid t)$ and $\hat{V}(\mu, \delta, r \mid t)/L(\mu \mid r)$ to be the limits of these ratios in the sequences. Such sequences can always be found because of the boundedness condition (4.4).)

So let us consider a weaker credibility criterion, which allows more statements to be accepted as credible and which will be easier to work with. We say that μ is *credible with respect to* w iff

$$\mu \in G, \tag{5.3}$$

$$L(\mu \mid t) > 0 \qquad \text{for at least one} \quad t \text{ in } T, \tag{5.4}$$

$$V(\mu \mid t) + (1 - L(\mu \mid t))\, w(t) \geqslant w(t), \qquad \forall t \in T, \tag{5.5}$$

$$V(\mu \mid t) + (1 - L(\mu \mid t))\, w(t) \geqslant \hat{V}(\mu, \delta, r \mid t) + (1 - L(\mu \mid r))\, w(t),$$

$$\forall t \in T, \quad \forall r \in T, \quad \forall \delta \in D. \tag{5.6}$$

Condition (5.3) asserts that μ is tenable, so that all the players moving after the negotiator would be willing to obey the requests in μ if they believed the negotiator's promise and allegation in μ.

We say that a statement μ in G is *null* iff $L(\mu \mid t) = 0$ for every t in T. Thus, a null statement could be interpreted as an assertion of the form "I would never make this statement..." Condition (5.4) asserts that a credible statement cannot be null.

Conditions (5.5) and (5.6) can be readily interpreted if we allow that the negotiator may direct a mediator or agent to negotiate on his behalf. Such a mediator might announce the statement μ on behalf of the negotiator as a part of to the following scheme. First, the negotiator confidentially reports his type to the mediator. For each type t, if the negotiator reports that his type is t then, the mediator will announce μ with probability

$L(\mu \mid t)$, otherwise he do something else (make some other statement or perhaps just be silent). We may let the reference payoff $w(t)$ represent the expected payoff to type t of the negotiator when the statement μ is not made. If the negotiator is honest and obedient and all other players are obedient then the expected payoff to type t from this scheme is

$$L(\mu \mid t)(V(\mu \mid t)/L(\mu \mid t)) + (1 - L(\mu \mid t)) \, w(t)$$
$$= V(\mu \mid t) + (1 - L(\mu \mid t)) \, w(t).$$

(Recall that $V(\mu \mid t)/L(\mu \mid t)$ is the expected payoff to type t from the terms of μ after it is announced.) On the other hand, if the negotiator's actual type is t but he pretends that his type is r and then, if μ is announced, disobeys the terms of his promise according to the manipulative strategy δ, then his expected payoff is

$$L(\mu \mid r)(\hat{V}(\mu, \delta, r \mid t)/L(\mu \mid r)) + (1 - L(\mu \mid r)) \, w(t)$$
$$= \hat{V}(\mu, \delta, r \mid t) + (1 - L(\mu \mid r)) \, w(t).$$

Thus, condition (5.5) asserts that, for any type t, the negotiator's expected payoff from this scheme should not be less than the reference payoff that he could have gotten by some other negotiation statement. In fact, (5.5) is equivalent to (5.1), and so (5.5) may be interpreted as a weak plausibility condition.

Condition (5.6) asserts that the negotiator's expected payoff under this scheme, implemented honestly and obediently. should not be less than what he could expect to get by lying and disobeying. Notice that, if $L(\mu \mid t) = 1$ for all t, then (5.6) is equivalent to (3.1). More generally, if μ satisfies (5.2) (letting the 0/0 ratios be defined as discussed parenthetically above), then (3.1) implies (5.6). Thus, (5.6) can be interpreted as a reliability condition that is weaker than (3.1) in many important cases. The difference between (3.1) and (5.6) is that (5.6) assumes that the negotiator can report his type to the mediator before any negotiation statement is announced and can allow the mediator to control the decision to announce μ according to the terms of μ itself. The reference payoffs are needed in (5.6) to account for the negotiator's payoff when μ is not announced under such a scheme.

Thus, (5.3)–(5.6) constitute a natural definition of credibility for mediated negotiation statements, once a reference allocation w has been specified. Given any w in $\mathbb{R}^T$, the set of all statements that satisfy (5.5) and (5.6) is a compact convex set, and so the set of credible statements with respect to w is convex. The central theoretical question that remains is how to determine the appropriate reference allocation w for our analysis.

With no loss of generality, we may assume that there is only one negotiation statement that is actually made by the negotiator with positive probability, so that this statement has likelihood one for all types. Any given theory that predicts that all the statements in some set $\{\mu_1, ..., \mu_k\}$ will be made with positive probability is equivalent to a theory that asserts that the negotiator's initial statement will be μ, where $\mu = \mu_1 + \cdots + \mu_k$ (so μ can be interpreted as "I or my agent will soon announce the one of the messages in the set $\{\mu_1, ..., \mu_k\}$, which should be interpreted according to its literal meaning"). In effect, we can assume without loss of generality that the fundamental negotiation statement made by the negotiator is actually uninformative, because any further informative communication could be subsumed by messages in a communication equilibrium that is established by the negotiation statement. This argument is called the *inscrutability principle* and is discussed further in [16]. Since, under the given theory, the statements in $\{\mu_1, ..., \mu_k\}$ were supposed to be the only statements used with positive probability by any type, their likelihoods must sum to one, so

$$L(\mu \mid t) = 1, \qquad \forall t \in T. \tag{5.7}$$

We define a *plan* to be any statement μ that satisfies condition (5.7).

Thus, a theory of negotiations should predict one credible plan that the negotiator should be expected to negotiate, no matter what his type is. In general, however, each type of the negotiator will have different preferences over the set of tenable statements. To compel all types to announce the same plan, the reference allocation must define a standard of credibility that accepts one plan but rejects all other statements that any types might prefer over it. This property is the key to determining the reference allocation.

We say that an allocation w in $\mathbb{R}^T$ is *strongly attractive* iff there are no credible statements with respect to w. That is, for any strongly attractive w, if we altered the game by giving the negotiator a new option, called "the easy way out," that would pay $w(t)$ to each type t, then the only credible negotiation statement for the negotiator would be "I am taking the easy out" (which would correspond to a null statement in the original game). Obviously, if the components $w(t)$ are all higher than the upper bounds on the utility functions (given in (4.4)), then w must be strongly attractive, by (5.4) and (5.5). It is straightforward to check that the set of strongly attractive allocations is an open subset of $\mathbb{R}^T$.

We say that w is *attractive* iff it is the limit of a sequence of strongly attractive vectors in $\mathbb{R}^T$. Thus, if w is attractive then any statement is not credible with respect to reference allocations that are arbitrarily close to w. Furthermore, as the following theorem asserts, for any attractive reference allocation and any reliable plan that any type might be tempted to advocate, there is a plausible inference that the other players could make about the negotiator's type after this plan is announced, such that this plan with this inference would not be tenable.

THEOREM 1. *Let w be an attractive reference allocation, and let μ be any plan that satisfies (5.7) and the reliability conditions (3.1) or (5.6). Suppose that $V(\mu \mid \hat{\imath}) > w(\hat{\imath})$ for at least one $\hat{\imath}$ in T (so that at least one type would find it profitable to announce μ, relative to w). Then there exists some likelihood vector λ in $[0, 1]^T$ such that $\lambda * \mu \notin G$ and, for every t in T,*

$$\lambda(t) \begin{cases} = 1, & \text{if} \quad V(\mu \mid t) > w(t), \\ = 0, & \text{if} \quad V(\mu \mid t) < w(t), \\ \in \{0, 1\}, & \text{if} \quad V(\mu \mid t) = w(t). \end{cases}$$

Proof. See Section 9.

We say that a statement μ is a *coherent plan* iff $L(\mu \mid t) = 1$ for every t in T and there exists some attractive reference allocation w such that μ is credible with respect to w. Thus, although μ may not be the unique credible statement with respect to w, if we allow that μ is judged with respect to w but every other statement is judged with respect to some strongly attractive vector arbitrarily close to w, then μ is the unique credible statement. (This may seem like a double standard, but it is only infinitesimally so.) Equivalently, we may suppose that the other players would accept the announcement of μ as inscrutable or uninformative about the negotiator's type; but, after the announcement of any other reliable plan that might tempt some of the negotiator's types, the other players would update their beliefs according to the plausible likelihood vector that is given by Theorem 1, which would destroy the tenability of the plan.

We can now state our general existence theorem.

THEOREM 2. *For any negotiation problem, as defined in Section 4, there exists at least one coherent plan in G.*

Proof. See Section 9.

We say that a plan μ is *incentive compatible* iff it is tenable and reliable, in the senses of (5.3) and (3.1). Notice that a plan μ is coherent iff it is incentive compatible and there exists some attractive reference allocation w such that $V(\mu \mid t) \geq w(t)$, for every t in T.

A plan μ is *strongly dominated* for the negotiator iff there is an incentive-compatible plan $\hat{\mu}$ such that $V(\hat{\mu} \mid t) > V(\mu \mid t)$, for every t in T. A coherent plan cannot be strongly dominated. (If $\hat{\mu}$ were an incentive-compatible plan such that $V(\hat{\mu} \mid t) > V(\mu \mid t) \geq w(t)$ for every t, then $\hat{\mu}$ would be credible with respect to any reference allocation sufficiently close to w.) Thus, the negotiator's expected payoff allocations that are generated by coherent plans must be in the undominated frontier of the incentive-feasible set, which is generally a $(|T| - 1)$-dimensional surface in $\mathbb{R}^T$.

In fact, there is reason to believe that the set of coherent plans is usually a small, zero-dimensional set (finite or countable). Notice that the set of attractive reference allocations is a $(|T| - 1)$-dimensional surface, since it is the boundary of an open set in $\mathbb{R}^T$. By definition, an attractive reference allocation is one that admits some credible statements but almost fails to admit any. So it is reasonable to expect that the set of statements that are credible with respect to an attractive reference allocation is minimal in size. Such a "minimal" set could not be a single point (since, for any α in $(0, 1]$, $\alpha\mu$ is credible with respect to w if μ is credible with respect to w), but a minimal credible set could be a segment of a one-dimensional ray. Then the condition that such a one-dimensional set should include statements that are plans, in the sense of having $L(\mu|t) = 1$ for all t, gives us $|T| - 1$ independent equations to satisfy. Thus, the set of attractive reference allocations that support coherent plans should usually be zero-dimensional. Obviously, this is not a rigorous argument, but it strongly suggests that the set of coherent plans is small for most negotiation problems.

To guarantee that coherent plans exist, we must allow that the attractive reference allocation w that supports a coherent plan μ may be different from the negotiator's expected payoff allocation from μ. (See the second example in Section 6.) In such cases, the attractive reference allocation may not coincide with the negotiator's expected payoffs from any incentive-compatible plan.

Strict inequality between expected payoffs from the coherent plan μ and reference payoffs from the attractive allocation w that supports μ can only occur for types that are, in a sense, free-riding on the other types in the negotiation of μ. To make this idea precise, let $\hat{T}$ denote the set of all types that get the same expected payoff from the coherent plan μ as from the attractive reference allocation w that supports it. Then $\hat{T}$ is nonempty and there is no other incentive-compatible plan that is strictly better than μ for all the types in $\hat{T}$. (If some incentive-compatible plan $\hat{\mu}$ were strictly better than μ for all the types in $\hat{T}$, then some convex combination of μ and $\hat{\mu}$ would be an incentive-compatible plan that was strictly better than w for all types, which would violate Theorem 1.) Thus, the desirability of μ for the negotiator would be evident even if we ignored the preferences of his types outside of $\hat{T}$.

The attractive reference allocation w that supports a coherent plan μ may be quite difficult to interpret when $w(t) < V(\mu|t)$ for some type t of the negotiator. The best general interpretation that we can offer is that the reference allocation represents a hypothetical conjecture that the followers make about what the negotiator would have expected to get, as a function of his type, if he had made some negotiation statement other than the one that he actually made. Such a conjecture is necessary to define a criterion for evaluating the plausibility of the negotiator's allegations.

A weaker concept of coherence may be defined that avoids the use of reference allocations, but it requires us to restrict the negotiator's statements to plans, which involve no nontrivial allegations. We may say that μ is a *semicoherent plan* (or that μ is *coherent in the weak sense*) iff μ is an incentive-compatible plan and, for any other incentive-compatible plan v such that $V(v|\hat{t}) > V(\mu|\hat{t})$ for some $\hat{t}$ in T, there exists some likelihood vector λ in $[0, 1]^T$ such that $\lambda * v \notin G$ and $\lambda(t) = \max_{r \in T} \lambda(r) > 0$ for every t in T such that $V(v|t) > V(\mu|t)$. That is, μ is semicoherent iff, for any other incentive-compatible plan v that the negotiator might prefer, there is an inherence that the followers might make about the negotiator, if he negotiated for v, such that they do not take his negotiation for v as evidence against any type that prefers v over μ, but they would not be willing to obey his requests in v after making this inference.

It is easy to see that a semicoherent plan cannot be strongly dominated for the negotiator by any other incentive-compatible plan. Furthermore, Theorem 1 implies that any coherent plan is semicoherent, so the set of semicoherent plans is nonempty. In Section 6, we show an example in which the set of semicoherent plans is much larger than the set of coherent plans, and we show another example in which the two sets coincide.

6. SENDER–RECEIVER EXAMPLES

Two-player sender–receiver games have been studied to gain insights into the problems of communication in games, since Crawford and Sobel [4]. In these games, one player, the sender, has all the private information and the other player, the receiver, has all the payoff-relevant actions. The sender moves first, sending some message or signal to the receiver, who then chooses an action. In analyzing sender–receiver games here, we assume that the sender is also the sole negotiator. A statement by the sender is tenable iff he is requesting the receiver to use only actions that maximize the receiver's expected payoff given the sender's allegation. In this section, we consider two sender–receiver games, to illustrate some of the key properties of coherent plans.

Throughout this paper, we have assumed that communication between a negotiator and the other players could be facilitated by a mediator. In fact, this assumption is crucial to our general existence theorem. Our first example illustrates the importance of this mediation assumption.

In this game (suggested by R. Aumann, based on a similar example studied by Moulin and Vial [14]), player 1, the sender, has a set of three possible types {1a, 1b, 1c} which are initially considered by player 2 to be equally likely. Player 2, the receiver, has a set of three possible actions {x, y, z}. The payoffs to players 1 and 2, respectively, depend on player 1's type and player 2's action according to Table I.

Notice that player 2 is initially indifferent between his three actions, since each type has probability $\frac{1}{3}$. Type 1a of player 1 would most prefer that 2 choose y, but player 2 would choose z if he were convinced that 1's type was 1a. On the other hand, y is also good for type 1c of player 1 (although x would be slightly better for 1c), and player 2 would be willing to obey a request to choose y if he believed that the request could have come from 1a or 1c with approximately equal likelihood. Thus, type 1a would like to be pooled with 1c, but distinguished from 1b, to be able to tenably request y. Similarly, 1c would like to be pooled with 1b but distinguished from 1a, to be able to tenably request action x; and 1b would like to be pooled with 1a but distinguished from 1c, to be able to tenably request z.

Suppose, for now, that player 1 can only communicate with player 2 by direct face-to-face communication, so that any signal that player 1 sends must be received unaltered by player 2. With such communication, there are only fully pooling equilibria in this game. That is, no matter what may be the set of signals available to player 1, in any equilibrium of the signalling game, player 2 must always have the same (uniform) posterior distribution over player 1's types after receiving any signal that has positive probability, and player 2's strategy must be independent of the signal sent by player 1. Thus, for any equilibrium, there must be some pair of 1's types which could both do strictly better (getting payoffs of 5 and 4) if, with equal likelihood, they would announce that the third type has likelihood zero and request that 2 should use his best action given this information. Furthermore, the third type would lose relative to the equilibrium from this request. Thus, for any reference allocation that is close to a feasible allocation (generated for player 1's types by a fully pooling equilibrium), there is a credible statement that at least two of player 1's types could more profitably use. In fact, there can be no coherent plans for this example without mediation.

TABLE I

Player 2's Actions

Player 1's types	x	y	z
1a	0, 0	5, 4	4, 5
1b	4, 5	0, 0	5, 4
1c	5, 4	4, 5	0, 0

Now suppose that player 1 can also send messages to player 2 through a mediator or noisy channel, as we have assumed throughout Sections 3–6. Then, as Theorem 2 guarantees, there does exist a coherent plan that would be implemented by a mediator as follows. First player 1 confidentially reports his type to the mediator. If 1 reports 1a then, with probability $\frac{5}{6}$, the mediator asks 2 to choose y, and, with probability $\frac{1}{6}$, the mediator asks 2 to choose z. If 1 reports 1b then, with probability $\frac{5}{6}$, the mediator asks 2 to choose z, and, with probability $\frac{1}{6}$, the mediator asks 2 to choose x. If 1 reports 1c then, with probability $\frac{5}{6}$, the mediator asks 2 to choose x, and, with probability $\frac{1}{6}$, the mediator asks 2 to choose y. In this coherent plan, each type of player 1 gets the payoff 5 with probability $\frac{5}{6}$ and gets the payoff 4 with probability $\frac{1}{6}$. The attractive reference payoffs that support this coherent plan are $4\frac{5}{6}$ for each of the three types of player 1. No two types could simultaneously get more than $4\frac{5}{6}$ by an allegation that assigns likelihood zero to the third type, since at least one of these types would get 4 from player 2's best response.

The mediator is needed in this plan because player 2 is not willing to obey any request to choose some action unless there is at least a $\frac{1}{6}$ probability that it is the second-most preferred action of player 1. So a mediator is needed to filter player 1's request and guarantee that there is always at least a $\frac{1}{6}$ probability that the request that 2 hears is for 1's second-most preferred action.

Mathematically, introducing mediation into the communication process helps to guarantee the existence of coherent plans, because mediation convexifies the set of credible statements. For example, without mediation, the reference allocation that gives 3.1 to each of plauer 1's types would allow a credible statement in which any pair of 1's types are given likelihood 1, but there would be no credible statement in which all three types have positive likelihood. Another useful mathematical analogy may be with the theory of the core. Coherent plans are similar to core allocations in traditional cooperative game theory, in that no coalition of types can block a coherent plan with a credible statement. Under this analogy, allowing mediated statements is mathematically analogous to taking the balanced cover of a game, which guarantees nonemptiness of the core.

The coherent plan described above is the unique coherent plan for this game. There are infinitely many semicoherent plans, however, including all incentive-compatible plans that are not strongly dominated for the sender and give an expected payoff greater than 4 to each type of the sender.

For a second example, consider the following sender–receiver game, proposed by Farrell [5]. Player 1, the sender, has two possible types, 1a and 1b, which player 2 initially considers to be equally likely. Player 2 has three possible actions, x, y, and z. The payoffs to players 1 and 2 respectively depend on 1's type and 2's action as in Table II.

TABLE II

Player 2's Actions

Player 1's types	x	y	z
1a	2, 3	$-1, 0$	0, 2
1b	1, 0	0, 3	2, 2

In this game, type 1a would like to reveal his type to player 2, but type 1b would prefer to not be distinguished from type 1a. Farrell [5] shows that this game has no neologism-proof equilibria, in the sense that he defines. However, there is a unique coherent plan for player 1 in this game, and it is also the unique semicoherent plan. In this plan, the probability distribution over player 2's actions depends on 1's type according to Table III.

This plan cannot be implemented without a mediator. (Indeed, Farrell has shown that direct face-to-face communication would only allow one pooling equilibrium in which player 2 chooses z for sure.) The plan in Table III is supported as a coherent plan by the attractive reference allocation that gives 1.6 to type 1a and gives 0 to type 1b.

Notice that this reference allocaton of 1.6 for 1a and 0 for 1b gives strictly less to type 1b than the expected payoff of 1.2 that 1b gets in the coherent plan itself. In fact, the coherent plan's actual payoff allocation of 1.6 for 1a and 1.2 for 1b is not attractive, because any reference allocation close to this would permit player 1 to credibly allege that he is type 1a and request that player 2 choose action x. The reference allocation (1.6, 0) can be attractive even though it is weakly dominated by (1.6, 1.2), because decreasing the reference allocation for type 1b makes it harder for player 1 to plausibly allege that he is type 1a. This example shows that, for a plan to be coherent, it may be necessary to use a reference allocation that is different from (and weakly dominated by) the actual expected payoff allocation from the plan.

Farrell [5] and Grossman and Perry [6] have defined solution concepts that are closely related to the coherent plans of this paper. Both of these

TABLE III

Player 2's actions

Player 1's types	x	y	z
1a	0.8	0	0.2
1b	0.4	0.2	0.4

papers assume that mediation is not used, and both implicitly equate reference payoffs with expected equilibrium payoffs. General existence theorems are not possible for the solution concepts developed in these papers, as the examples in this section would suggest.

7. SEQUENTIALLY COHERENT PLANS

When a player makes a negotiation move in a dynamic multistage game, the tenability correspondence F should be derived from an analysis of the game after his move. In Section 2, we simply assumed that this correspondence was exogenously given, but we can now show how this correspondence may be derived.

Let us consider a dynamic multistage game with n players, numbered 1 to n, who get to move in order of their numbers (player 1 first, n last). During each player's move, he can make public statements and choose some payoff-relevant action. To keep our notation from getting too complex, we assume in this section that each player moves only once, there are no simultaneous moves, and all statements are observed by all players. However, we do not assume that a player's payoff-relevant actions are necessarily observed by the other players.

Such a game may be formally described by a model of the form

$$\Gamma = (p_0, (\Theta_i, T_i, \tau_i, C_i, p_i, u_i)_{i=1}^n, \Theta_{n+1}),$$

where, each T_i, C_i, and Θ_i is a nonempty finite set, τ_i is a function from Θ_i into T_i, p_0 is a probability distribution over Θ_1, p_i is a function from $C_i \times \Theta_i$ into $\Delta(\Theta_{i+1})$, and u_i is a function from Θ_{n+1} into $\mathbb{R}$. We assume that

$$p_0(\theta_1) > 0, \qquad \forall \theta_1 \in \Theta_1,$$

and, for every i in $\{1, 2, ..., n\}$,

$$\forall t_i \in T_i, \quad \exists \theta_i \in \Theta_i \quad \text{such that} \quad t_i = \tau_i(\theta_i),$$

and

$$\forall \theta_{i+1} \in \Theta_{i+1}, \quad \exists (c_i, \theta_i) \in C_i \times \Theta_i \quad \text{such that} \quad p_i(\theta_{i+1} | c_i, \theta_i) > 0.$$

In the interpretation of this model, Θ_i is the set of all possible *states* of the game at the beginning of player i's move. Θ_{n+1} is the set of all possible final states or *outcomes* of the game. T_i is the set of possible *types* (or private-information states) for player i when he makes his move, and $\tau_i(\theta_i)$ is i's type if the state of the game is θ_i when he moves. C_i is the set of possible payoff-relevant *actions* that i can choose among. The probability that the initial state of the game will be θ_1 is $p_0(\theta_1)$. If θ_i is the state when i moves and i chooses action c_i then $p_i(\theta_{i+1} | c_i, \theta_i)$ is the probability that θ_{i+1} will be the state when $i+1$ moves. If the final outcome of the game is θ_{n+1} then the utility payoff for player i is $u_i(\theta_{n+1})$. The assumptions listed above guarantee that any state and type could occur with positive probability, if the players choose their actions appropriately.

For any finite set X, we let $\Delta^0(X)$ denote the set of all probability distributions on X that assign positive probability to every element in X, so

$$\Delta^0(X) = \{q \in \Delta(X) | q(x) > 0 \ \forall x \in X\}.$$

A *conditional probability system* on X is defined by Myerson [17] to be function $\bar{q}$ that maps nonempty subsets of X into probability distributions on X such that, for any sets Y and Z such that $\varnothing \neq Y \subseteq Z \subseteq X$,

$$\sum_{y \in Y} \bar{q}(y | Y) = 1,$$

and

$$\bar{q}(x | Z) = \bar{q}(x | Y) \sum_{y \in Y} \bar{q}(y | Z), \qquad \forall x \in Y.$$

We let $\Delta^*(X)$ denote the set of all conditional probability systems on X. Any probability distribution q in $\Delta^0(X)$ generates a conditional probability system $\bar{q}$ in $\Delta^*(X)$ by the formula

$$\bar{q}(x | Y) = \begin{cases} q(x) \Big/ \displaystyle\sum_{y \in Y} q(y), & \text{if} \quad x \in Y, \\[2ex] 0, & \text{if} \quad x \notin Y. \end{cases}$$

It can be shown (see Myerson [17]) that any conditional probability system in $\Delta^*(X)$ is the limit of a sequence of conditional probability systems that can be generated from distributions in $\Delta^0(X)$ in this way.

At the beginning of player i's move, the beliefs of all players about the state of the game are derived from some conditional probability system in $\Delta^*(\Theta_i)$. When player i announces an allegation and a promise, he is in effect announcing how to compute the new conditional probability system in $\Delta^*(\Theta_{i+1})$. For any π_i in $\Delta^*(\Theta_i)$, any allegation λ_i in $(0, 1]^{T_i}$, and any strategy γ_i in $\Delta^0(C_i)^{T_i}$, a conditional probability distribution $b_i(\pi_i, \lambda_i, \gamma_i)$ in $\Delta^*(\Theta_{i+1})$ is determined by Bayes' formula.

This function b_i can be defined precisely as follows. Suppose that π_i, λ_i, and γ_i are given as above. For any X that is a nonempty subset of Θ_{i+1}, let

$$Y = \{\theta_i \in \Theta_i | \exists c_i \in C_i \text{ and } \exists \theta_{i+1} \in X \text{ such that } p_i(\theta_{i+1} | c_i, \theta_i) > 0\}.$$

Then, for any x in X, let

$$\beta(x, X) = \sum_{y \in Y} \sum_{c_i \in C_i} \pi_i(y \mid Y) \lambda_i(\tau_i(y)) \gamma_i(c_i \mid \tau_i(y)) p_i(x \mid c_i, y).$$

Then, for any θ_i in Θ_i,

$$(b_i(\pi_i, \lambda_i, \gamma_i))(\theta_i \mid X) = \begin{cases} \beta(\theta_i, X) \Big/ \sum_{x \in X} \beta(x, X), & \text{if } \theta_i \in X. \\[2ex] 0, & \text{if } \theta_i \notin X. \end{cases}$$

This Bayesian-updating function $b_i: \Delta^*(\Theta_i) \times (0, 1]^{T_i} \times \Delta^0(C_i)^{T_i} \to \Delta^*(\Theta_{i+1})$ is continuous on its domain. However, λ_i must be in $(0, 1]^{T_i}$ and γ_i must be in $\Delta^0(C_i)^{T_i}$ (i.e., both λ_i and γ_i must have all strictly positive components) to guarantee that Bayes' formula never involves deviding by zero in the definition of $b_i(\pi_i, \lambda_i, \gamma_i)$. To define Bayesian updating when some components of i's allegation and promise may be zero, we must define

$$B_i: \Delta^*(\Theta_i) \times [0, 1]^{T_i} \times \Delta(C_i)^{T_i} \twoheadrightarrow \Delta^*(\Theta_{i+1})$$

to be the minimal upper-semicontinuous correspondence containing the graph of b_i. Then $B_i(\pi_i, \lambda_i, \gamma_i)$ is always a nonempty set of conditional probability systems on Θ_{i+1}, and

$$B_i(\pi_i, \lambda_i, \gamma_i) = \{b_i(\pi_i, \lambda_i, \gamma_i)\} \ \forall \lambda_i \in (0, 1]^{T_i}, \ \forall \gamma_i \in \Delta^0(C_i)^{T_i}, \ \forall \pi_i \in \Delta^*(\Theta_i).$$

To derive a model as in Section 2 to represent the negotiation problem faced by any player i in this game, we need to define the set of pure joint strategies for players after i. Player n has no followers, so let

$$S_n = \{\varnothing\}.$$

For any other player i, the set of pure joint strategies for players after i can be defined recursively by the formula

$$S_i = (C_{i+1} \times S_{i+1})^{T_{i+1}}. \tag{7.1}$$

That is, a joint strategy for the players after i is any rule for determining the action of player $i+1$ and the joint strategies for the players after $i+1$ as a function of the type of player $i+1$. (The choice of a joint strategy for the players after $i+1$ can depend on $(i+1)$'s type because his statement may convey information to them.)

We can recursively define utility functions for actions and strategies at earlier stages in the game by the formulas

$$U_i^n(c_n, \varnothing, \theta_n) = \sum_{\theta_{n+1} \in \Theta_{n+1}} p_n(\theta_{n+1} | c_n, \theta_n) u_i(\theta_{n+1}),$$

and, for any $j < n$,

$$U_i^j(c_j, s_j, \theta_j) = \sum_{\theta_{j+1} \in \Theta_{j+1}} p_j(\theta_{j+1} | c_j, \theta_j) U_i^{j+1}(s_j(\tau_{j+1}(\theta_{j+1})), \theta_{j+1}).$$

(Notice that $s_j(\tau_{j+1}(\theta_{j+1})) \in C_{j+1} \times S_{j+1}$ if $s_j \in S_j$.) Then $U_i^j(c_j, s_j, \theta_j)$ is the expected utility payoff for player i if, when j moves, the state is θ_j, j's action is c_j, and s_j is the joint strategy to be used by the players after j.

We now define $U_i: C_i \times S_i \times T_i \times \Delta^*(\Theta_i) \to \mathbb{R}$ by the formula

$$U_i(c_i, s_i, t_i | \pi_i) = \sum_{\theta_i \in \Theta_i} \pi_i(\theta_i | t_i) U_i^i(c_i, s_i, \theta_i),$$

where

$$\pi_i(\theta_i | t_i) = \pi_i(\theta_i | \{x \in \Theta_i | \tau_i(x) = t_i\}).$$

That is, $U_i(c_i, s_i, t_i | \pi_i)$ is the expected utility payoff for player i at his move if his type is t_i, his action is c_i, the joint strategy for the players following him is s_i, and conditional probability system π_i characterizes current beliefs about the state of the game.

We can now formulate the negotiation problem that player i faces in this game in the terms of the basic model that we developed in Section 2. Obviously, when the negotiator is player i, we should let $C = C_i$, $T = T_i$, and $S = S_i$ in the model of Section 2. Player i's negotiation problem depends on the current beliefs about the state of the game, which are characterized by some conditional probability system π_i in $\Delta^*(\Theta_i)$. Given such a π_i, the utility function $U(\cdot)$ in Section 2 should be identified with the function $U_i(\cdot | \pi_i)$. To complete the model, it now remains only to specify a tenability correspondence F.

When $i = n$, the set of follower's joint strategies S_n is a trivial one-point set (since there are no followers), and we may define F_n by the formula $F_n(\lambda_n, \gamma_n | \pi_n) = \Delta(S_n)$. Then, letting $F(\cdot) = F_n(\cdot | \pi_n)$ completes the formulation of the last player n's negotiation problem in the model of Section 2. Following the construction of Sections 2–5, let $\phi_n(\pi_n)$ be the set of coherent plans for player n, for any given conditional probability system π_n in $\Delta^*(\Theta_n)$. By Theorem 2,

$$\varnothing = \phi_n(\pi_n) \subseteq \Delta(C_n \times S_n)^{T_n}, \qquad \forall \pi_n \in \Delta^*(\Theta_n).$$

Now, for any player i, suppose inductively that a correspondence $\phi_{i+1}(\cdot)$ such that

$$\varnothing \neq \phi_{i+1}(\pi_{i+1}) \subseteq \Delta(C_{i+1} \times S_{i+1})^{T_{i+1}}, \qquad \forall \pi_{i+1} \in \Delta^*(\Theta_{i+1}), \quad (7.2)$$

has been defined to represent the set of coherent plans for player $i + 1$ when he moves in this game, as a function of the public information at his move. Notice that $\Delta(C_{i+1} \times S_{i+1})^{T_{i+1}}$ can be naturally embedded in $\Delta(S_i)$, by the recursive definition (7.1) of S_i. Using this natural embedding, we define the correspondence $\psi_{i+1} : \Delta^*(\Theta_{i+1}) \twoheadrightarrow \Delta(S_i)$ so that $\sigma_i \in \psi_{i+1}(\pi_{i+1})$ iff there exists some μ_{i+1} in $\phi_{i+1}(\pi_{i+1})$ such that

$$\sigma_i(s_i) = \prod_{t_{i+1} \in T_{i+1}} \mu_{i+1}(s_i(t_{i+1}) \,|\, t_{i+1}), \qquad \forall s_i \in S_i.$$

The sets $\phi_{i+1}(\pi_{i+1})$ and $\psi_{i+1}(\pi_{i+1})$ are obviously isomorphic, but they have different interpretations: $\phi_{i+1}(\pi_{i+1})$ is the set possible negotiation statements that player $i + 1$ could coherently make; whereas $\psi_{i+1}(\pi_{i+1})$ is a set of requests that player i could make as a part of his negotiation statement. Since tenable requests of one negotiator must correspond to plans that would be confirmed by the next negotiator, we should identify $\psi_{i+1}(\pi_{i+1})$ with the set of tenable requests that player i can make when π_{i+1} represents the updated beliefs generated by i's allegation and promise.

So let the correspondence $f_i : [0,1]^{T_i} \times \Delta(C_i)^{T_i} \times \Delta^*(\Theta_i) \twoheadrightarrow \Delta(S_i)$ be defined by the equation

$$f_i(\lambda_i, \gamma_i \,|\, \pi_i) = \{\sigma_i \,|\, \exists \pi_{i+1} \in B_i(\pi_i, \lambda_i, \gamma_i) \text{ such that } \sigma_i \in \psi_{i+1}(\pi_{i+1})\}.$$

That is, $f_i(\lambda_i, \gamma_i \,|\, \pi_i)$ is the set of all tenable requets by player i that would be conformed by player $i + 1$, with some Bayesian updated beliefs, after player i announced allegation λ_i and promise γ_i, if π_i represented the beliefs at the beginning of i's move. Our inductive assumption (7.2) implies that $f_i(\lambda_i, \gamma_i \,|\, \pi_i) \neq \varnothing$, as required by (2.1); and the definitions of b_i and B_i guarantee that $f_i(\alpha\lambda_i, \gamma_i \,|\, \pi_i) = f_i(\lambda_i, \gamma_i \,|\, \pi_i)$ for any scalar α in $(0,1]$, as required by (2.2). But we cannot guarantee that f_i is upper-semicontinuous, as required by (2.3). So, for any π_i in $\Delta^*(\Theta_i)$, we define $F_i(\cdot \,|\, \pi_i)$ to be the minimal upper-semicontinuous correspondence containing $f_i(\cdot \,|\, \pi_i)$. Then $F_i(\cdot \,|\, \pi_i)$ is nonempty-valued, homogeneous, and upper-semicontinuous, as conditions (2.1)–(2.3) require. Letting $F(\cdot) = F_i(\cdot \,|\, \pi_i)$ completes the formulation of player i's negotiation problem in the model of Section 2. Following the construction of Sections 2–5, let $\phi_i(\pi_i)$ be the set of coherent plans for player i, given the conditional probability system π_i in $\Delta^*(\Theta_i)$. By Theorem 2,

$$\varnothing \neq \phi_i(\pi_i) \subseteq \Delta(C_i \times S_i)^{T_i}, \qquad \forall \pi_i \in \Delta^*(\Theta_i), \quad (7.3)$$

which justifies the inductive assumption (7.2). Thus, we have recursively defined $\phi_i(\pi_i)$ to be the set of plans that player i could negotiate coherently, given beliefs π_i, when he and each of his followers take full account of the fact that a tenable request must be one that would not be renegotiated by subsequent players.

Let $\bar{p}_0$ be the initial conditional probability system on Θ_1 generated by p_0. Then $\psi_1(\bar{p}_0)$ may be called the set of *sequentially coherent plans* of the game Γ, and it represents our fundamental cooperative solution concept for this game. These are the randomized joint strategies for all players that could be coherently announced in the first stage of the game and would not be contradicted by any coherent negotiation statement by any other player. Notice that $\psi_1(\bar{p}_0) \subseteq \Delta(S_0)$, where (unwinding the recursive definition (7.1))

$$S_0 = \underset{i=1}{\overset{n}{\mathbf{X}}} \ C_i^{(T_1 \times \cdots \times T_i)}.$$

So any sequentially coherent plan describes how every player's action may depend on the types of all players before him. Because a coherent plan is incentive compatible for the negotiating player at every stage, any sequentially coherent plan is a sequentially rational communication equilibrium of Γ in the sense of Myerson [17].

Plans that are *sequentially semicoherent* or (*sequentially coherent in the weak sense*) may be similarly defined, by letting $\phi_i(\pi)$ be recursively defined as the set of semicoherent plans for player i, above formula (7.3).

In this construction, we twice took an upper-semicontinuous extension of a function or correspondence: in going from b_i to B_i, and from f_i to F_i. The extension from b_i to B_i is an application of the basic idea of Kreps and Wilson [10]: that Bayesian updated posteriors after events of probability zero should be computed by taking the limits of the posteriors that would be computed in a slightly perturbed system in which everything has positive probability.

The extension from f_i to F_i resolves a more novel technical problem, however. To see why this extension is needed, consider the following three-person game. First, player 1 chooses Heads or Tails. Then player 2 has an opportunity to negotiate, but he has only one trivial ("inaction") option in C_2. Then player 3 chooses Heads or Tails. Suppose that neither 2 nor 3 observes 1's action. The payoffs are as follows: player 1 gets \$1 if he matches 3 and gets \$0 otherwise; 2 gets \$1 if 3 chooses Tails and gets \$0 otherwise; and 3 gets \$1 if he does not match 1 and gets \$0 otherwise.

Let ρ denote the probability that 1 chooses Heads in this game. The coherent plans for player 3 are just his own best responses: Heads if $\rho < 0.5$; Tails if $\rho > 0.5$; and any randomized strategy if $\rho = 0.5$. These are also the tenable requests for player 2, so that his coherent plans must be to request Heads if $\rho < 0.5$, and to request Tails (which he prefers) if

$\rho \geqslant 0.5$. This discontinuity at $\rho = 0.5$ creates a serious dilemma for player 1. If 1 promises to use Heads with probability ρ such that $\rho \geqslant 0.5$, then 2 should tell 3 to choose Tails, in which case 1's promise to use Heads with positive probability is not reliable. On the other hand, if he promises to use Heads with probability ρ such that $\rho < 0.5$, then 3 must choose Heads, in which case 1's promise to use Tails with positive probability is not reliable. Obviously, the unique equilibrium of this game is when 1 and 3 independently randomize with equal probability between Heads and Tails (so $\rho = 0.5$), but 2's negotiation move seems to interfere with this plan (since 2 wants to steer 3 to Tails when 3 is indifferent). The technical resolution of this paradox is in our extension from f_1 to F_1. While $f_1(0.5)$ includes only the plan in which 3 obeys a request from 2 to choose Tails, $F_1(0.5)$ includes a plan in which 3 does Heads as well as a plan in which 3 does Tails, because for any positive ε, there are plans in $f_1(0.5-\varepsilon)$ in which 3 chooses Heads. Thus, 1 can promise to use Heads with probability 0.5 and tenably "request" that 3 should also randomize between Heads and Tails. To interpret this technical resolution, we might suppose that 3 has an inclination to obey 2's request as long as the expected cost to himself from doing so is less than some very small or infinitesimal number; and so 1 should choose Heads with a probability that is infinitesimally less than 0.5, to exactly counteract 3's inclination to obey player 2.

An alternative solution concept could be proposed in which the two upper-semicontinuous extensions are replaced by one. Given any π_i in $\Delta^*(\Theta_i)$, we could define $\hat{F}_i(\cdot \mid \pi_i)$ to be the minimal upper-semicontinuous correspondence on $[0, 1]^{T_i} \times \Delta(C_i)^{T_i}$ that extends $\psi_{i+1}(b_i(\pi_i, \cdot))$, which is defined only on $(0, 1]^{T_i} \times \Delta^0(C_i)^{T_i}$. Then, we could generate a somewhat different formulation of i's negotiation problem by using $\hat{F}_i(\cdot \mid \pi_i)$ as i's tenability correspondence instead of $F_i(\cdot \mid \pi_i)$. Using $\hat{F}_i$ in this way would be more in the spirit of Selten's [23] concept of trembling-hand perfect equilibrium, whereas our definition of sequential coherence using F_i is more in the spirit of Kreps and Wilson's concept of sequential equilibrium.

The assumption that players move one at a time, in a given order, is essential to the analysis of this section. For example, the analysis of the "Battle of the Sexes" game of Luce and Raiffa [12] depends on which player moves first, even if the player who moves second does not directly observe the action of the player who moves first. We only assume that the first player can commit to an action and make a negotiation statement before the second player can make any commitments. With this assumption, if the man moves first in the "Battle of the Sexes" then the unique sequentially coherent plan is for both players to choose the actions that he most prefers ("going to the prize fight"), because he will announce that he is using his action from this equilibrium and this statement will be credible. On the other hand, if the woman moves first, then the unique sequentially coherent plan is for both to choose the actions that she most prefers ("going to the ballet").

The above example suggests that there is often an advantage to moving first. On the other hand, there are games in which moving later may be an advantage. For example, consider a three-person game in which players 1 and 2 have no payoff-relevant alternatives, and player 3's alternative actions are Heads and Tails. Suppose that 3 is indifferent between Heads and Tails, but 1 prefers that 3 should choose Heads, while 2 prefers that 3 should choose Tails. Under the assumption that 2 gets to make the last negotiation statement before 1 moves, the unique sequentially coherent plan is for 3 to choose Tails. In the initial negotiation statement, player 1 would like to request that 3 should choose Heads, but this request would not be tenable because it would be immediately contradicted by player 2. Thus, when two players are both trying to influence a third player by their negotiation statements, the last person to speak before his move may have the advantage.

8. OTHER NEGOTIATION STRUCTURES

In Section 7, we assumed that a player has an opportunity to negotiate whenever he moves in a game. It is straightforward to relax this assumption, but we must then add to the structure of the game a specification of which moves are "negotiation moves" and which are not.

For example, we might assume that a particular player i can make mediated public announcements at his move, but that these announcements are not necessarily treated as negotiation statements. Substantively, this means either that player i cannot make his announcements in a language with given literal meanings (i.e., he can wave his arms or put lanterns in a church steeple but cannot say anything in English), or that he cannot be confident (for some exogenous reason) that the following players would attentively listen, understand, and respect literal meanings of his statements when they passed appropriate credibility tests. To take this revised assumption into account, the only change that is needed in the definition of sequentially coherent plans is, for such a nonnegotiating player i, to let $\phi_i(\pi_i)$ be the set of incentive-compatible plans (rather than the set of coherent plans) when this set is defined just above formula (7.3).

If it is assumed that some given players can neither negotiate nor communicate when they move, then other changes are needed in the definition of sequentially coherent plans for multistage games. For example, suppose that between the negotiation moves of players i and j, where i moves before j, there is a sequence of moves by other players who can not communicate when they move. Then the strategies for the players between i and j that are specified in a tenable request by player i must form a sequential equilibrium for these players, given the requested behavior for player j and his followers and given i's allegation and promise. Furthermore, the strategies for player j and his followers that are specified in a tenable request by player i must form a coherent plan for the game starting at j's move, given the allegation and promise by i and given the requested strategies for the players between i and j. Using such a notion of tenability, it should be possible to generalize the model in Section 7 to allow for such an exogenously given set of noncommunicative players.

One extension that is straightforward to make in the model of Section 7 is to allow that a player may have more than one move in a game. To reduce such games to the model of the Section 7, we can simply use the temporary-agent device suggested by Selten [23]. That is, each time a particular player moves again, we could suppose that he is represented by a different agent, who has the same utility function and the same type-information as the player, including a recollection of his past types and actions. Then treating these agents as the "players" gives us an equivalent game in which no one moves twice. (The only subtle point which needs to be checked, to verify this equivalence, is that there is no advantage for a player's later agent to know whether an earlier agent might have disobeyed or lied to the mediator who transmitted his public messages. Since the message that the mediator transmitted for the earlier agent are known by everyone, and since we assume that the later agent's type includes all information about the earlier agent's type and action, there is no advantage for the later agent to learn anything else about the earlier agent's private communications with his mediator.)

Although many of the most interesting models of bargaining (as, for example, the model of Rubinstein [21, 22]) do assume that players move one at a time, the assumption that there are no simultaneous moves is restrictive in general. It is not clear how our model could be extended to allow for two players to make simultaneous negotiation statements that are heard by all the other players. The problem is that each player's set of tenable requests must depend on what the other player is announcing. If they simultaneously make different contradictory requests on a later player who is willing to obey either one, which does he obey? (When the negotiators spoke one at a time, we assumed in Section 7 that the later request would be obeyed.)

One way to avoid this dilemma is to suppose that players who negotiate simultaneously must be speaking to different disjoint sets of players. A simple model with this kind of negotiation structure was considered by Myerson [15], in an analysis of equilibria among several principals who head separate corporations. In this model, the set of incentive-compatible (i.e., tenable and reliable) plans for each corporation depends upper-semi-continuously on the plans of other corporations. Consequently, each principal's optimal incentive-compatible plan (i.e., his coherent plan) for his corporation may depend discontinuously on the plans chosen by other principals for their corporations. This discontinuity may prevent the existence of any equilibrium in which each principal is negotiating his optimal incentive-compatible plan for his own corporation, given the plans that the other principals are simultaneously negotiating. However, a natural *quasi-equilibrium* concept can be defined, for which a general existence theorem can be proven (see [15]). The essential idea behind this quasi-equilibrium concept is that our definition of "optimality" or "coherence" must be weakened, so that the set of coherent plans for any negotiator is convex and depends upper-semicontinuously on the plans that are chosen simultaneously by other negotiators. This technical point is likely to be relevant in any model with simultaneous negotiation.

In the model of Section 7, the only communication between players was assumed to be in public statements and messages that all players observe. We may want to drop this assumption and allow a mediator to transmit different confidential messages to each player in the game. In [16], a model with such full communication potential is analyzed under the assumption that one player, called the *principal*, has all of the negotiating ability. That is, in the model of [16], confidential messages can be transmitted to and from any player, but only the credible public statements of the principal are necessarily interpreted according to their exogenous literal meanings.

To formulate this model in the current context, let $\{1, 2, ..., n\}$ be the set of players, and let player 1 be the principal. Let $\bar{C}_i$ be the set of actions available to player i, and let $\bar{T}_i$ be the set of his possible types. Let $\bar{C} = \mathsf{X}_{j=1}^{n} \bar{C}_j$, $\bar{C}_{-i} = \mathsf{X}_{j \neq i} \bar{C}_j$, $\bar{T} = \mathsf{X}_{j=1}^{n} \bar{T}_j$, $\bar{T}_{-i} = \mathsf{X}_{j \neq i} \bar{T}_j$. For any c in $\bar{C}$ and t in $\bar{T}$, let $u_i(c, t)$ denote the utility payoff i when c is the list of actions chosen by the players and t is the list of their actual types. Let $p_i(t_{-i} | t_i)$ denote the probability that player i would assign to the event that t_{-i} in $\bar{T}_{-i}$ is the list of types of the other players if t_i were i's own type.

A coordination plan or *mechanism* for this game is any μ in $\Delta(\bar{C})^{\bar{T}}$, specifying a probability distribution over the combinations of players' actions for any possible combination of players' types. For any such μ, any player i, any t_i and r_i in $\bar{T}_i$, and any function $\delta : \bar{C}_i \to \bar{C}_i$, let

$$\hat{V}_i(\mu, \delta, r_i | t_i) = \sum_{t_i \in \bar{T}_{-1}} \sum_{c \in \bar{C}} p_i(t_{-i} | t_i) \, \mu(c | t_{-i}, r_i) \, u_i((c_{-i}, \delta(c_i)), t).$$

(Here c_i is the i-component of the vector c in $\bar{C}$, $(c_{-i}, \delta(c_i))$ is the vector in $\bar{C}$ differing from c in that the i-component is changed from c_i to $\delta(c_i)$, (t_{-i}, r_i) is the vector in $\bar{T}$ with i-component equal to r_i and all other components as in t_{-i}, and $t = (t_{-i}, t_i)$.) Similarly, let

$$V_i(\mu | t_i) = \sum_{t_{-i} \in \bar{T}_{-1}} \sum_{c \in \bar{C}} p_i(t_{-i} | t_i) \, \mu(c | t) \, u_i(c, t).$$

Then a plan μ is *incentive compatible* iff, for every player i,

$$V_i(\mu \mid t_i) \geqslant \hat{V}_i(\mu, \delta, r_i \mid t_i), \qquad \forall t_i \in \bar{T}_i, \quad \forall r_i \in \bar{T}_i, \quad \forall \delta : \bar{C}_i \to \bar{C}_i. \quad (8.1)$$

The wide communication possibilities in this model cannot be subsumed in a model of the form considered in Sections 2 and 3, but they can be subsumed in the more general model considered in Section 4. To translate this model into the formulation of Section 4, when the negotiator is player 1, we equate the negotiator's set of types T and manipulative strategies D in Section 4 with the sets $\bar{T}_1$ and $\bar{C}_1^{\bar{C}_1}$ here, respectively. The set of possible negotiation statements (which is necessarily more general than the set of plans) for player 1 is

$$\Omega = \left\{ \mu \in \varDelta(\bar{C})^T \mid \exists \lambda \in [0, 1]^{\bar{T}_1} \text{ such that } \forall t \in \bar{T}, \sum_{c \in \bar{C}} \mu(c \mid t) = \lambda(t_1) \right\}.$$

(Here t_1 is the 1-component of $t = (t_i)_{i=1}^n$.) That is, a statement is any result of a star product between an allegation in $[0, 1]^{\bar{T}_1}$ and a plan in $\varDelta(\bar{C})^T$, where such a star product is defined by the formula

$$(\lambda * \mu)(c \mid t) = \lambda(t_1) \, \mu(c \mid t).$$

Notice that the formulas for V_i and $\hat{V}_i$ above can be applied to any statement μ in Ω. Thus, the negotiator's discounted-payoff functions V and $\hat{V}$ in Section 4 can be equated with the functions V_1 and $\hat{V}_1$ here, respectively. We may define the likelihood function L by the equations

$$L(\mu \mid t_1) = \sum_{c \in \bar{C}} \mu(c \mid t), \qquad \forall t_{-1} \in \bar{T}_{-1}.$$

Finally, the set of tenable statements G is the set of statements that satisfy the incentive constraints (8.1) for every player i other than player 1.

When we translate this principal's mechanism-design problem into the formulation of Section 4 in this way, then the set of coherent plans is exactly the set of *neutral optima* for the principal, as defined by in [16]. Similarly, the set of semicoherent plans coincides with the *principal's core* defined in [16]. To prove that the principal's neutral optima are coherent plans, notice that w is a strongly attractive reference allocation in this negotiation problem iff there are no nonnegative vectors λ and μ, other than the zero vectors, that solve the following system of constraints:

$$\sum_{c \in \bar{C}} \mu(c \mid t) = \lambda(t_1), \qquad \forall t \in \bar{T};$$

$$V_i(\mu \mid t_i) \geqslant \hat{V}_i(\mu, \delta_i, r_i \mid t_i), \qquad \forall i \neq 1, \quad \forall r_i \in \bar{T}_i, \quad \forall t_i \in \bar{T}_i, \quad \forall \delta_i : \bar{C}_i \to \bar{C}_i;$$

$$V_1(\mu \mid t_1) + (1 - \lambda(t_1)) \, w(t_1) \geqslant \hat{V}_1(\mu, \delta_1, r_1 \mid t_1) + (1 - \lambda(r_1)) \, w(t_1),$$

$$\forall r_1 \in \bar{T}_1, \quad \forall t_1 \in \bar{T}_1, \quad \forall \delta_1 : \bar{C}_1 \to \bar{C}_1;$$

$$V_1(\mu \mid t_1) + (1 - \lambda(t_1)) \, w(t_1) \geqslant w(t_1), \qquad \forall t_1 \in \bar{T}_1.$$

Using theorems of the alternative (see [20, section 22]), or the duality theorem of linear progamming, one can show that there are no nonzero solutions in the nonnegative orthants to these linear constraints iff there exist nonnegative vectors (l, a) such that, for every type t_1 in $\bar{T}_1$,

$$(l(t_1) + \sum_{r_1} \sum_{\delta_1} a(\delta_1, r_1 | t_1)) \, w(t_1) - \sum_{r_t} \sum_{\delta_1} a(\delta_1, t_1 | r_1) \, w(r_1)$$

$$> \sum_{t-1} v(t),$$

where, for every t in $\bar{T}$,

$$v(t) = \max_{c \in \bar{C}} l(t_1) \, p_1(t_{-1} | t_1) \, u_1(c, t)$$

$$+ \sum_{i=1}^{n} \sum_{\delta_i} \sum_{r_i} a_i(\delta_i, r_i | t_i) \, p_i(t_{-i} | t_i) \, u_i(c, t)$$

$$- \sum_{i=1}^{n} \sum_{\delta_i} \sum_{r_i} a_i(\delta_i, t_i | r_i) \, p_i(t_{-i} \lfloor r_i) \, u_i((c_{-i}, \delta_i(c_i)), (t_{-i}, r_i)).$$

These dual constraints, derived from the credibility conditions, are almost the same as the conditions in Theorem 7 of [16] that characterize the principal's neutral optima. Notice that, since all the inequalities constraining (l, a) are strict, we can always perturb l slightly to make its components strictly positive, instead of merely nonnegative. Then, by Lemma 1 of [16], for any incentive-compatible plan μ, a sequence of strongly attractive allocations can converge to an attractive reference allocation that supports μ as a coherent plan iff there exists a sequence of warranted claims that satisfy the conditions of Theorem 7 of [16] for the same plan μ.

9. Proofs

Proof of Lemma 1. Conditions (4.1), (4.4), and (4.6) follow easily from the definitions of L, V, and $\hat{V}$. (Notice that the V/L and $\hat{V}/L$ ratios in (4.4) are expected values of bounded payoffs in the finite range of $U(\cdot)$.) Conditions (4.2) and (4.3) follows straightforwardly from (2.2) and the way that $\hat{G}$ and G are derived from F. Compactness of G follows from upper-semicontinuity of F (2.3) and Caratheodory's theorem.

To show that (4.5) is satisfied, we use a fixed-point argument. Let λ be given as in (4.5). For any (γ, σ) in $\Delta(C)^T \times \Delta(S)$, define $K(\gamma, \sigma)$ so that $(\hat{\gamma}, \hat{\sigma}) \in K(\gamma, \sigma)$ iff $\hat{\sigma}$ is in the convex hull of $F(\lambda, \gamma)$, $\hat{\gamma} \in \Delta(C)^T$, and

$$\sum_{c \in C} \sum_{s \in S} \hat{\gamma}(c | t) \, \sigma(s) \, U(c, s, t) = \max_{c \in C} \sum_{s \in S} \sigma(s) \, U(c, s, t), \qquad \forall t \in T.$$

Using upper-semicontinuity of F, it is straightforward to show that K satisfies all the conditions of the Kakutani fixed-point theorem, so there exists some $(\bar{y}, \bar{\sigma})$ such that $(\bar{y}, \bar{\sigma}) \in K(\bar{y}, \bar{\sigma})$. Let $\mu = \lambda * \bar{y} * \bar{\sigma}$. Since $\bar{\sigma}$ is in the convex hull of $F(\lambda, \bar{y})$, μ is in G. Furthermore, $L(\mu \mid t) = \lambda(t)$ for every t, and

$$\sum_{c \in C} \sum_{s \in S} \mu(c, s \mid t) \, U(c, s, t)/\lambda(t)$$

$$= \sum_{c \in C} \sum_{s \in S} \bar{y}(c \mid t) \, \bar{\sigma}(s) \, U(c, s, t)$$

$$\geqslant \sum_{c \in C} \sum_{s \in S} \bar{y}(c \mid r) \, \bar{\sigma}(s) \, U(\delta(c), s, t) = \hat{V}(\mu, \delta, r \mid t)/\lambda(r)$$

for every t and r in T and every δ in D. Thus μ satisfies condition (4.5).

Q.E.D.

Proof of Theorem 1.   Let $\hat{w}$ be any strongly attractive reference allocation such that $|\hat{w}(t) - w(t)| < |V(\mu \mid t) - w(t)|$ for every t such that $V(\mu \mid t) \neq w(t)$. Let $\lambda(t) = 1$ if $V(\mu \mid t) \geqslant \hat{w}(t)$, and let $\lambda(t) = 0$ if $V(\mu \mid t) < \hat{w}(t)$. Condition (3.1) and the equations in (4.6) than imply that the statement $\lambda * \mu$ and the reference allocation $\hat{w}$ would satisfy conditions (5.5) and (5.6). Clearly $\lambda(\hat{t}) = 1$, so $\lambda * \mu$ is not null. If $\lambda * \mu$ were in G, then $\lambda * \mu$ would be credible with respect to the strongly attractive vector $\hat{w}$, which is impossible.

Q.E.D.

Given a negotiation problem as defined in Section 4, let M be a number such that

$$M \geqslant |V(\mu \mid t)/L(\mu \mid t)| \qquad \forall t \in T, \quad \forall \mu \in G \quad \text{such that} \quad L(\mu \mid t) > 0.$$

Such a bound M exists by condition (4.4).

LEMMA 2.   *Given any w in $\mathbb{R}^T$ and any $\hat{t}$ in T, if $w(\hat{t}) < -M$ then there exists some μ in G such that μ is credible with respect to w and $L(\mu \mid \hat{t}) = 1$.*

Proof of Lemma 2.   For any small positive number ε, define the correspondence $J_\varepsilon: [-M, M]^T \times [\varepsilon, 1]^T \twoheadrightarrow [-M, M]^T \times [\varepsilon, 1]^T$ so that $(z, m) \in J_\varepsilon(y, \lambda)$ iff

(1)   there exists some μ in G such that $L(\mu \mid r) = \lambda(r) \, \forall t \in T$, and $z(t) = V(\mu \mid t)/\lambda(t) \geqslant \hat{V}(\mu, \delta, r \mid t)/\lambda(r) \, \forall \delta \in D, \, \forall t \in T, \, \forall r \in T$,

and

(2) $m(t) = 1$ if $y(t) > w(t)$,

$\quad\quad m(t) = \varepsilon$ if $y(t) < w(t)$,

$\quad\quad m(t) \in [\varepsilon, 1]$ if $y(t) = w(t)$.

Condition (4.5) guarantees that $J_\varepsilon(y, \lambda)$ is a nonempty set. Condition (4.1) and the assumption that G is compact and convex guarantee that $J_\varepsilon(y, \lambda)$ is convex and that J_ε is upper-semicontinuous. Thus, by the Kakutani fixed-point theorem, there exists some $(y_\varepsilon, \lambda_\varepsilon)$ such that $(y_\varepsilon, \lambda_\varepsilon) \in J_\varepsilon(y_\varepsilon, \lambda_\varepsilon)$. Clearly, $\lambda_\varepsilon(\hat{t}) = 1$, since $y_\varepsilon(\hat{t}) \geqslant -M > w(t)$. Notice that $\lambda_\varepsilon(t) = \varepsilon$ if $y_\varepsilon(t) < w(t)$, and $\lambda_\varepsilon(t) = 1$ if $y_\varepsilon(t) > w(t)$. Let μ_ε be chosen to satisfy (1) when $z = y = y_\varepsilon$ and $m = \lambda = \lambda_\varepsilon$.

By compactness, we can assume that the sequences $\{y_\varepsilon\}$, $\{\lambda_\varepsilon\}$, and $\{\mu_\varepsilon\}$ are all convergent as ε goes to zero. We let $\bar{y}$, $\bar{\lambda}$, and $\bar{\mu}$ denote the limits of these sequences. Notice $\bar{\mu} \in G$, because G is compact. For any t in T, if $\bar{y}(t) < w(t)$ then $\bar{\lambda}(t) = 0$, and if $\bar{y}(t) > w(t)$ then $\bar{\lambda}(t) = 1$. Thus, for any t in T,

$$V(\bar{\mu} \mid t) + (1 - L(\bar{\mu} \mid t)) w(t) = (\bar{y}(t) - w(t)) \bar{\lambda}(t) + w(t)$$

$$= \max\{\bar{y}(t), w(t)\}.$$

Thus, (5.5) is satisfied by $\bar{\mu}$. Furthermore,

$$\bar{\lambda}(r) \bar{y}(t) = \bar{\lambda}(r) \lim_{\varepsilon \to 0} y_\varepsilon(t) \geqslant \bar{\lambda}(r) \lim_{\varepsilon \to 0} \hat{V}(\mu_\varepsilon, \delta, r \mid t) / \lambda_\varepsilon(r)$$

$$= \hat{V}(\bar{\mu}, \delta, r \mid t)$$

for any t, r, and δ. (Notice that, if $\bar{\lambda}(r) = L(\bar{\mu} \mid r) = 0$ then $\hat{V}(\bar{\mu}, \delta, r \mid t) = 0$, by continuity (4.1) and boundedness (4.4).) Thus,

$$\bar{V}(\bar{\mu} \mid t) + (1 - L(\bar{\mu} \mid t)) w(t) = \max\{\bar{y}(t), w(t)\}$$

$$\geqslant \bar{\lambda}(r) \bar{y}(t) + (1 - \bar{\lambda}(r)) w(t)$$

$$\geqslant \hat{V}(\bar{\mu}, \delta, r \mid t) + (1 - L(\bar{\mu} \mid t)) w(t),$$

so $\bar{\mu}$ satisfies (5.6). Finally, $L(\bar{\mu} \mid \hat{t}) = \bar{\lambda}(\hat{t}) = 1$, so $\bar{\mu}$ is not null. Thus, $\bar{\mu}$ is credible with respect to w.   Q.E.D.

Proof of Theorem 2. Notice first that, if a statement μ is credible with respect to w, then there exists a statement $\bar{\mu}$ that is credible with respect to w such that $\sum_{t \in T} L(\bar{\mu} \mid t) \geqslant 1$. To prove this, let

$$\bar{\mu} = (1/(\max\{L(\mu \mid t) \mid t \in T\})) \mu.$$

This $\bar{\mu}$ satisfies (5.5) and (5.6) by linearity. Condition (4.2) implies that $(1/(k \max\{L(\mu \mid t) \mid t \in T\})) \mu$ is in G, for some sufficiently large integer k, and then (4.3) implies that this $\bar{\mu}$ is in G.

Now, for any w in $[-(M+2), M+2]^T$, let $H_1(w) \subset \mathbb{R}^T$ be defined so that $y \in H_1(w)$ iff there exists some statement μ that is credible with respect to w such that $\sum_{r \in T} L(\mu \mid r) \geqslant 1$ and $y(t) = w(t) + L(\mu \mid t)$ for every t in T.

It is straightforward to check that $H_1(\cdot)$ is an upper-semicontinuous and convex-valued correspondence.

$H_1(w) = \emptyset$ iff w is strongly attractive. Let $H_2(w)$ be defined so that $H_2(w) = \{w - \mathbf{1}_T\}$ if w is strongly attractive, $H_2(w) = H_1(w)$ if w is not attractive, and $H_2(w)$ is the convex hull of $H_1(w)$ and $\{w - \mathbf{1}_T\}$ if w is attractive but not strongly attractive. It is straightforward to check that H_2 is nonempty-convex-valued and upper-semicontinuous. (Here, $\mathbf{1}_T$ is the vector in $\mathbb{R}^T$ in which all components are equal to one.)

For any w in $[-(M+2), M+2]^T$, $H_2(w) \subseteq [-(M+2), M+2]^T$. To verify this, notice first that, if $y \in H_2(w)$ then $|y(t) - w(t)| \leqslant 1$ for every t, so that $y(t)$ can fail to be in $[-(M+2), M+2]$ only when $|w(t)| \geqslant M+1$. If $w(t) > M$, then $L(\mu \mid t) = 0$ for any μ that is credible with respect to w (by (5.5) and the definition of the bound M), so that $y \in H_2(w)$ implies that $y(t) \leqslant w(t) \leqslant M + 2$. On the other hand, if $w(t) < -M$ for some t, then w is not attractive, by Lemma 2, and so $H_2(w) = H_1(w)$, and so $y \in H_2(w)$ implies that $y(t) \geqslant w(t) \geqslant -(M+2)$. Thus, $u \in H_2(w)$ implies that $y \in [-(M+2), M+2]^T$.

By the Kakutani fixed-point theorem, there exists some $\bar{w}$ in $[-(M+2), M+2]^T$ such that $\bar{w} \in H_2(\bar{w})$. Notice that $w \notin H_1(w)$ for every w in $[-(M+2), M+2]^T$, so $H_2(\bar{w}) \neq H_1(\bar{w})$, which implies that $\bar{w}$ is attractive. So $\bar{w}$ is a convex combination of the vector $\bar{w} - \mathbf{1}_T$ and a vector in $H_1(\bar{w})$. Therefore, by definition of H_1, there is some number α and some statement μ that is credible with respect to $\bar{w}$ and such that $L(\mu \mid t) = \alpha$ for every t in T. Let $\bar{\mu} = (1/\alpha)\mu$. Then $\bar{\mu} \in G$ (by conditions (4.2) and (4.3)), and $\bar{\mu}$ is credible with respect to $\bar{w}$. Furthermore, $L(\bar{\mu} \mid t) = 1$ for every t in T, so $\bar{\mu}$ is a coherent plan. Q.E.D.

References

1. R. AUMANN, Subjectivity and correlation in randomized strategies, *J. Math. Econ.* **1** (1974), 67–96.

2. J. BANKS AND J. SOBEL, Equilibrium selection in signalling games, *Econometrica* **55** (1987), 647–662.

3. I. CHO AND D. KREPS, Signalling games and stable equilibria, *Quart. J. Econ.* **102** (1987), 179–221.

4. V. CRAWFORD AND J. SOBEL, Strategic information transmission, *Econometrica* **50** (1982), 579–594.

5. J. FARRELL, "Meaning and Credibility in Cheap-Talk Games," to appear in *Mathematical Models in Economics*, (M. Dempster, Ed.) Oxford University Press.

6. S. GROSSMAN AND M. PERRY, Pzefect sequential equilibrium. *J. Econ. Theory* **39** (1986), 97–119.

7. E. KALAI AND D. SAMET, Persistent equilibria in strategic games, *Int. J. Game Theory* **13** (1984), 129–144.

8. E. KOHLBERG AND J.-F. MERTENS. On the strategic stability of equilibria, *Econometrica* **54** (1986), 1003–1037.

9. D. Kreps, "Signalling Games and Stable Equilibria," Stanford University working paper, 1984.

10. D. Kreps and R. Wilson, Sequential equilibria, *Econometrica* **50** (1982), 863–894.

11. P. Kumar, "Sequential Incentive Mechanism Design and the Incomplete Revelation Principle," Carnegie–Mellon University working paper, 1986.

12. R. Luce and H. Raiffa, "Games and Decisions," Wiley, New York, 1957.

13. A. McLennan, Justifiable beliefs in sequential equilibrium, *Econometrica* **53** (1985), 889–904.

14. H. Moulin and J.-P. Vial, Strategically zero-sum games: The class whose completely mixed equilibria cannot be improved upon, *Int. J. Game Theory* **7** (1978), 201–221.

15. R. Myerson, Optimal coordination mechanisms in generalized principal–agent problems, *J. Math. Econ.* **10** (1982), 67–81.

16. R. Myerson, Mechanism design by an informed principal, *Econometrica* **51** (1983), 1767–1797.

17. R. Myerson, Multistage games with communication, *Econometrica* **54** (1986), 323–358.

18. J. Nash, Noncooperative games, *Ann. of Math.* **54** (1951), 289–295.

19. M. Okuno–Fujiwara and A. Postlewaite, "Forward Induction and Equilibrium Refinement," University of Pennsylvania working paper, 1987.

20. R. Rockafellar, "Convex Analysis" Princeton Univ. Press, Princeton, NJ, 1970.

21. A. Rubinstein, Perfect equilibria in a bargaining model, *Econometrica* **50** (1982), 97–109.

22. A. Rubinstein, A bargaining model with incomplete information about time preferences, *Econometrica* **53** (1985), 1151–1172.

23. R. Selten, Re-examination of the perfectness concept for equilibrium points in extensive games, *Int. J. Game Theory* **4** (1975), 25–55.

JOURNAL OF ECONOMIC THEORY **48**, 304–332 (1989)

469-97

0261

0242

The Rate at Which a Simple Market Converges to Efficiency as the Number of Traders Increases: An Asymptotic Result for Optimal Trading Mechanisms*

Thomas A. Gresik

*John M. Olin School of Business, Washington University,
St. Louis, Missouri 63130*

AND

Mark A. Satterthwaite

*Kellogg Graduate School of Management, Northwestern University,
Evanston, Illinois 60208*

Received January 9, 1987; revised July 19, 1988

Private information in an independent, private-values market provides incentives to traders to manipulate equilibrium prices strategically. This strategic behavior precludes ex post efficient market performance. Increasing the number of traders improves the efficiency of some trading mechanisms by enabling them to better utilize the private information traders' bids and offers reveal. This paper shows that the expected inefficiency of optimally designed mechanisms, relative to ex post efficient allocations, decreases almost quadratically as the number of traders increases. *Journal of Economic Literature* Classification Numbers: 026, 022. © 1989 Academic Press, Inc.

1. Introduction

Private information prevents achievement of ex post efficiency within a small, private goods market. A trading mechanism's efficiency may improve as the number of traders increases because more traders may enable it to

* The participants of the Economic Theory Workshop at the University of Chicago helped this research materially by discovering a serious error in an early version of this work. We give special thanks to Larry Jones, Ken Judd, Ehud Kalai, Isaac Melijkson, Roger Myerson, and Roger Koenker for their help. This material is based upon work supported by the National Science Foundation under Grants SOC-7907542 and SES-8520247, the Center for Advanced Study in Managerial Economics and Decision Sciences at the Kellogg School, and the Health Care Financing Administration through a grant to Northwestern's Center for Health Services and Policy Research.

469

utilize more efficiently the private information traders' bids and offers reveal. This paper shows that within a simple market an optimally designed mechanism rapidly overcomes the constraints of private information as the market becomes large: the expected inefficiency of the mechanism's allocations relative to ex post efficient allocations is, at worst, $O((\ln \tau)/\tau^2)$ where τ is an index of the number of traders. This result provides a benchmark against which the rate other trading mechanisms converge to ex post efficiency can be compared.

That private information is responsible for small markets' inefficiency may be seen by considering an example. Let a single buyer and a single seller bargain over an indivisible object. Suppose the reservation value of the seller is $48, the reservation value of the buyer is $52, and these reservation values are common knowledge. Ex post efficiency requires that trade occurs because the object is more valuable to the buyer than to the seller.[1] Given the absence of private information, a mediator can be appointed who can use the common knowledge of the traders' reservation values to set a take-it-or-leave-it price of $50. The buyer and seller then agree to trade, and ex post efficiency is achieved.

If, however, each trader's reservation value is private to himself, then negotations on a satisfactory price may deadlock. If the buyer is confident that the seller's reservation value lies in the interval [25, 55], he may hold out for a price less than $50. If the seller is confident that the buyer's value is in the interval in [45, 75], he may hold out for a price greater than $50. Holding out is rational for each in terms of an expected utility calculation because not to hold out would allow the other trader to extract a disproportionate share of the expected gains from trade.

But if both hold out, no trade occurs and the outcome is ex post inefficient. Myerson and Satterthwaite [23] showed that, for bilateral trade in the presence of private information, this inefficiency is general: if trader participation is voluntary, no mechanism exists such that it always has an ex post efficient, Bayesian–Nash equilibrium. Thus incentives to engage in oppotunistic behavior are intrinsic to small markets whenever valuations are private.

In contrast to the small numbers case, this type of private information is not a problem within large markets. In the limit as a market becomes large each trader has no effect on the market clearing price. Therefore each trader reveals his true reservation value and an ex post efficient, competitive allocation results. These observations form the basis for economists' intuition that as a market grows in size the importance of private information as a source of inefficiency decreases.

---

[1] See Holmstrom and Myerson [17] for a definition and discussion of the three concepts: ex post efficiency, interim efficiency, and ex ante efficiency.

Our goal in this paper is to identify, as a function of the number of traders, an upper bound on the relative inefficiency in a market with private information. A reasonably precise statement of our result is this. The market we study consists of τN_0 sellers, each desiring to sell a single unit of traded good, and τM_0 buyers, each seeking to by a single unit of the good, where τ is an index of the market's size. Traders' preferences are fully described by their reservation values, which are independently drawn from the distribution F for buyers and the distribution H for sellers. Each trader's reservation value is private knowledge to him.[2]

For the moment, fix the value of τ. Construct a trading mechanism that is ex ante efficient in the sense that it

(a)   satisfies individual rationality and

(b)   maximizes the sum of buyers' and sellers' ex ante expected gains from trade.

Individual rationality means that the expected utility of a trader who knows his own reservation value but who does not yet know the reservation values of the other traders is nonnegative. Thus every trader, whatever his reservation value, wants to participate in the trading mechanism because participation offers him gain in expectation. The sum of the traders' ex ante expected utilities is the average gains from trade the mechanism would generate if

(a)   it were utilized repeatedly and

(b)   on each repetition every traders' reservation value were independently and freshly drawn from the distributions F and H.

For a given market size τ we define this optimal mechanism's relative inefficiency as follows. Compute the ex ante expected gains from trade that an ex post efficient mechanism would generate if it existed. While such mechanisms generally do not exist for the market we study, this measure is well defined and easily calculated. The optimal mechanism's relative efficiency is the ratio of its ex ante expected gains from trade to that of the ex post efficient mechanism. The optimal mechanism's relative inefficiency is then one minus its relative efficiency. Our main result is that, as τ becomes large, an upper bound on the optimal mechanism's relative inefficiency is $O((\ln \tau)/\tau^2)$.

Two caveats need emphasis. First, this is an optimal mechanism result. An optimal mechanism has the desirable property that it maximizes the sum of the traders' expected gains from trade. It has the undesirable property that the specific rules for trade vary as the distributions F and H

---

[2] This is the independent private values model that has been used in auction theory. See Milgrom and Weber [20].

vary. We do not observe trading institutions where rules vary in this manner; it is hard even to imagine such an institution. Trading rules that are invariant with respect to F and H are therefore unlikely to generate as great expected gains from trade as our optimal mechanism.[3] Nevertheless our conjecture is that realistic trading rules such as the sealed-bid double auction studied by Wilson [30, 31] may have relative inefficiencies of the same order as the optimal mechanism.[4]

The second caveat is that our results are derived in the context of a special model. Demand and supply are unitary, traders are risk neutral, and reservation values are independently distributed. It is hard to think of a market where this is a fully adequate abstraction of reality. For example, in many markets traders' reservation values are correlated with each other. This dependence enables each trader to infer information about the other traders' reservation values from his own reservation value. The extent to which our results hold when the specific assumptions of our model are relaxed is an open question.

This work is related to several sets of work in economic theory. First, and most directly related, is the work that Chatterjee and Samuelson [2], Myerson and Satterthwaite [23], Wilson [30, 31], Williams [29], Leininger *et al.* [19], and Satterthwaite and Williams [26] have done using the same basic model we use here. Chatterjee and Samuelson [2] showed with a bilateral example that one cannot expect ex post efficiency from the double auction. Myerson and Satterthwaite [23] showed that ex post efficiency is in general not achievable in bilateral trade if individual rationality is required. Williams [29] investigated ex ante efficient mechanisms where, instead of maximizing the expected gains from trade, the buyer and seller are assigned arbitrary welfare weights. Leininger *et al.* [19] and Satterthwaite and Williams [26] characterized the variety of equilibria that exist for the bilateral double auction. Wilson [31] studied double auctions with multiple buyers and sellers. He showed that if the number of traders is large enough and well-behaved equilibria exist, the double auction is interim efficient.

The second body of work to which this paper is related is auction theory. Auction theory is concerned with markets in which private information exists only on the buyer's side of the market, not on both sides as is the case in this paper. Our paper is most closely related to the normative work that Myerson [22] epitomizes. It is less closely related to the positive branch of auction theory such as Milgrom and Weber [20]. From the

---

[3] Satterthwaite and Wiliams [26] show that the bilateral sealed-bid double auction generically does not achieve ex ante efficiency.

[4] Satterthwaite and Williams [27] have recently shown this conjecture to be true for the buyers' bid double auction.

viewpoint of this work, auction theory is notable because it has been successful in relaxing the restrictive assumptions of private valuations and statistical independence. The presence of two-sided uncertainty creates technical difficulties that have prevented us from making a comparable relaxation of these assumptions.

The third body of work is general equilibrium theory. Roberts and Postlewaite [25] studied the noncooperative incentives that agents have to pursue strategic behavior within complete information exchange economies. They considered an exchange economy in which

(a)   agents report preferences,

(b)   a competitive equilibrium is computed based on the reported preferences, and

(c)   goods are allocated as prescribed by the computed equilibrium.

They show that as the economy becomes large each agent's incentive to misreport his preferences in order to manipulate the calculated price becomes vanishingly small. This formalizes the idea that for large, perfectly competitive economies strategic behavior is unimportant. It, however, is not comparable with our result for three reasons:

(i)   private information does not exist in their model,

(ii)   each agent's equilibrium misrepresentation is not calculated, and

(iii)   the rate at which the incentive to misrepresent vanishes is not calculated.

A number of authors including Hildenbrand [16], Debreu [5], and Dierker [6] have studied the rate at which core allocations within exchange economies converge to competitive allocations. Debreu, for example, showed that core allocations converge as the inverse of the number of agents. This can be interpreted as showing that the gains traders earn from engaging in strategic rather than price-taking behavior declines rapidly as the number of traders increase. Thus the spirit of these results is the same as in our results. The difference lies in the nature of the equilibrium concept used and the informational assumptions.

2. PRELIMINARIES

Model

There are $M = \tau M_0$ buyers each of whom seeks to buy a single unit of the traded good and $N = \tau N_0$ sellers each of whom seeks to sell the single, indivisible unit he owns of the traded good. Denote the total number of traders by $n = M + N$. Let x_i and z_j represent buyer i and seller j's reservation values, respectively. Buyers' reservation values are independently drawn from the distribution F, and sellers' reservation values are independently drawn from the distribution H. Both distributions have positive densities (f and h) on the bounded interval $[a, b]$. The realization of each trader's reservation value is private to that trader and unverifiable by anyone else. The initial numbers of buyers and sellers and the distribution functions of their reservation values constitute the essential data of the trading problem. Therefore we call the quadruplet $\langle M_0, N_0, F, H \rangle$ the trading problem.

A trading problem $\langle M_0, N_0, F, H \rangle$ is *regular* if

(i) F and H have continuous and bounded first and second derivatives on (a, b) and

(ii) the functions $x_i + (F(x_i) - 1)/f(x_i)$ and $z_j + H(z_j)/h(z_j)$ are both nondecreasing over the interval (a, b).

The purpose of these regularity assumptions is to restrict the set of admissible trading problems sufficiently to permit us to construct ex ante efficient mechanisms.

Before proceeding we need additional notation. Let $x = (x_1, ..., x_M)$, $z = (z_1, ..., z_N)$, $x_{-i} = (x_1, ..., x_{i-1}, x_{i+1}, ..., x_M)$, and $z_{-j} = (z_1, ..., z_{j-1}, z_{j+1}, ..., z_N)$. The density $g(x, z) = \prod_{i=1}^{M} f(x_i) \cdot \prod_{j=1}^{N} h(z_j)$ describes the joint density of all the reservation values, the density $g(x_{-i}, z) = g(x, z)/f(x_i)$ describes the density of reservation values buyer i perceives himself as facing, and the density $g(x, z_{-j}) = g(x, z)/h(z_j)$ describes the density of reservation values seller j perceives himself as facing.

For a particular trading problem $\langle M_0, N_0, F, H \rangle$, fix τ so that size of the market is $n = \tau(M_0 + N_0)$ traders. A trading mechanism consists of n probability schedules and n payment schedules that determine the final distribution of money and goods given the declared valuations of the traders. Let the probabilities of an object being assigned to buyer i and seller j in the final distribution of goods be $p_i^\tau(\hat{x}, \hat{z})$ and $q_j^\tau(\hat{x}, \hat{z})$, respectively, where $\hat{x}$ and $\hat{z}$ are the vectors of buyers and sellers' declared valuations. The declared valuation a trader reports need not be his true reservation value. Let the payments made to buyer i and seller j be $r_i^\tau(\hat{x}, \hat{z})$ and $s_j^\tau(\hat{x}, \hat{z})$, respectively. A negative value for r_i^τ indicates that buyer i plays $|r_i^\tau|$ units of money for the right to receive one unit of the traded object with probability p_i^τ. The r_i^τ and s_j^τ payments are not necessarily conditional on whether buyer i actually receives an object or seller j actually gives up his object.[5]

---

[5] We would like to regard the payments r_i and s_j to be certainty equivalents of payments that are made only when an individual is involved in a trade. Such a no-regret property seems desirable, but we have not identified the conditions under which it can be imposed.

We assume that the market size τ, the joint density of reservation values g, the probability schedules p and q, and the payment schedules r and s are common knowledge along all traders. The trading process is initiated when all players simultaneously declare reservation values in the interval $[a, b]$. Given these bids and offers, the N objects and money are reallocated as the trading mechanism (p, q, r, s) mandates.

Each trader has a von Neumann–Morgenstern utility function that is additively separable and linear both in money and in the reservation value of the traded object. Thus buyer i's expected utility, given that his true reservation value is x_i and the vectors of declared reservation values are $\hat{x}$ and $\hat{z}$, is

$$\bar{U}_i(x_i, \hat{x}, \hat{z}) = r_i^\tau(\hat{x}, \hat{z}) + x_i p_i^\tau(\hat{x}, \hat{z}). \tag{2.01}$$

Similarly, seller j's expected utility is

$$\bar{V}_j(z_j, \hat{x}, \hat{z}) = s_j^\tau(\hat{x}, \hat{z}) - z_j(1 - q_j^\tau(\hat{x}, \hat{z})). \tag{2.02}$$

Each trader's expected utility function is normalized so that if $(\hat{x}, \hat{z})$ are such that he is certain to neither trade an object nor make or receive a cash payment, then his expected utility is zero.

We constrain the trading mechanism in three ways to conform with our notions of voluntary trade among a set of independent buyers and sellers. First, in the final distribution of goods and money, the N objects are each assigned to a trader. Thus, necessarily, there is balance of goods in expectation:

$$\sum_{i=1}^{M} p_i^\tau(\hat{x}, \hat{z}) + \sum_{j=1}^{N} q_j^\tau(\hat{x}, \hat{z}) = N \tag{2.03}$$

for all $(\hat{x}, \hat{z})$. An allocation schedule achieves balance of goods in fact by making its assignment of objects correlated across traders.[6] Second, payments are constrained to offset receipts:

$$\sum_{i=1}^{M} r_i^\tau(\hat{x}, \hat{z}) + \sum_{j=1}^{N} s_j^\tau(\hat{x}, \hat{z}) = 0 \tag{2.04}$$

[6] Specifically for a given set of declared valuations, buyer 1 can be assigned an object with probability p_1 through an independent draw of a random number in the $[0, 1]$ interval. Buyer 2 can next be assigned an object with probability p_2 through a second independent draw, etc. This process of assigning objects through independent draws first to the M buyers and then to the N sellers can be continued until either (a) all N objects have been assigned or (b) K objects remain and exactly K buyers and sellers remain to have an object assigned to them. If eventually (a) occurs, then the remaining buyers and sellers should be excluded from receiving an object. If eventually (b) occurs, then the K remaining buyers and sellers should each receive an object. This rule guarantees that exactly N objects are distributed. The dependence that this rule induces between the probability of buyer 1 being assigned an object and seller N not being assigned an object has no effect on our results.

for all $(\hat{x}, \hat{z})$. The reason for this latter constraint is that trading connotes individuals freely cooperating with one another without subsidy or tax from a third party. Third, the mechanism must be individually rational.

In addition to these three constraints we also impose a fourth constraint on the mechanism: incentive compatibility. An incentive compatible mechanism never gives any trader an incentive to declare a reservation value different than his true reservation value, i.e., declaration of true values is a Bayesian–Nash equilibrium if the mechanism is incentive compatible.[7] Imposition of it is costless because the revelation principle states that for every mechanism an equivalent incentive compatible mechanism exists.[8] Therefore, even though we do not consider all conceivable mechanisms, we know that none of the mechanisms we overlook ex ante dominate the mechanisms we do consider.

Formalization of the individual rationality and incentive compatibility constraints requires additional notation and definitions. Let

$$\bar{p}_i^\tau(x_i) = \int \cdots \int p_i^\tau(x, z) g(x_{-i}, z) \, dx_{-i} \, dz, \tag{2.05}$$

and

$$\bar{r}_i^\tau(x_i) = \int \cdots \int r_i^\tau(x, z) g(x_{-i}, z) \, dx_{-i} \, dz. \tag{2.06}$$

Conditional on buyer i's reservation value being x_i, the quantities $\bar{p}_i^\tau(x_i)$ and $\bar{r}_i^\tau(x_i)$ are, respectively, his expected probability of receiving an object and his expected money receipts. The probabilities $\bar{q}_j^\tau$ and $\bar{s}_j^\tau$ have parallel definitions for seller j. The expected utilities of buyer i and seller j conditional on their reservation values are

$$U_i(x_i) = \bar{r}_i^\tau(x_i) + x_i \bar{p}_i^\tau(x_i) \tag{2.07}$$

and

$$V_j(z_j) = \bar{s}_j^\tau(z_j) - z_j(1 - \bar{q}_j^\tau(z_j)). \tag{2.08}$$

Individual rationality requires that, for all buyers i and all sellers j, $U_i(x_i) \geqslant 0$ for every $x_i \in [a, b]$ and $V_j(z_j) \geqslant 0$ for every $z_j \in [a, b]$. Incentive compatibility requires that, for every buyer i and all x_i and $\hat{x}_i$ in $[a, b]$,

$$U_i(x_i) \geqslant \bar{r}_i^\tau(\hat{x}_i) + x_i \bar{p}_i^\tau(\hat{x}_i) \tag{2.09}$$

---

[7] Harsanyi [15] introduced these concepts of Bayesian equilibrium.

[8] The revelation principle has its origins in Gibbard's paper [7] on straightforward mechanisms and was developed by Myerson [21, 22], Harris and Townsend [14], and Harris and Raviv [13].

and, for every seller j and all z and $\hat{z}$ in $[a, b]$,

$$V_j(z_j) \geq \bar{s}_j^\tau(\hat{z}_j) - z_j(1 - \bar{q}_j^\tau(\hat{z}_j)). \tag{2.10}$$

If (2.09) is violated for some x_i and $\hat{x}_i$, then buyer i has an incentive to declare $\hat{x}_i$ rather than his or her true reservation value, x_i. From this point forward we only consider incentive compatible mechanisms and we assume that traders always reveal their true reservation values.

Characterization of Incentive Feasible Mechanisms

A mechanism is called incentive feasible if it is both individually rational and incentive compatible. Theorem 1 characterizes all incentive feasible mechanisms. It exactly generalizes Myerson and Satterthwaite's [23] Theorem 1 from the bilateral case to the general case of multiple buyers and sellers.

THEOREM 1. *Consider a given replication τ of a trading problem $\langle M_0, N_0, F, H \rangle$. Let $p^\tau(\cdot, \cdot)$ and $q^\tau(\cdot, \cdot)$ be the buyers and sellers, probability schedules, respectively. Functions $r^\tau(\cdot, \cdot)$ and $s^\tau(\cdot, \cdot)$ exist such that $(p^\tau, q^\tau, r^\tau, s^\tau)$ is an incentive feasible mechanism if and only if $\bar{p}_i^\tau(\cdot)$ is a nondecreasing function for all buyers i, $\bar{q}_j^\tau(\cdot)$ is a nondecreasing function for all sellers j, and*

$$\sum_{i=1}^{M} \int \cdots \int \left(x_i + \frac{F(x_i) - 1}{f(x_i)} \right) p_i^\tau(x, z) \, g(x, z) \, dx \, dz$$

$$- \sum_{j=1}^{N} \int \cdots \int \left(z_j + \frac{H(z_j)}{h(z_j)} \right) [1 - q_j^\tau(x, s)] \, g(x, z) \, dx \, dz \geq 0. \tag{2.11}$$

Furthermore, given any incentive feasible mechanism, for all i and j, $U_i(\cdot)$ is nondecreasing, $V_j(\cdot)$ nonincreasing, and

$$\sum_{i=1}^{M} U_i(a_i) + \sum_{j=1}^{N} V_j(d_j)$$

$$= \sum_{i=1}^{M} \min_{x \in [a,b]} U_i(x) + \sum_{j=1}^{N} \min_{z \in [a,b]} V_j(z)$$

$$= \sum_{i=1}^{M} \int \cdots \int \left(x_i + \frac{F(x_i) - 1}{f(x_i)} \right) p_i^\tau(x, z) \, g(x, z) \, dx \, dz$$

$$- \sum_{j=1}^{N} \int \cdots \int \left(z_j + \frac{H(z_j)}{h(z_j)} \right) [1 - q_j^\tau(x, z)] \, g(x, z) \, dx \, dz. \tag{2.12}$$

This theorem is the key to constructing ex ante optimal mechanisms because it establishes that if the probability schedules (p^τ, q^τ) satisfy the relatively simple constraint (2.11), then payment schedules (r^τ, s^τ) exist such that the mechanism $(p^\tau, q^\tau, r^\tau, s^\tau)$ is an incentive feasible trading mechanism.[9]

Ex Ante Efficiency

A trader's ex ante expected utility from participating in trade is his expected utility evaluated before he learns his reservation value for the object. Thus $\tilde{U}_i = \int U_i(t) f(t) \, dt$ and $\tilde{V}_j = \int V_j(t) h(t) \, dt$ are buyer i and seller j's ex ante expected utilities, respectively. A trading mechanism is ex ante efficient if not trader's ex ante expected utility can be increased without either

(a) decreasing some other trader's ex ante expected utility or

(b) violating incentive feasibility.

We focus on a particular ex ante efficient mechanism: the one that places equal welfare weights on every trader and maximizes the sum of the traders' ex ante expected utilities. This maximiation is equivalent to maximizing the sum of all traders' expected gains from trade because each trader's utility function is separable in money and the object's reservation value. In contrast, ex post optimality requires that the mechanism, irrespective of incentive feasibility, exhausts the potential gains from trade by assigning the N objects to the N traders who have the highest reservation values.

Virtual Reservation Values and α-Schedules

Virtual reservation values play a crucial role in construction of ex ante efficient mechanisms.[10] Buyer i's virtual reservation value is

$$\psi^B(x_i, \alpha) = x_i + \alpha \cdot \left(\frac{F(x_i) - 1}{f(x_i)} \right), \tag{2.13}$$

and seller j's virtual reservation value is

$$\psi^S(z_j, \alpha) = z_j + \alpha \cdot \frac{H(z_j)}{h(z_j)} \tag{2.14}$$

where α is a nonnegative, scalar parameter. Let the vector of virtual reservation values be $\psi(x, z, \alpha) = [\psi^B(x_1, \alpha), ..., \psi^S(z_N, \alpha)]$.

---

[9] The assumption that trader's utility functions are linear in money is important in this simplification. Maximization of the expected gains from trade is dependent only on the final allocation of goods, not on the payments among the traders.

[10] Myerson [24] introduced the concept of virtual utility, A virtual reservation value is a special case of a virtual utility.

Define $R_i^B(x, z, \alpha)$ to be the rank of the element $\psi^B(x_i, \alpha)$ within ψ and define $R_j^S(x, z, \alpha)$ to be the rank of the element $\psi^S(z_j, \alpha)$ within ψ. For example, if $M = N = 1$ and $\psi = (0.4, 0.2)$, then $R_{i=1}^B = 2$ and $R_{j=1}^S = 1$.[11] Given this notation, a trading problem $\langle M_0, N_0, F, H \rangle$, and a value τ, we define a class of buyer and seller probability schedules that are parameterized by α:

$$p_i^{\tau\alpha}(x, z) = \begin{cases} 1 & \text{if} \quad R_i^B(x, z, \alpha) > M, \\ 0 & \text{if} \quad R_i^B(x, z, \alpha) \leqslant M, \end{cases} \quad i = 1, ..., M; \quad (2.15)$$

$$q_j^{\tau\alpha}(x, z) = \begin{cases} 1 & \text{if} \quad R_j^S(x, z, \alpha) > M, \\ 0 & \text{if} \quad R_j^S(x, z, \alpha) \leqslant M, \end{cases} \quad j = 1, ..., N. \quad (2.16)$$

Let $p^{\tau\alpha} = (p_1^{\tau\alpha}, ..., p_M^{\tau\alpha})$ and $q^{\tau\alpha} = (q_1^{\tau\alpha}, ..., q_N^{\tau\alpha})$. This pair of probability schedules, which we call an α-schedule, assigns the N available objects to those N traders for whom the objects have the highest virtual reservation values.

Before proceeding further we should discuss virtual reservation values and α-schedules. If $\alpha = 0$, then $\psi^B(x_i, 0) = x_i$ and $\psi^S(z_j, 0) = z_j$. The virtual reservation values equal the true reservation values and the N objects are assigned to the N traders who have the highest reservation values. If, however, $\alpha > 0$, then $\psi_i(x_i, \alpha) < x_i$ and $\psi_j(z_j, \alpha) > z_j$ almost everywhere. Thus, for $\alpha > 0$, buyers' virtual reservation values are distorted downward to be below their true reservation values and sellers' virtual reservation values are distorted upward to be above their true reservation values. Intuitively these distortions express the strategic behavior that traders exhibit under a mechanism such as the double auction that is not incentive compatible. In this case the possibility exists that the objects will not be assigned to the N traders whose reservation values are highest. Specifically, if $\alpha > 0$, then pairs of reservation values (x_i, z_j) exist such that $x_i > z_j$ and $\psi^B(x_i, \alpha) < \psi^S(z_j, \alpha)$. Trade fails to occur in such a case even though it should because the buyer values the object more than the seller. For this reason an α-schedule does not necessarily achieve ex post optimality whenever $\alpha > 0$.

---

[11] If several elements of ψ have the same value so that it is ambiguous which buyers and sellers should be classified as having virtual reservation prices as ranking within the top N, then the probability schedules should randomize among the several candidates so as to guarantee that exactly N traders are assigned an object. Thus if seller 2 and buyer 3 are tied for rank M, then each should be given a nonindependent probability of 0.5 for receiving an object in the final allocation.

3. RESULTS

Ex Ante Efficient Mechanisms and α*-Schedules

Fix the value of the parameter $\alpha \geq 0$ and consider the α-schedule $(p^{\tau\alpha}, q^{\tau\alpha})$. Theorem 1 states necessary and sufficient conditions for payment schedules (r, s) to exist such that the trading mechanism $(p^{\tau\alpha}, q^{\tau\alpha}, r, s)$ is incentive feasible. Central to the theorem's requirements is inequality (2.11), the incentive feasibility (IF) constraint. For the case of an α-schedule, substitution of (2.13) and (2.14) into (2.11) yields the requirement

$$
G(\alpha, \tau) = \int \cdots \int \left\{ \sum_{i=1}^{M} \psi^{B}(x_i, 1) \, p_i^{\tau\alpha}(x, z) \right.
$$

$$
\left. - \sum_{j=1}^{N} \psi^{S}(z_j, 1)[1 - q_j^{\tau\alpha}(x, z)] \right\} g(x, z) \, dx \, dz
$$

$$
\geq 0. \tag{3.01}
$$

This function $G(\alpha, \tau)$ plays a central role in the theorems that follow.

Let $\alpha^* = \min\{\alpha \in [0, 1) | G(\alpha, \tau) \geq 0\}$. An α-schedule $(p^{\tau\alpha}, q^{\tau\alpha})$ is an α^*-schedule if and only if $\alpha = \alpha^*$ and $\bar{p}_i^{\tau\alpha^*}(\cdot)$ and $\bar{q}_j^{\tau\alpha^*}(\cdot)$ are nondecreasing over $[a, b]$ for all buyers i and all sellers j. By definition, an α^*-schedule satisfies Theorem 1's requirements. Therefore payment schedules $(r^{\tau\alpha^*}, s^{\tau\alpha^*})$ exist such that the mechanism $(p^{\tau\alpha^*}, q^{\tau\alpha^*}, r^{\tau\alpha^*}, s^{\tau\alpha^*})$ is incentive feasible. We call this mechanism the α^*-mechanism for the trading problem $\langle M_0, N_0, F, H \rangle$ with a market size τ.

Theorem 2 states sufficient conditions for the α^*-mechanism—if it exists—to be an ex ante efficient mechanism. Theorem 3 states sufficient conditions for the α^*-mechanism to exist and be ex ante efficient for a trading problem with a given market size.

THEOREM 2. *Suppose an α^*-mechanism exists for market size τ of the trading problem $\langle M_0, N_0, F, H \rangle$. The α^*-trading mechanism $(p^{\tau\alpha^*}, q^{\tau\alpha^*}, r^{\tau\alpha^*}, s^{\tau\alpha^*})$ is ex ante efficient and has positive expected gains from trade.*

THEOREM 3. *If $\langle M_0, N_0, F, H \rangle$ is a regular trading problem, then, for every market size τ, the α^*-mechanism exists, is incentive feasible and ex ante efficient, and has positive expected gains from trade.*

Convergence to Ex Post Optimality

Before we determine the rate a which the ex ante optimal mechanism converges to ex post optimality, we need to show that it converges as

$\tau \to \infty$. Theorem 4 establishes this convergence both as it approaches the limit and in the limit. In order to understand the theorem, recall two facts. First, the closer the parameter α is to zero, the less virtual reservation values are distorted from true reservation values and the closer the α-schedule comes to achieving ex post optimal assignment of the objects. Second, for a given value of α and a given market size τ, if $G(\alpha, \tau) \geqslant 0$, then payment schedules (r, s) exist such that $(p^{\alpha\tau}, q^{\alpha\tau}, r, s)$ is incentive feasible.

THEOREM 4. *Pick an $\alpha \in (0, 1)$. If the trading problem $\langle M_0, N_0, F, H \rangle$ is regular, then a $\tau' > 0$ exists such that, for all market sizes $\tau > \tau'$, $G(\alpha, \tau) \geqslant 0$. Moreover $\lim_{\tau \to \infty} G(0, \tau) = 0$.*

The content of the theorem is that, no matter how close to zero we set α, if the market becomes large enough, then that α-schedule and its associated payment schedule is incentive feasible.

Rate of Convergence

We present two results. The first is an upper bound on the size of the parameter α^* as a function of τ. The magnitude of α^* as a function of τ is a measure of the mechanism's distance from ex post optimality.

THEOREM 5. *Consider a regular trading problem $\langle M_0, N_0, F, H \rangle$. The parameter α^* of the ex ante efficient α^*-mechanism is at most $O((\ln \tau)^{1/2}/\tau)$ for large τ.*

The second result, which is our main result, states an upper bound on the expected proportion of the gains from trade that the optimal mechanism fails to realize. Let $T^*(\tau)$ represent the expected gains from trade that the ex ante efficient α^*-mechanism realizes for the trading problem $\langle M_0, N_0, F, H \rangle$ with market size τ and let $T^0(\tau)$ represents the expected gains from trade that an ex post efficient mechanism (if one existed) would realize for the same trading problem and market size. Let $W(\tau) = 1 - [T^*(\tau)/T^0(\tau)]$ be a measure of the market's relative inefficiency.

THEOREM 6. *Consider a regular trading problem $\langle M_0, N_0, F, H \rangle$. For the ex ante efficient, α^*-mechanism, $W(\tau)$ is at most $O(\ln \tau/\tau^2)$, i.e., for large τ, a K exists such that*

$$W(\tau) = 1 - \frac{T^*(\tau)}{T^0(\tau)} \leqslant K \frac{\ln \tau}{\tau^2}. \tag{3.02}$$

Two comments about Theorem 6 are in order. First, the order of W as a function of τ indicates the mechanism's rate of convergence toward ex post optimality and is independent of the choice of the underlying distributions F and H. For a given value of τ, however, the absolute size of W is a function of F and H. Second, we conjecture that the bounds stated in Theorem 5 and 6 are not tight. Specifically, the example in the next section suggests that the true bounds are $O(1/\tau)$ for Theorem 5 and $O(1/\tau^2)$ for Theorem 6.

4. AN EXAMPLE

In this section we numerically calculate for varying market sizes τ the ex ante efficient α^*-trading mechanisms when $M_0 = N_0 = 1$ and traders' reservation values are uniformly distributed on the unit interval. This distributional assumption guarantees that the trading problem is regular as Theorem 3 requires. Therefore an α^*-mechanism exists for all market sizes τ.

The key step in constructing an efficient mechanism for a given number of traders is to calculate α^* as the solution of $G(\alpha, \tau) = 0$. Given that traders' reservation values are uniformly distributed over $[0, 1]$, $\psi^B(x_i, \alpha) = (1 + \alpha) x_i - \alpha$ and $\psi^S(z_j, \alpha) = (1 + \alpha) z_j$. Since $N_0 = M_0 = 1$, $G(\alpha, \tau) = 0$ reduces to

$$
G(\alpha, \tau) = \tau \left\{ \int_0^1 \psi^B(x, 1) \, \bar{p}^{\tau\alpha}(x) \, f(x) \, dx \right.
$$

$$
\left. - \int_0^1 \psi^S(z, 1)[1 - \bar{q}^{\tau\alpha}(z)] \, h(z) \, dz \right\}
$$

$$
= \tau \left\{ \int_0^1 (2x - 1) \, \bar{p}^{\tau\alpha}(x) \, dx - \int_0^1 2z(1 - \bar{q}^{\tau\alpha}(z)) \, dz \right\} = 0, \quad (4.01)
$$

where all i and j subscripts have been suppressed because all traders are symmetric with each other. It may be rewritten as

$$
\int_0^1 \left\{ [2x - 1] \, \bar{p}^{\tau\alpha}(x) - 2x[1 - \bar{q}^{\tau\alpha}(x)] \right\} \, dx = 0. \quad (4.02)
$$

Calculation of the marginal probabilities $\bar{p}^{\tau\alpha}(x)$ and $\bar{q}^{\tau\alpha}(z)$ is messy, but straightforward.[12]

Table I presents the results. The values of α^* have the following interpretation. If buyer i with reservation value x_i and seller j with reservation value z_j are each the marginal trader on his side of the market, then

---

[12] Details are in Gresik and Satterthwaite [9].

TABLE I

Properties of the α^*-Mechanisms as the Number Traders Increases

τ	α^*	$\alpha^*/(1+\alpha^*)$	$1/\alpha^*$	$T^*(\tau)$	$T^0(\tau)$	$W(\tau)$
1	0.3333	0.2500	3.00	0.14060	0.16667	0.1564
2	0.2256	0.1841	4.43	0.37746	0.39999	0.0563
3	0.1603	0.1382	6.24	0.62572	0.64286	0.0267
4	0.1225	0.1091	8.17	0.87527	0.88887	0.0153
6	0.0827	0.0764	12.09	1.37507	1.38462	0.0069
8	0.0622	0.0586	16.08	1.87504	1.88235	0.0039
10	0.0499	0.0475	20.04	2.37501	2.38095	0.0025
12	0.0416	0.0399	24.04	2.87501	2.88000	0.0017

necessarily i's virtual reservation value is greater than j's virtual reservation value, i.e., $\psi^B(x_i, \alpha^*) > \psi^S(z_j, \alpha^*)$. Substitution of explicit forms for ψ^B and ψ^S into this inequality followed by some algebraic manipulation shows that necessarily

$$x_i - z_j > \frac{\alpha^*}{1+\alpha^*}. \tag{4.03}$$

This required, positive difference in reservation values is the wedge that privacy of traders' reservation values creates within finite-sized markets. Its presence makes achievement of ex post efficiency impossible. Note that as α^* becomes small, the size of this wedge becomes essentially equal to the value of α^* itself. The fourth column displays $1/\alpha^*$ and shows that α^* is apparently bounded from below by $1/2\tau$. The last column shows for that $W(\tau)$, the relative inefficiency of this market, vanishes as $(1/\tau^2)$ for larger τ. Finally, note that by the time the market reaches 12 traders ($\tau = 6$) its relative inefficiency is down to the negligible level of less than 1%.

5. COMPARISON WITH A FIXED-PRICE MECHANISM

Theorem 6 serves as a benchmark for evaluating how well other mechanisms elicit and use private information as the market becomes large. Here we make this comparison for the fixed-price mechanism.[13] It works as follows. Price is fixed at the competitive price c that would obtain if our simple market had a continuum of buyers with reservation value dis-

---

[13] William Rogerson suggested to us that the fixed-price mechanism is an interesting alternative to the double auction. See Hagerty and Rogerson [11] for a discussion of its properties in the bilateral case.

TABLE II

Comparative Inefficiences of the Fixed Price
Mechanism (W') and the Optimal Mechanism (W)

τ	$W'(\tau)$	$W(\tau)$
1	0.2500	0.1564
2	0.2187	0.0563
3	0.1979	0.0267
4	0.1826	0.0153
6	0.1611	0.0069
8	0.1462	0.0039
10	0.1350	0.0025
12	0.1262	0.0017

tributed on F and a continuum of sellers with reservation values distributed on H. All buyers whose reservation values are greater than c indicate that they want to buy one unit and all sellers whose reservation values are less than c indicate that they want to sell one unit. The strategy of reporting honestly the desire to trade or not to trade is a dominant strategy for each trader because price is fixed. If the market does not clear, which is almost always the case, then rationing is done by random selection from among the traders on whichever side of the market is long.

The problem with random exclusion is that a buyer i whose gains from trade, $x_i - c$, are large is just as likely to be excluded as a buyer k whose gains from trade, $x_k - c$, are small. Therefore, as τ becomes large, the average loss per excluded trader remains a constant. This is unlike the optimal mechanism where, as τ becomes large, the average loss per unrealized trade declines rapidly because of the optimal mechanism's ability to use the private information it elicits.

Asymptotically for the fixed-price mechanism, the number of traders who wish to trade but who are excluded is $O(\tau^{1/2})$.[14] This is also the order of the gains from trade that the mechanism fails to realize. The number of traders who wish to trade at this fixed price c is $O(\tau)$. Therefore the gains from trade that a hypothetical ex post efficient mechanism would be expected to realize are $O(\tau)$. Dividing the order of the expected inefficiency by the order of the total gains available gives the result $W'(\tau) = O(1/\tau^{1/2})$ for the fixed-price mechanism, which contrasts starkly with $W(\tau) = O\{(\ln \tau)/\tau^2\}$ for the optimal trading mechanism. Further contrasting the

---

[14] This follows from the fact that the number of buyers who wish to trade at the fixed price c is a binomial variable that can be approximated asymptotically by a normal distribution with standard deviation $O(\tau^{1/2})$. This calculation is a special case of Bhattacharya and Majumdar's [1] Theorem 3.1.

performance of these two mechanisms is the fact that the magnitude of the inefficiency starts out larger for the fixed-price mechanism than for the α^*-mechanism. Table II, which shows $W(\tau)$ and $W'(\tau)$ for $M_0 = N_0 = 1$ and uniformly distributed reservation values, illustrates both these points. In fact, for the small values of τ shown on the table, $W'(\tau)$ converges to ex post efficiency at a rate noticeably slower than $O(1/\tau^{1/2})$. Both of these comparisons emphasize the benefit of eliciting valuation information from traders and—within the limits of incentive compatibility—using it to assign the objects appropriately.

6. FURTHER QUESTIONS

Our results are only a starting for understanding how fast market mechanisms converge to perfect competition in the presence of private information. Four of the more important questions that need attention are as follows. First, are asymptotic results useful when studying trading problems? While the numerical results of Section 4 are supportive of the idea that even for small numbers the asymptotic rate is a good approximation, we cannot conclude without further investigation that it is an equally good, small number approximation for prior distributions other than the uniform. Second, if traders are risk averse, does the $O((\ln \tau)/\tau^2)$ result continue hold? A recent paper of Ledyard [18] emphasizes the importance of this question. He shows, within the context of a somewhat different model, how careful selection of utility functions for a fixed set of agents can lead to almost any desired equlibrium behavior.[15]

Third, if agents' reservation values are not independent of each other, but rather are correlated, then does our convergence result hold? Milgrom and Weber [20] have shown in their studies of auctions that such distinctions are important. Gresik [8] employs a discrete distribution model of bilateral trade to show that the introduction of affiliated valuations can result in the existence of ex post efficient trading mechanisms. Whether these results carry over to models with continuous distributions is an open question. Fourth, is our focus on optimal mechanisms constructed using the revelation principle appropriate? In practice direct revelation mechanisms are seldom used to allocate goods. The reason is that a direct revelation mechanism's allocation and payment rules must be changed each time the traders' prior distributions concerning other traders' reservation values change. This cannot be done practically because traders' priors are unobservable. Consequently, the rules of a real trading mechanism are kept

---

[15] Ledyard's argument as it stands not address the focus of this paper: how does a Bayesian equilibrium converge toward the competitive allocation as the initial set of traders is replicated repeatedly.

constant and not changed each time traders' expectations about each others' reservation values change. This makes the result of Wilson [31] concerning the interim efficiency properties of the double-auction mechanism desirable.

7. PROOFS

Preliminaries

Detailed proofs of Theorems 1, 2, and 3 are contained in Gresik and Satterthwaite [9] and in less detailed form in Gresik and Satterthwaite [10] and Wilson [30]. The techniques of the proofs are a straightforward generalizations of Myerson and Satterthwaite's [23] treatment of the bilateral case.

Proofs of Theorems 4, 5, and 6 require a detailed understanding of the asymptotic behavior of the marginal distributions $\bar{p}^{\tau\alpha}$ and $\bar{q}^{\tau\alpha}$. We defined $\bar{p}^{\tau\alpha}(x_i)$ to be the marginal probability that a buyer i with reservation value x_i receives an object.[16] Its interpretation in terms of a simple random trial is this. Fix α. Draw independently $M - 1 = \tau M_0 - 1$ buyers' reservation values from F and $N = \tau N_0$ sellers' reservation values from H. Transform these reservation values into virtual reservation values using $\psi^B(\cdot, \alpha)$ and $\psi^S(\cdot, \alpha)$, respectively. The probability $\bar{p}^{\tau\alpha}(x_i)$ is the probability that buyer i's virtual reservation value $\psi^B(x_i, \alpha)$ is greater than the Mth-order statistic of the $M + N - 1$ virtual reservation values of the other traders.[17] If $\psi^B(x_i, \alpha)$ is less than the Mth-order statistic, then buyer i is not assigned an object. Denote with $\tilde{\xi}_{p\tau}$ this Mth-order statistic.[18] Then $\bar{p}^{\tau\alpha}(x_i) = \Pr\{\tilde{\xi}_{p\tau} \leqslant \psi^B(x_i, \alpha)\}$. Thus, in order to understand $\bar{p}^{\tau\alpha}$ we must understand the Mth-order statistic $\tilde{\xi}_{p\tau}$.

A standard result is that the Mth-order statistic of a sample of $n = \tau(M_0 + N_0)$ random variables independently drawn from a single distribution function is asymptotically normally distributed.[19] A second, less well-known result is that the expected value of the Mth-order statistic of a size n random sample drawn from a distribution converges asymptotically toward the population quantile of order $M_0/(M_0 + N_0)$ at a rate $O((\ln \tau)/\tau^2)$.[20] Two reasons exist why these results cannot be applied

---

[16] The i subscript identifying the buyer is suppressed because, given our assumption that each buyer's reservation value is drawn from F and given our focus on α^*-mechanisms, every buyer's $\bar{p}^{\tau\alpha}$ distribution is identical.

[17] The first-order statistic is the smallest element of the sample, the second-order statistic is the second smallest element, etc.

[18] The meaning of the p subscript on $\tilde{\xi}_{p\tau}$ is made clear later in this section.

[19] See Theorem 9.2 in David [4, pp. 254–255] and Theorem A of Section 2.3.3 in Serfling [28, p. 77].

[20] See Hall [12], David and Johnson [3], and expression (4.6.3) in David [4, p. 80].

directly to our problem. The first is this. The $M-1$ buyers' reservation values are drawn from the distribution F and transformed into virtual reservation values by ψ^B. Similarly the N sellers' reservation values are drawn from the distribution H and transformed by ψ^S. Therefore the resulting sample of virtual reservation values are not drawn, as the standard theorems require, from a single distribution; it is a sample of nonidentically distributed random variables. The second problem is that $\bar{p}^{\tau\alpha}$ is the distribution for the Mth-order statistic of a sample of size $n-1$, not a sample of size n. In other words, as τ increases the ratio of buyers to sellers in the sample underlying $\bar{p}^{\tau\alpha}$ changes. Theorem 7 below resolves both problems.

In order to state Theorem 7 some additional notation is helpful. Let $\{\psi_1^B, ..., \psi_{M-1}^B, \psi_1^S, ..., \psi_N^S\}$ denote the vector of virtual reservation values where each virtual reservation value ψ_i^B is drawn independently from $\tilde{F}$ and each ψ_j^S is independently drawn from $\tilde{H}$. The distribution $\tilde{F}$ is the distribution that is obtained by drawing a reservation value from F and then transforming that value into a virtual reservation value by means of $\psi^B(\cdot, \alpha)$. $\tilde{H}$ is similarly defined. Let $[a', b']$ be the union of the supports of $\tilde{F}$ and $\tilde{H}$. The dependence of $\tilde{F}$ on α is suppressed because we use only the asymptotic behavior of $\bar{p}^{\tau\alpha}$ for fixed values of α. Define, for any $t \in [a', b']$, the average distribution function to be $\Gamma(t) = p\tilde{F}(t) + (1-p)\tilde{H}(t)$ where $p = M_0/(M_0 + N_0)$. The population quantile of order p is $\xi_p = \inf_y\{y : \Gamma(y) \geqslant p\}$. Finally, define $\sigma(t) = M_0\tilde{F}(t)[1 - \tilde{F}(t)] + N_0\tilde{H}(t)[1 - \tilde{H}(t)]$. It is the standard deviation of the random number of virtual reservation values that are no greater than t whenever the sample is M_0 buyers and N_0 sellers.

THEOREM 7. *Let $\tilde{\xi}_{p\tau}$ be the Mth-order statistic of a sample $(\psi_1^B, ..., \psi_{M-1}^B, \psi_1^S, ..., \psi_N^S)$ where $M = \tau M_0$, $N = \tau N_0$, all ψ_i^B are drawn from the distribution $\tilde{F}$ and all ψ_j^S are drawn from the distribution $\tilde{H}$. Let $n = \tau(M_0 + N_0)$ and $p = M_0/(M_0 + N_0)$. In a neighborhood of ξ_p, Γ has positive continuous density Γ' and bounded second derivative Γ'', then, for any t,*

$$\lim_{\tau \to \infty} \Pr\left(\frac{[\tau(M_0 + N_0)]^{1/2}(\tilde{\xi}_{p\tau} - \xi_p)}{\sigma(\xi_p)/\{(M_0 + N_0)^{1/2}\Gamma'(\xi_p)\}} \leqslant t\right) = \Phi(t) \tag{7.01}$$

and, as $\tau \to \infty$,

$$|E(\tilde{\xi}_{p\tau} - \xi_p)| = O\left\{\frac{(\ln \tau)^{1/2}}{\tau}\right\}. \tag{7.02}$$

The theorem is stated from the buyer's point of view. A simple relabeling of the variables permits us to apply it to sellers. Its proof is found in Gresik and Satterthwaite [10, Th. 6.5]. The theorem is almost a restatement of the standard results for the special case in this paper. The aspect that differs from the standard results is that we have been unable to obtain the $O\{1/\tau\}$ bound on $|E(\bar{\xi}_{p\tau} - \xi_p)|$ that is found in the standard results and that, we conjecture, holds here. It is this inability that causes the bound in Theorem 6 to be $O((\ln \tau)/\tau^2)$ instead of $O(1/\tau^2)$.[21]

Proof of Theorem 4.   As the initial step in this proof we must show how Theorem 7 applies to $\bar{p}^{\tau\alpha}$ and $\bar{q}^{\tau\alpha}$. Consider some buyer i. For i to be assigned an object his virtual reservation value must be greater than the Mth-order statistic of the virtual reservation values of the N sellers and the other $M - 1$ buyers. Denote by $\psi_{(M)}^{B\alpha}$ this order statistic and let $\Lambda_\tau^{B\alpha}$ be its distribution function. *Theorem* 7 *applies to* $\psi_{(M)}^{B\alpha}$. It is asymptotic normal with an asymptotic expected value $\bar{\psi}_{(M)}^{B\alpha}$ and asymptotic variance σ_B^2/τ.

The density function $\bar{p}^{\tau\alpha}(\cdot)$ describes the distribution of the random variable $x(\alpha, \tau) = [\psi^B]^{-1}(\psi_{(M)}^{B\alpha})$ where $[\psi^B]^{-1}(\cdot)$ is the inverse of $\psi^B(\cdot, \alpha)$; it is the critical value that i's reservation value must exceed if i is to be assigned an object.[22] The variate $x(\alpha, \tau)$ is also asymptotically normal with asymptotic expectation $\bar{x}^* = [\psi^B]^{-1}(\bar{\psi}_{(M)}^{B\alpha})$ and asymptotic variance $J^2\sigma_B^2/\tau$ where $J = \partial[\psi^B]^{-1}/\partial x_i$ evaluated at $\bar{\psi}_{(M)}^{B\alpha}$. Consequently as τ becomes large the distribution of $x(\alpha, \tau)$ approaches a step function with the step at $\bar{x}^*$.

Define $\psi_{(M)}^{S\alpha}$, $\Lambda_\tau^{S\alpha}$, $\bar{\psi}_{(M)}^{S\alpha}$, σ_S^2, $z(\alpha, \tau)$, and $\bar{z}^*$ in parallel fashion. As τ becomes large the distribution $z(\alpha, \tau)$ approaches a step function with the step at $\bar{z}^*$ where $\bar{z}^* < \bar{x}^*$. The reason for the inequality $\bar{z}^* < \bar{x}^*$ is this. First, as τ becomes large, $|\psi_{(M)}^{S\alpha} - \psi_{(M)}^{B\alpha}|$ approaches zero because the samples that generate $\psi_{(M)}^{S\alpha}$ and $\psi_{(M)}^{B\alpha}$ become essentially identical as τ increases. Second, for all y in the ranges of $\psi^B(\cdot, \alpha)$ and $\psi^S(\cdot, \alpha)$, necessarily $[\psi^B]^{-1}(y) - [\psi^S]^{-1}(y) > 0$ because $\psi^B(x, \alpha) - x < 0$ and $\psi^S(x, \alpha) - x > 0$. Third, (2.13) and (2.14) imply that if $\alpha > 0$ and $w \in (a, b)$, then $\psi^S(w, \alpha) - \psi^B(w, \alpha) > 0$.

We can now prove the theorem's second part: $\lim_{\tau \to \infty} G(0, \tau) = 0$. One form in which (3.01), the IF constraint, can be written is

$$G(\alpha, \tau) = M \int_a^b \psi^B(x, 1) \, \bar{p}^{\tau\alpha}(x) \, f(x) \, dx$$

$$- N \int_a^b \psi^S(z, 1)[1 - \bar{q}^{\tau\alpha}(z)] \, h(z) \, dz$$

$$\geqslant 0. \tag{7.03}$$

Theorem 7 implies that, as τ increases, the variances of $\bar{p}^{\tau\alpha}(\cdot)$ and $\bar{q}^{\tau\alpha}(\cdot)$

[21] See (7.23) and (7.24).

[22] The inverses exist because regularity implies monotonicity of ψ^B and ψ^S.

approach zero. This means that in the limit, if $\alpha = 0$, both distributions become step functions with the step at the competitive price c. Thus

$$\bar{p}^{\infty 0}(x) = \begin{cases} 0 & \text{if} \quad x \leqslant c, \\ 1 & \text{if} \quad x > c, \end{cases} \tag{7.04}$$

and

$$\bar{q}^{\infty 0}(z) = \begin{cases} 0 & \text{if} \quad z \leqslant c \\ 1 & \text{if} \quad z > c. \end{cases} \tag{7.05}$$

Substitution of these into (7.03) and integrating the resulting expression shows that, for $\alpha = 0$ and $\tau \to \infty$, the IF constraint is satisfied:

$$\lim_{\tau \to \infty} G(0, \tau)$$

$$= M \int_a^b \psi^B(x, 1) \, \bar{p}^{\infty 0}(x) f(x) \, dx - N \int_a^b \psi^S(z, 1) [1 - \bar{q}^{\infty 0}(z)] \, h(z) \, dz$$

$$= M \int_c^b (xf(x) + F(x)) \, dx - N \int_a^c (zh(z) + H(z)) \, dz - M \overline{\int_c^b dx}$$

$$= M \int_c^b d[xF(x)] - N \int_a^c d[zH(z)] - M \int_c^b dx = 0 \tag{7.06}$$

because $H(a) = 0$, $F(b) = 1$, and $M(1 - F(c)) = NH(c)$. Therefore in the limit, when the number of traders becomes infinite, the competitive price c satisfies the IF constraint, describes the ex ante efficient mechanism, and is ex post efficient.

We now prove the first half of the theorem. Fix the value of α within $(0, 1)$. The resulting α-mechanism transforms the vector of traders' reservation values $(x_1, ..., x_M, z_1, ..., z_N)$ into a vector of virtual reservation values $(\psi^B(x_1, \alpha), ..., \psi^S(z_N, \alpha))$ and assigns the N objects to the N traders who have the highest virtual reservation values. Suppose, for some $\hat{\tau}$, $G(\alpha, \hat{\tau}) < 0$. As τ increases from $\hat{\tau}$ the distributions $\bar{p}^{\tau \alpha}$ and $\bar{q}^{\tau \alpha}$ approach step functions. Therefore, as with (7.06),

$$\lim_{\tau \to \infty} G(\alpha, \tau) = \lim_{\tau \to \infty} \left\{ M \int_a^b \psi^B(x, 1) \, \bar{p}^{\tau \alpha}(x) f(x) \, dx \right.$$

$$\left. - N \int_a^b \psi^S(z, 1)[1 - \bar{q}^{\tau \alpha}(z)] \, h(z) \, dz \right\}$$

$$= \int_{\bar{x}^*}^b dx F(x) - N \int_a^{\bar{z}^*} dz H(z) - M \int_{\bar{x}^*}^b dx$$

$$= M[bF(b) - \bar{x}^* F(\bar{x}^*)] - N\bar{z}^* H(\bar{z}^*) - M(b - \bar{x}^*)$$

$$= \bar{x}^* M(1 - F(\bar{x}^*)) - \bar{z}^* NH(\bar{z}^*)$$

$$= (\bar{x}^* - \bar{z}^*) M(1 - F(\bar{x}^*)) > 0 \tag{7.07}$$

because:

(a) asymptotically $M(1 - F(\bar{x}^*))$ is the expected number of buyers whose reservation values are greater than $\psi_{(M)}^{B\alpha}$ and are therefore assigned an object;

(b) asymptotically $NH(\bar{z}^*)$ is the expected number of sellers whose reservation values are less than $\psi_{(M)}^{S\alpha}$ and are therefore assigned to sell their objects;

(c) $M(1 - F(\bar{x}^*)) = NH(\bar{z}^*) > 0$ because the blance of goods constraint requires that supply equal demand; and

(d) $\bar{x}^* - z^* > 0$ is shown at the proof's beginning.

The asymptotic normality of $\Lambda_\tau^{B\alpha}$ and $\Lambda_\tau^{S\alpha}$ and the differentiability of $\psi^B(\cdot, \alpha)$ and $\psi^S(\cdot, \alpha)$ imply that, as τ increases, $G(\alpha, \tau)$ approaches $\lim_{\tau \to \infty} G(\alpha, \tau)$ continuously. Therefore, a τ' must exist such that, for all $\tau > \tau'$, $G(\alpha, \tau) \geqslant 0$.

Proof of Theorem 5. The proof is based on an analysis of the asymptotic properties of the IF constraint, $G(\alpha, \tau) = 0$. Recall that, for a given τ, the ex ante efficient mechanism is the α^*-mechanism where α^* is the root of $G(\alpha, \tau) = 0$. Rewriting (3.01) and reversing its order of integration gives

$$G(\alpha, \tau) = M \int_a^b I(t) \, \rho_B(t; \alpha, \tau) \, dt + N \int_a^b J(t) \, \rho_S(t; \alpha, \tau) \, dt - NK = 0 \qquad (7.08)$$

where

$$I(t) = \int_t^b \psi^B(x, 1) f(x) \, dx, \qquad\qquad J(t) = \int_t^b \psi^S(z, 1) h(z) \, dz,$$

$$(7.09)$$

$$\rho_B(x; \alpha, \tau) = d\bar{p}^{\tau\alpha}(x)/dx, \qquad\qquad \rho_S(z; \alpha, \tau) = d\bar{q}^{\tau\alpha}(z)/dz, \qquad (7.10)$$

$$\bar{p}^{\tau\alpha}(x) = \int_a^x \rho_B(t; \alpha, \tau) \, dt, \qquad\qquad \bar{q}^{\tau\alpha}(z) = \int_a^z \rho_S(t; \alpha, \tau) \, dt,$$

$$(7.11)$$

$$K = \int_a^b \psi^S(z, 1) h(z) \, dz = b. \qquad (7.12)$$

The functions ρ_B and ρ_S are probability density functions for $\bar{p}^{\tau\alpha}$ and $\bar{q}^{\tau\alpha}$, respectively. As the first part of the proof of Theorem 4 points out, $\bar{p}^{\tau\alpha}$ and

$\bar{q}^{\tau\alpha}$ are asymptotically normal distribution functions with variances that are $O(1/\tau)$; thus asymptotically ρ_B and ρ_S are normal densities.[23]

Taylor series expansions around c, the competitive price, may be taken of $I(t)$ and $J(t)$ and substituted into (7.08):

$$
\begin{aligned}
G(\alpha, \tau) = M \int_a^b & \left\{ I(c) + I'(c)(t-c) \right. \\
& \left. + I''(c) \frac{(t-c)^2}{2} + R_B(t) \right\} \rho_B(t; \alpha, \tau)\, dt \\
& + N \int_a^b \left\{ J(c) + J'(c)(t-c) \right. \\
& \left. + J''(c) \frac{(t-c)^2}{2} + R_S(t) \right\} \rho_S(t; \alpha, \tau)\, dt - NK \\
= 0 & \qquad\qquad\qquad\qquad\qquad\qquad\qquad\qquad (7.13)
\end{aligned}
$$

where $I'(c)$ and $J'(c)$ are first derivatives of I and J evaluated at c, $I''(c)$ and $J''(c)$ are second derivatives, and $R_B(t)$ and $R_S(t)$ are the remainder terms for the expansions. Two sets of terms may be dropped. First, a derivation similar to that of Eq. (7.06) shows that, for large τ,

$$
M \int_a^b I(c)\, \rho_B(t; \alpha, \tau)\, dt + N \int_a^b J(c)\, \rho_S(t; \alpha, \tau)\, dt - NK = 0; \quad (7.14)
$$

therefore these three terms may be dropped.[24] Second, the two remainder terms R_B and R_S may be dropped because, for large τ, they are inconsequential in comparison with the remaining terms. This follows from three facts:

(i) both terms are $O[(t-c)^2]$,

(ii) the densities $\rho_B(\cdot; \alpha, \tau)$ and $\rho_S(\cdot; \alpha, \tau)$ become spikes centered on c as τ becomes large and α approaches zero, and

(iii) the region of integration is a bounded interval.

---

[23] See footnote 24 for a qualification of this statement.

[24] The reason that we must make (7.14) conditional on τ being large is that $\bar{q}^{\tau\alpha}(a) > 0$ and $\bar{p}^{\tau\alpha}(b) < 1$ for small τ, i.e., they are improper distribution functions for small τ. As τ becomes larger, $\bar{p}^{\tau\alpha}(a) \to 0$ and $\bar{p}^{\tau\alpha}(b) \to 1$ very quickly. Specifically, Theorem 6.1 in Gresik and Satterthwaite [10] implies that both $\bar{p}^{\tau\alpha}(a)$ and $1 - \bar{p}^{\tau\alpha}(b)$ are $O(e^{-\tau})$. For large τ these quantities are negligible.

Integrating each remaining term and dividing both sides by τ gives

$$
\frac{G(\alpha, \tau)}{\tau} = M_0 \left\{ I'(c)[\bar{x}(\alpha, \tau) - c] + \frac{1}{2} I''(c)[(\bar{x}(\alpha, \tau) - c)^2 + \sigma_B^2(\alpha, \tau)] \right\}
$$

$$
+ N_0 \left\{ J'(c)[\bar{z}(\alpha, \tau) - c] + \frac{1}{2} J''(c)[(\bar{z}(\alpha, \tau) - c)^2 + \sigma_S^2(\alpha, \tau)] \right\} = 0
$$

$$(7.15)$$

where $\bar{x}(\alpha, \tau)$ is the mean of $\rho_B(t;, \alpha, \tau)$, $\sigma_B^2(\alpha, \tau)$ is the variance of ρ_B, $\bar{z}(\alpha, \tau)$ is the mean of ρ_S, and $\sigma_S^2(\alpha, \tau)$ is the variance of ρ_S.

Our target is how α varies with τ. Equation (7.15) implicitly defines α as a function of τ. Therefore let $\alpha = \alpha(\tau)$, $\alpha' = d\alpha/d\tau$, $\bar{x}_\alpha = \partial\bar{x}(\alpha, \tau)/\partial\alpha$, $\bar{x}_\tau = \partial\bar{x}(\alpha, \tau)/\partial\tau$, etc. Differentiation of (7.15) by τ gives

$$
M_0 \left\{ I'(\bar{x}_\alpha \alpha' + \bar{x}_\tau) + \frac{1}{2} I'' \left[2(\bar{x}(\alpha, \tau) - c)(\bar{x}_\alpha \alpha' + \bar{x}_\tau) + \frac{\partial \sigma_B^2}{\partial \alpha} \alpha' + \frac{\partial \sigma_B^2}{\partial \tau} \right] \right\}
$$

$$
+ N_0 \left\{ J'(\bar{z}_\alpha \alpha' + \bar{z}_\tau) + \frac{1}{2} J'' \left[2(\bar{z}(\alpha, \tau) - c)(\bar{z}_\alpha \alpha' + \bar{z}_\tau) + \frac{\partial \sigma_S^2}{\partial \alpha} \alpha' + \frac{\partial \sigma_S^2}{\partial \tau} \right] \right\} = 0
$$

$$(7.16)$$

where I' denotes $I'(c)$, etc. The plan is to solve this equation for α' and evaluate it as $\tau \to \infty$ and $\alpha = 0$. Setting $\alpha = 0$ is correct because, according to Theorem 4, as τ goes to infinity the ex ante efficient mechanism is the α-mechanism for which $\alpha = 0$. Solving for α' gives a differential equation whose solution can be approximated for large τ.

Note that, when $\alpha = 0$ and as τ becomes large, $\bar{x}(0, \tau) = \bar{x}^* \to c$ and $\bar{z}(0, \tau) = \bar{z}^* \to c$. Therefore, solving (7.16) gives, for large τ.

$$
\alpha'(\tau) = - \frac{M_0 I' \bar{x}_\tau + N_0 J' \bar{z}_\tau + \dfrac{1}{2} \left(M_0 I'' \dfrac{\partial \sigma_B^2}{\partial \tau} + N_0 J'' \dfrac{\partial \sigma_S^2}{\partial \tau} \right)}{M_0 I' \bar{x}_\alpha + N_0 J' \bar{z}_\alpha + \dfrac{1}{2} \left(M_0 I'' \dfrac{\partial \sigma_B^2}{\partial \alpha} + N_0 J'' \dfrac{\partial \sigma_S^2}{\partial \alpha} \right)}. \tag{7.17}
$$

We need to integrate its right-hand side.

Consider the $\bar{x}$ and σ_B^2 in the denominator. They respectively refer to the mean and variance of the random variable $x(\alpha, \tau)$ whose distribution is $\bar{p}^{\tau\alpha}(\cdot)$. Exactly as in the proof of Theorem 4, $x(\alpha, \tau) = [\psi^B]^{-1}(\psi_{(M)}^{B\alpha})$ where $\psi_{(M)}^{B\alpha}$ is the Mth-order statistic of the virtual utilities of $M - 1$ buyers and N sellers.

Let $\tilde{z}(\alpha, \tau) = [\psi^S]^{-1}(\psi^{B\alpha}_{(M)})$. Therefore $\psi^B[x(\alpha, \tau), \alpha] = \psi^S[\tilde{z}(\alpha, \tau), \alpha] = \psi^{B\alpha}_{(M)}$. The standard result that the asymptotic expectation of a function of a random variable equals the function of the variable's asymptotic expectation applies to $x(\alpha, x)$ and $\tilde{z}(\alpha, \tau)$. Therefore, for large τ,

$$\psi^B[\bar{x}(\alpha, \tau), \alpha] = \psi^S[\bar{\tilde{z}}(\alpha, \tau), \alpha] \qquad (7.18)$$

where $\bar{x}(\alpha, \tau)$ is the expected value of $x(\alpha, \tau)$, etc.

For any realization of reservation values, exactly M traders must have virtual utilities less than or equal to the realization of $\psi^{B\alpha}_{(M)}$. This means that the expected number of traders with virtual reservation values less than or equal to $\psi^{B\alpha}_{(M)}$ is M. Therefore, asymptotically,

$$(M-1) F[\bar{x}(\alpha, \tau)] + NH[\bar{\tilde{z}}(\alpha, \tau)] = M \qquad (7.19)$$

where $F[\bar{x}(\alpha, \tau)]$ is the probability that a buyer will have a reservation value such that $\psi^B(x_i, \alpha) < \psi^{B\alpha}_{(M)}$, $(M-1) F[\bar{x}(\alpha, \tau)]$ is the expected number of the $M-1$ buyers who will not be assigned an object because their virtual utility values are too low, etc.

Equations (7.18) and (7.19) implicitly define $\bar{x}(\alpha, \tau)$ and $\bar{\tilde{z}}(\alpha, \tau)$. Holding τ constant, they may be differentiated with respect to α:

$$(M-1) f\bar{x}_\alpha + Nh\bar{\tilde{z}}_\alpha = 0,$$
$$\bar{x}_\alpha + \frac{F-1}{f} + \alpha \frac{f^2 \bar{x}_\alpha - (F-1) f' \bar{x}_\alpha}{f^2} = \bar{\tilde{z}}_\alpha + \frac{H}{h} + \alpha \frac{h^2 \bar{\tilde{z}}_\alpha - Hh' \bar{\tilde{z}}_\alpha}{h^2} \qquad (7.20)$$

where $H = H(c)$, $F = F(c)$, $f = f(c)$, $h = h(c)$, $f' = df(c)/x_i$, $h' = dh(c)/dz_j$, $\bar{x}_\alpha = \partial\bar{x}(0, \tau)/\partial\alpha$, $\bar{\tilde{z}}_\alpha = \partial\bar{\tilde{z}}(0, \tau)/\partial\alpha$, and c is the competitive price. The derivatives are evaluated at $\alpha = 0$ and c because, as τ becomes large, $\alpha \to 0$, $\bar{x} \to c$, and $\bar{\tilde{z}} \to c$. Solving the system for $\bar{x}_\alpha$ and evaluating it for large τ at $\alpha = 0$ gives

$$\bar{x}_\alpha = \frac{N[fH - (F-1)h]}{Nhf + (M-1) f^2} \approx K' \qquad (7.21)$$

where K' is some constant. Similar calculations show that $\bar{\tilde{z}}_\alpha = K''$, $\partial\sigma^2_B/\partial\alpha = O(1/\tau)$, and $\partial\sigma^2_S/\partial\alpha = O(1/\tau)$. The denominator of (7.17) is therefore dominated by constant terms and, for large τ, is $O(1)$.

For large τ both sides of (7.17) can be integrated because its denominator is essentially constant:

$$\int_\infty^\tau \alpha'(\tau)\, d\tau = -\int_\infty^\tau \frac{M_0 I' \bar{x}_\tau + N_0 J' \bar{z}_\tau + \frac{1}{2}\left(M_0 I'' \dfrac{\partial \sigma_B^2}{\partial \tau} + N_0 J'' \dfrac{\partial \sigma_S^2}{\partial \tau}\right)}{M_0 I' \bar{x}_\alpha + N_0 J' \bar{z}_\alpha + \frac{1}{2}\left(M_0 I'' \dfrac{\partial \sigma_B^2}{\partial \alpha} + N_0 J'' \dfrac{\partial \sigma_S^2}{\partial \alpha}\right)}\, d\tau$$

$$= -\frac{1}{K}\left\{M_0 I' \int_\infty^\tau \bar{x}_\tau\, d\tau + N_0 J' \int_\infty^\tau \bar{z}_\tau\, d\tau\right\}$$

$$-\frac{1}{2K}\left\{M_0 I'' \int_\infty^\tau \frac{\partial \sigma_B^2}{\partial \tau}\, d\tau + N_0 J'' \int_\infty^\tau \frac{\partial \sigma_S^2}{\partial \tau}\, d\tau\right\} \qquad (7.22)$$

where $\bar{x}_\tau$, $\bar{z}_\tau$, $\partial \sigma_B^2/\partial \tau$, and $\partial \sigma_S^2/\partial \tau$ are evaluated at $\alpha = 0$ where $K = M_0 I'K' + N_0 J'K''$. Therefore, for large τ,

$$\alpha(\tau) = \alpha(\infty) - \frac{1}{K} M_0 I'(\bar{x}(0, \tau) - \bar{x}(0, \infty)) - \frac{1}{K} N_0 J'(\bar{z}(0, \tau) - \bar{z}(0, \infty))$$

$$-\frac{1}{2K} M_0 I''(\sigma_B^2(0, \tau) - \sigma_B^2(0, \infty))$$

$$-\frac{1}{2K} N_0 J''(\sigma_S^2(0, \tau) - \sigma_S^2(0, \infty))$$

$$= O\left(\frac{(\ln \tau)^{1/2}}{\tau}\right) + O\left(\frac{1}{\tau}\right)$$

$$= O\left(\frac{(\ln \tau)^{1/2}}{\tau}\right). \qquad (7.23)$$

This follows from three facts. First, when $\alpha = 0$, $x(\alpha, \tau) = \bar{z}(\alpha, \tau) = \psi_{(M)}^{B\alpha}$ and $\lim_{\tau \to \infty}(\psi_{(M)}^{B\alpha}) = c$. Second, Theorem 7 implies that

$$|E(\psi_{(M)}^{B\alpha} - c)| = O\left(\frac{(\ln \tau)^{1/2}}{\tau}\right). \qquad (7.24)$$

Third, Theorem 4 states that $\alpha(\infty) = 0$.

Proof of Theorem 6. A Taylor series expansion of the ex ante expected gains from trade, $T[\alpha(\tau), \tau]$, that an α*-mechanism realizes is

$$T(0, \tau) + \alpha(\tau)\frac{\partial T(0, \tau)}{\partial \alpha} + \frac{1}{2}[\alpha(\tau)]^2 \frac{\partial^2 T[\varepsilon(\tau), \tau]}{\partial \alpha^2} \qquad (7.25)$$

where $\varepsilon(\tau) \in [0, \alpha(\tau)]$. Three facts allow us to evaluate (7.25). First, for large τ, the ex post optimal mechanism assigns the N objects to those N

agents whose reservation values are greater than c, the competitive price. Therefore

$$T(0, \tau) \approx \tau M_0 \int_c^b (t - c) f(t) \, dt + \tau N_0 \int_a^c (c - t) h(t) \, dt = O(\tau) \quad (7.26)$$

for large τ.

Second, the last two terms on the right-hand side of (7.25) represent the ex post gains from trade that the ex ante optimal mechanism fails to realize as a consequence of $\alpha(\tau)$ being greater than zero. Let $S(\alpha, \tau)$ represent these two terms. S may be evaluated, for large τ, as follows. Recall from the proof of Theorem 4 the meaning of $\bar{x}(\alpha, \tau)$ and $\bar{z}(\alpha, \tau)$. For large τ the expected number of buyers excluded from trading as α increases from zero to $\alpha(\tau)$ is

$$\tau M_0 \int_c^{\bar{x}(\alpha, \tau)} f(t) \, dt \quad (7.27)$$

and the gains from trade that are lost from this exclusion are

$$\tau M_0 \int_c^{\bar{x}(\alpha, \tau)} (t - c) f(t) \, dt. \quad (7.28)$$

A similar expression exists for the gains from trade that the α^*-mechanism fails to realize on the sellers' side. Consequently, for large τ,

$$-S(\alpha, \tau) = \tau N_0 \int_{\bar{z}(\alpha, z)}^c (c - t) h(t) \, dt + \tau M_0 \int_c^{\bar{x}(\alpha, \tau)} (t - c) f(t) \, dt. \quad (7.29)$$

Differentiation gives

$$-\frac{\partial S(\alpha, \tau)}{\partial \alpha}$$

$$= -\tau N_0 [c - \bar{z}(\alpha, \tau)] h[\bar{z}(\alpha, \tau)] \bar{z}_\alpha + \tau M_0 [\bar{x}(\alpha, \tau) - c] f[\bar{x}(\alpha, \tau)] \bar{x}_\alpha \quad (7.30)$$

and

$$-\frac{\partial^2 S(\alpha, \tau)}{\partial \alpha^2}$$

$$= -\tau N_0 ((c - \bar{z})[h\bar{z}_{\alpha\alpha} + h'(\bar{z}_\alpha)^2] - h(\bar{z}_\alpha)^2)$$

$$+ \tau M_0 ((\bar{x} - c)[f\bar{x}_{\alpha\alpha} + f'(\bar{x}_\alpha)^2] + f(\bar{x}_\alpha)^2) \quad (7.31)$$

where $\quad \bar{z} = \bar{z}(\alpha, \tau), \quad h = h[\bar{z}(\alpha, \tau)], \quad \bar{z}_\alpha = \partial\bar{z}(\alpha, t)/\partial\alpha, \quad \bar{z}_{\alpha\alpha} = \partial^2\bar{z}(\alpha, \tau)/\partial\alpha^2,$
$h' = dh[\bar{z}]/dz$, etc. Evaluated for large τ and $\alpha = 0$ these derivatives are

$$\frac{\partial T(0, \tau)}{\partial\alpha} = \frac{\partial S(0, \tau)}{\partial\alpha} = 0 \qquad (7.32)$$

and

$$-\frac{\partial^2 T(0, \tau)}{\partial\alpha^2} = -\frac{\partial^2 S(0, \tau)}{\partial\alpha^2} = \tau(N_0 h(c)(\bar{z}_\alpha)^2 + M_0 f(c)(\bar{x}_\alpha)^2) = O(\tau) \quad (7.33)$$

because $\alpha(\tau) \to 0$, $\bar{x}(\alpha, \tau) \to c$, $\bar{z}(\alpha, \tau) \to c$, $\bar{x}_\alpha \to K'$, and $\bar{z}_\alpha \to K''$ as $\tau \to \infty$. Finally, the third fact is Theorem 5's result that for large τ, $\alpha(\tau) = O((\ln\tau)^{1/2}/\tau)$.

These facts are sufficient to evaluate the expression of interest:

$$1 - \frac{T[\alpha(\tau), \tau]}{T(0, \tau)} = 1 - \frac{T(0, \tau) + \alpha(\tau)\dfrac{\partial T(0, \tau)}{\partial\alpha} + \dfrac{1}{2}[\alpha(\tau)]^2 \dfrac{\partial^2 T(\varepsilon(\tau), \tau)}{\partial\alpha^2}}{T(0, \tau)}$$

$$= \frac{1}{2} \frac{[\alpha(\tau)]^2}{T(0, \tau)} \frac{\partial^2 T(0, \tau)}{\partial\alpha^2}$$

$$= \frac{\{O(\ln\tau)^{1/2}/\tau)\}^2}{O(\tau)} O(\tau) = O\left\{\frac{\ln\tau}{\tau^2}\right\}, \qquad (7.34)$$

which proves the theorem.

REFERENCES

1. R. BHATTACHARYA AND M. MAJUMDAR, Random exchange economies, *J. Econ. Theory* **6** (1973), 37–67.
2. K. CHATTERJEE AND W. SAMUELSON, Bargaining under incomplete information, *Oper. Res.* **31** (1983), 835–851.
3. F. N. DAVID AND N. L. JOHNSON, Statistical treatment of censored data, I. Fundamental formulae, *Biometrika* **41** (1954), 228–240.
4. H. A. DAVID, "Order Statistics," 2nd ed., Wiley, New York, 1981.
5. G. DEBREU, The rate of convergence of the core of an economy, *J. Math. Econ.* **2** (1975), 1–7.
6. E. DIERKER, Gains and losses at core allocations, *J. Math. Econ.* **2** (1975), 119–128.
7. A. F. GIBBARD, Manipulation of voting schemes: A general result, *Econometrica* **41** (1973), 587–602.
8. T. GRESIK, Efficient bilateral trade mechanisms for dependent-type markets, Washington University, 1987.
9. T. GRESIK AND M. SATTERTHWAITE, "The Number of Traders Required to Make a Market Competitive: The Beginnings of a Theory," CMSEMS DP. No. 551, Northwestern University, 1983.

10. T. GRESIK AND M. SATTERTHWAITE, "The Rate at Which a Simple Market Becomes Efficient as the Number of Traders Increases: An Asymptotic Result for Optimal Trading Mechanisms, CMSEMS DP No. 641, Northwestern University, 1985.

11. K. HAGERTY AND W. ROGERSON, Robust trading mechanisms, *J. Econ. Theory* **42** (1985), 94–107.

12. P. HALL, Some asymptotic expansions of moments of order statistics, *Stochastic Process. Appl.* **7** (1978), 265–275.

13. M. HARRIS AND A. RAVIV, A theory of monopoly pricing schemes with demand uncertainty, *Amer. Econ. Rev.* **71** (1981), 347–365.

14. M. HARRIS AND R. M. TOWNSEND, Resource allocation under asymmetric information, *Econometrica* **49** (1981), 33–64.

15. J. C. HARSANYI, Games with incomplete information played by Bayesian players, Parts I, II, and III. *Management Sci.* **14** (1967–68), 159–182, 320–334, 486–502.

16. W. HILDENBRAND, "Core and Equilibria of a Large Economy," Princeton University Press, Princeton, NJ, 1974.

17. B. HOLMSTROM AND R. B. MYERSON, Efficient and durable decision rules with incomplete information, *Econometrica* **51** (1983), 1799–1820.

18. J. LEDYARD, The scope of the hypothesis of Bayesian equilibrium. *J. Econ. Theory* **39** (1986), 59–82.

19. W. LEININGER, P. LINHART, AND R. RADNER, Equilibria of the sealed-bid mechanism for bargaining with incomplete information, *J. Econ. Theory* **48** (1989), 63–106.

20. P. MILGROM AND R. WEBER, A theory of auctions and competitive bidding, *Econometrica* **50** (1982), 1089–1122.

21. R. B. MYERSON, Incentive compatibility and the bargaining problem, *Econometrica* **47** (1979), 61–73.

22. R. B. MYERSON, Optimal auction design, *Math. Oper. Res.* **6** (1981), 58–73.

23. R. B. MYERSON AND M. A. SATTERTHWAITE, Efficient mechanisms for bilateral trading, *J. Econ. Theory* **29** (1983), 265–281.

24. R. B. MYERSON, Two-person bargaining problems with incomplete information, *Econometrica* **52** (1984), 461–488.

25. J. ROBERTS AND A. POSTLEWAITE, The incentive for price-taking behavior in large exchange economies, *Econometrica* **44** (1976), 115–128.

26. M. SATTERTHWAITE AND S. WILLIAMS, Bilateral trade with the sealed-bid *k*-double auction: Existence and efficiency, *J. Econ. Theory* **48** (1989), 107–133.

27. M. SATTERTHWAITE AND S. WILLIAMS, Rate of convergence to efficiency in the buyers bid double auction as the market becomes large, *Rev. Econ. Studies*, in press.

28. R. J. SERFLING, "Approximation Theorems of Mathematical Statistics," Wiley, New York, 1980.

29. S. WILLIAMS, Efficient performance in two agent bargaining, *J. Econ. Theory* **41** (1987), 154–172.

30. R. WILSON, Efficient trading, *in* "Issues in Contemporary Microeconomics and Welfare" (G. Feiwel, Ed.), Macmillan, London, 1985.

31. R. WILSON, Incentive efficiency of double auctions, *Econometrica* **53** (1985), 1101–1115.

Review of Economic Studies (1989) **56**, 477–498
© 1989 The Review of Economic Studies Limited

The Rate of Convergence to Efficiency in the Buyer's Bid Double Auction as the Market Becomes Large

MARK A. SATTERTHWAITE

and

STEVEN R. WILLIAMS

Northwestern University

First version received March 1988; *final version accepted March* 1989 (*Eds.*)

A trader who privately knows his preferences may misrepresent them in order to influence the market price. This strategic behaviour may prevent realization of all gains from trade. In this paper, trade in a simple market with an explicit rule for price formation is modelled as a Bayesian game. We show that the difference between a trader's bid and his reservation value is maximally $O(1/m)$ where m is the number of traders on each side of the market. Competitive pressure as m increases thus quickly overcomes the inefficiency private information causes and forces the market towards an efficient allocation.

1. INTRODUCTION

A goal of a market is to implement a Pareto efficient allocation of resources. Classical general equilibrium theory focuses on the existence of prices that implement an efficient allocation. Solving for such prices requires information about traders' preferences. This information is typically not possessed by any one individual or institution, for each trader typically has some private information about his own preferences. The market must somehow elicit the necessary private information if it is to implement an efficient allocation.

A major obstacle to accomplishing this is the incentive that traders may have to misrepresent their private information. In a market with prices this strategic behaviour takes the form of distorting supply and demand in order to influence price. This behaviour may cause ex post inefficiency, i.e. all potential gains from trade may not be realized. Intuitively, strategic behaviour is only significant in small markets, for the likelihood that a trader can affect price decreases as the number of traders in the market becomes large. In the limiting case of a market with a continuum of traders strategic behaviour vanishes and traders willingly reveal their private information. Appropriate prices can then be calculated and efficiency results.

This paper develops the intuition that the number of traders is critical to the performance of a market by using Harsanyi's notion (1967–68) of a Bayesian game to model the impact of private information upon a simple market. We consider an independent, private values model. There are m sellers, each having a single item to sell, and m buyers, each wanting to buy at most one item. Each trader has a reservation value for the item that is independently drawn from the unit interval; a seller's value is drawn from distribution F_1 and a buyer's value is drawn from distribution F_2. A trader privately knows his own reservation value. Each trader is risk neutral.

The items are reallocated according to the following rules. Sellers and buyers simultaneously submit offers and bids. These offers and bids determine a closed interval in which a market-clearing price can be selected. We choose as the price the upper endpoint of this interval. Trade then occurs at this price between those buyers whose bids are at least as great as it and sellers whose offers are strictly less than it. We call this procedure the *buyer's bid double auction* (BBDA) because in the one seller-one buyer case the buyer's bid determines the price whenever trade occurs.

We consider Bayesian Nash equilibria in which all sellers use one strategy and all buyers use a second strategy. Each seller in the BBDA has a dominant strategy to set his offer equal to his reservation value because he can not influence the price when he trades. In response to these dominant strategies, each buyer has an incentive to bid less than his reservation value, which causes the BBDA to be ex post inefficient. We show, however, that the amount of misrepresentation by buyers must be small when the market is large. In fact, we prove that in any equilibrium strategy of the buyers the difference between a buyer's bid and his reservation value is $O(1/m)$, regardless of the distributions of the reservation values. Thus, as the market grows, competitive pressures quickly force buyers towards truthful revelation and the equilibrium outcome towards an ex post efficient, perfectly competitive allocation.

Three aspects of our result deserve emphasis. First, it applies to all Bayesian Nash equilibria in which the buyers adopt the same response to the sellers' dominant strategy of truthful revelation. Large misrepresentation simply cannot be equilibrium behaviour in a large market regardless of which equilibrium is chosen. Second, the rules of the BBDA give each seller the incentive to honestly report his reservation value. Under other rules for selecting a market clearing price both sellers and buyers misreport in equilibrium. Third, numerical examples suggest that for m as small as six almost all gains from trade are realized, i.e. essentially ex post efficient outcomes are achieved. Consequently, for all but small m, it may not be worthwhile to use Holmstrom and Myerson's (1983) information-based concepts of incentive efficiency to evaluate the BBDA's equilibria.

The questions that give rise to this work were articulated by Hayek (1945), Arrow (1959), Hurwicz (1972), and others. Hayek emphasized the importance of modelling the impact of private information upon an economy: the resource allocation problem

> ... is thus in no way solved if we can show that all the facts, if they were known to a single mind (as we hypothetically assume them to be given to the observing economist), would uniquely determine the solution; instead we must show how a solution is produced by the interactions of people each of whom possesses only partial knowledge (1945, p. 530).

Arrow (1959) criticized general equilibrium theory for failing to explain how Walrasian prices are formed. Hurwicz has been a pioneer in formally evaluating the informational and incentive feasibility of economic mechanisms:

> On the informational side, the question is whether the mechanism allows for the dispersion of information and limitations on the capacity of various units to process information. On the incentive side, there is the problem whether the rules prescribed by the mechanism are compatible with either individual or group incentives (1972, p. 298-299).

Because we model the BBDA as a Bayesian game, our result reflects the role that private information and individual incentives play within an explicit process of price formation. We do not, however, deal with limitations on rationality and information processing. Nevertheless, our result that all equilibrium strategies of the BBDA in a large market are close to truthful revelation suggests that cognitive limitations are unimportant in large markets.

Our result is reminiscent of a classic result in general equilibrium theory. Building on Debreu and Scarf's (1963) result on the convergence of the core to the Walrasian allocations, Debreu (1975) and Grodal (1975) showed that as a regular Arrow–Debreu economy is replicated, the maximum distance between a core allocation and its nearest Walrasian allocation is $O(1/m)$, where m is the number of replications.[1] Beyond the obvious fact that the same rate holds, both results show that in a large market equilibrium outcomes are close to Walrasian outcomes. Some differences, however, between these results should be kept in mind. First, they are based upon very different notions about what happens in a market. The core convergence results assume that the outcome of trade is efficient no matter how many traders are present, while in our model private information and individual incentives cause inefficiency in any finite market. Second, the core convergence results neither explain how a core allocation is achieved nor how prices are formed. Our result concerns an explicit procedure for price formation. If "price-taking behaviour" means accepting prices rather than trying to manipulate them in one's favour, then our result provides insight into this topic, while the core convergence results cannot. It is important to note, however, that the Arrow–Debreu framework is much richer than our elementary model.

A precursor of our result is Roberts and Postlewaite's (1976) study of the non-cooperative incentive that an agent within an Arrow–Debreu exchange economy has to act strategically. In their model each agent first reports an excess demand function, a competitive equilibrium is computed based on the reports, and finally goods are allocated according to the computed solution. They show that as a generic economy becomes large each agent's maximal gain from misreporting his excess demand function vanishes. Their result, while related, is different from ours because it does not concern equilibrium behaviour by the agents, it does not model agents' preferences as private information, and it does not state a rate at which misreporting vanishes.

Most directly our work stems from earlier research on Bayesian game models of double auctions. Chatterjee and Samuelson (1983) and Leininger et al. (1986) analyzed bilateral double auctions. The mathematical approach of this paper follows naturally from Satterthwaite and Williams's (1987) analysis of the bilateral case. Wilson (1985) showed that double auctions achieve Holmstrom and Myerson's (1983) standard of interim incentive efficiency when the market is sufficiently large. This paper complements Wilson's result by showing that markets also converge at a specified, rapid rate to ex post efficiency as they grow larger.

Our work also stems from the analysis of trading from the mechanism design viewpoint. Myerson and Satterthwaite (1983) developed techniques for computing the optimal revelation mechanism when reservation values are private on both sides of the market. For given distributions F_1 and F_2 the optimal mechanism maximizes the ex ante expected gains from trade subject to the constraints of private information and strategic behaviour. Gresik and Satterthwaite (1986, Theorem 5) showed that if the optimal mechanism is used, then the maximal gap between the reservation values of a buyer and a seller who are ex post inefficiently excluded from trade is at most $O((\ln m)^{1/2}/m)$.

---

1. See Hildenbrand (1982) and Dierker (1982) for surveys of this topic.

They conjectured that the tighter $O(1/m)$ rate of our result holds. Our convergence result improves upon theirs in two ways. First, it verifies their conjecture, for the order of the optimal mechanism's bound must be as small as the order of the BBDA's bound. Second, our result concerns a realistic trading procedure. The rules of the BBDA are stated in terms of the offers and bids; the Bayesian game framework is used not to define the BBDA but to analyze the outcome of trade under this procedure when there is private information. By contrast, an optimal mechanism is defined in terms of the distributions F_1 and F_2; changing the distributions changes the optimal mechanism's rules for allocating the items. As Wilson (1987) has emphasized, the rules of real-world trading mechanisms are independent of the underlying distributions.

Finally, McAfee and McMillan (1987) have surveyed the literature on one-sided and double auctions.[2] Their survey shows both the debt that our paper and other papers on double auctions owe to the literature on one-sided auctions and the distance that the double auction literature has to go before it reaches an equivalent level of sophistication. For example, our results are for the independent, private values model only. Consideration of Milgrom and Weber's (1982) more general model of affiliated values has as yet proved intractable.

2. NOTATION, MODEL, AND PRELIMINARY OBSERVATIONS

Consider a market with m buyers ($m \geq 2$) and m sellers in which each seller wishes to sell an indivisible item and each buyer wishes to purchase at most one item.[3] Each seller has a reservation value independently drawn from the distribution F_1 and each buyer has a reservation value independently drawn from F_2. A trader's reservation value is his own private information. Each distribution F_i is a C^1 function whose density $f_i = F_i'$ is positive at every point in $(0, 1)$ and zero outside $[0, 1]$. The distributions F_1 and F_2 are common knowledge among the traders. We use v_1 to denote a seller's reservation value and v_2 to denote a buyer's reservation value. A seller's utility is zero if he fails to sell his item and $p - v_1$ if he does sell and the market price is p. Similarly a buyer's utility is zero if he fails to buy and $v_2 - p$ if he does buy.

These are the common knowledge rules of the BBDA. Every trader simultaneously submits an offer/bid. These offers/bids are arrayed in increasing order $s_{(1)} \leq s_{(2)} \leq \cdots \leq s_{(2m)}$ and the price p is set at $s_{(m+1)}$. Trade occurs among sellers whose offers are strictly less than p and buyers whose bids are greater than or equal to p. When ties occur, p may not be a market-clearing price. In order to explain exactly who trades under the BBDA we refer to Table 2.1.

TABLE 2.1

Determination of the market price

	Sellers	Buyers
No. offers/bids $> s_{(m+1)}$	s	t
No. offers/bids $= s_{(m+1)}$	k	j
No. offers/bids $< s_{(m+1)}$	$m - s - k$	$m - t - j$

2. In a one-sided auction a seller with a known reservation value is attempting to maximize his revenue in selling an object(s) to a set of buyers whose reservation values are private. Thus the distinction between a one-sided auction and a double auction of the type we are studying is that in a double auction both buyers and sellers have private information while in a one-sided auction only the buyers have private information.

3. We have excluded the bilateral case ($m = 1$) because its analysis is different from the $m \geq 2$ case. See Satterthwaite and Williams (1987).

Let s be the number of sellers whose offers exceed p, k the number of sellers whose offers equal p, t the number of buyers whose bids exceet p, and j the number of buyers whose bids equal p. There are $(m-s-k)$ offers and $(m-t-j)$ bids less than p. Note that $(s+k+t+j) \geqq m$ traders offer/bid at least as much as p, since $p = s_{(m+1)}$. Therefore

$$t + j \geqq m - s - k, \tag{2.1}$$

which means the demand $(t+j)$ at the price p is necessarily at least as large as the supply $(m-s-k)$.

Consider the case in which a single offer/bid uniquely determines $s_{(m+1)}$, i.e. $j + k = 1$ and $t + s = m - 1$. In (2.1) bring $s + k$ to the left-hand side; the left-hand side then sums exactly to m and (2.1) holds with equality. In this case, supply exactly equals demand and every buyer whose bid is at least p purchases an item and every seller whose offer is less than p sells his item. Next consider the remaining case in which at least two offer/bids equal $s_{(m+1)}$, i.e. $j + k \geqq 2$ and demand $t + j$ may strictly exceed supply $(m - s - k)$. The BBDA then prescribes that the supply of $(m - s - k)$ items is allocated beginning with the buyer who bid the most and working down the list of buyers whose bids are at least p. If in this process a point is reached where two or more buyers submitted identical bids and the remaining supply of unassigned items is insufficient to serve them, then the available supply is rationed among these bidders using a lottery that assigns each an equal chance of receiving an item. This completes the definition of the BBDA.

We adopt the Bayesian game framework to analyse the outcome of trade. Within this framework a trader's reservation value is his *type* and his *strategy* is a function that specifies an offer/bid for each of his possible types. An *equilibrium* consists of a strategy for each trader such that, for each of his possible reservation values, the offer/bid his strategy specifies maximizes his expected utility given the other traders' strategies and the distributions of their reservation values.

We now identify some basic properties of equilibria in the BBDA. The most funda-mental property is that a seller can not influence the price p at which he trades by altering his offer. This follows from the BBDA's rule that a seller only sells if his offer is strictly less than the price $p \equiv s_{(m+1)}$. As noted by Wilson (1983), it follows that sellers have no incentive to act strategically, i.e. each seller's dominant strategy is to submit his reservation value as his offer.[4] Let $\tilde{S}$ denote this strategy:

$$\tilde{S}(v_1) = v_1 \tag{2.2}$$

for all $v_1 \in [0, 1]$.

Theorem 2.1. *In the BBDA, $\tilde{S}$ is a dominant strategy for each seller.*

Proof. Select a strategy for each buyer and for all but one of the sellers, and let v_1 be the reservation value of the exceptional seller. This seller would be no worse off by submitting an offer of $b = v_1$ rather than $b' > v_1$ because: (i) if he sells the item with the offer b' at a price $p > b'$, then he also sells it with the offer of $b = v_1$ at the unchanged price p; and (ii) if he fails to sell the item with the offer $b' \geqq p$, he can only gain if he instead offers $b = v_1$, for the price whenever he trades necessarily exceeds his offer. A similar analysis shows that the seller is no worse off with the offer of $b = v_1$ than an offer $b'' < v_1$. ‖

We assume throughout this paper that all sellers adopt the strategy $\tilde{S}$. We also assume that all buyers use the same strategy. Let B denote the common strategy of buyers and let $\langle \tilde{S}, B \rangle$ denote a set of strategies in which each seller plays $\tilde{S}$ and each buyer plays B.

---

4. A stand-off equilibrium also exists in which all buyers bid zero, all sellers offer one, and no trade occurs.

In order to further establish the properties of equilibria $\langle \tilde{S}, B \rangle$ we need additional notation:

$\pi(v_2, b; B) =$ a buyer's expected utility when v_2 is his reservation value, b is his bid, and B is the common strategy of the other buyers;

$P(b; B) =$ the probability a buyer will trade when b is his bid and B is the common strategy of the other buyers;

$C(b; B) =$ the expected payment of a buyer when b is his bid and B is the common strategy of the other buyers.

Note that $\pi(v_2, b; B) = v_2 P(b; B) - C(b; B)$ and that $P(\cdot; B)$ is a probability distribution on the interval $[0, 1]$. Finally, $P(\cdot; B)$ is strictly increasing on this interval because (i) the density f_1 is positive on $(0, 1)$ and (ii) each seller uses his dominant strategy $\tilde{S}$.

Theorem 2.2. *If $\langle \tilde{S}, B \rangle$ is an equilibrium in the BBDA, then the function B has the following properties:* (i) $0 < B(v_2)$ *for all* $v_2 \in (0, 1]$; (ii) $B(v_2) \leq v_2$ *for all* $v_2 \in [0, 1)$; (iii) $B(v_2)$ *is strictly increasing on* $[0, 1]$ *and differentiable almost everywhere.*

Proof. An important preliminary observation is this. Select a buyer. Suppose each seller uses $\tilde{S}$ and the other $m - 1$ buyers use the strategy B, where no restriction is placed on B. For any $p \in (0, 1)$, if the selected buyer bids p, then there is a positive probability that the price will be p and the selected buyer will receive an item at this price. This is true because, given any array of bids from the $m - 1$ buyers using B, a positive probability always exists that the offers of the m sellers will fall such that exactly m of the offers/bids of these $2m - 1$ traders are strictly less than p, i.e. $p = s_{(m+1)}$.

This observation immediately implies (i) and (ii). If a buyer with reservation value $v_2 > 0$ bids $b'' \leq 0$, then his expected utility is zero because no seller's offer will be less than b''. Bidding $b' \in (0, v_2)$, however, provides him with a positive probability of a profitable trade. This proves (i). If a type v_2 buyer ($v_2 < 1$) bids $b > v_2$, then a positive probability exists that the price will be in $(v_2, b]$ and he will trade at a loss. Reducing his bid to $b = v_2$ eliminates these losses without eliminating any profitable trades. This proves (ii).[5]

An argument from Chatterjee and Samuelson (1983, Theorem 1) shows that B must be non-decreasing. Let $v_2'' > v_2'$. Because $\langle \tilde{S}, B \rangle$ is an equilibrium,

$$\pi(v_2', B(v_2'); B) - \pi(v_2', B(v_2''); B) \geq 0 \tag{2.3}$$

and

$$\pi(v_2'', B(v_2''); B) - \pi(v_2'', B(v_2'); B) \geq 0. \tag{2.4}$$

Adding these inequalities produces

$$\pi(v_2'', B(v_2''); B) - \pi(v_2', B(v_2''); B) + \pi(v_2', B(v_2'); B) - \pi(v_2'', B(v_2'); B) \geq 0. \tag{2.5}$$

Recall that $\pi(v_2, b; B) = v_2 P(b; B) - C(b; B)$. Using this formula, (2.5) reduces to

$$(v_2'' - v_2') P(B(v_2''); B) + (v_2' - v_2'') P(B(v_2'); B) \geq 0. \tag{2.6}$$

or equivalently

$$(v_2'' - v_2')[P(B(v_2''); B) - P(B(v_2'); B)] \geq 0. \tag{2.7}$$

---

5. We can not rule out extremely small bids (e.g. $b = -1000$) for a type-zero buyer and extremely large bids for a type-one buyer. These are probability zero cases that do not affect the expected utilities of other traders and therefore do not affect equilibrium calculations.

By assumption, $v_2'' > v_2'$; therefore, $P(B(v_2''); B) \geq P(B(v_2'); B)$. Since $P(\cdot; B)$ is increasing, we conclude that $B(v_2'') \geq B(v_2')$.

We now show by contradiction that B cannot be constant over any interval with non-empty interior. Suppose that $B(v_2) = b'$ for all v_2 in such an interval I. The bounds that we have derived upon B imply that $0 < b' < 1$. Our argument rests upon the following point: the probability of trade $P(b; B)$ is discontinuous at $b = b'$. This is true because the following events occur simultaneously with positive probability: (i) each buyer's reservation value is in I and therefore all buyers bid b', (ii) at least one seller's offer is less than b', and (iii) at least one seller's offer is greater than b'. Note that (ii) and (iii) require that $m \geq 2$. Stipulations (i)–(iii) imply that the market price is b', the market fails to clear at this price, and the available units are allocated randomly among the buyers. Raising the selected buyer's bid from b' to $b'' > b'$ ensures that he receives an item with probability one in the stipulated situation rather than with some probability less than one under the random allocation rule. Therefore an $\varepsilon > 0$ exists such that $P(b''; B) > P(b'; B) + \varepsilon$ for all $b'' > b'$.

We next bound the change in the buyer's expected payment when he raises his bid from b' to b''. The change in his bid increases his payment only if either: (i) he trades with the bid b'' but would fail to trade with the bid b'; or (ii) the bid b' would be the market price, and he just drives up the price by raising his bid. In event (i), his payment is no more than b'', and in event (ii), the change in his payment is no more than $b'' - b'$. This implies the following bound on the change in the expected payment:

$$C(b''; B) - C(b'; B) \leq b''[P(b''; B) - P(b'; B)] + (b'' - b'). \qquad (2.8)$$

Because $B(v_2) \leq v_2$ for all v_2, there exists a v_2' in I such that $B(v_2') = b' < v_2'$. To obtain a contradiction we show that the type v_2' buyer has an incentive to incrementally raise his bid above b'. The change in his expected payoff from increasing his bid from b' to some $b'' \in (b', v_2')$ is

$$\pi(v_2', b''; B) - \pi(v_2', b'; B) = v_2'[P(b''; B) - P(b'; B)] + C(b'; B) - C(b''; B)$$

$$\geq (v_2' - b'')[P(b''; B) - (P(b'; B)] + (b' - b'')$$

$$> (v_2' - b'')\varepsilon + (b' - b''). \qquad (2.9)$$

For b'' near b', (2.9) is positive, which contradicts the assumption that $\langle \tilde{S}, B \rangle$ is an equilibrium.

Finally, the existence of B' almost everywhere follows from the monotonicity of B by a well-known theorem in analysis (e.g. see Royden (1968, p. 96)). ‖

Two points should be emphasized about the monotonicity of the buyers' strategy in an equilibrium $\langle \tilde{S}, B \rangle$. First, it implies that the probability of ties in the array of offers and bids is zero. Consequently we can ignore ties and the randomized allocations that they may necessitate. Second, the argument in Theorem 2.2 can be applied to double auctions besides the BBDA to show that when $m \geq 2$ an equilibrium common strategy of either side of the market must be increasing over all intervals in which the probability of trade is positive. Equilibrium strategies in the bilateral case may not be increasing; Leininger, Linhart, and Radnar (1986), for instance, have derived step-function equilibria in the bilateral split-the-difference double auction. Such equilibria, however, do not exist in this double auction when $m \geq 2$.

3. THE FIRST-ORDER APPROACH

This section concerns a buyer's first-order condition for maximizing his expected utility conditional on his reservation value v_2, the use of a common strategy B by the other $m-1$ buyers, and the use of $\tilde{S}$ by each seller. If $\langle \tilde{S}, B \rangle$ is an equilibrium, then this conditional expected utility is maximized at $B(v_2)$. We interpret the first-order condition as a differential equation that must be satisfied almost everywhere by any function B that defines an equilibrium $\langle \tilde{S}, B \rangle$. Conversely, we show that any increasing function B defines an equilibrium $\langle \tilde{S}, B \rangle$ if (i) B satisfies the differential equation, (ii) B respects the bounds $0 < B(v_2) < v_2$ for all $v_2 \in (0, 1]$, and (iii) the distribution F_1 of each seller's reservation value satisfies a monotonicity condition.

The first-order condition is formally derived in the Appendix. Here we state the condition and explain it intuitively. In order to state it we must define three probabilities:

K_m = the probability that bid b lies between $s_{(m-1)}$ and $s_{(m)}$ in a sample of $m-1$ buyers using strategy B and $m-1$ sellers using $\tilde{S}$.

L_m = the probability that bid b lies between $s_{(m-1)}$ and $s_{(m)}$ in a sample of $m-2$ buyers using strategy B and m sellers using $\tilde{S}$.

M_m = the probability that the bid b lies between $s_{(m)}$ and $s_{(m+1)}$ in a sample of $m-1$ buyers using strategy B and m sellers using $\tilde{S}$.

Recall that $s_{(k)}$ is the kth-order statistic (i.e. the offer/bid that ranks kth from the bottom) in the specified sample.

Suppose a type v_2 buyer considers raising his bid by Δb above the value b, which may or may not equal the value $B(v_2)$. Assuming that $b = B(\bar{v}_2)$ for some $\bar{v}_2$ and that $B'(v_2)$ exists, his incremental expected utility is

$$\left[m f_1(b) K_m \Delta b + (m-1) \frac{f_2(\bar{v}_2)}{B'(\bar{v}_2)} L_m \Delta b \right] (v_2 - b - \Delta b) - M_m \Delta b. \tag{3.1}$$

The buyer has two considerations in raising his bid. First, it may increase his probability of obtaining an item and, second, it may increase by Δb the price he pays for an item that he would have received at price b. These two considerations correspond respectively to the two terms in (3.1), which we now explain in detail.

The term in brackets represents the probability that the selected buyer obtains an item by raising his bid. If initially he does not receive an item, then some buyer or seller's offer/bid above b determines the price p. If raising his bid is to benefit the buyer, then p must be in $(b, b + \Delta b)$, i.e. p must be just above b so that he surpasses it and becomes one of the buyers who purchases an item.

Select a seller in addition to the selected buyer. The probability that this seller's bid falls in the interval $(b, b + \Delta b)$ is $f_1(b)\Delta b$. Conditional on it falling in the interval and on the selected buyer bidding b, the probability that this offer determines the market price is K_m. Note that this probability is calculated on a sample of the remaining $m-1$ bids and $m-1$ offers because the selected buyer's bid and the selected seller's offer are fixed. Any of the m sellers could have been selected, so the probability that by increasing his bid the selected buyer jumps over a price-determining seller's offer is $m f_1(b) K_m \Delta b$. A similar argument shows that $(m-1)f_2(\bar{v}_2)L_m \Delta b / B'(\bar{v}_2)$ is the probability that the selected buyer jumps over a price-determining buyer's bid as he increases his bid. The density of a buyer's bids at b is $f_2(\bar{v}_2)/B'(\bar{v}_2)$, not $f_2(\bar{v}_2)$, because the distribution of a buyer's bids is different from the distribution of his reservation values. Finally, the selected buyer's expected gain from obtaining an item by raising his bid is the term in brackets times the gain $v_2 - b - \Delta b$ when this happens.

On the other side of the ledger is $M_m \Delta b$. If the buyer is the trader whose bid determines the price, then raising his bid Δb increases the price that he pays for an item by Δb. The expected cost of raising his bid is therefore Δb times the probability M_m that he is in fact the price-determining trader.

From (3.1) we obtain the formula for the marginal expected utility of a type v_2 buyer whose bid is b:

$$\frac{d\pi(v_2, b; B)}{db} = \left[mf_1(b)K_m + (m-1)\frac{f_2(\bar{v}_2)}{B'(\bar{v}_2)} L_m \right] (v_2 - b) - M_m. \tag{3.2}$$

If $\langle \tilde{S}, B \rangle$ is an equilibrium, then B satisfies the first-order condition $d\pi(v_2, B(v_2); B)/db = 0$ at all reservation values v_2 where B' exists.

To obtain a differential equation in the strategy B we must define the probabilities K_m, L_m, and M_m so that their values are functions only of the point (v_2, b):

$$K_m(v_2, b) = \sum_{i=0}^{m-1} \binom{m-1}{i}^2 F_1(b)^{m-1-i}(1 - F_1(b))^i F_2(v_2)^i (1 - F_2(v_2))^{m-1-i}, \tag{3.3}$$

$$L_m(v_2, b) = \sum_{i=1}^{m-1} \binom{m}{i}\binom{m-2}{i-1} F_1(b)^{m-i}(1 - F_1(b))^i F_2(v_2)^{i-1}(1 - F_2(v_2))^{m-i-1}, \tag{3.4}$$

$$M_m(v_2, b) = \sum_{i=0}^{m-1} \binom{m-1}{i}\binom{m}{i} F_1(b)^{m-i}(1 - F_1(b))^i F_2(v_2)^i (1 - F_2(v_2))^{m-1-i}. \tag{3.5}$$

The probabilities K_m, L_m, and M_m in (3.1-3.2) are obtained by evaluating (3.3-3.5) at $v_2 = B^{-1}(b)$.

That $K_m(B^{-1}(b), b)$ is the probability that the bid b lies between $s_{(m-1)}$ and $s_{(m)}$ in a sample of $m - 1$ buyers using strategy B and $m - 1$ sellers using strategy $\tilde{S}$ can be seen as follows. The statement that b lies between $s_{(m-1)}$ and $s_{(m)}$ means that $m - 1$ offers/bids are below b and that the remaining $m - 1$ offers/bids in the sample are above b. We sum the probabilities of all possible events in which exactly $m - 1$ offers/bids are less than b. A total of $m - 1$ offers/bids less than b may be obtained by i bids and $(m - 1 - i)$ offers less than b. For a particular selection of i buyers and $(m - 1 - i)$ sellers, the probability that only their offers/bids are less than b is $F_1(b)^{m-1-i}(1 - F_1(b))^i \times F_2(v_2)^i (1 - F_2(v_2))^{m-1-i}$ where $v_2 = B^{-1}(b)$. $F_1(b)$ is the probability that a particular seller (using strategy $\tilde{S}$) offers less than b, and $F_2(v_2) = F_2(B^{-1}(b))$ is the probability that a particular buyer (using strategy B) bids less than b. The term

$$\binom{m-1}{i}^2 = \binom{m-1}{i}\binom{m-1}{m-1-i}$$

is the number of ways of simultaneously choosing i buyers from $m - 1$ buyers and $(m - 1 - i)$ sellers from $m - 1$ sellers. Similar arguments show that L_m and M_m are given by (3.4) and (3.5).[6]

A differential equation in the strategy B is obtained by setting (3.2) equal to zero and regarding K_m, L_m, and M_m as functions of v_2 and b. Suppose $\langle \tilde{S}, B \rangle$ is an equilibrium.

_____

6. See David (1981, Chapter 2) for a discussion of this type of probability calculation.

Because B is necessarily increasing we can invert B and regard a buyer's reservation value v_2 as a function of his bid b, i.e. $v_2 = v_2(b) \equiv B^{-1}(b)$ and $\dot{v}_2 \equiv dv_2(b)/db = 1/B'(v_2)$. Substituting $\dot{v}_2$ into the differential equation and solving gives

$$\dot{v}_2 = \frac{M_m(v_2, b) - mf_1(b)K_m(v_2, b)(v_2 - b)}{(m-1)f_2(v_2)L_m(v_2, b)(v_2 - b)} \tag{3.6}$$

$$\dot{b} = 1 \tag{3.7}$$

where the tautology $\dot{b} \equiv db/db = 1$ has been added. Written in this form, the differential equation defines a vector field $(\dot{v}_2, \dot{b})$.

If $\langle \tilde{S}, B \rangle$ is an equilibrium, then (3.6-3.7) hold at every point $(v_2, B(v_2))$ at which $B'(v_2)$ exists. To establish a converse, we assume that the distribution F_1 of a seller's reservation value satisfies the following monotonicity property:

$$v_1 + F_1(v_1)/f_1(v_1) \text{ is increasing for } v_1 \in [0, 1]. \tag{3.8}$$

Given (3.8), if a solution curve to (3.6-3.7) defines an increasing function $b = B(v_2)$, then $\langle \tilde{S}, B \rangle$ is an equilibrium in the BBDA.

Theorem 3.1. *If $\langle \tilde{S}, B \rangle$ is an equilibrium in the BBDA, then $B(v_2) = b$ and $\dot{v}_2 = 1/B'(v_2)$ satisfy (3.6-3.7) at every $v_2 \in [0, 1]$ at which $B'(v_2)$ exists. Conversely, suppose (3.8) holds and B is a C^1 function on $[0, 1]$ such that (i) $B'(v_2) > 0$ and $0 < B(v_2) < v_2$ for all $v_2 \in (0, 1]$ and (ii) $B(v_2) = b$ and $\dot{v}_2 = 1/B'(v_2)$ satisfy (3.6-3.7) at every $v_2 \in (0, 1]$. Then $\langle \tilde{S}, B \rangle$ is an equilibrium of the BBDA.*

Proof. See Appendix. ‖

We do not address the existence of equilibria here; Williams (1988) shows that an equilibrium $\langle \tilde{S}, B \rangle$ exists for a generic choice of the distributions F_1, F_2.

4. THE GEOMETRY OF SOLUTIONS

Theorem 2.2 states that if $\langle \tilde{S}, B \rangle$ is an equilibrium, then $0 \le B(v_2) \le v_2 \le 1$. The graph of an equilibrium strategy B therefore lies within the triangle $0 \le b \le v_2 \le 1$ (see Figure 4.1). Following an approach developed in Satterthwaite and Williams (1987), we describe the vector field (3.6-3.7) on this triangle in order to gain insight into the equilibria of the BBDA.

Formula (3.6) defines $\dot{v}_2$ as a real number at every point in the triangle except along the edges XY where $b = 0$ and XZ where $v_2 = b$. At points X and Z, $\dot{v}_2$ is indeterminate; between X and Y it is negative infinity and between X and Z it is positive infinity. To obtain well-defined values for the vector field $(\dot{v}_2, \dot{b})$ everywhere except X and Z we consider the field's normalization $\bar{v} = (\dot{v}_2, \dot{b})/|(\dot{v}_2, \dot{b})|$. Normalization does not alter the solution curves. Note that $\bar{v}$ is non-singular at every point in the triangle except X and Z.

Inspection of the field along the edges and at the vertices allows us to identify three sets where solution curves enter the triangle and one set where they leave the triangle. A solution curve enters at each point where the field points inward. Solutions may enter through X where $\dot{v}_2$ is indeterminate. The field $\bar{v}$ equals $(1, 0)$ and therefore points into the triangle along the edge XZ. It also points inward along the edge YZ at points where $F_1(b) > f_1(b)(1 - b)$. A solution curve exits at any point where the field points outward. This occurs only on YZ (perhaps including vertex Z) at points where $F_1(b) < f_1(b)(1 - b)$.

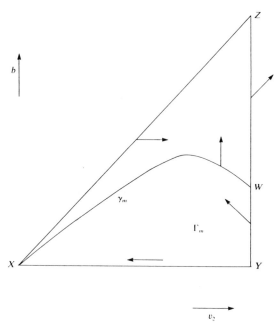

FIGURE 4.1

If $\langle \tilde{S}, B \rangle$ is an equilibrium then the graph of B lies in the triangle XYZ defined by the inequalities $0 \leq b \leq v_2 \leq 1$. The arrows show the direction of the vector field $(\dot{v}_2, \dot{b})$ on the edges and at a point on γ_m

Figure 4.2 shows three solution curves for the case in which F_1 and F_2 are uniform and $m = 2$. Curve ρ_1 enters from the edge XZ, ρ_2 enters from the vertex X, and ρ_3 enters from the lower half of the edge YZ. All exit along the upper half of edge YZ. Curve ρ_2 meets the conditions of Theorem 3.1 and therefore defines an equilibrium $\langle \tilde{S}, B \rangle$. Curve ρ_1 may be a segment of an equilibrium strategy B, but it is unclear how to complete its definition for reservation values that lie to the left of the point on XZ where it enters the triangle.[7] Finally, curve ρ_3 does not determine an equilibrium because it does not define the buyer's bid b as an increasing function of v_2, i.e. $\dot{v}_2$ is negative along a segment of ρ_3.

The failure of ρ_3 to determine an equilibrium illustrates an extremely important property of $\dot{v}_2$. Inside the triangle an open region necessarily exists where $\dot{v}_2$ is negative; formally we define this region as

$$\Gamma_m(F_1, F_2) \equiv \{(v_2, b): \dot{v}_2 < 0\}. \tag{4.1}$$

where the dependence in (3.6) of $\dot{v}_2$ on (v_2, b), F_1, F_2, and m is suppressed. Let γ_m denote the upper edge of Γ_m. The set Γ_m always contains the edge XY and some portion of the edge YZ. Figure 4.1 shows Γ_m as the region below the curve γ_m connecting X and W. The set Γ_m is important because the graph of any function B that defines an equilibrium $\langle \tilde{S}, B \rangle$ must lie outside Γ_m at every point where B is differentiable. In the

---

7. Extending B's graph down along the edge XZ towards X does not define an equilibrium. At each point on this extension B' exists and yet (3.5) is not satisfied. This violates Theorem 3.1.

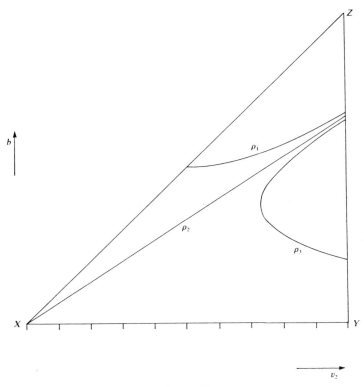

FIGURE 4.2

The curves ρ_1, ρ_2, and ρ_3 are solutions to the differential equation (3.6)–(3.7) when $m = 2$ and reservation values are distributed uniformly. Only ρ_2 defines an equilibrium

next section we show that as m increases Γ_m grows and forces all equilibrium strategies towards edge XZ, which corresponds to truthful revelation. Figure 4.3 illustrates this. It graphs γ_m, the upper boundary of Γ_m, for values of m equal to one, eight, and sixteen when F_1 and F_2 are the uniform distribution. This property of Γ_m is the fundamental insight that underlies our convergence result.

The set Γ_m can be interpreted in terms of marginal expected utility. Choose a point (v_2, b) in Γ_m and suppose an equilibrium $\langle \tilde{S}, B \rangle$ did exist such that $B(v_2) = b$ and B is differentiable at v_2. Theorem 2.2 states that $B'(v_2) \geqq 0$. Select a buyer. If the other traders use their equilibrium strategies, formula (3.2) implies that the selected buyer's marginal expected utility is necessarily positive at (v_2, b) because by the definition of Γ_m, a negative number would be needed in place of $B'(v_2)$ in (3.2) in order to make his marginal expected utility zero. The selected buyer therefore has an incentive to raise his bid above $B(v_2) = b$, which contradicts the assumption that $\langle \tilde{S}, B \rangle$ is an equilibrium.

5. CONVERGENCE TO TRUTHFUL REVELATION

The complement of Γ_m in the triangle $0 \leqq b \leqq v_2 \leqq 1$ contains the edge XZ where the buyer's bid b equals his reservation value v_2. In this section we show that as m increases

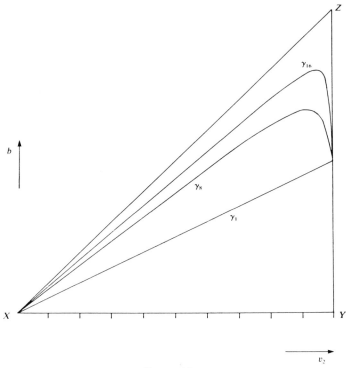

FIGURE 4.3

The boundaries γ_1, γ_8, and γ_{16} are shown for the uniform case. The graph of any equilibrium strategy B in a market with $2m$ traders must lie above γ_m almost everywhere. The edge XZ corresponds to the strategy of truthful revelation

the vertical distance between the boundary γ_m and the edge XZ is $O(1/m)$. The graph of an equilibrium strategy B must lie between γ_m and XZ at almost all values of v_2. This permits us to show that in equilibrium the difference between a buyer's reservation value and his bid is $O(1/m)$, no matter what his reservation value and no matter which equilibrium $\langle \tilde{S}, B \rangle$ is chosen.

Rearrangement of (3.6) produces an inequality defining the region in which $\dot{v}_2$ is non-negative:

$$\dot{v}_2 \gtreqless 0 \quad \text{if and only if} \quad v_2 - b \lesseqgtr \frac{1}{f_1(b)} \times N_m(v_2, b) \tag{5.1}$$

where N_m is the ratio

$$N_m(v_2, b) \equiv \frac{M_m(v_2, b)}{mK_m(v_2, b)}. \tag{5.2}$$

The left-hand side of the second inequality in (5.1) is the amount by which the buyer's bid misrepresents his reservation value. Only the right-hand side depends on the number of traders. We therefore focus on the behaviour of N_m as m increases.

Recall that K_m is the probability that bid b lies between $s_{(m-1)}$ and $s_{(m)}$ in a sample of $m-1$ buyers and $m-1$ sellers, and M_m is the probability that bid b lies between $s_{(m)}$ and $s_{(m+1)}$ in a sample of $m-1$ buyers and m sellers. These two probabilities are almost the same; consequently one expects that, for each (v_2, b) pair, as m grows tht the ratio M_m/K_m approaches some constant. If this is so, then substitution into (5.2) gives our main result. Two theorems, whose proofs are in the Appendix, confirm this intuition.

Theorem 5.1 *For each pair of numbers* $0 < b \leq v_2 < 1$ *and all* $m \geq 1$, *the ratio* $N_m(v_2, b)$ *is strictly decreasing in* m.

The functions K_m, L_m, M_m, and hence N_m are well-defined in the $m = 1$ case, which permits us to state Theorem 5.1 using $m = 1$. The statement of Theorem 5.2 uses the notation

$$z(v_2, b) = \frac{F_2(v_2)(1 - F_1(b))}{F_1(b)(1 - F_2(v_2))}.$$
(5.3)

Theorem 5.2. *If* $m \geq 2$ *and* (v_2, b) *satisfies* $0 < b \leq v_2 < 1$, *then*

$$N_m(v_2; b) < \frac{2F_1(b)}{m} \max[1, z(v_2, b)].$$
(5.4)

These theorems have the following interpretation. Consider $m' < m''$. If, for m', $\dot{v}_2$ is negative at some point (v_2, b), then Theorem 5.1 implies that it is also negative for m''. The region Γ_m therefore grows monotonically in m, i.e. for $m' < m''$, $\Gamma_{m'} \subset \Gamma_{m''}$. Theorem 5.2 describes the rate at which this region grows.

The main result of the paper follows from substituting the inequalities of Theorem 5.2 into (5.1).

Theorem 5.3. *Consider the BBDA when sellers' reservation values are drawn from* F_1 *and buyer's reservation values are drawn from* F_2. *A continuous function* $\kappa(v_2; F_1, F_2)$ *of* v_2 *exists such that, for any* $m \geq 2$ *and any equilibrium* $\langle \tilde{S}, B \rangle$ *in a market of size* m,

$$v_2 - B(v_2) \leq \frac{\kappa(v_2; F_1, F_2)}{m}$$
(5.5)

at every v_2 *in the open interval* $(0, 1)$.

Proof. We first show that B satisfies (5.5) at all reservation values $v_2 \in (0, 1)$ where $B'(v_2)$ exists. Fix v_2 and let $\bar{b}$ denote $B(v_2)$. From (5.1) and Theorem 5.2 we have

$$v_2 - \bar{b} \leq \frac{N_m(v_2, \bar{b})}{f_1(\bar{b})} < \frac{2}{m} \frac{F_1(\bar{b})}{f_1(\bar{b})} \max[1, z(v_2, \bar{b})].$$
(5.6)

A finite bound on $v_2 - \bar{b}$ that does not involve $\bar{b}$ is obtained by maximizing the right-hand side of (5.6) over a closed interval that contains $\bar{b}$. The bid $\bar{b}$ is bounded above by v_2 and below by zero. The right-hand side, however, may be infinite at $\bar{b} = 0$. This complication is sidestepped by bounding $\bar{b}$ away from zero. The region Γ_2 is an open set that contains the triangle's lower edge XY. Theorem 5.1 implies that the point $(v_2, \bar{b})$ lies above the region Γ_2. Choose a continuous function μ on $(0, 1)$ such that the graph of μ lies within Γ_2 and μ is greater than zero. The bid $\bar{b}$ therefore satisfies $\mu(v_2) \leq \bar{b} \leq v_2$. Define

$$\kappa(v_2) \equiv \max_{\mu(v2) \leq b \leq v_2} \frac{2F_1(b)}{f_1(b)} \max [1, z(v_2, b)]. \tag{5.7}$$

For convenience, we suppress the dependence of κ on F_1 and F_2. Note that κ is continuous in v_2 because μ is continuous. With this definition of κ, (5.5) holds at all points where B' exists.

We now show that (5.5) also holds at reservation values in $(0, 1)$ where B' does not exist. Consider the set D_m of reservation values v_2 and bids b that violate (5.5):

$$D_m \equiv \{(v_2, b): 0 < b \leq v_2 < 1 \text{ and } v_2 - \kappa(v_2)/m > b\}. \tag{5.8}$$

The set D_m is open because κ is continuous. Suppose, contrary to the theorem, that some $(v_2, B(v_2)) \equiv (v_2, b)$ is an element of D_m. A rectangle within D_m exists whose base is on the edge XY and whose upper right corner is (v_2, b). Because B is increasing, the graph of B must pass through the rectangle. Somewhere on this segment of the graph B' must exist, which contradicts the above result that (5.5) holds wherever B is differentiable. ‖

As an illustration, we follow the proof of Theorem 5.3 to compute a suitable function κ for the case in which each trader's reservation values are uniformly distributed. To bound b away from zero, we choose a positive function $b = \mu(v_2)$ on $(0, 1)$ whose graph lies within Γ_2. Formula (3.6) for $\dot{v}_2$ implies that

$$\gamma_1 = \{(v_2, b): v_2 = b + F_1(b)/f_1(b)\}. \tag{5.9}$$

In the uniform case, γ_1 is the graph of the function $b = v_2/2$. Let μ be this function. We now compute κ using (5.7). From (5.3), $z(v_2, b) = v_2(1-b)/(1-v_2)b$. Note that $z(v_2, b) \geq 1$ for $v_2/2 \leq b \leq v_2$. Formula (5.7) therefore simplifies to

$$\kappa(v_2; F_1, F_2) = \max_{v_2/2 \leq b \leq v_2} \frac{2bv_2(1-b)}{(1-v_2)b} = \frac{v_2(2-v_2)}{(1-v_2)}. \tag{5.10}$$

which means that in the uniform case, the difference between a buyer's reservation value v_2 and his bid is less than or equal to $v_2(2-v_2)/(1-v_2)m$.

In the uniform case direct substitution shows that the strategy

$$B(v_2) = \frac{m}{m+1} v_2 \tag{5.11}$$

satisfies the first-order condition (3.6) and hence defines an equilibrium $\langle \tilde{S}, B \rangle$ for the market with m sellers and m buyers. Inspection shows that this equilibrium satisfies the bound $v_2(2-v_2)/(1-v_2)m$. While the bound in Theorem 5.3 is loose, this example shows that the rate of convergence $O(1/m)$ is sharp as a description of how fast all sequences of equilibria converge.

Curve ρ_2 in Figure 4.2 depicts this solution for $m = 2$. Substitution of $m = 1$ in (5.11) defines the equilibrium that Williams (1987) computed for the bilateral BBDA in the uniform case. Table 5.1 compares the total ex ante expected gains from trade that this sequence of equilibria generates with (i) the expected gains from the optimal mechanism (which was defined in the Introduction) and (ii) the expected gains that would be realized if all traders honestly reported their reservation values. The table shows the rapidity with which allocations in the BBDA approach ex post efficiency.

TABLE 5.1

Relative efficiency of the BBDA as the market grows: uniform case

m	T_B	T^*	T_0	$1 - T_B/T_0$	$1 - T^*/T_0$
2	0·37037	0·37746	0·39999	0·07415	0·05633
3	0·62227	0·62572	0·64286	0·03203	0·02666
4	0·87333	0·87527	0·88887	0·01748	0·01530
6	1·37421	1·37507	1·38462	0·00751	0·00690
8	1·87454	1·87504	1·88235	0·00415	0·00388
10	2·37470	2·37501	2·38095	0·00263	0·00249
12	2·87479	2·87501	2·88000	0·00181	0·00173

Notes. T_B is the total ex ante expected gains from trade that the equilibrium (5.11) of the BBDA generates, T^* is the total ex ante expected gains that the optimal mechanism generates, and T_0 is the total ex ante expected gains from trade that would be generated if traders honestly reported their reservation values. The values for T^* and T_0 are from Gresik and Satterthwaite (1986, Table 1).

6. ADDITIONAL COMMENTS

1. Insight into the effectiveness of the BBDA is obtained by comparing it to a plausible alternative, the fixed-price mechanism, that Hagerty and Rogerson (1985) and Gresik and Satterthwaite (1988) studied. This mechanism *a priori* fixes price at the value p that would be the competitive price if there were a continuum of sellers with reservation values distributed according to F_1 and a continuum of buyers with reservation values distributed according to F_2. In the uniform case, for instance, the price p is fixed at 0·5. In equilibrium each trader honestly reports his reservation value and sellers whose values are less than p trade at this price with buyers whose values are greater than p. If, as is likely for finite markets, supply does not equal demand, then whichever side of the market is long is randomly rationed. The combination of the fixed price and random rationing among all traders on the long side of the market is what makes honest reporting a dominant strategy for each trader.

This rationing creates inefficiency because a buyer whose gain from trade is large is just as likely to be excluded as a buyer whose gain is small. Table 6.1 illustrates the seriousness of this inefficiency by comparing this mechanism's performance with the BBDA's performance in the uniform case. Informally the reason for the poor performance of the fixed price mechanism is that it only uses traders' reports to determine who is willing to trade at the specified price p. The BBDA, on the other hand, extracts more information from the traders' reports by rank-ordering them according to their expressed desire to trade. Despite the misrepresentation that the BBDA induces, its more thorough use of the agents' reports results in dramatically better performance.

TABLE 6.1

Relative efficiency of the fixed price mechanism and the BBDA

m	2	4	6	8	10	12
$1 - T_F/T_0$	0·2187	0·1826	0·1611	0·1462	0·1350	0·1262
$1 - T_B/T_0$	0·0742	0·0175	0·0075	0·0042	0·0026	0·0018

Notes. T_B is the total ex ante expected gains from trade that the equilibrium (5.11) of the BBDA generates, T_F is the total ex ante expected gains that the fixed price mechanism generates, and T_0 is the total ex ante expected gains from trade that would be generated if traders honestly reported their reservation values. The values for T_0 and T_F are from Gresik and Satterthwaite (1988, Tables 1 and 2).

2. For finite markets the BBDA and other double auctions are ex post inefficient, i.e. when the market closes potential gains from trade may be "left on the table". Equilibrium strategies are fully revealing of traders' reservation values; consequently when the market closes the traders know if further gains from trade are possible. Cramton (1984) criticized one-shot double auctions on this point. Specifically, he argued that the use of a one-shot double auction implicitly assumes that traders pre-commit not to reopen the market even when it is common knowledge that further gains from trade exist. Such pre-commitment may be difficult or impossible to maintain. Our results suggest that this criticism of one-shot double auctions lacks force in large markets because the expected value of the unrealized gains from trade rapidly vanishes as the market grows.

3. A simple partial equilibrium calculation provides insight into our convergence result. It reveals that the driving force behind the $O(1/m)$ rate is the relative rates at which the likelihood of obtaining an item by increasing one's bid and the likelihood of simply driving up price go to zero as the number of traders increases. Consider the BBDA for a market with $2m$ traders in which $F \equiv F_1 \equiv F_2$ (with density f). Select a buyer with reservation value v_2. Suppose he believes the non-equilibrium conjecture that all other buyers will truthfully report their reservation values. In the sample of offers and bids from the $2m - 1$ other traders, let g be the density of the critical offer/bid $s_{(m)}$ that the selected buyer must beat with his bid b in order to receive an item. As before, let M_m be the probability that the bid b lies between $s_{(m)}$ and $s_{(m+1)}$ in this sample and thus determines the market price. Adapting (3.2) to this simplified situation, the buyer chooses his bid to satisfy

$$(v_2 - b)g(b) = M_m. \tag{6.1}$$

When the buyer considers raising his bid, the left-hand side is his marginal expected gain from increasing his likelihood of receiving an item and the right-hand side is his marginal expected cost from driving up the price. Formulas in David (1981, p. 9) give

$$M_m = \binom{2m-1}{m} F(b)^m (1 - F(b))^{m-1} \tag{6.2}$$

$$g(b) = (2m-1)f(b)\binom{2m-2}{m-1} F(b)^{m-1}(1 - F(B))^{m-1}. \tag{6.3}$$

Substitution into (6.1) implies

$$v_2 - b = \frac{F(b)}{mf(b)}. \tag{6.4}$$

which is the same rate that we obtained in Theorem 5.3.

4. A basic insight of the literature in social choice theory on strategy-proofness is that strategic behaviour is only avoidable in mechanisms in which individuals can not affect each other's allocations.[8] In the BBDA traders affect each other's allocations by affecting the expected price. The ability to affect price vanishes rapidly as the market grows. The social choice results therefore suggest that strategic behaviour should vanish as the market grows large. Our result shows that this in fact happens.

5. Williams (1988) generalized the results of this paper to the case in which the number of sellers may differ from the number of buyers. He showed that for any

---

8. See, for example, Satterthwaite and Sonnenschein (1981). The one important exception is the family of Groves mechanisms.

equilibrium $\langle \tilde{S}, B \rangle$ in the market with n sellers and q buyers

$$v_2 - B(v_2) \leqq \frac{\kappa(v_2; F_1, F_2)}{\min(n, q)}, \tag{6.5}$$

where $\kappa(v_2; F_1, F_2)$ is the same function as in (5.5). The proof of this more general result is obtained using the approach of our paper and its convergence result.

6. The BBDA is one example of the sealed-bid k-double auction. The more general formulation of the k-double auction is to set price equal to $(1 - k)s_{(m)} + ks_{(m+1)}$ where k is a fixed parameter in the interval $[0, 1]$. The BBDA is the k-double auction in which $k = 1$. All the results of this paper have exact parallels for the seller's offer double auction in which $k = 0$. Our analysis of these two extreme cases is greatly facilitated because in each case traders on one side of the market truthfully reveal their reservation values. The analysis becomes more difficult when k is in the open interval $(0, 1)$ because then a trader on either side of the market can affect the price at which he trades; as a consequence all traders misrepresent their reservation values. As of this writing we have been unable to obtain the $O(1/m)$ convergence result for this more general case. We conjecture, however, that it is true for two reasons. First, regions analogous to Γ_m exist in the general case that bound equilibrium strategies. The key insight in our analysis of the BBDA thus generalizes to all k-double auctions. Second, numerical computation of equilibria in the general case supports the conjecture that all differentiable equilibria converge to truthful revelation as $O(1/m)$.

APPENDIX

Proof of Theorem 3.1. To prove the necessary part of the theorem, it is sufficient here to derive formula (3.2) for $d\pi/db$. The result in the theorem concerning (3.6–7) then follows from the discussion in the text. We derive the marginal expected utility at bid b of a type v_2 buyer who is bidding against m sellers, each using strategy $\tilde{S}$, and $m - 1$ buyers, each using an increasing function B as his strategy. Let $x = s_{(m)}$ and $y = s_{(m+1)}$ in the array of $2m - 1$ offers/bids received from the other traders and let $e(x, y)$ denote the joint density of x and y. Note that $e(x, y) = 0$ whenever $x > y$. Table A.1 catalogues the three distinct utility consequences of the bid b. For example, if b should be greater than y, then the selected buyer receives an item at price y and has utility $v_2 - y$.

The expected utility of bidding b is

$$\pi(v_2, b; B) = \int_b^1 \int_0^b (v_2 - b)e(x, y)dxdy + \int_0^b \int_0^y (v_2 - y)e(x, y)dxdy \tag{A.1}$$

where the first integral is the expected gain from the case II outcomes and the second integral is the expected gain from the case III outcomes. Differentiating with respect to b, produces

$$\frac{d\pi}{db} = -\int_0^b (v_2 - b)e(x, b)dx + \int_b^1 (v_2 - b)e(b, y)dy$$

$$- \int_b^1 \int_0^b e(x, y)dxdy + \int_0^b (v_2 - b)e(x, b)dx. \tag{A.2}$$

TABLE A.1

Possible outcomes of a bid b

Case no.	Case definition	Ex post utility
I	$b < x < y$	0
II	$x < b < y$	$v_2 - b$
III	$x < y < b$	$v_2 - y$

Note: Ties are a probability zero event because all traders use increasing strategies.

The first and fourth terms cancel, $(v_2 - b)$ factors out of the second term, and the remaining integrals have straightforward probability interpretations:

$$d\pi/db = (v_2 - b)g(b) - \Pr(x < b < y) \tag{A.3}$$

where $g(b)$ is the density of the order statistic x evaluated at b. This density can be shown to equal the term in brackets in (3.2) using the standard technique in David (1981, p. 9). Similarly, $\Pr(x < b < y) = M_m(B^{-1}(b), b)$, which completes our discussion of the theorem's necessary part.

Sufficiency of the first-order approach is proven as follows. Given a function B that meets the theorem's requirements, we must show that $\pi(v_2, b; B)$ is maximized at $b = B(v_2)$. Arguments in the proof of Theorem 2.2 show that we can restrict attention to $b \in (0, v_2]$. Two cases must be considered; $b \in (0, B(1)]$ and $b \in (B(1), v_2]$. The first case is facilitated by defining

$$J_m(v_2, b; B) \equiv mf_1(b)K_m(v_2, b) + (m-1)f_2(v_2)L_m(v_2, b)/B'(v_2). \tag{A.4}$$

Formula (3.2) then becomes

$$d\pi(v_2, b; B)/db = J_m(B^{-1}(b), b; B)(v_2 - b) - M_m(B^{-1}(b), b) \tag{A.5}$$

and the differential equation (3.6) is equivalent to

$$J_m(v_2, B(v_2); B)(v_2 - B(v_2)) - M_m(v_2, B(v_2)) = 0. \tag{A.6}$$

Formula (A.5) can be rewritten as

$$d\pi(v_2, b; B)/db = J_m(B^{-1}(b), b, B)(v_2 - B^{-1}(b))$$
$$+ J_m(B^{-1}(b), b; B)(B^{-1}(b) - b) - M_m(B^{-1}(b), b). \tag{A.7}$$

If we evaluate the differential equation (A.6) at $v_2 = B^{-1}(b)$, we obtain the last line in (A.7). We therefore have $d\pi/db$ equal to the top line. Note that (i) $J_m(B^{-1}(b), b; B)$ is positive for all $0 < b < B(1)$, (ii) $d\pi(v_2, b; B)/db$ is zero at $b = B(v_2)$, and (iii) the function B^{-1} is increasing since B is increasing. The marginal expected utility $d\pi(v_2, b; B)/db$ therefore changes from positive to negative at $b = B(v_2)$, which establishes that $\pi(v_2, b; B)$ is maximized on $(0, B(1)]$ at $b = B(v_2)$.

Consider now the remaining case of $b \in (B(1), v_2]$. While the marginal expected utility $d\pi(v_2, b; B)/db$ is discontinuous at $b = B(1)$, the expected utility $\pi(v_2, b; B)$ is continuous in b on $[0, 1]$ because B is a C^1 function. It is therefore sufficient to prove that $d\pi(v_2, b; B)/db$ is negative over $(B(1), v_2]$. For a bid b in this interval (A.3) is

$$\frac{d\pi(v_2, b; B)}{db} = (v_2 - b)mf_1(b)K_m(1, b) - M_m(1, b)$$

$$= (v_2 - b)mf_1(b)[1 - F_1(b)]^{m-1} - mF_1(b)[1 - F_1(b)]^{m-1}$$

$$= mf_1(b)[1 - F_1(b)]^{m-1}\left[v_2 - b - \frac{F_1(b)}{f_1(b)}\right]. \tag{A.8}$$

Consider the last line of (A.8). The monotonicity property (3.8) implies that the expression in brackets is decreasing in b, and it is also increasing in v_2. Consequently if some line of (A.8) is negative at $v_2 = 1$ and $b = B(1)$, then each line is negative for any v_2 over the entire interval $(B(1), v_2]$.

We show that the first line is negative at $v_2 = 1$ and $b = B(1)$ by considering the solution B at that point. By hypothesis $\dot{v}_2$ is positive at all points $(v_2, B(v_2))$. The numerator of the right-hand side of (3.6) determines the sign of $\dot{v}_2$; at $(1, B(1))$ this numerator is $-[1 - B(1)]mf_1(B(1))K_m(1, B(1)) + M_m(1, B(1)) > 0$. The negative of this expression is the first line of (A.8) evaluated at $v_2 = 1$ and $b = B(1)$. ‖

In proving Theorems 5.1 and 5.2 we use the following formula for $N_m/F_1(b)$:

$$\frac{N_m(v_2, b)}{F_1(b)} = \frac{\sum_{i=0}^{m-1} \binom{m-1}{i}\binom{m}{i}z^i}{\sum_{i=0}^{m-1} \binom{m-1}{i}\binom{m}{i}(m-i)z^i}. \tag{A.9}$$

The right-hand side has been derived from (5.2) by (i) factoring out F_1 from $M_m(v_2, b)$ and cancelling, (ii) dividing the numerator and denominator by $[F_1(b)(1 - F_2(v_2))]^{m-1}$, and (iii) substituting

$$m \binom{m-1}{i}^2 = \binom{m-1}{i}\binom{m}{i}(m-i) \tag{A.10}$$

into the denominator.

Proof of Theorem 5.1. It is sufficient to prove that N_m / F_1 is strictly decreasing in m. Substitute j for i as the index of the terms in the formula for N_{m+1}/F_1 that is given by (A.9). Next, compute the numerator of $(N_m - N_{m+1})/F_1$:

$$\left[\sum_{i=0}^m \binom{m-1}{i}\binom{m}{i} z^i\right]\left[\sum_{j=0}^m \binom{m}{j}\binom{m+1}{j}(m+1-j)z^j\right]$$

$$-\left[\sum_{i=0}^{m-1}\binom{m-1}{i}\binom{m}{i}(m-i)z^i\right]\left[\sum_{j=0}^m \binom{m}{j}\binom{m+1}{j}z^j\right]. \tag{A.11}$$

The proof will be completed by showing that all of the coefficients of this polynomial are non-negative, and some are strictly positive.

For $0 \le k \le 2m - 1$, the coefficient of z^k is

$$\sum_{i+j=k,\, 0 \le i \le m-1,\, 0 \le j \le m} \binom{m-1}{i}\binom{m}{i}\binom{m+1}{j}(i+1-j). \tag{A.12}$$

We now pair terms in this expression with the following formula: the $i = u$, $j = v$ term is paired with the $i = v - 1, j = u + 1$ term. Some terms may be left out by this pairing; there is no term to pair with the $i = k, j = 0$ term (if such a term exists for the given value of k), and a term of the form $i = u, j = u + 1$ is paired with itself. It is easy to see from (A.12), however, that a term with $j = 0$ is positive, and a term with $i + 1 = j$ is zero. Except for these special cases, the formula pairs each term in (A.12) with a different term. This pairing is well-defined, i.e. if i', j' is assigned to i'', j'' by the formula, then i'', j'' is assigned to i', j'.

We now rewrite the sum of $i = u, j = v$ term and the $i = v - 1, j = u + 1$ term. Factoring out the $i = u, j = v$ term, we have

$$\binom{m-1}{u}\binom{m}{u}\binom{m}{v}\binom{m+1}{v}(u+1-v)+\binom{m-1}{v-1}\binom{m}{v-1}\binom{m}{u+1}\binom{m+1}{u+1}(v-u-1)$$

$$=\binom{m-1}{u}\binom{m}{u}\binom{m}{v}\binom{m+1}{v}(u+1-v)\left\{1-\left[\frac{v}{u+1}\right]^2\right\}. \tag{A.13}$$

The signs of the last two terms of the product on the second line of (A.13) are the same. The expression (A.13) is therefore positive except when $u + 1 = v$, which is a case that was discussed above. ∥

Proof of Theorem 5.2. The inequality (5.4) is equivalent to the following pair of inequalities: (i) if $z(v_2, b) \le 1$, then $N_m(v_2, b)/F_1(b) < 2/m$, and (ii) if $z(v_2, b) \ge 1$, then $N_m(v_2, b)/F_1(b) < 2z(v_2, b)/m$. We begin by proving the first inequality. Using (A.9), it is sufficient to show that

$$\sum_{i=0}^{m-1}\binom{m-1}{i}\binom{m}{i}\left[1-\frac{2(m-i)}{m}\right]z^i \tag{A.14}$$

is negative for $0 < z \le 1$. Multiplying through by m, we obtain

$$\sum_{i=0}^{m-1}\binom{m-1}{i}\binom{m}{i}(2i-m)z^i. \tag{A.15}$$

Note that the coefficient of z^i is positive if $i > m/2$, zero if $i = m/2$, and negative if $i < m/2$. Excluding the $i = m/2$ term (if it is present) and the $i = 0$ term (which is clearly negative), we now pair the remaining terms with the following formula: for $1 \le u < m/2$, the $i = u$ term is paired with the $i = m - u$ term. The sum of the $i = u$ and $i = m - u$ terms reduces as follows:

$$\binom{m-1}{u}\binom{m}{u}(2u-m)z^u+\binom{m-1}{m-u}\binom{m}{m-u}(m-2u)z^{m-u}$$

$$=\binom{m-1}{u}\binom{m}{u}(2u-m)z^u\left[1-\frac{u}{m-u}z^{m-2u}\right]. \tag{A.16}$$

Since $u < m/2$, and $z \leq 1$, it is true that (i) $(2u - m) < 0$, (ii) $u/(m - u) < 1$, and (iii) $z^{m-2u} \leq 1$. The second line of (A.16) is therefore negative, and it follows that (A.15) is also negative. This completes the proof of the first inequality.

We now turn to the second inequality. Again using (A.9), it is sufficient to show that

$$\sum_{i=0}^{m-1} \binom{m-1}{i} \binom{m}{i} z^i - \frac{2}{m} \sum_{i=0}^{m-1} \binom{m-1}{i} \binom{m}{i} (m-i) z^{i+1} \tag{A.17}$$

is negative when $z \geq 1$. After reindexing the right-hand summation by replacing i with $i - 1$ and then multiplying (A.17) by m, we obtain

$$m - 2mz^m + \sum_{i=1}^{m-1} \left[m\binom{m-1}{i}\binom{m}{i} - 2(m-i+1)\binom{m-1}{i-1}\binom{m}{i-1} \right] z^i. \tag{A.18}$$

Since $z \geq 1$, $m - 2mz^m$ is negative. It is thus sufficient to focus on the remaining summation.

By factoring, this summation can be rewritten as

$$\sum_{i=1}^{m-1} \binom{m-1}{i} \binom{m}{i} \left[m - \frac{2i^2}{m-i} \right] z^i. \tag{A.19}$$

The coefficient of z^i is negative when $i > m/2$, zero when $i = m/2$, and positive when $i < m/2$. Excluding the $i = m/2$ term (if it exists), we pair terms as in the proof of the theorem's first part: for $1 \leq u < m/2$, the $i = u$ term is paired with the $i = m - u$ term. The sum of these terms is

$$\binom{m-1}{u}\binom{m}{u}\left[m - \frac{2u^2}{m-u} \right] z^u + \binom{m-1}{m-u}\binom{m}{m-u}\left[m - \frac{2(m-u)^2}{u} \right] z^{m-u}. \tag{A.20}$$

The proof is completed by showing that the sum (A.20) is negative. Since $z \geq 1$ and the $i = m - u$ term is negative, it is sufficient to show that

$$\binom{m-1}{u}\left[m - \frac{2u^2}{m-u} \right] + \binom{m-1}{m-u}\left[m - \frac{2(m-u)^2}{u} \right] \tag{A.21}$$

is negative. By factoring out $\binom{m-1}{u}/(m-u)$, this reduces to

$$\binom{m-1}{u}[m(m-u) - 2u^2 + mu - 2(m-u)^2]/(m-u). \tag{A.22}$$

The expression in brackets equals $-(m-2u)^2$, which shows that (A.20) is negative. ‖

Acknowledgement. We thank John Moore for encouraging us to investigate the special case of the buyers bid double auction, and Michael Chwe for his assistance. This material is based upon work supported by the National Science Foundation Nos. SES-8520247 and SES-8705649. We also acknowledge the support of Northwestern University's Research Grants Committee and its Center for Advanced Study in Managerial Economics and Decision Sciences.

REFERENCES

ARROW, K. (1959), "Towards a Theory of Price Adjustment", in Abramovitz, M. (ed.), *The Allocation of Economic Resources* (Stanford: Stanford University Press), 41-51.
CHATTERJEE, K. and W. SAMUELSON (1983), "Bargaining Under Incomplete Information", *Operations Research*, **31**, 835-851.
CRAMTON, P. (1984), "Bargaining with Incomplete Information: An Infinite-Horizon Model with Two-Sided Uncertainty", *Review of Economic Studies*, **51**, 579-593.
DAVID, H. (1981) *Order Statistics (2nd ed)* (New York: John Wiley & Sons).
DEBREU, G. (1975), "The Rate of Convergence of the Core of an Economy", *Journal of Mathematical Economics*, **2**, 1-8.
DIERKER, E. (1982), "Regular Economies", in Arrow, K. and Intriligator, M. (eds.), *Handbook of Mathematical Economics, Vol. II* (Amsterdam: North-Holland), 795-830.
GRESIK, T. and SATTERTHWAITE, M. (1986), "The Rate at which a Simple Market Becomes Efficient as the Number of Traders Increases: An Asymptotic Result for Optimal Trading Mechanisms", *Journal of Economic Theory* (forthcoming).
GRODAL, B. (1975), "The Rate of Convergence of the Core for a Purely Competitive Sequence of Economies", *Journal of Mathematical Economics*, **1**, 279-294.

HAGERTY, K. and ROGERSON, W. (1985), "Robust Trading Mechanisms", *Journal of Economic Theory*, **42**, 94-107.

HARSANYI, J. (1967-68), "Games with Incomplete Information Played by Bayesian Players, parts I, II, and III", *Management Science*, **14**, 159-182, 320-334, 486-502.

HAYEK, F. (1945), "The Use of Knowledge in Society", *American Economic Review*, **35**, 519-530.

HILDENBRAND, W. (1982), "Core of an Economy", in Arrow, K. and Intriligator, M. (eds.), *Handbook of Mathematical Economics, Vol. II* (Amsterdam: North-Holland), 831-878.

HOLMSTROM, B. and MYERSON, R. (1983), "Efficient and Durable Decision Rules with Incomplete Information", *Econometrica*, **51**, 1799-1820.

HURWICZ, L. (1973), "On Informationally Decentralized Systems", in Radner, R. and McGuire, C, (eds.), *Decision and Organization* (Amsterdam: North-Holland), 297-336.

LEININGER, W., LINHART, P. and RADNER, R. (1986), "The Sealed-Bid Mechanisms for Bargaining with Incomplete Information", *Journal of Economic Theory* (forthcoming).

MCAFEE, R. P. and MCMILLAN, J. (1987), "Auctions and Bidding", *Journal of Economic Literature*, **25**, 699-738.

MILGROM, P. and WEBER, R. (1982), "A Theory of Auctions and Competitive Bidding", *Econometrica*, **50**, 1089-1122.

MYERSON, R. (1981), "Optimal Auction Design", *Mathematics of Operations Research*, **6**, 58-73.

MYERSON, R. and SATTERTHWAITE, M. (1983), "Efficient Mechanisms for Bilateral Trade", *Journal of Economic Theory*, **29**, 265-281.

ROBERTS, J. and POSTLEWAITE, A. (1976), "The Incentive for Price-Taking Behavior in Large Exchange Economies", *Econometrica*, **44**, 115-128.

ROYDEN, H. (1968) *Real Analysis* (New York: Macmillan).

SATTERTHWAITE, M. and SONNENSCHEIN, H. (1981), "Strategy-Proof Allocation Mechanisms at Differentiable Points", *Review of Economic Studies*, **48**, 587-597.

SATTERTHWAITE, M. and WILLIAMS, S. (1987), "Bilateral Trade with the Sealed Bid Double Auction: Existence and Efficiency", *Journal of Economic Theory* (forthcoming).

WILLIAMS, S. (1987), "Efficient Performance in Two Agent Bargaining", *Journal of Economic Theory*, **41**, 154-172.

WILLIAMS, S. (1988), "The Nature of Equilibria in the Buyer's Bid Double Auction" (Northwestern University CMSEMS DP No. 793).

WILSON, R. (1983), "Efficient Trading" (Stanford University IMSSS Technical Report No. 432).

WILSON, R. (1985), "Incentive Efficiency of Double Auctions", *Econometrica*, **53**, 1101-1115.

WILSON, R. (1987), "Game-Theoretic Analyses of Trading Processes", in Bewley, T. (ed.), *Advances in Economic Theory, Fifth World Congress* (Cambridge: Cambridge University Press), 33-70.

JOURNAL OF ECONOMIC THEORY **47**, 307–333 (1989)

Pollution Claim Settlements under Private Information

Rafael Rob*

University of Pennsylvania,
Philadelphia, Pennsylvania 19104–6297

Received January 9, 1987; revised June 15, 1988

The classical problem of resolving a nuisance dispute between a pollution-generating firm and nearby residents is modelled here as a mechanism-design problem. We assume that the designer of the mechanism is the firm, that it is uncertain about the actual losses suffered by residents and that the initial assignment of property rights is one where each resident is entitled to prevail. We derive a profit-maximizing scheme under the individual-rationality and incentive-compatibility constraints and examine its properties. It is shown that the outcomes it yields are sometimes inefficient. Moreover, when many residents are affected by pollution and the degree of uncertainty with respect to the losses they suffer is large, these inefficiencies become rampant. *Journal of Economic Literature* Classification Numbers: 025, 026, 722. © 1989 Academic Press, Inc.

1. Introduction

It has long been recognized that external effects drive a wedge into the price system and that in such cases the market mechanism cannot be relied upon to efficiently allocate resources (see [14]). In many economists' eyes, the government's role in the regulation of pollution has developed in response to this type of market failure.

That traditional view, however, is not shared by Ronald Coase [2] and his followers. Their basic argument is that an inefficiency is equivalent to the existence of profitable opportunities, that the gains from trade have not

* First manuscript dated February, 1984. The author gratefully acknowledges the financial support of NSF under Grant SES-84-16191 and a scholarship from the American Association for the Advancement of Sciences. This paper was previously presented at the Department of Justice, EPA, the University of Minnesota, NYU, Carnegie-Mellon University, and the 1986 Summer Meetings of the European Econometric Society in Budapest, Hungary. I thank participants at these seminars for useful remarks and two anonymous referees for many helpful suggestions. Typing facilities from the Foerder Institute for Economic Research are gratefully acknowledged. All remaining errors are my sole responsibility.

been fully exhausted and that by arranging side payments all parties could benefit. Furthermore, such rearrangements could take place until no gains remain unexploited, i.e., until a fully efficient outcome has been attained.

The mechanism which the latter literature suggests for implementing these improvements is that of bargaining between affected parties. However, the specifics of this mechanism are not provided. That is, it is not stated which strategies are available to the bargainers, what are the rules of the "bargaining game" in which they are involved, how outcomes in that game are determined, and so on. Hence, the Coase argument is more in the spirit of cooperative game theory where efficiency is being postulated as an axiom, rather than being shown to emerge as an outcome of some non-cooperative procedure.

The purpose of the present paper is to specify exactly one such procedure (mechanism, scheme, or process interchangeably). The inputs of the procedure are decision-relevant characteristics, namely, the pollution-related monetary damages suffered by potential victims. The outputs are two. First, there is a zero-one decision—accept or reject the construction of a pollution-generating plant (the obvious extension to the case where the firm chooses an activity or output level is not pursued here). Second, compensatory payments are determined. This bargaining process is meant to **describe** an actual procedure for internalizing external costs and is, hence, modelled as a non-cooperative game. An essential feature of our formalism is that we do not restrict (a priori) outcomes to be Pareto-optimal. On the contrary, the primary goal is to examine the efficiency of one of the equilibria of the bargaining process. In other words, our goal is to examine the Coase argument in a non-cooperative setting.

Our results in that regard are as follows: (1) inefficiencies do emerge as equilibrium outcomes; and (2) when the number of participants is large, inefficient outcomes are, in fact, much likelier than efficient ones. These results run counter to some recent studies on the allocation of **private** goods in large economies (see Gresik and Satterthwaite [6] and Wilson [16]). Thus, with regard to the attainability of social optima by means of non-cooperative procedures, our model highlights a fundamental difference between private and public goods environments.

The basic reason for the emergence of inefficient equilibria runs as follows. We assume that external damages are publicly unobservable; that is, that the loss suffered by an individual is private information to him. Given that the firm is unsure about the actual losses, each participant has an incentive in the negotiations to overstate his damages, so as to receive more compensation. Therefore, it is conceivable that even though the total sum of **true** damages is less than the firm's profits, the **stated** damages (or demands) exceed these profits, making it financially impossible for the firm to compensate individuals. As a result, it is possible that a project will not be undertaken, even when it is socially desirable. Thus, our analysis focuses on uncertainty-based misallocations.

The plan of the paper is as follows. The section below formulates the mathematical structure. Section 3 analyses the model, deriving a closed-form solution to the maximization program of the firm. Section 4 offers an example and discusses various features of the firm's policy. Section 5 deals with the issue of mechanism performance in large groups. Section 6 relates our work to mechanism theory. Section 7 concludes the paper.

2. FORMULATION

Our formulation closely follows the Myerson model [12] of optimal auction design, the crucial element of similarity being the uncertainty about individual types.

Consider a firm having to decide on the construction of a plant. There are n individuals who reside on the site where construction is contemplated. Index individuals by i, $i = 1, ..., n$. An "operate" decision carries a benefit of $R > 0$, R being the incremental profit of the firm over and above what it could earn in its next best alternative (construct and operate the plant on another site, for instance). On the other hand, operation imposes external costs because it entails the unavoidable release of toxic substances which are harmful to the residents. We assume that residents are risk neutral, that the pollution-related losses they suffer vary from person to person and that they are only privately known. Let x_i denote the loss to person i.

There are many reasons for differential effects of pollution: proximity to the factory, sensitivity to smoke, quality of built-in devices reducing the effects of pollution, age distribution of household members, differential information about the health effects of hazardous substances, and so on. Suppose that individual i understands the impact of these factors on himself (summarized by x_i) but is uncertain about their aggregate effect on his neighbors. Adopting the Harsanyi approach [8], we assume that each individual acts as a Bayesian decision maker and regards the damages to others as independent draws from the cumulative distribution functions (cdf),

$$F_j(x_j), \qquad j = 1, ..., n. \tag{2.1}$$

We also assume (continuous) differentiability of these cdf's and denote their respective densities by

$$f_j(x_j), \qquad j = 1, ..., n. \tag{2.2}$$

The supports of the $F_j(\cdot)$'s are assumed to be non-degenerate, bounded intervals:

$$D_j = [\underline{x}_j, \bar{x}_j], \qquad j = 1, ..., n, \qquad (2.3)$$

where $0 \leqslant \underline{x}_j < \bar{x}_j < \infty$.

While x_i is private information to resident i, we assume that R, and the $F_j(\cdot)$'s are common knowledge. For future reference, let us adopt the following notation:

$$D \equiv X_{i=1}^n D_i \qquad (2.4a)$$

$$D_{-i} \equiv X_{j \neq i} D_j \qquad (2.4b)$$

$$x \equiv (x_1, ..., x_n) \qquad (2.4c)$$

$$x_{-i} \equiv (x_1, ..., x_{i-1}, x_{i+1}, ..., x_n) \qquad (2.4d)$$

$$(x \mid y_i) \equiv (x_1, ..., x_{i-1}, y_i, x_{i+1}, ..., x_n) \qquad (2.4e)$$

$$f(x) \equiv \prod_{i=1}^n f_i(x_i) \qquad (2.4f)$$

$$f_{-i}(x_{-i}) \equiv \prod_{j \neq i} f_j(x_j). \qquad (2.4g)$$

The vector of external costs, x, completely summarizes the economic state. No uncertainty about the best course of action would arise if x were (publicly) known. The first-best decision would then be to operate the plant if and only if

$$\sum_{i=1}^n x_i \leqslant R, \qquad (2.5)$$

and the first-best social surplus would be

$$S(x) = \text{Max} \left\{ 0, R - \sum_{i=1}^n x_i \right\}. \qquad (2.6)$$

We are modelling, however, a second-best world in which no single participant knows x. Decision-making procedures in such settings should first elicit information on x and then choose an action based on it. The specific procedure we look at is one where the **firm** is designing a mechanism and is subject to certain constraints (to be specified momentarily). The firm is assumed to be risk-neutral and its objective is to maximize expected profits. (See, however, the discussion in Section 5 where an alternative formulation is briefly discussed.)

The choices available to the firm are announcements of decision rules

$$0 \leqslant p(\cdot) \leqslant 1, \tag{2.7}$$

and

$$c_i(\cdot), \qquad i = 1, ..., n, \tag{2.8}$$

where $p(\cdot)$ is the **probability** of operating the plant (randomization is permissible) and $c_i(\cdot)$ is the **expected** compensation to individual i. Let

$$c(\cdot) \equiv (c_1(\cdot), c_2(\cdot), ..., c_n(\cdot)), \tag{2.9}$$

and define a **mechanism** as an $(n+1)$ tuple of plans

$$(p(\cdot), c(\cdot)). \tag{2.10}$$

The strategies available to individuals, on the other hand, are **reports**

$$y_i \in D_i, \tag{2.11}$$

of losses (which may or may not coincide with their actual losses, x_i). The decision rules (2.7) and (2.8) are functions of the vector of **reported** losses, $y \equiv (y_1, ..., y_n)$.

The scenario considered in this paper is one where the firm moves first. Its choice is assumed to be binding, i.e., it must carry out (ex-post) the decision rules it selected (ex-ante)—no matter what the actual configuration of (reported) losses, y, turns out to be (the significance of this point will become clear as we proceed). Residents move subsequently and non-cooperatively, making their reports in full knowledge of the firm's plans but without cooperation or sharing of information. In other words, when residents are called upon to move, each is informed of his own loss x_i and of the $(p(\cdot), c(\cdot))$ mechanism, but not of the losses to others, x_{-i} (or their reports y_{-i}).

We impose two constraints on the class of mechanisms among which the firm may choose. First is the incentive compatibility (IC, hereafter) constraint which requires that truthtelling (i.e., $y_i = x_i$) be a Bayesian equilibrium point of the revelation game played by the n residents. The reason for placing this restriction is the well-known revelation principle according to which the outcome of **any** (static) game can be mimicked as a truthtelling equilibrium of some revelation scheme. One (general) limitation, however, of the revelation principle is that the revelation schemes it suggests typically have multiple equilibria; yet the analysis focuses on the truthful one and no justification is provided as to why that equilibrium is more likely to prevail than the non-truthful ones. We shall further discuss and illustrate this difficulty in Section 4.

Expressing the IC constraint mathematically, fix a mechanism, (p, c) and let $U_i(x_i; p, c)$ denote the **net** (of pollution losses) payoff to individual i when both his true and reported loss is x_i (and when the remaining residents are also acting truthfully). Then,

$$U_i(x_i; p, c) \equiv \int_{D_{-i}} [c_i(x) - p(x) x_i] f_{-i}(x_{-i}) dx_{-i}. \qquad (2.12)$$

(In cases where it is well understood which underlying mechanism we have in mind, we shall abbreviate and write $U_i(x_i)$ instead of $U_i(x_i; p, c)$.)

When individual i, on the other hand, misrepresents his actual losses and reports y_i, two changes take place: the expected compensation he receives becomes $c_i(x \mid y_i)$, and the probability of the plant operating becomes $p(x \mid y_i)$. The incentive compatibility constraint requires that the payoff associated with a false report be no greater than the one associated with a truthful one, i.e., we must have:

$$U_i(x_i) \geqslant \int_{D_{-i}} [c_i(x \mid y_i) - p(x \mid y_i) x_i] f_{-i}(x_{-i}) dx_{-i}. \qquad (2.13)$$

Second is the individual rationality constraint (IR, hereafter) which requires that no individual be forced to participate in the mechanism or that the expected payoff to all resident **types** be non-negative. That is,

$$U_i(x_i) \geqslant 0, \qquad x_i \in D_i, \qquad i = 1, ..., n. \qquad (2.14)$$

The notion underlying this constraint is that the status quo ante is one where no plant is operating (and thus each resident enjoys "clean air") and that individuals are entitled to maintain that status quo. Alternatively stated, each resident is granted veto power. This requirement and its implications are further discussed in Sections 4 and 6.

These are then the only constraints imposed on the firm's program. We do **not**, in particular, place the break-even requirement:

$$\sum_{i=1}^{n} c_i(x) \leqslant p(x) R, \qquad x \in D. \qquad (2.15)$$

A mechanism satisfying (2.13) and (2.14) is said to be **feasible**.

3. ANALYSIS

As previously stated, the problem studied in this paper is that of maximizing the **firm's** expected profit subject to the IC and IR constraints.

Formally written, we have

$$\underset{p,c}{\text{Max}} \int \left[p(x) R - \sum_{i=1}^{n} c_i(x) \right] f(x) \, dx, \tag{3.1}$$

s.t. (2.13) and (2.14).

Denote the firm's objective, (3.1), by U_0.

3.1. Finding a Solution to the Firm's Problem

An extremum to this program is found using two lemmas which are slight modifications of similar results proven in Myerson's [12] paper—see his Lemmas 2 and 3 (the adaptation to the present context is worked out in a discussion paper version which is available from the author).

The first lemma is concerned with the residents' revelation game. It gives conditions under which residents voluntarily participate in that game and are induced to truthfully report their losses. The advantage of these conditions is that they are equivalent to but simpler than the IR and IC constraints. As a by-product, they show that residents are capturing "informational rents" (which are due to the costliness of eliciting their private information), and that these rents increase as individual losses decrease.

LEMMA 1.   *The mechanism* $(p(\cdot), c(\cdot))$ *is feasible if and only if*:

(a) $0 \leqslant p(x) \leqslant 1, \qquad x \in D.$ \hfill (3.2a)

(b) $U_i(\bar{x}_i) \geqslant 0, \qquad i = 1, ..., n.$ \hfill (3.2b)

(c) $Q_i(y_i)$ *is monotonically decreasing,* \hfill (3.2c)

   where $Q(y_i) \equiv \int_{D_{-i}} p(x \mid y_i) f_{-i}(x_{-i}) \, dx_{-i},$ \hfill (3.2d)

(d) $U_i(x_i) = U_i(\bar{x}_i) + \int_{x_i}^{\bar{x}_i} Q_i(y_i) \, dy_i.$ \hfill (3.2e)

The second lemma deals with the firm's maximization program. The simplified version of the constraints it is facing (as stated in Lemma 1) enables us to reduce that program to one involving only one choice variable: namely the $p(\cdot)$ function.

LEMMA 2.   *Assume* $p: D \to [0, 1]$ *maximizes*

$$\int_D p(x) \left\{ R - \sum_{i=1}^{n} \left[x_i + \frac{F_i(x_i)}{f_i(x_i)} \right] \right\} f(x) \, dx - \sum_{i=1}^{n} U_i(\bar{x}_i) \tag{3.3}$$

subject to (3.2c). *Assume also that*

$$c_i(x) = p(x) x_i + \int_{x_i}^{\bar{x}_i} p(x \mid y_i) \, dy_i, \qquad i = 1, ..., n. \tag{3.4}$$

Then (p, c) *maximizes the firm's expected profit.*

Under one further distributional assumption, a particular solution to the firm's program can be identified from expression (3.3).

ASSUMPTION A.1. $x_i + F_i(x_i)/f_i(x_i)$ *is monotonically increasing for all* $i = 1, ..., n$.

Remarks. 1. The above assumption is satisfied by any uniform distribution on an interval $[\underline{x}_i, \bar{x}_i]$, $0 \leqslant \underline{x}_i < \bar{x}_i < \infty$. It is also satisfied by the exponential, Pareto, and positive normal (the density, f, of which is defined by $f(x) = 2\varphi(x)$, $0 \leqslant x \leqslant \infty$, where φ is the density of a normal variate) and by their truncated (from above) versions. All these distributions conform to all the remaining assumptions, as stated in Section 2 above.

2. When the monotonicity assumption is violated, a solution is still obtainable, but it involves "bunching" of types (i.e., individuals with different x_i values receiving the same compensation). This case is fully treated in Myerson's paper [12]. The adaptation to the present context is not spelled out here.

THEOREM 1. *Under Assumption* A.1, *the following is a profit-maximizing scheme*:

$$p^*(x) = \begin{cases} 1, & \text{if } \sum_{i=1}^{n} [x_i + F_i(x_i)/f_i(x_i)] \leqslant R \\ 0, & \text{otherwise;} \end{cases} \tag{3.5}$$

$$c_i^*(x) = p^*(x) x_i + \int_{x_i}^{\bar{x}_i} p^*(x \mid y_i) \, dy_i, \qquad x \in D, \ 1 \leqslant i \leqslant n. \tag{3.6}$$

Proof. p^* certainly satisfies (3.2a) and is monotonically decreasing in each of its arguments. From its definition, (3.2d), we see that $Q_i(\cdot)$ is monotonically decreasing as well, i.e., that (3.2c) is satisfied. Substituting (3.6) into (2.12) we see, next, that (3.2b) holds and that each $U_i(\bar{x}_i)$ attains its lowest possible value—zero. A fortiori, $-\sum_{i=1}^{n} U_i(\bar{x}_i)$ attains its maximal value. Finally, p^* maximizes the expression under the integral sign of (3.3) subject to the probability constraint, $0 \leqslant p(\cdot) \leqslant 1$. Hence all the assumptions of Lemma 2 are satisfied and the theorem is proven.

Remarks. 1. The above solution involves no randomization; that is, the p^* function does not assume any values strictly between zero and one.

2. Theorem 1 identifies only one solution. The analysis and discussion from this point on, and, in particular, that which is contained in Section 5 below pertain to that solution. Regrettably, I was unable to determine whether other maxima exist.

Next, let us rewrite the solution expressed by Theorem 1 in a more explicit form. Define first the "virtual social loss" function, $h(x)$, as

$$h(x) \equiv \sum_{i=1}^{n} \left[x_i + \frac{F_i(x_i)}{f_i(x_i)} \right]. \tag{3.7}$$

Second, for a fixed x_{-i}, consider $h(x \mid y_i)$ as a function of the ith variable (y_i) only. Then we can write the firm's optimal decision rules as follows:

— Operate the factory if and only if $h(x) \leqslant R$. $\tag{3.8a}$

— In case the factory operates, pay the ith resident, the maximum amount, $\tilde{x}_i$, for which $h(x \mid \tilde{x}_i) \leqslant R$. $\tag{3.8b}$

— In case the factory does not operate, pay zero.

3.2. *Comparison to the Demand Revealing Mechanism*

Expressions (3.8a) and (3.8b) are particularly convenient for the purpose of contrasting the firm's maximizing scheme with the demand revealing mechanism (DRM, hereafter) which was previously suggested as a scheme for public decision-making under private information (see Groves and Loeb [7] and Green and Laffont [5] for a comprehensive study of the latter mechanism and its properties).

There are several differences between our setup and that which underlies the DRM. For one thing, we are concerned with the firm's profits whereas the DRM solves a social planner's program. Second, the DRM imposes no IR constraints (or even lower bound constraints on individual wealth levels), whereas we do. Third, the equilibrium concept which underlies the DRM is stronger than ours—it requires that truth be a **dominant strategy** (i.e., be a best-response—no matter what other individuals are reporting), whereas in our setup it need only be a **Bayesian** equilibrium point.

Despite these differences, the incentive structures (i.e., the compensations received by individuals) which the two procedures yield are very similar. The common idea behind them is that each individual be paid as though he was a "pivotal player," that is, as though his (virtual) loss made the firm just indifferent between operating the plant and moving to another site (this is exactly what the decision rule (3.8b) specifies). The difference between the two schemes is in the "social loss" function used for determin-

ing these payments. The DRM relies on the actual loss, $\sum_{i=1}^{n} x_i$, whereas, in the present setting, we use the virtual loss, $h(x)$, as defined in (3.7).[1]
We shall pursue this comparison further in Section 6 below.

4. An Example and Discussion

4.0. To develop some intuition for the working of the optimal mechanism, (3.8), consider the following example. Assume that all the densities $f_1(x_1), ..., f_n(x_n)$ are identical and equal to the uniform on $[0, 1]$, i.e., that

$$f_i(x_i) = \begin{cases} 1, & x_i \in [0, 1] \\ 0, & \text{otherwise.} \end{cases}$$

This assumption corresponds to the case of complete ignorance, since all damages are equally likely. The common "hazard ratio" is then $F_i(x_i)/f_i(x_i) = x_i$, and, thus, $x_i + (F_i(x_i)/f_i(x_i)) = 2x_i$, $i = 1, ..., n$. Applying (3.8) to this example, the firm's decision rules take on the following form:

—   Operate the factory if and only if $\sum x_i \leqslant R/2$.   (4.1)

—   In case the factory operates pay individual i

$$\tilde{x}_i = \text{Min} \left\{ 1, R/2 - \sum_{j \neq i} x_j \right\}. \tag{4.1b}$$

Suppose now, in addition, that there are only two individuals ($n = 2$) and that $R = 1$. Lemma 1 shows then that individuals' net payoffs (at the optimum) are

$$U_i(x_i) = \begin{cases} \frac{1}{2}(\frac{1}{2} - x_i)^2, & 0 \leqslant x_i < \frac{1}{2} \\ 0, & \frac{1}{2} \leqslant x_i \leqslant 1, \ i = 1, 2. \end{cases} \tag{4.2}$$

Hence, averaging with respect to the prior (or "interim stage") probabilities, average individuals' payoffs are

$$U_i^* = \int_0^1 U_i(x_i) f_i(x_i) \, dx_i = \tfrac{1}{48}, \qquad i = 1, 2. \tag{4.3}$$

On the other hand, using expression (3.3) of Lemma 2, the **firm's** average profit is

$$U_0^* = \int_{x_1 +} \int_{x_2 \leqslant 0.5} [1 - 2(x_1 + x_2)] \, dx_1 \, dx_2 = \tfrac{1}{24}. \tag{4.4}$$

---

[1] Our distributional specifications (2.1)–(2.3) are embedded in the virtual loss function, $h(x)$. These specifications play no role in the DRM literature.

Thus, the average **realized** surplus is

$$U_0^* + U_1^* + U_2^* = \tfrac{1}{12}. \tag{4.5}$$

We see that 50% of the rent goes to the firm while 50% goes to the two residents (in an expected value sense). In the next section, we shall systematically examine how the division of rents varies as we increase the number of residents.

Next let us define the (ex-ante) **potential** surplus as the expected value of expression (2.6) with respect to the prior $\prod_{i=1}^{n} f_i(x_i)$ (this is appropriate since (2.6) gives the **maximum** attainable welfare for a **given** realization of damages, x, and we are taking the expected value of that with respect to the ex-ante probabilities),

$$V \equiv \int_A \left(R - \sum x_i \right) f(x)\, dx = \int_{nx}^{R} (R - s)\, g_n(s)\, dx, \tag{4.6}$$

where $A \equiv \{(x_1, ..., x_n) \mid \sum x_i \leqslant R\}$ and where $g_n(s)$ is the density of $\sum_{i=1}^{n} x_i$. Specializing this to our example we have

$$g_2(s) = \begin{cases} s, & 0 < s < 1, \\ s - 2, & 1 < s < 2, \end{cases} \tag{4.7}$$

and thus,

$$V = \int_0^1 (1 - s)\, g_2(s)\, ds = \tfrac{1}{6}. \tag{4.8}$$

Comparing (4.8) with (4.5), we see that welfare performance in the case of two residents is not very high: only 50% of the potential surplus is actually realized. Further analysis of welfare performance and, in particular, how it relates to the number of residents is given in Section 5.

Expressions (4.1)–(4.5) give us a complete solution to the firm's maximization problem. We next discuss several features of that solution. No claim, however, is made with regard to the robustness of these features since other maxima may exist (see Remark 2 following Theorem 1) in which these problems are avoided.

4.1. Ex-post inefficiency. From (4.1a) we see that the firm will build the plant on an alternative site whenever the configuration of losses, $x = (x_1, ..., x_n)$, is such that $\sum_{i=1}^{n} x_i > R/2$. This decision rule is clearly different from the ex-post optimal one—as specified in (2.5) above, and it leads to inefficient outcomes when (and only when) $R/2 < \sum_{i=1}^{n} x_i < R$. In such instances, it would be in the best interest of all parties to deviate from what the rule dictates, arrange for compensatory payments, and have the plant operate. Thus, the inefficiency that arises in our model is that the plant should operate but in actuality it does not. The firm nonetheless chooses this inefficient rule because deviations from it are incompatible with the residents' incentives (i.e., truthtelling will no longer be an equilibrium strategy if these "deviations" are fully anticipated). Moreover, such deviations are incompatible with the firm's objective (which, to repeat, is the maximization of ex-ante **expected** profits).

Similar inefficiencies were pointed out in a variety of related setups. Proposition 1 in Samuelson [15], for instance, is exactly in this spirit. Likewise, Green and Laffont [5, Theorem 6.2(1), p. 27] have shown that no truthful (in dominant strategies) and efficient mechanisms exist if individual rationality constraints are insisted upon. Laffont and Maskin [11] have proven an analogous result in the **Bayesian** setting. The revenue maximizing auction in Myerson's paper [12] is inefficient because the seller (sometimes) retains an item despite the fact that it is worth more to one of the buyers than it is to him. And finally, Myerson and Satterthwaite [13] have proven (in the private goods case) the impossibility of attaining ex-post efficiency by means of an incentive-compatible, individually rational mechanism.

4.2. Bankruptcy. Consider the following configuration. $R = 4$, $n = 10$, and $x_i = 0$ for $i = 1, ..., 10$. Since $\sum_{i=1}^{10} x_i = 0 < 2 = \frac{4}{2}$, the firm decides to build the plant. From (4.1b), compensatory payments are $\tilde{x}_i = \text{Min}\{1, 2 - 0\} = 1$, $i = 1, 2, ..., 10$. Thus, total payments, $\sum_{i=1}^{10} \tilde{x}_i = 10$, exceed the profit, 4, so the firm is sustaining a loss.

At the same time, configurations $x = (x_1, ..., x_n)$ do exist where the firm's realized return is positive. More importantly, the firm's **expected** profit, U_0^*, is positive since it can always choose inaction, i.e., set $p = c_i \equiv 0$ and make zero profits. Hence, if the mechanism is to be applied repeatedly and independently over time, reserves could be set aside to alleviate the bankruptcy problem.

On the other hand, if the location decision is to be made exactly once, a possible remedy would be to impose a break-even constraint—as specified in (2.15) above. Note, however, that such constraint is socially costly because both the firm's (optimum) profit and the residents' (optimum) payoff would be smaller when that constraint is added.

4.3. Coalitional manipulations. While no single individual can do better than tell the truth, a coalition of individuals **can** swing the outcome to the benefit of all of its' members. In other words, our mechanism is **not** immune to coalitional manipulations. To show that, consider the following configuration: $R = 8$, $n = 10$, and $x_i = 0.5$ for $1 \leqslant i \leqslant 10$. By (4.1a), the firm decides to locate elsewhere (since $\sum x_i = 5 > 4 = \frac{8}{2}$) and makes no compensatory payments. Consider now a maneuvre whereby a group of four individuals ($i = 1, 2, 3, 4$, say) decides to falsely report $y_i = 0$. Under these reports, we have $\sum_{i=1}^{10} y_i = 3 < 4 = \frac{8}{2}$, so that the firm decides to operate, and it pays each coalition member $\tilde{y}_i = \text{Min}\{1, 4 - 3\} = 1 > 0.5$. Each of these individuals is thus getting a compensation which exceeds his true loss, making him better off than he was at the truthful equiluibrium.

Coalitional manipulations of this sort, however, are hard to put into effect. They require, first, that coalitions be formed, agreements be reached and agreed-upon actions be carried out. Second and more importantly, the choice of (coalitional) reports requires credible sharing of information among coalition members. But the essence of our formulation is that information is private and hence that sharing it is a costly undertaking. For these reasons, the **net** returns to coalitional maneuvres might not be very high and, thus, neither will be the incentives to form coalitions.

4.4. Uniqueness. Given the firm's optimal polity, (4.1), a truthful response ($y_i = x_i$, $1 \leqslant i \leqslant n$) is a Bayesian equilibrium point of the subgame played by the residents (by design), but it is not a unique one. For example, the n-tuple of "understatements" $y_i \equiv 0$ is also an equilibrium (for **any** $x \in D!$) and, moreover, it dominates the truthful one from the standpoint of all residents.

Three ways of dealing with this difficulty spring to mind. First, one can search for other optimal decision rules (recall that (4.1) is only one maximum to the firm's program) for which truthfulness is a **unique** equilibrium. Second, one can consider criteria for selecting among multiple equilibria. And third, there is the possibility of designing multi-stage games which avoid the multiplicity problem. I will not pursue the uniqueness issue in this paper.

5. MECHANISM PERFORMANCE IN LARGE ECONOMIES

Up until now we have studied a victim compensation scheme in the "finite" case, i.e., have assumed a fixed number of residents. Our analysis has shown that inefficient outcomes might very well occur, and the example in Section 4.0 exhibts a situation where these inefficiencies amount to 50% of potential welfare. The present section is concerned with the case of a large economy, i.e., where the number of residents tends to infinity and considers the issues of welfare losses and the division of rents in that context. The results we present here constitute the bulk of this paper's contribution.

Our primary result is that, under certain restrictions, welfare losses are maximal in large economies, or in other words, that the potential "gains from trade" are completely dissipated in the negotiations. The main restriction needed for that proposition is that there be a minimal degree of uncertainty with respect to residents' losses (for otherwise the firm would have a good knowledge of these losses, be able to bid the residents down to their reservation values, and, thus, be able to avoid the ex-post inefficiencies which give rise to the dissipation of rents). With regard to the gains which are realized we show, by means of an example, that the group of residents is capturing a substantial portion of them. Both conclusions pertain to the **firm's** optimal mechanism, not to the one which a **social planner** would have chosen.

To be more specific, we consider a sequence of economies indexed by the number, n, of residents. For each economy, we have an expression for the firm's optimal mechanism ((3.5)–(3.6)), and, thus, can define a numerical welfare-performance measure corresponding to it. Call it W_n.[2] We thereby get a sequence of numbers, $\{W_n\}$; the essence of our analysis is to evaluate the limit of that sequence.

To make comparisons between different size economies meaningful, however, some normalization is necessary. The one adopted here is very simple: we assume that per-person profits and losses are both held constant along the sequence. No claim is made as to the robustness of our results with respect to other normalizations.

We are assuming then that $R_n = r \cdot n$, where R_n is the firm's total profit in a size n economy and r is its **per-person** profit. The **expected** per-person loss is μ, whereas **specific** individual losses $(x_1, x_2, ..., x_n)$ are, as before, assumed to be independent draws from certain (and publicly known) distribtions. We now add the further assumption that these distributions be **identical**. Slightly abusing our previous notation, we let F be the common cdf of that distribution, f be the corresponding density, and $[\underline{x}, \bar{x}]$ $(0 \leqslant \underline{x} < \bar{x} < \infty)$ be the support. Let $\tilde{x}$ be a random variable corresponding to the distribution F and let $\tilde{z} \equiv F(\tilde{x})/f(\tilde{x})$. We assume that $E\tilde{z}^2 < \infty$ and use the notation

$$\mu \equiv E\tilde{x} \equiv \int_{\underline{x}}^{\bar{x}} x\, dF(x)$$

$$\lambda \equiv E\tilde{z} = \int_{\underline{x}}^{\bar{x}} F(x)\, dx$$

$$\sigma^2 \equiv \mathrm{Var}(\tilde{x}) = \int_{\underline{x}}^{\bar{x}} (x - \mu)^2\, dF(x),$$

$$\tau^2 \equiv \mathrm{Var}(\tilde{x} + \tilde{z}) = \int_{\bar{x}}^{\bar{x}} \left[x + \frac{F(x)}{f(x)} - (\mu + \lambda) \right]^2 dF(x).$$

By the integration by parts formula we have: $\mu + \lambda = \bar{x}$.

---

[2] Actually, we shall consider two alternative measures.

Next, we introduce a welfare-performance measure, W_n^1. From the discussion in Section 4.1, we know that the only inefficiency which arises under the firm's optimal mechanism, (3.8), is the one where the plant is **not** constructed even though it should be, and that occurs whenever $\sum_{i=1}^{n} x_i \leqslant R_n$ but $\sum_{i=1}^{n} [x_i + F(x_i)/f(x_i)] > R_n$. W_n^1 is defined then as the **probability** of the complementary event (i.e., as the probability that an inefficient outcome does **not** occur). Formally,

$$W_n^1 \equiv \Pr \left(\sum_{i=1}^{n} \left[x_i + \frac{F(x_i)}{f(x_i)} \right] \leqslant R_n \,\middle|\, \sum_{i=1}^{n} x_i \leqslant R_n \right).$$

Our next proposition is concerned with the asymptotic behavior of this welfare measure (i.e., the limit of W_n^1). Two assumptions are used in its proof.

ASSUMPTION A.2. $\underline{x} < r < \bar{x}$.

ASSUMPTION A.3. $(\mu - \underline{x})/\sigma < (\bar{x} - \underline{x})/\tau$.

Remarks. 1. Assumption A.2 focuses attention on the case which is of greater interest: namely, where the firm is uncertain about the net profitability of building the plant. In the reverse case it is a priori known what action is optimal (build the plant if $r \geqslant \bar{x}$; locate elsewhere if $r \leqslant \underline{x}$) and hence there is little room for making the wrong decision. The role of A.2 is to rule out these situations. Assumption A.3, on the other hand, is technical and, admittedly, harder to interpret. Roughly speaking, what it ensures is that the firm is (sufficiently) uncertain about individual damages. A simpler but stronger condition is that the variance, σ^2, be sufficiently large—see the Appendix for an exact statement and proof.

2. Both A.2 and A.3 are invariant with respect to linear changes in the monetary unit of measurement. For instance, if they hold when damages are measured in dollars, they would also hold when we measure them in cents.

3. Assumptions A.2 and A.3 are satisfied by the parametric family of distributions,

$$F(x_i) = x_i^\theta, \qquad 0 \leqslant x_i \leqslant 1, \ \theta > 0 \tag{5.1}$$

(θ being the parameter). By Remark 2, these assumptions are also satisfied by the distributions which are generated from (5.1) by linear transformation of x_i, i.e., by

$$F(x_i; \theta, \underline{x}, \bar{x}) = \left(\frac{x_i - \underline{x}}{\bar{x} - \underline{x}} \right)^\theta, \qquad \underline{x} \leqslant x_i \leqslant \bar{x}.$$

Note that any uniform distribution on an interval, $[\underline{x}, \bar{x}]$, is a member of this family.

4. Assumptions A.2 and A.3 are only sufficient, not necessary.

THEOREM 2. *Under Assumptions A.2 and A.3,* $\lim_{n \to \infty} W_n^1 = 0$. (*That is, if we let* $\varepsilon > 0$ *be given, then the probability of an ex-post **efficient** decision is **smaller** than* ε, *provided the number of residents is sufficiently large*).

Proof. Since $z_i = F(x_i)/f(x_i)$ is a positive random variable we have

$$W_n^1 = \Pr\left(\sum_{i=1}^n \left[x_i + \frac{F(x_i)}{f(x_i)} \right] \leq R_n \,\bigg|\, \sum_{i=1}^n x_i \leq R_n \right)$$

$$= \frac{\Pr(\sum_{i=1}^n [x_i + z_i] \leq R_n)}{\Pr(\sum_{i=1}^n x_i \leq R_n)} \equiv \frac{A_n}{B_n}.$$

Approximating the above terms by the central limit theorem we get

$$A_n \equiv \Pr\left(\sum_{i=1}^n [x_i + z_i] \leq R_n \right)$$

$$= \Pr\left(\frac{\sum [x_i + z_i] - n\bar{x}}{\sqrt{n}\,\tau} \leq \frac{nr - n\bar{x}}{\sqrt{n}\,\tau} \right)$$

$$= \Pr\left(\frac{\sum [x_i + z_i] - n\bar{x}}{\sqrt{n}\,\tau} \leq \sqrt{n}\,\frac{r - \bar{x}}{\tau} \right) \approx \phi\left(\sqrt{n}\,\frac{r - \bar{x}}{\tau} \right),$$

where ϕ is the cdf of a standardized normal variate. And,

$$B_n \equiv \Pr\left(\sum_{i=1}^n x_i \leq R_n \right)$$

$$= \Pr\left(\frac{\sum x_i - n\mu}{\sqrt{n}\,\sigma} \leq \sqrt{n}\,\frac{r - \mu}{\sigma} \right) \approx \phi\left(\sqrt{n}\,\frac{r - \mu}{\sigma} \right).$$

Therefore,

$$\lim_{n \to \infty} \frac{A_n}{B_n} = \lim_{n \to \infty} \frac{\phi(\sqrt{n}\,a_r)}{\phi(\sqrt{n}\,b_r)}, \tag{5.2}$$

where $a_r \equiv (r - \bar{x})/\tau$ and $b_r \equiv (r - \mu)/\sigma$.

Distinguish now between the following two cases:

(1) $b_r \geq 0$ (i.e., $r \geq \mu$). In this case the numerator of (5.2) converges to zero (by A.2, a_r is always negative), while the denominator converges to a positive constant (either $\frac{1}{2}$ or 1). The ratio, thus, converges to zero.

(2) $b_r < 0$. In that case, both the numerator and the denominator converge to zero. However, we shall show that the numerator does so more rapidly than the denominator. Indeed, by A.2 and A.3, $|b_r| < |a_r|$, $\underline{x} < r < \mu$. Thus, using L'Hôspital's rule, we get

$$\lim_{n \to \infty} \frac{A_n}{B_n} = \lim_{n \to \infty} \frac{(a_r/2\sqrt{n}) \, \varphi(\sqrt{n}\, a_r)}{(b_r/2\sqrt{n}) \, \varphi(\sqrt{n}\, b_r)} = \frac{a_r}{b_r} \lim_{n \to \infty} e^{-n(a_r^2 - b_r^2)} = 0.$$

The proof is now complete. ∎

Our second welfare-performance measure, W_n^2, is defined as the ratio of **realized** to **potential** welfare. Explicitly, letting $V(n)$ denote potential welfare (see Eq. (4.6) and the discussion preceding it) we have

$$V(n) \equiv \int_{\Sigma x_i \leqslant R_n} \left(R_n - \sum_{i=1}^{n} x_i \right) \prod_{i=1}^{n} f(x_i) \prod_{i=1}^{n} dx_i$$

$$= \int_{nx}^{nr} (nr - s) \, dG_n(s), \tag{5.3}$$

where $G_n(s)$ is the cdf of the sum $\sum_{i=1}^{n} x_i$ (i.e., the n-fold convolution of $F(\cdot)$).

Let $U_0^*(n)$ and $U_i^*(n)$ denote the firm's and the residents' (respectively) realized gains. Then

$$U_0^*(n) \equiv \int_D \left[p^*(x) \, R_n - \sum c_i^*(x) \right] \prod_{i=1}^{n} f(x_i) \prod_{i=1}^{n} dx_i, \tag{5.4}$$

and

$$U_i^*(n) \equiv \int_{D_i} U_i(x_i; c^*, p^*) \, f(x_i) \, dx_i, \tag{5.5}$$

where (p^*, c^*) is the optimal mechanism—as defined in (3.5) and (3.6) above—and where expected values are taken with respect to the prior, $f(\cdot)$. Using (5.3)–(5.5) we now **define**

$$W_n^2 \equiv \frac{U_0^*(n) + \sum_{i=1}^{n} U_i^*(n)}{V(n)}.$$

The following assumption is needed for our next proposition.

ASSUMPTION A.4.   *There exists an $\alpha > 0$ so that*

$$\frac{F(x_i)}{f(x_i)} \geqslant \alpha(x_i - \underline{x}), \qquad \underline{x} \leqslant x_i \leqslant \bar{x}.$$

Remarks. (1) As is the case with Assumptions A.2 and A.3, Assumption A.4 is invariant with respect to rescalings of the unit of measurement.

(2) All the examples mentioned in Remark 1 following Assumption A.1 and the parametric family of distributions, (5.1), **do** satisfy Assumption A4.

THEOREM 3. *Assume that F satisfies* A.4 *and that* $\underline{x} < r < \mu + \alpha(\mu - \underline{x})$. *Then* $\lim_{n \to \infty} W_n^2 = 0$.

Proof. In the Appendix.

Discussion. 1. According to Theorem 3, rents need **not** dissipate for **all** values of the parameter r. In particular, if the maximal α which satisfies Assumption A.4 is such that $\mu + \alpha(\mu - \underline{x}) < \bar{x}$, then for $r \geqslant \mu + \alpha(\mu - \underline{x})$, we need not have complete dissipation, or we might even have convergence to **full efficiency** (the "opposite" result). However, that the conclusion of Theorem 3 could hold in the strongest possible sense can be seen from the parametric example, (5.1). For that family of distributions one has $F(x_i)/f(x_i) = (1/\theta) x_i$. Thus, choosing $\alpha_\theta = 1/\theta$ we see that A.4 **is** satisfied. Furthermore, as one can easily verify the expected value under $F(\cdot | \theta)$ is $\mu_\theta = \theta/(\theta + 1)$. Hence, $\mu_\theta + \alpha_\theta(\mu_\theta - \underline{x}) = 1 = \bar{x}$ and so, by Theorem 3, rents do dissipate for **all** values of r in the relevant range $(0 < r < 1)$.

2. As previously mentioned, Theorems 2 and 3 refer to the **firm's** optimal rules and hence their impact is weaker than it would be if they referred to the **planner's** program. The latter program can be formulated as the maximization of a weighted sum, $\beta U_0 + (1 - \beta) \sum_{i=1}^n U_i$ (for some exogenously determined $\beta \in [0, 1]$), under the constraints (2.13) and (2.14), and it can be analyzed using the techniques of Section 3 (details are omitted). The solution to that program, as one would expect, yields outcomes which are more efficient than those implied by the firm's optimum, (3.8). Hence, the analogous asymptotic inefficiency results would be **weaker**.

Notwithstanding this, observe that the planner's ability to improve upon (3.8) is limited to the extent that the firm's profit might also be subject to an individual-rationality-type constraint (namely, that its expected profit must be non-negative) or to the extent that the provision of subsidies to make up for the firm's losses is a distortionary activity. Either one of these two considerations implies that the planner's choice of β is restricted to those exceeding some threshold level, β_0 and, thus, that there is an upper bound on the extent to which his solution can differ from that of the firm.

3. Theorems 2 and 3 match the experimental study by Isaac, McCue, and Plott [10] of group behavior within a traditional model of public

goods provision. In that study it is demonstrated that the private provision of public goods is deficient. On the other hand, the experimental results reported by Hoffman and Spitzer [9] tend to support the opposite hypothesis, namely, that group members **do** cooperate and, thus, that efficient outcomes do emerge in those situations. However, as the latter authors note (see Footnotes 14 and 15 in their paper), their experimental setup does **not** incorporate the informational gaps which are the essence of our formulation, and it does not invoke IR constraints (the "controllers" in their study are not required to behave in a self-regarding manner). Moreover, the bargaining groups they have studied contained no more than 20 participants.

Our last proposition is concerned with the division of **realized** rents. Here I was regrettably unable to obtain a general result which holds under mild distributional assumptions (such as those which underlie Theorems 2 and 3 above). Nonetheless, for the **specific** family of distributions (5.1), it is the case that the group of residents captures most of the rents.

THEOREM 4.   *Let $\theta > 0$ be given and assume that the x_i's are independent draws from $F(x_i) = x_i^\theta$, $0 \leqslant x_i \leqslant 1$. Then*

$$\lim_{n \to \infty} \frac{U_0^*(n)}{\sum_{i=1}^n U_i^*(n)} = 0.$$

Proof.   In the Appendix.

We close this section with a worked numerical example. Table I reports figures for our welfare-performance measure, W_n^2 and for the surplus-division ratio, $U_0^*/(U_0^* + \sum U_i^*)$. The numerical simulations were carried out for several values of the parameters n and r. The distribution of

TABLE I

n	W_n^2			$U_0^*/(U_0^* + \sum U_i^*)$		
	$r = 0.25$	$r = 0.50$	$r = 0.75$	$r = 0.25$	$r = 0.50$	$r = 0.75$
2	0.50000	0.50000	0.54000	0.50000	0.50000	0.50000
4	0.15625	0.17857	0.28835	0.38400	0.40000	0.42820
6	0.05490	0.08252	0.22215	0.27513	0.28783	0.31291
8	0.01785	0.03753	0.16882	0.22222	0.22581	0.24572
10	0.00557	0.01686	0.12004	0.18182	0.18650	0.23424
12	0.00169	0.00754	0.10116	0.15384	0.15906	0.18852
14	0.00050	0.00336	0.07925	0.13333	0.13876	0.16754
16	0.00015	0.00150	0.06245	0.11514	0.12312	0.15102

damages which underlies the calculation is uniform on $[0, 1]$. As these numbers indicate, welfare losses could amount to more than 90% of potential welfare even when the number of individuals is as small as ten.

6. COMPARISON TO THE LITERATURE

In relating the present paper to mechanism theory it would be useful to distinguish between the public and private goods cases.

Starting with allocation mechanisms for public goods we observe that the negative spirit of Theorems 2 and 3 runs counter to propositions proved by Green and Laffont [5], Arrow [1], or D'Aspremont and Gerard-Varet [4]. In Green and Laffont it is shown that the DRM is asymptotically efficient while Arrow's mechanism is fully efficient (the two approaches use different equilibrium concepts). Apart from some technical discrepancies between the various models (see also Section 3.2 above), the fundamental difference in results is essentially due to the individual rationality requirement, a condition imposed in our structure but not in Arrow or Green and Laffont.

This observation has both positive and normative implications. From a positive standpoint, the above difference might explain why a "rigid" preassignment of property rights to residents (which is what the IR constraints amount to) is rarely invoked in the real world. Our analysis suggests that such preassignment is simply too costly in terms of attained welfare. Relatedly, from a normative standpoint, the comparison between the three mechanisms shows that a trade-off between efficiency and the preservation of (residents') property rights exists. This trade-off had previously been highlighted by Samuelson [15] and it had, moreover, been suggested that an assignment of property rights via a competitive bid can increase efficiency. We complement Samuelson's results by exhibiting an example where an increase in efficiency can be accomplished by using a majority rule, rather than preassigning property rights to all residents (which, in effect, endows each of them with veto power).

Indeed, consider the example of Section 4 and the following version of the DRM applied to it:

— Build the plant if and only if $x_1 + x_2 \leqslant 1$.   (6.1a)

— Pay the ith resident $\tilde{x}_i = 1 - x_j$.   (6.1b)

— Regardless of whether the plant operates or not, charge a $\frac{1}{12}$ flat fee from the residents. Transfer the proceeds to the firm.   (6.1c)

By (6.1a) this scheme is fully efficient. The flat tax is designed to bridge the gap between compensatory payments and the firm's profits, enabling it to break even (in expected value sense). Verifying this, observe that the firm's net profits (including the subsidy) are

$$\int_0^1 \int_0^{1-x_1} (x_1 + x_2 - 1)\, dx_2\, dx_1 + 2\tfrac{1}{12}$$

$$= \int_0^1 (s-1)\, g_2(s)\, ds + \tfrac{1}{6} = 0,$$

where $g_2(s)$ is defined in (4.6) above. On the other hand, the gain to individual i is

$$\int_0^{1-x_i} (1 - x_i - x_j))\, dx_j - \tfrac{1}{12} = \tfrac{1}{2}(1 - x_i)^2 - \tfrac{1}{12}$$

(this being positive for all $x_i < 0.59$), whereas the average (ex-ante) gain is

$$\tfrac{1}{2}\int_0^1 (1 - x_i)^2\, dx_i - \tfrac{1}{12} = \tfrac{1}{6} - \tfrac{1}{12} = \tfrac{1}{12} > 0.$$

Thus, individuals are better off "on average" and a majority of 59% is better off "in actuality." The main point of this example is to show that social welfare can be increased as soon as one relaxes the individual rationality constraints for a **minority** of the group of residents, i.e., as soon as not all residents are granted veto power.

Next, let us compare our large numbers propositions to parallel results in the private-goods case, or more precisely, in the private-values auction setting. We have already noted that in that setting efficiency losses arise as well (see end of Section 4.1). However, they tend to vanish as we increase the number of bidders to infinity (see Gresik and Satterthwaite [6], Wilson [16] and Cramton, Gibbons, and Klemperer [3]), whereas in our setting they tend to increase, instead, to their maximal value.

The apparent reason for these diametrically opposed results lies in the different types of allocation decisions which underlie them: joint vs individualized. In our setting, individuals are imposing negative externalties on each other via their control on the **joint** probability, $p(\cdot)$, of operating the plant. On the other hand, in the auction setting these externalties do not emerge since shading one's valuation affects only **that person's** probability, $p_i(\cdot)$, of receiving the item.

7. Summary and Conclusion

In the absence of transaction costs, negotiations would be frictionless and recontracting would proceed until all the gains from trade have been exploited. When many people are involved, however, and a joint (i.e., public) decision has to be made, transaction costs could be substantial. It is then necessary to explicitly account for them. In the above model, we represented a specific bargaining process and formalized the frictions which surround the negotiations as uncertainty about the magnitude of residents' damages. The addition of this element was shown to alter the full-efficiency conjecture quite dramatically. It was shown, in particular, that negotiations might very well generate inefficient outcomes and, moreover, that for large economies these inefficiencies are substantial. On the other hand, we have argued that these negative results do depend on the initial assignment of property rights.

These conclusions should not be construed as a recommendation for a direct governmental intervention because policymakers are subject to the same (and possibly more) uncertainties as is the firm. What they do suggest, instead, is that attention should be paid to the choice of property rights or, more generally, to the design of an institutional framework within which firms and residents can interact. The example (in Section 6) suggests, moreover, that the judicious use of familiar policy instruments (such as voting procedures and tax/subsidy schemes) could be welfare-improving.

Appendix

LEMMA 3. *Assume the random variable $\tilde{x} + \tilde{z}$ has a bounded support $[\underline{x}, \hat{x}]$. Then Assumption A.3 is satisfied if*:

$$\sigma^2 > \left(\frac{\hat{x} - \bar{x}}{\bar{x} - \underline{x}}\right)(\mu - \underline{x})^2. \tag{A.3}'$$

Note. (A.3)' is invariant with respect to changes in the unit of measurement.

Proof. First, observe that the variance, τ^2, of $\tilde{x} + \tilde{z}$ can be no larger than $\hat{\tau}^2$, where

$$\hat{\tau}^2 \equiv w(\hat{x} - \bar{x})^2 + (1 - w)(\underline{x} - \bar{x})^2$$

and $\tag{B.1}$

$$w \equiv (\bar{x} - \underline{x})/(\hat{x} - \underline{x}).$$

This is so because the latter is the variance of a discrete distribution which puts the entire mass on the two endpoints, $\underline{x}$, $\hat{x}$, and which has the same expected value, $\bar{x}$, as $\tilde{x} + \tilde{z}$ (second-order stochastic dominance argument). Therefore, in order for (A.3) to hold, it would suffice to have

$$\left(\frac{\sigma}{\mu - \underline{x}}\right)^2 > \left(\frac{\hat{t}}{\bar{x} - \underline{x}}\right)^2.$$

But, substituting in from (B.1), we get

$$\left(\frac{\hat{t}}{\bar{x} - \underline{x}}\right)^2 = \frac{w(\hat{x} - \bar{x})^2 + (1 - w)(\bar{x} - \underline{x})^2}{(\bar{x} - \underline{x})^2}$$

$$= \frac{(\bar{x} - \underline{x})(\hat{x} - \bar{x})^2 + (\hat{x} - \bar{x})(\bar{x} - \underline{x})^2}{(\bar{x} - \underline{x})^2}$$

$$= \frac{\hat{x} - \bar{x}}{\bar{x} - \underline{x}}.$$

And the claim follows.

Proof of Theorem 3. We start out by proving the following:

CLAIM. $U_0^*(n) + \sum_{i=1}^n U_i^*(n) = \int_{D_0^n} [R_n - \sum x_i] f(x) \, dx$, where

$$D_0^n = \left\{ x \in \mathbb{R}_+^n \; \middle| \; \sum_{i=1}^n \left[x_i + \frac{F(x_i)}{f(x_i)} \right] \leqslant R_n \right\}. \tag{B.2}$$

Proof of claim. Substituting in from Lemma 1 and using $U_i(\bar{x}) = 0$ (as implied by Theorem 1), we have

$$U_i^*(n) = \int_{D_i} U_i(x_i) f(x_i) \, dx_i$$

$$= \int_{D_i} \int_{x_i}^{\bar{x}} Q_i(y_i) f(x_i) \, dy_i \, dx_i$$

$$= \int_{D_i} \int_{x_i}^{\bar{x}} \int_{D_{-i}} p^*(x \mid y_i) f_{-i}(x_{-i}) f(x_i) \, dx_{-i} \, dy_i \, dx_i.$$

Therefore,

$$U_i^*(n) = \int_{D_{-i}} \int_{\underline{x}}^{\bar{x}} \int_{\underline{x}}^{y_i} p^*(x \mid y_i) f_{-i}(x_{-i}) f(x_i) \, dx_i \, dy_i \, dx_{-i}$$

$$= \int_D p^*(x \mid y_i) F(y_i) f_{-i}(x_{-i}) \, dy_i \, dx_{-i}$$

$$= \int_D p^*(x) \frac{F(x_i)}{f(x_i)} f(x) \, dx,$$

where the first equality follows by changing the order of integration and the two succeeding it are obtained by rearrangements of terms. Thus,

$$\sum_{i=1}^{n} U_i^*(n) = \int_D p^*(x) \left(\sum_{i=1}^{n} \frac{F(x_i)}{f(x_i)} \right) f(x)\, dx. \tag{B.3}$$

Also, by Lemma 2 and the fact that $U_i(\bar{x}) = 0$ at the optimum,

$$U_0^*(n) = \int_D p^*(x) \left\{ R_n - \sum_{i=1}^{n} \left[x_i + \frac{F(x_i)}{f(x_i)} \right] \right\} f(x)\, dx. \tag{B.4}$$

The claim now follows by adding up the last two terms ((B.3) and (B.4)) and substituting in for $p^*(x)$ from Theorem 1 (see, in particular, expression (3.5)).

Continuing now with the proof of the theorem note that, by Assumption A.4, $\sum_{i=1}^{n} [x_i + F(x_i)/f(x_i)] \geq (1+\alpha) \sum_{i=1}^{n} x_i - \alpha n\underline{x}$. Hence, D_0^n is contained in the region $\{x \in \mathbb{R}_+^n \mid \sum_{i=1}^{n} x_i \leq nq\}$, where $q \equiv (\alpha/(1+\alpha))\,\underline{x} + (1/(1+\alpha))\,r$. Thus,

$$U_0^*(n) + \sum_{i=1}^{n} U_i^*(n) \leq \int_{\Sigma x_i \leq nq} \left[R_n - \sum x_i \right] f(x)\, dx$$

$$= \int_{n\underline{x}}^{nq} (nr - s)\, dG_n(s)$$

$$= n(r - q)\, G_n(nq) + \int_{n\underline{x}}^{nq} G_n(s)\, ds \equiv K_n^1 + K_n^2,$$

where the first equality follows from the change of variables $\sum_{i=1}^{n} x_i = s$ and the second from the integration by parts formula.

On the other hand, substituting in from (5.3) and using again the integration by parts formula we get

$$V(n) = \int_{n\underline{x}}^{nr} (nr - s)\, dG_n(s) = \int_{n\underline{x}}^{nr} G_n(s)\, ds \equiv L_n.$$

It now suffices to show that $\lim_{n \to \infty} (K_n^1/L_n) = \lim_{n \to \infty} (K_n^2/L_n) = 0$. Proceeding as in Theorem 2, we first approximate K_n^1, K_n^2, and L_n using the central limit theorem,

$$K_n^1 \approx n(r - q)\phi\left(\frac{nq - n\mu}{\sqrt{n}\,\sigma} \right) = n(r - q)\phi(\sqrt{n}\,l),$$

$$K_n^2 \approx \int_{n\underline{x}}^{nq} \phi\left(\frac{s - n\mu}{\sqrt{n}\,\sigma} \right) ds = \sqrt{n}\,\sigma \int_{\sqrt{n}\,m}^{\sqrt{n}\,l} \phi(t)\, dt,$$

$$L_n \approx \int_{n\underline{x}}^{nr} \phi\left(\frac{s - n\mu}{\sqrt{n}\,\sigma} \right) ds = \sqrt{n}\,\sigma \int_{\sqrt{n}\,m}^{\sqrt{n}\,k} \phi(t)\, dt,$$

where

$$k \equiv \frac{r - \mu}{\sigma}, \qquad l \equiv \frac{q - \mu}{\sigma}, \qquad m \equiv \frac{x - \mu}{\sigma}, \tag{B.5}$$

and where the change of variables $t = (s - n\mu)/\sqrt{n}\,\sigma$ had been used to derive the last two equalities. Note from (B.5) that $k > l > m$ and from the assumptions underlying Theorem 3, that $l < 0$. Next, considering $\lim_{n \to \infty} (K_n^1/L_n)$, we have

$$\lim_{n \to \infty} \frac{\sqrt{n}\,\phi(\sqrt{n}\,l)}{\int_{\sqrt{n}\,m}^{\sqrt{n}\,k} \phi(t)\,dt} = \lim_{n \to \infty} \frac{\phi(\sqrt{n}\,l) + \sqrt{n}\,l\,\varphi(\sqrt{n}\,l)}{k\phi(\sqrt{n}\,k) - m\phi(\sqrt{n}\,m)},$$

using L'Hôspital's rule. If $k \geq 0$, the above ratio converges to zero (since l, $m < 0$ as we have just noted), and, thus, $\lim_{n \to \infty} (K_n^1/L_n) = 0$. Otherwise (i.e., if $k < 0$), we apply L'Hôspital's rule again and obtain

$$\lim_{n \to \infty} \frac{l\varphi(\sqrt{n}\,l) + l\varphi(\sqrt{n}\,l) + \sqrt{n}\,l^2\varphi'(\sqrt{n}\,l)}{k^2\varphi(\sqrt{n}\,k) - m^2\varphi(\sqrt{n}\,m)}$$

$$= \lim_{n \to \infty} \frac{\varphi(\sqrt{n}\,l)(2l - nl^3)}{k^2\varphi(\sqrt{n}\,k) - m^2\varphi(\sqrt{n}\,m)},$$

using the fact that $\varphi'(x) = -x\varphi(x)$. Now, since $\varphi(x) = (1/\sqrt{2\pi})$ $\exp[-x^2/2]$ we have

$$\lim_{n \to \infty} \frac{K_n^1}{L_n} = \frac{l(r - q)}{\sigma} \lim_{n \to \infty} \frac{(2 - nl^2)\exp[-nl^2]}{k^2\exp[-nk^2] - m^2\exp[-nm^2]}$$

$$= \frac{l(r - q)}{\sigma} \lim_{n \to \infty} \frac{(2 - nl^2)\exp[-n(l^2 - k^2)]}{k^2 - m^2\exp[-n(m^2 - k^2)]} = 0,$$

since k is assumed now to be negative and, thus, $l^2 > k^2$ and $m^2 > k^2$ (see note following (B.5)).

Turning next to $\lim_{n \to \infty} K_n^2/L_n$ we have

$$\lim_{n \to \infty} \frac{K_n^2}{L_n} = \lim_{n \to \infty} \frac{\int_{\sqrt{n}\,m}^{\sqrt{n}\,l} \phi(t)\,dt}{\int_{\sqrt{n}\,m}^{\sqrt{n}\,k} \phi(t)\,dt}$$

$$= \lim_{n \to \infty} \frac{l\phi(\sqrt{n}\,l) - m\phi(\sqrt{n}\,m)}{k\phi(\sqrt{n}\,k) - m\phi(\sqrt{n}\,m)} = 0,$$

where the second equality follows from L'Hôspital's rule and the steps involved in proving the one following it are exactly those which are contained in the proof of $\lim_{n \to \infty} (K_n^1/L_n) = 0$ (i.e., distinguishing between the

$k \geq 0$ and $k < 0$ cases and applying L'Hôspital's rule for the latter). Our proof is now complete.

Proof of Theorem 4.   For this family of distributions we have

$$\frac{F(x_i)}{f(x_i)} = \frac{1}{\theta} x_i,$$ (B.6)

$$x_i + \frac{F(x_i)}{f(x_i)} = \frac{\theta + 1}{\theta} x_i \equiv \gamma x_i,$$ (B.7)

and

$$D_0^n = \left\{ x \in \mathbb{R}_+^n \,\middle|\, \sum_{i=1}^n x_i \leq \gamma n r \right\},$$ (B.8)

where D_0^n is defined in (B.2) above. Thus,

$$\sum_{i=1}^n U_i^*(n) = \int_{D_0^n} \left[\sum_{i=1}^n \frac{F(x_i)}{f(x_i)} \right] f(x) \, dx$$

$$= \frac{1}{\theta} \int_{D_0^n} \left(\sum_{i=1}^n x_i \right) f(x) \, dx$$

$$= \frac{1}{\theta} \int_0^{\gamma n r} s \, dG_n(s)$$

$$= \frac{1}{\theta} \left[\gamma n r G_n(\gamma n r) - \int_0^{\gamma n r} G_n(s) \, ds \right],$$

where the first equality follows from (B.3) (of the previous theorem), the second from (B.6), the third from the change of variables $\sum x_i = s$, and the fourth from the integration by parts formula. Similarly,

$$U_0^*(n) = \int_{D_0^n} \left\{ R_n - \sum_{i=1}^n \left[x_i + \frac{F(x_i)}{f(x_i)} \right] \right\} f(x) \, dx$$

$$- \int_{D_0^n} \left[n r - \gamma \sum_{i=1}^n x_i \right] f(x) \, dx$$

$$= \int_0^{\gamma n r} (n r - \gamma s) \, dG_n(s)$$

$$= \int_0^{\gamma n r} G_n(s) \, ds.$$

Therefore,

$$\frac{\sum_{i=1}^{n} U_i^*(n)}{U_0^*(n)} = \frac{1}{\theta} \left[\frac{\gamma nr G_n(\gamma nr)}{\int_0^{\gamma nr} G_n(s)\, ds} - 1 \right]. \tag{B.9}$$

The proof can now be completed following the steps of Theorem 3. More specifically, the bracketed term of (B.9) can be approximated using the central limit theorem and then shown to converge to infinity by an application of L'Hôspital's rule. The details are omitted. ∎

References

1. K. J. Arrow, The property rights doctrine and demand revelation under incomplete information, in "Economics and Human Wealth" (M. Boskin, Ed.), Academic Press, New York, 1979.
2. R. H. Coase, The problem of social cost, *J. Law Econ.* **3** (1960), 1–44.
3. P. Cramton, R. Gibbons, and P. Klemprer, Dissolving a partnership efficiently, *Econometrica* **55** (1987), 615–632.
4. C. D'Aspremont and L. A. Gerard-Varet, Incentives and incomplete information, *J. Pub. Econ.* **11** (1979), 25–45.
5. J. Green and J. J. Laffont, "Incentives in Public Decision Making," North-Holland, Amsterdam/New York, 1979.
6. T. A. Gresik and M. A. Satterthwaite, "The Number of Traders Required to Make a Market Competitive: The Beginning of a Theory," Discussion Paper 651, Northwestern University, 1983.
7. T. Groves and M. Loeb, Incentives and public inputs, *J. Pub. Econ.* **4** (1975), 211–226.
8. J. C. Harsanyi, Games with incomplete information played by Bayesian players, *Manage. Sci.* **14** (1967), 159–189; 320–334; 486–502.
9. E. Hoffman and M. L. Spitzer, Experimental tests of the Coase theorem with large bargaining groups, *J. Legal Stud.* **15** (1986), 149–171.
10. M. R. Isaac, K. F. McCue, and C. R. Plott, Public goods provision in experimental environment, *J. Publ. Econ.* **26** (1985), 51–74.
11. J. J. Laffont and E. Maskin, A differential approach to expected utility maximizing mechanisms, in "Aggregation and Revelation of Preferences" (J. J. Laffont, Ed.), North-Holland, Amsterdam, 1979.
12. R. B. Myerson, Optimal auction design, *Math. Oper. Res.* **6** (1981), 56–73.
13. R. B. Myerson and M. A. Satterthwaite, Efficient mechanisms for bilateral trading, *J. Econ. Theory* **29** (1983), 265–281.
14. A. C. Pigou, "Economics of Welfare," 4th ed., Macmillan & Co., London, 1952.
15. W. Samuelson, A comment on the Coase theorem, in "Game Theoretic Models of Bargaining" (A. E. Roth, Ed.), Cambridge Univ. Press, Cambridge, 1985.
16. R. Wilson, Incentive efficiency of double auctions, *Econometrica* **53** (1985), 1101–1115.

Index

ECONOMIC THEORY, ECONOMETRICS, AND MATHEMATICAL ECONOMICS

Series Editor: Karl Shell

CORNELL UNIVERSITY
ITHACA, NEW YORK

Erwin Klein. Mathematical Methods in Theoretical Economics: Topological and Vector Space Foundations of Equilibrium Analysis

Paul Zarembka (Ed.). Frontiers in Econometrics

George Horwich and Paul A. Samuelson (Eds.). Trade, Stability, and Macroeconomics: Essays in Honor of Lloyd A. Metzler

W. T. Ziemba and R. G. Vickson (Eds.). Stochastic Optimization Models in Finance

Steven A. Y. Lin (Ed.). Theory and Measurement of Economic Externalities

Haim Levy and Marshall Sarnat (Eds.). Financial Decision Making under Uncertainty

Yasuo Murata. Mathematics for Stability and Optimization of Economic Systems

Jerry S. Kelly. Arrow Impossibility Theorems

Peter Diamond and Michael Rothschild (Eds.). Uncertainty in Economics: Readings and Exercises

Fritz Machlup. Methodology of Economics and Other Social Sciences

Robert H. Frank and Richard T. Freeman. Distributional Consequences of Direct Foreign Investment

Elhanan Helpman and Assaf Razin. A Theory of International Trade under Uncertainty

Edmund S. Phelps. Studies in Macroeconomic Theory, Volume 1: Employment and Inflation. Volume 2: Redistribution and Growth

Marc Nerlove, David M. Grether, and José L. Carvalho. Analysis of Economic Time Series: A Synthesis

Michael J. Boskin (Ed.). Economics and Human Welfare: Essays in Honor of Tibor Scitovsky

Carlos Daganzo. Multinomial Probit: The Theory and Its Application to Demand Forecasting

C. W. J. Granger and Paul Newbold (Eds.). Forecasting Economic Time Series, Second Edition

Marc Nerlove, Assaf Razin, and Efraim Sadka (Eds.). Household and Economy: Welfare Economics of Endogenous Fertility

Thomas Sargent (Ed.). Macroeconomic Theory, Second Edition

Yves Balasko (Ed.). Foundations of the Theory of General Equilibrium

Jean-Michel Grandmont (Ed.). Temporary Equilibrium: Selected Readings

J. Darrell Duffie (Ed.). An Introductory Theory of Security Markets

Ross M. Starr (Ed.). General Equilibrium Models of Monetary Economics

Peter Diamond and Michael Rothschild (Eds.). Uncertainty in Economics, Second Edition

S. C. Tsiang (Ed.). Finance Constraints and the Theory of Money: Selected Papers

M. Aoki (Ed.). Optimization of Stochastic Systems: Topics in Discrete-Time Dynamics, Second Edition

P. Diamond and M. Rothschild (Eds.). Uncertainty in Economics: Readings and Exercises, Revised Edition

M. J. Osborne and A. Rubinstein (Eds.). Bargaining and Markets

T. Ichiishi, A. Neyman, and Y. Tauman (Eds.). Game Theory and Applications

B. D. Presman and J. M. Sonin (Eds.). Sequential Control with Incomplete Information

M. Itoh, K. Kiyono, M. Okuno-Fujiwara, and K. Suzumura (Eds.). Economic Analysis of Industrial Policy

A. Takayama, M. Ohyama, and H. Ohta (Eds.). Trade, Policy, and International Adjustments

John M. Letiche (Ed.). International Economic Policies and Their Theoretical Foundations: A Source Book, Second Edition